Phillip Kerman

{ ActionScripting
in FLASH MX™ }

New Riders

A Division of Pearson Education
201 West 103rd St. • Indianapolis, Indiana, 46290 USA

Copyright © 2003 by Phillip Kerman

Trademarks

Warning and Disclaimer

Publisher
David Dwyer

Associate Publisher
Stephanie Wall

Production Manager
Gina Kanouse

Executive Editor
Jeff Schultz

Acquisitions Editor
Kate Small

Development Editor
Damon Jordan

Product Marketing Manager
Kathy Malmloff

Publicity Manager
Susan Nixon

Project Editors
Stacia Mellinger
Beth Trudell

Copy Editor
John Sleeva

Technical Editor
Matthew Manuel

Indexer
Chris Morris

Manufacturing Coordinator
Jim Conway

Book Designer
Alan Clements

Cover Designer
Aren Howell

Proofreader
Linda Seifert

Composition
Amy Parker

Overview

Contents

Dedication

Dedicated to my entire family, including our newest member, Savannah—and to the canine Kerman, Max, who deserved more walks than he got during the writing of this book.

Acknowledgments

The hardest part of writing a book is attempting to acknowledge all those who helped, but knowing that you'll fail to mention everyone. Here is my attempt to acknowledge everyone.

First, the people at New Riders. You'll find a list of the key players in the credits column on the copyright page, but even they would acknowledge that others helped them. After seeing my first book become a reality, I realized that even if I could write a perfect book on my own (which, of course I can't), it would never get printed because so much work is involved in preparing the files for the printer. Although I can't say I know how every publisher works, I can say that New Riders is professional, responsive, and fun. Of particular note, Kate Small and Damon Jordan made the book flow. Everything seemed to make sense when I wrote it, but after Kate and Damon reorganized parts, it made much more sense. Matthew Manuel used his Flash experience both to ensure that technical details were correct and exercises could be performed, as well as to suggest countless additional facts that were included in the text. A copy editor like John Sleeva is doubly valuable because he eliminates errors that would otherwise make the book difficult to read, and he makes me a better writer! Reviewing his edits is like a free English class. Obviously, there are many others who work behind the scenes for whom I am grateful.

Macromedia continues to amaze me with its forthcoming and approachable style. The company is totally involved in email lists and Flash community sites. The folks who seem to go way beyond the call of duty by providing help to all include Jeremy Allaire, Brad Bechtel, Damian Burns, Mike Chambers, Jeremy Clark, Henriette Cohn, John Dowdell, Ken Eckey, Allen Ellison, Gary Grossman, Erica Norton, Nigel Pegg, Peter Santangeli, Sharon Selden, Christopher Thilgen, Michael Williams, Eric J. Wittman, and Matt Wobensmith.

I subscribe to many email lists, but three in particular have been most helpful: those run by Branden Hall, Jon Warren Lentz, and Darrel Plant. There are countless instances when a thread on one of these lists has helped me.

One last acknowledgment for some authors of other Flash books. I'm proud of this book, but it contains only my style of communication. For some different perspectives on Flash, check out books containing contributions by the following authors:

Joshua Davis, Brendan Dawes, David J. Emberton, Bruce Epstein, Derek Franklin, Garo Green, Branden Hall, Andreas Heim, Jon Warren Lentz, Kim Markegard, Colin Moock, Robert Penner, Darrel Plant, Robert Reinhardt, Crissy Rey, Gary Rosenzweig, Nik Schramm, Glenn Thomas, Phillip Torrone, Bill Turner, and Samuel Wan.

I can't vouch for books I haven't reviewed, but I can say these folks know their stuff. They've also provided direct help on various Flash-related matters to myself and others for years.

—*Phillip Kerman*

About the Author

Phillip Kerman is an independent programmer, teacher, and writer specializing in Macromedia products. His degree in Imaging and Photographic Technology from the Rochester Institute of Technology was earned back when "multimedia" had a different meaning than today. One of Phillip's internships, for example, involved programming multiple slide projector presentations with dissolves synchronized to a sound track—the multimedia of the 1980s. In 1993, he found Macromedia Authorware a natural fit for his interest and skills. After getting his start at The Human Element, Inc., he moved back to Portland, Oregon to work on his own.

Phillip has transitioned his expertise from Authorware to Director, and now, to Flash. Over seven years, he has had to adapt to a total of 16 version upgrades—Flash MX being the most significant of them all! In addition to retooling and building his own skills, Phillip finds teaching the biggest challenge. He has trained and made presentations around the world, in such exotic locations as Reykjavik, Iceland; Melbourne, Australia; Amsterdam, Holland; and McAlester, Oklahoma. He is also the best-selling author of *Sams Teach Yourself Macromedia Flash MX in 24 Hours* (that is the title, not how long it took to write). His writing has also appeared in publications such as *Macworld*, *Macromedia User Journal*, and his self-published *The Phillip Newsletter* (www.phillipkerman.com/newsletter).

In addition to showing others how to create multimedia, Phillip has had plenty of opportunities to get his hands dirty in programming. You can see a recent Flash site he programmed at www.allsteeloffice.com/number19.

Feel free to email Phillip at flash6@phillipkerman.com.

Tell Us What You Think

As the reader of this book, you are the most important critic and commentator. We value your opinion and want to know what we're doing right, what we could do better, what areas you'd like to see us publish in, and any other words of wisdom you're willing to pass our way.

As the Associate Publisher for New Riders Publishing, I welcome your comments. You can fax, email, or write me directly to let me know what you did or didn't like about this book—as well as what we can do to make our books stronger.

Please note that I cannot help you with technical problems related to the topic of this book, and that due to the high volume of mail I receive, I might not be able to reply to every message.

When you write, please be sure to include this book's title and author as well as your name and phone or fax number. I will carefully review your comments and share them with the author and editors who worked on the book.

Fax: 317-581-4663

Email: stephanie.wall@newriders.com

Mail: Stephanie Wall
           Associate Publisher
           New Riders Publishing
           201 West 103rd Street
           Indianapolis, IN 46290 USA

Foreword

You might not think that the upgrade to Macromedia Flash MX is quite as significant as the upgrade to Flash 5. For a programmer, however, it's certainly the biggest upgrade ever. Whereas anything was possible before, now it's also elegant, efficient, and easy. Of course, you have to become a programmer first. If you just organize your goals and translate them into the language of a programmer, you can make Flash do precisely what you imagined. But therein lies the problem: Not everyone can translate goals into a programming language.

This book targets the reader who can assemble a basic Flash movie and who knows what he or she wants to achieve. I'll help you divide your goal into individual tasks that can then be translated into ActionScript. Naturally, this will involve teaching you how to "program" (and even how to think like a programmer). This book, however, is not a general programming book; *every* topic is related to and applied to Flash. Naturally, if you are already an experienced programmer, you might find parts of this book to be a review. But for you programmers, I'll show you how to apply your programming knowledge to make Flash perform. All the programming skill in the world (whether I teach it to you or you bring it with you) won't help you if you can't apply it to Flash.

Although this book definitely does not shy away from advanced topics, it isn't an exhaustive reference to every detail in the ActionScript language. The truth is that there are countless other resources for advanced programming topics. That's not what this book is about. It's about giving you the skills so that you can apply any idea you have to Flash. When you're equipped with the knowledge I cover, you'll be able to meet any challenge. It might involve researching an esoteric formula for physics or applying a unique math calculation. If that means you have to research a specific topic, this book will give you the skills to figure out how to apply it to Flash.

This book is an overhaul of *ActionScripting in Flash* (covering Flash 5). Believe me, I didn't just do a "find-and-replace" to change all the *5*s to *MX*s! (I wish it were that easy.) For the most part, this book is just *more*. I cut out plenty, but added much more. The general programming topics didn't change much, but anything specific to Flash (most of the book) went through significant changes. I think readers can learn two things from this book: how to be a programmer and how to harness Flash's ActionScript language. The major difference between this book and the previous one on Flash 5 is that harnessing ActionScript is much different now.

The book is organized in two parts. The chapters in Part I, "Foundation," are like chapters in a textbook. Plenty of examples are interspersed, but you don't need to follow along with Flash running. (I suspect that you'll be inspired to try things out often, however.) Part II, "Workshops," features hands-on tutorials. They offer you a chance to apply what you've learned in Part I. If you prefer, you can jump right into the workshop chapters. (References are made to the chapters in Part I when further explanation might be helpful.) You'll find the workshop chapters to be quite useful. In many of them, I even guide you down the wrong path so that we can discuss the solution that follows. I find that this is more true-to-life than some tutorials that seem to prove only that it's *possible* to achieve a particular result with very few steps. Real life is often frustrating, and perhaps the simulated reality of these workshop chapters will help you avoid frustration when you go on your own.

One last note before we get rolling: Flash MX was such a change from Flash 5 that I chose to cover *only* Flash MX. It turns out that there are a few ancillary mentions of older versions of Flash in this book. By and large, however, this book is for Flash MX only. Workshop Chapter 1 provides information about ensuring that your users have the correct Flash Player. Naturally, I'll show you how to upgrade those users so that they can see your Flash MX creations.

Now get ready to transform yourself from a Flash user to an ActionScripter!

{ Part I }

Foundation

{Foundation} Introduction

The following 16 chapters cover practically every detail of ActionScript. Although the content is organized like a textbook, I've included several examples along the way. You are encouraged to break from the reading and try out any topic that interests you. Generally, however, this is the part of the book that you read. In the second half (the workshop chapters), you can follow along with the 18 detailed tutorials.

Here's a quick rundown of the topics explored in this part of the book:

1. "Flash Basics" includes the prerequisites that I expect every reader to bring with him or her. Even if you consider yourself a Flash expert, you should read this chapter as both a review and an insight into some of the terms that I'll use throughout the book.

2. "What's New in Flash MX" introduces you to the key features in Flash MX that pertain specifically to ActionScript. In addition to changes in the programming language, features that affect how you build a Flash movie are discussed. Finally, this chapter includes some guidelines and a legend for the rest of the book.

3. "The Programmer's Approach" is a very general chapter that lays the groundwork for your programming career. Topics such as writing specifications, prototyping, and exactly what "good style" means are covered.

4. "Basic Programming in Flash" introduces you to the terminology and basic elements of ActionScript, such as data types and variables. It's impossible to discuss these elements without showing how they work, but the goal of this chapter is just to introduce all the pieces that will be incorporated in later chapters.

5. "Programming Structures" is a huge chapter that explains all the ways ActionScript is structured. If Chapter 4 was the building materials (wood, bricks, and concrete), this chapter is the framework and architectural styles. You also get a peek at both the Math and Number objects because they're so integral to the structural elements covered.

6. "Debugging" offers a chance to catch your breath (after Chapter 5) and take the time to learn ways to ensure quality programming before you go too far in the wrong direction. The revised Flash Debugger is explained, as well as some general programming techniques to avoid or remove bugs.

7. "The Movie Clip Object" introduces a familiar component of Flash, but in a way that will help you understand other "objects" that come up in later chapters. In this way, you can leverage your existing knowledge when learning advanced topics.

8. "Functions" shows you how to use the built-in functions as well as how to write your own functions. It turns out that homemade functions prove to be much more involved than the ones that come with Flash. This is possibly the most valuable chapter because it can save you a ton of time.

9. "Manipulating Strings" looks at how to manipulate string data. Often, the user will end up seeing this text onscreen—but not necessarily. The ability to manipulate strings before the user sees them is very powerful.

10. "Keyboard Access and Modifying Onscreen Text" makes the leap to how text is displayed onscreen. Flash MX's new TextField and TextFormat objects are explored as well as listeners and keyboard control.

11. "Arrays" explores how to make, access, and manipulate arrays, which are simply a great way to organize complex information.

12. "Objects" introduces the general form of objects, shows you how to use the built-in objects Sound, Color, and Date, and teaches you new ways to use the familiar Movie Clip. This chapter also covers the new runtime drawing functions.

13. "Homemade Objects" shows you how to apply the knowledge you already have to make complex objects in Flash. If arrays are a way to store complex information easily, objects are a way to store *really* complex information.

14. "Extending ActionScript" introduces all of the new ways you can modify ActionScript to make it behave as you want. You should definitely check out this chapter because you'll learn a few simple techniques that will save a ton of time.

15. "Components" walks through all the ways to build and use components, from ways of making standard components work for you to creating custom User Interfaces (custom UIs).

16. "Interfacing with External Data" shows you many of the ways that Flash can "talk" to outside applications. Topics include reading text files, interacting with server applications, exchanging XML-structured data, exchanging data through the new LocalConnection object, and saving data on the users local machine with the local SharedObject. I didn't have time to actually show you how to use outside tools, but this chapter shows you practically everything else.

It's amazing to think that there's so much to say about Flash and I don't even say it all. I could probably double the size of this book and there'd be still more! However, I'm sure that if you grasp all the content I've organized in these 16 chapters, you'll be able to adapt quickly to any new situation that arises.

{Chapter 1}

Flash Basics

Flash professionals are a strange breed. Some have traditional animation and graphics skills. Others come to Flash from a programming background. Still others are so young they don't have *any* professional background—they're straight out of college (or younger)! It doesn't matter where you come from because Flash is approachable *and* powerful.

For this book to serve as the bridge between intermediate Flash and advanced programming, it is best that you start at the same level. Intermediate Flash users, who are familiar with drawing, tweening, and sound effects, are about to embark on programming; already experienced programmers are about to apply their skills to Flash. But we all need to start at the same level.

This chapter is an important link to the material that follows. It isn't a recap of drawing, tweening, and sound effects; rather, it's a quick overview of foundational knowledge unique to Flash scripting. If the material in this chapter looks familiar, good. If not, you should make sure that it all makes sense before attacking the rest of the book.

Specifically, this chapter covers:

- The timeline hierarchy of nested Movie Clips.
- The Stage coordinate system.
- Traditional Flash tricks, such as invisible buttons and empty Movie Clips.
- The places where scripting occurs.

I'd like to think that most of this chapter is a review, but it's okay if some material is new to you. If nothing else, you should begin to approach the concepts in the way they're presented here. For example, if you've never heard of invisible buttons, that's fine—just try to start using them.

Timeline Hierarchy

A key concept that is critical to understanding Flash is nested timelines. Any time you select a shape and Insert, Convert to Symbol (F8), the shape is placed in the Library and you're left with an instance of the symbol on the Stage. You also can select an instance of a symbol and Insert, Convert to Symbol, which nests an instance of the selected symbol inside a new symbol. The main thing to remember is that F8 takes whatever is selected and places it in the Library as a new symbol (even if you have a symbol instance selected). Such nesting of symbols has implications for both programming and animation structure.

Implications for Animation and Filesize

To see how nesting symbols applies to animation, consider how to create a symbol of a car containing moving wheels. First, draw a wheel and convert it to a Movie Clip symbol called "Wheel." To create a rotating wheel symbol (that is, a Movie Clip containing an animation), you can convert an instance of the Wheel symbol to another Movie Clip called "Rotating Wheel." Then edit the contents of the Rotating Wheel by making a simple Motion tween that rotates the Wheel symbol. Because only symbol instances can be used in a Motion tween, the extra step of placing the Wheel symbol inside the Rotating Wheel symbol is necessary. Finally, use two instances of the Rotating Wheel clip inside a third clip, "Car." Then you can animate the car across the main timeline.

In the end, your car is a symbol containing two instances of the Rotating Wheel clip, which both contain an instance of the plain wheel. When building such nested symbols, it's usually best to work from the "inside out" or "specific to general." Regardless of how you approach it, be sure to monitor the address bar that appears above the Stage, as shown in Figure 1.1. The address bar begins with the name of the scene that you're currently editing, and shows the hierarchy of symbol nesting as well. In Figure 1.1, the address bar indicates that you're editing the "Wheel" symbol inside "Rotating Wheel," which in turn is nested inside "Car." Of course, you can make more complex nested symbols than a car with rotating wheels—you just have to keep track of what you're doing.

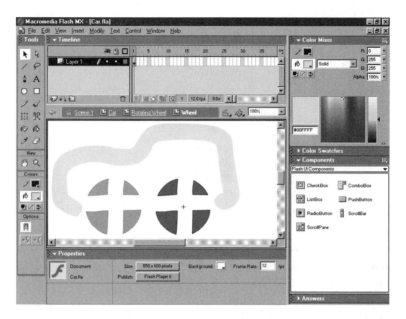

Figure 1.1   *The address bar shows the hierarchy of nested symbols.*

Besides enabling complex effects, nested symbols can reduce your movie's file-size by recycling graphic components. You can actually take this seeming advantage too far, and it will begin to work against you. Take the absurd example of a single-pixel symbol that is recycled and nested to make a line…and then four lines are used to make a square…and so on. Generally, however, the benefits of recycling symbols are significant.

In addition to filesize savings, careful use of symbols generally (and Movie Clips specifically) can help your productivity. For example, when a change is made to the master symbol, that change is reflected in each instance already in use. Also, when you duplicate a shape that hasn't been converted to a symbol, you encounter two problems: the obvious filesize contribution and the fact that Flash might not render the "identical" shapes the same way. Because you can position graphics in fractional locations, Flash often needs to round off when drawing every pixel. The bottom line is that two different shapes of the same size can easily appear slightly differently, whereas multiple symbols look the same (unless they're scaled differently).

Implications for Programming

Finally, nested symbols can be useful for programming tasks. For one thing, nesting symbols makes your Flash file more modular and manageable. Imagine if our entire money supply were based in pennies. It would certainly be possible to carry out any transaction, but it'd be a pain. You could nest one hundred pennies in a "dollar" symbol. A ten-dollar bill is like 10 instances of the "dollar" symbol. Sometimes such nesting is simply more convenient.

In addition to modularization, clips and buttons are the primary ways to include interactivity in your movies. If you want to respond to user's mouse click, you can use a button that can "trap" a user's press. If you want a script to execute the moment a movie is fully loaded, you can use Flash's load event that's made for Movie Clips. Throughout this book you'll see that there are countless ways to make your movie respond to user interaction—but they nearly always involve a clip or button instance.

Addressing (or Targeting)

When creating nested symbols, it's important to pay attention to the address bar. When programming, it's just as important to understand the concept of *addressing* (also called *targeting*)—that is, which clip you want to affect. Say you intend to move a Movie Clip instance when the user clicks a button. The instance could be in the main timeline or nested inside another clip (perhaps many levels deep). Before you say "move," you have to address the correct clip. It's like in real life. If you want someone in a crowd to move, for example, you can't just say, "Hey, move." You must first address the person you're targeting by saying "Hey, Phillip, you move."

Another way to envision addressing is to think of the folder (and subfolder) structure on your computer. You can have symbols inside symbols just like folders inside folders. (I'll use this analogy throughout the description and tie it to Flash at the end of this section.) If you are browsing one folder and you want to open a file in a subfolder, you simply "address" the subfolder you want to browse. When you decide to address another file or folder, you have two basic ways to do so: relatively and absolutely. Take a quick look at Figure 1.2. Starting from the folder "Flash MX," if you want to go into a folder "Help" and then into a subfolder "Flash," the relative target can be expressed as *go into the folder "Help" and then into the subfolder "Flash."* Consider that you can only be "in" (browsing) one folder at a time, so when you begin by saying *go into the folder*

"Help," you're assuming that a folder called "Help" is present within the current folder. This is relative addressing because it's relative to where you are. (In Chapter 7, "The Movie Clip Object," you'll learn that Flash uses the reserved word "this" to mean "this timeline.")

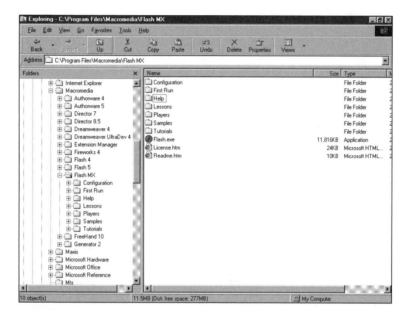

Figure 1.2   *Relative and absolute addressing are similar to browsing files and folders on your computer.*

In addition to relative addressing that "dives" down into subfolders, relative addressing can go up too. That is, if you're inside one folder (or Movie Clip), you can refer to the folder that contains the folder you're in. For example, if you were browsing the "Flash MX" folder inside the "Macromedia" folder, you could refer to the "Macromedia" folder with a relative target: "go up one level" (the same way you could click "Up" in Figure 1.2). In Flash, such a relative reference involves the term _parent; in HTML, the characters . . / are used. You'll learn more about this later in this chapter, but the important concept to remember is that relative references can go "up" or "down."

Absolute addressing is an alternative to relative addressing. Absolute addresses specify the entire address of the item (or folder) that you're targeting. As such, absolute references are unaffected by which folder you're currently "in." In the case of browsing folders, an absolute path would include the drive letter. For example: C:\Program Files\Macromedia\Flash MX is an absolute path. You also can compare a phrase such as "next door" or "down the street" to a relative address, and "1234 SW Whatever St., Portland, OR 97214" to an absolute address.

It's a subjective decision as to which references are better: absolute or relative. But, generally, relative references are desirable because you aren't restricted in changing the hierarchy. Imagine that you wanted to move your "Flash MX" folder to a different hard drive? All of a sudden, the absolute address C:\Program Files\Macromedia\Flash MX won't work. However, if you're using a relative target, such as Macromedia\Flash MX (which is really *go inside the folder "Macromedia"—adjacent to where I am—and then go into the folder "Flash MX"*), it isn't tied to any particular drive or folder. The only disadvantage of relative references is that they require you to be "in" a particular folder (in this case, the "Program Files" folder). The absolute reference C:\Program Files\ Macromedia\Flash MX works no matter where you are (as long as the folder hasn't moved).

Although the decision between relative and absolute addressing is subjective, you'll often find that relative targets become quite complicated when you have to go both "up" and "down" to find the target. For example, if you wanted to address the folder called "Flash 4" (which is inside your "Macromedia" folder) if you were in the "Flash MX" folder, a relative target would be go *up one folder, and then down into "Flash 4."* It's not impossible to make relative references that change direction like this, but an absolute address is often easier.

Just so we don't drift too far from Flash, let's look at addressing in Flash. You often need to address clip instances (and their timelines). Using the earlier car example, if I were in a "wheel," I could use a relative address to refer to the car in which I was contained. It helps greatly to name the instances of each nested Movie Clip. For example, if I wanted to address the front wheel instance inside my car, I would want to make sure that both the car and the wheel had an instance name. Because you might have several instances of the original "car" symbol on the Stage, you definitely cannot address a clip by its master name in the Library. You can address only one clip instance at a time—so you'd have to specify which car instance you were targeting.

Relative addressing in Flash is pretty simple. You just begin with `this` and follow it by the instance name of the clip you're addressing. If the instance name is "BigCar," for example, you just use `this.bigCar`. To address instances inside

instances, you simply separate each instance name with a dot (that is, a period
"."—but people say *dot*). this.BigCar.FrontWheel will address the
"FrontWheel" instance inside the "BigCar" instance that is present in the current
timeline. If you are writing a script from inside the "FrontWheel" instance and
want to target the "BigCar" instance, use _parent. The term _parent means the
clip that contains the clip you're in. (Think "up one level.") You can also use
_parent._parent (and so on) to "go up" more than one level at a time. You can
also target an instance that's "up one level." Say, from inside the "FrontWheel"
instance, you want to address "BackWheel" (which is contained in "BigCar," the
same clip containing "FrontWheel"), you can use _parent.BackWheel.

Absolute addresses in Flash almost always begin _root, which addresses the
main timeline. For example, _root.BigCar.FrontWheel will address the instance
named "FrontWheel" inside "BigCar," which is in the main timeline. The only
exception to beginning absolute addresses with "_root" is when addressing
levels. Using the loadMovie method, you can play .swf files inside clips or level
numbers. To address a clip (or the entire .swf file) absolutely that's been loaded
via loadMovie, begin with _level1 (use _level2 for level 2, _level3 for 3, and
so on). If you see an address that begins with _root, you know it's absolute. If it
begins with _parent or this, you know it's relative. Finally, if you don't see
_root, _parent, or this, then the this is implied (and can always be added for
clarity) and therefore you have a relative address.

Addressing clips might sound like an exercise in futility, but there are actually
several reasons to do so. You can address a clip to change one of its properties.
For example, you could address the front wheel in the car to change its alpha
property. For example, the script _root.BigCar.FrontWheel._alpha=50 would
set the front wheel's alpha to 50%. Not only can you change properties of an
individual instance, but you can also make instances change more significantly.
For example, _root.BigCar.FrontWheel.gotoAndStop(10) will go to frame 10
(in the FrontWheel instance) and stop. Such a script is called a *method* of the
instance. We'll discuss both changing properties and using methods (plus much
more) in Chapter 4, "Basic Programming in Flash," and Chapter 7, "The Movie
Clip Object." It's just important to understand *why* you'd need to address a clip in
the first place. (Again, if you addressed me by saying "Hey, Phillip," you probably had something more to say.)

This section provides the basics of addressing. You might want to practice, however. A great way to learn is by using Flash's Target Path Editor. Any time you see the Insert Target Path button (see Figure 1.3), you can explore your entire file and Flash will write the target reference for you. What's more, you can experiment with both relative and absolute targets.

Finally, although the old "slash" reference is also supported (and might be familiar to those with HTML experience), I recommend using only the dot notation. You can see the Target Path Editor in Figure 1.4.

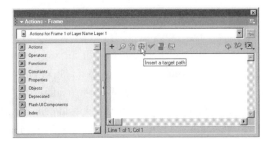

Figure 1.3   *The Insert Target Path button helps you compose a target path.*

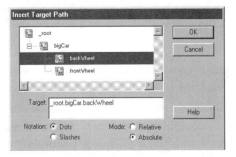

Figure 1.4   *The Target Path Editor enables you to choose between relative and absolute paths and dot and slash notation.*

Script Locations

All your scripts are written in the Actions panel, but there are three places you can attach scripts: keyframes, button instances, and Movie Clip instances. You can also place scripts inside a master Movie Clip, but still attach scripts only to keyframes, button instances, and clip instances that are inside the Movie Clip.

Flash is "event-driven," meaning that events trigger scripts to execute. Even after you write a script (an instruction for Flash to follow), you must select an event to trigger that script.

Keyframe scripts are probably the easiest to understand. You simply select a keyframe and open the Actions panel to create a script. When the frame is reached, a frame script is triggered. That is, if you put a script on frame 10, it will execute when the playhead reaches frame 10. Keep in mind that Flash executes the script first and then draws the onscreen contents. This becomes important if your script's instructions are to jump to another frame; you might never see the onscreen contents of the frame where the script is written.

Button and Movie Clip scripts are attached to instances of buttons or Movie Clips—but not contained inside the master symbol of a button! If you place a script anywhere inside a button's symbol, it will be ignored. If you place a script inside a Movie Clip symbol, it will work fine; but consider such a script is placed in a keyframe, button instance, or nested clip instance. To attach a script to a button or clip instance, select an instance on the Stage and then use the Actions panel to write a script. Button and clip instance scripts differ from frame scripts in one interesting way: They are always contained within an event. Buttons respond to mouse events (such as `press`, `release`, and `rollOver`) and clip instances respond to clip events (such as `load`, `unload`, and `enterFrame`). (In Chapter 14, "Extending ActionScript," you'll see that Flash MX also enables you to make Movie Clips respond to mouse events—a task previously reserved for buttons.) When comparing buttons and clips to keyframes, remember that keyframe scripts execute in the event that the frame is reached, whereas button scripts respond to mouse events, and clip instance scripts respond to clip events. For example, you can't simply make a button `gotoAndPlay(1)`. You have to specify exactly what event will trigger that script—a `press` mouse event, a `rollOver` event, or other. Chapter 4 discusses events in greater detail, but you should have a clear understanding of these three script locations.

Another very important concept related to addressing is that button and keyframe scripts both perform as though you were "in" the timeline in which they reside. Scripts attached to clip instances perform as though you were "in" the Movie Clip's timeline. For example, if your script `gotoAndStop(1)` were attached to a keyframe or button (within a mouse event), it would cause the playback head to jump to frame 1 within the timeline in which the button or keyframe resides. (If it helps, just add the implied "this," as in `this.gotoAndStop(1)`.) If the same script were attached to a clip instance, the playback head would jump to the first frame *within the clip* unless you changed the script to _parent.gotoAndStop(1). This topic will be fully explored in many of the workshop portions of this book.

One last point about script locations: You can display the Actions panel in Normal Mode or Expert Mode. This is set through the options menu (at the top-right of the Actions panel) or the new View options menu (see Figure 1.5).

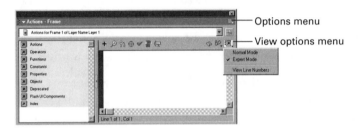

Figure 1.5   *The View options menu enables you to change from Normal Mode to Expert Mode.*

New to MX

I used to switch between Expert Mode and Normal Mode quite frequently. It can be nice the way Normal Mode not only ensures proper syntax but often lists a choice of options (see Figure 1.6). With Flash MX's new code hints feature, however, you can get that same list of options automatically. In Chapter 2, "What's New in Flash MX," I'll go over all the tricks to using code hints, but the bottom line is that I'd strongly recommend that you simply leave the Actions panel set to Expert Mode. For a quick taste, click the first cell in the timeline, open the Actions panel, set it to Expert Mode (Ctrl+Shift+E), and then press the following three keys in sequence (but not all at the same time): Esc, O, C. You should see a drop-down list of options for the "On Clip" events. Start a new line, and then press Esc, O, N for a list of "On Mouse" events. (Forget for a moment that you're not allowed to put mouse or clip events on keyframes.) Once you learn how to use code hints, you'll find the correct script elements with little effort.

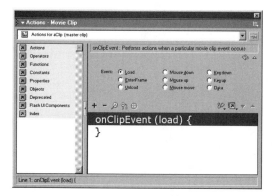

Figure 1.6   *Normal Mode provides a list of options (as does the new code hints feature).*

Always Movie Clips

Every time you create a symbol, you have a choice between Movie Clip, Button, or Graphic behavior. Selecting the Button symbol is often convenient because an instance automatically causes the cursor to change to a "finger" (for the user), and the symbol has provisions for various visual states plus a "hit" state. Buttons are great when you need buttons.

The choice between the Graphic and Movie Clip symbols isn't as clear. I used to believe, incorrectly, that Graphic symbols were appropriate for static graphics and Movie Clips for multi-frame clips. However, a Graphic symbol should be used in one of only three cases: when you're creating a multi-frame clip that you want locked to its parent timeline (so that you can scrub—by dragging the red current frame marker—to preview its behavior); when you're planning to take advantage of one of the special loop settings available only to Graphic symbols (See Figure 1.7); or when you want Flash to stream the contents of the Graphic symbol (instead of loading all frames before proceeding the way Movie Clips do).

Basically, if those cases don't exist, use Movie Clips. Only Movie Clip and button instances can be named, which means that only they can be addressed to have their properties changed or ascertained. (You must know the name of a clip to address it, after all.) There are other features of clip instances—just remember the cool stuff that can be done only with clip instances. Now that Flash MX lets you name button instances (and, for that matter, text objects), many of the ways that you can affect a clip instance now also apply to buttons. In practice, however, the fact that Movie Clips can now perform button-related tasks (such as use mouse events and the hand cursor), there are even fewer reasons to use buttons.

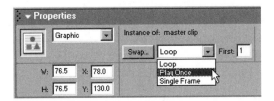

Figure 1.7 *Use a Graphic symbol only when you need to preview in the timeline or use one of the Loop options found in the Properties panel.*

Nested Movie Clips not only have the ability to be addressed, but they almost always contribute less to filesize. A simple test in which you compare nesting Graphic symbols inside Graphic symbols to clips inside of clips will show a dramatic filesize difference. To offer a bit of balance, nested Graphic symbols will tend to perform slightly better (and stream differently), although this is usually of negligible benefit compared to the filesize bloat they cause.

Realize that the behavior you select when you make the symbol or if you change a Library symbol's properties later will affect only the default behavior for created instances. By using the Properties panel, you can change a particular instance's behavior, as shown in Figure 1.8. A symbol that was originally a button can "act" like a Movie Clip, for example. Changing an instance's behavior makes that instance perform as selected—the only difference is that the original symbol (and subsequent instances) might have a different default behavior.

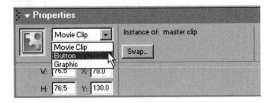

Figure 1.8 *You can change the behavior of any instance on the Stage through the Properties panel.*

Coordinate System

On the Stage, Flash considers the x and y coordinates to begin at the top-left corner. The x coordinate increases as you move to the right. The y coordinate increases as you move down. This might be familiar to you, and you just accept that "0, 0" is the top-left corner. In the case of clip instances, position is based on the center registration point of that clip. If you use `someClip._x=100`, the clip will move so that its center appears at position 100x. Whenever you're inspecting the coordinates of clips on the Stage, use the Info panel and be sure to click the center box, as shown in Figure 1.9 (so that you're not viewing the top-left corner of the clip). (By the way, the coordinates that appear in the Properties panel reflect either the center point or the top-left corner, depending on the current setting in the Info panel.)

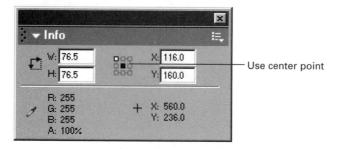

Figure 1.9   *The center option on the Info panel reflects the location a clip will move to when using ActionScript.*

Similarly, when you are inside a clip, "0, 0" is the center of the clip, as shown in Figure 1.10. The best way to understand coordinates is to select View, Rulers and edit a symbol by double-clicking the symbol item in the Library.

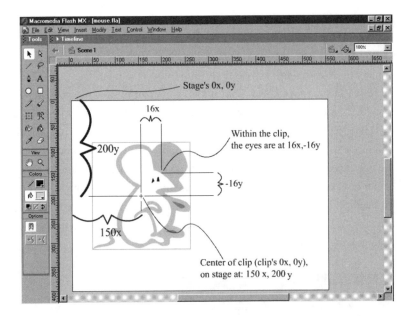

Figure 1.10   *The position of objects on the Stage is based on the top-left corner being 0x, 0y. Within Movie Clips, objects are based on the center being 0x, 0y.*

Tricks of the Trade

As I mentioned, Flash-heads tend to be strange characters. Perhaps they've turned out that way while developing creative and resourceful solutions to control Flash. Some of the tips that I'm about to disclose might seem wacky on first look, but they're all very useful.

Invisible Buttons

Buttons are cool because you can automatically create an Over-and Down-state. However, they also offer something else: access to mouse events. There are situations when you want or need access to a mouse event (such as Roll Over, for example), but you don't need or want all the pretty graphic features of a button. (Chapter 3, "The Programmer's Approach," discusses the value of code-data separation—that is, separating the generic programming code from the specific graphic content so that you can easily extract the programming and use it again with different content.) An invisible button is perfect for this. What is an invisible button? Simple: a button that has no graphic contents except a shape in its hit state (see Figure 1.11). I don't know how many times I've drawn a shape, converted it to a button symbol, and then double-clicked the button instance to edit its contents by dragging the first frame to the Hit-state—but it's a lot of times! The coolest part of invisible buttons is that Flash will display (while authoring) a semi-transparent cyan shape, so it's easy to position the button.

Figure 1.11   *An invisible button is simply a button with graphics in the Hit-state only.*

Let me give you a couple examples of when an invisible button might be useful. Say you have several words that you intend to act as clickable buttons. It might seem easiest to have a separate button for each word, whereas nesting the text inside the button would be clumsy. Each word would be a separate button, editing the words would require going into the button, and each one would need a hit state that's larger than the word (or they would be hard for the user to click). Compare this to having several instances of an invisible button that contains a rectangle in its Hit-state. All the text can be in the main timeline where it's easy to edit, you can resize the invisible buttons as needed, and overall it will be easier to maintain.

You also can use invisible buttons in conjunction with clip instances. I often find that a button with just an Over-and Down-state isn't enough; sometimes a "selected" state is necessary to show the user which buttons have been selected. One Movie Clip could contain different frames for Up, Over, and Down (similar to a button). Additionally, the clip could contain graphics to communicate "selected" (perhaps a checkmark). Just place an invisible button in the clip (or on top of the clip), and by jumping to the appropriate frames within the clip, you can make a much more sophisticated button.

I can think of many more times when invisible buttons would be useful. Any time that you simply want something "clickable" but don't want to put all the graphic content inside a button, invisible buttons can help.

Empty Movie Clips

Similar to the reasons for invisible buttons, empty Movie Clips are useful when you want to take advantage of some benefit of a Movie Clip but don't have a need or desire for any graphics. A Movie Clip can do "Movie Clip things," regardless of whether the clip has any graphic contents. You can put extra frames and keyframes within an empty clip to write scripts; you can attach scripts to instances of empty Movie Clips; you can even give names to empty clip

instances so that they can be addressed. And now Flash MX enables you to create empty clip instances entirely in script (that is, never dragging from the Library). The easiest way to create an empty Movie Clip is to select Insert, New Symbol; name it; and click OK. When you're taken inside the clip to edit its contents, simply return to your main scene. The trick to remember is that you'll need to drag an instance of this empty clip from the Library window. Unlike invisible buttons, empty Movie Clips are displayed as a white dot while you are authoring (see Figure 1.12).

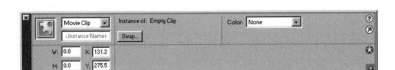

Figure 1.12 *Empty Movie Clips appear as a small white dot when on stage.*

Perhaps even more common than empty Movie Clips are Movie Clips that have contents in all their frames *except* the first frame. While you are authoring, such a clip appears as an empty Movie Clip; that is, as a white dot. (Actually, because the dot is so cryptic, I often place *something* in the first frame of every clip—I just move it off the Stage so that the user won't ever see it, but I'll be able to easily grab it while authoring.) There are situations in which you don't want to display the contents of a clip until a certain event occurs. Just create a blank keyframe in the first frame of the clip with a `stop()` script. Then, perhaps when the user clicks the correct button, you can use a script such as `_root.clipInstanceName.play()`, which causes the instance (called "clipInstanceName" in this case) to play. You'll see exactly how this works in more detail in Chapter 4, but you should have an idea how such clips can be used.

Empty Layers and Keyframes

A really great technique is to create an extra layer for no other purpose than to contain blank keyframes. These keyframes are strategically placed wherever you want a label or script. You could actually have one layer for all your keyframe scripts and another for all your labels. It's nice to separate these keyframes from your graphics (and tweens) because they won't disrupt anything visual. For example, if you want a keyframe script that stops your animation right in the middle of a tween, inserting a keyframe script on the same layer as the tween will disturb your tween. Instead of only two keyframes (one at the beginning and one at the end), you'll have three keyframes. If, later in the project, you want to move the middle keyframe (where the stop occurs), you can't do it without changing the tween. Putting a stop script on a dedicated script layer solves this problem. Figure 1.13 shows a real project with separate layers for scripts and labels.

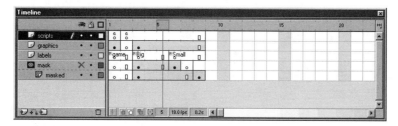

Figure 1.13   *A typical project's timeline will include layers that contain only labels and scripts.*

I have another trick that combines layers with empty Movie Clips. Empty clips are difficult to select because you need to grab a tiny white circle (refer to Figure 1.12). If you have several empty clips near each other, it can be impossible to select the correct one. To keep things organized, I often create a new layer for each empty clip (or group of clips). Because I know that when I click the layer in the timeline it will select all the contents of that layer on the Stage, I can quickly determine which empty clip is which by clicking the layer that I've named to match the clip. The nice thing about layers is that they don't add to the exported .swf's filesize.

You'll find many more tips and tricks throughout this book. However, I expect the tricks I've shown so far are familiar, if not "old hat," to you. At least make sure that you understand how they work and why they're helpful.

Summary

Depending on your past experience, this chapter was either a review, all new, or a mix thereof. In any case, this is the starting point from which we will program advanced Flash scripts. It's fair to assume that you know how to draw and animate in Flash. However, I think this chapter was a good way to get everyone oriented. If some of the material was new to you, that's fine. If it's all new to you, I suggest that you first read a basic Flash MX book, such as *Sams Teach Yourself Macromedia Flash MX in 24 Hours*, which I wrote before this book.

The critical concepts that you really must understand to get the most out of this book include timeline hierarchies (nested clips), addressing (or "targeting"), script locations (keyframes, button instances, and clip instances), and the coordinate system. In the "Tricks of the Trade" section, you learned helpful (but not required) information about making invisible buttons and empty Movie Clips. Additionally, a method to use a whole layer for keyframes containing scripts or labels was discussed.

{ Chapter 2 }

What's New in Flash MX

This chapter would have been easier to write if I had called it "What's Not New in Flash MX." The Flash MX upgrade is huge! I can't cover everything that's new, of course, but this chapter covers the main highlights of Flash MX and provides a course outline for the rest of the book. That is, I'll cover as much as I can, but most topics will be introduced only, with references to upcoming chapters that cover them in full.

Although I don't recommend skipping any chapter (this book does follow a sequence), you certainly should read the last section in this chapter, "Book Conventions and Expectations." It discusses how to get the most out this book as well some tricks to help you learn programming.

In this chapter, you'll learn:

- The most significant product enhancements.
- How the programming language has been improved.
- How to use this book.

I've actually saved this chapter to write last. This way, I know which topics are covered, where they're covered, and how. If you like to know where you're headed, this chapter should be revealing. It turns out the first section, "General Enhancements," has little to do with scripting, so I've kept it brief. You can pick

up some tips and ideas in this section. The second section, "Programming
Enhancements," introduces topics that we'll revisit throughout the book. Let's
start with a quick rundown of the "non-programming" enhancements.

General Enhancements

In my opinion, the "killer feature" of Flash MX isn't actually video; it's work-
flow. Nearly every nook and cranny has some touch-up to usability. Small, subtle
features are scattered around, but they result in improvements to productivity. In
Flash 5, for example, when you select a fill color and then select an already filled
shape, the Fill Color tool loses the color you selected. What if you want to *use*
that color? That task is simple in Flash MX, which includes a ton of tiny such
changes. I used to like to make fun of the peculiar quirks in Flash, but frankly,
I'm running out of comedy material.

Video

Like I said, video might not be the "killer feature," but it's still pretty killer. You
can import and compress videos of nearly any source data type by using
Sorenson Spark (a compression technology built into Flash with matching
decompression capabilities in the Macromedia Flash Player 6). Basically, this
means that you can import video, set the best compression balance of filesize
and quality, and then use the video as though it were any other Library symbol.

It's usually best to place your videos inside a Movie Clip. You can then mask the
Movie Clip to reveal only parts of the video frame. Also, because videos are
synchronized to their timeline (the way multiple-frame graphic symbols are), you
can end up with long timelines.

Really, to get the most out of video in Flash, you need to understand the rules
that apply to compression. Start with the best quality video footage as possible;
when selecting compression options, consider the nature of your content; and
realize the trade-offs between quality and filesize (such as high frame rates,
which result in larger files). A third-party product is available, called Sorenson
Squeeze, which, like Flash, uses Spark to compress videos. Sorenson Squeeze
offers other better-quality compression settings and features, including batch pro-
cessing (which compresses several files in sequence rather than individually).

Finally (and I really wish I could explore this topic fully), Macromedia has server products in development that—through the Flash Player 6—will allow two-way communications, including voice, video, and shared data between multiple users. Now that might really be the "killer feature." (Alas, you won't hear any more about those products specifically in this book.)

Workspace

Even though the subtle features are what really enhance your productivity, the obvious changes in Flash's interface are what you notice first. Flash MX's entire screen is cleaner because panels are snapped into panes, where they can take up the most screen space without overlapping other panels. Even if you undock a panel to make It float, other panels docked with a floating panel will expand to fill the space efficiently. Ultimately, though, the panels are less cumbersome because there are fewer of them. Less clutter is a good thing.

The newly added Properties panel takes the place of 12 panels that have either been removed or replaced because the Properties panel contains so much information. Gone are the panels for Character, Paragraph, Text Options, Stroke, Fill, Instance, Effect, Frame, and Sound. How can the Properties panel replace all those panels? Simple: It changes to reflect the properties of whatever you have selected. I don't need to walk through how this works—it's very intuitive. I'm sure you'll keep the Properties panel open most of the time.

I have only a few tips for the new panel design (including the Properties panel). Realize that some panels have expand/collapse arrows so some parts can be hidden from you. Also, be sure to play with all the organization options: the "gripper" area (to dock panels), the minimize/maximize arrow (in the panel's title), and the super-mini "window shade" mode (which appears when you double-click the title bar on a floating panel). You can also save panel layouts, like you could in Flash 5.

There are plenty of other interface changes. A really big one that is the timeline now has folder layers into which you can nest multiple layers. The cool thing here is that making a folder invisible or visible affects all the nested layers. Related to layers is the Distribute to Layers command under the Modify menu. When you combine that feature with the new way a block of text breaks into individual characters (the first time you select Modify, Break Apart), you can quickly make sophisticated animations.

Shared Libraries

If you thought shared libraries were half-baked in Flash 5, you really ought to give them another try. The entire feature has been overhauled, making it easier to understand and to use.

There are two confusingly similar features: runtime sharing and authortime sharing. Runtime sharing involves storing symbols in a source movie (that gets exported to an .swf), and then giving many other movies access to the media in that shared file. Shared libraries have worked this way since version 5. Now, however, you have a couple of extra options, including the decision of whether or not the shared item must download completely before the first frame appears (an old requirement that made the user sit through downloading all shared items even if the items weren't needed right away).

Authortime sharing is similar in that you have one source movie with shared symbols, but at the time a movie using the shared items gets exported, those items are copied into the user movie. This isn't quite as efficient because you have to re-export all user movies after you edit the shared item. There are no complex download issues, however.

{ Note }

Authortime sharing is really quite useful and a vast improvement over Flash 5. All you do is create a symbol in one movie, save that movie, and then either copy and paste that symbol or drag it into a new movie. Then, in the new movie, you can select Properties for the duplicate symbol in the Library (from the options menu). In the "Advanced" section of the Properties dialog box, you should see that the Source section provides a way for you to automatically re-import (that is, "update") the symbol every time you publish or test the movie (see Figure 2.1). You'll find additional options to "link" to other symbols in other source .fla files. Just remember it's only linked while authoring; once you publish, all symbols are embedded as though you copied and pasted.

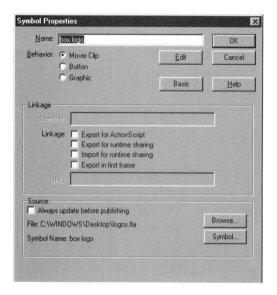

Figure 2.1   *The new Advanced Symbol Properties dialog includes options for authortime sharing*

{ Note }

Another feature (that works regardless of the authortime sharing feature) is the way duplicate symbols are handled. Actually, because each symbol must have a unique name, you can't have duplicates. Now in Flash MX, however, when you paste a symbol that matches the name of one already in your movie, you're given the option to either replace or keep the original (just like what happens when you copy a same-named file into a folder on your computer). This is one of those small touches that makes Flash MX so much more usable than Flash 5.

The bottom line is that shared library items (and, for that matter, the new template feature) are worth learning because they will make you more productive.

Ready-Made Components

Components replace the old Smart Clip feature. The components that ship with Flash MX include interface widgets, such as buttons and drop-down menus. A second set has shipped (since Flash was released), and I suspect many more are to come. You'll learn how to make your own components in Chapter 15, "Components." One of my favorite new ones is "Tree," a hierarchical-view component that makes a folder-selection interface a snap (see Figure 2.2).

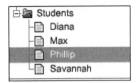

Figure 2.2 *The Tree component (downloaded for free from Macromedia Exchange)
helps you create graphical views of complex, nested data.*

My natural tendency is to suggest that you try only to learn from the built-in
components (as source files are available). However, because they're so well
made and useful, I'd say to go ahead and use them in your projects. You can still
snoop through the source files to see how they tick. I'd never criticize something
that works—and these work great. There are many additions to the ActionScript
language, especially for making components. This means that not only will you
see some cool components that others make, but you'll be able to make your own
as well.

Flash Player Performance

The performance of the Flash Player has been improved in several ways. First,
operations involving strings and XML data are much faster because all the code
was re-written in a low-level language (whereas scripting languages are considered to be "high-level"—like you're at a higher level than the computer).
Anyway, there is always more than one way to solve a programming task. In past
versions of Flash, you often could see a huge performance difference, depending
on which solution you used. People would often test different solutions to see
which was the fastest. Although you might still see a few milliseconds difference
between the available options for some string operations, there are no longer
extreme cases.

Another improvement is in the compressed size of your .swf files. Under the
Flash tab in Publish Settings, you'll see an option for "Compress Movie" when
you export as Flash Player 6. This applies compression to your scripts (but only
the Flash Player version 6 can uncompress them). Movies with a ton of scripts
export to much smaller .swfs.

Although Flash MX has a ton of other new features, I think all of these are interesting because they save you time. As you may or may not know, one of the
ultimate ways to save time is to program solutions that would otherwise take a
great deal of effort to create. That's really what this book is about, so let's take
a tour of the features for programmers.

Features for Programmers

The vast majority of the new features in Flash MX are geared towards programmers (lucky us!). Not only are there countless additions to the programming language itself, the improvements to the interface make programming easier. Sure, creating a complex web site using components is a snap, but that's not what I mean when I say programming is easier. Complex programming is still complex, but the new features mean that you'll spend less time creating workarounds or fixing stupid mistakes. For example, you can now set the Actions panel preferences to any font, whereas before the font made a "0" look nearly the same as "()"—and the font was so small that you couldn't tell the difference. There are a ton of things like this, but I'll try to stick to the biggies.

Revised Actions Panel

All scripting gets typed into the Actions panel. Anything that saves you time while editing scripts is a good thing. Even after you become a proficient programmer, it's likely that you won't be able to just type in some code and see it work. The process involves constant refining—either to fix bugs or to add features. The last thing you need is stupid mistakes like typos and improper syntax. The features in the Actions panel should help reduce errors.

Code Hints and Auto Completion

Code hints and Auto Completion are probably my favorite features in Flash MX because they help you every time you script. As soon as you start to type a recognizable word from the ActionScript language, a tooltip appears with the proper syntax to guide you along (see Figure 2.3). Code hints are almost like quickly referencing the help files automatically while you type.

```
my_mc.attachMovie("symbolID",
```
`MovieClip.attachMovie( idName, newName, depth [, initObject] )`

Figure 2.3   *Code hints pop up as you type to guide you along.*

Auto Completion is similar to code hints. A host of properties and methods are made for any given object type. (Don't worry if you don't recognize every vocabulary word in that last sentence; you'll learn them all soon enough.) For example, a Movie Clip instance has a `gotoAndStop()` method that causes a clip to jump to a particular frame. When you type "my_mc.", you'll see a list appear as soon as you type the period (see Figure 2.4). You just select the gotoAndStop method, and Flash automatically completes the code for you. (Actually, the code hint for gotoAndStop() appears to help you further.) To see this for yourself, select a frame in the timeline, open the Actions panel (F9), make sure the Actions panel is in Expert Mode (Ctrl+Shift+E), and then type my_mc. The list appears from which you can select gotoAndStop. All you have to do is to memorize the designated suffixes that Flash uses. (Movie Clip instances use the _mc suffix.) I'll be sure to use the default suffixes throughout the book as new object types are introduced—but as you'll see next, you can change the "recommended" suffixes to whatever you prefer.

Figure 2.4 *The Auto Completion feature provides a list of appropriate options once it can determine the context of your script.*

Extensible Configuration

I think the easiest misconception about the Actions panel is that it represents the entire ActionScript language. In fact, the entire contents of the Actions panel are extensible. For example, if you want to change the suffix that triggers the Auto Completion for Movie Clip from _mc to _movie, you can edit an XML text file called "AsCodeHints.xml" that was installed on your computer when you installed Flash MX. You'll need to know how and where, of course (and I'll show that shortly).

You can customize more than just the Auto Completion rules. A bunch of other parts can be adjusted to fit your work-style. The Actions panel has a "toolbox" list on the left. Well, the folders, organization of those folders, and the contents of the folders can all be edited or added to. Code hints for any element, including things you add, can be edited. Finally, you can change the words that automatically change color as part of Flash's "Syntax Coloring" feature to whatever you want.

Without fully documenting every detail of how to make adjustments, let me start you in the right direction and give you a few pointers. First, the actual location for these configuration files varies based on operating system. Just look in the Configuration folder (adjacent to your installed version of Flash MX) to find the "Readme" file, which explains where to find the *other* Configuration folder. Anyway, once you find the right Configuration folder, there's a folder called ActionsPanel, inside of which you'll find several XML files—these are the ones to edit. Naturally, you really should keep a backup of these files before you edit them, but Flash is smart enough to restore the default set if they are missing. (This is not true for the files inside the "Custom Actions" subfolder, which are created when you install new components—so don't remove them.) To get an idea how you can change the Auto Completion feature, open the file AsCodeHints.xml using a text editor. Scroll to the end and you'll see several lines that all begin "<typeinfo" (see Figure 2.5). You should see the pattern matches that trigger Movie Clip methods (*_mc), arrays (*_array), and so on. You can change *_mc to read *_movie, if you like. Then, any time that you end a Movie Clip instance name with _movie, you'll see the automatic completion list appear (as soon as you type a period).

```
<typeinfo pattern="*_mc" object="MovieClip" />
<typeinfo pattern="*_array" object="Array" />
<typeinfo pattern="*_str" object="String" />
<typeinfo pattern="*_btn" object="Button" />
<typeinfo pattern="*_txt" object="TextField" />
<typeinfo pattern="*_fmt" object="TextFormat" />
<typeinfo pattern="*_date" object="Date" />
<typeinfo pattern="*_sound" object="Sound" />
<typeinfo pattern="*_xml" object="XML" />
<typeinfo pattern="*_xmlsocket" object="XMLSocket" />
<typeinfo pattern="*_color" object="Color" />
<typeinfo pattern="_level*" object="MovieClip" />
<typeinfo pattern="_parent" object="MovieClip" />
<typeinfo pattern="_root" object="MovieClip" />
</codehints>
```

Figure 2.5   *At the end of the AsCodeHints.xml file, you'll see all the default suffixes (where you can optionally edit them).*

Obviously, there are more details to the configuration files. For example, you can see that the "ActionsPanel.xml" file (in which you can change the contents of folders that appear in the Actions panel toolbox area) is a much more complex file. Generally, though, I've found that you can edit or supplement any of these files by modeling after what's already in the file. In the case of the ActionsPanel.xml file, you can copy an entire "folder" or a single "action" node, and then make edits to the properties name, tiptext, and text. However, if you create any new entries, remove the properties for `helpid` and `quickkey` so that your additions don't conflict with other elements. All of this makes more sense if you understand the XML data structure (which is covered in Chapter 16, "Interfacing with External Data"). To give you a practical example, the following is a line of text that I inserted between lines 783 and 784 of the ActionsPanel.xml file:

```
<string name="allowDomain" tiptext="Allows another domain to load
➥this movie" text="System.security.allowDomain()" version="6" />
```

All I did was to copy line 783, remove the references to `helpid` and `quickkey`, and then make a few edits. Now, whenever I begin by typing "System.", the Auto Completion dialog box appears, and I can even find `allowDomain` in the Actions panel under Objects, Movie, System. Basically, `allowDomain` is a feature in ActionScript that wasn't included in the Actions panel—so I added it to mine. (By the way, you'll hear more about allowDomain later in this chapter, and in Chapter 7, "The Movie Clip Object," you'll see how it works.)

Presumably, Macromedia will fully document the format of these configuration files—but they're not too difficult to deconstruct. Realize, too, that I've mentioned only one rather involved extensibility feature. There are other very powerful, yet approachable, options for the Actions panel. Specifically, check out all the Preferences and Auto Format Options found under the Actions panel's options menu (see Figure 2.6).

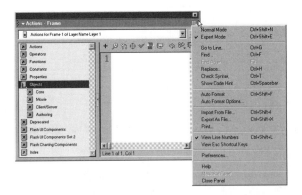

Figure 2.6   *There are many other nice options available from the Actions panel's options menu. (Click where the pointer is shown.)*

A True Debugger

Although Flash 5's Debugger was quite useful, it wasn't really a "debugger." I'd call it a "watcher" or an "inspector." Flash MX has a *true* debugger. If you're having trouble with your code (and, I'm sorry, you will—everyone does), you can set breakpoints (that cause the file you're testing to pause) and then step through the code one line at a time to investigate (and solve) the problem. The Flash MX Debugger not only has more features than the Flash 5 Debugger, it was redesigned and makes more sense. In addition, the remote debugging option is well thought out and very usable. You'll learn much more about the Debugger in Chapter 6, "Debugging."

New Objects

In programming, *objects* are sets of related features that all follow consistent rules. Sometimes objects relate to something onscreen (such as the Movie Clip object), and sometimes they're more ephemeral (such as the Sound object). Anyway, there are a bunch of new ones in Flash MX. Let me run down a few of the more significant objects and tell you how they will affect your life.

Not only do instances of buttons and text onscreen now have instance names (such as "Movie Clips"), they have most of the same properties. For example, you can set a button's position onscreen using script (whereas in the past only Movie Clip instances could be affected in this way). And just like there's a Movie Clip object, there are Button and TextField objects as well. (Note that Static text is excluded—only Dynamic Text and Input Text are instances of the TextField object.)

Whereas clips, buttons, and text are pretty concrete, the new TextFormat object is not. Basically, the TextFormat object is a pretty powerful way to store detailed formatting information. You'll need to *apply* it to onscreen text, however, to see anything. You'll see how it works with the TextField object in Chapter 10, "Keyboard Access and Modifying Onscreen Text."

Another new object, called LoadVars, effectively replaces both the Movie Clip method `loadVariables()` and the confusingly similar `loadVariables()` function. The benefit to using the LoadVars object is that you can now determine how much data has loaded and even automatically trigger a function when all data has loaded. You'll learn about LoadVars in Chapter 16.

The Stage object gives you a way to both gain information about a movie's set-tings (its dimensions, for example) as well as to monitor whether the Stage size is changing. Once you learn about "listeners" (in Chapter 10), you'll be able to figure out the Stage object. You'll also see some applications of this feature in Workshop Chapter 13, "Drawing Graphs."

Finally, although I don't want to go into detail here, let me mention that the whole object-oriented design of ActionScript has been revisited and improved. One big enhancement is that you can create your own classes based on the built-in Movie Clip object. Specifically, you can make your own Movie Clip that inherits all the basic features of regular clips and then adds more homemade properties and methods. It's not as though you have to use this feature in every project (it can actually mean a lot of upfront planning), but in addition to making programming geeks happy, it means complex components can be mixed and matched and everything works without conflicts.

Understanding objects isn't terribly difficult; knowing how to apply them to your projects is a bit more work. You'll learn all about objects through this book—I promise. Just realize that they don't have to be difficult to use (I promise that, too).

Runtime Drawing

Flash MX adds the ability to draw lines, curves, and solid, radial, or linear fills. When you see how, it might appear like a ton of programming that's good only for drawing primitive shapes or really cheesy gradients. In nearly every case, it will seem easier to just draw the graphic by hand. However, the power of runtime drawing is that it happens at runtime, so it can be based on timely information or specific preferences of the user. In Workshop Chapter 13, for example, you'll see how to draw customized graphs for the user. Basically, instead of manually draw-ing every permutation of possible results (ahead of time), you can create draw-ings dynamically.

Major Changes to ActionScript Events

Obviously, we've already seen many major changes. The following section will quickly look at major changes to the way scripts can respond to various events. The idea of an event driven-language such as ActionScript is that scripts are writ-ten to respond to specific events (the user clicking a button, for example). Flash MX offers additional ways for your scripts to tap in to those events.

Callback Functions

Callback functions are a new way for you to define which scripts should execute when a particular event occurs. You can still use the old (and perhaps more intuitive) way of placing code right on a button. For example, you can type the following code into the Actions panel while a button instance is selected:

```
on(press){
  play();
}
```

This translates to, "On the event that the button is pressed, do the script `play()`." Actually, you could even write the preceding script in one line, as follows:

```
on(press){play();}
```

It's the same thing. It turns out that a named instance of a button also has an `onPress` event to which you can assign a function. For example, if your button instance is named `my_btn` (the default Auto Completion suffix for buttons is `_btn`), you can use the following code in a keyframe (in the timeline where the button is present):

```
my_btn.onPress=function(){play();}
```

It looks sort of the same as our one-liner in the preceding example, and the effect is the same. We'll cover all the syntax details later, but for now, just consider why this might be useful. The first benefit I see is that all the code can be consolidated in one place—a keyframe—instead of being scattered all over on separate button instances. Another benefit is that you can change the `onPress` event to trigger a different function later. For example, if you later execute the script `my_button.onPress=function(){stop();}`, the same button will now make the movie stop (rather than play). Again, we'll go over all the details, but I've found this new way of writing scripts in a keyframe instead of on separate instances to be very addictive.

Listeners

Listeners are confusingly similar to callback functions because they also enable you to define which scripts are to occur when certain events happen. However, listeners are easier to mix and match because you can have several different scripts all listening for the same event. In the preceding example using the `onPress` event, we could have only one callback function defined at a time. Assigning a new callback function would erase the old one. With listeners, it's cumulative; you can add or remove listeners at will.

Now, one tricky limit is that not all events can be "listened" for. That is, my comparison to onPress isn't totally fair because an onPress listener is not available. (It's still a good example, though.) You'll find that there are only a few listeners available for any particular object. Perhaps the easiest one to understand is the onChanged listener for the TextField object. It enables you to trigger a script any time the contents of a specified text field change. Say you have an input field into which you want users to type a number. You can add a listener that executes a script every time they type into the field. Perhaps you want to determine whether the value is too high or too low. You can later remove this listener or add another—perhaps one that checks whether users actually typed a number. Although there are other ways to restrict what users type, listeners are a convenient way to automatically trigger scripts at the right time. You'll learn more about listeners in Chapter 10.

Watchers

Callback functions and listeners give you a way to trigger scripts any time an event occurs. In comparison, watchers let you trigger scripts any time a specified variable changes. *Variables* are just a way for you to store information for later retrieval. For example, you might have a username variable that contains the current user's name (the name typed in, that is). Maybe you have a million different places in your movie where the username variable can be changed. It's very simple to add a script that effectively says, "Any time the username variable changes, I want you to do these things." Naturally, you'll need to learn the details of exactly *how* this works—and you will in Chapter 14, "Extending ActionScript."

Timing Controls

Even though ActionScript is an event-driven language, you can still write scripts that appear to trigger automatically instead of waiting for a particular event. Really, the best way to think of this is that the passing of time is really an event. Each time the second hand on the clock ticks is an event. With Flash, you can actually write scripts that get triggered more frequently than that.

SetInterval

In Flash 5, you could trigger a script every enterFrame, meaning that if the frame rate was 12 frames-per-second, the script would execute every 1/12 of a second. It was kind of a pain because you always needed a Movie Clip instance on which to attach such a script. In addition, you were always limited by the movie's frame rate, which should always be kept at a reasonable level. Anyway, the new `setInterval()` and `clearInterval()` functions enable you to indicate a script that you want to trigger automatically as frequently as you specify. We'll get into the syntax later, but you can just type the following script into a keyframe, and provided that you have a clip on the Stage with the instance name "clip," you'll see it move to the right every second:

```
setInterval(function(){clip._x+=20},1000);
```

The first parameter is the script that you want to execute (here, a script that increases the clip's _x property by `10`), and the second parameter is the interval (in milliseconds) between each execution. If you change the `1000` to `100`, it will move every 100 milliseconds. (That's 1/10 of a second.) You'll learn more about the `setInterval()` function in Chapter 14.

{ Note }

It might seem as though most of the cool stuff doesn't come up until later chapters. That's only partially true. First of all, there's plenty of new stuff in every chapter. Ultimately, though, to really exploit the timing features, watchers, listeners, and callback functions (not to mention objects), you really need a solid foundation of the basics. This is not one of those deals where you must first pay the price of long, hard work. It's more like this: Once you get the basic idea, you'll be able to apply the same techniques to many concepts. That is, it's super consistent, so you'll reach a point where things start to really make sense.

Sound Duration and Position, and the `onComplete` Event

Three new features of the Sound object make it much more usable than before. Specifically, you can access any sound's total duration and current position, which simplifies tasks such as displaying the visual progress of a sound. Of course, if you continually check to see if the current position is equal to the total duration, you'll know the sound has finished. However, there's an even better way: the `onComplete` event. That is, you can define a script to execute the instant a particular sound finishes playing. These are great additions.

Oh, and if you haven't heard, Flash MX lets you load external .MP3 audio files! This means that your movies can remain small and load sounds only when the user requests.

Web-Specific Features

I suppose nearly everything is web-specific in Flash. It's just that a few new ActionScript features are particularly web-centric.

`allowDomain` Method

There are a few objects that I didn't mention earlier—specifically, the System object. The current documentation doesn't reveal a whole lot here, but within the System object is a method called `allowDomain()`. This particular method overcomes an old security limitation in Flash that made it impossible to load movies that reside on other web domains. In Chapter 7, you'll see how it works.

Local SharedObject

Simply put, local SharedObjects are like cookies—but much more. Now it's simple to store data on the users' computers so that the next time they visit your site you can "remember" anything you bothered to save. For example, you can save their preferences. Perhaps you let them select a background color for your Flash movie and you want it to restore when they come back. Or, you can track the "history" of which parts of your site they've visited. That way, you can show them an introductory animation just once. Subsequent visits will bypass the animation. The coolest part is that the data stored remains in its original data type. You don't have to convert string data (the way you do with nearly every other option). You'll learn about SharedObjects first in Chapter 16, "Interfacing with External Data," and then revisit them in Workshop Chapter 17, "Using the LocalConnection Object for Inter-Movie Communication."

Local Connection

The LocalConnection object gives you an easy way to let one movie trigger scripts in another movie. For example, your web site can include two Flash movies in different cells of a table, and those two movies can communicate. Even if one Flash movie pops up in a separate window, it can send data to another window. This feature will blow your mind! Whenever I demonstrate just a simple example of using the mouse to drag a box in one movie and having another movie's box move at the same time, the audience goes wild. You'll learn all about the LocalConnection object in Chapter 16.

Book Conventions and Expectations

It might seem weird to put this information at the end of Chapter 2, but this is more than just a legend explaining the icons used in this book. Think of this section as "what's new in this edition." Chapter 3, "The Programmer's Approach"—the first "real" chapter—is where we really start rolling.

New for MX

A "New to MX" icon will appear any time a new Flash MX feature is discussed (see Figure 2.7). This icon will be most interesting to those of you who've used Flash 5. You should see a lot of those icons when you flip through the book! The thing is, I didn't include the icon for *everything*. This entire chapter would be pretty messy if we had a million such icons—so we left them out. Anyway, you'll see the icon for the major changes.

Figure 2.7   *Look for the "New to MX" icon to see features new to Flash MX.*

Handy-Dandy Formulas

I wrote this book as much for me as for everyone else. That is, I present the information in a way that I would like to see it. After the first edition of this book, I found myself bookmarking certain pages that contained formulas that I use frequently. For example, I can tell you the page where the formula to calculate the distance between two points appears in my old book.

Instead of making a separate index of such handy formulas, I call them out in the text. In most instances the formula is first derived, but if you want to come back to it later, it's nice to see it highlighted in some way. In addition, when you encounter a formula in the text, you should realize that it might be useful later.

Separating ActionScript from "PhillipScript" (and What's a "Foobar?")

One of the hardest things about learning a programming language when you look at examples is separating the elements that are part of the language from the homemade parts the programmer added. If you were learning English, for example, you might have a hard time with the sentence: "Phillip Kerman has a dog named Max." The names "Phillip," "Kerman," and "Max" are not really part of

English the same way the other words are. The same issues can come up in ActionScript. Nearly every line of code will have a mix of built-in elements and homemade pieces that the programmer added.

When you see script inside Flash, the Syntax Coloring feature helps by changing ActionScript elements to specific colors—but it can still be difficult (especially in a book). As much as possible, I prefix homemade names with "my" (for example, "mySound" or "myText"). The idea is that you will understand this is not some feature of Flash, but something I came up with when making the example. I'm sure you'll start to recognize what's homemade and what's part of the language, but I know (from experience) that it can be difficult at first.

{ Note }

Programmers often use the term "foobar" (or just "foo" and "bar") whenever they are trying show an example with absolutely no context. For example, if you were learning the form of a function, I might show you: `function goPlay(frame){}`. But there's no indication of what's part of the language and what's part of my example. To separate the form from the content, I could instead use `function foo(bar){}`, in which case you would know that only the word `function` is part of the language. I don't think you'll see "foobar" in this book, but it comes up in many programmers' examples. You may be interested in researching the history of "foobar" and its Army-speak ancestor, the crude acronym FUBAR. Although "foobar" is cleaned up for programming, it's utterly meaningless.

Prerequisites

Now I tell you about the prerequisites? Well, really, there aren't many. It's quite possible to go through this book and learn ActionScript without a base knowledge in Flash. It sure helps if you can build the basic framework of a Flash movie. Even more important is that you see the application for scripting. That is, if you know what's involved doing things by hand in Flash, you'll better appreciate how scripting makes things easier.

I see the ideal reader as someone who is familiar with drawing, animating, and structuring a Flash movie. You should be able to make nested Movie Clips and keep track of where you are (whether you're nested in a clip or in the main timeline, for example). You don't need to be a math wiz, but if you are, you might get bored with a few of my explanations. My goal is to turn Flash users into Flash programmers. I'm sure if you have the same intention, you'll do fine.

Summary

All this new stuff might appear to be overwhelming. Just remember that you can learn only one thing at a time. ActionScript really has never been more empowering. It's still work, but hopefully the way this book is presented will help things make sense and provide plenty of practical applications.

If you already have experience programming in Flash, you really should try to open up to some of the new techniques that are now possible. In a way, learning new things means breaking old habits, but I can assure you that every minute invested will pay back in hours of time saved.

In any event, you should see all these killer features not as "a ton of stuff to learn," but rather as a huge opportunity to reach a higher potential. I'm excited, partially because I'm nearly done writing the book, but mainly because I can see myself getting more efficient every time I script a project. It's true that you never stop learning!

{Chapter 3}

The Programmer's Approach

This chapter might appear to be the most ambiguous and vague in the book. However, it's probably the most valuable chapter because it can save you time. Effective programming requires you to have more than just brute force, math skills, and technical ability (which are all important); you must also be efficient. For any programming task, you can do it the hard way or you can do it the easy way. This chapter will help you find the easy way. I don't want to suggest that there are always shortcuts that make anything easy—only that avoiding overly complex solutions can save you a lot of grief.

This chapter explains conventional programming philosophies to help you:

- Write specifications.
- Prototype your creations quickly for initial review.
- Develop good style.
- Keep code and data separate.

Specification

It might sound cavalier, but after you finish a detailed specification, 95 percent of your work is through. When a client asks me whether something is possible, I always answer that if he can describe it in detail, I can program it. That's all a specification is—a detailed description of exactly how the Flash movie is to appear and perform. A good specification can take a lot of time and work, but when it's finished, it serves as the blueprint from which to work. It's like creating an outline for a term paper. After you know where you're headed, it's just a matter of filling in the outline.

One person's idea of the necessary level of detail might vary from another's. The more detail, however, the better. When you invest additional work upfront, it not only saves time down the road, but it reduces the chances of rework because everyone involved presumably reads the "spec" and raises necessary objections early. Another value of a specification is that it makes estimating the total cost easier because the task is clearer.

As you'll see in the following section on prototyping, the problem in writing a super-detailed specification is that you will fail to fully describe the final program because a written spec's form is different from the final media. That is, it's impossible to describe the colors in a painting using only words or the sound of a song without some kind of musical device—there's a translation error. This doesn't mean that you should just forgo the specification process entirely. Rather, just write enough detail to get rolling. In addition, be sure to leverage previous work of your own, and the work of others. For example, part of your specification might say that you're going to build something "like the project we did last year," but with these differences. Do whatever you need to make it clear. Include tables, figures, and pictures—whatever helps.

Writing specifications takes practice. An interesting exercise to improve your specification writing skills is to go back and look at any description or specification you were given early in a project that is now finished. Identify the types of details that were missing or would have helped were they given to you. Without providing a lesson on how to write specifications, let me just say that those details make a big difference.

Prototyping

A good specification makes you more efficient because it defines the course you'll take before you start. Even though this means that you want to wait to start programming, there is one type of programming that can start early, even while you write the specification: prototyping. A *prototype* is a quick and dirty sample that you create in Flash to get an idea of how the final project might look and feel. No matter how great a specification on paper might be, it will never compare to the real thing. It's sort of like learning to swim. You can read books, watch people swimming on television, even hang out at the pool—but eventually, you'll have to actually get in the water to swim! Prototypes are the best "simulation" of your final movie because they are produced in Flash.

One way to produce a great site involves first roughly defining the objectives and then starting the prototyping right away. You make a few quick prototypes and then analyze the results. Let everyone play with the prototypes so that they can get a feel for the direction the site is taking, and then go back to the drawing board and elaborate on your specification. This cyclical process (defining, prototyping, redefining, and so on) might seem slightly inefficient, but it usually results in a better end product.

If ever there were a place where being sloppy is okay, it is while prototyping. The goal of prototyping is to get something up and running quickly. The prototype doesn't have to be pretty. Check out Figure 3.1, for example, which shows an early prototype of part of a larger project.

Your prototypes will not only look rough, but you can allow the programming to slip a bit too. Let's look at a few prototyping techniques that—during any other stage of programming—could be considered bad style.

Figure 3.1 *A prototype doesn't have to be pretty—it just has to communicate the idea. You can even use a picture of your dog as a placeholder.*

Hard Wiring

Hard wiring is generally a big no-no. *Hard wiring* is using an explicit value instead of a variable or reference to other values. For example, imagine that your program is supposed to display the message "Welcome <User>," where "<User>" would be replaced by whatever name the user used when logging in. Instead of actually doing the work to display the user's name dynamically, you could hard wire the screen to read "Welcome Phillip," and then any time you demonstrate the prototype, you make sure to log in as "Phillip." Of course, if you logged in differently, the program would still display "Welcome Phillip," because it's hard wired. This is perfectly acceptable because likely everyone can just imagine how this will work in the final project. Sometimes you'll want your prototype to really do the work—especially if you're sending the prototype to a client who might not understand that it's just a prototype. Depending on who is judging the prototype, you can do more or less hard wiring as appropriate. Just remember the term "hard wiring" because in later chapters I'll refer to it as a bad thing. Ideally, everything is dynamic.

Pseudo-Code

Unlike hard wiring, pseudo-coding is always a good thing. The only problem is that you'll need to replace all your pseudo-code eventually. *Pseudo-coding* is the process of writing scripts using your own words, not the ActionScript language, as instructions. Then you can replace your completed pseudo-code with components of ActionScript. The truth is that really detailed and clear pseudo-code can be quickly and easily translated to functioning ActionScript. I often say that if you can pseudo-code well, you can get a monkey to clean it up ("cross all the *t*s and dot all the *i*s," as it were). You might find that you can clearly state what you want your interactive movie to do, but you need help from an experienced programmer to translate your pseudo-code. But the process of pseudo-coding actually makes you a better programmer by forcing you to sort out the details of the task you're solving.

Pseudo-code should be very detailed and written in clear English. That is, you want to say *everything* necessary, but you don't need to use any words from the ActionScript language. For example, imagine you plan to program a button that will convert a dollar amount from one field and display the equivalent value in Euros in another field. (By the way, the preceding description is suitable as part of a specification—it provides enough information to start programming.) The pseudo-code for such a button might look like this:

```
When user presses button
    dollars=text in field
    exchangeRate=.5
    euros=dollars multiplied by exchangeRate
    euros=euros rounded off to two decimal places
    put euros into another field
end
```

After you know a little bit of ActionScript, you can easily translate this pseudo-code into a working script. The first step, however, is to sort things out in your own words.

Good Style

If this chapter is ambiguous, this section is downright subjective. *Good style* means programming in a way that's easy to maintain. Your code should be easy enough for anyone to understand. Not because others need to see what you've programmed (which could happen), but so that you can quickly interpret what you've produced when you need to make adjustments or fix bugs. It's easy to get carried away trying to build something and ignore good housekeeping practices. Before you know it, your code resembles a plate of spaghetti (hence the term *spaghetti code*). In fact, haste makes waste, so you should always try to follow the rules of good style.

Even though the value of good style is easy to understand, the concept itself is subjective. Here are a few characteristics of good style; call them *rules*, if you will.

Less Is More

Consider that every line of code you read has to be translated in your mind. You have to figure out what it really means. The fewer lines you must read, the better. Generally, any time you can do something in fewer steps or less code, do it. It's almost never too late to use less code. For example, I often start programming and then come up with a better (more concise) solution while implementing the original idea. Even if it means going back and starting over, it's usually worth the resulting compact code. Compare the two code segments in Figures 3.2 and 3.3; both achieve the same effect, but the code in Figure 3.3 is much more concise.

```
on (release) {
  setProperty("highlight",_x, getProperty("highlight", _x)+10);
  tellTarget("highlight"){
    gotoAndStop(getProperty("",_currentframe)+1);
  }
}
```

Figure 3.2

```
on (release) {
  highlight._x+=10;
  highlight.nextFrame();
}
```

Figure 3.3   *The script in Figure 3.2 achieves the same effect as the script in Figure 3.3, but with unnecessary complexity.*

You can take this rule too far. The appeal of concise code should not outweigh legibility. You can easily get carried away and end up with code that you can't even read. I would never fault a finished piece of code that worked—so, really, that's the number one priority. Furthermore, you must be able to maintain your code. Remember to write code that you can read. For example, in Chapter 4, "Basic Programming in Flash," you'll learn that `count++;` is equivalent to `count=count+1;`. Although the latter takes more typing, it might be easier for you to read. By all means, use what you understand. If this occasionally means that your code is a little bit wordier, so be it. Take it one step at a time, and you should see your code shrinking in size.

Comments

Comments are lines of code that are ignored by Flash. Text preceded by `//` is ignored. Actually, if you start a block of text with `/*`, all lines are ignored until `*/` is reached. The idea is that you can write notes to yourself (or anyone reading your code) that explain—in normal English—what's going on in the code. Actually, you'll often find that comments help you discover bugs. You might see a comment that says `//loop through all the answers` and then notice that the code doesn't really do that!

I suppose that I'm a bad boy because I often don't fully comment my code until right after I get a program running. However, it's important for me not to delay this step because I will forget everything about the code days after writing it. Without comments, code is much more difficult to interpret. So, just take the time to comment your code, even if it's after you've finished and when the incentive to do so is reduced. Compare the uncommented code in Figure 3.4 to the same code with comments in Figure 3.5. Even though you might not understand the details of the code, if there were a problem, you could easily identify the portion containing the problem.

```
onClipEvent (keyUp) {
  if (Key.getAscii() == 13 || Key.getAscii() == 0){
    return;
  }
  if (Key.getAscii() == 8 ){
    if(cur.charAt(cur.length-2)==" "){
      _root.wordsThisTime--;
    }
    cur = cur.slice(0, cur.length-2)+mbchr(8);
    if(_root.wrongPlaces[_root.place-1] == "X"){
      _root.wrongPlaces.pop();
      _root.wrongs--;
    }
    _root.place>0 && _root.place--;
    return;
  }
}
```

Figure 3.4   *Code that has not been commented is difficult to understand.*

```
onClipEvent (keyUp) {
  //ignore these characters
  if (Key.getAscii() == 13 || Key.getAscii() == 0){
    return;
  }
  //if they click backspace
  if (Key.getAscii() == 8 ){
    //remove a blank space?
    if(cur.charAt(cur.length-2)==" "){
      _root.wordsThisTime--;
    }
    //remove the last character (but put a box at the end)
    cur = cur.slice(0, cur.length-2)+mbchr(8);
    //did they fix a mistake?
    if(_root.wrongPlaces[_root.place-1] == "X"){
      _root.wrongPlaces.pop();
      _root.wrongs--;
    }
    //set place one lower
    _root.place>0 && _root.place--;
    //and leave
    return;
  }
}
```

Figure 3.5   *A few comments can make things clearer, even if you don't understand the underlying code.*

Finally, comments are of great assistance while you create a prototype. Instead of building *everything,* you can just place a comment that says something such as //check their answers here, and then come back later to actually write the code that does. This technique also exposes errors in logic flow. Remember that specifying exactly what a Flash movie is supposed to do is most of the work. A comment can be a way of specifying the tasks that need to be implemented.

Magic Numbers, Constants, and Variables

A *magic number* is an explicit value used within a formula. For example, to calculate the page count for any chapter in this book, I use this formula: characters/1900=pages. I know there are approximately 1900 characters per printed page. Of course, if the margins or page size were different, I'd have to use a different magic number than 1900 in my formula. An example of a constant is pi. To calculate the area of a circle, use pi times radius squared (πr^2). Generally, magic numbers should be avoided because they're dangerous. At a minimum, they should be commented.

Consider what happens if I use my magic number for characters per page in many places and then the book layout changes—maybe we change the paper size. I would need to replace every instance of 1900 with the new number. The ultimate solution in this case is to use a variable (discussed in Chapter 4) like a constant. At the very beginning of my movie, I could establish a variable "charsPerPage" as 1900 (charsPerPage=1900;). Then, instead of using 1900 in several locations, I could use charsPerPage instead of my constant. If charsPerPage were to change, every instance would reflect the change. Compare magic numbers to a gotoAndPlay(2) Action (where 2 is the magic number). A better solution is to use a frame label (which you can think of as a constant), as in gotoAndPlay("loopFrame"). If you move the "loopFrame" label, you won't need to go and fix your scripts in any way.

It's very easy to think that a magic number will *never* need to change, so it doesn't seem worth the effort to create a variable that can be used like a constant. In reality, magic numbers are not evil. You just need a bit of foresight to realize whether such a number could potentially change—in which case, you should use a variable instead.

Repeated Code

To put it simply: Every programming task should appear only once in your movie. If you have the same code in two places, you'll have twice the work to make updates or fix bugs. You'll learn ways to achieve this—such as keeping scripts in the Library, in functions, or external to the movie itself—but for now, just make sure that anytime you copy and paste code, a bell rings in your head to notify you that there must be a better way.

In Flash MX, it's now possible to put nearly all your code in a single keyframe (instead of having some code on buttons, some on clips, some in clips, and so forth). For example, instead of writing a mouse event right on a button, such as on(press){play()}, you can instead put (in a keyframe) myButtonInstance. onPress=function(){play()} (where "myButtonInstance" is the instance name for a button). In Chapter 14, "Extending ActionScript," you'll see more advanced techniques like this. The value is that your code is not spread out. (The disadvantage, however, is that it may be less intuitive to you.)

You'll probably develop more techniques that exemplify good style. Remember, it's subjective and based on personal preference. Although there are definitely methods that *should* be employed by all programmers, you only need to acquire skills as you become comfortable. I know that if I looked at anything I programmed even just a few months ago, I'd question the approach I took—but that's because I'm always improving. If you waited until your skills were perfect, you'd be waiting a long time. Just jump in, but take the time to be self-critical so that you can improve.

Code Data Separation

All programmers should strive to keep code (that is, the programming scripts) separate from the data (or the project-specific content such as text and graphics). By keeping code separate from data, you enable all your programming efforts to transfer easily to other projects. Similarly, when you want to make a major change to the content—say, redo the entire project in a different language—you just need to replace data without touching (or breaking) the code. It's a great concept that is sometimes difficult to achieve.

Imagine a factory that produces furniture with a wide selection of fabric upholstery. Likely the upholstery (think "data") is kept separate from the furniture and padding (think "code") until an order is placed. The benefit of code data separation (in this analogy) is that the factory can easily produce furniture as its customers request it and never have additional stock that's already upholstered. Applying this to Flash isn't much different. Assume that your Flash site has graphic buttons that display a floating tooltip whenever the user places his cursor over the button. If you kept the code (the script that makes the tooltip appear) separate from the data (the actual text or words that appear in the tooltip), you could easily translate this to another language by replacing the text for the tooltips. Ideally, you would keep *all* the text for all the tooltips in one location to make translation that much easier. The main idea is that you want to be able to make significant changes to either the code or data without affecting the other.

You can think of code data separation as a form of modularization. Other forms of modularization are available—including Flash's `LoadMovie()`, which enables you to play separate .swf files within a larger movie. Modularization has many benefits in addition to those mentioned for code data separation. For one thing, by modularizing your Flash movie, users won't have to wait for the entire site to download. They can selectively download just the portions in which they are interested. Also, modularizing makes working with others easy and efficient. Consider that if you just had one master file for the entire site, only one person could work at a time. So, there are a ton of benefits to code data separation and other kinds of modularization. Without providing a lot of details now, just realize that throughout this book I'll try to emphasize solutions that exhibit such modular attributes.

Summary

This chapter explored the attributes that make up the "programmer way." In my experience, it seems as though programmers tend to fit the same profile. For example, they often work in darkened offices that lack windows and subsist on soft drinks.

You don't have to become a geek to be a good programmer. Just concentrate on the approach discussed in this chapter. Try to develop a good style by striving to write concise code with a lot of comments and avoid magic numbers and repeated code. Realize, too, that your programming style should continually improve. The best programmers in the world know they have room to improve further.

The process you undertake can also make programming easier (and better). Creating a specification and quickly producing prototypes might seem like additional up-front work, but they will save you time later. Finally, always try to separate code from data. In no time, you'll start "feeling it," and before you know it, you can call yourself a "programmer" with pride.

{Chapter 4}

Basic Programming in Flash

Although you don't have to know traditional programming concepts to use ActionScript, they will help you greatly in Flash. If you're experienced in another programming language, this chapter might look familiar to you. Flash's ActionScript language is based on the same standard used by JavaScript (called *ECMA-262*; see www.ecma.ch). As such, many aspects are similar or identical. This chapter is a good introduction for both experienced programmers as well as those with basic Flash skills. I'll explain some general programming concepts, but with specific attention to how they apply to Flash.

In this chapter, you will:

- Learn basic programming terms.
- Recognize built-in script elements.
- Get an overview of traditional concepts such as variables and data types.

Terminology, Special Characters, and Formatting

The terms and rules in programming are very strict. This can actually be helpful. Unlike in English, where the meaning of a sentence can be ambiguous or vague, in programming there are absolutes. After you fully understand what a "property" is, for example, you never need to wonder what kind of property—as you would with the word *property* in English, which has multiple meanings. Not only do terms in programming have absolute meanings, they're usually closely related to the word's meaning in English. Be careful, however; sometimes your first impression of a term could carry a special meaning to you that is unrelated to the true meaning. Luckily, most terms are very easy to learn.

Events

Everything that happens in Flash is the result of an event that causes a script to execute. Even for such a simple example as the user clicking a button that causes the movie to skip ahead, the instructions (to skip ahead) resulted from the click "mouse event."

There are three types of events in Flash: keyframes, mouse events, and clip events. Notice that these correlate to the three places you can place scripts (keyframes, button instances, and clip instances). If you place a script in a keyframe, the script will execute as soon as Flash reaches the keyframe. In the case of buttons, you must always specify the mouse event to which you want to respond. Similarly, scripts on clip instances need to include a clip event. Figure 4.1 shows the available mouse events and clip events.

I like to think of an event as the wrapper of the scripts that it contains. Consider that you can't just have a `stop()` Action attached to a button; you must wrap it within a mouse event. I suppose that it makes sense to think the `stop()` action *follows* the mouse event. But because you can have several actions follow one event (maybe the button causes both `stop()` and `stopAllSounds()` to execute), you need some indication of where the results of an event end. In Flash, the event wrapper starts with an opening curly brace ({) and ends with a closing curly brace (})—sort of like a "script sandwich" with two curly braces for bread and scripts in the middle. Even if that corny analogy doesn't help, you should see that scripts are wrapped inside events. (See Figure 4.2.)

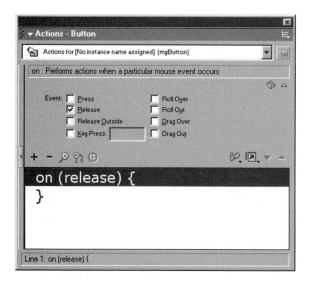

Figure 4.1   *The mouse events (for buttons) on the top and the clip events (for clips) on the bottom include all the events available in Flash.*

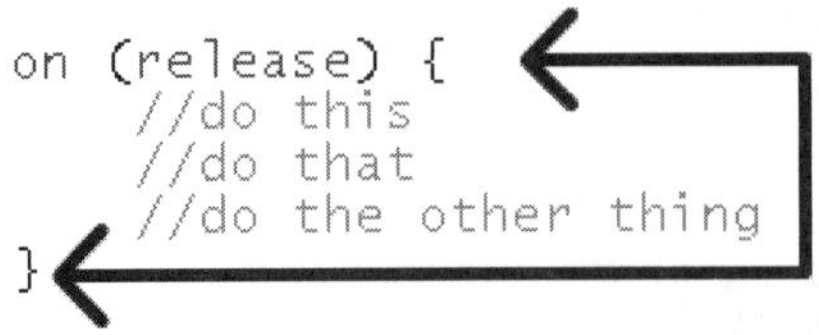

```
on (release) {
    //do this
    //do that
    //do the other thing
}
```

Figure 4.2 *Everything between the two curly braces will be performed when the event occurs.*

Results of Events

After an event happens, a script is executed. The instructions that Flash follows can range from simple to complex. Let's start by thinking about the results of events in very general terms. First, we'll look at the five types of tasks that happen as the result of an event:

1. A script can do something that is invisible or unimportant to the user (such as add to a counter that is tracking how many times a button is clicked). Think of this type as laying the groundwork or defining what can happen later.

2. The script can do something visual (such as change the rotation of a Movie Clip).

3. The script can trigger another script to execute—effectively behaving like a homemade event. Perhaps the script attached to one button causes another script to rotate a Movie Clip. In this way, several buttons can trigger the same "rotate the clip" script and your code can be modularized.

4. Scripts can "ask" other scripts for information (the part that's said to be "returned") and use the result to do one of the other tasks here. For example, one script could ascertain the current exchange rate from another script and use that information to translate a price from yen to dollars.

5. Finally, the fifth result of an event is nothing. That might seem odd, but events happen all the time and nothing happens. For example, a linear movie with no buttons will have no response to the mouseDown event (despite the fact that it happened). It's kind of like a tree falling in a deserted forest; that's an event despite whether anyone reacts to it.

Terms

We can't go much further without defining a few terms.

Syntax

Syntax is the way any sentence is organized. In programming, a "sentence of code" is called a *statement*. The syntax, or the form of your statements, must adhere to strict syntax rules. One simple rule (that works in English, too) is that any parenthetical statement that you start with an opening parenthesis must be followed by a closing parenthesis. If your statement's syntax is incorrect, your code will perform unexpectedly (at best) or not at all (at worst).

There are many ways that Flash helps you follow perfect syntax. While you are working in Normal Mode, the Actions panel will all but ensure that your syntax is perfect. Actually, as soon as your statement contains an error, it is highlighted in bright red. An explanatory message appears to guide you along, and often a code hint appears to help you with the proper syntax. Figure 4.3 shows a statement that isn't complete. Remember that even after your syntax is perfected, it doesn't mean your Flash movie will play the way you want it to. The script could still contain logical errors. The first step is to fix the syntax, and then you can ensure that it performs correctly.

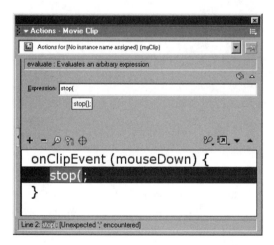

Figure 4.3   *When you edit your script in Normal Mode, errors are highlighted while you type.*

Another way that Flash helps you produce perfect syntax is by color-coding certain terms. The Syntax Coloring option in the ActionScript Editor's Preferences dialog box (accessed via the Actions panel's options menu and shown in Figure 4.4) is a great way to learn to type (and spell) terms correctly.

Keywords and identifiers (which, for now, you should simply consider as built-in terms of ActionScript) are colored dark blue. Comments (which are ignored by Flash and enable you to write notes to yourself or others reading your code) are colored gray by default. Finally, anything you type between quotation marks is blue. This is particularly useful because you must remember to end any quotations you start (just like parenthetical statements). If you start a quotation, everything that follows will turn gray until you type another quotation mark. You'll find out more about keywords, properties, comments, and strings later this chapter.

New to MX

Figure 4.4   *The ActionScript Editor's Preferences dialog box enables you to change syntax coloring and fonts, in addition to other settings.*

I wanted to mention the Syntax Coloring feature because it's a great way to learn. For example, when you look through someone else's finished code, it's easy to separate the elements that are built-in to Flash (they'll be blue) from the code that the programmer created (left in black). Possibly the most frustrating syntax rule in Flash is that all keywords are case sensitive. For example, `goToAndPlay(2)` won't turn blue (only `gotoAndPlay(2)` will). Throughout this book, you'll see many places where syntax is important. Syntax Coloring is just one little helper available to you.

Because Syntax Coloring is a preference, you can change any color to meet your needs. (Only the settings are saved with Flash MX, not the file). There's also a new Auto Format feature that helps your code look neat. The Auto Format

Options shown in Figure 4.5 are accessible from the Actions panel's options menu. While we're on the subject of "built-in features that help you learn," be sure to study the way code hints work. There's an explanation and table in Chapter 2, "What's New in Flash MX." All these helpers are by no means "cheating" because they help you to become a better programmer.

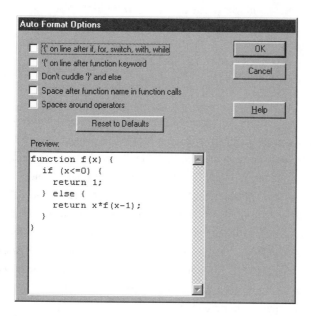

Figure 4.5   _Auto Format Options specify how Flash MX cleans up your code as you type._

Objects, Instances, Instance Names, and Properties

In Flash, there are many types of objects, but the easiest kind to understand are Movie Clip instances. Every Movie Clip you drag from the Library onto the Stage becomes a separate instance. Properties are attributes of objects. In real life, you could compare properties of objects to personal attributes and characteristics of people. People have an eye color property, a height property, a weight property, and so on. If you have two instances on the Stage, they're both based on the original master symbol but each is most likely positioned differently; that is, they'll have different _x and _y properties. Not only can you change properties of individual clip instances while editing, but through scripting you can change each instance's properties at runtime. This is easiest if the clip instance has been given an instance name (via the Properties panel). In pseudo-code, you'd say something like this: *Set the _x property of the instance named "box_1."* Just remember that the instance name is what matters (not the master name in the Library).

> **{ Note }**
>
> By the way, Flash MX enables you to give instance names to several other types of objects, including buttons, text, and video. You'll see this first in Chapter 10, "Keyboard Access and Modifying Onscreen Text," but realize they have a few limits. For example, text must be set to Dynamic or Input. For now, just remember that a Movie Clip is no longer the only object with an instance name.

After you fully understand how to access clip instance properties, it will be easy to understand other objects. In Chapter 7, "The Movie Clip Object," you'll learn how to access and change instance properties. You will use the same techniques in Chapter 9, "Manipulating Strings," Chapter 10, "Keyboard Access and Modifying Onscreen Text," Chapter 11, "Arrays," and Chapter 12, "Objects," to control the sound object, string object, and color object (among others). Finally, in Chapter 13, "Homemade Objects," you'll create your own objects. The reason the Movie Clip is so much easier to understand is that it's an object that you can see and touch. All the other objects are just as real, but you may never grab one with your mouse or see it onscreen. It's sort of like how you can have a picture in your mind. Think of a physical printed photograph as the Movie Clip object— you can fold it, frame it, or hang it on the wall. Now, consider a picture in your mind as any of the other objects. Even though there's no physical evidence, you can still manipulate the picture in your mind—picture it being folded, framed, and so on.

Statements, Expressions, and Operators

The entire block of text in the Actions panel is a script, where each line is a statement. As mentioned earlier, statements are "sentences of code." It's not so critical if you interchange the terms *script* and *statement*. But if a statement of code is like an entire sentence in speech, an expression is like a phrase. In speech, you might use the phrase *as slow as molasses*. First of all, you'd create an entire sentence (a statement), such as *His computer is as slow as molasses.* You can see that the expression (or phrase) is only part of the statement.

Expressions in Flash are evaluated. For example, an entire statement might read: `halfprice=price/2`. The part on the right of the equals sign is an expression and it will be evaluated (that is, a result will be placed in that spot). If it helps, think of evaluated expressions as having "math" done on them. Now, imagine that "as slow as molasses" is an actual speed (say 1 mile-per-hour). If you evaluated the expression, you'd be left with the result "1 MPH." The original sentence would become *His computer is 1 MPH*. This analogy is beginning to fall apart, but it's a good way to learn about statements and expressions (as well as the standard terms *evaluate* and *result*).

Finally, operators perform specific (usually math) operations. They always need at least one number, called an *operand*, on which to work. For instance, "+" is an operator that performs addition. The "+" addition operator requires two operands to work. Get it? There's the operator (doing the work) and the operands (getting work done on them). The thing to remember is that operators are used within expressions. Therefore, they're evaluated and their results appear in their place. For example, saying `whatever=2+2` is the same as saying `whatever=4`. The expression on the right is evaluated and turns into 4. This might seem simple. Just think of expressions morphing into their results.

Operators are pretty easy to understand when you consider familiar math operators—such as multiplication (*), division (/), and subtraction (–). Others aren't so easy to figure out and might even seem arbitrary. For example, one deceptively useful operator uses the percent sign (%), but not to calculate a percent. It's called the *modulo* operator and results in the remainder of two numbers. `10%2` is evaluated into `0`. Ten divided by 2 has 0 for a remainder. This can be useful to determine whether a number is odd or even (or evenly divisible by any other number, for that matter); that is, if the number % 2 is 0, it's an even number because it's evenly divisible by 2. Anyway, I don't recommend memorizing all the operators. We'll use many of them in the Workshop section, especially when we make sliders and the currency exchange calculator. However, after you understand the form—that operators create an expression that's evaluated and they always require at least one operand—you can learn them gradually.

Actions and Functions

In Flash, "actions" have many meanings. I think it's best to think of actions as Flash-unique commands that execute specific tasks. For example, the `stop()` action is a command that causes the playback head to stop. The `gotoAndPlay` ("framelabel") action is another command that jumps to a frame number or label and plays. These actions do things specific to Flash. However, the Actions panel lists many "actions" that are, technically, statements (or elements of statements). Figure 4.6 shows some actions that are really statements. For example, if is a piece of code that creates a statement. You have to specify additional details (such as, "If *what?*"), but if was around way before Flash—and in my book, it's a statement. For the sake of understanding, I'll try to avoid the term "actions" completely.

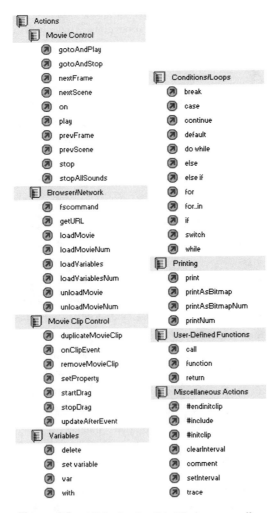

Figure 4.6 *All the "actions" in Flash are actually a mix of statements and Flash-unique commands.*

Keep in mind that although the term "actions" is made up, actions behave in a consistent manner. All the actions in Flash are one of two types. They're either specific Flash commands (such as stop, duplicateMovieClip, and play), or they are statements (such as if or break). (Actually, you'll learn in the next chapter that a more common name for many actions is *method*.) Many actions (of either type) need additional parameters provided—for instance, gotoAndPlay() requires a frame label or number. Another consistent attribute of all actions is that they're never evaluated; they do things. Actions have consequences. (To avoid confusion, don't call them "results.") The script you create using actions doesn't morph into a result the way that expressions do. Actions simply "do things." Either they help construct a statement or they do a Flash-unique task.

Although Flash's built-in functions are easy to confuse with actions, they are different in a profound way. A function always returns a value. That is, a built-in function's job is to calculate an answer. Similar to how an expression is evaluated, a function "returns" a value, which, in turn, is placed where the function was called. For example, the function getTimer() returns the total number of milliseconds elapsed since the movie started. It's almost like a "what time is it?" function. But consider if you asked someone, "What time is it?" That person might look at her watch, but unless she "returns" the answer, you might never know what time it is. Similarly, if you just wrote the script getTimer(), it would be meaningless. The getTimer() would turn into a number—maybe 10200, but so what? If, however, you wrote elapsedTime=getTimer()/1000 + " seconds", the getTimer() part would turn into 10200 and the expression on the right side of the equation would evaluate as 10.2 seconds.

All the built-in functions behave this way. Consider these real-life activities as actions: drive a car, stop the car, fill the car with gas. Now consider these as functions: getting today's price of gas, determining how many liters fit in a 20-gallon gas tank, determining how many yen are equal to 10 dollars. The functions always result in an answer (which can be used within a bigger calculation). Notice, too, that some functions just provide an answer (such as "getTimer" or "getting today's price of gas"). However, other functions (such as "converting gallons to liters") require additional data to be provided (that is, "How many gallons?"). In these cases, you need to provide a parameter.

In Chapter 8, "Functions," you'll learn all about functions—both the built-in functions and homemade functions. For now, just understand that actions are either Flash-unique commands (also called *methods*) or statements, and that built-in functions always return values. The big difference is that an action can be used by itself, whereas a function is always used within a larger script.

Special Characters and Formatting

As part of the many syntax rules in Flash, certain characters have special meanings. Additionally, the layout or format of your scripts must follow some rules. Parentheses are a perfect example of this point. Any parenthetical statement must start with an opening parenthesis and must always end with a closing parenthesis. The reason this is important is that you can have nested parentheses like this: `((6+2)*3)/2`, which results in 12. That's different than `6+((2*3)/2)`, which results in 9. The innermost expressions are evaluated first, followed by expressions in outer parentheses. The point is that anything you start, you have to finish. For example, `((6+2)*3/2` will cause an error because there's an extra open parenthesis.

There are identical rules for quotation marks (`"`), brackets (`[` and `]`), and curly braces (`{` and `}`). Quotation marks are a little different because apostrophes will work the same as quotation marks. This way you can nest quotations in quotations. You can't mix and match, however. For example, all of these are legitimate:

```
"This is 'cool' "
'Flash version "MX" is More eXemplary than "5"'
"Phillip's dog is named Max"
```

But these won't work:

```
"What you "start" you have to "finish""
"Mixing will not work'
```

It's interesting because in the case of `"Phillip's dog... "`, you might think that the apostrophe would cause problems. It works fine, however. Also, nested quotation marks are different than nested parentheses. You can have two open parentheses in a row, and as long as you eventually close what you open, they will work fine. However, two quotation marks in a row will cause Flash to think that the second one is closing what the first one opened. So, if you have to nest quotations in quotations, you must use quotations for one and apostrophes for the other. (By the way, the curly, or "smart," quotation marks, " and ", won't work in the Actions panel.)

Generally, spaces and return characters (at the end of a line) are ignored by Flash. If you start a parenthetical statement and close it five lines later, there's no problem. Because you can't simply create a new line to represent a new thought, every line of code can be terminated with a semicolon. For example, look at this piece of code:

```
if (age>18){
    voter=1;
    draftable=1;
}
```

Even though we haven't looked at the `if` statement yet, you can see that the open curly brace is followed (three lines later) by a closing curly brace. Also, there are two separate lines of code, each ending with a semicolon. Actually, the following is also totally legitimate:

```
if (age>18){voter=1;draftable=1;}
```

The first example was easier to read. In either case, the semicolon clearly ended individual statements. Occasionally you can be sloppy and, based on context, Flash will figure out what you intended. It's best to deliberately use semicolons to end each line, however.

One of the best character sequences to learn is the double forward slash (`//`), which creates a comment. Comments are ignored by Flash, so you can write anything you want. You can use comments as notes to yourself (or anyone else who might be viewing your code). The phrase "commenting your code" means that you include all the information necessary to make sense of your code through comments. Also, comments are useful to cause Flash to temporarily ignore part of your code—effectively removing the code, but leaving it so that you can restore it easily.

Everything that follows `//` (on the same line) is ignored. You'll see the commented text turn pink, which makes it very easy to recognize. The following code sample includes comments:

```
//This button makes the movie stop
on (release) {
    stop(); //don't go any further
}
```

Normally, comments automatically end at the end of a line. (Notice that there's no "closing" comment mark in the code.) However, you can use /* to start a block of comments that will continue until a */ is reached.

```
/* Comments:
    This is a comment.
    This is another comment.
*/
```

We'll encounter other special formatting and new terms throughout this book, but this should give you a good start. Now, with the terms and other technical matters out of the way, we can move on to variables and how to use them.

Data Types and Variables

It's difficult if not impossible to discuss either data types or variables without mentioning the other. We'll discuss both here.

Variables' Names and Values

Variables are a way that you can safely—yet temporarily—store data. Think of variables as individual whiteboards. You can write someone's telephone number on one whiteboard and refer to it later. You can easily change the telephone number on the whiteboard. Variables are similar in that you can store information in a variable for later reference or change it any time. You can have as many variables as you choose. To return to our whiteboard analogy, you could have one for telephone number and one for address. Every variable has two parts: a *name* (so that you can keep track of which variable is which) and a *value* (what is stored in the variable). For example, the name of the telephone number whiteboard (or variable) could be "phonenumber," but the value might be "800-555-1212." To assign the value of phonenumber, you could write the script phonenumber="800-555-1212" (which, translated, reads "the variable named phonenumber is assigned the value "800-555-1212""). We'll discuss variables at length later in this chapter, but you really just need to understand the concepts of value and name first.

String and Number Data Types

The type of data that is stored in a variable's value is important. The type of data that goes into a variable can be one of many types. Just as you can store paper in an envelope, you can also store paper clips, money, even sand. This concept is easiest to understand when you compare two common data types: string and number.

A string is always expressed between quotation marks. "Phillip," "David," and "Kerman," for example, are all strings. (Remember that we're talking about the values contained in a variable, not the variable's name.) You can do interesting maneuvers with strings, such as converting them to all uppercase letters and determining the number of letters in a string (using the techniques you'll learn in Chapter 9).

Numbers (such as 13 and 35) are a different data type. Numbers are as difficult to compare to strings as apples are to oranges. You can also do interesting things with numbers, such as add them together and find their difference. However, you wouldn't mix them. "Phillip" plus 35, for example, doesn't make sense.

The good news about ActionScript is that it's *untyped*—meaning that you don't have to decide ahead of time the data type for each variable's value. From context, Flash figures it out. If you said username="Phillip", Flash would treat the value of username like a string because "Phillip" is contained within quotation marks. If you said age=35, Flash would treat age as a number. (No, Flash doesn't know what a username or age is; it just figures out the data type from how you've used the word.) Because ActionScript is untyped, you can change the data type in a variable. Maybe in the first frame you said score="untested" (at which point the value in the score variable would be a string: "untested"). Later, you could say score=85 (and the value of score would become a number). Despite the freedom to change data types, it's still important to understand each data type.

More About Strings

In Chapter 9, you'll learn all about manipulating strings. There are two tricks you should understand now, however. Concatenating two strings is just a matter of using the *concatenate* character +. For example, "Phillip"+"Kerman" would evaluate as "PhillipKerman". A more practical situation might be that you have an input text field onscreen (with the variable name "username"), and after the user types her name, you could use the script message="Welcome " + username + "!" and make sure to display a dynamic field containing the variable message. Notice the variable message is having its value set to a string that combines the word "Welcome " (with an extra space) plus the value of username plus an exclamation point. Figure 4.7 shows part of such a "Hello World" exercise.

Figure 4.7 *Dynamic text (based on user input) can appear by modifying strings.*

Another interesting trick to understand is how to include characters that would otherwise be difficult or impossible to include inside a string. For example, what if you want your string to contain a double quotation mark, such as `"Phillip is "old""`? Forgetting for a moment the way you learned to nest quotation marks (inside apostrophes), the difficulty here is that the quotation mark right before the letter "o" would act like an end-quote for the quotation mark at the beginning. Instead of letting Flash get confused, you can use a backslash in front of any quotation mark you want to be used verbatim. So, `"Phillip is \"old\""` works fine. This is called an *escape sequence.* You'll find a table of escape sequences in Flash MX's online help under "Understanding the ActionScript Language, About Data Types, String." For example, `\r` creates a return, and `\t` makes a tab.

More About Numbers

Manipulating numbers will probably look familiar to you because it works the same as traditional math. Something simple like `10-2` evaluates to 8. It might seem strange that `10+2` evaluates to 12 because we just learned the plus sign (+) is the concatenation character for strings. The plus sign acts as an addition operator only when both operands are numbers. But, something odd like `"Phillip"+2` evaluates to "Phillip2", because one of the operands is a string, so the plus sign concatenates the two. Often, depending on context, Flash will use the same symbols differently.

Other number operators are pretty easy to figure out. Common arithmetic operators such as / (divide) and * (multiply) are all listed in the Operators section in the Actions panel. Remember that an expression by itself won't do anything. For example, `2+2` evaluates to `4`—but so what? If, however, you wrote `myAge=2+2`, the variable myAge would be assigned the value 4. You can also use variables within expressions, as in this example: myAge=myAge+1. The right side is evaluated first, and the result is placed in the value of myAge. That is, myAge is incremented (one more than it is currently).

It is good to know a few powerful shorthand operators for numbers. They're not called "shorthand," but rather they are categorized as "assignment operators" (and listed that way in the Actions panel) because they perform complex tasks, including assignments. One operator (the double plus sign, ++) is used to increment a variable. For example, myAge++ increases myAge by one. To decrement, use, -- (for instance, myAge--). Consider that you can write both these statements in "long hand," as follows:

```
myAge=myAge+1   //performs the same thing as myAge++

myAge=myAge-1   //same as myAge--
```

Finally, if you want to increase or decrease a variable's value by more than one, you can use += or -=. For example, myAge+=5 adds five to the current value of myAge, whereas myAge-=5 subtracts five.

By the way, "3" and 3 are different; one's a string and the other is a number. Consider the following example:

```
myAge="3";
myAge=myAge+1;
```

The variable myAge would become the string "31" (because the plus sign concatenated the string). This situation would easily happen if myAge were a variable associated with an Input Text field. The contents of Dynamic Text and Input Text are always treated as strings. Without fully exploring functions, I will introduce one that enables you to convert any variable into a number. It's pretty simple: Number(myAge) will result in a number version of myAge (or whatever you put in the parentheses). So, to be sure that you have a number, you could use the assignment statement myAge=Number(myAge)+1. This example should really demonstrate how data types make a difference. (In Chapter 10, you'll learn that associating a variable with a Text Field is not even necessary and often undesirable.)

Other Data Types

There are only a few other data types to learn. Boolean is one that's fairly easy. The values in Boolean variables are either true or false. Perhaps you start your movie with passedTest=false, and then after the user finishes the test, you write the script `passedTest=true`. There are slight efficiency benefits to Booleans. You only need to consider them, however, when appropriate. Examples where Booleans make sense include `PassedTest`, `seenIntro`, and `SoundOn`.

Primitive Data Types Versus Reference Data Types

The data types discussed so far (string, number, and Boolean) are all considered *primitive* data types(sometimes called *value variables*). The other data types that you're about to see (array and object) are called *reference* data types. Understanding the difference between primitive and reference data types is good for more than impressing people at parties.

A variable in a primitive data type (say a string `username=":Phillip"`) copies the actual value into the variable. A variable of the reference data type only holds a pointer to the actual data. It's sort of like the way a shortcut on Windows (or an alias on Macintosh) works—it doesn't contain the actual data; it contains only a reference to the real thing. The difference becomes important when you begin to copy the contents of one variable into another. If the data type is primitive, copy-ing will duplicate the contents of the variable at the time of copying. If you change the original variable's contents, the new variable remains unchanged. In the case of a reference type, if you copy a variable and then change the original, the copy also changes. Look at the following example of copying by value (that is, using primitive data types):

```
myPaint="brown";      //myPaint contains "brown"
myHouseColor=myPaint; //myHouseColor contains "brown"
myPaint="blue";       //now myPaint contains "blue"
                      //but myHouseColor is unchanged (it's still "brown")
```

Now, consider this example of copying by reference:

```
myFavoriteFoods=["Pizza", "Hot dogs", "Waffles"];
childhoodFoods=myFavoriteFoods;
/*childhoodFoods now contains a reference to myFavoriteFoods
(which currently contains "Pizza"...etc.)
*/
myFavoriteFoods=["Tiramisu", "Bitter Chocolate", "Falafel"];
/*
Not only does this mean that myFavoriteFoods has changed, but since a
➥reference to myFavoriteFoods is contained in childhoodFoods
➥(not a copy but a reference) childhoodFoods now contains
➥"Tiramisu" etc.—and will change any time myFavoriteFoods
➥changes again.
*/
```

There are other subtle differences between primitive and reference data types, but if you simply understand how "copying by value" (primitive) and "copying by reference" (reference) works, you will understand the important difference.

Objects and Arrays

You might have noticed in the preceding examples of primitive and reference data types that the `myFavoriteFoods` variable was given a value containing more than one item (pizza, hot dogs, and waffles). That's another data type called an *array*. An array simply contains several items. If you think of most variables as an empty whiteboard onto which you can write a value, an array is like a whiteboard with permanent horizontal lines separating many pieces of information. The cool part is that you can selectively find out what's in each spot, add items, sort all the items, shuffle them, and so on. Usually, the different items are accessed by their *index* (that is, the position in the array). You'll discover all the ins-and-outs of arrays in Chapter 11, but there are a couple points we can cover now so that you become familiar with what arrays look like.

You can create an array with a statement as simple as `myFirstArray=` `["Phillip", "Kerman", 36]`. In this case, you're creating the array and populating it all in one move. Notice that the creation process involves surrounding the data with brackets and separating each item with a comma. Also, notice that any data type can go into any index; the example has two strings and one number. (You'll see in Chapter 11 that you can even put arrays into arrays to create a matrix.) Finally, if you're not sure what items you plan to put in the array, but you want to create an empty array that can be populated later, you simply use `new Array()`, as in `myFirstArray=new Array()`.

There's a simple technique to manipulate arrays. You might want to access certain items in an array (by index), change the value in a particular index, or simply insert a value in a specific index. The form is `arrayName[index]`. But watch out: Arrays' indexes start counting with zero. The first item is 0, and then 1, and so on. So, to write an expression that returns the third item in `myFirstArray`, you can write `myFirstArray[2]`. (Remember that because this is just an expression, it evaluates as `36` in this case; by itself, however, it doesn't really *do* anything.) To change the third item, you could say `myFirstArray[2]="age"`. Finally, you can insert an item in the 99th index position by saying `myFirstArray[98]="way out"`. This will create at least 98 blank positions, if necessary.

Now, just to leave you with a tiny applied script, here's a case in which I'm going to increment the value in the third index. I have to first access the item in the third position (to increment it) and set the value in the third position.

```
myFirstArray[2]=myFirstArray[2]+1;
//also could have used: myFirstArray[2]++;
```

The last data type is *object*. And because Flash has many built-in objects (including Array, Math, Sound, etc.), we should call this type of object a "generic object" (also called a "homemade" or "short" object). Generic objects are similar to arrays in that you can store more than one piece of data in a single object. Whereas arrays use indexes to contain multiple numbered items, an object contains multiple named items (called *properties*). In addition, you can design these objects to use methods. The big difference between objects and arrays is that when you put data in an array, there's just one copy of that array. If you change the contents in an index, it changes in the one copy. After you construct an object and the properties and methods it will contain, you can make as many duplicates as you want. Even though each instance of an object is based on the same design, each instance can maintain different values for each property.

Remember that Movie Clip instances are really objects. It's easy to understand how each Movie Clip instance has unique properties. For example, each instance of a clip on the Stage can have a different _x property and _y property. There are several built-in properties of clips that can vary between each instance. Objects also have methods. Methods are commands or functions that operate on an individual object instance. A great example of a method is the gotoAndStop() action. If you said someClip.gotoAndStop(2);, for example, the clip instance named "someClip" would jump to frame 2. gotoAndStop() is a method of the Movie Clip object.

As stated earlier, there are other built-in objects and even a way for you to create your own objects, but none has such a physical presence as a clip instance. Many of the other objects require you to first create an instance of the object (called *instantiating*) by assigning the value of a variable to an Object data type—maybe oneObject=new Color(). Then you can change properties of the oneObject instance or apply methods to it. (Color happens to be one of the built-in objects and it comes standard with many properties and methods.) If you were making your own object, you'd first have to define the properties and methods you plan to have. It gets very involved, which is why I have several chapters on the subject, but the usage of objects is always the same: You put the Object data type into a variable, and then you act on that variable instance. If you want more copies of the object, just stuff them into other variables. Each variable's value is an object. It's pretty weird because you never "see" anything unless you proceed to affect something onscreen. Just return to the concept that a clip instance is an object and you should have an easier time.

Using Variables

After you stuff a particular data type into your variable's value, there are only a few things you can do with the variable. You can access its value (just to look at it or use it within an expression), change its value (that is, *assign* a new value—which is really what you do when you set its initial value), compare its value with another variable or expression, or pass the value to a function for the function's use. It might sound as though that's a lot of maneuvers to learn, but it's really not that bad.

Assigning and Accessing Variables

You've already seen how to assign values to variables many times in this chapter, but it doesn't hurt to go over the details. The most common form is variableName=newValue. You can translate this to read "the variable named 'variableName' *is assigned the value of* newValue." If, whenever you read the equals sign, you say to yourself, "...is now equal to..." or "...is assigned the value of...," it should make sense. This means that no matter what the value the variable (on the left side) contains before this statement is encountered, it is now assigned the value of whatever is on the right side. If an expression such as price/2 is on the right side in the code halfPrice=price/2, the right side is evaluated first and the result is placed in the variable on the left.

You actually saw another way in which variables are assigned values—namely, with assignment operators, such as ++ (which increments the variable to the left of the operator). The confusing part is that many operators don't actually change the contents of their operands. For example, discountPrice= (0.15*originalPrice) won't change the value of originalPrice—originalPrice is just being referenced so that it can be used within an expression. But a statement such as age++ will change the value of _age by increasing it by one. The most common way in which variables are assigned values is through the equals sign—just don't forget the assignment operators (++, --, +=, and -=).

One last point to remember when assigning values: If you want to copy the value of one variable into another (for instance, `myName=username`), just remember the difference between primitive and reference data types. If `username` contains a string (primitive), a duplicate of its contents is placed into the value of `myName`. However, if `username` contains an array (that is, a reference data type), only a reference is placed into the variable `myName`. After that, if `username` changes, so does the value in `myName`.

Accessing variables can be very simple. You just use the variable's name. Variables are evaluated wherever they're used. That is, if you say `username`, the value of `username` is used in that place. Just as 3+2 evaluates to 5, using a variable's name evaluates to its value. This might seem very simple, because it is! The tricky part is making sure that you're referring to the right variable name (which is covered in more detail later in this chapter).

Comparing and Passing Values

Quite often, you'll find the need to compare or check whether a variable's value either matches, is greater than, or is less than another variable's value. Sometimes you compare a variable's value to an expression, such as:

```
if (age>17){
    canVote=true;
}
```

In this case, we're simply checking whether the value of `age` is greater than 17. (We'll cover the `if` statement in detail in Chapter 5, "Programming Structures.") Consider that, in this case, 17 is "hard wired." What if the minimum age to vote changes? If you expect there's a chance of changes, you could first assign the value to another variable (`minimumAge`) and create a slightly more dynamic solution:

```
minimumAge=18;
if (age>minimumAge-1) {
    canVote=true;
}
```

In this case, we're comparing the value of `age` to the expression "minimumAge minus 1." You'll do a lot of this kind of thing in any programming language, but there are two important concepts to remember. First, such comparisons never

change any variable's values. If you're checking whether two variables happen to
be equal, use the following:

```
if (oneVariable==otherVariable){
//then... do whatever
}
```

The double equals sign doesn't change oneVariable or otherVariable. In
Chapter 9, you'll also learn about Flash MX's new strict equality comparison
operator (===). (That's three equals signs.). The regular equality operator (==)
just compares two values, whereas the strict equality operator (===) also compares two variables' data types. Again, only the regular assignment operator (=)
actually changes variables. The second concept to remember is that when comparing two primitive variables, the contents of each are compared—number for
number or letter for letter. (This is likely the way you expect.) However, if you're
comparing two variables that contain (references to) reference variable types, the
comparison checks only whether both variables point to the same original. For
example:

```
oneArray=["Phillip", "Kerman"];
anotherArray=["Phillip", "Kerman"];
oneRef=oneArray;
//that line only placed a reference to "oneArray" in "oneRef"
otherRef=anotherArray;
if (oneRef==otherRef){
//they match!
}
```

The expression after the if statement's condition (oneRef==otherRef) evaluates
as false. Even though the actual contents of both variables look identical, they're
pointing to two different arrays (which, remember, are reference data types). The
entire subject of "primitive versus reference" might seem esoteric (and I suppose
it is in many ways). However, you'll find arrays so powerful that the last thing
you'll need is to hunt down a bug that's caused by this (less than intuitive) behavior. The two points to remember from this section so far are that comparing variables in an expression doesn't actually change them, and that different data types
behave differently.

Finally, let's consider passing variables. When you write your own functions in
Chapter 8, you'll see that there's an opportunity to write a function that accepts
parameters. This concept is similar to how gotoAndStop() requires that you provide a parameter—namely, a frame number or label name to *go to*. Often you'll
write functions that will act differently depending on parameters that are

received. For example, you might write a custom `exchangeCurrency()` function that accepts one price and determines the price in another currency (like we'll do in Workshop Chapter 8, "Creating a Currency Exchange Calculator"). To use this (yet-to-be-created) function, you'd simply say `exchangeCurrency(1.95)`. If you provided a different parameter (the part in the parentheses), such as `exchangeCurrency(14.50)`, you'd get a different answer. Instead of a hard-wired number, you could *pass* a variable instead—for example, `exchangeCurrency (currentPrice)`. In this case, the value for `currentPrice` would be passed. As long as the value of `currentPrice` contained a primitive data type, the original can never be changed by the function. If the `currentPrice` were a reference data type, you *could* write the function to change the original value. Only reference type variables can be changed in this way. Often you'll pass variables of the primitive data type (see Workshop Chapter 8) and hence only pass copies of the variable. However, in Workshop Chapter 6, "Working with Odd-Shaped Clickable Areas," you'll actually pass references to Movie Clips (which is a reference data type—object). In that workshop, changing the parameter received will most definitely change the original Movie Clip instance. (You'll learn much more about functions in Chapter 8.)

Scope and Variable Collision

As stated earlier, when you place a variable's name in a script, the variable's value is used in its place. I said it was easy as long as you used the correct variable name. Certainly, you'll need to remember which variable is which. It's just as if you have several children with different names; you need to keep track of which one is which. With kids, it's pretty easy because you memorize their names. You can name your children (and your variables) anything you want. Although some people name their children with their own name, most people tend to use a unique name for each child. You can imagine the problems that would arise if you named two of your children with the same name. In Flash, you can't exactly get away with giving two variables the same name—but almost.

{ Note }

Actually, you can't really name your variables just anything. Variable names must start with a character other than an underscore (`_myAge`, for example, won't work) or a number (`2Cool` won't work, either). Also, you can't include spaces in a variable name— only one word per variable, although people often use uppercase characters to make a variable seem like two words (`myVariable`, for example).

In traditional programming the *scope* of a variable (either local or global) defines the area in which that variable has influence—sort of like a sheriff's jurisdiction is his scope. In Flash MX, there are really three types of variables: true globals, true locals, and then all the rest, which are called *timeline variables*. Unless you specify a variable as global or local, it falls into the timeline category. (If I don't call a variable global or local in this book, you can count on it being a normal timeline variable.)

In actuality, timeline variables are like traditional global variables because they can be accessed from any script. It's just that with timeline variables you must be explicit in order to avoid variable collision. Variable collision occurs when you try to have two variables with the same name, but expect them to maintain separate values. For example, it's perfectly logical to have a variable called "president" that stores the name of the President of the United States. However, what if you want another variable called "president" that stores the name of the president of your club? Obviously, the two variables would collide if you said president="George" and then later said president="Mary". In Flash, however, you simply need to be explicit, and instead, store each variable in it's own clip instance. Say you had two clip instances, one with an instance name "usa" and the other called "club." You could be explicit and say usa.president="George" and club.president="Mary".

You'll learn the details of this syntax in Chapter 7, but for now just realize that two variables in different Movie Clip instances don't collide because their explicit location (clip address) is unique. To understand variables better, compare them to properties. Variables unique to a clip instance are the same as how the _y property of one clip instance (oneInstance._y) can be uniquely different from the _y property of another instance of the same clip (otherInstance._y). Anywhere inside a Movie Clip, referring to _y refers to the _y of that clip, just like president refers to that clip's president. There's only one version of _y anywhere inside the clip, but as soon as you need to write an explicit reference to one of the clip's properties or variables, you need to precede the property or variable with the clip instance name.

Finally, I should note that keeping variables with the same name inside multiple clip instances could be very useful. Think of such timeline variables as similar to the properties unique to clip instances. For example, assume that you create a Movie Clip that uses the variable speed. You can drag multiple instances of that clip on the Stage and each instance will have its own speed, just as each instance maintains its own _alpha property, _x property, and so on. The only concern is to be clear which clip's variable you're referring to so that you don't get mixed up.

Global Variables

New to MX

Flash MX added true global variables. There's only one copy of any global variable. In the case of "president," if this were a global variable, you'd never need to wonder, "Which president?" Using global variables is easy. The name of any global variable always begins _global. For example, you could use _global.president to refer to the global variable called president. It's like there is an imaginary clip called _global in which you can store variables. Just remember that you can have only one version of any named global variable. Global variables are really not much different from normal variables that are unique to a timeline. It's just that every time you refer to a global variable, you should be explicit and use the _global. prefix.

Global variables make keeping track of variables easy. You never have to remember which clip they're stored in, or whether there's another variable with the same name. As such, they're only appropriate for certain types of data storage. Variables are a way to store data. Global variables are appropriate for data of which there's only one copy (_global.totalScore or _global.todaysDate, for example). However, if you built a game with two players, you couldn't have one global variable called _global.score because you wouldn't be able to store a value for each player. We'll get into the practical use of all variable types later. Just remember that global variables always start "_global." and that there's only one copy of each.

Local Variables

Even though most of your work won't involve local variables, they're good to understand—if, for nothing else, comparison. Local variables are used within custom functions and exist only for the short duration while they're used. The benefit is that local variables are always removed from the user's computer memory when they're not being used. Other variables take up space in RAM and will never "let go" of that memory unless you use delete (as in delete someVarName). You can also just assign a value that's practically insignificant, such as someVarName=0, which isn't the same thing but perhaps is easier to understand.

Local variables have to first be declared, using either of the following forms:

```
var counter;
```

or

```
var counter=0;
```

In the second case, not only is the local variable (`counter`) created, but it's assigned a value from the start. In the first example, you'd have to eventually assign a value to the variable before it could be used. Just remember that such a variable is still useful to temporarily hold a value to be used later, but it only "lives" within the function (that is, between the { and } curly braces). You can practice with local variables when you learn all about functions in Chapter 8.

Dot Syntax

ActionScripting uses what's called *dot syntax*. You've already seen this in effect throughout this chapter. When we used `someClip._y`, it could be translated to "someClip's _y property." (Think of the dot as a possessive *s*.) In this way, the dot separates a clip instance name from its property. If you have clips nested inside of other clips, you can use dots to separate the nested clip names (`_root.someClip._y` or `someClip.subClip._y`, for example). You can also use dots to separate clip names from their respective variables. (This fact is probably easiest to learn if you think of variables as custom properties.) Finally, the dot is used to separate a clip name from the method (or action) when you want to apply the method to an individual clip (`someClip.gotoAndPlay(2)`, for example).

The form of dot syntax is interesting because it always reads left to right, from general to specific. In speech, we usually refer to things from specific to general. For example, "The age of the mayor of Portland, Oregon" reads from specific to general. If these were nested clips in Flash, however, it would read the other way: `Oregon.Portland.Mayor.age`. Depending on whether your target path is relative or absolute, the length might change, but it's always from general to specific. (Chapter 7 discusses relative and absolute paths in greater detail.)

Dot syntax is quite easy to learn. Just remember that you can't name variables or clips with periods in their name. Also, although you're allowed to name clips with spaces (but you shouldn't), you can never name variables with spaces in their names. You might imagine if your clip name were "clip.one," there would be no way to tell whether `clip.one._y` referred to the _y property of the clip "one" inside the clip "clip" or to the _y property of a clip named "clip.one." By avoiding periods and spaces in clip and variable names, you avoid this issue. Finally, you shouldn't name clips or variables beginning with a numeral. To summarize: Clip instance names and variable names should include no spaces, no periods, and never start with a number.

Summary

This chapter has consolidated practically every component of ActionScript. Naturally, it's more of a starting point rather than the last word. It's fair to say that everything covered will be revisited—in much more detail—throughout the rest of the book.

Everything was important in this chapter, of course, but you should retain a few concepts in particular. For example, you should be comfortable with all the terms used, even if you don't fully understand their application. You should understand the basic purposes of "events," "properties," "syntax," "statements," and "expressions." The concept of data types is very important, but the good news is that you'll hear more about it later. Regarding variables, if you only grasp that they are a safe—yet temporary—storage mechanism, you'll be fine.

Just treat this chapter as an overview of the basic programming skills that you're about to develop.

{ Chapter 5 }

Programming Structures

I suspect that the overview of programming from the previous chapter has made you eager to start scripting. (I hope so anyway.) The last chapter briefly touched on practically every concept from ActionScript. In this chapter, we'll start by exploring the structural elements necessary to write any script. Just as a house is built from the ground up by first laying down the foundation and then the framework, Flash scripts require a design and a framework. We're about to explore the structural elements of ActionScript that hold your scripts together.

This chapter covers:

- How to write expressions and statements.
- How to use operators in expressions.
- How to use conditions (such as `if`) and loop structures.
- How to practice using this knowledge.

Statements, Expressions, and Operators

To quickly review, statements are complete "sentences of code" that usually do something. Expressions are more like "phrases" because they don't *do* anything by themselves, but rather are used within statements. Expressions also result in a value when they're evaluated. For example, if you were to evaluate the expression "slow as molasses," it would have an actual value (perhaps 1 inch per hour).

It works the same in Flash—the expression `price/2` results in a value. Finally, operators, as part of an expression, perform an operation (often math) on one or more operands. For example, the "plus" operator (+) performs the addition operation on two numbers (operands). The expression 2+2 results in a value (4). Finally, the statement `quad=2+2` actually *does* something (namely, assigning the value of 4 to the variable `quad`). Now that we know the terms, we can explore each concept in detail.

Writing Expressions

The key to writing expressions is to always remember that you're only writing part of a larger statement. By themselves, expressions don't *do* anything; rather, expressions result in a value because they are evaluated. That is, expressions are evaluated and become their result. An expression from real life might be, "The shirt's price minus the discount." If you said, "My credit card's balance is now increased by the cost of the shirt (minus its discount rate)," it becomes a statement that does something. After you can write expressions (segments), you'll have no trouble writing statements.

Let's use the discounted shirt price for practice. Imagine that you previously assigned the variable `price` to the cost of the shirt. It doesn't matter what the `price` was—but let's just say $25 (that is, `price=25`). Also, consider that the discount rate is 10 percent. Interestingly, I'll bet everyone who's ever gone shopping already knows the shirt will cost $22.50, which just goes to show that you can write expressions! You just have to take one step at a time. Say the variable containing the discount rate is called "discount" (or `discount=0.1`). The final expression looks like this:

```
price-(price*discount)
```

You can think of this as a mathematical formula. No matter what the values of `price` and `discount` are, the formula works. It always results in the discounted price.

Precedence

We'll get to statements later in this chapter (in the section, "Types of Statements"). For now, however, there's more to learn about expressions. Notice in the earlier expression about price, I placed parentheses around `price*discount`. In the version with no parentheses—`price-price*discount`—you might think that Flash will execute the first two elements (`price-price`) first—the result of that portion would be zero. Then zero multiplied by `discount` would always equal zero. (What a sale… "All Shirts $0.") So, putting parentheses around the expression `price*discount` tells Flash to execute this expression first. It turns out this wasn't necessary. The expression `price-price*discount` results in the same value as `price-(price*discount)`. That's because the precedence for multiplication is greater than for subtraction; multiplication is executed first, and then subtraction.

Of course, if you want to force Flash to execute the subtraction operation first, you could rewrite the expression as `(price-price)*discount`. Personally, instead of memorizing the precedence for each operator (also called *order of operation*), any time there's a question as to how Flash will interpret my expression, I simply place parentheses to make the expression not only clear when reading, but crystal clear to Flash despite the fact the extra parentheses are unnecessary. Flash always executes the expressions in the most-nested parentheses first. Look up "Operator Precedence and Associativity" in Flash's ActionScript Reference (from the Help menu).

Interestingly, operators each have an associativity of either "right-to-left" or "left-to-right," which determines the order of execution when two of the same operators appear and therefore have the same precedence. For example, because addition has left-to-right associativity, `2+3+4` is the same as `(2+3)+4`. Although this example doesn't demonstrate a different result, remember that parentheses can override associativity (as in `2+(3+4)`). Associativity is not usually a critical issue, but it's covered in Flash's ActionScript Reference along with all the operators and their precedence.

Balancing Parentheses

Parentheses in an expression must balance. That is, for every open parenthesis, you must have a closing parenthesis. This holds true for the entire statement—but that doesn't mean you can't create errors within an expression. While you are in Expert Mode, you need to ensure that the parentheses balance. One way you can do that is to read your scripts (from left to right) and count up for every opening parenthesis and count down for every closing parenthesis. After reading the entire statement, your count should be at zero, proving everything balances. While you are in Normal Mode, any errors in balance will be highlighted in red, and Flash will provide limited information about the error in the parameters area (see Figure 5.1).

Figure 5.1   *The Actions panel will draw your attention to missing parentheses while you are in Normal Mode.*

It is important to understand that just because you balance your parentheses, there's no guarantee that your code will work as expected. For example, the expression `(price-price)*discount` balances just as well as `price-(price*discount)`, but with entirely different results. So, balancing parentheses is just a technical requirement (like spell-checking a document)—making your code logical or work for your purpose is still necessary. Here's a great tip that I personally guarantee will help you: Any time you type an opening parenthesis, immediately type a closing parenthesis and then backspace to complete the parenthetical portion of the expression. This way you're sure to balance all parentheses. Finally, everything just discussed about parentheses also applies to quotation marks (`"` or `'`), brackets (`[` and `]`), and curly braces (`{` and `}`—also called *curly brackets*).

Using Operators in Expressions

Instead of listing every operator here, we'll first look at how operators work, and then explore the ones that operate within expressions (operators categorized as *arithmetic*, *comparison*, and *logical*). Finally, after the upcoming section on statements, we can look at operators that perform assignments.

I've said several times that operators operate on one or more operands. To be technical, when an operator operates on a single operand, it is called *unary* (like "uni-cycle"). When operating on two operands, it's called a *binary* operator. Finally, one operator (`?:`) is considered *ternary* because it operates on three operands. (Because there's just one such operator, "ternary" may only come up on a quiz show for geeks.) What makes this important is that *some* operators can act as either a unary operator or a binary operator. One example is -, which is both a "unary minus" and a "subtract" operator. When used on a single operand (as with -direction or within a statement such as oppositeDirection = -direction), it simply results in an inverse (or minus version) of its operand. But as a binary operator (as in price-couponValue), the entire expression is converted into the result of subtracting the second operand from the first.

The fact is that operators operate differently depending on the context. Even though it's pretty easy to see and understand how operators act differently based on the number of operands because you can quickly see how many operands are present, some operators also perform differently based on the data type of their operands. That is, the same operator can perform a different operation on different data types. Recall from Chapter 4, "Basic Programming in Flash," that the value of a variable can be one of several data types. Let's just consider the Number and String data types (probably the most common and familiar data types). The + operator is either an addition operator or a concatenate (meaning to connect) operator, depending on its operands. If one or both operands are strings, + is a concatenate operator, as in:

```
first="Phillip";
last="Kerman";
wholeName=first+last;
```

The expression first+last results in "PhillipKerman".

If both the operands are numbers, the + operator performs the addition operation, as in:

```
previousScore=10
currentScore=2
totalScore=previousScore+currentScore;
```

The expression previousScore+currentScore results in 12.

This issue can become quite frustrating if you think a variable (say previousScore) contains a number, but it actually contains the string ("say 10"). The expression previousScore+2 will result in the *string* "102" because + acts as the concatenate operator when one or more of the operands are strings. This is likely to happen in Flash when you use a Dynamic (or Input) Text field to display the value of a variable. Even though the field might read 10, it's actually the string "10" because the data type of fields is string. By the way, in Chapter 8, "Functions," you'll learn how to treat a string like a number by using the Number() function. Also, later in this chapter, you'll see how certain operators will actually change the data type of their operands in the section, "Using Assignment Operators to Create Statements."

There's no need to get freaked out about operators. Just remember that operators often behave differently depending on their position in an expression and on their operands' data types. In practice, you'll usually select the correct operator without fail. Just learn to recognize the symptoms of such problems. For example, if the numbers you were expecting to grow end up getting longer (such as 10 turning into 101) or if your strings are appearing as NaN (meaning "not a number"), you're likely mixing data types or using the operators incorrectly.

Finally, even though an operator operates only on one or two operands, the operand could actually be an expression (really, the result of an expression). This might have been particularly obvious when we discussed parentheses earlier. The example price-(price*discount) has the minus operator operating on the result of an expression (the multiplication part in the parentheses). Figure 5.2 shows how an operand can actually be the result of an expression.

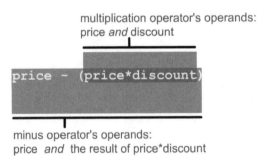

multiplication operator's operands:
price *and* discount

price - (price*discount)

minus operator's operands:
price *and* the result of price*discount

Figure 5.2   *An operand can be the result of an expression.*

Arithmetic Operators

Let's look at the operators used to perform simple arithmetic. These won't change their operands and (when used on number operands) will have expected results.

- Add numbers (+) results in the sum of two number operands.
- Multiply numbers (*) results in the product of two number operands.

- Subtract numbers (-). As a binary operator (that is, with two operands), it results in the difference by subtracting the second number from the first. It can also be used as a unary operator (on one operand) by placing it before the operand (as in -myNum), in which case it will result in the inverse of the operand. If it's positive, the result is negative; if it's negative, the result is positive.

- Divide numbers (/) results in the quotient of two numbers. That is, it divides the first number by the second.

- Modulo (%) results in the remainder when you divide the first number by the second. For example, 20%7 results in 6 because after you divide 7 into 20 (two times), you're left with a remainder of 6.

In addition to these, there are two operators (++ and --) that also perform simple arithmetic. Because they both *change* their operands, I've decided to discuss these in the "Assignment Operators" section later in this chapter.

Flash enables you to perform many additional math operations through the Math object (discussed later this chapter), but don't discount how such simple operators can be used in expressions. When you look at the following examples, keep two things in mind: All the variables' values are assumed to have been previously set to numbers and these are just expressions—so, by themselves, they don't do anything.

Average (mean):	`sum/total`
Half:	`full/2`
Average (median— that is, the midpoint):	`lowest+((highest-lowest)/2)`
Price when discounted:	`price-(price*discount)`
Compounded interest:	`principal+(principal*interestRate)`
Seconds (with milliseconds known):	`milliseconds/1000`

These examples all use simple arithmetic operators on homemade variables. You can certainly combine built-in properties in expressions (for example, use _currentFrame+1 to express the frame number of the next frame). You'll see more of this in Chapter 7, "The Movie Clip Object."

Finally, I didn't provide any examples of the modulo (%) operator—but it is one of the most powerful operators available. It seems so innocuous, the remainder. But consider how you determine whether a number is even—it has to be evenly divisible by two. Or, when divided by two, the remainder is zero. Similarly, to determine whether something is evenly divisible by five, there just has to be no remainder when dividing by five. This is where the modulo operator can help. If you just use `anyNumber%2` and find the expression results in `0`, you know the number is even. Later in this chapter (in the "Applied Expression Writing" section), you'll see an example that uses the modulo operator to make a loop execute every *other* time (that is, when `loopCounter%2` equals 0).

Comparison Operators

Comparison operators are used to write expressions that evaluate to either true or false. That's it. You might understand the need for such expressions if you remember that they'll usually reside within a larger statement. For example, by itself the word "true" doesn't mean anything. However, an entire statement that makes sense might be "If your age is greater than 21, you can purchase alcohol." The expression "is greater than 21" always evaluates as either true or false. To make the statement even more explicit, you could say "If the expression 'your age is greater than 21' is true, you can purchase alcohol." This example is a conditional statement. Such statements are covered in detail later this chapter in the section "Conditional and Loop Statements."

The comparison operators by themselves are pretty easy to understand. All these operators require two operands in the form *first operand, operator, second operand* (such as `12>4`, where 12 is *first operand*, > is the *operator*, and 4 is *second operand*). Let's look at them all.

- Greater than (>) results in true when the first number is greater than the second.

- Less than (<) results in true when the first number is less than the second.

- Greater than or equal to (>=) results in true when the first number is greater than or equal to the second.

- Less than or equal to (<=) results in true when the first number is less than or equal to the second.

- Not equal to (!=) results in true when the first number is not the same value as the second.

- Equality(==) results in true when the value of the first and second numbers are equal.

- Strict equality (===) results in true when both the value and data type of the first and second numbers are equal. (See Flash MX's Reference entry for a full description of how the different data types vary.)

You'll see the most practical examples of the comparison operators later in this chapter, but there are several interesting points to make now. Remember that the result of any expression you write with these operators is always either true or false. That is, they can result in nothing except true or false, and false is a perfectly fine possibility. An expression such as 12<25 is perfectly legitimate—it just happens to evaluate to false.

It's interesting that true and false are the two variations of the Boolean data type. However, you can use them within expressions as though they were numbers. True is 1 and false is 0. For example, the expression score*(timesCheated<1) will automatically reduce the value of score (no matter what it is) to 0 if the timesCheated variable is greater than 0. That is, the portion timesCheated<1 evaluates to either true or false (1 or 0). If timesCheated is 0, that portion is true and score is multiplied by 1—and thus is unaffected. If timesCheated is not less than 1, that portion is false and multiplies score by 0 (bringing it down to 0). This is a form of a conditional statement—but much simpler.

The regular equality operator is formed by two equals signs (==)—and the strict equality operator with three equals signs (===). A single character (=) is a different operator entirely. The single equals sign performs an *assignment* (as you'll see later in this chapter). That is, the variable to the left of = is assigned the value of the expression on the right. It actually creates a complete statement (because it *does* something), rather than an expression as the == or === operators do. Not only does this mean that the variable on the left side changes, but if you intended to create an expression that resulted in true or false, you'd find it always results in true. That is, age=21 assigns 21 as the value of age, and this statement will be evaluated as true. On the other hand, age==21 will be either true or false (depending on what the age variable's value happens to be). In addition, age will not change value when you use ==. The first case said, "age now equals 21;" the second said, "Does age happen to equal 21?" You'll see more about assignments, but just don't forget this operator is a "double equal."

Finally, string manipulation is covered in much more detail in Chapter 9, "Manipulating Strings," but it's worth mentioning that the comparison operators work perfectly well on strings. To work intuitively, both operands must be strings. But the expression `"a"<"b"` evaluates as true because `"a"` is earlier in the alphabet. (Uppercase letters are considered less than lowercase, which might be counterintuitive.) The truth is, you'll see such amazing ways to manipulate strings in Chapter 11, "Arrays," that it's not worth discussing much here. Just don't expect all the comparison operators to act differently depending on the data type of their operands (the way that many of the arithmetic operators do).

Logical Operators

Logical operators are used to compare one or two Boolean values—expressions that result in either true or false. (Operators "and," and "or," use two operands, whereas "not" uses one.) Commonly you will extend the comparison operators with logical operators to make compound expressions such as "age is greater than 12 *and* age is less than 20" ("and" being the logical operator in this case). You're actually comparing two expressions (not two single values), but the result of the entire expression must be either true or false. If you use these logical operators on non-Boolean values (such as numbers), any number except 0 will be considered true. If you use them on strings, each string will be true as well.

- The "and" operator (`&&`) results in true if both operands are true.

- The "or" operator (`||`) results in true if either (or both) operands are true.

- The "not" operator (`!`) results in true when the operand (following `!`) is not true (that is, it's false).

Here are a few common examples:

True if age is a "teen":	`(age>12) && (age<20)`
True if either age is greater than 15 or `"accompaniedByAdult"` is true:	`(age>15) ||(accompaniedByAdult==true)`
True if age is anything except 21:	`!(age==21)`
True if age is not a "teen":	`!((age>12) && (age<20))`
True if age is not equal to 21:	`age != 21`

Even though these expressions should be easy to figure out, there are some interesting elements to note. I included additional parentheses to make these expressions clear. But because the logical operators have very low precedence, the expressions on each side will be evaluated first. That is, `age>12&&age<20` works just as well as `(age>12) && (age<20)`, although it might not be as easy to read. Also notice that both operands of the "and" and "or" operators must be a complete expression. For example, `age>12 && <20` won't work. It sounds okay in speech (as in "age is greater than 12 and less than 20,"), but in ActionScript, you want to say "age is greater than 12 and age is less than 20."

Finally, there's one trick that is commonly used to abbreviate scripts—but it might not be intuitive to you. The expression `accompaniedByAdult==true` is the same as `accompaniedByAdult` (by itself). So, in this example, I could have said `age>15||accompaniedByAdult`. If you don't say "==true," it's implied. Of course, you can still get messed up (in either case) if the value of `accompaniedByAdult` is a number or string—but that's another issue (discussed earlier).

You'll get plenty of practice writing expressions. Remember that they'll always be contained within bigger statements. These concepts should begin to make more sense as you write statements. The best way to learn to write statements and expressions is to first write your objectives and then start to program in pseudo-code (as discussed in Chapter 3, "The Programmer's Approach"). You might notice that in many of my examples, I actually include the pseudo-code version as well.

Types of Statements

As I've mentioned countless times, statements *do* things. Often statements do one of two things: either assign values or compare values. A statement could assign a value to the variable `score`. Another statement might compare the user's score to a set of values to determine a grade. Realize that when comparing values, the end result of a statement could be that no action is taken. For example, a statement could compare the user's score to a minimum and then, if the score is not high enough, do *nothing*. Only when the score is high enough would this comparison (or "conditional") statement *do* something—perhaps display a message. We'll look at such conditional statements (that is, the kind that compare values) in the "Conditional and Loop Statements" section later in this chapter. There's a lot of material to discuss related to assigning values.

Using Assignment Operators to Create Statements

The granddaddy of the assignment operators is the equals sign (=). When this operator appears in a statement, you can read = as "…is assigned the value of…."

That is, username="Phillip" can be translated and read aloud as "username *is assigned the value of* 'Phillip.' " The truth is that you don't need any assignment operator other than =. The others just make certain tasks easier. For example, the increment assignment operator (++) can be used to increment its operand, as in age++. That's the same as saying age=age+1. So, if you just understand how the plain old = assignment operator works, the others are variations on the same theme.

Here are the basic assignment operators:

- Assignment (=) places the value of the expression on the right into the variable on the left.

- Increment (++) increments the variable on the left by 1 (that is, it's increased by 1).

- Decrement (--) decrements the variable on the left by 1 (that is, it's reduced by 1).

- Addition and assignment (+=) increases the variable on the left by an amount equal to the expression on the right. (counter+=10 will increase counter by 10.)

- Subtraction and assignment (-=) decreases the variable on the left by an amount equal to the expression on the right.

- Multiplication and assignment (*=) multiplies the variable on the left by an amount equal to the expression on the right.

- Divide and assignment (/=) divides the variable on the left by an amount equal to the expression on the right.

- Modulo and assignment (%=) assigns the variable on the left a value equal to the remainder of dividing the value of the expression on the right into the value of the variable on the left. It sounds worse than it is; it just tries dividing the second number into the first and assigns the variable on the left what's leftover. For example, if your variable counter happens to equal 10, counter%=3 will assign counter the value 1 because 3 goes into 10 three times (3*3=9) with 1 leftover.

If these are starting to seem a bit complicated, remember that you only *need* =. All the other operations can be achieved with =. For example, counter+=10 will increase counter by 10—but so will counter=counter+10. It's not important that you memorize these now. Ultimately, the only thing that matters is getting your movie to do what you want. After you sort that out, you can reach for whichever operators you want.

Possibly the best thing about the all the assignment operators (except +=) is that they actually change the operand being assigned (usually on the left side) to a Number data type. Realize that these operators don't serve double duty (that is, they perform only mathematical assignments and don't work with strings). As such, they try to convert their operand into a number. For example, if you had a variable count that contained a string "12" and you wrote the script count++, the value of count would become 13 (the number, not the string). So, unlike some operators that operate differently based on the data type of the operands, these attempt to convert operands to numbers.

The two assignment operators = and += can work with strings as well. For example, if name="phillip" and then you executed name+="kerman", the current value for name would be "phillipkerman". So, here, the += operator performs like the concatenate version of +. (That is, when either operand is a string, + is "concatenate," not "add.") Obviously, the simple statement name="phillip" assigns the name variable the value of a string; therefore, = is not just for numbers.

Although the data type of operands won't make some of the assignment operators perform different operations, the operator's placement (before or after) the operand can make a difference. You can actually place the ++ or -- in front of or behind the operand, as in ++counter or counter++. The difference is subtle but important. Placing the operator after the operand (counter++, called *post-increment*) increments counter "returns" the value of the operand *before* the increment happened. When your entire statement is only counter++, this issue doesn't matter. However, when you say otherVariable=counter++, otherVariable will turn into the value of counter *before* it gets incremented. On the other hand, if you say otherVariable=++counter, otherVariable turns into the incremented (higher) value of counter. In either case, the variable counter increments (sooner or later). It's not that one variation is better than the other; it just depends on your intent.

Although the difference between pre- and post-decrement and increment might seem very subtle, there's actually a particular situation in which you might have to use the pre-decrement or pre-increment option. Specifically, when the operand is a value that you're not allowed to change, only pre-decrement or pre-increment makes sense. For example, the _totalFrames property of a Movie Clip cannot be changed with ActionScript. (You can "get" it, just not "set" it.) If you want to use a value that's one less than _totalFrames, you must use --_totalFrames. Although Flash "wants" to decrement _totalFrames, it can't, but at least the expression results in a number that's one less than _totalFrames. Realize that both pre and post options do two things: change the value of the operand and return the value (either before or after the change). Even if the operand is an unchangeable value (such as _totalFrames), the pre-increment or pre-decrement options will still return the value as if it could change. Consider these two statements:

```
oneMore=_totalFrames++;
oneMore=++_totalFrames;
```

In either case, _totalFrames can't change. But only the second statement will assign the oneMore variable a value that's one greater than _totalFrames.

Here are a few examples of typical statements that assign values. (Notice that I've thrown in plenty of expressions within the statements.)

- Reduce price to half: price=price/2; (You could also use price/=2;)

- Calculate a percent correct based on a number of questions: percentCorrect=(numberCorrect/totalQuestions)*100;

- Apply a discount to price if age is greater than 64: price=price-(discount*(age>64));

Notice that I ended each statement with a semicolon. Flash understands the end of your statement is reached when the semicolon is used. You can't just type a return at the end of the line because both blank spaces and returns are ignored when Flash reads your script. You could actually run all your code along one long (difficult-to-read) line if you separated distinct statements with semicolons.

The Thought Process

Writing statements takes the same skill as writing expressions. Similarly, the skill will come with practice. Most people write any such code in segments. That is, it's difficult to write a statement in the same way that you might compose a sentence in speech (in which you almost talk without thinking—let alone thinking about the composition of your sentence). Rather, to write a script statement, first think of your general objective, write it out in pseudo-code, and then break down your pseudo-code into discrete elements that can be expressed in script. For example, it's unrealistic to simply think "double score when they get the bonus question" and then immediately type score*=(1+(bonusQuestion==true)). Even though this example is intentionally complex, you're unlikely to create such a statement without breaking down the task into smaller parts. Your thought process might follow this order:

"Okay, I want to double their score if they got the bonus question right. Well, what if they got it wrong? In that case, just leave `score` alone. What can I do to `score` that will leave it untouched? Either add 0 or multiply by 1. Since doubling involves multiplying by 2, I've got an idea: I'll either multiply by 2 or multiply by 1 (depending on the outcome of the bonus question). So far, I have the statement `score*=` in mind. That is, `score` is assigned the value of `score` multiplied by blank. I want "blank" to be either 1 or 2. That is, either `1+0` or `1+1`. For the second number (`+0` or `+1`), I can simply write an expression that evaluates as either false or true. The expression `bonusQuestion==true` will always evaluate as 0 (when `bonusQuestion` is *not* true) or 1 (when `bonusQuestion` *is* true). The part on the right (`(1+0)` or `(1+1)`) can be replaced with `(1+(bonusQuestion==true))`. So, the entire statement `score*=(1+(bonusQuestion==true))` makes complete sense now."

Perhaps your brain works differently than mine, but this was just a sample of my thought process. By the way, the same exact task could be expressed with countless variations of statements—this is just one solution. Generally, when you're starting out, your expressions will tend to be wordy—that's fine. You'll get more practice writing expressions and statements at the end of this chapter.

Built-In Statements

Although I've probably said that "statements *do* things" enough times so that you'll never forget, what I failed to mention is that there are built-in statements that also do things. Consider that ActionScript and JavaScript are practically identical, but there are a few Flash-centric actions that only ActionScript contains, such as `gotoAndPlay()`. The ambiguous term *actions* is left over from older versions of Flash. Realize that everything listed in the Actions section of the toolbox list (some of which are shown in Figure 5.3) is either a Flash-centric feature (a command or method) or a true built-in statement. Think of them all as statements if you want. (By the way, another way in which ActionScript and JavaScript vary is in the events to which they respond—Flash has `on(release)`, and JavaScript has `onClick`, for instance.)

We don't need to step through each statement now. You'll pick them up as you write blocks of code. For example, you'll see both `return` and `break` in the upcoming section about conditional and loop statements. The point is that all built-in statements are listed under Actions—and that some of them are unique to Flash.

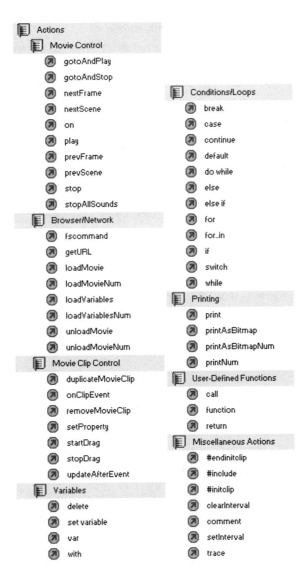

Figure 5.3 *Flash actions are either Flash-specific features or built-in statements.*

Simple Objects in Statements

It's only fair to introduce you to objects now. Even though there are seven other chapters dedicated to the finer points of objects (Chapter 7, "The Movie Clip Object;" Chapter 9, "Manipulating Strings;" Chapter 10, "Keyboard Access and Modifying Onscreen Text;" Chapter 11, "Arrays;" Chapter 12, "Objects;"

Chapter 13, "Homemade Objects;" and Chapter 14, "Extending ActionScript"), there are a couple of simple objects that will help you immensely as you write statements—namely, the Math object and the Number object. Instead of providing detailed information about objects here, I'll simply show you how to use the Math and Number objects. They're so easy that you really can use them without fully understanding objects. When you get to the workshop chapters, you'll find the Math Object useful in almost every exercise. You'll use it in Workshop Chapter 3, "Creating a Horizontal Slider," (to help determine the percentages) and in Workshop Chapter 11, "Using Math to Create a Circular Slider," (to help determine the angles). In fact, you'll find the Math Object invaluable if you ever want to go beyond simple addition, subtraction, multiplication, and division.

Using the Math Object

The Math object will give you access to both common mathematical functions as well as a few constants (such as pi). The functions in the Math object (called *methods*) are almost like the buttons on a scientific calculator; actually, they're practically identical. For example, my calculator has a square root button (that looks like this: √). If I first type a 9 and then press the square root button, my calculator "returns" (into the display field) the square root of 9—that is, 3. Within an expression in Flash, you can also type a 9 (or a variable whose value happens to equal 9) and use the Math object's square root method to return the square root into the expression where you used it. The expression looks like this: `Math.sqrt(9)`. (Remember that as an expression, this evaluates to 3, but it doesn't do anything unless you use it in a statement, such as `answer=Math.sqrt(9);`.)

The form for all the Math object methods is `Math.methodName()` where `methodName` is the function that you want to use. The parentheses are required for all methods because they often accept parameters. For example, you can't just say `Math.sqrt()`. Flash needs to know, "Square root of what?" You put the number (or expression that evaluates out as a number) into the parentheses— for example, `Math.sqrt(9); Math.sqrt(6+3);` `Math.sqrt(oneVar+((someExpression*2) +whatever))`. Flash will take the result of the expression in the parentheses, calculate the square root, and finally put the answer in place of the entire expression. (Remember that it's an expression.)

In addition to methods that perform mathematical operations, the Math object has constants. You can tell them apart from the methods because they're listed in all uppercase letters, such as `E` (Euler's constant—for use in natural logarithms) and

PI (the ratio of a circle's circumference to its diameter—used in trigonometry and geometry). They're used like methods except that because they don't accept parameters, the parentheses aren't used. That is, `Math.PI` (not `Math.PI()`) turns into 3.14159... and `Math.E` into 2.718.... You could probably live your entire life without ever really *needing* constants. For example, you could just hard-wire 3.14159 every time you needed to use pi in a formula (for example, if you wanted to calculate the circumference of a circle, `PI` times radius). It's just that the constants are built into ActionScript and they're very accurate—so you might as well use them when you need them. Just remember the constants are all upper-case and don't need or accept parameters; therefore, they don't use parentheses.

Instead of going through all the Math object features (see Figure 5.4)—effectively providing a recap of the last trigonometry course you took (and possibly awakening the long repressed anxieties associated)—we'll just start using them in statements.

Here are a few fun examples of the Math object:

- `Math.abs(number)` Absolute value. Returns a non-negative version of number. For example, `Math.abs(startPoint-endPoint)` returns the distance between `startPoint` and `endPoint`, and it will always be a positive number even if the `endPoint` is a greater number (which would otherwise cause `startPoint-endPoint` to be a negative number).

- `Math.max(x,y)` returns the value of either x or y (whichever is greater). For example, the statement `bestScore=Math.max(writtenScrore, verbalScore);` will assign the value of `bestScore` to equal the value of either `writtenScore` or `verbalScore` (whichever is greater).

- `Math.floor(number)` returns the integer portion of a number. (That is, it rounds it down.) For example, given the number of minutes I've worked on this chapter, I can calculate how many full hours that is by using `hours=Math.floor(minutesWorked/60);`. I can combine this with the modulo operator (%) we looked at earlier to express a string that shows the total time in hours and minutes (instead of just minutes): `Math.floor(minutesWorked/60) + " hour(s) and " + (minutesWorked%60) + " minute(s)"`.

- `Math.round(number)` rounds off number to the closest integer. For example, `Math.round(1.9)` returns 2; `Math.round(1.1)` returns 1; and `Math.round(1.5)` returns 2. Note that computers have an inherent "rounding error" that crops up with many floating-point numbers (that is, decimal numbers). Consider the fact that 1/3 + 1/3 + 1/3 equals 1. When a computer tries to represent 1/3 in a decimal form, however, it can't just use 0.3333 (with threes repeating forever). Instead, it rounds off—and eventually this type of thing will cause errors. Don't lose any sleep over it, but do be sure to check out Workshop Chapter 8, "Creating a Currency-Exchange Calculator," for an application of the issue.

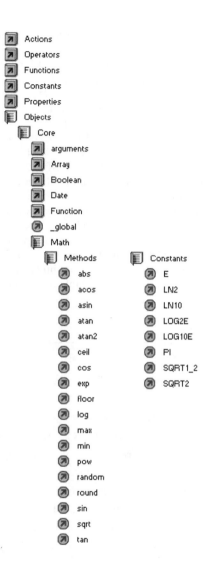

Figure 5.4   *You'll find all the components of the Math object under Objects>Core in the Actions panel's toolbox.*

- `Math.random()`returns a random decimal number between 0 and 1 (but not including 0 or 1—that is, literally *between* 0 and 1, not inclusive). For example, if you want to return a number between 1 and 100 (inclusive), first set min=1 and max=100 and then use this expression: `Math.floor(Math.random()*((max-min)+1))+min`. This might not be easy to read, but the idea is that you multiply the random decimal number by 100 (that is, the difference between the max and min plus 1— that's the part that reads `Math.random()*((max-min)+1)`). Assume that `Math.random()` returns 0.56899. It will turn into 56.899 when multiplied by 100. You take that whole expression and strip off the excess decimals (using the `floor` method), resulting in 56. Finally, you add the min (at the end of the expression) because it's quite possible that the random number could be 0.00000000001, which turns into 0 even after you multiply by 100 and use the Floor method (and that's lower than our min). Also consider that if you multiply the random decimal by 100 (the max) you'll never quite get to 100 because the random number is always *lower* than 1. That last +min eliminates the possibility of going lower than the min (1) and makes sure that it's possible to reach the max (100).

Handy Formula

To return a random integer between min and max, use
`Math.floor(Math.random()*((max-min)+1))+min`

Just to make things fun, the Math object's trigonometry functions (`Math.sin (angle)`, `Math.cos(angle)`, and `Math.tan(angle)`) expect the angle provided to be expressed in radians (not in degrees with which you might be more familiar). Radians and degrees are simply different measurement units— like miles and kilometers. A half-circle has 180 degrees but only pi radians, whereas a whole circle is 360 degrees, or 2 pi (see Figure 5.5.) Therefore, any time you need to convert degrees to radians, you must *multiply* by `Math.PI/180`. That is, 90 degrees is `(Math.PI/180)*90` radians (or 1.57....) (Just multiply your degrees by `Math.PI/180` to get radians.)

Whereas the trig functions accept angles (in radians, not degrees), the inverse functions (`Math.asin()`, `Math.acos()`, and `Math.atan()`) return angles (natu- rally, in radians as well). If you want to convert a value represented in radians to degrees, just *divide* by `Math.PI/180`. That is, 1.57 radians is `1.57/(Math.PI/180)` degrees (or 90). Even though all this might seem like a sick joke from a sadistic mathematician, the truth is that you can usually do all your calculations in radians; you might never need to convert between radians to degrees. An exception would be if you want to display—for the user—a found angle in degrees, or you want to set the _rotation property of a clip to an angle you calculated. Generally, do all the calculations in radians and then (if you need to) convert the values to degrees at the last minute. If nothing else, just be aware of the difference.

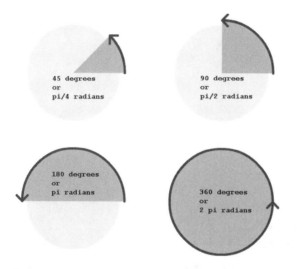

45 degrees
or
pi/4 radians

90 degrees
or
pi/2 radians

180 degrees
or
pi radians

360 degrees
or
2 pi radians

Figure 5.5   *A full circle contains 360 degrees or 2 pi radians—two units of measure that can lead to confusion.*

Handy Formula

To calculate radians from a given value in degrees, use

```
radians=degrees*(Math.PI/180)
```

To calculate degrees from a given value in radians, use

```
degrees=radians/(Math.PI/180)
```

Flash provides one trig function that you might never have seen in math class: Math.atan2(). As you might know, the plain Math.atan() function (or "arc tangent") will help you determine the angle of a corner in a right triangle. Just provide the length of the triangle's opposite side divided by the length of the adjacent side, and Math.atan() will then return the angle. For example, if one side is 70 pixels and the other side is 200 pixels, the angle is 30 degrees (well, .528 radians, because Math.atan(70/120) returns .528). Figure 5.6 has a couple of examples.

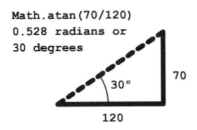

```
Math.atan(70/120)
0.528 radians or
30 degrees
```

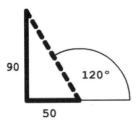

```
Math.atan(90/50)
1.064 radians or
60 degrees (180-60 is 120)
```

Figure 5.6 *The regular arc-tangent function (`Math.atan()`) enables you to calculate angles given two sides of a right triangle.*

The plain `Math.atan()` function is fine and dandy when you're in the real world (where moving up increases values). But consider the coordinate system in Flash. The y values decrease when you go up! Consider the second example in Figure 5.6; both the x and y values are really negative numbers. In addition, you have to remember in that case to subtract the value you find from 180. It becomes even more of a hassle when you move into the other quadrants (from 180 degrees to 270 degrees and from 270 degrees to 360 degrees). Luckily, `Math.atan2()` resolves the entire mess! You just provide `Math.atan2()` with two parameters: one for the y value and one for the x value. That's it. You'll notice in Figure 5.7 that all the issues with positive and negative values are handled automatically by `Math.atan2()`. In Workshop Chapter 11, you'll learn how `Math.atan2()` can make calculating angles a snap.

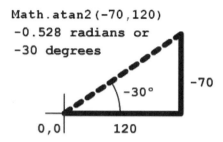

Math.atan2(-70,120)
-0.528 radians or
-30 degrees

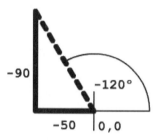

Math.atan2(-90,-50)
-2.078 radians or
-120 degrees

Figure 5.7   *When you consider Flash's coordinate system,* Math.atan2() *is a life-saver because it handles all issues with positive and negative numbers.*

By now you see how the Math object's methods can be used within expressions. Basically, you're given a suite of mathematical functions through this object. It's pretty easy to use the Math object, but that doesn't mean all your expressions will be easy to write. It also doesn't mean all the other objects are as easy either. For now, just realize that the Math object provides you with many useful functions.

Using the Number Object

The Number object and Math object are similar in that you can use both of them in expressions without having an intimate understanding of objects. You simply say Number.methodName() or Number.CONSTANT_NAME. As you can see in Figure 5.8, the Number object consists mainly of constants (uppercase items). I suspect that you'll most often use the Number object for its constants only, so at this point we'll focus on them. (When we discuss objects in Chapter 11, the Number object's methods—toString() and valueOf()—will be covered.)

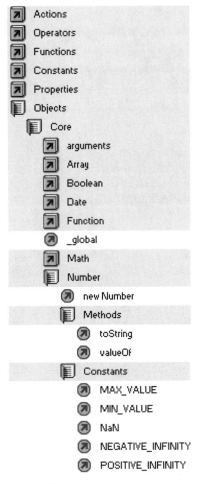

Figure 5.8 *The Number object is primarily used for the constants (all listed in upper-case).*

I've included this brief discussion now, however, because—in addition to being a simple object—there's another part of ActionScript with the *same* name. In addition to the Number object, there's a function called `Number()` that we touched on earlier this chapter. Even though we won't discuss functions fully until Chapter 8, using the `Number()` function is easy: `Number(expressionOrVariable)` attempts to convert the value of `expressionOrVariable` into a number and return the result. So, `myNum=Number("100")+1;` will convert the string `"100"` to a number, add 1 to it, and place `101` into `myNum`. Remember that the addition operator will act differently if one operand is a string (and in our case, turn `myNum` into `"1001"`). Because the word *Number* is used in both the case of a Number object and the Number function, it can be confusing. The weird part is that if you use the new constructor in front of Number(), you'll be creating a new instance of the Number object—a different thing entirely, and something that you probably don't want to do. (At least wait until you learn all about objects in upcoming chapters.)

The Number object's constants are easy to use, albeit not particularly exciting. Here they are:

- Number.MAX_VALUE is the "largest representable number," meaning a very high number, but one from which you can subtract. For example, you might initialize a variable to equal MAX_VALUE (as in bigNumber= Number.MAX_VALUE). Then you could subtract from your variable (for a very long time—but not forever).

- Number.MIN_VALUE is the smallest number (actually, a negative number).

- Number.NEGATIVE_INFINITY is so far into the negative that you can't even add numbers to ever get out. You can use this constant in comparison expressions, but you can't perform operations on "infinity" the way you can with Number.MAX_VALUE and Number.MIN_VALUE.

- Number.POSITIVE_INFINITY is like Number.NEGATIVE_INFINITY but positive. Because you can't perform calculations on variables that contain Number.POSITIVE_INFINITY, the most likely usage would be in a comparison expression (such as an if statement—discussed later this chapter). For example, you could check whether a variable or expression is equal to Number.POSITIVE_INFINITY. For example, 1/0 is Number.POSITIVE_INFINITY.

- Number.NaN means "Not a Number." You'll probably see "NaN" by accident more often then you'll need to select it by choice. When you try performing a math operation on a string, you'll get "NaN" for an answer—meaning the operation failed. Number.NaN can be used in comparison expressions such as (aVariable==Number.NaN). Often, however, there are alternatives that might work better (for example, undefined, which all variables have for a value before you ever use them). Probably a better way to determine whether you've got NaN is to use the function isNaN(expression), which return false if expression is a number (or true if it's not a number). Because variables all equal undefined before they are assigned, you can use a conditional (for example, an if statement) to check whether a variable is undefined—in which case you could take corrective action, such as assigning it a legitimate value.

We've looked at a lot so far in this chapter: expressions, statements, and the operators that hold them together. Also, the Math object was included because it gives you a different set of operators. There's more. Despite the fact that we've seen some perfectly complete statements, we haven't looked at conditional statements (that execute only when certain conditions exist) or loop structures (that repeatedly execute scripts). Loops and conditionals will round out your knowledge, and then you can start practicing everything at the end of the chapter.

Conditional and Loop Statements

Flash executes every line of script that it encounters. If a script is never encountered, it's never executed. And, if a script is encountered repeatedly, it is executed over and over. Using conditional statements, you can control what part of your script is executed or skipped. Obviously, if you place a script on a button and the user never clicks the button, the script won't execute. However, after a button is clicked, a conditional statement can control what portion of the contained script executes. This way, you can write scripts that behave differently depending on outside conditions.

Looping is a way to make a particular script execute repeatedly—either a certain number of times or until a condition is met. This is helpful when you have a lot of code to process, but also when you're not sure how many times the code needs to execute. In the upcoming section on loops, you'll find that loops can save you a lot of typing. Compare the following two pseudo-code descriptions in which a loop would help:

The long way:

```
Attention Dasher; Attention Dancer; Attention Prancer; Attention
Vixen; Attention Comet; Attention Cupid; Attention Donder; Attention
Blitzen.
```

Using a loop:

```
All reindeer... Attention.
```

Although this might not explain the ActionScript syntax (it's just pseudo-code after all), the second choice (the loop) is obviously easier to use.

Conditional Statements: `if, if else, if else if, switch`

These four structural conditional statements are really variations on the same concept: If a condition is true, Flash should execute a block of code. At the core of all four variations is a kind of "if"—and it's the easiest. Consider my wife instructing me, "If they have jellybeans, get me some." The condition is that "they have jellybeans," and the result—if they do—is that I'm supposed to "get some" for her. More technically, *if* the condition "they have jellybeans" is true, I execute the second part of my wife's instructions.

A plain `if` statement will execute the consequences only when the statement is encountered and the condition is true—nothing more. Realize that unless my wife specifies what to do in the event that they're out of jellybeans, I don't need to do anything (of course, I know better). Had she said, "If they have jellybeans, get some; otherwise, get some chocolate," it's clear that I'll be purchasing one item or the other. If the condition is false (that is, if they don't have jellybeans), I am to automatically follow the second part (the "otherwise" or the `else` statement, if you will). In reality, I can't get chocolate unless they have some, but that's not at issue. In this case, when the initial condition is false, the second part (the `else`) is executed every time.

You can make the `else` statement conditional, too. That is, "If they have jellybeans, get some; otherwise, if chocolate is on sale, get some of that." Realize that there's a distinct possibility that I will come home empty-handed. A plain `if` statement can skip part of the code; an `if else` statement will do one or the other instructions; and an `if else if` statement could easily skip all the code. Let me show the three real-life statements in actual ActionScript—using a few homemade variables (that are assumed to have previous values).

A plain `if`:

```
if (jellybeans>0) {
    // buy some
}
```

A regular `if else`:

```
if (jellybeans>0) {
    // buy some
} else {
    // get chocolate
}
```

An `if else if`:

```
if (jellybeans>0) {
    // buy some
} else if (chocolateOnSale == true) {
    // get chocolate
}
```

Even though you *can* write an `if` statement with the Actions panel in Normal Mode, I'd recommend (even if just temporarily) going into Expert Mode to do so. I always start by typing the structure of the `if` statement—no conditions, no results... just a skeleton—as follows:

```
if (condition){
}
```

This way I won't forget to satisfy any parentheses or curly braces I start. Then I go back through and replace `condition` with an expression that results in true or false (1 or 0). Then, finally, after the opening curly brace, I make a new line and type the script I want to be executed (when the condition is true).

If I decide I need to add an `else` catch-all statement when the condition is not true, I'll add `else {}` at the end. That is, the code

```
if (jellybeans>0){
    //buy some
}
```

can have an `else` provision added, like this:

```
if (jellybeans>0){
    //buy some
} else {
}
```

Then I'll go back through and make a new line after the opening curly brace that follows the `else` statement. Adding an `else if` statement is not much different. Simply add `else if (condition){}` instead of `else {}`.

Finally, `else if` statements can be nested. That is, when one condition is not met (because it's false), another condition is not met, and you can keep adding `else if` *ad infinitum*. As such, nested `else if` statements can become unwieldy. Although it's not as eloquent (or efficient for the computer), I recommend avoiding deeply nested `else if` statements and instead using a series of independent `if` statements. For example, you could use all three `if` statement in sequence, as follows:

```
if (jellybeans>0){
    //buy some
}
if (!(jellybeans>0)){
    //buy chocolate
}
if (chocolateOnSale==true){
    //buy chocolate
}
```

There's a logical problem with this code as *each* `if` statement is encountered (and potentially entered), meaning that it's possible that I come home with both jellybeans and chocolate. (Not necessarily a problem, but remember that this is supposed to serve as an alternative to a nested `if else if` statement.) If the various conditions were exclusive—that is, when one is true, the others are necessarily false—then there's no problem with this method. Notice that's the situation with the first two conditions. That is, there's no possible way that `(jellybeans>0)` and `!(jellybeans>0)` could both be true—they're mutually exclusive. However, the first and third conditions could both be true, and thus both conditional scripts would be executed. In the case of nested `if` statements, if one condition is met, the others aren't even considered—they're simply skipped.

Even if multiple `if` statements aren't all exclusive (which is the problem here), you can still use this more readable format with a little extra work. The `return` statement will cause Flash to bypass the rest of the script in a block of code. Realize that the code could be enclosed within a larger block of code—perhaps within an `on (press){ }` mouse event of a button. As soon as Flash encounters `return`, it will skip the rest of the code. So, if you type `return` right before the closing curly brace in each `if` statement, you can be assured that once an `if` statement's condition is met, the rest will be ignored.

My suggestion for a series of `if` statements is beginning to look like a real pain, considering that even *after* one condition is met, you want the rest of the `if` statements to be skipped but you might have more code (at the end) that you want to execute; therefore, you can't simply use `return` within each `if` statement. Just to carry this through, one solution would be to set a "flag" variable. That is, above all the `if` statements, you can type `notDone=1;`. Then each condition can be expanded from `if(mainCondition){}` to read `if((mainCondition)&&notDone)){}`. This script says that if *both* the original condition (such as `jellybeans>0`) *and* the condition `notDone==1`, then execute the code. Finally, instead of using `return` within (but at the end of each) `if` statement, use `notDone=0;`, which will effectively cause Flash to skip the rest of the conditions. The result would look like this:

```
1 notDone=1;
2 if (jellybeans>0){
3      //buy some
4      notDone=false;
5 }
6 if (!(jellybeans>0)&&notDone){
7      //buy chocolate
8      notDone=false;
9 }
```

```
10 if (chocolate=="on sale"&&notDone){
11     //buy chocolate
12     notDone=false;
13 }
14 //the rest of the code
```

(Recall that the expression including notDone on lines 6 and 10 is the same as notDone==true.) I'll be the first to admit that this solution is not eloquent, nor is it particularly efficient for the computer. I would argue, however, that compared to a deeply nested if else if statement, it's probably easier to read. The sacrifice of making slightly less concise code is worth it if it means the code is more readable. Feel free to use else if when you're able to keep track of everything. Keep in mind that this discussion hasn't been wasted because we got to talk about the return statement as well as a little bit about solving a problem.

New to MX   There's another statement (called switch) that can be used like the variations of the if statement. The switch statement enables you to avoid deeply nested if else if statements—but only when you're trying to match one of many specific results of a single expression. Consider that my wife gave me these instructions: "If jellybeans cost $1 per pound, get 2 pounds plus a chocolate bar; if jellybeans cost $2 per pound, just get one pound of jellybeans; finally, if jellybeans cost $3 per pound, only get one-half pound." Although you could express this by using a nested if else if statement, notice that all the conditions are based on the same expression: "The cost of one pound of jellybeans."

The switch statement uses the following form:

```
switch (expression){
    case value1:
        //do this
        break; //to skip the rest
    case value2:
        //do that
        break; //to skip the rest
}
```

Where expression is a single expression that could have a variety of different values. For each possible value you expect, replace value1 or value2. The great thing about switch is that you can account for as many different unique values as you want. Consider the following finished version from my practical example of jellybeans:

```
switch (pricePerPound){
    case 1:
        //buy 4 lbs. and buy a chocolate bar
        break;
```

```
        case 2:
            //buy one pound
            break;
        case 3:
            //buy one-half pound
            break;
}
```

Notice that cases 1, 2, and 3 don't indicate a sequence but rather specific values for the `pricePerPound` variable. Also, `break` in the last case is unnecessary. (You'll learn more about `break` later this chapter.) Finally, this analogy might not be the most appropriate for the `switch` statement because it's possible the cost is $2.95 per pound (although I suppose you could include `Math.round()` in one of the cases). Consider the following example for something a little more useful:

```
switch (username){
    case "admin":
        //do admin stuff
        break;
    case "customer":
        //do customer stuff
        break;
    case "supplier":
        //do supplier stuff
        break;
}
```

Ignore, for the time being, the fact that the value for `username` could be `"ADMIN"` (all uppercase) and this example would fail to recognize that value. (In Chapter 10, you'll see how to control strings to handle that kind of thing.) However, do notice that if `username` is not one of the three explicit cases shown, nothing happens. That could be what you want, but there's a feature of `switch` that enables you to include a "catch-all" at the end. It looks just like any case, but it reads `case default:` (no quotes around `default`). Here's a modified version of the preceding example:

```
switch (username){
    case "admin":
        //do admin stuff
        break;
    case "customer":
        //do customer stuff
        break;
    case "supplier":
        //do supplier stuff
        break;
    case default:
        //do catch all stuff
}
```

You'll get more practice at the end of the chapter in the "Applied Expression Writing" section. For now, however, I recommend that you study the skeleton form of each version of the `if` statement as well as of the `switch` statement.

Loop Statements: `for, for in`

Any loop will execute the same script as many times as you specify, or until a condition you specify is met. Often you don't know exactly how many times you need the code to execute, but you can still refer to the number of loops by reference, such as, "Keep rinsing the spinach until there's no more dirt in the water" and, "For every envelope in that stack, please address, seal, and stamp each one." If there are 100 envelopes, you'll repeat the process 100 times—but you don't have to explicitly specify 100 iterations. You'll see how to specify the number of iterations this way. In addition, realize that you won't always execute the same exact code repeatedly. For example, when you address, seal, and stamp several envelopes, you're following the same instructions (the same "script," if you will), but with slight variations. You don't put the same address on each envelope, but you do put *some* address on each envelope. When structuring the loop you're writing, consider two issues: How many times should the script execute and how do I write the script (that executes) so that it behaves differently for each iteration?

If you only learn one loop statement, it should be the `for` loop. Here's the skeleton:

```
for (init; condition; next) {
    //do statement(s) here
}
```

Let's use the following example for our discussion:

```
for (n=1; n<11; n++) {
    trace("Current iteration is "+n);
}
```

You can read the skeleton form of this `for` loop as: Starting with `init`, repeat the following while `condition` is true, and on each iteration, do `next`. Therefore, the example says, "Starting with n=1, keep doing the `trace` action while n<11..., each time incrementing n." The `trace` action is executed 10 consecutive times, but the string that is formed looks slightly different on each loop. In the Output window, you'll see "Current Iteration is 1," and then "Current iteration is 2," and so on. Imagine walking through this loop—the `init` says "n starts at 1," so the first time the trace action is encountered, n is 1. Look at the next expression to see what will happen the next time through, and you'll see n++ (meaning that n is incremented by 1) and n becomes 2. The trace action is executed again. It keeps doing this while the condition—n<11—is true. When n reaches 10, the condition is still true. The next time through, n is 11, so the condition is false and Flash jumps past the closing curly brace to continue any scripts that follow. (Go ahead and type this for loop in the first keyframe of a new Movie Clip instance, and then select Control, Test Movie.)

One tip (just like writing if statements) is that you should start by typing the skeleton and then replace init; condition; next. Another tip is to remember that the condition is the condition that keeps them *in* the loop—not the condition to get out of the loop. That is, repeat *while* the condition is true, not repeat *until* the condition is true. In the earlier example, we wanted to repeat until n reached 11, but the following (updated) script has a problem:

```
for (n=1; n==11; n++) {
    trace("Current iteration is "+n);
}
```

The problem is that n starts at 1, but the condition is looking for 11, so it doesn't have a chance to ever get to 11—and the entire loop is skipped.

Probably the biggest warning I can give you is to make sure that your loops eventually finish. It's easy to accidentally produce a script that, in theory, loops forever. While testing a movie, if the Flash Player ever remains stuck in a loop for more than 15 seconds, it displays a warning to the user (see Figure 5.9).

Because each iteration of a script takes a tiny fraction of a second, 15 seconds is a very long time! Generally, being stuck in a script is likely a symptom of an infinite loop (also called an *indefinite loop*). Here's a perfect example of just such a loop:

```
for (n=1; n>0; n++) {
    //anything because this is an infinite loop!
}
```

The condition (n>0) is true from the beginning and remains so forever! If the "next" expression *decremented* n instead of *incrementing* it, this would not be a problem.

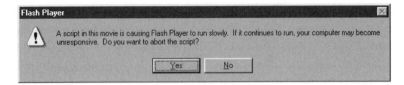

Figure 5.9   *This dialog box appears when the Flash Player remains stuck in a script for more than 15 seconds.*

Another way to inadvertently create an infinite loop is to forget how = differs from ==. Only init and next are assignments (and, therefore, they're state-ments), but "condition" is just an expression. Therefore, the following example probably doesn't do what the programmer intended (unless she was trying to make an infinite loop):

```
for (n=1; n=11; n++) {
    //Help, I'm stuck in an infinite loop
}
```

The problem is that "condition" is n=11 (an assignment). The entire n=11 state-ment, if evaluated, is 1 (or true). This code loops forever because the condition (n=11) is true and remains so forever. (This mistake messes me up all the time!)

As I mentioned, learning the plain for loop is all you really *need*. However, the variation for in is also useful. Unlike the if, if else, and if else if state-ments, the for in loop is not an extension of the plain for loop. The two are entirely different statements. To fully utilize for in loop, it's best to understand arrays and objects—two subjects covered in later chapters. The idea is that the loop will continue to loop "for all the items in the object." Here's an example: "For all the envelopes in that box, do whatever." I'll just show you the skeleton form and one example without fully explaining arrays or objects.

Skeleton form:

```
for(iterant in object){
    //do statement(s) here
}
```

Example:

```
allNames=["Dasher", "Dancer", "Prancer", "Vixen", "Comet",
➥"Cupid", "Donder", "Blitzen"]
for(n in allNames){
    trace("On "+allNames[n]);
}
```

The skeleton form has two elements for you to replace: `iterant` and `object`. Give iterant any name you want and it becomes a variable that automatically increments from the highest down to the lowest. If there are eight things in your object (as in my example), it starts at 7, returns the value of the 7th item in the array (in my example: Blitzen), and then decreases in every loop until it reaches 0. (Because arrays start counting from 0, the range is 7 down to 0 rather than 8 to 1, as you might expect.) `object` is the name of your object or array (in this case, the variable `allNames`, which happens to contain an array of eight items). You don't have to understand arrays fully to imagine how this example works. For now, notice that one way to populate a variable with an array is shown in the first line of the example (use brackets and separate individual values with commas). If you ever need to grab individual elements from an array, you can use the form: `arrayName[index]`, where `index` evaluates as 0 through the total number of items in the array (minus 1, because arrays count 0,1,2,3, and so on).

Unlike the plain `for` loop, the `for in` loop doesn't require that you specify what is supposed to happen on every loop (that is, the "next"). That's because the variable name you use for the iterant automatically goes through all the items in the object (starting at the highest and incrementing down). The two advantages of the `for in` loop are that you don't have to define the "next" and you don't have to specify a condition to control the number of times the loop repeats. Here's an example of using a plain `for` loop to achieve nearly the same result as the `for in` example I showed. Notice that it's not quite as clean, but it works basically the same way.

```
allNames=["Dasher", "Dancer", "Prancer", "Vixen", "Comet",
➥"Cupid", "Donder", "Blitzen"]
for(n=0; n<8; n++){
    trace("On "+allNames[n]);
}
```

(By the way, instead of hard-wiring 8 in the condition, I could have used `allNames.length`, which returns the length of the array—but that's something you'll learn in Chapter 11.) Notice that this example is equivalent to, but not the same as, the `for in` loop. The `for in` version effectively goes in reverse order (starting with "Blitzen" rather than "Dasher," as is the case here).

Let's look at the statements that execute every time the loop repeats. You can put any statement (or statements) within the loop. You don't have to use the iterant at all. If you want the statement that executes to vary every time the loop repeats, however, the trick is to *use* the iterant within the statement. All my examples use a plain trace command. However, the string that appears is different in each iteration because the iterant variable is used—either explicitly, as in trace ("Current iteration is "+n); or within an expression, as in trace("On "+allNames[n]);. (This won't reveal the value of n; rather, it uses n to extract an element in the allNames variable.)

Also realize that you can include as many statements as you want within a loop. You could even make your own iterant or counter that you maintain. You can nest other statements, such as if statements. See whether you can figure out the result of the following nested statement:

```
for(n=1; n<11; n++){
    if(n%2==0){
        trace(n+" is even");
    } else {
        trace(n+" is odd");
    }
}
```

The variable n starts at 1 and iterates through 10. If the expression n%2 happens to equal 0 (that is, zero is the remainder when dividing n by 2), the trace command displays "n is even" (but n is replaced by the value of n). Otherwise, the trace command "n is odd" appears. By the way, I wrote out this example by first typing the skeleton of the for loop, and then inserting a skeleton of the if else statement. Finally, I came back through and filled in the data. (And naturally, I had to test it a few times to weed out the bugs; one of the semicolons in the for statement was a comma, and my if condition was mistyped as an assignment: n%2=0.)

while

If nothing else, while loops are the easiest to accidentally turn into infinite loops. Basically, you say, "Repeat while this condition is true." If the condition never becomes false, you'll repeat forever. You have to make sure that the condition eventually turns out to be false. The while loop is *not* suitable for repeating statements while you wait for the user to do something (or to stop doing something). For example, "While the user has the mouse pressed" is a perfectly legitimate concept, but you have to use a different solution for that objective—while loops are just not made for that. A while loop gives you a way to write a script that will repeatedly execute a statement, but because you might not know exactly how many times it is supposed to execute, you can use a while loop *while* a condition is true. Remember, both for and for in statements require that you specify the number of loops—even if that specification is in reference to a variable, length of an array, or number of items in an object. If, for example, the task is that you keep looping while a variable called found is 0 (or while(found==0)), the while loop is perfect. (Just make sure that found will eventually become something other than 0, or you'll be stuck in the loop forever.)

Here's the form:

```
while (condition) {
    //do this statement
}
```

The following example shows that you must take precautions to ensure that the condition eventually becomes false (so that you can get out of the loop):

```
allNames=["Dasher", "Dancer", "Prancer", "Vixen", "Comet",
➥"Cupid", "Donder", "Blitzen"]
found=0;
n=0;
while (found==0 && n<allNames.length){
    if (allNames[n]=="Rudolf"){
        found=1;
    }
    n++;
}
if (found){
    trace("Rudolf found in spot " + n);
}
```

The form is simple: Statements will repeatedly execute while the condition is true. The preceding example is a bit complex, but instead of contriving an unrealistically simple example, it accurately shows the types of provisions necessary when you use the while loop.

Basically, I want the loop to repeat until I find the string "Rudolf"—so the initial condition is while found==0 (or false). Before the loop, both found and n are initialized. Because my basic condition is found==0, I want to make sure that it's 0 from the start. The variable n serves as an iterant. (You'll almost always need your own iterant in while loops.) This iterant must be initialized before the loop, so that I can increment n at the end of each statement in the loop. The if statement just checks to see whether the nth index of allNames contains the string "Rudolf." If so, found is set to 1—and that gets us out of the loop. Notice that even if found were set to 1, the last statement in the loop (n++) would still execute once before getting kicked out of the loop on the next iteration. So, if n were 4, when Rudolf was found, n would be 5 by the time the loop was exited. I'm taking advantage of the fact that n is always greater than the index where Rudolf was found. My trace command doesn't refer to the array index where Rudolf was found but rather to the made-up term "spot," which is more intuitive than array's indexes (that count 0,1,2…). Finally, it's quite possible that "Rudolf" is never found! To ensure that the loop would exit after each index was checked, I added && n<allNames.length to the condition (found==0). Translated, the entire condition reads: "While both found is zero and n is less than the total number of items in allNames." (Notice that I didn't have to say n<=allNames.length because the length is 8 and I only needed to check through the last item—at index 7.)

The previous example shows how while loops require extra maintenance in the form of your own iterating variable that you first initialize and then increment. This is almost always necessary, although occasionally you don't need to do it. For example, if you're trying to create two random numbers, the following statement should work fine:

```
oneNum=0;
otherNum=0;
while (oneNum==otherNum){
    oneNum=Math.random();
    otherNum=Math.random();
}
```

There's a theoretical possibility that on every iteration, both oneNum and otherNum will be assigned the same random number. The two variables contain the same value at the start (0) and will then repeat while they remain the same. Likely, this loop will execute only once, but even if the two random numbers came out the same, it would take only a fraction of a second to loop 1,000 more times. On my old 450MHz Pentium III, for example, a loop like this will iterate more than 10,000 times per second! The point is that there's a high likelihood that two different random numbers will be found before Flash reaches its 15-second timeout. Unless you include a "way out" in the condition, however, a while loop could try looping forever. (This just means that Flash will reach the timeout dialog box—refer to Figure 5.9—but that is a bad thing because the user sees the dialog.)

Let's review a few final points about loops. The user won't see any visual change on the Stage *during* the loop. For example, consider the following statement:

```
for (n=1; n<6; n++){
    someClip._x= n*5;
}
```

You might expect to see someClip's x position appear at 5, 10, 15, 20, and then 25. It actually does move to those five locations, but you won't see it move. When the loop is finished, you'll see it in the final resting position of 25—but the Stage does not refresh after each loop. (By the way, you can certainly animate a clip by using scripts, as we'll do in the Workshop Chapter 14, "Offline Production," and Workshop Chapter 15, "Creating a Dynamic Slide Presentation"—you just can't do it by using loops.)

Finally, there are two interesting statements that change the flow of a loop. Similar to the way return will skip out of any function or enclosed event (such as on(press)), both break and continue can make a loop change course. Specifically, the break statement will jump out of any loop (actually, it jumps to the end of the loop), and the continue statement will immediately jump to the top of the loop (that is, iterate) by skipping any further statements within the loop.

Here's an example that shows how the continue statement jumps to the top of a loop:

```
for (n=1; n<6; n++){
    if (n==3){
        continue;
    }
    trace ("A number that's not three is " + n);
}
```

If the condition (n==3) is true, the continue statement jumps to the top of the loop (to continue) while bypassing the trace statement below. The continue statement effectively says, "Skip the rest of the statements, but continue looping."

The following example shows how the break statement will jump out of a loop:

```
n=1;
while(true){
  //do something
  if (n>10 && n%2==0){
    break;
  }
  n++;
}
trace ("The first even number past ten is "+n);
```

Without the break statement, this loop would repeat forever. When break is executed, Flash jumps to the end of the loop where it is currently enclosed (that is, to where the trace statement appears in this example). This is just a quick way to get out of a loop. Notice, too, that break will jump past the n++ statement (that is, right outside the enclosing curly brace). You also use break in the switch statement. There, it will cause only the remaining cases to be skipped—but any code following the closing brace of the switch statement itself will be encountered. Compared to return, the break statement only jumps past the end of an enclosed loop, whereas return jumps out of the function or the event that started it all (as with on (press))—most likely skipping a lot more code than a break statement would. For example, if return were used in this example instead of break, the trace statement would be skipped as well.

Applied Expression Writing

This chapter is packed with concepts that relate to composing scripts. You've seen a couple of previews of concepts that will come up later (such as arrays and functions), but for the most part, everything in this chapter has to do with writing expressions and statements. The remaining pages provide a chance to practice writing more complex expressions. I'll provide the objective and you should at least try to write the pseudo-code and then (if you can) the actual script. I'll provide my solution with a translation. You should remember two things while you work through these challenges. First, my solution is just one of countless possible solutions. You might very well find a better way to solve the problem. Second, I include many made-up variables. In a real project, these variables would necessarily have their values set earlier or within a different part of the movie. For example, I might use the expression score>=80. The idea is that the variable score is one that I've been tracking. Perhaps, attached to the button for each correct answer, I used the script: score=score+10;. I'm just assuming that such variables have had their values set properly already. You can make up variables to use in expressions—just realize that you'll have to take care of them by changing their values, as necessary.

Objective:

Given a minimum (x location, for example) and a maximum x, write an expression that uses a given percent to return an integer midpoint based on percent. That is, if the west coast is at 100 miles longitude and the east coast is at 3100 miles longitude, a location 50 percent across the country would be at longitude position 1600 miles. Even though most people can figure that out in their head, it's more difficult to write the expression (using variables named high, low, and percent).

Solution:

```
low+ Math.floor((high-low)*(percent/100));
```

Translation:

Calculating 50 percent of 3000 is easy. Just use `3000*(50/100)`. To determine
the width of the United States, for example, you can subtract the longitude
of the east coast (`high`) from the west coast (`low`). Our formula so far:
`(high-low)*(percent/100)`. That will usually result in a decimal answer, and
using `Math.floor()` returns the integer portion. Finally, the entire expression is
added to `low` (or the west coast) because you'll want to start counting from there.
For example, if the longitude of west coast is 5000 and the east coast is 8000,
50 percent of the difference is still 1500. If you want to end up in the middle of
the country, however, you need to add 1500 to 5000—that is, 6500 (by counting
from the west coast). Figure 5.10 should help you visualize this problem.

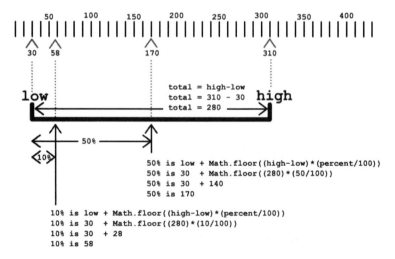

Figure 5.10   *A visual representation of the problem might help you solve the expression
for percent.*

Handy Formula

To determine a proportional x position between two points, use:

```
xLoc = low + Math.floor( (high-low) * (percent/100) )
```

Objective:

Build an array that contains the days of the week, as follows:

```
daysOfWeek=["Sunday","Monday", "Tuesday", "Wednesday",
➥"Thursday", "Friday", "Saturday"];
```

Then write a loop that displays all the days of the week in the Output window (using the `trace` statement).

Solution:

```
daysOfWeek=["Sunday","Monday", "Tuesday", "Wednesday",
➥"Thursday", "Friday", "Saturday"];
for (n=0; n<7; n++){
    trace(daysOfWeek[n]);
}
```

Translation:

After populating the array, our `for` loop initializes n to 0 (because, remember, the first item in an array is in index 0). Then, while n is less than 7 (the last item in the array is at index 6), our `trace` statement displays the nth item in the array. Notice that the following also works, but displays the days in reverse order:

```
for (n in daysOfWeek){
    trace(daysOfWeek[n]);
}
```

Objective:

Write a statement (using `if`, `if else`, or `if else if`) that sets a variable called grade to A, B, C, D, or F, based on a variable called score, using a scale in which 90–100 is an A, 80–89 is a B, 70–79 is a C, 60–69 is a D, and 0–59 is an F.

Solution:

```
grade="F";
if (score>=60){
    grade="D";
}
if (score>=70){
    grade="C";
}
if (score>=80){
    grade="B";
}
if (score>=90){
    grade="A";
}
```

Translation:

Granted, this isn't the eloquent solution; there are many other possibilities. The way I solved it was to first award an F (sort of discouraging, I suppose), and then if score was high enough (score>=60) I give a D, and so on. Even though this isn't a super-efficient solution—after all, if a score were 95, the grade would be assigned F, D, C, B, and then finally A—I used it because it's easy to read, not because it shows off every component of ActionScript.

Summary

What a chapter! Believe it or not, there's more. However, the topics covered in this chapter cover almost all the typical programming tasks that you'll be doing day in and day out. Although many upcoming chapters have interesting and valuable information, this chapter summarizes the core skills.

{ Chapter 6 }

Debugging

Bugs are a fact in any programming. Even if you could write code that—by itself—was bug-free, outside influences can cause your movie to fail. Such basic issues as the user's computer configuration, the operating system, the browser, and even the Flash player all have *some* bugs. You don't need any help creating bugs, of course, because if you're human, you'll create many on your own. Actually, you, not the underlying software, will likely be the source of most bugs. A bug can be a flaw in your flow of logic or an error in the syntax of an expression. Regardless, bugs will crop up with unpredictable results that are invariably undesirable.

Debugging, or finding bugs and fixing them, poses an interesting dilemma. The premise of debugging is that you (the one who created the bug in the first place) are supposed to uncover where the flaw in logic or syntax error appears. Naturally, this is quite difficult because it requires that you find a problem in a script you thought was perfectly logical and legitimate at the time you wrote it. Despite this difficulty, Flash has both practical methods and built-in features to help you squash bugs.

In this chapter, you will:

- Interpret syntax errors that Flash provides.
- Develop methods to identify and document bugs.
- Learn conventional debugging techniques.
- Use the Flash Debugger to watch properties and variables.

Compared to previous chapter's intensity and length, this chapter is pretty mild. You should find it a good reprise.

General Approaches to a Bug-Free Life

While programming Flash, your life will never be truly "bug-free." There are, however, many steps you can take to uncover bugs, fix them, and ensure that there are no obvious ones waiting to reveal themselves at the least opportune time. Most of these quality assurance techniques apply to any process—not just Flash programming. We'll cover built-in Flash features later this chapter in the section, "Using the Debugger." First, let's look at a few general ways to find, define, fix, and prevent bugs.

Finding and Defining Bugs

The first—and most important—step in debugging is to find the bug. Some bugs will prove to be elusive, whereas others will be so significant that you won't be able to make the movie run. I classify bugs into three categories: those that prevent the movie from even starting, those that cause the movie to effectively stop running, and those with an error in logic that—while still allowing the movie to run—displays inaccurate results. The first type is the easiest to find; the third type is the most difficult.

Find the Bugs That Prevent Your Movie from Starting

When you select Control, Test Movie, Flash will export an .swf. If there are any syntax errors (or other critical problems) in your script, however, you will see a full listing of the problems in the Output window (see Figure 6.1). Although the offending script will be ignored (after all, Flash can't figure out what you meant), other scripts might still work. Regardless, the appearance of any syntax error is effectively a "show stopper." A script you wrote is not being interpreted and that is a problem that must be fixed.

Errors that appear in the Output window usually look worse than they are. Sometimes something as simple as a missing semicolon at the end of a line will display a long-winded error message. Fortunately, that's easily fixed. Let me explain some of the more common errors you're likely to see and how to resolve them.

```
Output                                                                    ×
                                                                    Options
Scene=Scene 1, Layer=Layer 1, Frame=1: Line 2: Unexpected ';' encountered
    err((;

Scene=Scene 1, Layer=Layer 1, Frame=1: Line 3: ')' expected
    )

Scene=Scene 1, Layer=Layer 1, Frame=1: Line 1: Statement block must be terminated by ')'
    onClipEvent (load) (

Scene=Scene 1, Layer=Layer 1, Frame=1: Line 4: Syntax error.
```

Figure 6.1   *When you test your movie, all syntax errors will appear in the Output window.*

First, to digest an error message, you should understand the form shown in Figure 6.2. The exact location in your script where the error occurs is shown first. You can fix the problem only when you track down the script's scene, layer, frame, and line number—luckily, it's all listed clearly. After the address, the generic Flash error message describes the nature of your problem. The text following the figure describes some of the more common errors. (You can find all the error messages in a table in Flash's ActionScript Reference Manual and help documents.) Finally, a quote—or partial quote—of your script is displayed on a new line.

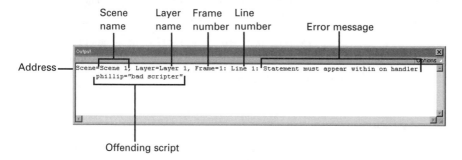

Figure 6.2   *Error messages are detailed, including where the error occurred and the nature of the problem.*

Here are the errors that seem to appear most often.

Balancing Errors

As you learned in Chapter 5, "Programming Structures," anything you start (such as a quote or parenthetical statement) must be finished properly. You'll see one of the following errors if you follow this rule.

```
string literal was not properly terminated
```

```
')' expected
```

```
';' expected
```

`Unexpected '}' encountered` (This is usually caused by forgetting to include a semicolon at the end of a line.)

```
Statement block must be terminated by '}'
```

Right Church, Wrong Pew

These errors appear when you have script—which might be perfectly legitimate—but it's in the wrong place. For example, you can't use an "onClipEvent" anywhere except clip instances. If you use an "onClipEvent" on buttons or keyframes, you will get an error.

`Statement must appear within on handler` (This occurs when you place a script on a button without surrounding it with an "on" mouse event.)

`Statement must appear within onClipEvent handler` (This occurs when you place a script on a clip instance without surrounding it with an "onClipEvent.")

`Mouse events are permitted only for button instances` (This occurs when you try to use an "on" mouse event in a keyframe.)

`Clip events are permitted only for movie clip instances` (This occurs when you try to use an "onClipEvent" on something other than a clip instance—for example, a button or keyframe.)

Catch All

Although several other specific error messages are available, if your problem doesn't clearly fit into one of those, the following catch-all message will appear:

```
Syntax error
```

FLASH MX   { Note }

> Although the "right church, wrong pew" errors will appear as
> described, Flash MX has a new feature that enables you to make clips
> behave like buttons—that is, include mouse events such as rollOver
> and rollOut. It's as simple as putting an "on" mouse event on a clip
> instance. There are many other ways you can extend buttons, clips,
> and text to go even further. Chapter 14, "Extending ActionScript,"
> explains exactly how.

Fixing the problem is usually easy after you know the cause. Keep in mind that
the Output window will often display several errors. Instead of trying to fix them
all, repair them one at a time (starting at the top of the list). You'll find that fixing
one problem often resolves others.

By the way, the same error messages sometimes appear in the Output window
while you are authoring. This happens when you try to paste a bogus script (from
your Clipboard) into an Actions panel set to Normal Mode. When the error is in
your Clipboard, the "address" of the error is shown as "Clipboard Actions" rather
than the familiar scene, layer, and frame format. Additionally, the Actions panel's
options menu has a "Check Syntax" feature (Ctrl+T) that provides a similar listing of errors.

Any errors that reveal themselves in the Output window are critical, and you
should deal with them before moving on to other tasks. Also, be sure to clear the
Output window (or just close it) before each test movie so that you'll see only
errors. (It's easy to become distracted by old errors that could have been fixed if
they still appear in the Output window.)

Repeat and Isolate the Bug

The syntax errors that appear in the Output window might seem overwhelming,
but such errors will—in the long run—prove to be the least of your problems. It's
just that they're critical, so you have to deal with them first. Most of your bugs
will just cause your movie to play incorrectly or display erroneous data. Because
these errors appear only while you're testing your movie (maybe you click a button and nothing happens), you might believe they are intermittent. Very rarely is
a bug truly intermittent and usually only when something outside your control
(such as an Internet server or user's computer hardware) is the cause. Even
though bugs might appear to be intermittent, to fix them you need to learn the
cause, and to find the cause, you must be able to repeat the bug.

I know it sure helps when a client describes precisely how he caused a bug to appear. Often, a good description of the cause will enable me either to think of the solution on the spot or at least to have a good idea of which script I need to resolve. Spending time both to repeat a bug and to clearly specify the steps necessary to make that bug appear is time well spent. It's easy to fool yourself, though. The *post hoc, ergo propter hoc* ("after this, therefore because of this") fallacy can mess you up. For example, if you wash your car and then it rains, you could use *post hoc, ergo propter hoc* reasoning to mistakenly attribute washing your car to causing the rain to fall.

While tracking the cause of a bug, try to find the fewest steps necessary. For example, imagine that you're testing a movie you made and, after twice clicking a button you labeled "Help" followed by a click of the "Sound Off" button, you find that your "Search" doesn't work. You might be convinced that those were the steps that caused the problem, but you should start over and try just the last step (pressing the "Search" button). That could be the only problem! If the "Search" button works, start over and try again by just clicking "Sound Off" and then "Search." This is really just basic troubleshooting. However you do it, make sure that you can repeat the bug, because the next step is to clearly document the bug.

Document and Analyze the Bug

This is probably the stage that will require the most restraint. The natural tendency when you find a bug is to try to fix it. Don't! It's possible, I suppose, when the bug is acute and clear, to simply fix it. More often, when you prematurely attack a bug, you'll find yourself opening a can of worms. It's like starting to bake without a recipe or trying to assemble shelves without reading all the instructions first. You want to first have a clear plan of attack and know where you're headed—and then you'll likely fix the bug accurately and efficiently. The way to achieve this is to document the bug.

Simply knowing the bug is half the work. Depending on whether you uncover the bug early or late in a project, you should usually attempt to fix the bug with the least disruption to the rest of the code. Obviously, if the bug is rampant or fundamentally intertwined in your program, you'll want to consider rebuilding from scratch. Consider that fixing one thing often causes other things to break. Therefore, when you narrow the bug, you'll be able to fix it better. Imagine you have a toothache. Surely, the dentist could simply remove the tooth and place a crown in its place, but this would probably be unnecessary. If the dentist found the precise location of a cavity, he could fill the cavity instead.

Also realize that with any problem, doing _nothing_ is a viable alternative. This comes up all the time in medicine when performing an operation is too great a risk compared to doing nothing. The same is true with bugs. Not only should you implement only the necessary changes and nothing more, but you should always consider doing nothing as a suitable option. You should document and categorize every bug. Some bugs might be critical and prevent the movie from functioning. Other bugs might occasionally cause a display to blink for a second. Certainly I would always prefer to fix every bug, but you can viably opt to "punt" (just not fix a bug) if the bug isn't very important compared to a looming deadline or if fixing the bug will potentially break many other parts of the movie. I can't establish a set of guidelines for you to use, but if you first document and categorize each bug, you'll be able to set an appropriate course of action.

Fixing Bugs

An entire chapter on debugging and only now we talk about fixing bugs? Yep. I can't stress enough that after you know exactly what your objectives are, you can swiftly achieve them. It's true with converting detailed pseudo-code, and it's true when you fix bugs. Sincerely, that's all there is to it. Of course, I have a couple tips for how you should fix bugs, but the truth is that if you know what the bug is, you're 95 percent of the way to fixing it.

Have the Humility to Call Yourself a Fool

Most bugs are the result of a stupid mistake. You need to have the humility to realize that you could be overlooking something obvious. I once heard that the majority of the tech help calls to a sound card manufacturer were resolved simply by turning up the volume. Just because a bug is causing you a great deal of grief, it doesn't necessarily require a lot of work to fix. Later in this chapter, you'll learn how to use Flash's Debugger to focus in on exactly what your movie is doing. When you walk through the steps that reveal the bug, leave no stone unturned. That is, don't take for granted the "easy" scripts. They're just as likely to have an error that causes the bug as more complex scripts.

Try Being a Cynic

Not only do you need humility, but a good dose of cynicism will also help. The best quality assurance people often come across as cynical people. When applied to finding and fixing bugs, this is a good personality trait. Don't believe *anything* unless it can be proven. Even though part of your movie might appear to be working, a cynic will find a way to trip it up. For example, the movie might start with the user typing his name and pressing a "continue" button. When looking for a bug, you should try everything to break the movie! What happens when you type nothing and click "continue"? What about when you press the Enter key—does it make a new line and move the first thing typed out of view? It's as though you're *trying* to make it break. Good programmers can do most of this themselves, but because of the need for this cynical attitude, it sometimes helps for someone else to test your creation.

This cynicism can help to do more than uncover bugs. When you're trying to fix a bug, step through the entire code and question the logic every step of the way. Don't just try to translate the code to English, however, because you'll likely just repeat the intention you had in the first place. Rather, read each line with cynicism—as though someone were trying to trip you up and you have to find the flaw in the logic. If a line can be justified, move to the next line. If a block of code stands the "is it logical?" test, you can move on. It's difficult because you're effectively calling yourself a liar. Opposite to the United States' courts, your code is guilty (of bugs) until proven innocent.

Ensuring That All Bugs Are Squashed

The joy you feel after fixing a bug is a feeling like no other. Don't get too happy, however. (Remember, you're a cynic.) I think the greatest error programmers make is that they don't retest after fixing a bug. Because it's quite possible that fixing one bug causes other bugs to appear, consider retesting everything after you implement a supposed fix. It's difficult because in the process of fixing a bug, you've developed a pattern of steps to re-create the bug. The tendency is simply to follow those exact steps to see whether the bug is still present. Consider that after fixing one bug, if another bug was created you'll probably have to follow a different set of steps to see it. Although it might be impossible to retest everything after every minor bug is fixed, you should at least consider testing at logical milestones. You can also send the file back to your trusty cynic. Realize that even if you tell the testy testing person to check only whether certain bugs are fixed, if she does a good job, she'll actually test everything—not just the things that are supposed to be fixed.

Preventing Bugs

I suppose it's obvious that your life programming in Flash will be better if you simply prevent any bugs from the start. Even though this is wishful thinking, if not pure fantasy, there are several steps you can take while working in Flash that will reduce the likelihood of bugs.

Version Control

One form of documentation that's helpful while programming is version control. Although some people use sophisticated software packages, you can still take advantage of the benefits of tracking versions as you develop a Flash site. The simplest form of version control is to do a "Save As" periodically. For example, you can start each day by saving a copy of your movie with the date in the name plus a letter of the alphabet (starting with "a")—such as "4_March_2002-a.fla." Every time you add a feature or squash a bug, save the movie with the next letter of the alphabet ("4_March_2002-b.fla"). If you're really organized, you'll keep a paper log that documents exactly which features were added or which bugs were fixed in each revision. That way, if you find that a major bug has appeared that wasn't in an older version, you can go back through the revisions to find the latest version without the problem. Then you can redo the same edits—and test the site after each one. You'll uncover what caused the bug and your document will help you restore everything else.

Avoiding Bugs in the First Place

A related technique is to build new scripts and resolve bugs "offline." For example, if you intend to add a sophisticated feature to a Flash movie, you can try to work out the solution in a new separate file. After you get it working in the new file, you can add the script you developed to the main file. Sometimes working offline involves so much extra work just in laying the foundation that you might consider using the main file. However, before going wild trying different solutions, you should first save the main file, and then save as "working.fla." Do what it takes to find a solution, but when you do, go back to the original and carefully implement the scripts you developed (in "working.fla"). Even though this seems like extra work, realize that in the process of trying different solutions, you might make several attempts that don't work. Even though you might _think_ you were careful to dispose of any failed attempts, there's a chance they're still present. By determining the solution "offline" and then implementing it "online," you're more likely to create a script that's more streamlined and less buggy. Compare this process to the way an artist will work on several "studies" before creating his masterpiece. (Remember that this technique is useful both for building scripts and for fixing broken scripts.)

The only other tip I can offer that tends to avoid bugs is to build your movies in pieces. No matter how large the task, it's always just a collection of subtasks. When you approach a large Flash project, try to break it down into pieces. Get each element to work before moving on to the next task. You can even modularize scripts by using functions (as you'll see in Chapter 8, "Functions"), and build building blocks of code by using objects (as you will in Chapter 12, "Objects," and Chapter 13, "Homemade Objects"). Regardless of the technical solution you apply, you should try to break down your task into pieces.

Using the Debugger

When it comes to finding the bugs you've created, Flash does offer help in the form of the Debugger. This special window enables you to view variables or properties while a movie plays. You can also change most properties of any Movie Clip. In addition, Flash MX adds several options that make this a true "debugger." The name "Debugger" might be deceptive. It won't "de-bug" (that is, remove bugs from your movie). Later in this chapter you'll see the new options, including setting breakpoints (which are points in the script where the program will pause), the Step Over/Step In/Step Out buttons (which enable you to selectively skip parts of the script or to execute only one line at a time), and the Call Stack (which reveals "how you got there" when you encounter a breakpoint).

Despite the fact that the Debugger won't *fix* your problems, it's still very useful. We'll first look at how to use the Debugger, and then we'll consider strategies to apply its features.

Viewing and Setting Properties and Variables

Flash's Debugger enables you to view and set both properties and variables—while the movie plays. To view the Debugger, select Control, Debug Movie (rather than Control, Test Movie). When the Debugger first appears, your movie will pause until you click the Continue button (see Figure 6.3). (It might seem like a pain to have to click Continue each time; however, as you'll learn later, you can navigate to any script to insert breakpoints while the movie is paused.)

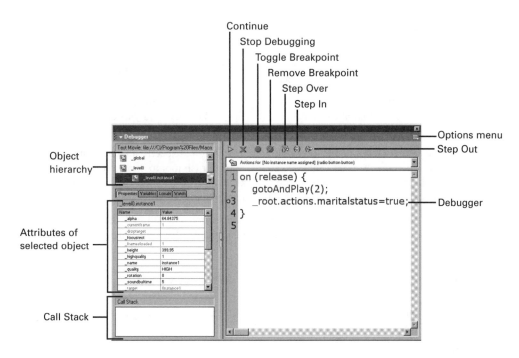

Figure 6.3   *The Debugger requires that you press Continue to begin debugging.*

Once you have your movie playing in the Debugger, you'll see a hierarchy of your movie and all its Movie Clip instances in the white area at the top left. To view properties or variables, first select the Movie Clip instance that you want to analyze. Selecting _level0 will enable you to see properties of and variables in the main timeline. Similarly, selecting _global gives you access to variables stored in the new common area for global variables. (Global variables—and local variables for that matter—were covered in Chapter 4, "Basic Programming in Flash.") You will also see any unnamed clips, but Flash assigns seemingly arbitrary names to them. Regardless, each clip in the hierarchy appears with its full path, always starting with _level0 (except, of course, movies that you've loaded into other level numbers, which appear starting with "_levelx"—where "x" is the level number). Despite how complex your hierarchy becomes, all you do is select the clip (or _level0 for the main timeline) you want to inspect and then click the Properties tab or the Variables tab.

You can test out what's been covered so far by following these steps:

1. Create a text field with some text in it and use the Properties panel to set the field to Dynamic Text. Also, specify a variable name in the panel's "var" field—maybe someVar. Leave this text on the main timeline.

2. Draw a box and convert it to a symbol (Movie Clip). Use the Properties panel to give it an instance name "boxClip" and use Color Styles drop-down to set the alpha to 50%.

3. Create another Dynamic Text field with text in it and specify a memorable variable name. (I used "anotherVar.") Use the Brush tool to draw a rough circle around the text. Select both the text and the drawn circle and convert to symbol (Movie Clip). Give this instance the name "textClip."

4. Finally, select Control, Debug Movie. The hierarchy should look like Figure 6.4. (You might need to resize and adjust the different panes inside the Debugger.)

Figure 6.4   *The hierarchy of our exercise includes the two clip instances, "boxClip" and "textClip."*

At this point, you can first select a clip and then click either the Properties tab or the Variables tab. For example, if you click the _level0.boxClip clip instance and then view its properties, you'll see _alpha listed as 50. Because the _alpha property is not grayed out, you can change it. Double-click the 50, type a new number, and then press Enter. You should see the clip change onscreen. Select the instance of _level0.textClip and change the _y property. When you press Enter, you should see the property change onscreen. Notice that both the _xmouse and _ymouse properties are grayed, meaning that you can't change them, but while you move your cursor around the movie, you'll see these properties update (see Figure 6.5).

Figure 6.5   *Selecting an instance enables you to view properties, including the current _y.*

Now try viewing and changing the custom variables. Select _level0 and click on the Variables tab. You should see the name and value of your variable someVar that's stored in the main timeline. If you want to change this variable's value, remember that because this variable is a string, you need to include the quotation marks or it won't work. (You can view the variable contained in your clip _level0.textClip—but don't try to change the variable; you'll do that in the next section.)

To review: The basic process is to select the clip you want to inspect and then select either the Properties or the Variables tab. In practice, the idea is that you might expect to see a clip's _alpha change and you should be able to (while the movie plays) see this property change. Or, if there's a variable in a clip (which isn't always shown to the user in a text field), you might want to monitor the current value—that is, make sure that it's changing when you expect it to. You'll see how this will be useful in the section, "Using Dynamic Text to Watch Variables or Expressions," later in this chapter.

Watching Variables

Selecting individual clip instances is a necessary step before viewing their properties or variables because the Debugger can show you only one clip's _x property at a time (because different clips might have different values for this property). It was easy in our case because we just had two clips plus the main timeline. In a real project, it can be a lot more complex. Figure 6.6 shows how complex a real project can become.

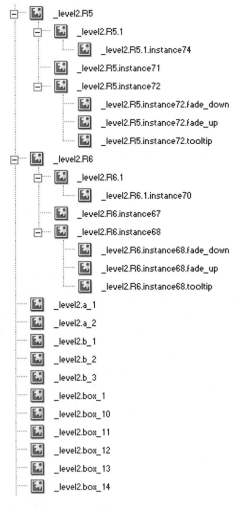

Figure 6.6 *A real project can become quite complex with countless clip instances.*

So, instead of weaving through a complex hierarchy, the Debugger enables you to "watch" the variables of certain clips. All you need to do is select the variable that you want to monitor and either right-click it (control+click on Macintosh) and then select Watch, or select Add Watch from the Debugger's options menu. You'll see a blue dot next to the variable. Also, when you select the Watch tab, your variable will be visible at all times (regardless of which clip you happen to select in the top-left pane of the Debugger). Under the Watch tab, you can also select "add watch" (or simply "add"), and then type the path and variable name you want to watch. It's a little tricky because you have to begin each variable name with an explicit address (that is, timeline) for that variable, starting with `_level0`. I think it's easiest to first find the variable you want to watch (under the Variables tab), and then add it from there.

If you want to test it out, just create two buttons and two Movie Clip instances. Name one Movie Clip instance `box1` and the other `box2`. Then attach a script on one button that reads `box1.count++` and have the other button's script read `box2.count++`. (Both scripts will need to be within a mouse event, such as `on (release){ }`.) Now when you select Control, Debug Movie, even though you the user won't "see" each clip's `count` variable, you'll be able to with the Debugger. In addition, you can monitor both `count` variables if you first use the Debugger to find `box1`, select `count` and then select Add Watch from the options menu. Do the same for `box2` and you won't need to keep finding `box1` or `box2` to view their respective `count` variables.

Keep in mind that the Debugger is a runtime-only feature. That is, you can make changes while your movie plays, but if you re-export your movie (by selecting Control, Test Movie), all variables will reinitialize regardless of the changes you made in the Debugger the last time it ran.

Stepping Through Code

The feature that makes Flash MX's Debugger the "real deal" is its capability to step through code. It's almost as though you can make the frame rate come to a halt while you step through one line of code at a time. As you step, you can watch variables and see the sequence of events in slow motion. The way it works is you first set a breakpoint on any line of code you want to analyze. While debugging, if that line of code is encountered, the Debugger pauses the movie and displays the line of code in context in the right-side pane (see Figure 6.7).

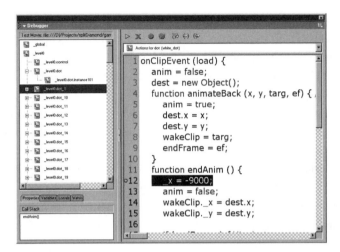

Figure 6.7   *The Debugger pauses when it encounters a line of code on which the author set a breakpoint (line 12).*

Once your movie is paused on a breakpoint, several additional pieces of data may be revealed. You'll always see the line of code in question on the right side. If your breakpoint is inside a function, you'll see additional variables listed under the Locals tab. These variables are specific to the function in which you've just paused. For example, some functions may operate on a temporary variable just while inside the function. Or, if your breakpoint is inside a loop, the iterant variable could be local; this way, you can reveal its current value. (Chapter 8 discusses functions in detail.) Finally, if you're paused inside a function and you arrived at that function by way of another function, the Call Stack pane will be filled with a history—or "how you got here" information. Figure 6.8 shows information from the upcoming example.

Even though we haven't discussed functions yet, you can type the following code into the first keyframe of a movie as an introduction to the Locals tab and Call Stack pane:

```
function tellOneFriend(){
    andTheyTell("a", "b");
}
function andTheyTell(){
    for(var i=0; i<arguments.length; i++){
        andSoOn(arguments[i]);
    }
}
function andSoOn(which){
```

```
        trace(which);
}
tellOneFriend();
```

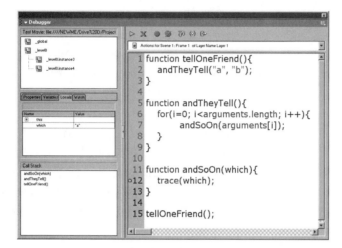

Figure 6.8   *The Debugger can display variables local to the current function and the Call Stack (like a recent history).*

Before you debug this movie, set a breakpoint on the line that executes the `trace` command. First, click that line in the script, and then either right-click or click the Debug options menu (the stethoscope icon) and select Set Breakpoint. Now debug the movie. After pressing the green Continue button in the Debugger, you should see a display like Figure 6.8. By the way, any time you debug a movie, before you click the Continue button, you can insert temporary breakpoints by first navigating to a script (through the Debugger drop-down list at the top right) and then right-clicking or clicking the Toggle Breakpoint button (the red dot).

Let's walk through the Debugger for the example in Figure 6.8. First, notice the entries in the Call Stack pane. In a way, the order might appear to be backward. The most recent function in the sequence (`andSoOn(which)`), which is really the current function) is listed on top. That's where we are paused, but right before that, the function `andTheyTell()` was triggered—and before that, the `tellOneFriend()` function. It all started with `tellOneFriend()`, which you can see at the bottom of the stack. Even though it might seem backward, consider the result if you placed the daily newspaper on a stack every night. You'd find the most recent paper on top, and then the previous day's paper underneath. Anyway, the Call Stack is useful because it answers, "How did I get here?"

As you'll learn, an advantage of functions is that multiple places in your code can invoke the same function. Maybe when you page forward you have an additional function that plays a sound. You may want to invoke the same sound-play function when you page back. If you set a breakpoint and the Debugger pauses, you can look at the Call Stack to determine the sequence that got you to where you are. Unfortunately, only homemade functions appear in the Call Stack—not internal events. That is, you won't see on (press) at the very bottom of the Call Stack even if that was the "thing that started it all." Nevertheless, the Call Stack is interesting.

In the example that you're currently debugging, select the Locals tab. You'll see which (and its value of "a"). The point is that at this frozen moment in time, the which variable has a value of "a". But which really isn't a variable, but rather a name given to the parameter received. It's effectively a local variable because as soon as the andSoOn() function is done, it will vanish out of memory—but while you're debugging, it may be useful to know its value. Anyway, go ahead and click the Continue button again. The Debugger appears to have not changed even though when you're paused and then click Continue, you'd expect the movie to continue on its way. It did! Actually, you should see the Output window with "a" (from your trace command). What happened? You continued, but Flash encountered your breakpoint again. The andTheyTell() function includes a loop that repeatedly calls the andSoOn() function where you have a breakpoint. Notice that this time around the value for which is "b". So, if there were any question as to which loop iteration you're in, the Locals tab helped you figure it out. You can also try this with a breakpoint in the for loop and use the Locals tab to see the value of i (the iterant variable).

Finally, once you're paused on a breakpoint, you can do more than just view the Call Stack and local variables. There are other buttons besides Continue, including Step Over, Step In, and Step Out. Basically, these give you the option (when stopped at a breakpoint) to step through one line of code at a time. Normally, when a breakpoint is encountered, a little yellow arrow points to the line of code in question. Clicking Continue will make the movie play until the next breakpoint is reached. However, if you click the Step In button (think "baby step"), the arrow moves to the very next line of code, at which point you can keep clicking Step In and monitor how variables or properties are changing. Step Out is slightly different, because when you're paused within a homemade function, it will step right outside the currently enclosed function. Step Over is similar, but it just jumps over the very next line of code. In any event, your code isn't really skipped. (Every line will always execute no matter what.) However, the little yellow line can jump a little bit further ahead and pause if you want.

In practice, I find myself clicking Step In first, but then if I find that I'm stepping into a repetitive loop, I might use Step Over or even Step Out. The differences are really subtle, but the general idea is the same: you can step through one line at a time and check out what's happening.

Remote Debugging

One of the coolest features of the Debugger is that you can debug movies playing in a browser. This means that even after you upload a finished movie, it's possible to debug it remotely. When you see the steps involved for this to work, you might think it's a pain, but the steps are necessary for good reason. For example, you might not want others to be able to debug your movies.

To debug a movie remotely, the following conditions must be met:

- The original .fla needs to have its Publish Settings set to Debugging Permitted. Optionally, you can also specify a password (see Figure 6.9).

- You must store an .swd file adjacent to the .swf on your server. (You'll create an .swd file automatically any time you test, debug, or publish a movie with the Debugging Permitted option selected in Publish Settings.)

- Finally, the Debugger must have the options menu set to Enable Remote Debugging (see Figure 6.10). (This makes Flash act like a server, so you might need to adjust firewall settings.)

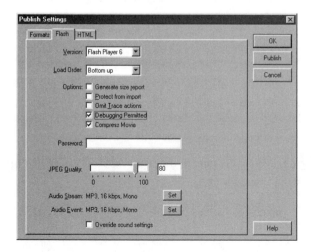

Figure 6.9   *The movie's Publish Settings must allow for debugging.*

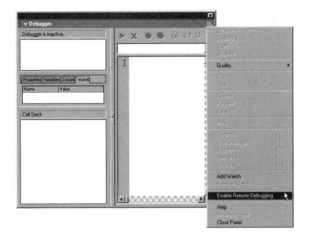

Figure 6.10 *Because you'll be debugging while Flash is running, you must set the Debugger to Enable Remote Debugging.*

To debug a movie, first open Flash, start a new movie, and then select Window, Debugger. From the Debugger's options menu, select Allow Remote Debugging. Then just launch your browser and right-click a movie that has been set to permit debugging when it was published. If you're running the correct version of the Flash player (the Debug version), you can select Debugger from the menu that appears. (Users who have downloaded the free player from Macromedia won't see this option.) First you need to specify where your version of Flash MX is running (that is, the one with its Debugger set to enable remote debugging). Normally, you'll just accept the default Localhost option. Then you can return to Flash, enter the password (or simply click OK if you have no password), and you'll be able to debug the movie like normal.

One frustrating fact is that—as with any application—when you make Flash active (by clicking on the Debugger, for example), the entire Flash application comes to the front and may cover your web browser that contains the move being debugged. You'll just need to resize the Flash application to take up less space, and then arrange it so that it doesn't cover your browser (see Figure 6.11).

Remote debugging has been vastly improved in Flash MX; if you found it funky before, you really should consider trying it again.

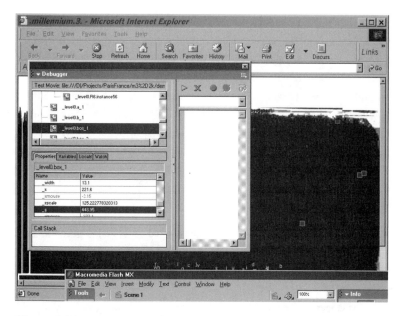

Figure 6.11 *Although Flash comes to the front when it's the active application, you can arrange windows so that it won't cover up too much of your browser.*

Strategies of Debugging

After you've found, documented, and determined to fix a bug, the approach you take can involve many different avenues. You can't just select Debug Movie and expect the solution to fall into your lap. You have to be deliberate in your quest. If you need to see whether a variable or property is changing as you expect, the Debugger is great. If you've *really* narrowed down the problem, it might even be appropriate to set breakpoints so that you can step through the script. However, you often need to first determine that the script you believe is in error is being encountered at all, and then you must determine that it's producing the expected results. There are several ways to check your scripts.

The `trace` Command

Sometimes you'll have a script that—for the life of you—appears to be perfect. But that script has to be encountered in order to execute. Often, the script isn't even being reached. Perhaps it's contained within an `if` statement whose condition is false. Or, you keep checking a script that's inside a Movie Clip that isn't used on the Stage. There are many ways for this to happen, so you need a quick way to confirm that a script is reached. The `trace` command is the perfect solution.

When you're testing a movie (or debugging, for that matter), any time Flash encounters trace("whatever"), the Output window will pop up (if it's not already open) and display "whatever." If you place trace("hi") inside a loop that repeats 10 times, hi will appear 10 times in a row. So, if you have a block of script that appears to be ineffectual, just throw a trace("hi mom") right before the script. It's sort of a sanity check to see whether a script is even being used. For example, assume that you have the following script attached to a button:

```
on (release) {
    if (age<12&&age>21) {
        age++;
    }
}
```

Now say that you've tested the movie with the Debugger and noticed that age doesn't increment (as you expect) when the button is pressed. So, you can insert trace("I'm incrementin' here") at the beginning of the if statement, as follows:

```
on (release) {
    if (age<12&&age>21) {
        trace("I'm incrementin' here");
        age++;
    }
}
```

When you test or debug the movie again, if the script is reached, an Output window pops up and displays, "I'm incrementin' here." To your surprise (or maybe not), the Output window doesn't appear. At this point you know that it doesn't matter whether the age++ statement is legitimate, because it's not even being encountered. What's interesting about the trace statement is that you can actually put an expression in the parentheses (rather than a hard-wired string). For example, if the statement trace("Age is "+age) is reached, the Output window will show the result of the expression "Age is "+age. The problem at hand, however, is that our trace statement is never reached. Try the following script instead:

```
on (release) {
  trace("Age is "+age);
  if (age<12&&age>21) {
        age++;
    }
}
```

This will display the value of the expression "Age is "+age (that is, "Age is " followed by the value of age). This way, the message that appears in the Output window will be much more informational. (Remember that the + operator concatenates when either operand is a string.) You could keep trying different expressions, such as:

```
trace("age: " + age + " part a: " + (age<12) );
trace("age: " + age + " part b: " + (age>21) );
```

Eventually, you should narrow down the crux of the bug (that age cannot be both less than 12 and greater than 21 and, therefore, our if statement's condition is never true and we never reach the part that reads age++). Granted, this bug was rather obvious, but the idea was to show the process of using the trace command. trace is a great way to quickly see that a script is being reached as well as displaying the results of an expression right in the Output window. You can use trace quite liberally and your audience will never see the Output window after you publish the movie. (And, if you want to turn it off while you're testing, there's an option in the Flash tab under Publish Settings to "Omit Trace actions.")

Using Dynamic Text to Watch Variables or Expressions

The Debugger is great for watching variables and properties change, but you need to make an effort to first activate the Debugger, select Debug Movie, find the clip whose variables or properties you want to watch, and then set up a watch. Often, you'll have a specific variable that you need to watch quite a lot and it will become a hassle to always use the Debugger. Also, the Debugger enables you to watch only a single property or variable. What if you want to "watch" an expression? You'll need to devise another way to monitor the values that interest you.

You can quickly monitor any variable just by creating a Dynamic Text field. (Remember, you'll likely have many variables that won't be visible to the user—this is a case where you want to temporarily view these variables.) If you want to "watch" a variable named score in a Dynamic Text field, you just associate that variable name in the Properties panel. Of course, the text needs to be placed in the timeline or clip that you want to monitor. If you want, you can even precede the name of the variable with the path to that variable—such as _root.score or _root.someClip.score—depending in which timeline the variable resides. Keep in mind that creating a Dynamic Text field will initialize the variable as a string (even if you type a number into the text field). You might need to make sure that the variable gets converted to 0 or some other number immediately after such a field is displayed onscreen. Because the Dynamic Text field will try to make a

variable a string, you can place a script in the first frame that reads
`score=Number(score)` to reassign the variable to a number data type. The weird
part is that a Dynamic Text field will properly display the value of a number.
(Therefore, you never need to change it back to a string.)

This technique of watching variables in text fields works great. If you keep all
such variables in a separate layer, it's easy to effectively remove them before
publishing by simply changing the layer to Guide. This way, you can just as
quickly restore all the variables that you were watching by resetting the layer to
Normal.

In addition to convenience, Dynamic Text fields have another benefit over the
Debugger. Namely, you can use them to constantly monitor the current value of
an expression—not just a variable. Unfortunately, you can't just type an expression in the Text Options panel. Rather, you can use this simple workaround:

1. Create a Dynamic Text field associated with a variable named `result`.

2. Use the Arrow Tool to select the text field and then convert it to a Movie
   Clip symbol (by pressing F8).

3. Attach a script to the instance of your Movie Clip now on the Stage that
   keeps setting `result` on the `enterFrame` event. For example, try this script:

```
onClipEvent (enterFrame) {

        result=_root._ymouse;

}
```

Although this example—to monitor the _y property of the mouse—isn't performing anything you couldn't do with the Debugger, consider that you can set the
`result` variable to anything you want. A much longer expression could show the
result of an expression that calculates the user's current average, using variables
called `sum` and `questionsAnswered`:

```
onClipEvent (enterFrame) {
    result=_root.sum/_root.questionsAnswered;
}
```

Again, this is a rather simple expression—but it doesn't have to be. Keep in mind
that because this script is attached to a clip, it behaves as if it were *in* the clip.
You need to pay special attention to the target paths for variable names. If you
can keep that straight, this is a great way to monitor complex expressions.
Because this is just for testing purposes, you can ignore the fact that using the
`enterFrame` event might put a heavy load on the computer processor.

Here's another example. On a button, attach the following script:

```
on (release) {
    lastClick=getTimer();
}
```

Then on the Movie Clip that contains the Dynamic Text field displaying the variable `result`, attach this script:

```
onClipEvent (enterFrame) {
    result=Math.floor((getTimer()-_root.lastClick)/1000);
}
```

You'll constantly monitor how long (in seconds) it has been since the user clicked the button. In the `release` event, our custom variable `lastClick` is assigned the value of `getTimer()`, which is the precise number of milliseconds since the movie started. Then in the `enterFrame` clip event (which executes repeatedly), we assign the variable `result` the value of `getTimer()` (that is, the current time) minus `lastClick` (the start time). It doesn't matter when you started; you can always determine the elapsed time by finding the difference between the current time (`getTimer()`) and the start (`lastClick`). Finally, we divide by 1000 (which converts milliseconds—for which each second has 1000—into seconds). Finally, the whole expression is inside a `Math.floor()`, which returns the integer portion of the expression.

New to MX

Because I can't restrain myself—and because it fits so well here—I have to tell you about a new Flash MX feature: watch. In a nutshell, the `watch` method enables you to identify a single variable that, when changed, causes another function to be triggered. That is, you can "watch" the variable. In the example above where we wanted to see the time constantly change, it was necessary to use the `enterFrame` event even though this forced the computer to work harder. If you're just watching for one variable to change and want to trigger a result, there's another way. In practice, this means you can actually display the result of an expression without using the `enterFrame` event unnecessarily.

Although you'll find the most complete coverage of the watch method in Chapter 14, "Extending ActionScipt," here's something to give you a taste of its power. Consider an Input Text field for `price`. Any time `price` changes, you want to display the `actualPrice` with 8 percent sales tax added. You certainly could set up an `enterFrame` script like we did earlier, but you don't really want to monitor the value of price *constantly*—only when it changes. This is a perfect situation for `watch`. You can trigger a function any time that `price` changes.

Assuming you have an Input Text field associated with `price` and a Dynamic Text field with the variable `actualPrice`, type the following code into a keyframe:

```
watch('price',function(id,oldVal,newVal){actualPrice=newVal*1.08});
```

It really is amazing. I won't explain `watch` fully now; Chapter 14 covers it in detail. However, you can use the general form above to redisplay the value of an expression any time a specified variable's value changes. Just replace `'price'` with the variable you want to watch, and then the part inside the curly braces can perform an assignment to the onscreen variable (in this case, `actualPrice`). It's weird, but the variable appears as `'price'` (that is, like a string) when inside the `watch` method. Just realize that within the expression, use `newVal` in place of the trigger variable. That is, you don't have access to `price` inside the formula (as in `actualPrice=price*1.08`) but instead have to use `newVal` because that's the parameter name given in the function. I know that doesn't explain everything, but it really is easy to adapt for the purpose of seeing an expression onscreen.

Quality Assurance and Productivity Scripts

It might be discouraging to find a bug, but when you're aware of a bug (and what causes it) you can at least take the time to address the bug. ("The devil you know is better than the devil you don't.") Compare that to bugs you don't find. They're worse because the user might be the first to uncover them. Ideally, you can provide some level of assurance that the quality of your movie is high—that is, has few if any bugs. As you'll see, it's possible to write scripts that provide a level of quality assurance.

A quality assurance script is a script that serves no purpose except to prove the program is working. For example, imagine you're making a reference site with information about the Olympics. Assume that your interface includes a column of 10 buttons for 10 different years and a row of buttons for 10 different events, plus three buttons ("photos," "stats," and "winners"). The user could click any year and any event to see photographs, statistics, and medal winners for each combination. The 100 combinations of year/event, multiplied by the three bits of content means a total of 300 discrete pieces of information. Although you don't have to step through 300 combinations to test that it's basically working, you do need to proof all 300 pages of content. Instead of stepping through every combination by hand (and probably missing a few due to human error), you can write a script that does this for you! I would use a couple of temporary buttons ("reset" and "next"), plus a Dynamic Text field that constantly displays the combination of year/event/media-type (for "photos," "stats," or "winners"). To proof all the content, you just click "reset," and then keep clicking "next." If you find a page that has bogus information or doesn't work, just note the data in the Dynamic Text field. Figure 6.12 shows what I have in mind.

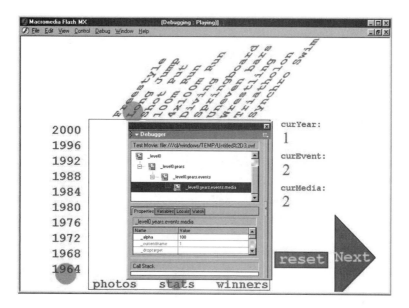

Figure 6.12   *The multitude of options in this matrix calls for a quality assurance script that steps through all 300 combinations.*

To construct this script requires using homemade functions, which we haven't discussed yet. (We'll get to them in Chapter 8.) By using functions, you can access the same function from several buttons, including the "next" button. Without explaining the code, imagine that all the content is in a clip called `years`. The `years` clip contains 10 frames, one for each Olympic year. Every frame in `years` has a unique master clip (with content from a different year), but all clip instances are named `events`. Finally, each `events` clip contains 10 frames for the 10 different events. On each frame of each `events` clip there's a clip called `media` that contains three frames—one each for photos, stats, and winners. Every clip in this movie has a `stop()` script in the first frame. Figure 6.13 shows a portion of the hierarchy in the Movie Explorer.

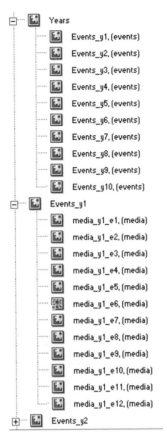

Figure 6.13   *The Movie Explorer shows the basic architecture used for the Olympics example.*

Here's the script that can be placed in the main movie's first keyframe:

```
reset();
function reset(){
    curYear=1;
    curEvent=1;
    curMedia=1;
    goUpdate();
}
function goNext(){
    curMedia++;
    if (curMedia>3){
        curMedia=1;
        curEvent++;
    }
    if (curEvent>10){
```

```
        curEvent=1;
        curYear++;
    }
    if (curYear>10){
        reset();
        trace("You're done");
    }
    goUpdate();
}
function goUpdate(){
    _root.years.gotoAndStop(curYear);
    _root.years.events.gotoAndStop(curEvent);
    _root.years.events.media.gotoAndStop(curMedia);
}
```

The reset() function (which is executed at the very start) simply sets the variables (containing current year, event, and media) to 1. Then, it calls the function goUpdate(). This is the same function that is called when the user clicks any button (year, event, or media)—but after the variable for curYear, curEvent, or curMedia is set. For example, if the user clicks year 2000, curYear is set to 10 and the goUpdate() function is called. If the user clicks the Freestyle event, curEvent is set to 1 and the goUpdate() function is called. When the Next button is pressed, the quality assurance function (goNext()) tries to go to the next media element. If doing so puts curMedia higher than 3 (for three types of media), it's set back to 1 and curEvent is incremented. If curEvent is greater than 10 (the total number of events), it's set back to 1 and curYear is incremented. Basically, the goNext() function starts in the first year and steps through all the media in the first event, and then through all the media of the next event. When it's done with the events in one year, it moves on to the next year.

Even though you might not understand every detail of this script, the concept should start to make sense. You can write a script that serves no other purpose than to aid in the testing process.

It's easy for me to say, "Oh, just write a quality assurance script." Obviously, this will take additional effort, which might seem like time away from your main goal. In fact, the time investment necessary isn't that great, and if it means that you can save time on another stage of the production (proofing, in this case), it's likely worth the investment. In this not-so-contrived example, it turns out this script could have another use. Maybe you think it might be nice to provide the user with an "auto slide show mode" that steps him through all the combinations. You'll already have the script. I don't want to suggest that every quality assurance script will turn out to have other value, but even if it doesn't, it's probably still worth the investment.

Another reason why you might want to write an extra script is to aid in the production of your project. Unlike a quality assurance script, which might have practical use in the final movie (the way the "next" button turned out to have a secondary use as a slide show), a productivity type of script will *never* be useful in the final movie—but it can still be very valuable. Quite often the process of assembling a project can be tedious. It's possible to invest a little bit of time writing a "productivity script" that will pay back in time saved later.

I had a great opportunity to write a productivity script when I programmed part of the 2000 edition of the site www.m3snowboards.com. In one section, individual letters would scatter and assemble themselves to spell the name of each snowboarder on the team. (Figure 6.14 shows a sequence of the movie.) Each letter was a separate movie clip. Without explaining how I made each letter move, it's obvious that I needed to know the x and y coordinates of each letter in the final arrangement for each snowboarder. With all the different team members and the multiple use of several letters (that is, there weren't just 26 letters—letters such as "s" were used many times), the total number of coordinates was more than 1,400!

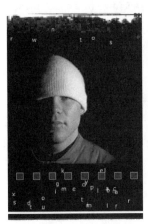

Figure 6.14 *Because each letter arranges itself, I needed to gather the coordinates for each snowboarder's name. (From www.m3snowboards.com—screen shots courtesy of Paris France Inc., copyright MLY Snowboards.)*

You can see just half of one page (of five pages) of data in Figure 6.15. At first, I thought that someone would simply need to position the letters in the arrangement he wanted and then—one by one—use the Info panel to ascertain the x and y positions. Then that person (I sure didn't want to be the one) would simply type these numbers into the text file (the result for which is shown in Figure 6.15) and that would be loaded using Flash's `loadVariables` command. Calculating the 1,400 individual coordinates by hand would not only be tedious, but fraught with potential errors. Instead, I wrote a productivity script that would make the process relatively simple.

```
co_a_1x=549.15&co_a_1y=79.5&co_a_2x=392.6&co_a_2y=364.05&co_b_1x=509.05&co_b_1y=
399.25&co_b_2x=460.55&co_b_2y=405.4&co_b_3x=561.9&co_b_3y=392.95&co_c_1x=372.4&c
o_c_1y=364.1&co_c_2x=419.45&co_c_2y=73&co_d_1x=402.55&co_d_1y=364.05&co_e_1x=455
.65&co_e_1y=363.35&co_e_2x=522.6&co_e_2y=78.8&co_f_1x=507.3&co_f_1y=393.7&co_g_1
x=442.55&co_g_1y=77.65&co_h_1x=382.5&co_h_1y=364.2&co_i_1x=291.1&co_i_1y=404.55&
co_i_2x=449.3&co_i_2y=77.3&co_i_3x=488.5&co_i_3y=396.8&co_j_1x=286.9&co_j_1y=404
.6&co_k_1x=348.35&co_k_1y=78.9&co_k_2x=526.65&co_k_1y=399.4&co_l_2x=534.75&co_l_
2y=397.65&co_l_3x=433.6&co_l_3y=79.25&co_m_1x=513.55&co_m_1y=363.5&co_m_2x=505.5
5&co_m_2y=401.75&co_n_1x=437.15&co_n_1y=404.25&co_n_2x=586.7&co_n_2y=238.4&co_o_
1x=426.7&co_o_1y=363.35&co_o_2x=503.9&co_o_2y=363.35&co_p_1x=451.45&co_p_1y=74.2
&co_q_1x=491.3&co_q_1y=400.35&co_r_1x=464.8&co_r_1y=363.5&co_r_2x=493.75&co_r_2y
=363.5&co_s_1x=474.85&co_s_1y=363.35&co_s_2x=289.9&co_s_2y=75.8&co_s_3x=424.6&co
_s_3y=397.95&co_t_1x=445.95&co_t_1y=363.4&co_t_2x=484.55&co_t_2y=363.4&co_t_3x=4
36.3&co_t_3y=363.4&co_t_4x=217.15&co_t_4y=292.6&co_u_1x=411.9&co_u_1y=400.8&co_v
_1x=460.7&co_v_1y=394.1&co_w_1x=548.25&co_w_1y=402.6&co_x_1x=219.95&co_x_1y=230.
35&co_y_1x=580.6&co_y_1y=255.05&co_z_1x=375.9&co_z_1y=71.6&mm_a_1x=549.15&mm_a_1
y=79.5&mm_a_2x=341.2&mm_a_2y=364.45&mm_b_1x=513.2&mm_b_1y=399.95&mm_b_2x=460.55&
mm_b_2y=405.4&mm_b_3x=561.9&mm_b_3y=392.95&mm_c_1x=332.45&mm_c_1y=364.5&mm_c_2x=
382&mm_c_2y=364.25&mm_d_1x=216.8&mm_d_1y=253.3&mm_e_1x=545.85&mm_e_1y=403.15&mm_
e_2x=522.6&mm_e_2y=78.8&mm_f_1x=507.3&mm_f_1y=393.7&mm_g_1x=389.8&mm_g_1y=364.7&
mm_h_1x=350.1&mm_h_1y=365.2&mm_i_1x=325.95&mm_i_1y=364.6&mm_i_2x=396.55&mm_i_2y=
364.35&mm_i_3x=417.85&mm_i_3y=364.35&mm_j_1x=286.9&mm_j_1y=404.6&mm_k_1x=348.35&
mm_k_1y=78.9&mm_l_1x=526.65&mm_l_1y=399.4&mm_l_2x=534.75&mm_l_2y=397.65&mm_l_3x=
352.2&mm_l_3y=405.6&mm_m_1x=317.5&mm_m_1y=364.6&mm_m_2x=374.6&mm_m_2y=364.35&mm
_n_1x=410.95&mm_n_1y=364.35&mm_n_2x=403.45&mm_n_2y=364.35&mm_o_1x=286.05&mm_o_1y
=80.6&mm_o_2x=383.25&mm_o_2y=406.1&mm_p_1x=537.1&mm_p_1y=379.35&mm_q_1x=518.45&m
m_q_1y=400.35&mm_r_1x=585.6&mm_r_1y=247.85&mm_r_2x=258.55&mm_r_2y=81.35&mm_s_1x=
230.95&mm_s_1y=402.3&mm_s_2x=271.85&mm_s_2y=80.6&mm_s_3x=432.25&mm_s_3y=404.9&mm
_t_1x=454.5&mm_t_1y=403.55&mm_t_2x=390.45&mm_t_2y=405.55&mm_t_3x=278.95&mm_t_3y=
80.65&mm_t_4x=424.1&mm_t_4y=364.25&mm_u_1x=431.4&mm_u_1y=403.6&mm_v_1x=453.75&mm
_v_1y=405.95&mm_w_1x=530.15&mm_w_1y=403.3&mm_x_1x=219.95&mm_x_1y=230.35&mm_y_1x=
432.2&mm_y_1y=364.15&mm_z_1x=375.9&mm_z_1y=71.6&boxA_1x=619.45&boxA_1y=360.05&bo
```

Figure 6.15   *1,400 individual coordinates is a lot of data to type by hand—the production script meant we didn't have to.*

I made a separate Flash movie that enabled the production author to individually align—by hand or with the Align panel—each letter visually. Then the production author would test the movie and press a button in the Flash movie that ran my script. My script would loop through every letter and ascertain the x and y property of each one. This data would be formatted the way the external text file needed to be (URL encoded, as you'll learn in Chapter 16, "Interfacing with External Data"). Finally, the script would use the `trace` statement to display all this data in the Output window. The production author simply copied this text and pasted it into a text file.

The process was repeated for each snowboarder—but it was a simple process: Just line up all the letters while authoring in Flash, test the movie, press the button, and then copy and paste the contents of the Output window. Multiply that process by each team member and you can well imagine that it is way less time (and more accurate) than using the Info panel to determine the coordinates of 1,400 letters! It might have taken an hour or two to write the script, but that investment was well worth it.

Summary

This chapter introduced you to many debugging techniques. If you've ever done any kind of troubleshooting, this chapter was not all new. Even though the focus was on applying such skills to fixing or preventing bugs in Flash, it's not much different than fixing or preventing problems with your VCR. In any case, there are no hard-and-fast rules, but rather a general approach you must take.

Finding and documenting bugs is always the first step. You learned how to use the Debugger, but you must first know what you're looking for before you can fix it. I suggested that you could try to develop personality attributes (such as cynicism and humility) that make finding or testing for bugs easier. Ultimately, you'll develop skills that will reduce bugs in the first place. By writing quality assurance scripts and productivity scripts, you'll be well on your way.

By the way, you'll learn more details about the topics in this chapter in Workshop Chapter 14, "Offline Production," and Workshop Chapter 18, "Fixing Broken Scripts." Of course, you'll get plenty of practice fixing bugs, because they're just a fact of programming. Perhaps realizing this will make the debugging process part of the entire production rather than something extra that you hadn't expected to do.

{ Chapter 7 }

The Movie Clip Object

The Movie Clip object is the most prevalent and most understandable of all Flash objects. Even the most novice Flash user knows more about objects than he might realize. Although you might not use the words *instance*, *class*, and *object*, you've experienced the concepts. By dragging a Movie Clip onto the Stage, changing its alpha, and then dragging another one and scaling it, you experience the concept of multiple instances of the same master—each with different properties. Each instance (Movie Clip on the Stage) of the class (the master symbol) is an object that has properties (such as `_alpha` and `_scale`).

We'll cover all these details in this chapter. After you understand the Movie Clip object, you'll not only be able to change any property of a clip with scripting, but you'll understand objects generally. As you read this chapter, don't think that "now I'm learning the complicated concept of objects;" rather, think that "now I'll be able to modify every aspect of a movie clip using scripting!" Although you are indeed learning about objects, it's the application of making Movie Clips do cool things that's most interesting.

In this chapter, you will:

- Access and modify built-in properties of clip instances.
- Create custom variables that act like homemade properties.
- Learn the concept of, and how to use, "methods" of Movie Clip objects.
- Address clips dynamically in addition to absolute and relative addressing.

Properties of Clips

When you drag a Movie Clip from the Library onto the Stage, you have already set the _x and _y (position) properties of the instance created. Each instance on the Stage will have its own set of properties. The available built-in properties are the same for every instance, but the actual settings for each vary. Properties such as _scale, _rotation, and _alpha are examples of other built-in properties that you can modify. Although you can set properties of instances of Graphic symbols while authoring, you can only access properties of instances of objects (such as Movie Clip instances) with scripting. You can both ascertain the current values of a clip's properties and change them through scripting. Flash MX gives you access to instances of clips, buttons, and dynamic or input text. A simple way to understand this fact is that you can't name instances of Graphic symbols—only clips, buttons, or (non-static) text.

New to MX

Here's the form that a script takes to access a clip's properties:

```
clipInstanceName.theProperty
```

Notice that this is only an expression that results in the value for whatever property you put in the position, "theProperty."

To set a clip's property, the form is:

```
clipInstanceName.theProperty=newValue;
```

The form is always "object-dot-property" (or, really, "address to object-dot-property"). Even though you can often refer to the object (that is, the clip instance) by its instance name (which is set through the Properties panel), you'll want to make sure that such a clip has been addressed correctly. It is often easier to understand when you precede "clipInstanceName" with a relative or absolute address reference. The section "Relative and Absolute Referencing" later in this chapter covers this in more detail, but realize that if you don't qualify the instance name with an address, Flash assumes the clip you're addressing resides in the same timeline in which you write this script.

The property (shown as theProperty earlier) is whatever property you want to reference. The list of built-in properties is available in the Actions panel (see Figure 7.1).

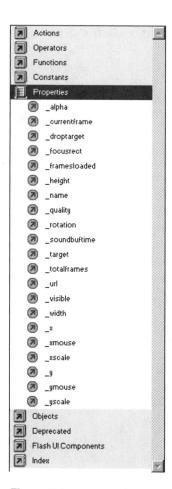

Figure 7.1 *Flash's built-in properties as listed in the Actions panel.*

You'll notice that all the built-in properties start with an underscore (as in _alpha—not alpha). So, an actual script that changes the alpha of a clip named "box" to 50 percent would look like this:

```
box._alpha=50;
```

Pretty simple, eh? It really is. After you understand the concept of "object-dot-property," you'll understand a lot of other topics that come later in the book.

You Can Get Them All, But You Can't Set Them All

One issue that might be initially frustrating is that although you can *always* ascertain the value of any property of a particular clip, you can set the values of only certain properties. For example, you can set the _alpha property of a clip (as in box._alpha=50), but you can't set the _currentframe property of a clip. The best way to learn which properties are both "set-able" and "get-able" is to look at the Properties tab of the Debugger. As you can see in Figure 7.2, the properties in gray are only available to view (not to change). This makes sense when you look at a property such as _totalframes (which contains the total frames in a clip) because you can only add frames to a clip while authoring—not while watching a movie. Other non-settable properties, however, don't make sense. For example, I constantly find myself trying to *set* the _currentframe property of clips, as in box._currentframe=12. As much as I try, it doesn't work because _currentframe is just one of the properties you can only ascertain and cannot set. By the way, you achieve the same result by using the method box.gotoAndStop(12), which is covered later in this chapter.

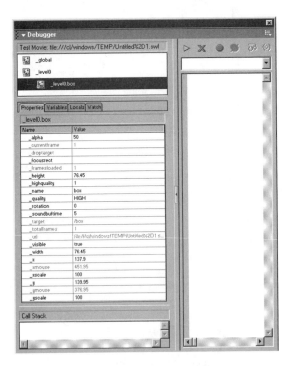

Figure 7.2 *The Debugger displays the non-settable properties in gray.*

Anonymous Targeting

I mentioned that you can refer to a clip's property (for example, `instanceName.property`) only when the instance (`instanceName`) is in the same timeline in which this script is written. I think the easiest way to understand this concept is to realize that, unless otherwise specified, Flash always assumes the address `this` precedes any reference to an instance. That is, saying `clip._alpha=50` is the same as saying `this.clip._alpha=50`. The keyword `this` means "this timeline." Translated, `clip._alpha` is assumed to refer to the alpha of an instance named "clip" in the current timeline where `this.clip._alpha` is just more explicit. In either case, these are "relative" addresses; that is, "relative to the current timeline." If you don't specify "this" (or let it be assumed), you must target the clip instance by preceding its name with the full path to that clip. We'll discuss addressing clips in more detail later this chapter, but what about referring to a property without specifying a clip at all? That is, what will `_alpha=10` (or `this._alpha=10`) do?

It's actually quite simple. When you refer to a property with no clip name, Flash assumes that you are referring to the clip where you are currently; that is, `this` is implied. If you're in the main timeline, you can actually set and get properties of the main timeline. Think of real life. You can say "the hair color of that kid" like `this.kid.haircolor`, if you will. (This assumes that there's a "kid" right in front of you—otherwise, you'd have to precede your reference with an address other than `this`, such as "look across the street at the kid's hair color.") But if you just said "hair color" or "this hair color is brown" without specifying an object (or clip instance), you'd assume that it was the person speaking whose hair color was in question. The main point I'm making here is that if you don't use "object-dot-property" and just use "property," you'll be referring to the property of the timeline in which the script resides. Personally, I've only recently gotten into the habit of always including `this` instead of assuming Flash knows that's what I mean. Remember, too, from Chapter 1, "Flash Basics," that scripts in keyframes or buttons are "in" (that is, their `this` is) the timeline in which the button or keyframe resides, but scripts attached to clip instances are "in" the clip itself (not the timeline in which the instance resides).

The idea of anonymous targeting is that you leave off the object part of the form object-dot-property and use just this-dot-property. By doing this, you're implying that you want the current timeline to be used. Even though this isn't always necessary (and will often be assumed if you leave it off), I think it helps to understand when you include it and think "this timeline." Actually, you'll see in later chapters, as well as in the "Dynamic Referencing" section later in this chapter, that you often need this to identify the current clip and then refer to the object that you are currently "in." In the case of clip instances, each instance is an object. You'll see other kinds of objects in which you can similarly use this to point to the current object. I recommend including this when addressing clips anonymously, but just realize that you are implying it when you leave it out.

Variables in Clips (or "Homemade Properties")

If you understand how the built-in properties of clips can be ascertained and often changed through the dot syntax (object-dot-property), you'll have no problem understanding how to reference the variables you create in clips. Actually, you should think of homemade variables (in clips) as homemade properties of those clips. Not only is the syntax similar (object-dot-variable), but variables are conceptually the same as properties. Built-in properties include _x and _alpha. If you use a variable inside a clip, say age, you can think of the age property of that clip. Of course, you could say this.box.age=21 in the same way that you could say this.box._alpha=50. There are slight differences with variables (oh, I mean "homemade properties") in that all can be both seen and changed (unlike properties, some of which can only be seen and not changed). In addition, you shouldn't name your variables with an underscore. Finally, another difference is that only built-in properties cause an immediate and obvious visual change. If your clip's "age" variable is higher or lower, you won't "see" anything unless you write a statement that affects a built-in property. Perhaps use clip._alpha=100-clip.age and then if the clip is older (its age is a higher number), it will be more transparent.

Variables exist inside clips as soon as you start using them. If you had the script this.age=1; on the first keyframe inside a clip, every instance of that clip would have its own "age." This is identical to how every clip has its own _alpha (and every other property). You have to create and maintain the custom variables, whereas properties are built-in, but the concept is the same. Suppose, for example, that you had two instances of this clip (with the this.age=1 script in frame 1). From the main timeline, if you name one instance "brother" and the other "sister" and then select Debug Movie, you would be able to see each clip's variables (see Figure 7.3). Back on the main timeline, you can place a button that includes the script _this.sister.age=12 (within a mouse event, of course)—and then perhaps another button with this.brother.age=this.sister.age-2. Notice that both are statements that assign a value to the age variable unique to one clip. The second example assigns brother's age to the result of the expression this.sister.age-2 (or two less than sister's age). These examples don't have an immediate and clear practical use, but they serve to show how you can treat custom variables just like properties.

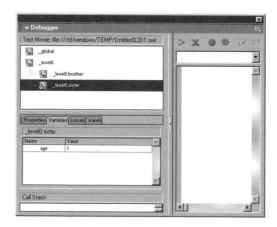

Figure 7.3 *Think of custom variables as homemade properties (despite the fact the Debugger lists them as variables).*

To sneak in a quick example of how you might apply this, consider a script attached to a clip that reads

```
onClipEvent (enterFrame) {
    this._x+=this.speed;
}
```

Every time the screen refreshes (12 times a second if the frame rate is 12fps), this will assign the _x property to "speed" more than it is currently (that is, _x+=speed). First, whose _x property? When you don't specify a clip (that is, you use this), the script refers to the _x property of the timeline in which it resides— or, inside the clip itself. So, this._x is just the _x property of the clip itself. Because it's anonymous, the same script will work on as many instances that you can attach this script to. Second, speed is a custom variable. Because it's being used "inside" the clip (remember that scripts attached to clips act as though they are inside the clip), the variable speed is this clip's speed (like this clip's _x). If speed is not defined anywhere, it will be "undefined" and will evaluate as 0 when used in a mathematical expression; thus, it will have no visual effect (just as adding zero to the clip's _x property will have no effect). However, if you had two clips with this script (with instance names thing1 and thing2, respectively), you could place a script in the first frame of the main timeline that reads:

```
this.thing1.speed=5;
this.thing2.speed=10;
```

Now, the movie should move the two clips to the right. The one with a higher "speed" will appear to go faster (that is, in bigger steps). You can think of speed either as a variable or a property—I don't care. Because it behaves and follows the same syntax of properties, maybe it's just easier to think of variables as properties unique to the clip where they're used.

Methods of Clips

This is really starting to get fun! After you understand the concept of object-dot-property, you can use the same syntax on variables. Now you're going to learn how methods follow a similar syntax: object-dot-method. A method is easy to confuse with a property, but they are quite different. Think of real-life properties first: hair color, height, weight, tooth count... whatever. Although these properties can change, at any instant, they're basically static. As humans, we are given these properties and they can change (sort of like the built-in properties or custom variables in Flash). There's not much more to say about properties.

As humans, we also have certain activities that we can perform—for example, combing our hair, brushing our teeth, running... whatever. The point is that these behaviors are analogous to the concept of methods. A method performs an operation on an individual object. Even though "brushing teeth" is a method, it can be applied to you or me. The method does its "thing" on me or on you. I brush my teeth; you brush your teeth.

In Flash, it's even easier to understand. The simplest method (of clips) is gotoAndStop(). By itself, a script that says gotoAndStop(3) will jump to frame 3 in the timeline where the script is written. However, that's just because there's no object specified and the code really says this.gotoAndStop(3). If the script says `this.box.gotoAndStop(3);`, the clip with the instance name "box" in the current timeline jumps to frame 3. Does it look familiar? Object-dot-method is the same as object-dot-property and object-dot-variable! You're pretty much done with the book now. Obviously, there's more, but after you get it, you *really* get it.

There are many built-in methods made for clip instances. Most are listed under Actions in the Actions panel—but remember that many "actions" are really statements. Most of the methods for clips are probably very familiar to you: `stop()`, `play()`, `gotoAndPlay(num_or_label)`, `gotoAndStop(num_or_label)`, `nextFrame()`, `prevFrame()`, for example. I'll bet you've used most—if not all— of these. But now you know that they're methods that can apply to unique clips, as in `this.box.stop()` or `this.slideShow.nextFrame()`.

One thing you should notice is that all methods have parentheses that follow the method name. This is required (and a good way to recognize methods). Some methods accept parameters between the parentheses—as in `gotoAndStop(12)`. You can't just say `gotoAndStop()`—you have to specify which frame number (or string label name) you want to go *to*. The concept of parentheses for parameters will come up again in Chapter 8, "Functions." The word *function* is probably better suited to thinking of human functions such as brushing teeth or combing hair. Think *method* or *function*—it doesn't matter. The difference is that methods are functions that apply to one object (or clip, in this case) at a time. (If you think the list of methods for clips is short, just wait until next chapter, when you write your own functions that can be used as methods of clips.)

Although you'll find only a few of the Movie Clip's methods listed under Actions, Movie Control (such as `stop()`, `play()`, and `gotoAndPlay()`), you'll find them all under Objects, Movie, Movie Clip (see Figure 7.4). Keep in mind that when you understand the way to use methods, you can figure out all these. That is, you always use the form `clipName.method(parameters)` (or just `this.method(parameters)` when addressing the current clip). However, it makes sense to step through a few of the more interesting Movie Clip methods now.

Figure 7.4   *All of the Movie Clip's built-in methods (listed under Objects>Movie in the Actions panel).*

`attachMovie()`, `createEmptyMovieClip()`, `createTextField()`, `duplicateMovieClip()`, and `removeMovieClip()` enable you to create (and delete) clip instances at runtime. In the case of `createTextField()`, you can create new Text Field instances. You'll see how to use all these in Chapter 10, "Keyboard Access and Modifying Onscreen Text" and Chapter 12, "Objects," as well as in Workshop Chapter 15, "Creating a Dynamic Slide Presentation."

`getBounds()` will return any clip's dimensions, which effectively ascertains a clip's size. Because a clip's dimensions include four values (`xMin`, `xMax`, `yMin`, and `yMax`), `getBounds()` actually returns a value in the form of a generic object (which contains all four values in a single variable). You'll learn how a generic object maintains multiple values in later chapters (including Chapters 11, 12, and 13). In Workshop Chapter 5, "Mapping and Scripted Masks," you'll use `getBounds()` in a practical exercise.

`getBytesLoaded()` and `getBytesTotal()` are used to ascertain filesize information on `.swf files` being loaded dynamically through `loadMovie()` or the main movie itself when you use `_root.getBytesTotal()`.

`globalToLocal()` and `localToGlobal()` are fancy ways to convert a point (x and y coordinates) in one clip instance to the equivalent point in another clip instance. As you recall from Chapter 1, different clips' coordinate systems vary. These methods perform a sort of "exchange rate" on coordinates. Just as you could ask, "How many dollars is 100 yen worth?," `globalToLocal()` answers the question, "If a point is 100x 100y in this clip, what coordinates is that same point in another clip?" The catch is that the parameter you supply must be in the form of a generic object because it contains two values (one for x and one for y). You can avoid `globalToLocal()` by making calculations manually—it's just harder that way.

`hitTest()` is used to determine whether one point is within the shape or bounds of a particular clip. For example, you can determine whether the user has clicked on a graphic portion of a movie clip—effectively making a clip act like a button. Also, `hitTest()` can tell you whether one clip is currently intersecting another. (We'll use `hitTest()` in Workshop Chapter 2, "Creating Custom Cursors," and Workshop Chapter 6, "Working with Odd-Shaped Clickable Areas.")

New to MX

`swapDepths()` and `getDepth()` can control the visual stacking (or layering) of multiple clips. Once you place clips on the Stage (or create them using a `loadMovie()`, `attachMovie()`, or similar script), they'll remain in front of or behind other clips. You can swap the stacking depth on any two clips. (I used this feature extensively on my homepage at: `www.phillipkerman.com`.)

`loadMovie()` enables you to download and play separate .swf files inside your main (host) movie. That is, if you had a clip with the instance name "clip" in your main movie, you could load a file called "other.swf" in place of "clip" with this code:

`clip.loadMovie("other.swf")`. One thing to realize is the top-left corner of the loaded movie will align with the center point of the clip it's replacing. When creating the original clip (that gets replaced), just use the top-left default center point in the Convert to Symbol dialog box (see Figure 7.5). Also, you need to wait until the movie is fully loaded before you start applying a method such as `gotoAndStop()`. You can't jump to frame 10 until the movie has loaded completely. You can, however, use the methods `getBytesLoaded()` and `getBytesTotal()`, which return information about the loaded movie (as in `clip.getBytesLoaded()`), and which enable you to determine how much has been downloaded. (We'll do this type of thing in several workshops.)

Figure 7.5 *Using the top-left default center option makes registration for loadMovie() easier.*

The address of the `.swf` that you're loading can be relative or absolute. If an absolute address points to a `.swf` residing at a different domain (than the host movie), however, the .swf being loaded has to give permission to the host movie. The new Flash MX feature "allowDomain" lets a `.swf` say, "It's okay for another domain to load me into their movies." Luckily, the code is more concise. Place the following in a keyframe (of the move being loaded—"other.swf" in the preceding example):

`System.security.allowDomain("phillipkerman.com");`

Naturally, you need to replace `phillipkerman.com` with the domain where the movie executing the `loadMovie()` method resides.

`setMask()` enables you to specify dynamically that one clip masks another. For example, `myPicture.setMask(shapeClip)` causes the clip instance "shapeClip" to act as though it were in a mask layer above the "myPicture" instance (in a masked layer). Another advantage of this great addition to Flash MX is that you can now control objects acting as masks by using script—just as you can control any clip. Workshop Chapter 13, "Drawing Graphs," discusses a few cool applications of these features.

That pretty much covers the more interesting Movie Clip methods. Obviously, learning which one is which is just a start. You'll get plenty of practice with practically all these methods in upcoming chapters and workshops.

Referencing Clips and Addressing

Now that you know about accessing a clip's properties, variables, and methods, you need to make sure that you address (or "target") the correct clip. Although Chapter 1 offered a general discussion of addressing, it won't hurt to revisit the topic and apply it to what you've learned in this chapter. Basically, you can set/get properties and variables or assign methods to any clip you want—you just need to be clear which clip (or which timeline) you are addressing.

Relative and Absolute Referencing

The section on addressing in Chapter 1 was extensive in covering the concept. Now we'll look at addressing (or referencing) clips very specifically. As anyone who's studied physics knows, "Everything is relative." When you're in a car driving beside a train, it can seem as though the train is barely moving—or even moving backward. The train could be going backward relative to your perspective, when in fact relative to the Earth, the train is moving forward quite fast— just not as fast as your car. The concept is called *frame of reference*, or *starting point*. "Frame of reference" applies to Flash when you think about a script's starting point. If you put a script in a keyframe, your starting point (the "this," if you will) is the timeline in which the keyframe resides. If that's inside a clip, your starting point is the timeline inside that clip. Placing a script on a button is similar to keyframes because your starting point is the timeline where the button is placed. It gets a little weird when you place a script on a clip instance. A scripts *on* a clip instance behaves the same as though it were *in* the clip (like a keyframe or button in that clip). It makes sense when you think about it, but it's also easy to incorrectly assume that you're starting at the timeline in which the clip is sitting. Figures 7.6 and 7.7 show how frames of reference work.

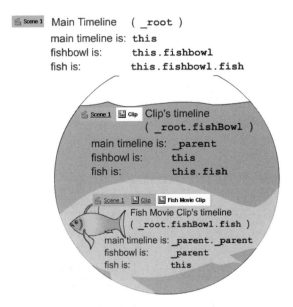

Figure 7.6 *Because your frame of reference is from outside the bowl, the fish appears to be "in water, in the bowl."*

Scripts on buttons or keyframes are "in" the main timeline.

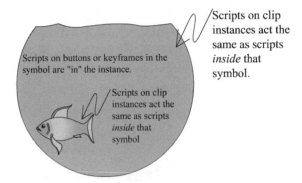

Figure 7.7 *Scripts attached to clip instances (or to keyframes in the clip) act as though they are "in" that timeline.*

Now that you know to be clear about your starting point (that is, where the script is written), you can explore the different types of relative and absolute references. The following list shows several ways to address the rotation property of a frontWheel clip instance that happens to be inside the "car" clip instance. Inside frontWheel are many instances of a Spoke symbol, named spoke1, spoke2, and so on (see Figure 7.8). Remember, it's the instance names—not the symbol names—that matter when you address clips.

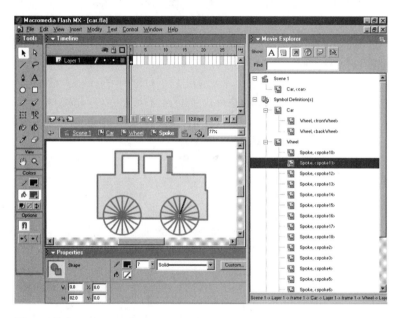

Figure 7.8   *Regardless of how many times the Spoke symbol is used, you can target an individual instance by its instance name.*

From a button or keyframe script on the main timeline:

- Relative: this.car.frontWheel._rotation
- Absolute: _root.car.frontWheel._rotation

From a button or keyframe in the Car symbol or from a script that's attached to the car instance in the main timeline:

- Relative: this.frontWheel._rotation
- Absolute: _root.car.frontWheel._rotation

From a button or keyframe in the `frontWheel` symbol or from a script that's attached to the `frontWheel` instance inside the car instance:

- Relative: `this._rotation`
- Absolute: `_root.car.frontWheel._rotation`

From a button or keyframe in the Spoke symbol or from a script that's attached to one of the `spoke` instances in the `frontWheel` instance:

- Relative: `_parent._rotation`
- Absolute: `_root.car.frontWheel._rotation`

It might seem that I was redundant by including the way to express an absolute reference in each example, but this will drive home the point that absolute paths are identical no matter what your frame of reference. They're hard-wired in that they will break if the hierarchy changes. Most people pooh-pooh absolute references for this reason, but absolute paths have a very definite advantage when relative references would otherwise be quite complex. For example, if you wrote a script attached to a clip inside one Spoke symbol inside `frontWheel` that was supposed to address a `spoke` instance inside the `backWheel` instance, a relative reference would look like this:

```
_parent._parent._parent.backWheel.spoke1
```

That is, from the clip inside a `spoke` instance, go up once to the instance of the spoke, go up again to the wheel that contains the `spoke` instance, go up again to the car that contains the wheel that contains the `spoke`, go down into `backWheel`, and then down into `spoke1`. This is arguably more complex than the following absolute reference:

```
_root.car.backWheel.spoke1
```

Relative references work great when the resulting path is short or direct. I could target a neighbor's house relatively as "down the block and across the street." But to use a relative reference to my friend across the country, it would become a nightmare—an absolute reference would probably be better.

Another attribute of relative references arises when you place a script inside a master symbol, because the same script will be present in every instance you create. Remember, you can only address instances of clips. If a script is addressing another clip relatively, each instance (of the master symbol) will do the same thing. If a script addresses one clip instance absolutely, multiple copies of the script (caused from multiple instances of that symbol on the Stage) might be redundant, but it won't address more than one clip. Let's say you put a script in the first frame of the master Wheel symbol. Consider a relative script: `this.spoke1._xscale=200`. This will cause the "spoke1" in both the `frontWheel` and `backWheel` instances to get wider. Actually, if you use the wheel symbol *any-where* else in the entire movie, its "spoke1" will grow too. Compare this to using the absolute reference `_root.car.frontWheel.spoke1._xscale=200`. Naturally, this script will execute once for every instance of the master Wheel symbol used, but the result is that it will affect only one thing: the `spoke1` that's inside the `frontWheel` that's inside the `car` that's placed in the main timeline. It's not that one method is better than the other; it's just that they have different results. As much as this might sound like a defense of absolute references, that's not the case. There's a need for both absolute and relative references. That being said, I definitely try to use relative references as much as possible. They tend to enable you to make drastic changes to your movie at the last minute without extensive script rewrites.

Here are a few reminders. Any reference that begins with `_root` is absolute and cannot be preceded with `this` or `_parent`. Starting a reference with `_root` means that you're writing an absolute reference. Also, any reference that doesn't already begin `this`, `_parent`, or `_root` can have `this` added to the beginning. Actually, it's implied and, personally, I find it the best way to learn.

Dynamic Referencing

When you know a clip's instance name or relative location, absolute and relative addressing is suitable. However, you might not be able to or want to hard-wire every reference. For example, assume that you have seven box clips (one for each page of a slideshow) and that you want them moved to the right when the appropriate page of a slideshow is active. In other words, you have something like Figure 7.9 where invisible buttons are placed on top of the seven box clips. Users will be able to jump to any page (by clicking a box on the left) or they'll be able to advance to the "next" (or "previous") page by clicking the arrow buttons. The clip instances are named `box_1`, `box_2`, and so on. It's easy enough to address each box from the individual invisible buttons placed on top of each one. But the arrow buttons must be able to address clips dynamically. If you're on page 1 and you click the right arrow button, you want `box_1` to move to the left and then `box_2` to move to the right. But when you're currently on page 2, the same right arrow button should then move `box_2` to the left and `box_3` to the right. (All this in addition to telling the slideshow Movie Clip to go to the next frame.) The point is, the right arrow button will need to do the same basic operation (move boxes), but it should do so slightly differently depending on the current page. You need to refer to a "box_x" clip dynamically (where "x" depends on the current page).

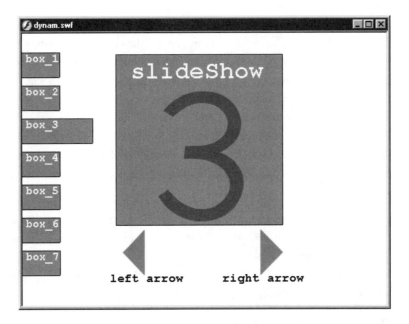

Figure 7.9 *In this example, the arrow button will dynamically target an individual box clip in the left column.*

In pseudo-code, the script on the right arrow button should be

```
Set box_currentFrame's _x to 0
//current Frame being the current frame in the slideShow
Make the slideShow go to the next Frame
Now, set box_currentFrame's _x to
50 //now that "currentFrame" has increased.
```

But you can't just say `this.box_currentFrame._x=0` because the clips are only named `box_1`, `box_2`, and so on. You can ascertain the `_currentframe` property of the slideshow clip (using `this.slideShow._currentframe`). The closest guess that makes sense (but won't actually work) is

`(this.+"box_"+slideShow._currentframe)._x=0;`.

The only problem is that although `"box_"+slideShow._currentframe` indeed evaluates to "box_1" (if the current frame of `slideShow` is 1), this result is a string (not a reference to a clip instance). That is, we don't say `"box_1"._x=0`, we say `box_1._x=0`. Sorry to show all these ways that *don't* work, but it helps to see the issue at hand.

The solution is easier than the explanation of how it works. Here's how you do it:

```
this["box_"+slideShow._currentframe]._x=0;
```

If you said `this["box_"+2]`, notice the result of concatenating `"box_"` and 2 will be a string `"box_2"`, but when this string is placed in brackets that immediately follow a target path (`this`, in this case), Flash will try to find the clip instance with that name in the path given. By the way, you can include any path (`_root`, `_parent`...whatever); you just have to precede the brackets with a path because you can't assume `this` will be added for you if you leave it blank). In actuality, every timeline has a special kind of array (called an *associative array*) that contains the name of each clip present. In Chapter 11, "Arrays," you'll learn more about arrays and associative arrays.

Naturally, you don't need to know that much about associative arrays to start referring to clips dynamically. Just specify the path (like `_root`) and follow that—not by a dot—but by a square bracket that contains an expression that results in a string matching the name of the clip you want to address (`_root["box_"+2]`). Notice that addressing the `_root` timeline is an explicit target. If the clip whose name you were building dynamically existed in a nested clip, you could use `_root.subClip[stringExpression]` (where "stringExpression" resulted in a string that matched a clip name in the `subClip`'s timeline. After you have addressed your target clip, you can continue with the "... dot-property," "... dot-variable," or "... dot-method." The finished script (shown earlier in pseudo-code) looks like this:

```
on (release) {
  this["box_"+this.slideShow._currentframe]._x=0;
  slideShow.nextFrame();
  this["box_"+this.slideShow._currentframe]._x=50;
}
```

This code first figures out which box instance to target by combining `"box_"` with the value of `this.slideShow._currentframe`, and then it sets the `_x` of the correct box clip to 0. Next, it makes `slideShow` advance to the next frame. Finally, it targets another `"box_x"` in `_root` to set its `_x` to 50. But at this point (now that slideShow has advanced), the value for this.slideShow._currentframe has increased, so a different box is targeted (and moved to an x position of 50).

The more streamlined version that follows is a lot less complex than the solution I originally developed. Just to see another way to solve this task (and to review other concepts, such as loops), check out this other solution:

```
on (release) {
    this.slideShow.nextFrame();
    for(i=1;i<8;i++){
        this["box_"+i]._x=0;
    }
    this["box_"+this.slideShow._currentframe]._x=50;
}
```

In this solution, the first line sends slideShow to the next frame. Then, in the for-loop statement, I set *all* seven "box_" clips' _x back to zero. Finally, I set the correct box's _x to 50. I admit that this solution isn't eloquent, but it's still good for review.

As I said, you can start writing expressions that result in a dynamic clip name and, as long as you put it between brackets that immediately follow a path, it works great. You'll learn more about what's really happening when you study arrays. Just don't forget the syntax is:

```
path[string].property
```

not

```
path.[string].property
```

Notice that you don't use a dot after the path when the brackets are present.

It might look as though we're addressing clips by name, but notice that their names are never between quotes. This is because clips are a different data type. You can only address a clip with a string using the bracket reference technique described previously. Realize, too, that as a data type, clips can be stored in variables. For example, you could have one variable containing a string (myName="phillip"), another containing a number (myAge=36), and still another containing a Movie Clip reference (myClip=_root.someClip). I say "reference" to a clip because, like other reference data types discussed in Chapter 4, "Basic Programming in Flash," (compared to "value" or "primitive" data types), Movie Clips are objects. After you assign myClip to reference the someClip instance, you could say myClip._alpha=50 and the original *would* change. I mention this because you'll quite often want to store references to clips in variables, but you need to remember those variables contain only "pointers" to the original. We'll store clip references in variables in Workshop Chapter 6 (as well as other times throughout the book).

Summary

Although it might seem as though you learned several aspects of Movie Clips in this chapter, the truth is that you learned one basic concept: the syntax `targetPath.clipInstanceName.property`. The part "dot property" could change to "dot variable" or "dot method" for slightly different purposes. Actually, home-made variables are best understood as homemade properties. And methods are just functions that are assigned to individual clips. (Properties just *are*; methods *do something*.)

You also learned how each timeline (or target path) contains an array full of all the clips present. This enables you to dynamically refer to clips by building their names dynamically with an expression. The syntax is `path[stringName].property`.

The best part of this chapter was that every concept about Movie Clip instances is totally transferable to the concept of objects generally. When you learn more about objects in Chapter 12, "Objects," and Chapter 13, "Homemade Objects," you'll see the same concepts of instances, properties, and methods. From now on, each chapter will continue to expand on the same themes.

{Chapter 8}

Functions

Now that you can write complex statements and affect clip instances by changing their properties, it's time to learn to modularize your scripts. Placing the same (or very similar) script on several buttons is a cry for help. Every time you copy and paste the same block of code, a little voice should be saying, "No!" In Chapter 3, "The Programmer's Approach," we discussed *why* you want to reduce repeated code. Now you'll see one great way to do it: functions.

Among all the benefits of functions, the core benefit is that you can store code in one place and access it as much as you want. Type it once, use it a million times. This chapter will introduce other benefits as well as show you how to create functions.

In addition to learning how to use homemade functions just as you use Flash's built-in functions, in this chapter you will write functions that do the following:

- Act as subroutines, thus eliminating repeated code.
- Accept parameters so that they can perform differently based on different situations.
- Return values so that they can be used within expressions.
- Act as custom methods (for your own purposes).

You'll see all three uses for functions (running subroutines, returning values, and acting like methods). As you might have noticed, functions can do more than simply reduce repeated code—but that's the main thing. Regardless of how you use them, functions always take the same form.

How to Use Functions

Functions involve two steps: writing the function and then using the function. I'm going to discuss using functions first, which might seem like I'm putting the cart before the horse. However, because Flash's built-in functions are already written, it's easy to look at using those. Also, this way, when you do write your own functions, you'll already know how to use them. Suffice it to say that you can't start using a homemade function unless you write it first…and if you just write a function (but never use it), nothing happens.

Using Built-In Functions

To get this far in the book, you've already learned *something* about the built-in functions. In addition to the brief explanation in Chapter 4, "Basic Programming in Flash," you actually used a few functions in Chapter 5, "Programming Structures." For example, to ensure that an expression was treated like the number data type, we used the `Number()` function, as in `Number(anExpression)`. This evaluates the string "anExpression" as a number. If the expression in parentheses evaluated as `"112"`, the entire expression (`Number("112")`) would evaluate as `112`.

In Chapter 5, we also looked at the suite of methods for the Math object (square root and sine, for example). These are—at their core—functions too, but we'll return to methods later in this chapter. For now, let's consider only the conventional functions listed in the Actions panel (see Figure 8.1).

Regarding all the built-in functions, consider two things: how they are used in expressions or statements and what they do. Any time you want to call (that is, execute or invoke) a function, you type its name and parentheses using the following form:

```
functionName()
```

Figure 8.1   *Flash's conventional functions as listed in the Actions panel.*

Functions' names are always followed by parentheses. Not only does this make them easy to identify, but—more importantly—the parentheses provide a means for you to provide an optional parameter (also sometimes called an *argument*). The getTimer() function is complete without parameters. getTimer() returns the elapsed milliseconds since the movie started, so it doesn't need any additional information. The Number() function, however, requires a parameter. It needs to know what expression to evaluate as a number. String(expression), another function that requires a parameter, returns a string version of expression.

Now you know how to use a function: call its name followed by parentheses, which may or may not accept parameters. As for what they do, it's important to understand that the built-in functions do *nothing* except return values. They don't perform an assignment as a statement does. That is, if myVar equals the string "11", the expression Number(myVar) not only has no effect on myVar (it'll stay "11"), but by itself Number(myVar) is practically meaningless because it's only an expression and not a statement. The function only *returns* a value so you can use the function within a larger expression or statement. For example, myVar= Number(myVar) will first perform the function on the right side of the equals sign and return (in its place) a number version of myVar (so the statement becomes `myVar=11`). Then the equals sign will perform the assignment (and `myVar` is changed). It's simply a way to write an expression that changes depending on what the function returns.

Imagine a function that returned the effective temperature based on the wind chill. (By the way, we could write such a homemade function.) In that case, you'd need two parameters: current temperature and wind speed. Multiple parameters are separated by commas. Calling the homemade function would look like this:

`effectiveTemp(40,20)`

We could build the function so that it arbitrarily establishes that the first parameter is current temperature and the second is wind speed. Even after we build such a function, we can't just call the function because we need a place for the answer to go—that is, by itself `effectiveTemp(40,20)` doesn't really *do* anything. One logical thing we could do is to call this function within a larger expression, which would look like this: `"It's only 40 degrees, but it feels like it's "+effectiveTemp(40,20)+"!"` (if the wind were blowing at 20 mph, for example). We could also call the function within a statement to assign the result that's returned to a variable `realTemp=effectiveTemp(40,20)`. The thing to remember is that all built-in functions do one thing: return values.

{ Note }

In the next section, "Using Homemade Functions," you'll see that whereas built-in functions always return values, homemade functions don't necessarily have to.

Another point that should be clear is that the parameters you provide can be hard-wired (such as `40` or `20`), or they can be variables (such as `curTemp` or `curSpeed`) and the value of the variables will be used instead. The parameters could actually be the result of expressions (such as `TempSum/NumSamples` or `speedInKilometersPerHour*.62`). Whatever is placed in the parentheses will be evaluated. Finally, consider that expressions can include calls to functions that, in turn, return values. Therefore, one parameter might invoke a function and whatever is returned from that function would be used in its place. The following examples are completely legitimate:

`realTemp=effectiveTemp(curTemp,speedInKilometersPerHour*.62)`

`realTemp=effectiveTemp(Number(temperatureString),_Number(windSpeedString))`

Notice the `Number()` function that's nested in place of a parameter. Just remember all that you learned in Chapter 5 about writing complex expressions, and the nested parentheses should be easy to track.

Using Homemade Functions

Using homemade functions is practically identical to using built-in functions. You call homemade functions in the same way that you call built-in functions: `functionName(optionalParams)`. The difference is that homemade functions can do other things besides *just* return values. You can design your homemade functions to return values if you want. Also, if you want your function to accept parameters, you need to build them that way. So, calling homemade functions is identical to calling built-in functions. However, when we get to writing our functions (later this chapter), you'll find that homemade functions can do a lot more than the built-in ones—you just have to write the script to make them perform the operation that you have in mind.

There is one slight difference in how you call homemade functions. In the case of the built-in functions, you can call them any time, any place—on a button, in a clip's keyframe, wherever. Homemade functions are written in keyframes. It can be a keyframe in the main timeline or inside a nested clip. Because homemade functions are "in" a particular timeline, they need to be addressed. If you are calling the function from any keyframe or button located in the same timeline as your function, you can call that function just by typing its name (`functionName()`)—or, if you want to be more explicit, by including the implied `this` (as in `this.functionName()`). (That is, technically, a relative reference.) If you are "in" another timeline, however, you have to precede the name of the function with a target path. Maybe you have a function in the main timeline and you want to call it from inside a clip. Just use the absolute reference `_root.functionName()`. If the clip is only nested one level deep, you could alternatively call the function with the relative reference `_parent.functionName()`.

The concept of addressing should be very familiar to you. All the same information you learned about addressing properties, variables, or methods of clips in Chapter 7 applies to calling functions including relative and absolute references. (You can learn more about targeting in Chapters 1, "Flash Basics," and Chapter 7, "The Movie Clip Object.")

In Chapter 7, you also learned that many built-in actions are really methods of the Movie Clip object. Methods are functions that are applied to individual instances (of clips, in this case). For instance, as a method, `someClip.gotoAndStop(2)` will cause an instance named "someClip" (in the current timeline) to jump to frame 2. When you write homemade functions, you can choose to write them in a keyframe of the main timeline or in a keyframe of any master symbol. Naturally, you'll need an instance of the clip containing the function if you want to call it. When calling such functions, you always precede the function name with a path to that function. The syntax of such a call looks the same as when you are applying methods to clips. That is, `someClip.gotoAndStop(2)` is the same form as `someClip.myFunction()` (where "myFunction" is the name of a homemade function that exists in a keyframe of the clip, "someClip"). Not only do they "look" the same, but homemade functions can act like built-in methods if that's how you design them. This is a great way to leverage the knowledge you already have. Rather than trying to learn a lot of different things, I think it's best to learn a few things really well, and then everything else can be understood in relative terms.

Creating Homemade Functions

Now that you know how to call functions (that is, how to use them), we can look at how to write them. The concepts of accepting parameters, returning values, and acting like methods should start to really make sense when you apply them to a purpose. You'll learn not only how to write functions, but also how they can help you. It's not as though this were an exercise in learning vocabulary words such as *parameters* and *methods*; rather, you will get to the point where you can reach for these tools as needed to solve problems.

Basics

Functions are written in keyframes. I find it much easier to type in the basic form while in Expert Mode. Here's the skeleton form:

```
function myFunction(){
}
```

The word "function" is *always* used as is. Next, you type the name for your function—anything you want as long as it's one word and doesn't start with a number. (Keep in mind, you also can't use words that are already part of the ActionScript language for your function name.) Parentheses always follow the function name. If you expect to receive any parameters, you must provide each with a temporary one-word name (separated by commas when you have more than one parameter). Finally, the opening and closing curly braces enclose your entire script. Within the script for the function, you can use the name given for any parameters and it will evaluate as the value for that parameter. For example, consider this start of a function that accepts a parameter:

```
function doubleIt(whatNum){
}
```

In this case, the function name is "doubleIt." If you call this function (from else-where), you'd say `doubleIt()`. But because this function can accept a parameter, the call would actually look like `doubleIt(12)` or like `doubleIt(getTimer())`. Calling the function effectively jumps to the function, sending with it the value of the parameter. Once at the function's script, the value of a parameter is accessed by using the parameter name (in this case, `whatNum`). If the parameter's value happens to be `12`, `whatNum` is `12`; if the parameter is `1203`, `whatNum` is `1203`. This is just like any variable. (You refer to their values by referring to their name.) In the preceding example, you can refer to `whatNum` anywhere within the function, and you'll be referring to the value of whatever was passed as a param-eter. You'll see how to apply parameters in a moment, but for now, just under-stand these two basic forms (functions that accept parameters and those that don't).

You're about to see the four basic applications of homemade functions. Then you'll have a chance to create functions that solve problems.

Functions as Subroutines

The first type of function we're going to write is unlike built-in functions because it won't return a value. A *subroutine* is one or more lines of code that you want to execute from more than one place in your movie. Perhaps you have several buttons that do the same basic thing. Rather than putting the same script on each button, you can call the same function from each button. The advantage (in addi-tion to reducing the amount of typing) is that your code is centralized. If there's a bug or you want to make an adjustment, you need to do it in only one place (in the master function) and not on each button's call to the function.

Consider the example from the "Dynamic Referencing" section in Chapter 7 (shown in Figure 8.2).

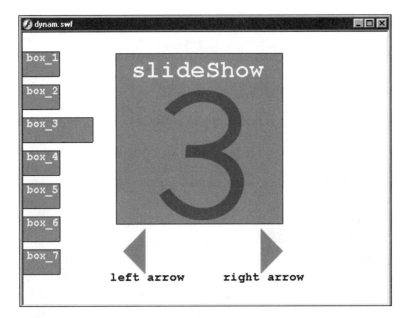

Figure 8.2 *Moving all seven "box_" clips can be done in a* for *loop that references them dynamically.*

That example has "forward" and "back" buttons that, in addition to moving to the next or previous frame of a clip, also set the _x position of seven clips ("box_1," "box_2," and so on) to zero. The code for the "forward" button was as follows:

```
on (release) {
    this.slideShow.nextFrame(); //move slide show ahead
    //Move all the boxes back to 0
    for(i=1;i<8;i++){
        this["box_"+i]._x=0;
    }
    this["box_"+this.slideShow._currentframe]._x=50; //set cur box to 50
}
```

Notice that the "back" button code was nearly identical:

```
on (release) {
    this.slideShow.prevFrame(); //move slide show back
    //Move all the boxes back to 0
    for(i=1;i<8;i++){
        this["box_"+i]._x=0;
    }
    this["box_"+this.slideShow._currentframe]._x=50; //set cur box to 50
}
```

In addition to the "back" and "forward" buttons, there were seven invisible buttons on top of the box clips that had code that was nearly identical. Each of the seven buttons covering the box clips had code like this (although the parameter for gotoAndStop() was different for each button):

```
on (release) {
    this.slideShow.gotoAndStop(1); //move slide show to frame 1
    //Move all the boxes back to 0
    for(i=1;i<8;i++){
        this["box_"+i]._x=0;
    }
    this["box_"+this.slideShow._currentframe]._x=50; //set cur box to 50
}
```

The only difference in each of the seven buttons was that the frame number used in the gotoAndStop() method was different: 1, 2, 3, and so on. But the rest of this code is the same as the "forward" and "back" buttons.

This is clearly a case in which a function can serve to eliminate redundant code. The script in each button is identical except for the first line (and, as you'll see later, the first line is even similar enough to be moved into a function that accepts a parameter). For now, let's move the identical code from each button into a function. In place of the code that's moved, we simply call our function. So, you can simply create a function in frame 1 of the main timeline:

```
function moveBoxes(){
}
```

Then, paste (between the curly brackets) the code taken from each button. The finished function will look like this:

```
function moveBoxes () {
    for(i=1;i<8;i++){
        this.["box_"+i]._x=0;
    }
    this["box_"+this.slideShow._currentFrame]._x=50; //set cur box to 50
}
```

Finally, you simply need to call this function from each button. The "next" button becomes

```
on (release) {
    this.slideShow.nextFrame(); //move slide show ahead
    this.moveBoxes();
}
```

The "back" button becomes

```
on (release) {
    this.slideShow.prevFrame(); //move slide show back
    this.moveBoxes();
}
```

And each invisible button looks like this:

```
on (release) {
    this.slideShow.gotoAndStop(1); //the 1 is different in each button
    this.moveBoxes();
}
```

Notice that in place of the code that was moved to the function, a call to the function is used instead. That is, `this.moveBoxes()` is used in place of the code that was removed.

Because the code is in only one place, you can modify it quickly. For example, if it turns out that there are more than seven "box" clips to move, you can modify that `for` loop in the function.

The process of writing a function is to first identify a need and then solve it. In the case of a function that serves as a subroutine, the need is to reduce redundant code. The solution involves extracting that portion of the code that's repeated, moving it into a function, and—in the place from which it was extracted—calling the function. It's fine to start scripting and later notice that some code is repeated. When you find yourself copying and pasting code, bells should ring in your head saying, "Time to consider a function." I often build my first version of a script using a rather hard-wired approach. After I get it working, I walk through the code and try to identify portions that are duplicated. Then, I try to move the duplicated code into a function instead.

As you're about to see, the repeated code doesn't even have to be identical. It can just be similar. The bells that ring in your head can also be useful if they identify portions of your code that follow the same pattern. Think about pseudo-code. If the explanation of what's being achieved in your code (the pseudo-code) can be generalized, you can probably write a function instead. For instance, in the preceding example, we didn't extract the very first line in each button because they were different. One used `nextFrame()`, another used `prevFrame()`, and each of the seven invisible buttons used a different parameter for `gotoAndStop()`. Although this might seem unique for each button, it can actually be generalized. In pseudo-code, the general version of the first line for *each* button is "jump

slideShow to a new frame." The trick is translating the pseudo-code. You'll see
that the solution is to use a parameter.

Making Functions That Accept Parameters

Writing a function that accepts parameters is quite easy. Doing it effectively is
just a bit more work. First, consider the form

```
function myFunction(param){
}
```

Whatever value is sent as a parameter when calling this function (as in
myFunction(12)) can be referred to by using the variable name param. Inside the
function (between the parentheses), you can refer to that parameter name (param,
in this case) and you are really referring to the value sent from the function call.
It's like when you order a steak cooked "well done." Consider that the cook
always performs the "cookIt" function. The parameter is "doneness." It doesn't
matter whether you call this function by saying cookIt("wellDone") or
cookIt("rare"), there's always a "doneness" parameter. It just happens that the
value for "doneness" varies.

One common reason to make your function accept parameters is that you don't
really want to perform the *exact* same procedure every time, but rather you want
to perform a slightly different procedure each time. Just like the "cookIt" function, you'd like some variation available. Let's try to further consolidate the script
in each button from the last example. The "next" button uses this.slideShow.
nextFrame(), the "previous" button uses this.slideShow.prevFrame(), and the
seven other buttons use this.slideShow.gotoAndStop(x) (where "x" is 1
through 7). Although this might look like three distinct scripts, they can easily be
consolidated. Without changing what we've already coded in moveBoxes, we can
add a feature to this function. Namely, we can make it accept a parameter
that serves as the destination frame for the slideShow clip. That is,
_this.slideShow.gotoAndStop(destinationFrame) will work great if
"destinationFrame" evaluates to the correct number. We'll just send a number
when we call the moveBoxes() function (as in moveBoxes(2)) and refer to the
parameter once in the function as destinationFrame. Check out the finished
function:

```
function moveBoxes (destinationFrame) {
    this.slideShow.gotoAndStop(destinationFrame);
```

```
    for(i=1;i<8;i++){
        this["box_"+i]._x=0;
    }
    this["box_"+this.slideShow._currentFrame]._x=50; //set cur box to 50
}
```

Notice that only the very first line and the second line have changed. (The rest remains untouched.) Now that this function accepts parameters (namely, the frame to which you want slideShow to jump), we can adjust the various calls to this function. (By the way, only when you make a significant change to the function—such as adding a parameter—do you need to modify every call to that function; edits usually will occur only in the function itself, not in the calls to the function.) The seven buttons are easy to adjust. In each button, remove the line that starts this.slideShow.gotoAndStop() and change this.moveBoxes() to this.moveBoxes(1) for the first button, this.moveBoxes(2) for the second button, and so on. For the "forward" and "back" buttons, you need to first remove the first line (either this.slideShow.nextFrame() or this.slideShow.prevFrame()). Then when calling moveBoxes(), you need a value for the parameter. You can't just hard-wire something like moveBoxes(2), because that will *always* jump to frame 2. The "forward" button should (in pseudo-code) "jump to the current frame plus one," and the "back" button should "jump to the current frame minus one." We can write an expression in place of the parameter that results in the frame to which we want to jump. The call from the "forward" button will look like this: this.moveBoxes (this.slideShow. _currentFrame+1). The "back" button will use this.moveBoxes (this.slideShow._currentFrame+1). The expression this.slideShow. _currentFrame+1 can be translated as "slideShow's current frame plus one."

Finally, there's one slight problem with the solution I've outlined. Namely, it's possible to press the "forward" button when you're already on the last frame of "slideShow" or press the "back" button when you're on the first frame. Therefore, the value that is sent as a parameter can be too high or too low. Inside the function, the line this.slideShow.gotoAndStop(destinationFrame) will attempt to jump to frame zero or to a frame number greater than the maximum. Often nothing detrimental happens, but it's worth addressing this issue—for practice, if nothing else. (Ideally, we'd just make the buttons dim out and become inactive appropriately—and you'll do just that in Workshop Chapter 4, "Building a Slide Show.") Without going through the work to inactivate buttons, there's another simple fix for this issue. Inside and at the top of the `moveBoxes()` function, add the following two `if` statements:

```
if(destinationFrame<1){
  destinationFrame=1;
}
if(destinationFrame>this.slideShow._totalframes){
  destinationFrame=this.slideShow._totalframes;
}
```

Translated, the first `if` statement says that if the value for `destinationFrame` is less than 1, reset `destinationFrame` to equal 1. The second `if` statement checks whether `destinationFrame` is greater than the `_totalFrames` property of `slideShow` and if so, it assigns `destinationFrame` the value of `_totalframes`. (By the way, the first `if` statement's condition could be `destinationFrame==0`, but using `destinationFrame <1` instead is "safer" in that it will account for *any* improper value.)

Just because `destinationFrame` is a parameter that's accepted doesn't prevent us from changing its value after we're inside the function. This solution resolves the minor flaw in the original function. Here's the final function, in case you want to attempt to rebuild the example from Chapter 7:

```
function moveBoxes (destinationFrame) {
  if(destinationFrame<1){
    destinationFrame=1;
  }
  if(destinationFrame>this.slideShow._totalframes){
    destinationFrame=this.slideShow._totalframes;
  }
    this.slideShow.gotoAndStop(destinationFrame);
    for(i=1;i<8;i++){
        this["box_"+i]._x=0;
    }
    this["box_"+this.slideShow._currentframe]._x=50; //set cur box to 50
}
```

It's both typical and desirable to put the bulk of your code in functions and then make the calls to that function as minimal as possible. Remember, you can invoke any function as many times as you make calls to it.

Even though this sample function accepted a parameter and used that parameter's value directly (as the frame to which we jumped), parameters don't have to be used so directly. The parameter can control what part of a function to skip or execute. For example, a function could perform several very different procedures depending on the parameter accepted. Consider this example:

```
function doSomething(whatToDo){
  if (whatToDo=="eat"){
    //place code for "eating" here
  }
  if (whatToDo=="sleep"){
    //place code for "sleeping" here
  }
}
```

If the function is called with doSomething("eat"), just the code within the first if statement is executed. Notice, too, that if you called doSomething("cry"), neither if statement will be entered. Of course, you could also write nested if-else or if-else-if statements. The point I'm making here is that you can use the parameter to affect which part of the function is executed, rather than using the parameter's value directly within an assignment inside the function. I use this technique often for multi-purpose functions, which act like a clearing house. Several different procedures go through the same function, but only execute a small portion of the function.

Making Functions That Return Values

Making a function that returns a value is as simple as adding a line that starts with the keyword return. Following the word return, you can type a hard-wired number, a variable, or an expression—the value of which will be "returned" to wherever the function was called. Consider this basic form:

```
function doubleIt(whatNum){
  return whatNum*2;
}
```

Now, from anywhere in your movie, you can call this function. Because this function returns a value, the place where you call the function turns into the value that's returned. So, trace(doubleIt(12)) will display 24 in the Output window. You could also say the following:

```
theAnswer=this.doubleIt(22);
trace("Two times 22 is "+theAnswer);
```

One important note about the word return: In addition to specifying what is returned (to wherever the function is called), this will jump out of the function. That is, if there are more lines of code after return is encountered, they'll be skipped. This is actually kind of nice even if you're not trying to write a function that returns a value. For example, an `if` statement at the top of a function could cause the rest of the function to be skipped when a particular condition is met. We looked at this technique in Chapter 5 and compared it to `break`—which only jumps out of an enclosed loop or switch statement (not the entire function the way that `return` does).

The main thing to remember about functions that return values is that you'll probably want to call them from within a statement. Simply writing the script `doubleIt(12)` doesn't really do anything because the answer (the value `24` that is returned) is not being used anywhere. There's no rule that says you have to use what's returned from a function. It's just more likely that when you call a function that returns a value, you will want to use that value somehow. Compare it to using a slot machine: You "call" the slot machine function by pulling the arm. Normally, you would take the winnings that are "returned," but if you want, you can just watch the pretty shapes spinning.

Let's look at a more practical example than my `doubleIt()` function. We can write a simple function that uses a currency exchange rate to calculate the value in U.S. dollars for a price given in Canadian dollars. The idea is that anytime you're given a price in Canadian dollars, you can call the `convert()` function (with the value in Canadian dollars as a parameter), and the value in U.S. dollars will be returned into the place the function is called. For example, you can call this function as follows:

```
Trace("20 dollars Canadian is really "+convert(20)+" in US dollars");
```

This function is explored in great detail in Workshop Chapter 8, "Creating a Currency-Exchange Calculator," but here's a finished version:

```
function convert(amountInCAD){
  exchangeRate= 0.62;
  return amountInCAD*exchangeRate;
}
```

The only reason I use the variable `exchangeRate` is that I want a clear and easy way to adjust that value (because it obviously varies). You could consolidate this into one line if you simply used `0.62` in place of `exchangeRate` in the second line. Actually, you could also add some fancy features that rounded off the answer. Workshop Chapter 8 discusses all kinds of fancy features, including how to make the answer appear in "money format" ("$1.50," not "1.5," for example). The methods of the Math object explored in Chapter 5 (as well as those of the

String object, which you'll see in Chapter 9, "Manipulating Strings") will make this process relatively simple. As with all functions, those that return values aren't particularly difficult to write. The effort comes in designing good ones. You'll build your skills with practice.

Another point: It's not necessary that a function that returns a value must also accept parameters. It just makes sense when you want the function to do something *with* a value you provide.

Finally, there are situations when even if your function's main goal is to act as a subroutine, you'll want to additionally return a value that reports whether the expected outcome was successful. For example, suppose that every time your function triggers, it moves a clip a given number of pixels to the left. However, you may want to prevent the clip from moving too far to the left. Here's the start of such a function:

```
function moveLeft(howMuch){
  clip._x=clip._x-howMuch;
  if(clip._x<0){
    clip._x=0;
  }
}
```

This function can be triggered repeatedly (perhaps from within a button's press event) with the code moveLeft(10). However, a button that's invoking this function may never know that you've reached the end. You can report back to the button itself (in the form of a returned value) the success or failure of the moveLeft operation—that is, whether the clip reached 0. Here's a modified version of the function:

```
function moveLeft(howMuch){
  clip._x=clip._x-howMuch;
  if(clip._x<0){
    clip._x=0;
    return "failure";
  }
  return "success";
}
```

Now if you change the code where this function is called to actually use the returned value, you can just check whether "success" or "failure" was returned. For example, you could put this code on a button:

```
on (press){
  if (moveLeft(10)=="failure"){
```

```
    gotoAndPlay(2);
  }
}
```

Even though the if statement's condition looks innocent, the part moveLeft(10) actually turns into the string "success" or "failure." It calls the function and gets a value returned, but the function also moves stuff on the screen. Really, it just comes down to what you want to happen and how you write code. The idea of a function returning information (as to the success or failure of an operation) happens to be a quite common technique among programmers.

Using Functions as Methods

You can call built-in functions from anywhere by referring to the function name (as in Number(anExpression)). Unlike built-in functions, for homemade functions, you have to address the timeline where the function exists. Often, I write all my general-purpose functions in a keyframe of the main timeline. If I want to call such a function from within a clip or nested clip, I have to remember to include _root. in front of the function's name (as in _root.convert(12)). As previously mentioned, a function that's written in a keyframe of a different timeline needs to be addressed as well. You could actually have two different Movie Clips, each with a function named myFunction() in the first keyframe. These functions could produce entirely different results. Within either clip, simply calling the function (as this.myFunction()) would work great. If you were outside the clip or wanted to invoke the myFunction() of another clip, you'd have to precede the name with a path. For example, _root.someClip.myFunction() would execute the myFunction inside the clip with an instance name of "someClip."

To understand creating functions that perform like methods, recall what a method is. A method is a function that is applied to a single instance of a Movie Clip. (Actually, methods are functions that affect objects—but the object with which we're most familiar is a Movie Clip instance.) The "action" gotoAndStop(1) is really a method because it is applied to the timeline in only one clip at a time. If you design them right, custom functions can act just like methods.

Let's write a function that serves as a method. I'd like a method called grow() that will increase both the _xscale and the _yscale properties of a clip. (It's always such a pain to set *both* of these because there's no _scale property.) First, make a clip by drawing a circle, selecting it, and choosing Convert to Symbol. Then go inside the master clip and attach the following script to the first frame:

```
function grow(){
  this._xscale+=10;
  this._yscale+=10;
}
```

Translated, this says, "Set the _xscale to 10 more and set the _yscale to 10 more." Which _xscale? This clip's _xscale. This is an anonymous reference to the instance in which this code resides. Now, we can call this function from anywhere inside the clip by saying this.grow(), but we want to do it from the main timeline. Drag a few instances of this symbol to the main timeline, and then name each instance something unique (such as circle_1, circle_2, and so on). Now, in the main timeline, create two buttons, one with this script:

```
on (release) {
  this.circle_1.grow();
}
```

The other button's script can be

```
on (release) {
  this.circle_2.grow();
}
```

Check out Figure 8.3.

It looks exactly like applying a method to a clip (like you might do circle_1. nextFrame()). This example really does behave like a method for one important reason: The function refers (relatively) to the clip in which it is contained. I don't think this is a hard-and-fast rule of what makes a custom method, but for a function to act like a method, I think it's fair to say that the function has to affect the clip it's inside. All methods are functions—not all functions are methods. When functions are unique to the clip in which they're contained, you can think of them as methods.

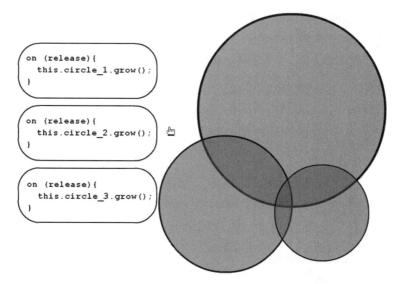

```
on (release){
   this.circle_1.grow();
}
```

```
on (release){
   this.circle_2.grow();
}
```

```
on (release){
   this.circle_3.grow();
}
```

Figure 8.3 *A function inside the master symbol acts like a method of each instance.*

Local Variables

The variations of functions (acting like methods, returning values, accepting parameters, and acting like subroutines) are all part of the same thing: functions. They're not even exclusive concepts. For example, you can have a subroutine that accepts parameters. The differences are in the way you use the functions you create. Local variables are another concept related to functions. You can use local variables in any type of function, but you don't have to.

Local variables are used just like any other variable except they exist only while inside the function. Similar to the way a named parameter has a value only while you're inside the function, local variables can be accessed only from within the function. The only real benefit of local variables is that they cease to occupy any memory after they're used. This concept of "good housekeeping" is not terribly important until your movies become very complex—and even then, it's likely that the user's computer memory (RAM) is large enough to make the issue almost nonexistent. But it's worth understanding, because there's no reason to use more memory than you have to.

Normally, after you assign a value to a variable (such as username="phillip"), a small portion of RAM is dedicated to that variable. At any time, you can ascertain the value of username. Even if you're in another timeline, you can access the variable by preceding its name with the path to the variable. That variable will "live" forever—even if you reassign it to an empty string (as username="", for example). If you are done with the variable, you can use the delete statement to remove it from memory (delete username). Depending on your application, you might want the variable to "live" forever. Perhaps you're tracking a user's score and you don't want to flush it from memory. Just remember that even if you stop using a variable, it's still occupying a portion of RAM (unless you delete it). Such normal "timeline" variables can be considered global variables in that they're available at any time and from anywhere (that is, they're not "local"). It's just that in Flash MX there are now true globals (that effectively "live" in an imaginary clip called _global—don't use _root._global.someVar, use _global.someVar).

New to MX

All variables are safe, yet temporary, storage for data. They are temporary in that when you restart the movie, they are gone (or at least reinitialized). Some variables are used so briefly that you should consider making them local variables. A local variable does occupy RAM, but as soon as you leave the function that RAM is released and the variable ceases to exist. The way that you declare a local variable in a function is by using var. There are two ways: You can either say var tempVar (where tempVar will be the local variable) or var tempVar="initial" (where tempVar is the local variable and you're assigning a value from the get-go—to, in this case, the string "initial"). Then, from anywhere inside the enclosed function, you can refer to the variable by name. (You don't need to proceed with var.)

A perfect example of where I should have used a local variable was for the exchangeRate variable in the following function:

```
function convert(amountInCAD){
  exchangeRate= .62;
  return amountInCAD*exchangeRate;
}
```

Because `exchangeRate` was used only once for convenience—and never again outside the function—a local variable would have been more appropriate. It would look like this:

```
function convert(amountInCAD){
    var exchangeRate= .62;
    return amountInCAD*exchangeRate;
}
```

Just that simple `var` before the first use of the variable makes it local. (Also, remember that you won't be able to access the value of a local variable from outside the function's curly braces.)

Here's a great analogy to understand local variables. Just remember that variables are for storage. If you're baking a cake, you'll likely need to mix all the dry ingredients before combining them with the wet ingredients. The bowl that you use to temporarily hold the flour, salt, baking powder, and so on can be considered a local variable. You put all the dry ingredients in one bowl, mix them, and then finally pour the whole bowlful into *another* bowl that contains your eggs, milk, vanilla, and the rest. The dish in which you bake the cake is more like a timeline or global variable. You pour the whole cake mixture into this dish, bake, and serve inside the dish. You want the baking dish to stick around for a while. This analogy is best for thinking about how local variables are different than all others. Often you want a place to temporarily store information (the dry ingredients or the exchange rate, for example). Then when you're done, you don't need the variable (or bowl) anymore. The truth is that if you never use a local variable, you'll probably never know the difference. It becomes an issue only when you're storing (unnecessarily) an enormous amount of data in a timeline variable. In any case, now you know how to declare a local variable!

Applying Functions to Previous Knowledge

Now that you've seen most of the ways that built-in and homemade functions behave, it makes sense to review some previously covered concepts, which happen to apply seamlessly to functions. This section is almost a summary of functions—and that's how you should see it. Here's a chance to solidify a few concepts you've heard over and over.

Review Built-In Functions

All built-in functions return values. Some people actually define a "function" as only something that returns values. But we've seen that homemade functions don't have this requirement—Flash's built-in functions do. If you just remember that all built-in functions return values, you'll also remember that they are used within expressions or statements. They don't create statements by themselves.

All the built-in functions follow the form `functionName(optionalParam)`. Some accept more than one parameter. An interesting (and useful) fact is that you can use built-in functions any place, any time; you don't need to precede their names with a path to a particular timeline the way you do with homemade functions.

Finally, there are quite a few built-in methods. Under Actions, Movie Control, you'll find standard "Flash Centric" Movie Clip methods, such as `play()` and `stop()`. I suppose it's fair to call these "commands" because they perform a special Flash feature, but I think lumping them in with all methods makes more sense. Think of these as "methods" because they're functions that apply to a specific Movie Clip instance. In my thinking, methods don't necessarily have to return a value—they simply have to do whatever they're going to do *to* a specific instance. Compare `clip.gotoAndPlay(2)` to `clip.getBytesLoaded()`, for example. The first (gotoAndPlay) acts on the instance called "clip" and the second (getBytesLoaded) returns a value based on how much of that clip has downloaded. To be technical, the first is a command and the second a method—but I just think of them as the same.

There are some methods of objects that may appear to act like regular functions and are not really methods-applied specific objects. For example, nearly all the Math object's methods return a value based on the value passed as a parameter. But since you always begin with "Math.," you wouldn't say `oneObject.sqrt(4)` or `otherObject.sqrt(4)` (if you wanted the square root of 4). Instead, you would always say `Math.sqrt(4)`. I suppose `sqrt()` is really a function and would appear to be more streamlined if the "Math." part was unnecessary. However, that's not the way it works. Simply put: There are some built-in Flash objects that require something such as "Math." or "Number." verbatim. For example, methods for objects Math, Number, Key, and Selection—plus others, such as Stage and System—always begin "Math." or "System." At their core, these objects are nothing more than a suite of functions that come in the form of methods. It's really not that weird. (You'll learn more in the next five chapters.) Just realize that sometimes a method's object (on which it's operating) is a unique object (such as `someClip.play()`) and other times it's just a built-in "simple" object that Flash provides for your convenience and that behaves more like a function (such as `Math.random()`).

Things to Remember

There are many things to remember when writing or calling functions. I think the most important concept is that homemade functions are called by preceding the function name with a path to that function. Because functions are written in keyframes, you just need to address the timeline where it resides.

Naturally, functions that return values should be called from within an expression because the value that is returned will be returned to wherever the function was called. This concept has been explained, but realize that just because your function returns values, that doesn't mean it can't do other things too. That is, a function can act as a subroutine (maybe setting the `_alpha` property of several clips), and when it's done, it can return a value. There's also no rule that says if a function returns a value, you have to _use_ that value. You might have a function that does several things and then returns a value. If you simply call it by name—for example, `doit()`—the value that's returned never gets used, but the function still executes (including all contained scripts). Because the function returns a value, you might normally use it within a statement, such as `theAnswer=doit()`, but you don't have to.

Finally, don't forget all that you learned about data types in Chapter 4. When passing values as parameters, pay attention to the data type sent to and expected by the function. Also realize functions that return values only return values of the type you specify. For example, if you call the following function by using `doit("one")`, you'll have trouble because the parameter being sent is a string and the function almost certainly expects a number:

```
function doit(whatNum){
  var newLoc=whatNum*10;
  someClip._x=newLoc;
}
```

Similarly, consider the following function, which returns a string. If you call it within an expression that treats the result as a number, you'll get unexpected results:

```
function getAlpha(){
  return "The alpha is "+curAlpha
}
```

You'll also have trouble if you call the preceding function with:

```
_someClip._alpha=getAlpha()
```

The problem is that you're trying to set the _alpha of "someClip" to a string (where you can only set _alpha to a number). This is just a case of mixing data types. You're trying to use apples in the orange juice maker, if you will.

While we're on the topic of data types, remember that there's a Movie Clip data type. You refer clips by name but not a string version. That is, simply typing someClip._x=100 will set the _x property of a clip instance called someClip. Notice that there are no quotation marks. The reason I'm reminding you of this now is so that you can store a reference to a clip instance in a variable or as a parameter. For example, the following function accepts—as a parameter—a reference to a clip:

```
function moveOne(whichOne){
  whichOne._x+=10;
}
```

This function will work only when you send the Movie Clip data type as a parameter. For example, if you have a clip instance named "red," you can use moveOne(_root.red). If the clip is in the same timeline from which you call this function, you could use moveOne(this.red). But notice that it's a reference to the clip (data type Movie Clip), not a string, that is being passed as the parameter. Remember, too, that numbers and strings are primitive (or "value") data types, whereas objects (including clip references) are reference data types. This means when I said earlier in this chapter that the "value of a parameter can be used in a function," that's true only when the data type of the parameter is primitive (a number or string). If the parameter is a clip reference, the function has the power to change the clip itself. That is, a reference to the original clip is used instead of just its value. As you just saw, saying moveOne(someClip) means that the moveOne function can affect (say, change a property of) someClip because it's being passed by reference (not by value).

Finally, an esoteric point should be made about the terms *argument* and *parameter*. In my opinion, they can be used interchangeably. Some people define "parameter" as the general term and "argument" as the specific term. That is, when you're not sure what the parameter's value is, it's still a "parameter." After you are done analyzing and know the value, you call it an "argument." So, a function can accept parameters, but when you call the function, you'll use a particular value as an argument. I'm only mentioning this definition so that you'll know *argument* and *parameter* are really the same thing. I'll try to use "parameter" throughout the book, but don't be surprised when you hear someone else say "argument."

There are countless other things to remember, of course, but at this point, I think it makes the most sense to practice. Try to analyze a Flash movie you made in the past to see whether a function can reduce redundant code. Naturally, if it "ain't broke," there's little incentive to fix it. However, recognizing places in your own code that can be optimized is a great skill. If you're having a hard time finding flaws in your own movies, here are a few exercises to try out:

- Write a function that moves a clip instance (maybe a box) 10 pixels to the right. Create two different buttons that call this function.

- Adapt the preceding function to accept a parameter so that it can move the clip instance 10 pixels to the right or to the left—depending on the value of a parameter received. Make one button move the clip to the right, the other to the left.

- Write a different function that returns half of the value provided as a parameter. That is, if the function is called `half()`, calling the function with `trace ("Half of 4 is "+half(4))` will result in "Half of 4 is 2" appearing in the Output window.

- Write another function that acts like a method inside a clip. Make one that reduces the clip's `_alpha` or increases it. You can write two methods or one that accepts a parameter. In the end, you should be able to use buttons in the main timeline to target any particular instance (of this clip with the method) and you can reduce or increase the `_alpha`.

Summary

Functions are so useful that it's hard to imagine programming without them. It's possible (after all, you couldn't write functions in Flash 4), but functions mean that repeated code can be consolidated; that one block of code can behave slightly differently depending on the value of a parameter received; that values can be returned; and that you can create your own methods.

Throughout all these techniques, one thing remains consistent: The form of a function is always the same. Additional parameters will sometimes appear in the parentheses following the function name, and sometimes you'll return values, but the form is always the same. Just like `if` statements and `for` loops, you should start every function by typing the core form (in a keyframe script), as follows:

```
function anyName(){
}
```

Then you can fill in the space between the curly braces or parameters in the parentheses if you want. Practically every workshop chapter involves a function, so get used to it! You'll learn to love the way that functions minimize typing.

{Chapter 9}

Manipulating Strings

Whereas storing the string data type in a variable is straightforward enough, manipulating a string can be much more difficult. After you have a string, you'll often want to change it, extract just a portion, or analyze the characters contained within it. Perhaps you want to automatically capitalize the first letter in each word of a string. Or maybe you want to compare the user's input text to a list of correct answers. Using the features of Flash's String object, you can manipulate strings the way a word processor can "find and replace"—and much more.

Often the values for your string variables will come from the user; that is, a user will type text into an input text field. Gathering such string data is explained in detail in Chapter 10, "Keyboard Access and Modifying Onscreen Text," when the Key, TextField, TextFormat, and Selection objects are covered. (The order I chose might seem backwards; you can't manipulate a string before you acquire it.) In any event, just realize that you need to populate your variables with strings first. In fact, it's realistic that your string variables can be populated without the user. For example, you may have a list of cities that populates an array. You could hard-wire this at the beginning of your movie. The point is that there's a lot you can do with strings—with or without the user's input.

In this chapter you will:

- Learn the basics of the String object.
- Integrate the String object's methods for advanced applications.
- Leverage your knowledge by comparing the String object to other objects.

String Object Form

I'll first explain the easy way to think of the String object, and then I'll provide the messy details that—although important—will probably never affect you in any practical manner. The String object has several methods and one property (length)—see Figure 9.1.

Figure 9.1 *All the String object's methods (and one property) are found in the Toolbox list of the Actions panel.*

You can write an expression using the methods or property in this form:

```
anyString.method()
anyString.property
```

Recall that methods (like functions) always include parentheses that will hold optional parameters. The preceding example shows a variable (anyString) that contains a string for a value can be used with any method or property. For example, the toLowerCase() method converts the string to all lowercase characters and returns the result. If anyString happens to equal "Phillip", the following expression would return (that is, "turn into") "phillip":

```
anyString.toLowerCase()
```

You could actually use the literal version `"Phillip".toLowerCase()`, but more likely you'd want to write an expression that changes based on the value of a variable (`anyString`). Either way, the form is quite simple.

The only property is `length`. (And, unlike properties of clips, this one doesn't have an underscore at the beginning of its name.) Using `anyString.length` returns the number of characters in the string (`anyString`).

It doesn't get much harder than that. Some methods require a parameter or two. For example, `charAt(index)` requires the parameter (`index`) to specify which character you're trying to get. For example, `"Phillip".charAt(2)` returns `"i"` (because the first character is located in "index" 0—it counts 0, 1, 2, 3, and so on). We'll look at some practical uses for the different methods in the next section. Notice, it really is pretty simple.

Esoteric String Object Details

Before moving on to a more practical discussion, I should explain a few details. First, all methods of objects require that an object has to be instantiated. In the case of the Movie Clip object, it simply requires that you have an instance on the Stage before you can refer to any properties or methods. The methods of the String object are special, however, because you don't have to first instantiate the object manually. When you use a method (or property) on a variable or string literal (like all the earlier examples), Flash automatically instantiates a temporary String object, does the method's operation, and then discards the object. You don't have to care because it's automatic. When you learn more about objects in Chapter 13, "Homemade Objects," you might learn to love this feature of the String object.

You *can* instantiate a String object if you want. (But I can't think of a practical reason why you'd want to.) The way you instantiate any object (except a Movie Clip object, which you just drag onto the Stage) is by using the `new` constructor. (Think of a "constructor" as something that constructs a new instance of object type—in this case, String.) Here's an example of creating a new String object and placing it entirely within a variable:

```
myObjectVar=new String("phillip")
```

Even though I don't have a practical reason to actually instantiate a String object, I want to point out something confusing. The *function* called `String()` is completely different from `new String()`. `String()` simply returns a string version of whatever is passed as a parameter (between the parentheses). When you preface `string ()` with the word new, you get a completely different result: a new String object. Just as the `Number()` function ensures that you have a number data type, `String()` ensures that the expression in the parentheses is in the string data type form.

Another very similar method is the `toString()` method, which is used like `whatever.toString()` to return a string version of `whatever`, as long as the data type of `whatever` is an object. The `toString()` method is almost identical to the `String()` function, except that (as a method) it operates only on objects (Array, Color, and so on, as you'll see in Chapter 12, "Objects"). Depending on the type of object you're using the `toString()` method on, it will behave slightly differently. For example, when you use `toString()` on an array, each item *in* the array will be converted to a string individually (instead of just one big string). You'll learn more about arrays in Chapter 11, "Arrays." The point is that `toString()` is a little more refined in its behavior than `String()`. Generally, most of these details are very intuitive if you avoid using the new constructor and simply think of the `String()` function and `toString()` method as ways to ensure that a variable is of the string data type.

While we're on the subject of confusing topics, there are several older functions that have the same or similar names as Flash MX's new methods, including those of the String object. Consider, for example, the (old) *function* `length()`. `length(myString)` returns the number of characters in the `myString`'s value. Bear in mind that Flash's older functions are considered to be "deprecated," which basically means that you should avoid them because they're being phased out. (They're leftover from Flash 4.) It's actually easy to tell the older functions from the newer functions because they're listed in the "Deprecated" folder of the Actions panel.

Methods always operate on an object—a given String, in the preceding example. The form is always either `object.method()` or `object.property` (just like clip instances!). In this case, the "object" is simply the variable that contains the string on which we're operating—such as `myString.length` or `myString.substring()`. The functions just stand alone and accept a string for a parameter: `length(myString)` or `substring(myString)`, for example. The cool thing is the rigid rules in ActionScript make phasing out the old stuff easy. That is, the old function `random()` is totally different from `Math.random()`, and it's easy to tell which one is which. (`Math.` clearly follows the new form `object.method()`.)

Methods of the String Object Explored

You can use the String object to do some pretty fancy maneuvers. After walking through a few definitions, we'll look at a few examples of how to use it for practical tasks. You can actually learn quite a bit by exploring the Tooltip and code hints that appear in the Actions panel (see Figure 9.2), not to mention the new Reference panel. The following discussion should give you a good background to the String object's methods before we exercise our expression-writing skills to use the String object.

Figure 9.2   *In addition to information provided in the Tooltip and code hints, the reference panel is also available.*

Zero-Based System

While playing with the String object, you must remember that (as with arrays) counting begins with 0 (not 1). This is called a *zero-based system*. That is, the characters in `"Phillip"` are `"P"` in the zero index, `"h"` in the first index, `"i"` in the second index, and so on. Any time you specify an index in a string, you must start by counting 0, 1, 2, and so on. This "counting from zero" technique can mess you up when you consider the only property of strings: `length`. (The others are methods.) The expression `"Phillip".length` will return `7` even though the last character is in the sixth index. Although it's obvious when you think about it, it can often trip you up.

Extracting Portions of Strings

On with the fun! The three methods slice(), substr(), and substring() are different versions of the same basic method. These methods will return a portion of the string being operated on. Even though they're practically equivalent, each has a unique feature or two that makes it interesting. It might make sense to become familiar with one and then realize that the other two are available when your favorite becomes unwieldy.

For the following examples, assume that the variable myString equals "ABCDEFGHI".

slice(start,end) returns all the characters from "start" to (but not including) "end." myString.slice(2,4) returns "CD". That is, the character in the second index ("C") to—but not including—the fourth index ("E"). Special feature 1: If, in either parameter, you want to include a number equal to the index of the last character but you don't know how many characters are present, just use -1. For instance, if you want all the characters from the second index through (but not including) the end, you could use myString.slice(2,-1)—which, in our example, would equal "CDEFGH". Special feature 2: If you leave out the second parameter, you'll get all the characters from start through (and including) the last character. That is, myString.slice(2) returns "CDEFGHI".

substr(start,length) returns a total of "length" characters starting with the one in the "start" index. myString.substr(2,4) returns "CDEF". That's because the second parameter (4) specifies that a string of four letters will be returned, starting with the character in the second index ("C"). Special feature: If you leave out the second parameter, you'll get all characters from "start" through (and including) the last character—just like the slice() method. (Like I say, it some-times makes sense to use one of these until you find a need for the others.)

substring(from,to) returns all the characters from "from" to (but not including) "to." myString.substring(2,4) returns "CD" because (just like the slice() method) the second index is "C", and all the characters to (but not including) the fourth index ("E") would include only indexes two and three. The substring() method is the same as slice, except the special features vary. Both have the option of leaving the second parameter blank (and getting a string from the one parameter provided through the end of the string). But only substring() has the feature that when you accidentally use a higher number for the first parameter, the higher and lower numbers are swapped automatically. That is, `myString.substring(4,2)` also returns `"CD"`. Also, negative parameters will behave as though they were zeros. That is, you cannot specify a "from" or "to" that are below the first index (`0`) or above the top index (`length-1`).

Just to make it confusing, there's an old deprecated *function* called `substring()`. The best way to avoid confusion is to make sure that you never use this function. Remember that you can tell the difference because methods always appear after the string (`myString.substring()`, `for example`), whereas the `substring()` function's form is `substring(string,start,length)`. Just so you know what it does, the `substring()` function returns a total of "length" characters from the "start" spot (not index) in "string." Therefore, `substring(myString,2,4)` returns `"BCDE"`. Notice that the 2 parameter is not an index but rather the second character (counting the way you would normally—starting with 1). As I said, just avoid using the `substring()` function, and you won't get confused.

Extracting Characters, Changing Case, and Searching

Before we do a few exercises, let me introduce a couple other methods. When you only want one character, you can use the `charAt()` method. `charAt(index)` simply returns the character in the "index" position. Therefore, `myString.charAt(2)` will return `"C"`. It's pretty simple, really.

`charCodeAt()`, a sister method, is identical, except instead of returning an actual string version of the character in the particular index, it returns the ASCII code for that character. The ASCII value for "A" is 65, "B" is 66, and so on. The code for "a" is 97, "b" is 98, and so forth. By the way, the old way to convert a string to uppercase was to find its ASCII value, (assuming it was greater than 96) subtract 32 (the difference between 97 and 65), and then convert back to the string value for the resulting code. (You're about to see that this is unnecessary now.) To convert an ASCII number back to a string, use `String.fromCharCode(65)`. Notice you don't use `fromCharCode()` in the same way you use other methods (attaching it to a particular string), because you're not operating on a specific string. But just to be consistent, you should begin with `String`. In this way, `fromCharCode()` acts like all the Math object methods (which always appear as `Math.method()` but with `String` verbatim).

The method `toLowerCase()`returns an all-lowercase version of the string being operated on. `myString.toLowerCase()` will return `"abcdefghi"`. Remember that none of these methods actually change the string itself. An assignment like this will, however: `myString=myString.toLowerCase()`. Naturally, `toUpperCase()` will return an all-uppercase version of the string.

Finally, perhaps the most powerful methods of the String object are `indexOf()` and `lastIndexOf()`. These methods will search through your entire string for a pattern (either a sequence of characters or a single character) that you pass as a parameter. They will then return the index at which the pattern is first found. The difference between `indexOf()` and `lastIndexOf()` is that `indexOf()` starts at the beginning and searches forward, whereas `lastIndexOf()` starts at the end and searches backward. For example, `myString.indexOf("A")` will return `0` because `"A"` was found in the zero index. If the pattern provided as a parameter doesn't appear in the string, `-1` is returned. Optionally, you can specify that the search should start at a different spot from the very beginning or very end. You just include an additional parameter, as in `myString.indexOf("xx",2)`, which starts from the second index and searches for `"xx"`. Using these methods, you can quickly find where any particular sequence of characters appears within a larger string. The following example shows how you could first determine where the colon appears in the string `"username:phillip"` and then use `substr()` to extract just the characters before or after the colon:

```
theString="username:phillip";
var spot=theString.indexOf(":");
if (spot!=-1){
  firstPart=theString.substr(0,spot);
  secondPart=theString.substr(spot+1);
}
```

Notice that because `substr()` includes characters only from its first parameter *to* (but not including) its second parameter, I could use `spot` (the `spot` found using `indexOf()`) when assigning the value for `firstPart`. But when assigning `secondPart`, I wanted to start with one character past the colon (`spot+1`). Also, because I didn't include a second parameter, `secondPart` included everything from `spot+1` through the end. Notice that this code works no matter what the value for `theString`. For example, `"city:Portland"` works just as well. Finally, the `if` statement uses the expression `spot!=-1` for a condition. Translated, it says "If it's true that `spot` is not equal to `-1`, then proceed." Recall that `-1` is returned when the `indexOf()` method can't find the character for which you're searching.

String Object Methods Applied

That was a nice warm-up example. Let's look at a few more complex solutions that involve a taste of some of the other things you've learned so far.

Let's say you want to ensure that the first letter in each word of a string is capitalized. The toUpperCase() method by itself won't work because it will change every character! The following two functions achieve this goal. In pseudo-code: "Loop for as long as it takes to find all the blanks, and then whenever you find a blank, use the toUpperCase() method on just the character that follows the blank." Check out the two functions here:

```
function capitalizeWords(theString){
  var blankFound=-1;

  while ( true ) {
    theString=capitalize(blankFound+1,theString);
    blankFound=theString.indexOf(" ",blankFound+1);

    if (blankFound==-1){
      return theString
    }
  }
}

function capitalize(index, aString){
  return aString.substr(0, index) + aString.charAt
➥(index).toUpperCase()+aString.substr(index+1)
}
```

This actually took me quite some time to program, but (as always) I just did it one step at a time. I first built the function capitalize(), which will replace an individual character within a string (and return the result). The capitalize() function receives parameters for both an index (that is, which character you want capitalized) and a string (that's the string you want changed). The one-line function builds a string by combining three parts: first, the characters in front of the index (aString.substr(0, index)); then, an uppercase version of just the one character in the index (aString.charAt(index).toUpperCase()); finally, all the characters after the index (aString.substr(index+1)). The last substr() method doesn't include two parameters because I wanted everything from just past the index to the end. (When you leave the second parameter blank, the method returns all characters through the end.) Basically, the capitalize() function combines three parts: before the character, the character, and after the character. Only the character is turned into uppercase. Before I proceeded, I tested the function with a button containing the following (hard-wired) script:

```
on (release) {
  trace(capitalize(7,"phillipkerman"));
}
```

Once complete, this will display "phillipKerman" in the output window. I tried a few more options, such as capitalizing the first letter or the last letter—the point being that I tested this function before moving on to the more complicated `capitalizeWords()` function.

After I got the `capitalize()` function working, I built `capitalizeWords()`. I wanted a loop that would go through an entire string and capitalize every letter that appeared after a blank. Because I didn't know exactly how many times the loop would repeat, I made a loop that "while true" will loop forever. Notice within the loop that if the variable `blankFound` ever equaled `-1` (the if statement `if(blankFound==-1)`), the line `return theString` would execute, which jumps out of the function. (Without this escape route, we could have had a true infinite loop on our hands—as discussed in Chapter 5, "Programming Structures.") Remember that when using `indexOf()` and no match is found, `-1` is returned. So, the second line in the loop—the one that assigns `blankFound` to the index where a blank is found (`theString.indexOf(" ",blankFound+1)`)—will turn into `-1` when no more blanks are found. Notice that the optional parameter `blankFound+1` is provided in this `indexOf()` method (specifying where the search for blanks should start—not at the beginning). Without this, `indexOf()` would keep finding the *first* instance of `" "`, but I wanted it to find one, and then find the next. To make sure that it doesn't find the same blank twice, I simply say "start searching on spot past the last one found." On each iteration of the loop, I reassign `theString` (the string passed as a parameter) to a new value. Specifically, I capitalize the character just past the last blank found using the `capitalize()` function created earlier (`theString=capitalize(blankFound+1,theString)`). The only funky thing is that in the first line I initialize the value of `blankFound` to `-1` so that the first time in the loop (when I capitalize character `"blankFound+1"`), I'm actually capitalizing the character in the `0` position (the first character).

Naturally, this is easier to explain than it is to write (or to interpret). It's interesting, though, that when I explained how it works, I did so in almost the reverse of the order in which it appears. That's not a requirement, but in the case of the "while true" loop, I think the very first thing you must establish is a "way out."

I've heard robbers always establish their exit route before proceeding. It's practically the same thing with loops. (You don't want to be stuck in an infinite loop.) Also, because Flash doesn't read the script in a linear order, you shouldn't try to interpret my finished code that way, either. You can go through line by line, but just realize that certain parts might repeat (in a loop) and you might need to jump around to other parts of the script (anytime a function is called).

Alright, that example was a bit of a doozy. Here's one that's a bit less involved.

The getInfo() function accepts a filename (such as "sunrise.bmp") and returns a string in the form "The file sunrise is a bitmap" (or "jpeg" or "text file," and so on). The basic approach is to cut the string into two parts: the part before the period (the prefix) and the part after the period (the extension). Then we use a series of if-else statements to determine what file type the particular extension matches. Finally, we create the string "The file BLANK is a BLANK," but replace the two BLANKs with the prefix and file type, respectively. Here's the code:

```
function getInfo(filename){
  var dotLoc=fileName.lastIndexOf(".");
  var prefix=filename.substr(0,dotLoc);
  var extension=filename.substr(dotLoc+1);
  var filetype;
  if (extension=="bmp"){
    filetype="a bitmap";
  }else if (extension=="txt"){
    filetype="a text file";
  }else{
    filetype="an unknown file type";
  }
  return "The file \"" + prefix + "\" is " + filetype + ".";
}
```

Notice that I save a few local variables that I'll need within the function but nowhere else: dotLoc (containing the "last index of" the period); prefix (using substr() to extract all characters from index 0 through dotLoc); and extension (using substr() again, but from the index dotLoc+1 through the end). Then the if-else sequence checks extension against a few known file types and sets the filetype variable accordingly. The last else is a catch-all that simply sets filetype to "unknown." Also, just so that the string follows proper English and uses "a" and "an" appropriately, I included that part in the filetype variable. (Even though it's not really accurate, it's just the way I designed it—it's my variable after all.) This technique is also useful when you're building plural or singular words on-the-fly; it eliminates the need for funky things such as "page(s)," for example.

To test this function, make a button with the following code:

```
on (release) {
  trace(getInfo("sunrise.txt"));
  //or
  //onScreenVariable=getInfo("sunrise.txt");
}
```

You can probably see that what you've already learned about code structures (statements such as `if` and `while`), plus homemade functions will all come in handy when you try to perform elaborate maneuvers with the String object.

There are a couple methods of the String object that I've left out. In particular, I've left out the method `split()`, which is quite cool. It will convert a string into an array. You just specify a delimiter as a parameter (`myString.split(delimiter)`). If `myString` is `"phillip,david,kerman"`, `myString.split(",")` will return an array with three items (`"phillip"`, `"david"`, and `"kerman"`). We'll look at this method more in Chapter 11, when we look at arrays.

Finally, I left out the `concat()` method. It does the same thing as the + concatenation character, except that it will never act like an addition operator (as + will when both operands are numbers). If `myString` is `"Phillip"`, `myString.concat("David","Kerman")` will return `"PhillipDavidKerman"`. By the way, you can have as many parameters as you want—just be sure to separate each with a comma.

Summary

Wow, each chapter is more fun than the last! Perhaps the best part of this chapter was that we got to apply our previous knowledge to more practical maneuvers. This was our first introduction to an object other than the all-to-familiar Movie Clip object: the String object. In the past, we played with the Math and Number objects a bit—but those are a bit different because they're not much more than a suite of functions. That is, you always begin with `Math.` or `Number.` The String object is different because the methods operate on specific instances of strings (just like the Movie Clip methods).

Perhaps the String object is a bit unique because there's no "instantiation" step with strings, which, as you'll see, is required with other objects. In any event, it's still a good object because some powerful and useful methods are available. Using any string value as the object gives you access to some very fancy methods. Extracting substrings and changing case are just a couple things you can do to strings. If this isn't fun, I don't know what is!

{ Chapter 10 }

Keyboard Access and Modifying Onscreen Text

In the preceding chapter, we explored how to manipulate strings. However, each example used either a literal (hard-wired) string or a variable that we assumed had been previously populated. This certainly is a common technique—perhaps you fill an array with several words and then extract just one at a time. Quite often, however, you'll want to let users supply the string data (perhaps letting them type in their name and password). There are actually a lot of subtleties to how users can use their mouse and keyboard to input text. In addition, you have nearly infinite possibilities as to how you present that text onscreen (regardless of whether it's taken from the user). In this chapter, you'll learn both how to gather text the user inputs and how to display any text onscreen.

In this chapter, you will:

- Use the TextField object to manipulate text fields the same way you can with the Properties panel, but instead using script.

- Define format characteristics for displayed text using the TextFormat object.

- Use the Key object to determine which keys are being pressed.

- Ascertain and set the selected area of a text entry field.

- Use "listeners" to respond (by running a script) any time a specified event occurs.

The countless details of text field instances, formatting, selection, and keyboard access might seem at times to be excessive or just plain confusing. Here's a quick overview of where we're heading so that you won't get too bogged down by details as we step through.

The TextField object is a set of methods and properties (and listeners) to manipulate instances of text onscreen. When authoring, you can create a block of text, set its attributes, and even give it an instance name—all by using the Properties panel. The features of the TextField object give you a way to do all that (and more) through script. When you do stuff to a TextField (for example, change its width), you're doing it to one specific instance at a time.

The TextFormat object is comparable to Movie Clips (that have a lot of built-in properties), but an instance of the TextFormat object has properties for all kinds of visual text settings: the color, the font, and the font size. The funky thing about the TextFormat object is that you won't see anything until you apply a TextFormat object (with all its properties) to an individual TextField instance on the Stage. Think of the TextFormat as a style guide. You can apply it to any part of any field.

The Selection object enables you to determine either the portion of a field that's selected or which field has focus (that is, the one currently being accessed). It might seem to be an esoteric and useless detail, but believe me, it's useful. You can use the Selection object to build a really usable data-input screen for your viewers.

The Key object is just a way to determine what the user is doing with his keyboard. In fact, you don't even need any onscreen text to use the Key object—for example, consider a game that uses the four arrow keys to control a car's movement.

I find it interesting that the Key object is the only one that really requires the user. That is, you can set a selection, change the format, or modify a field's properties with or without the user. Although you'll write scripts that respond to user interaction, preparing and displaying text often occurs before the user does anything.

New to MX   Finally, this chapter introduces you to another new Flash MX feature: listeners. Several objects (including Key, TextField, and Selection) have specific events that you can cause to trigger a script. Just like how a button has a press event (for which your script can respond), a text field has an onChanged event for which you can trigger a specified script.

The Two "Text" Objects: TextField and TextFormat

As I just explained, there are two similarly named text-related objects, although they have totally different purposes. The TextField object enables you to manipulate properties for any individual text instance. (Only Dynamic and Input text can be affected; Static text has no option to be given an instance name.) The TextFormat object is stored in a variable, and that variable has named properties that you can change (just like how you change a clip's properties). After the variable's properties' values are set the way you want, you can finally apply it to a particular text instance onscreen. You could actually have several variables, each containing a TextFormat object with slightly different values. Then, you could decide to apply only one particular format to the onscreen text. You'll see some examples of this in the section "Using the TextField and TextFormat Objects" later in this chapter.

TextField Object

Basically, the TextField object is a way to control a text instance the way the Properties panel does—except by using script. (You can actually do additional things, such as change the background color.) You can give any field on the Stage (Dynamic Text or Input Text) an instance name by using the Properties panel (see Figure 10.1).

Figure 10.1   *You can name a text field instance through the Properties panel.*

TextField Properties

Once you have a named instance, you can change any property by using the following syntax:

```
my_txt.property=newValue
```

`my_txt` is the text's instance name (`_txt` is the code hint suffix), and you replace `property` with the desired TextField property, and `newValue` with an appropriate value. For example, the following code will set the `border` property to true:

```
my_txt.border=true;
```

This is basically the same as if you had clicked the "Show Border Around Text" option while authoring. The difference here is that you're using script; therefore, the border can appear or disappear any time you specify. In addition, you actually have much more control with script. The "Show Border" option is more appropriately called "Show Border *and Background*." You can't use the Properties panel to set only the border (with no background). This is just a taste of the way the TextField object lets you do a bit more than the Properties panel alone. (By the way, just use `my_txt.background=true` to reveal the background as well.)

> Before we dive right into a quick rundown of the properties available for the TextField object, an issue about variables is worth discussing. You may be familiar with the way Dynamic or Input Text fields can be associated with a variable. By filling in the "Var:" field in the Properties panel, you effectively link the variable to the onscreen text. That is, if the variable changes, you'll see the onscreen text change, and if the user changes the onscreen text (in the case of input text), he is effectively changing the variable. Although this feature is useful, you'll see that now there is another (arguably better) way. Specifically, any text field has a `text` property. That is, `my_txt.text` contains the value currently in the field instance "my_txt." You can change onscreen text by saying `my_txt.text="new stuff"`.
>
> I often still feel attracted to the old way of associating a variable through the "Var:" field. However, I really think it's best to keep your variables as variables, and your text fields as text fields. Just think of them as separate things. There's nothing wrong with using the value of a variable when you assign the `text` property of a text field (as in `my_txt.text=myVar`). Realize, however, that associating a variable with a text field will tend to turn that variable's data type to String. For example, a field may look like it contains a `3` when in fact the associate variable's value becomes `"3"`.

Finally, there is one advantage to associating a variable with a text field. Any time the variable changes, the text field automatically updates to reflect the change. Even though I'd recommend avoiding the associated variable feature, its convenience is hard to resist. The thing is, Flash MX has an alternative to associated variables that's even better. It's called a *watch*. Basically, you specify that you want to watch a particular variable and invoke a function (that you specify) any time it changes. You include code to update the text field's text property inside the function that gets triggered by the variable changes. In fact, a watch can be complex; therefore, I'd say it's okay to use the "Var:" option for simple cases. As you'll see in Chapter 14, "Extending ActionScript," watches can be really powerful as well.

Just understand a text field can have a text property and it can also have a variable associated with it. The two are not the same thing. My recommendation it to try to avoid the "Var:" option to associate a variable.

The form `textInstance.property` should look strikingly familiar to `clip.property` or `object.property`. These are all the same. Once you understand this form, you can explore all the TextField properties (see Figure 10.2) and, for that matter, the methods. Just remember that these are always specific to an instance. That is, you always say "instanceName.property," not "TextField.property," the way you might expect if you compare to objects such as Math or Number. Those objects always include the object name verbatim (as in `Math.random()`). With the TextField object, you always address an individual text instance.

Also, you don't need to instantiate the TextField object; having an instance on the Stage is enough. By the way, the Movie Clip object even has a method to create text fields on-the-fly. It's just like `attachMovieClip()`, but it's called `createTextField()`. The syntax is nearly the same:

```
this.createTextField("my_txt", level, x, y, width, height);
```

Figure 10.2 *The properties for the TextField object include many that are inaccessible through the Properties panel.*

This preceding code creates a new text field with the instance name "my_txt". You just need to replace level, x, y, width, and height with suitable numbers. For example, the following code places a new text field (instance name "my_txt") in level 1 of the this timeline at the top-left corner (0,0) with a width of 300 pixels and height of 100:

```
this.createTextField("my_txt", 1, 0,0,300,100);
```

You might not see anything if you place the preceding code in the first keyframe of a movie; however, you can follow the code with this simple script to assign a value to the text property:

```
my_txt.text="This is new text";
```

Without carrying this example any further, just realize that once you have a field, you can start affecting it or changing it. It doesn't matter if that field was drawn by hand while authoring or spawned at runtime using the createTextField() method. The text simply needs an instance name—that's all.

At this point it should be pretty clear that you can access and set any property of a text field. The following discussion of nearly every property available should be approached rather casually. That is, it's not as though you have to memorize every property. For one thing, that's impractical because there are so many properties (including quite a few more for the TextFormat object). Just try to get a sense for the possibilities; in the case of the TextField object, that's mainly the stuff you do with the Properties panel. When you have a practical objective, you might still need to come back to reference this material or reach for the Flash manuals.

I keep saying that the properties available are like a script version of the Properties panel. In Figure 10.3, I've labeled most of the buttons on the Properties panel with the corresponding script property. You can easily explore each button by drawing some text and experimenting. The idea is that anything you can do by hand during authoring, you also can do with script at runtime.

Most of these are pretty straightforward; however, I have a few notes. All the properties for any attribute that uses a toggle button (pressed or not pressed) are Boolean (that is, either true or false). For example, my_txt.selectable is either true or false (and, yes, you can *set* these properties—for example my_txt.selectable=false). Interestingly, the embedFonts property is either true or false; it doesn't consider whether you embedded all the font outlines or just some of them. Anything except the default "No Characters" is considered true.

- type has a string value of either "dynamic" or "input."

- password, multiLine, and wordWrap are all part of the Line Type drop-down. For example, you could effectively select the "Multiline no wrap" option with two lines of script: multiLine=true; and wordWrap=false;.

- `variable` is a property that's always in the form of a string. That is, you can't set a field's variable by saying: `my_txt.variable=myVar` because the value of myVar would be used. Instead, you could say `my_txt.variable="myVar"`. (Similarly, when you ascertain the `variable` property, you're given back a string version of the variable name.)

- `textColor` is returned in an integer form. You'll learn more about what that means, as well as how to convert such integers to hex or RGB form, in Chapter 12, "Objects."

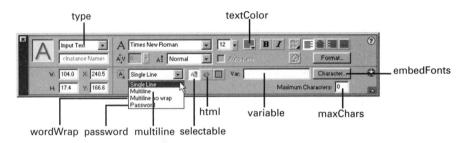

Figure 10.3   *All the standard Text Field properties have equivalent script property names.*

Wow, the preceding were just the properties that have a direct relationship to the Properties panel. Without going through every remaining detail, I do have a few comments to add, so let's go through them quickly.

- `textHeight` and `textWidth` have nothing to do with font size, but rather the size of the box drawn around the text. If you set background or border to `true`, you'll see a box with the same width and height.

- `autoSize` is pretty cool. Normally, text fields have an `autosize` of `"none"` (a string value), which means the margins don't move. If you set `autoSize` to `"center"`, you see both margins expand (or contract) whenever the field's text changes. It's easiest to understand when you see it. Make an Input Text field called "my_txt" and put this script in frame 1: `my_txt.autoSize="center"`. Then test the movie and type into the field. You can also try `autoSize="right"` or `autoSize="left"`.

- `background`, `border`, `backgroundColor`, and `borderColor` are cool because they let you create settings that are otherwise impossible through the Properties panel. (They're also dynamic, of course, which is why scripting is cool.) Anyway, `background` and `border` are independent in that you can have one with or without the other. Changing the color with script accepts either an integer color value or a hex value (more about this in Chapter 12). If you want to use a hex value, just precede it with `0x` (and don't use a string). For example, `my_txt.backgroundColor=0xFFFF00` makes a yellow background. (Be sure that the `my_txt` instance either has a background set manually or that its `background` property is set to `true`).

- bottomScroll, maxscroll, and scroll are ways to determine or control which portion of a multiline field is visible. The scroll property actually causes the visible portion to change. Suppose, for example, that your text field is vertically big enough to show just two out of a total of four lines of text. The code my_txt.scroll++ will make the text appear to scroll up; That is, lines 2 and 3 will be visible rather than lines 1 and 2. maxscroll and bottomScroll are read-only. (You can't set them.) maxscroll indicates the highest number scroll will ever reach (that is, the line number of the line at the top when the text is scrolled all the way up). In the case of two lines showing out of a total of four, the maxscroll is three lines because when it's scrolled all the way up (to show lines 3 and 4), line 3 is on top. Similarly, bottomScroll is the line number of the text currently showing in the last line. When the sample two lines showing out of four begins, bottomScroll is 2 because line 2 is sitting at the bottom. scroll might seem to be the most complex property, but it's really simple: It's the line number of the text at the top of the field. Because it's the one you *set*, it seems more complex.

- restrict is pretty fancy. You can specify either the characters you want to allow the user to type or the characters you want to prevent the user from typing. You can assign the restrict property to a string that lists several characters (such as my_txt.restrict="abc") or a range (such as my_txt.restrict="a-c"). In either case, the user will be able to type only a, b, or c. If you want to exclude characters, just begin with a caret (^). For example, use my_txt.restrict="^aeiou" to allow all characters except for lowercase vowels. Remember from Chapter 4, "Basic Programming in Flash," that you can use a double-backslash to escape characters. If you want to specify ^, -, or \ as characters that are being included or excluded, you need to use the following sequences instead: \\^, \\-, or \\\\, respectively. (The double backslash means that the second one is to be taken verbatim; the quadruple backslash is really just two double backslashes, which are necessary to escape a backslash.)

Again, don't try to memorize all the properties. Notice, however, that all the properties affect the entire text field instance. It's not so much for making subtle changes to the appearance; rather, the changes affect the entire field in a functional way (such as changing its "type" from "Dynamic" to "Input"). Also, as static properties, they aren't as involved as the methods, events, and listeners you're about to see.

Callback Functions for Events

Before we get to the methods, let me introduce events and listeners. You should be familiar with events by now—but only a button's mouse events and a clip's clip events. In the case of both clips and buttons, you place scripts inside an event attached right to the instance. In this section, you'll see how you can trigger events another way: by using callback functions.

Callback functions can take one of two basic forms; in either case, you'll assign a function as the value for an available event. In the first form, you just cram the function definition right where you assign the event's value, as follows:

```
instance.onEvent=function(){trace("do script");}
```

In the second form, you define the function first and then point to it by name when assigning the event's value, as follows:

```
function myFunction(){
  trace("doing a script");
}
instance.onEvent=myFunction;
```

The two forms shouldn't look terribly different. The second form exposes myFunction() so that you can use it in other places; however, it also takes up a bit of memory. Therefore, if you're not using the code anywhere else, the first form is more efficient. In both cases, you have to replace both instance with the button, clip, or text instance name, and onEvent with a legitimate event that's available for that object type. For example, onPress is an event available to only clips and buttons, so the following is legitimate:

```
myButton.onPress=function(){trace("you pressed")}
```

This is the same as placing the following code right on a button instance:

```
on (press){
  trace("you pressed");
}
```

Why haven't I shown you this way to avoid putting code right on button and clip instances? Well, you'll actually learn even more about callback functions in Chapter 14. It's just appropriate in order to learn about the various events and listeners available to the objects discussed in this chapter.

The following events are available to text field instances:

- onChanged triggers every time the field's text changes.
- onKillFocus triggers when the text field loses focus (such as when the user tabs out of the field).
- onScroller triggers every time the field scrolls.
- onSetFocus triggers when the field receives focus (such as when the user tabs into the field).

It's really pretty simple to specify which function you want to be triggered when any one of these events occurs to a text instance. For example, the following code will trigger the homemade `checkit()` function every time the contents of an Input Text field called `my_txt` changes:

```
1 function checkit(){
2   trace("checking what you typed...");
3   if(my_txt.text=="flash"){
4     trace("You typed 'flash'!");
5   }
6 }
7 my_txt.onChanged=checkit;
```

Although this isn't very practical as is, it shows how you can trigger a function any time the user types into the field. By the way, you can actually change the condition in line 3's `if` statement from `my_txt.text=="flash"` to `this.text=="flash"`, because in this case, `this` is `my_txt`. This way, you can share `checkit()` (that is, also trigger it with other text field instances) with the following code:

```
other_txt.onChanged=checkit;
```

Although this quick explanation of callback functions is good for a general understanding, there's another confusingly similar feature, called *listeners*. Before we look at listeners, understand that for any one text field, you can assign only one function per event. (This is also true for clips, buttons, and any other object that accepts callback functions.) For example, if you have another function like `checkit()` (say `checkitAgain()`), the following code will override whichever function currently is residing in the `other_txt` instance's onChanged event:

```
other_txt.onChanged=checkitAgain;
```

The point is, just like when you replace the value in a variable, the new function replaces whatever used to be in that event. Saying that "this instance's onChanged event now equals this function" also implies that you mean to wipe away any function that happens to already be present in the onChanged event. Actually, turning off the callback function involves reassigning the event to `null`. For example, the following code will stop triggering any callback function for the `other_txt` instance:

```
other_txt.onChanged=null;
```

It's not that having one function per event is really that big of a deal. After all, if you want additional scripts to execute, you could just add more code to the function when you define it. However, this approach is not particularly modular and particularly problematic if you want to write code (for a component, for example) that has no chance of breaking other stuff. That is, it's not ideal if your component overwrites an `onChanged` event that a user had planned on using herself. Again, this scenario is not the end of the world, but it provides a good segue to listeners.

Listeners

Listeners are similar to callback functions except that listeners are easier to turn on and off; in addition, listeners are cumulative in that one text field could have several listeners that all "listen for" the same event. The confusing part is that in the case of text fields, there are four events (to which you can attach a callback function), but there are only two listeners available (`onChanged` and `onScroller`). I suppose it's also confusing because they have the same name as two of the events! You sure don't need memorize which one is which (you can see them listed in Figure 10.4), but realize as you discover listeners and events for other objects that you might find apparent inconsistencies and limitations. You can usually find a workaround, but note the differences. For now, we're just going to cover text fields, but remember that there are several other objects that can use their own listeners.

Figure 10.4 *Listeners are similar to (and even share names with) callback functions.*

{ Note }

Although I haven't covered so called "generic objects" yet, you'll learn everything there is to know throughout the next few chapters. For now, realize they're just variables. Unlike most variables, which contain a single value, generic objects can maintain as many values as you want. Each one is given a name. Whereas a plain variable has a name and a value, a generic object has a name and many named properties—each with its own value. You can also compare generic objects to clip instances; the syntax is the same. That is, a clip named "myClip" could have a property called "myProperty" (`myClip.myProperty`), and the syntax would look the same as the a generic object named "myObject" and it's "myProperty" property (`myObject.myProperty`). The only difference is that Movie Clips become instantiated when you drag an instance from the Library. Generic objects always need to be instantiated with the code `new Object()` verbatim. For example, to create a generic object in the variable `myObject`, use

```
myObject = new Object();
```

After completing that step, you can start to add properties using the same syntax as clips. That is, `myObject.myProperty="myValue"` will store the string `"myValue"` into the `myProperty` property of the `myObject` generic object. You'll hear this explanation several more times throughout the book.

It always takes three general steps to add a listener. (It's cumulative, so you're "adding.") You create a generic object with a named property for the event you want to listen for, assign a function to that event, and then add that generic object as a listener to your text field instance (or to whichever object you're adding a listener).

Here's a simple example that displays a message in the Output window any time the user changes the text in the Input Text field "my_txt":

```
1 //define the function that gets triggered
2 function myFunction(){
3   trace("some text changed");
4 }
5 //create a generic object that becomes our listener
6 myListener = new Object();
7 //make an onChanged property point to our function
8 myListener.onChanged=myFunction;
9 //add the listener to the my_txt instance
10 my_txt.addListener(myListener);
```

Notice that I broke it up so that first the function is defined (lines 2–4), and then the generic object variable myListener has its onChanged property assigned to that function (line 8). I could have crammed the entire function definition into line 8 (as in myListener.onChanged=function(){trace("some text changed");}) and forgone the separate function declaration. Finally, once the function and listener property are fashioned properly, the addListener method identifies which listener will be added to my_txt—that is, the addListener's parameter is the generic object myListener in line 10.

Now that we have constructed the listener, we can do a few really interesting things. First, it's easy to share the myListener variable by adding it (as a listener) to other text fields. For example, other_txt.addListener(myListener) will trigger the same function when the field called other_txt is changed. Furthermore, because myListener is an object variable (that is "reference," not "primitive"), if we change its value, we effectively change all the added listeners. For example, myListener.onChanged=function(){trace("new version");} will overwrite the function stored in myListener's onChanged property and, therefore, change both text instances' listeners. (Chapter 4 covers reference and primitive data types.)

In addition to sharing or changing the myListener object, we can add more listeners to an individual text instance (to listen for the same event but trigger different functions). Recall that you can have only one callback function per event for a single text instance. With listeners, you just keep adding as many callback functions as you want. For example, say you have three input fields (firstName, lastName, and phoneNumber) and you want a clip instance (clip) to blink every time the user changes any field. Additionally, you want the clip to rotate any time the number field changes (but you also want the clip to blink). Despite being somewhat impractical, this is a good example to see how easy such a task is when you use listeners. (More practical examples appear later.) Consider that "clip" contains a different graphic in each of its two frames and a stop() in frame 1. Check out the following code, and then I'll explain it:

```
1 //make a listener called "playClip"
2 playClip=new Object();
3 playClip.onChanged=function(){clip.play()};
4
5 //make a listener called "rotateClip"
6 rotateClip=new Object();
7 rotateClip.onChanged=function(){clip._rotation+=5};
8
9 //add the play clip listener to all three fields
```

```
10 firstName.addListener(playClip);
11 lastName.addListener(playClip);
12 phoneNumber.addListener(playClip);
13
14 //additionally, add the rotateClip listener to number
15 number.addListener(rotateClip);
```

These two listeners (playClip and rotateClip) have names that refer to the function they trigger rather than the event for which they are listening. Also (in lines 3 and 7), I use the technique of defining the function in one line instead of pointing to a predefined function. The two points to understand in this example are that all three fields share the playClip listener and that the phoneNumber field has an additional listener called rotateClip. Typing in any field makes the clip play and, additionally, typing into the phoneNumber field makes the clip also rotate. If you decide that the phoneNumber field should include only the rotateClip listener and not the playClip listener, you can use the removeListener() method, as follows:

```
number.removeListener(playClip);
```

The fact that you can easily share, add, or remove listeners makes them much more convenient than plain callback functions.

TextField Methods

We've covered the TextField object's properties, events, and listeners. The only thing left is its methods. We've seen a couple already (addListener() and removeListener()), but the rest are easiest to understand after you learn about the other objects in this chapter. For example, replaceSel() makes more sense after you see how the Selection object works.

There's one method that will answer the burning question you should have. That is, how do you manipulate other properties, such as fonts, italic, bold, and so on? The TextField object really only showed us how to control attributes of the entire field—not subtle formatting issues within the field. The answer is the TextFormat object. As you're about to see, the TextFormat object enables you to set all kinds of formatting properties; however, nothing really happens unless you apply that formatting to a particular text field. Specifically, you use the TextField method called setTextFormat() to apply formatting to all or part of a field. (You can format part of a field differently than the rest.) Before you can use setTextFormat(), you have to fashion a variable (which will contain an instance of the TextFormat object). For example, the following code will cause an entire text field instance (my_txt) to be formatted, but it assumes the myFormat variable has been previously assigned:

```
my_txt.setTextFormat(myFormat);
```

There are a couple of more details to the setTextFormat() method (such as how you can provide optional parameters to format only certain characters). Also, there's a setNewTextFormat() method, which specifies how any new text that's about to appear in the field will be formatted—much like how you can change the font in your word processor and then begin typing. Simply changing the font (without selecting anything) is like setting the new text format. However, for any of these examples, you must first create a TextFormat variable with the properties you desire—so we'll just jump into that next.

TextFormat Object

Luckily, when you explore the properties for the TextFormat object, you'll find familiar terms, such as align, font, italic, and so on (see Figure 10.5). Furthermore, the TextFormat object has only one method and no events or listeners. After all, a variable containing a TextFormat object is nothing more than the data describing a particular style; there's no instance on the Stage to which it's linked.

Figure 10.5 *The TextFormat object's properties should look familiar because most are common formatting terms.*

Once you learn the TextFormat object's syntax, you'll find it's very easy to use. There are three basic steps: store an instance of the TextFormat object in a variable, modify the named properties of that variable, and then apply the format to some or all of a text field by using the TextField object's `setTextFormat()` method. Here's an example:

```
1 myText.text="My name is Phillip Kerman";
2 myFormat = new TextFormat();
3 myFormat.bold=true;
4 myFormat.italic=true;
5 myFormat.underline=true;
6 myText.setTextFormat(myFormat);
```

Line 1 stores some text in the text field instance called `myText`. Line 2 creates a variable called `myFormat` that will contain an instance of the TextFormat object. I use lines 3–5 to individually set the `bold`, `italic`, and `underline` properties to `true`. Finally, line 6 is necessary in order to see anything onscreen. You can define a format in a variable, but you must take that final step to see anything onscreen.

It turns out that when you call the `new TextFormat()` constructor function, there a ton of optional parameters—nearly one for each property available. Personally, I like doing it the way I showed above even though it takes three lines to set three properties. And because the optional parameters have an expected order (`font`, `size`, `color`, `bold`, `italic`, `underline`, `url`, `target`, `align`, `leftMargin`, `rightMargin`, `indent`, and `leading`), if you plan to set only `bold` and `italic` (the fourth and fifth parameters), you need to make sure to fill in the first three parameters with a value or `null`. For example, I could modify my earlier example by changing the second line to:

```
myFormat=new TextFormat(null, null, null, true, true, true)
```

Sure, I could then skip the next three lines (3–5), but it's so cryptic to have to decode which parameter is which.

By the way, you can change just part of the text field when using `setTextFormat()`. Consider the following example in which I format my last name differently than the rest of the field:

```
1 myText.text="My name is Phillip Kerman";
2 main_fmt = new TextFormat();
3 main_fmt.bold=true;
4 main_fmt.italic=false;
5 main_fmt.underline=true;
6 other_fmt = new TextFormat();
```

```
 7 other_fmt.bold=false;
 8 other_fmt.italic=true;
 9 other_fmt.underline=false;
10 myText.setTextFormat(0,10, main_fmt);
11 myText.setTextFormat(11,myText.length, other_fmt);
```

Notice that I'm creating two format variables: main_fmt and other_fmt. (_fmt is the suffix to trigger TextFormat code hints.) Then, in line 10, I'm using the optional parameters to apply main_fmt only to characters 0 through 10. Finally, in line 11, I apply the other_fmt format to characters 11 through the end (that is the length of the text field's contents). The setTextFormat() can accept a single parameter for format and the entire field gets formatted, or two additional parameters (in the first two slots) for start and end index, or even just one extra parameter to format a single character. In every case, the last parameter is the variable containing the TextFormat object. Finally, I wasn't just trying to show off with the myText.length parameter in line 11—I just got tired of counting characters! (I mean, I could have used something like myText.text.indexOf("Phillip") in place of the 10 and 11 if I wanted to be more dynamic.) In addition, it should jog your memory of the String object. If you're really astute, you'll wonder why I didn't use myText.text.length because, after all, it's the length of the text string *in* the field that I was trying to reference. This is a logical and totally accurate interpretation. It turns out, however, that text fields also have a length property, which is not only easier to use (less typing), but it performs faster.

There's one important issue to always remember: You can only format text that exists. This may seem obvious, but it's easy to think, "I'll make a field, then I'll format the field, then I'll set the field's text property to populate it with some words." It just won't work in that order.

There really isn't much more to say about the TextFormat object. You'll find some powerful properties, such as tabStops, leading, and bullet. Most are pretty easy to work through, but some require that you learn about arrays and generic objects. For example, you can easily assign the font property to an instance of the TextFormat object—but it won't display properly unless the user has that font on her computer (or, if you embed all the font outlines, which adds to the file size). Fortunately, the TextField object has a method called getFontList() that returns an array containing every font installed on the current computer. Once you learn about arrays, you can easily confirm that a desired font

is available before you set the `font` property. I'd suggest revisiting the
TextFormat object with the Reference panel after you read the next few chapters
or when you have a project at hand. For more practical examples, see the section
"Using the TextField and TextFormat Objects" later in this chapter.

HTML Formatting

Just when you thought you learned everything about text formatting, there's actually another way! Provided that your text field has the option selected to "Render
text as HTML" in the Property panel (or has its `html` property set to true, which
is the same thing), you can use a limited set of basic HTML tags. This option
was shown earlier in Figure 10.3.

Only the following HTML tags are supported: `<A>`, `<B>`, `<FONT COLOR>`, `<FONT
FACE>`, `<FONT SIZE>`, `<I>`, `<P>`, and `<U>`.

In addition, the following attributes are supported: `LEFTMARGIN`, `RIGHTMARGIN`,
`ALIGN`, `INDENT`, and `LEADING`.

There's really not too much to it, but I do feel compelled to mention one other
detail. In addition to requiring a text field with the `html` property set to `true`,
you'll want to be sure to assign the value of the text field's `htmlText` property
(not the `text` property we've been using). For example, only the first example
shown here will work:

```
myText.htmlText="This is <i>cool</i>"
myText.text="This <b>won't</b> work"
```

If you've got a ton of existing content already in HTML format, it might make
sense to use this feature. It is a standard after all. Also, it's sort of nice the way
you can intuitively format portions of a string by using the standard tag system.
However, the TextFormat object has a simplicity, beauty, and consistency with
the rest of ActionScript that makes it desirable. There certainly is some redun-
dancy in that both HTML text and the TextFormat object can do similar things.

Using the TextField and TextFormat Objects

The preceding examples were pretty impractical. While learning, it makes sense
to remove unnecessary complexity. The following examples should help you see
that the TextField and TextFormat objects have great power. I'll reveal the solutions for several tasks and then walk through the code.

Example: Search and Highlight

In this example, the user will be faced with an Input Text field into which he can type a search term. The code will then highlight (really, format) each word that matches the pattern he types. Only three pieces are onscreen: a large multiline Dynamic Text field (instance name `main`), a small Input Text field (instance name `search`), and a button instance called `my_btn`. (`_btn` is the code-hint suffix for buttons). Because I want to show how button instances can have callback functions, all the following code (even that for the button) will go inside a keyframe:

```
 1 //fill the onscreen text
 2 main.text="The quick brown fox jumps over the lazy dog.";
 3 main.text+=" Then, I take a rest because I'm lazy.";
 4 main.text+=" Finally, I mention my dog Max.";
 5 main.text+=" He's not brown but he is lazy.";
 6
 7 //create a "plain" format
 8 plainFormat=new TextFormat();
 9 plainFormat.underline=false;
10 plainFormat.italic=false;
11 plainFormat.color=0x000000;
12
13 //create a "highlight" format
14 hiFormat=new TextFormat();
15 hiFormat.underline=true;
16 hiFormat.italic=true;
17 hiFormat.color=0xFF0000;
18
19 //define the function that searches
20 function doSearch(){
21    main.setTextFormat(plainFormat);
22    var pat=search.text.toUpperCase();
23    var allText=main.text.toUpperCase();
24    var found=allText.indexOf(pat);
25    while (found!=-1) {
26       main.setTextFormat(found, found+pat.length, hiFormat);
27       found=allText.indexOf(pat, found+1);
28    }
29 }
30
31 //set the button's callback function to our function
32 my_btn.onPress=doSearch;
```

If you're a real geek, you should love the fact that this entire script is placed in a single keyframe. Of course, it's possible to just fill the `main` text field by hand and skip the first 5 lines (which, I broke up into 5 lines for readability). Lines 8–11 create and fashion the `plainFormat` TextFormat variable. Then, in lines 14–17, I create another similar format variable called `hiFormat`. (Notice, too, in lines 11 and 17, that I specify a `color` by using the hex string format preceded by `0x`, which tells Flash that I'm specifying a hex value.) Line 32 makes the `my_btn` button trigger our custom function `doSearch` whenever the `onPress` event occurs. (Notice that when pointing to a callback function, you don't invoke the function by saying `functionName()`, but rather by using `functionName` with no parentheses.) The `doSearch()` function is where things get just a bit tricky. In line 21, I just reformat the entire `main` instance (to clear any formatting that might be left over from the last time the user searched). The next two local variables (`pat` and `allText`) are created for convenience. (They're nice, short names that are easier to type and to read when they appear several times later.) Into `pat` I store the "pattern" that I'm searching for—that is, the text of the `search` field. Into `allText` I just place the whole `main` text field. I change both `pat` and `allText` to uppercase so that this feature will be case-insensitive. Line 24 does the first search (using `indexOf()`)and places the result (that is the character position where the pattern is found) into the variable `found`. Then the `while` loop (lines 25–28) keeps doing two lines of code while `found` is not equal to `-1` (which is the code for when `indexOf()` finds no match). The first of two lines in the loop (line 26) applies the `hiFormat` format to certain characters in the field `main`. Specifically, all the characters from `found` (where the match was found) through `found+pat.length` (the `found` location plus however many characters are in the pattern). Then line 27 sets `found` for the next match. Notice that the optional second parameter for `indexOf()` (the "begin index") is provided (`found+1`) so that the next match is found—that is, it starts searching just past where the last match was found.

You can probably find a few tiny issues with this example, including that it doesn't search for whole words. (Try searching for "the," and you'll match the first three characters in "then.") Go ahead and play around with other formatting properties, however, where the `plainFormat` and `hiFormat` variables are defined.

Example: Dynamic Roster

For the next example, I wanted to use the `createTextField()` method (even though it's a Movie Clip method). Basically, the example lets you add names to a list. Actually, every time you enter a new name, a new Input Text field is created and placed on the Stage (underneath the last one). In fact, the basic operation could have been much simpler if I had just concatenated the text in a Dynamic Text field, but this example explores more new concepts from this chapter. All you need is two Input Text fields with instance names `firstName` and `lastName`, as well as a button with the instance name add_btn. Then, the following code can go in the first frame:

```
1 myFormat=new TextFormat();
2 myFormat.size=38;
3
4 count=0;
5 left=0;
6 top=0;
7 width=500;
8
9 function addOne(){
10   add_btn._visible=false;
11   count++;
12   var y=top+(count*(myFormat.size+4));
13   var h= myFormat.size+4;
14   var thisOne="field_"+count;
15   _root.createTextField(thisOne, count, left, y, width, h);
16   thisOne=_root[thisOne];
17   thisOne.text=firstName.text + " " + lastName.text;
18   thisOne.type="input";
19   thisOne.border=true;
20   thisOne.setTextFormat(myFormat);
21 }
22
23 add_btn.onPress=addOne;
24 add_btn._visible=false;
25
26 myListener=new Object();
27 myListener.onChanged=function(){ add_btn._visible=true};
28 firstName.addListener(myListener);
29 lastName.addListener(myListener);
```

The first two lines fashion the myFormat variable that's used for the text that gets created. Then, in lines 4–7, a few variables are initialized (outside of any function so that they get assigned only once). The variable count increments every time a field is created so that we can give each a unique name ("field_1," "field_2," and so on). Also, each new field has to reside in a new level number. The variable left designates the side of each new field (always the same); top is for the starting point for the first field (and then new ones appear spaced below that); width is simply the width of each field. Finally, lines 9–21 define the addOne() function. This is the function that gets triggered by the button add_btn's onPress event (as you can see in line 23).

Let me walk through addOne(). In line 10, add_btn is made invisible (so that a user can't press it twice). Line 11 increments count. Then, in lines 12 and 13, I create two local variables: h and y (for height and vertical location, respectively).

These get used at line 15 in the `createTextField()` method, which needs values for the vertical location and total height, among other things. It's just easier to read this way. The value for `h` is based on the format's `size` (specified earlier in line 2)—plus a little bit (to accommodate a lowercase *j* that appears below the baseline). In line 13, I calculate `y` by adding to `top` a space for each line (that is, `count*h`). Finally, in line 14, I create another local variable (`thisOne`) that contains a dynamic string based on `count` so that when I create the text field, I have a unique name. The createTextField() method in line 15 is pretty easy to read with all the previously assigned variables (instead of explicit values). Notice that I must say `_root.createTextField()` (not this) because the `this` of this function is the `onPress` event of the button. Then, in line 16, I convert `thisOne` into an instance reference by placing the current value (a string) in brackets preceded by the path to that instance. In line 17, I create the text that goes into the field. Next, in lines 18 and 19, I just adjust this newly created text field's properties for `type` and `border`. Finally (and now that the field has some text), I set the text field's format to `myFormat` (defined much earlier).

In line 24, I hide the button right from the start (and in line 10, I hide it every time the user creates a new field). I just thought it would be nice to prevent the user from accidentally creating duplicates. But we need the button to reappear any time the user changes the `firstName` or `lastName` fields. A listener is perfect for this. Line 26 initializes the `myListener` variable and then sets the `onChanged` property of `myListener` to a function that sets the button's `_visible` property to `true`. Then, in lines 28 and 29, I add this listener to both the `firstName` and `lastName` fields. If you had any doubts as to the value of listeners, this example should prove that they're super powerful.

It would be fun to continue with these kinds of examples, but we've got plenty of workshop chapters later in the book—and they'll combine more topics than just the TextField and TextFormat objects. Listeners and callback functions appear in a lot of the workshop chapters. The TextField and TextFormat objects appear in Workshop Chapter 13, "Drawing Graphs."

Selection Object

The Selection object enables you to control selectable text fields. Input Text fields are automatically selectable, but you can also set the Selectable option for Dynamic Text fields by using the Properties panel (see Figure 10.6) or by setting the field's `selectable` property to `true`. You can control selectable fields in several ways. First, you can set or ascertain which field currently has focus. Only one field can be actively selected at a time, and that field is said to "have focus." In addition to setting or finding out which field has focus, you can also specify (or find out) which portion of that field currently is selected. The most obvious application for this is a situation in which you want to help a user fill out a form. Instead of making the user fill in a blank field, you can preselect a portion so that typing automatically replaces the selected text. Maybe the field says "Enter Name" and instead of making the user select the text (so the user can replace it with his name), you can select it for him.

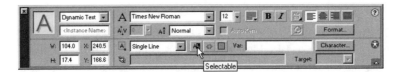

Figure 10.6   *You can turn a Dynamic Text field's selectable properties on or off by using the Properties panel (or by writing a script).*

Knowing and setting the selection is also useful when combining the powers of the TextFormat object with the TextField object. For example, you could build a mini word-processor entirely in Flash! You might want to let the user select some text to change its format. You'll need to know which part is selected before you can use `setTextFormat()` on the field.

Additionally, the Selection object has one event for which you can add a listener: `onSetFocus`. Any time the focus changes, this listener reports which field just received focus and which one used to have focus. With this, you can determine everything the user is doing and guide him accordingly.

Like the Math object, you never need to instantiate the Selection object. You just use `Selection.` verbatim for every use: `Selection.oneMethod()` or `Selection.otherMethod()`. There aren't multiple instances of "selection" because only one thing can be selected at time. The list of methods for the Selection object is quite short. You can only set or determine which field has focus, set or determine the portion that's selected in a field, and add or remove an `onSetFocus` listener. We'll look at setting and getting focus first.

Getting and Setting Focus

`Selection.getFocus()` returns the field name of the currently focused text field. The only catch is that the name returned is in the form of a string (not the actual field instance reference), and it always includes the absolute path to that field. On top of that, the path doesn't start with "`_root.`" but with "`_level0.`" (or `_levelx`, where x is the level number in which the field resides). Simply finding the name of a field (in string form) might be all you need. And, if you use the following code, you can extract just the field name at the end of the string:

```
wholeThing=Selection.getFocus();
justVarName=wholeThing.substr(wholeThing.lastIndexOf(".")+1);
//or in one line:
justVarName=Selection.getFocus().substr(Selection.getFocus().lastIndexOf
➥(".")+1);
```

The fact that `getFocus()` always returns the string name for your field means that you cannot do something like this:

```
Selection.getFocus().text="Something new";
```

Although it might seem logical that you want to replace the `text` property of the field that currently has focus, `getFocus` returns a string—not a reference to a text instance. Suppose that the currently selected field instance were `myText`; the preceding code would translate to this meaningless line:

```
"_level0.myText".text="Something new";
```

But you intended:

```
_level0.myText.text="Something new";
```

The quick solution to this is to use the function `eval()`. That is, `eval("_level0.myText").text="Something new"` will assign the string `"Something new"` to the value of the field itself. Therefore, the following line works as you might expect:

```
eval(Selection.getFocus()).text="Something new";
```

The last point regarding `getFocus()` is that if no field has focus, it will return `null`.

There is one funky thing about getting focus. If you put the preceding code within a `press` mouse event, you'd find that regardless of which field *had* focus, as soon as you click the button, it loses focus! We'll deal with this in the examples, but realize that clicking out of a field causes no field to have focus.

As for the `setFocus()` method, you must specify a string form of the field you want to set focus to. For example, to set focus on the field instance `myText` (that resides in the root, not in a clip's timeline), use:

```
Selection.setFocus("_root.myText");
```

Notice that the field instance name is in quotation marks. Although `getFocus()` returns a string form starting with the level number, you can (if you want) use the hierarchy starting with _root (or, for that matter, relative references such as `this` and _parent). Notice, too, that the preceding method doesn't return a value; rather, it goes ahead and sets the focus.

Setting and Getting Selections

After you're sure which field has focus, you can set (or find out) which portion of the field is selected. Before you use any of the following Selection object methods, make sure that there is a currently focused field (that is, just click on the field while testing the movie). Otherwise, the `setSelection()` method will have no effect, and the various `getSelection()` calls will return -1.

The `setSelection()` method is the easiest method to understand. The form is `Selection.setSelection(start,end)`, where `start` is the index at which you want the selection to start, and `end` is the last character that is also selected. (Unlike `substr(start,end)`, which is not inclusive of the last parameter, `setSelection()` includes all the characters inclusively.) As with all the String object methods, the Selection object methods are zero-based (meaning they start counting the first character as index 0).

To find out which portion of a field is selected, you can use the methods `Selection.getBeginIndex()` and `Selection.getEndIndex()`. These two are pretty self-explanatory, but just remember that if no field had focus or no characters are selected, these methods will both return -1 (rather than the index at which the selection starts or ends).

Finally, there's another method called `getCaretIndex()`, which returns the index in front of the blinking cursor. That is, if you click to start typing at the very beginning of a field, `Selection.getCaretIndex()` will return 0. You can think of this as the index into which the user will start typing (when she starts typing).

The Selection object might not seem terribly exciting. It comes in handy only when you are controlling selectable text fields—often in conjunction with the Key object. Just remember that when using the Selection object, you must first have a focused field before you can select text. And, selecting a field (or finding out which fields are selected) uses a string version of the variable name.

Selection Object Listeners

Adding listeners is new to Flash MX, so naturally, adding listeners to the
Selection object is new as well. The process is nearly identical to that of adding
listeners to text fields. With text fields, however, you add a listener to any one
text field instance at a time. But there are no instances of the Selection object
rather only one "selection" at any given time. Therefore, the listeners you're
about to see could be considered as being "global"—that is, they will listen to
any selection regardless of where it might be.

Using the Selection object's `onSetFocus` listener (there's only one) looks similar
to the TextField object's listeners, but it's actually different in two ways. First,
you always add the listener to the Selection object (not an individual instance)
and, second, the function that gets triggered will automatically receive two
parameters (one for the name of the field that used to have focus, and one for the
field getting focus). The following is a simple example that reports the name of
fields involved any time one gets or loses focus:

```
1 myListener=new Object();
2 myListener.onSetFocus = report;
3
4 function report(oldFocus, newFocus) {
5   trace("the old focus was " + oldFocus);
6   trace("the new focus is " + newFocus);
7 }
8
9 Selection.addListener(myListener);
```

Line 1 assigns the `myListener` variable the value of a generic object so that we
can then (in line 2) set the `onSetFocus` property equal to the forthcoming function, `report`. (Actually, I was surprised this worked because normally you want
to declare your functions before referring to them—but it does work and is easier
to explain this way.) Anyway, the `report()` function is different than any you've
seen applied to a listener's properties because it expects to receive two parameters. This is just a special arbitrary feature of the Selection object's `onSetFocus`
listener. The first parameter contains the name of the field that used to have focus
(or `null` if there was none). The second parameter is the name of the field getting
focus (or, `null` when no field is getting focus). Finally, line 9 adds the listener
`myListener` (fashioned earlier) to the Selection object. Notice that nowhere in
this example do you need to specify a field name. The two `trace` statements will

report information into the Output window regardless of how many fields you have onscreen. Also, when you test the movie, you'll notice the values for oldFocus and newFocus are the long string version names of the instances (that start "_level0")—similar to what we saw earlier.

Without walking through a practical example, I can give you an idea how you might put this to use. Say you're building a site that includes a custom calculator that shows a user how much she will save by buying whatever product you're selling. Many compelling sales arguments are based on a return on investment (that is, you buy something, and over time, you'll actually save money). You can build what amounts to a spreadsheet into which the user enters numbers based on her situation. To make the result better than a real spreadsheet, you can limit her entries to ranges that make sense. For example, you might not want any fields to accept numbers above 1000. All you need is a function that checks the value of what the user just entered and warn her if she does something out of the range. For example, you can use the following to replace the report function in the preceding code:

```
function report(oldFocus, newFocus) {
  if(eval(oldFocus).text>1000){
    eval(oldFocus).text=1000;
  }
}
```

(Remember that you need the other code to create and add the listener in order for this to work.) The idea is that if the text in oldFocus is greater than 1000, we change it back to 1000. You could add more useful features, such as a clip that appears to tell the user what's going on. Also, notice that the eval() function had to convert the string name for oldFocus into an actual text field instance name. If you want a different range (other than 1000) for other fields, you could create a case statement that checks oldFocus against a long list of different fields, each with a different limit. It turns out that the TextField object's onChanged listener may or may not be more appropriate because you can add a listener to each text field instance. You really can do a lot with this object.

Finally, just to tie the Selection object back to the text fields, there's a method of the TextField object called replaceSel() that replaces the currently selected text with whichever value is passed as a parameter. For example, the following will replace the current selection in the field my_txt with "new stuff":

```
my_txt.replaceSel("new stuff");
```

Again, you'll need to have a practical application to really understand much of this material, but the range of possibilities is pretty limitless.

Key Object

The Key object consists of just a few methods, several constants, and a couple of listeners. The methods primarily just enable you to ascertain whether a particular key is currently being pressed (whether it "is down") or, in the case of Caps Lock or Num Lock, whether a key "is toggled." The constants (simply properties that never change) are all associated with particular keys. That is, to check whether a key is pressed, you need to specify which key. Each key is a constant (such as Shift, Left Arrow, Delete, and so on).

Using the Key Object

To use the Key object, use the form `Key.isDown(whichKey)`, which returns either `true` or `false` and in which `whichKey` is either the Key object constant for that key or the "virtual key code" for that key. Virtual key codes are almost identical to ASCII. However, whereas ASCII applies only to numbers and characters that appear in strings, virtual key codes are extended to include other keys, such as Shift and Ctrl. What's really funky is that the virtual key code for an alphanumeric key happens to be the same as that key's uppercase ASCII. Although ASCII distinguishes between uppercase and lowercase, it includes only letters and numbers. Virtual key codes, on the other hand, include all keys but don't recognize any difference between uppercase or lowercase. The ASCII for "A" is 65 (as is the virtual key code for the "A" key). However, the ASCII for "a" is 97, whereas 97 happens to be the virtual key code for the "1" on a keyboard's number pad. You'll see that it's easy to determine any key's ASCII or virtual key code. For a practical example of the `isDown()` method, consider that the virtual key code for the Tab key happens to be 9. Both of the two following expressions will return `true` if the user happens to press the Tab key:

```
Key.isDown(9);
Key.isDown(Key.TAB);
```

Notice that the form for a Key object constant is `Key.THEKEY` (where `THEKEY` is `TAB`, `SHIFT`, `ENTER`, and so on). Figure 10.7 shows a full list of the Key objects. You'll notice that all the constants are in uppercase. The Key object constants (as opposed to virtual key codes) make your code a little bit more readable. However, only a handful of Key object constants are available (the ones you'll probably use most commonly).

Figure 10.7   *All the Key object features. (Notice that most are just constants—the all-uppercase items.)*

An important detail when using a Key object to check whether a key is down is to think about *when* you're checking. One logical place to check is within a keyDown clip event (see Figure 10.8). That is, when the user presses a key, you can check whether one key or the other is being pressed. You could also use the isDown() method within an enterFrame clip event (where you'd keep checking at all times). It turns out that using a listener is vastly easier and less processor-intensive. In any event, realize that these methods return TRUE or FALSE based on the status of the user's keyboard at the time the script is executed.

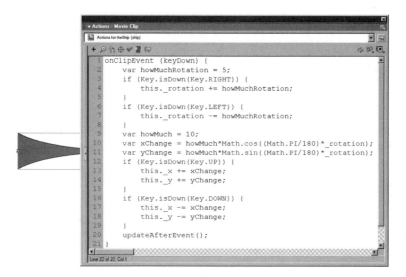

Figure 10.8   *A script that checks whether a particular key is currently pressed is logically placed within a* KeyDown *clip event.*

The other primary feature of the Key object is the isToggled() method. Similar to isDown(), this method tells you whether the Num Lock or Caps Lock key is currently engaged. For example, each of the following expressions return true when the Caps Lock is on:

```
Key.isToggled(20);
Key.isToggled(Key.CAPSLOCK);
```

Because there's no constant for the Num Lock key, you must use the virtual key code (144) to determine whether the Num Lock is on:

```
Key.isToggled(144);
```

By the way, you can determine the virtual key code for any key you'd like to trap by using the getCode() method. This method will return the virtual key code of the last key pressed. For example, the following script (attached to a clip instance) will display onscreen the virtual key code for any key pressed:

```
onClipEvent (keyUp) {
  trace (Key.getCode());
}
```

How do you think I determined that the Caps Lock key was 144? I just used this script, pressed the Caps Lock key, and then saw a 144 display in the Output window.

By the way, there's a similar method that lets you learn what the ASCII value for the last key pressed: Key.getAscii().

Key Object Examples

Let's look at a simple example first and then move on to something more advanced. Suppose that you want to let the user move a Movie Clip around the Stage by pressing the arrow keys on his keyboard. The up arrow key moves the clip up, the down arrow key moves it down, and so forth. You can place the following code on the clip instance:

```
1 onClipEvent (keyDown) {
2 var howMuch=2
3   if(Key.isDown(Key.DOWN)){
4      _y+=howMuch;
5   }
6   if(Key.isDown(Key.UP)){
7      _y-=howMuch;
8   }
9   if(Key.isDown(Key.RIGHT)){
10      _x+=howMuch;
11   }
12   if(Key.isDown(Key.LEFT)){
13      _x-=howMuch;
14   }
15   updateAfterEvent();
16 }
```

You'll notice that I used a local variable, howMuch, in line 2 so that if I wanted to change the amount the clip moves for each keypress, I could change it in one place. I threw in updateAfterEvent() at the end so that regardless of the movie's framerate, this script would update the onscreen contents every time a key was pressed. (By the way, updateAfterEvent() only affects key and mouse clip events.) Also, because this clip event waits for a "keyDown," the speed of execution is directly related to the "repeat rate" of the user's keyboard settings. You could change the clip event to enterFrame, in which case the script would check which keys were down as frequently as the framerate (that is, 12 fps would "enter frame" 12 times a second).

You may have noticed if you tried the sample code that you can hold two arrow keys at the same time (for instance, down and right) to make the clip move diagonally. Let's add a feature that makes the clip move twice as fast when both the Shift key is pressed and an arrow key is pressed. Replace the line var howMuch=2 with the following code:

```
var howMuch;
if (Key.isDown(Key.SHIFT)){
  howMuch=4;
}else{
  howMuch=2;
}
```

Notice that in this case I chose to establish howMuch as a local variable in the first line (without assigning it), and then I assigned it a value of 4 or 2 based on whether the Shift key is selected.

That was a pretty easy exercise. A challenging exercise you can try—which would involve some major adjustments to this script—involves using the left or right arrows to rotate the clip and then using the up and down arrows to make the clip move forward or back. When the clip is rotated 180 degrees, make it move down; when it's rotated 0 degrees, make it move up. The solution lies in considering that every time you move the clip, you really move it some x and some y. It just happens that (based on the rotation) sometimes the x is 0 or negative. All you need are the trigonometry methods of the Math object.

Here's the code:

```
 1 onClipEvent (keyDown) {
 2   var howMuchRotation=5;
 3     if(Key.isDown(Key.RIGHT)){
 4       this._rotation+=howMuchRotation;
 5     }
 6     if(Key.isDown(Key.LEFT)){
 7       this._rotation-=howMuchRotation;
 8     }
 9   var howMuch=10;
10   var xChange=howMuch*Math.cos ((Math.PI/180)*_rotation);
11   var yChange=howMuch*Math.sin ((Math.PI/180)*_rotation);
12     if (Key.isDown(Key.UP)){
13       this._x+=xChange;
14       this._y+=yChange;
15     }
16     if (Key.isDown(Key.DOWN)){
17       this._x-=xChange;
18       this._y-=yChange;
19     }
20   updateAfterEvent();
21 }
```

Most of this is fairly straightforward, except lines 10 and 11 where I assign the value for xChange and yChange, respectively (the variables used to change the _x and _y positions of the clip). Basically, both Math.sin() and Math.cos() return a number between -1 and 1. The cosine of 0 degrees is 1; the cosine of 180 degrees is -1. Any midpoint is a fraction thereof. The cosine of 90 degrees (halfway between 0 and 180) happens to equal 0. The Movie Clip has a shape that appears to be pointing to the right (refer to Figure 10.8). If it's rotated 180 degrees (pointing left), I want the change in _x position (when moving "forward") to be -1*5 (5 being "how much"—that is, the full amount in the negative direction). If the rotation stays at 0 degrees, I want the change in _x to be 1*5 (so that it moves to the right). When it's 90 degrees, I don't want to change the _x at all, so 0*5 gives me zero. I can easily determine the factor to multiply howMuch by (between 1 and -1) just by calculating the cosine of the current rotation. If the rotation is less than 180 degrees, cosine will return a fraction of 1, which causes howMuch to be multiplied by a smaller number (meaning, the change in _x is proportionally less). The only hairy part is that you have to translate _rotation from its value in degrees to the equivalent value in radians (because Flash's Math object uses radians). As you recall from Chapter 5, "Programming Structures," you can translate degrees into radians by multiplying by (Math.PI/180). The change in _y is calculated the same way, but with sine. If the user presses the down arrow, I reduce the values for _x and _y instead of adding to them—as is the case with the up arrow. This explanation should give you an idea of what went into the solution even if you can't immediately understand the code. Realize that you're coming in after the code is written, and in reality, you'll need to write the code from the ground up— so try to first just get the gist.

There are so many more things we *could* do by combining all the objects covered in this chapter. Instead of doing any more examples, however, let me just remind you that you can also use listeners with the Key object. For example, the following code serves as a substitute to the virtual key code gathering script shown earlier:

```
myListener=new Object();
myListener.onKeyUp=function(){trace(Key.getCode())}
Key.addListener(myListener);
```

It's a lot like using the Selection object's listeners—you don't add the listener to a particular key, but to the Key object. For a nice exercise, try converting either of the preceding two examples to use listeners instead. Basically, you won't have to put any code on the clips themselves. (I have my solution to this exercise, as

well as many others, at the companion site for this book:
`www.phillipkerman.com/actionscripting`)

Summary

Wow, I think this chapter might be the most fun so far because not only did we explore new concepts, they were easy to apply using our existing base knowledge. You got to see four unique Flash objects: TextField, TextFormat, Selection, and Key. It turns out that they share some similarities, but they're all unique objects.

The material in this chapter is a good follow-up to the String object from last chapter. You should notice that many String object methods came in handy. We got to create, modify, and populate text fields (as well as format the text they display). The Selection object was all about finding or setting focus, and finding or setting the portion of a selectable field that currently is selected. Finally, the Key object enables you to find out which key (or keys) is pressed at any given time.

You know this is fun when you can think up your own exercises or you're so excited to go try this stuff out for your own projects. (Hopefully, you're feeling like that now.) I know I'd go play (with Flash MX) right now if I didn't have the rest of the book to write!

{ Chapter 11 }

Arrays

Using and understanding arrays is a milestone concept that will catapult you into another level of programming skill. It's almost like the difference between riding a one-speed and a 10-speed bicycle… between a piece of toast and a waffle… or between playing checkers and chess. I'm just saying arrays are a big deal. Your programming career can be separated as "before arrays" and "after arrays." Unlike the way we've used variables so far (to store one value at a time), arrays enable you to store as many individual values as you want—and of any data type. In addition to storing a lot of information in one place (an array variable), you can quickly access any individual item to see or change its value. Furthermore, the Array object has a host of methods that let you perform fancy operations on the contents of an array. For example, you can—almost instantaneously—sort the contents alphabetically if you want.

Although arrays are not the most advanced feature of ActionScript, they are perhaps the most valuable because they're so easy to use. If storing values in variables is convenient, storing lots of values in one array is invaluable. In addition to the useful operations you can do with arrays, you'll find that the syntax you learn (as with so much other syntax) is easily applicable to other parts of ActionScript.

In this chapter, you will:

- Learn how arrays work and their benefits.

- Build arrays using several techniques.

- Access individual items in arrays (to ascertain or change their values).

- Explore all the methods for the Array object.

- Learn how to create and use associative arrays (also called *generic objects*).

Unlike many topics covered in this book, we'll actually go through practically every detail of using arrays in ActionScript. For example, I've left many topics out of this book because they are either unlikely to ever serve you or they can be picked up easily based on the foundation knowledge you're acquiring. In the case of arrays, it's quite possible you'll use every conceivable aspect. For that reason, this chapter is quite detailed.

Array Overview

Arrays are just another data type. Variables can contain strings, numbers, or other data types, including arrays. Just as you can do "string" types of things to variables containing strings and "number" types of things to variables containing numbers, when your variable's value is an array, there is a unique set of "array" operations that you can execute. Strings and numbers are very familiar. Let's take an overview of the way arrays work.

The idea with arrays is that any one variable can contain multiple values—each in a unique address within the variable. Compare a plain variable containing a number or string to a studio apartment or single-person home. Assuming that only one person lives in any given apartment at a time, it's like a variable containing a string. You can replace the value in the variable or replace the person living in the apartment—but only one is in the variable or apartment at a time. If a regular variable is like a single apartment, an array is like an apartment building (see Figure 11.1). There might be 50 individual apartments in an entire building. Similarly, an array can have 50 individual locations for data (called *indexes*). Replacing the value in any one index is like replacing the resident in any one apartment.

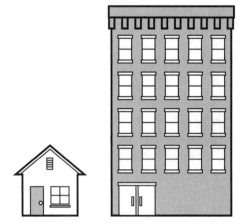

Figure 11.1 *If a variable is like a house that holds one person, an array is like an apartment building that holds many individuals.*

To continue with the apartment building analogy, it's possible to put different types of people in the different apartments. One apartment could even be used to store cleaning supplies. The storage concept is similar with an array. You could store a string in the first index of an array. In the second index, you could store a number. What's really wild is that you can store any kind of data type in the individual indexes of an array—including arrays! That is, in the third index, you might have an array of 10 separate numbers. Compare this to one apartment being converted to bunk beds where four separate people could sleep (see Figure 11.2).

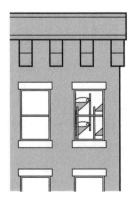

Figure 11.2 *Each apartment (or index of an array) can contain several people (just as one index of an array can contain another array).*

Unlike apartment buildings, you can structure arrays without regard to physical limits. Your master array, for example, could be made up of 10 arrays, each containing 3 items. Each of the 10 arrays could contain students' personal information—for example, first name, last name, and age. If you decide to add a forth piece of information for each student, your 10 arrays will simply contain four items each. Consider the data in the table shown in Figure 11.3. All this data can be stored in one array variable. You could store an array of information in that fourth index—perhaps all the individual scores that each student has received on tests taken. Even if you don't have the same number of scores for each student, an array is perfectly suitable.

First name	Last name	age	score
Phillip	Kerman	37	100
Joe	Smith	28	89
Sally	Smith	30	91
Sam	Jones	19	74
Sandy	Miller	29	99
Bart	Brown	12	60
Andy	Anderson	29	80
Cindy	Corrigan	25	93
Damion	Dinkens	29	82
Mary	Miller	32	98

Figure 11.3   *All 10 rows of four columns each can be stored in one array variable.*

Arrays full of arrays (or "nested arrays") might seem complicated, but they actually help keep things organized in a couple of ways. First of all, you can structure the data however you choose. You could have an array with 10 sub-arrays, each of which contain 4 items (as in the 10 rows of 4 columns in Figure 11.3). Or, if you choose, you could have an array containing 4 items, which each contain 10 items each (as Figure 11.4 illustrates with its 4 rows of 10 columns). In this way, you structure data in a way that makes the most sense based on the nature of the data.

Phillip	Joe	Sally	Sam	Sandy	Bart	Andy	Cindy	Damion	Mary
Kerman	Smith	Smith	Jones	Miller	Brown	Anderson	Corrigan	Dinkens	Miller
37	28	30	19	29	12	29	25	29	32
100	89	91	74	99	60	80	93	82	98

Figure 11.4   *You can structure data in any format you want.*

Another way that arrays (and nested arrays) keep things organized is by reducing the need for superfluous variables. Consider the relatively simple idea of 10 students each with 4 bits of information. To store all that information without arrays, you'd need 40 separate variables—perhaps something like:

```
firstName_student1="Phillip";
lastName_student1="Kerman";
age_student1=37;
score_student1=100;
firstName_student2="Joe";
lastName_student2="Smith";
age_student2=28;
score_student2=89;
//and so on
```

Not only do you need to develop a workable naming convention, but you have to keep track of it. That is, you can't try to use the variable `student1_firstName` because the earlier convention was `firstName_student1`. With 40 separate variable names, there's a lot to track and many places to have problems. Arrays eliminate such issues entirely.

Array Creation and Manipulation

When you can see the benefits of arrays and you decide how to structure the data, you need to learn how to populate the array with the various values. After an array is created, you'll need to learn how to manipulate its contents. Not only can you search and sort an array, but you also can add more items. This section covers how to create and manipulate arrays.

Creating and Populating Arrays

There are several ways to create a variable that contains an array. You can simply initialize a new variable as an array without contents, and populate the array later. Similarly, you can initialize an array of a specific dimension (that is, with a certain number of indexes available). Finally, by assigning a variable's value to data that's in the form of an array, you can create and populate an array in one move. We'll look at all three ways to create arrays as well as how to add to an array already in existence.

The most basic form to make a variable become an array is:

```
myArray=new Array();
```

This assigns the custom variable `myArray` the value of an empty array. The only thing this accomplishes is to prepare `myArray` so that you can start populating it. Although it's not the same thing, I think of this method as similar to the statement `var myLocalVariable`. All that statement does is say, "I'm about to start using a variable called `myLocalVariable` and it's going to be local." It only makes sense to use the `new Array()` technique when you know you're going to need an array, but you don't know any of its contents yet. This just gets you set up with an array that you can mess with later.

Another—and, in my opinion, counterintuitive—way to initialize an array is the form:

```
myArray=new Array(totalItems);
```

For example, `dozenThings=new Array(12)`. The parameter passed in parentheses establishes how many items are in this array. The 12 items in `dozenThings` are null. The reason that I find this technique counterintuitive is that (as you'll see shortly) when you include multiple parameters in the parentheses, it behaves as if you were creating and populating it in one step.

To create a new array *and* populate it with two or more items, use:

```
stackedArray=new Array("first item", "second item", "third");
```

You can include as many initial values in the array as you want, but you must have more than one because a single item would indicate that you want to specify how many items an empty array should have (as above). For example, `unluckyNum=new Array(13)` could have unexpected results (because it will just create a new array with 13 empty items).

Finally, the most direct (and probably the most intuitive) way to put an array into a variable is in the literal form:

```
myArray=["item1","item2","item3"];
```

The brackets say to Flash, "These items are in the form of an array." You could also initialize an empty array as `myArray=[]`. This literal technique is the way that I usually create arrays (and it's the way I'll do it throughout the rest of this book).

Before we move on to accessing information stored in an array, let's talk about the data types you can put into the various indexes of an array. So far, I've been placing strings and numbers (strings being shown between quotation marks). Naturally, you can use variable names instead, and the current value for those variables will be in their place. For instance, `names=[firstname,lastname]` places the value for the variables `firstname` and `lastname` into the two indexes of the array `names`. You can also put references to clip instances, as in `myClips=[box,circle,_root.otherClip]`. If `box` and `circle` are clip instance names (in the current timeline) and a clip called `otherClip` exists in the main timeline, you've just stored references not to the string versions of clip names, but to the clips themselves. When you learn in the next section ("Accessing Array Contents") how to access one index at a time, you'll be able to refer to those clips and perform any operation that you can do when referencing clips directly.

In addition to strings, numbers, and instance references, you can add references to arrays. In this way, you can make an array full of arrays! Consider the following code sequence:

```
washingtonPolitics=["Governor Hansen", "Sec. White", "Attorney Meier"];
oregonPolitics=["Governor Jones", "Sec. Stevens", "Attorney Philips"];
californiaPolitics=["Governor Black", "Sec. Jackson", "Attorney Smith"];
westCoast=[washingtonPolitics,oregonPolitics,californiaPolitics];
```

In the last line, the variable `westCoast` is assigned the value of an array with three items. It just so happens that the data type for each of these three items is array. As you're about to learn, you can quickly refer to the Governor of California by saying you want the first item in the third index of the `westCoast` array. (In reality, because arrays are zero-based, you start counting with zero, so you'd have to retrieve the zero item in the second index.) With this first example of an array full of arrays, I feel compelled to remind you that because arrays are reference variables (not primitive), they're copied by reference. Therefore, in this example, even after the variable `westCoast` is assigned, if you ever change any of the three "politics" arrays, you'll also be changing the contents of the respective index in `westCoast`. (If necessary, you can review the differences between primitive and reference variables in Chapter 4, "Basic Programming in Flash.")

Accessing Array Contents

As you just saw, populating arrays is pretty easy. Accessing the contents of previously created arrays is even easier. To access a particular array's contents, you need to be familiar with how that array is structured. For example, Figure 11.5 shows (on top) how our previous west coast politician example was structured: three arrays, one for each state. Just as easily, we could have had three arrays, but one for each job title instead. It doesn't really matter how we structure it, but when accessing individual items, it's important to first know the structure.

```
[["Governor Hansen", "Secretary White", "Attorney Meier"],
 ["Governor Jones", "Secretary Stevens", "Attorney Philips"],
 ["Governor Black", "Secretary Jackson", "Attorney Smith"]]


[["Governor Hansen", "Governor Jones",  "Governor Black"],
 ["Secretary White", "Secretary Stevens", "Secretary Jackson"],
 ["Attorney Meier", "Attorney Philips", "Attorney Smith"]]
```

Figure 11.5   *You can structure the same data however you want. The example on top is no better or worse than the one on the bottom.*

Now that you are familiar with the array's structure, you'll find accessing items in the array (to see their values or change them) is very easy. We'll look at how to access individual indexes directly, and then look at how to use loops to step through all the indexes of an array.

Direct Access

Array items are accessed using what's called *bracket access*. The following expression will return the item in the first (the zero) index:

```
myArray[0];
```

Therefore, if `myArray` is first assigned the values using `myArray=["apples","oranges","bananas"]`, the expression `myArray[0]` returns `"apples"`. Simple, isn't it? The only thing to mess you up is the fact that you must start counting with zero. I probably don't need to remind you (but I will) that this bracket access simply produces an expression that returns the value in that index—but there's no assignment or change to the array. You could copy the second thing in `myArray` into another variable, as follows:

```
secondFruit=myArray[1];
```

secondFruit will be assigned the value "oranges", but nothing changes in myArray.

To access the contents of an index in an array that's inside another array, the form is extended to:

```
mainArray[indexOfSubArray][indexInSubArray];
```

Consider the following example:

```
bookDataOne=["Teach Yourself", 587, 24.99];//title, page count, price
bookDataTwo=["ActionScripting", 618, 39.99];
allBooks=[bookDataOne,bookDataTwo];
```

After you understand the structure used (title, page count, price) to access the price for the first book, you can use allBooks[0][2], or for the price of the second book, use allBooks[1][2]. To access the title of the first book, use allBooks[0][0]. If this way of referencing items in arrays inside arrays is confusing, consider looking at it in pieces. For example, to access the entire array for book 2, you'd simply use allBooks[1]. To access just the price from the simple array bookDataTwo, you'd use bookDataTwo[2]. But what is allBooks[1], anyway? It's the same thing as bookDataTwo. Because allBooks[1] and bookDataTwo are interchangeable, you can say allBooks[1][2], and it's the same as saying bookDataTwo[2]. Because such nested bracket references use left-to-right associativity, allBooks[1][2] first performs the first part (allBooks[1]) and that turns into the array that then has its second index referenced.

What's cool about bracket reference is that you can use it for more than just accessing the contents of arrays. You can also refer to items and change them through assignments. For example, allBooks[1][1]=525 assigns the value of 525 to the second item in the second array, so that 500 changes to 525.

There's not much more to say about accessing the contents of arrays. Perhaps a few examples will solidify these points. Using the original data in allBooks, consider the following maneuvers.

The following expression returns a number that is 10 percent less than the price of the first book:

```
allBooks[0][2]*.9;
```

If you want an expression that rounds off to the nearest cent (that is, the one-hundredth decimal), use:

```
Math.round(100* allBooks[0][2]*.9)/100;
```

Notice that I multiply by 100, round off, and then divide by 100. The only flaw in this solution is that there are no trailing zeros; for 24.50, you'll get 24.5. To pad with trailing zeros, you'll have to convert to a string (and possibly use the String object's lastIndexOf() method and length property). Workshop Chapter 8, "Creating a Currency Exchange Calculator," covers how to perform these tricks.

The following statement takes 10 percent off the price of the first book and changes it in the array:

```
allBooks[0][2]= Math.round(100* allBooks[0][2]*.9)/100;
```

Loops

Even though accessing individual items in arrays is quite common, you'll also have the need to access each item in sequence. You already saw how to create an empty array or populate one. Later in this chapter, you'll learn all the methods available to add to, or otherwise change, arrays. If you populate your array by hand, going through each item is not much of a challenge because you'll know how many items are present. However, you might often add to arrays and never know precisely which items are present. In such cases, it's easiest to use a loop to go through each item. Even when you know how many items are in your array, a loop is often more efficient than writing a separate line of code to access each item individually.

Suppose, for example, that you have an array called vowels that is initialized as follows:

```
vowels=["A", "E", "I", "O", "U"];
```

A hard-wired loop (not ideal) could look like this:

```
for(i=0;i<5;i++){
  trace ("One vowel is " + vowels[i]);
}
```

Notice that using vowels[i] will extract items 0 through 4 from the vowels array as i varies from 0 through 4. This example is hard-wired because the 5 means that the loop will always repeat five times (even if you add more items to the array later). You can improve upon this loop by using the for in loop instead. A for in loop will automatically step through all the items in an array.

```
for (i in vowels){
  trace ("One vowel is " + vowels[i]);
}
```

This alternative is easier because you don't have to include the three elements in a regular `for` loop—namely, "init" (or `i=0`), "condition" (`i<5`), and "next" (`i++`). (We covered these when we first looked at the `for` loop in Chapter 5, "Programming Structures.") The `for in` loop has a couple of funky attributes. First, nowhere do you specify that the iterant (`i` in these cases) will increment. In fact, the iterant actually decrements. It automatically begins at the highest index value (`4`, in the case of the `vowels` array) and then decrements through all the items in the array to zero. Often the fact that a `for in` loop goes through the array in reverse order is not an issue. Just realize it works this way. Finally, to be fair, the initial `for` loop I showed could be less hard-wired if, in place of `5`, you used an expression that resulted in the number of items in the array. You'll see later in this chapter that you can use the `length` property (which you learned with the String object) in exactly this way; `vowels.length` results in `5`.

Here's a quick example of a function that goes through the string passed as a parameter and replaces all vowels with an uppercase version of that character. So, `changeVowels("Phillip Kerman")` turns into `"PhIllIP KErmAn"` (notice that `"P"` and `"K"` were already uppercase).

```
1 function changeVowels(aString){
2   var vowels=["A", "E", "I", "O", "U"];
3   var total= aString.length;
4   for (var spot=0; spot<total; spot++){
5     var aLetter=aString.charAt(spot).toUpperCase();
6     var vowelFound=0;
7
8     for (var i in vowels){
9       if (aLetter==vowels[i]){
10        vowelFound=1;
11        break;
12      }
13    }
14    if (vowelFound){
15      aString=
        ➥aString.substr(0,spot) + aLetter + aString.substring(spot+1);
16    }
17  }
18  return aString;
19 }
```

This example is worth walking through despite having arguably no practical use. (I mean, how many times will you need to capitalize all the vowels in a string?) Anyway, after the array of vowels is created in line 2, I store the string's length in a variable `total`. Then, a `for` loop in line 4 goes through all the characters in the provided string (aString), one spot at a time. The only reason I used the variable total instead of an expression (aString.length) in the "condition" of the loop is that Flash will actually calculate that value in every iteration. It's faster this way. For every iteration of the main for loop, the charAt the current spot is converted to uppercase and placed in the variable aLetter. Then the variable vowelFound is set to 0 (assuming at the start that the aLetter is not a vowel—but, of course, if it is, we'll find out shortly). While this one letter (aLetter) is being analyzed, we start another loop. This time, we use a for in loop to go through all the items in the array of vowels (vowels). For every item in vowels, we check whether aLetter==vowels[i] (where i iterates from 4 down to 0). Who cares that it's going backwards because as soon as we find a match, we set vowelFound to 1 and break out of the current loop (the one looping through all the items in the vowels array). So every time, the loop either finishes naturally and leaves vowelFound set to 0, or finishes early and vowelFound is set to 1. In any case, the next if statement performs a string replacement (of the letter in the current spot) if vowelFound is 1. Notice that I don't bother extracting the letter in the current spot and changing it to uppercase, because I already did that when I first assigned aLetter's value. Also notice that even letters that turned out not to be vowels were converted to uppercase because when comparing them to each item in vowels, they needed to be uppercase to match (as the vowels array contained all uppercase).

As an overview, this function steps through each character in the given string, compares this character to each item in an array of vowels, and when a match is found, makes a replacement to the given string. You'll have many more opportunities to write loops that work on strings (including the one that turns a number into a dollar value—in Workshop Chapter 8) and loops that work on arrays (when you need to loop through every clip on the Stage to see which one the mouse is covering—in Workshop Chapter 6, "Working with Odd-Shaped Clickable Areas").

Array Object Methods

Populating arrays and accessing their contents is quite convenient because you can store many different items in one variable. In addition, arrays are convenient because after they're created, ActionScript offers a host of methods that can perform very interesting modifications on that array (see Figure 11.6). Besides the one property (length), almost all the Array object methods will actually modify the array itself. That is, myArray.someMethod() won't return a value; rather, it will *change* the contents of the array. Of course, `"someMethod()"` doesn't exist, but the types of methods available can be broken down into three general types: string-related methods, which convert arrays into strings or vice versa; populating methods, which add to or subtract from arrays; and sorting methods, which reorder the contents of your array. We'll look at the methods and related topics in that order.

Figure 11.6 *All the methods and properties for the Array object are listed in the Actions panel.*

String-Related Methods (`length`, `toString()`, `split()`, `concat()`, `join()`)

You won't find a listing of string-related array methods anywhere in the Flash help files. The topics you're about to learn are grouped together because I think they are either similar to String object methods or they involve converting strings to or extracting strings from arrays.

The only property available for arrays happens to be the same as the only property available for strings: length. Although this might appear confusing, it's actually quite useful. If the object for which you're trying to get the length happens to be a string, you'll get a count of the number of characters. When the object is an array, you'll get the count of items in the array. Consider assigning a string to a variable as myString="hot" and assigning an array to a variable myArray=["waffles", "pancakes", "cereal"]. The following two expressions return 3:

```
myString.length;
myArray.length;
```

There's not much more to it, except to remember two points for both arrays and strings. First, length is a property (not a method) and, as such, doesn't include the parentheses that always follow methods. Second, because both arrays and strings are zero-based, the last character in a string with a "length" of 3 (or the last item in an array with a "length" of 3) is character (or item) 2. Or, for creating dynamic expressions, you can think of the last item in an array as being at the index "length minus 1."

The method called toString()—when attached to an array—will return a string version of the array. For instance, if a variable contains an array, such as myArray=[1,2,3,4], the expression myArray.toString() will return the string "1,2,3,4". One thing you can do with this method is to quickly take an entire array and get a string that can be placed into a Dynamic Text field. Naturally, you could (with little more work) loop through the entire array and convert each item to a string. Perhaps you want to separate each item (being extracted from the array) with returns so that it appears in a Dynamic Text field like a column of data. As always, you can solve one task in several different ways. You could either use a loop and concatenate each item with "\r" (for return) or write a function that replaces each comma with "\r". The toString() method just gives you a quick and easy way to make a string. (By the way, objects introduced in Chapter 12, "Objects," can also use the toString() method.)

The split() method is actually a method of the String object. The reason I waited until now to introduce it is because this method takes a string (as its object) and returns an array. That is, if you take a string such as myString="Phillip,David,Kerman" and use this method (as in newArray=myString.split()), the result is that newArray is assigned the array value ["Phillip","David","Kerman"]. The split() method uses commas (as a default) to separate the items in the string that is being operated on. If you want the `split()` method to use a different character as a delimiter instead of the comma, just supply the character as the parameter when using `split(delimiter)`. That is, if your string uses `"#"` for a delimiter (as in `myString="Phillip#David#Kerman"`), you can create the same array shown earlier by using `newArray=myString.split("#")`. This comes in handy when you have an external source of data that you want to use in an array.

In Chapter 16, "Interfacing with External Data," you'll learn how to load variables from server scripts, XML data sources, and text files. With the exception of XML data, external sources provide data in the form of strings (not arrays). (Even if you want to load in the numerical value 2, you'll actually get "2"—which needs to be converted to a number.) If you simply separate items with commas (or another delimiter), you can use `split()` to quickly and easily convert this loaded data into an array. In the previous edition of this book, I had to explain that although split() is powerful, it was so slow that sometimes it was problematic to use. Not in Flash MX! All the string, array, and XML parsing routines have been optimized by being written in low-level code. Before, `split` used actual ActionScript that couldn't be optimized very much. Now, all these methods perform lightning fast.

The last two methods we'll explore in this section might seem identical, but they're actually quite different: `join()` and `concat()`. The `join()` method performs the opposite operation that `split()` does. That is, `join()` takes an array, converts each item to a string, separates each item with an optional separator (or comma), and finally returns the string. Actually, `join()` is almost the same as the `toString()` method except that with `join()`, you can optionally specify a different separator besides a comma. So, if a variable is assigned an array value, as in `myArray=[1,2,3,4]`, you perform the assignment `stringVersion=myArray.join("_")`. The result is that `stringVersion` will equal `"1_2_3_4"`. If you used `stringVersion=myArray.join("\r")`, each item would appear on a new line (that is, separated by returns). (When you use `join()` without a parameter, a comma will be used as the separator.)

The `concat()` method will either concatenate additional items onto the end of an array or will concatenate two or more arrays (merging them into one). As a method, `concat()` is always attached to one array and takes (as parameters) the items you want to add to the array. If the parameters are individual values, they are added to the end of the array being operated on. For example:

```
odds=[1,3,5,7,9];
oddEven=odds.concat(2,4,6,8);
```

This creates an oddEven array with the value [1,3,5,7,9,2,4,6,8]. I suppose simply adding to the end of an array using concat() is convenient because you can use one line of code to add as many items listed as parameters.

The other way to use concat() is to concatenate one or more entire arrays to the end of another array. Consider this code:

```
vowels=["a","e","i","o","u"];
other=["y"];
odd=["q","z"]
all=vowels.concat(other,odd);
notOdd=vowels.concat(other);
```

First, notice that the first three variables contain arrays (even though other is an array with only one item). In the end, the variable all will equal ["a","e","i","o","u","y","q","z"], and notOdd will equal ["a","e","i","o","u","y"]. Notice also that when the parameters are arrays, the items in that array are added to the end of the array being operated on. Finally, you should notice too that the concat() method doesn't actually change the array, but rather returns a new array. I always find this method strange in that regardless of whether I want to add one item, several items, an array, or multiple arrays, I always must concatenate onto a base array. That is, you can't treat concat() like a function and say concat(oneArray,otherArray). Because it's a method, you must say something more like oneArray.concat(otherArray). (By the way, there's an identical concat() method that's used with strings.)

Populating in Order (pop(), push(), shift(), unshift())

The rest of the methods we'll look at are different than all the others discussed so far this chapter. Both the populating methods (this section) and the sorting methods (next section) will actually change the array that they operate on. The methods described earlier in this chapter will return values (either string or array data), but they don't actually change the array at hand.

The best way to understand these methods (pop, push, shift, and unshift) is to think of a spring-loaded tray dispenser that you might find in a cafeteria. You can take a tray from the top of the stack and the next tray below rises to the surface for someone else to take. To replenish the dispenser, you can place one or more trays on top of the stack. Every time a tray is placed back on the stack, all the trays below are pushed down. Think of a starting array like a stack of trays (each item is a separate tray). Then the methods perform the following operations. Taking a tray from the top of the stack is equivalent to the pop() method because it will remove the last item in your array and return it. (That item is returned and the array has that item removed.) Placing trays on the top of the stack is the same as the push() method because it accepts one or more parameters that are placed at the end of the array. The shift() method is the same as pop() except that it removes the first item and returns it (from the bottom of the stack). Finally, unshift() is like push() except that it will add an item (or items) to the beginning of an array and push everything else to later indexes in the array. Check out Figure 11.7.

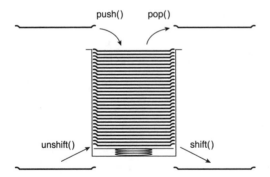

Figure 11.7   *To understand* pop, push, shift, *and* unshift, *you should think about a stack of trays.*

Although these four methods might seem useful only for a cafeteria simulation, they're actually quite helpful. A great application to consider—and one that will help you understand how to *use* these methods—is a universal "Back" button (such as on a browser). Imagine that you give your users the ability to navigate to any section in your movie. For this example, let's say that each section is on a different frame number. In theory, this would be a simple case of pushing the frame number into an array any time a destination was navigated to, and popping the last value off the end of the array any time we wanted to go "back." Of course, it is slightly more involved, but here's what I came up with:

There is a button for each section to which the user can navigate as well as a "Go Back" button. Each navigation button invokes the custom function go() by providing the frame number to navigate to, as follows:

```
on (release) {
    go(5);
}
```

The "Go Back" button invokes another function, as follows:

```
on (release){
  goBack();
}
```

Then, I have the following code in the first frame of the movie:

```
history=new Array();

function go(where){
  history.push(where);
  gotoAndStop(where);
  onScreen_txt.text=history.join("\r");
}

function goBack(){
  if (history.length<2){
    return;
  }
  var discardCurrent=history.pop();
  go(history.pop());
}
```

Let me explain. First, the variable history was initialized as an empty array when this frame was reached. (Because the first line is not contained within a function, it executes when the frame is reached.) We will be populating the history array via the go and goBack functions. Then any time the go function is called, the destination frame (given the parameter name where) is pushed onto the end of the history array. The same parameter's value is used to navigate (using gotoAndStop(where)) to the desired section of the movie. Finally, the history array is converted to string (separated by returns) and placed into a Text Field instance named onScreen_txt for testing.

The goback function (with no parameters) starts off with a couple of error checks. First, if the length of the history array is less than 2 (that is, it only has one item), the function is exited using return. If there's only one item in the array, the user is currently in that section and there's nowhere to goBack to.

Next, we strip off the last item in the array (which is the frame that the user is currently viewing) and place it in a local variable, discardCurrent. Actually, I could have just used history.pop() with no assignment, but I want you to remember that the pop() method returns a value regardless of whether you plan to use that value. Lastly, I call the regular go function and pass (as a parameter) the value of the last item in the array. Notice that by using pop() to grab the last item in history, I'm also removing it. If you don't remove the last item, it will be put in there twice because part of the go function's script involves pushing back the item onto the end of the history variable.

Sorting

You just saw how pop(), push(), shift(), and unshift() can add or remove items from an array. Even though the sorting methods that follow don't change how many items are in an array, they most certainly change the array—because they reorder it. There are three sorting methods: sort(), sortOn(), and reverse(). (We'll look at sortOn() in the following section, "Associative Arrays.") First, the easy one: reverse(), which simply reverses the order of the items in the array.

```
myArray=[1,2,3,4];
myArray.reverse();
```

After these two lines execute, the value of myArray is [4,3,2,1]. Generally, I can't think of many uses for reverse(). First of all, you're the one who designs the structure of the array. You can always deal with an array no matter whether it's forward or reverse. For example, you can choose between pop() and shift() to delete items or between for loops and for in loops. If an array needs to be reversed, I just wonder who put it in the wrong order, but now you know how to reverse the order in one swift move.

The sort() method is actually very powerful. Without any parameters provided, the sort() method will reorder your array in alphabetical order. It's pretty cool.

```
myFriends=["Dave","Graham","Chandler","Randy","Brad","Darrel"];
myFriends.sort();
```

After these two lines, myFriend's value becomes ["Brad","Chandler", "Darrel","Dave","Graham","Randy"]. If sort() worked so easy in practice, this would be the end of the section. However, it's super funky in the way it sorts arrays. Specifically, it always sorts alphabetically even if your array contains numbers. For example:

```
someNums=[4,2,1,444,2222,11111];
someNums.sort();
```

This turns `someNums` into `[1,11111,2222,2,444,4]`, which is not exactly numerical order.

Another counterintuitive fact about the `sort()` method is that it treats uppercase letters with greater importance than lowercase. Consider the following example:

```
someWords=["Zimbabwe", "zebra", "cat", "apple", "Arizona"];
someWords.sort();
```

This turns `someWords` into `["Arizona","Zimbabwe","apple","cat","zebra"]`.

I'm sure that I don't need to provide more examples to make you want to learn how to make the `sort()` method perform the way you want. I thought it was confusing at first to really understand how to control the `sort()` method. The good news is that you can make the `sort()` method reorder your array by following elaborate rules that you provide. For example, in addition to sorting numerically, or without regard to uppercase and lowercase, you'll see how you can make up your own sorting rules such as sorting by length, or putting all the even numbers first and then the odd numbers. You can make `sort()` follow any rule you can think of.

The way to write a customized `sort` is to provide a homemade function as a parameter. One way is to call another function from inside the parameter, as follows:

```
myArray.sort(customFunction);
```

Notice that (normally) you always call functions by including opening and closing parentheses after the function name, but not when providing a function as a parameter of the `sort()` method. The job of `customFunction` is to set up the rule for comparison (when sorting), and you don't really "call" it the way you normally call a function. In Chapter 13, "Homemade Objects," you'll learn more about supplying a function definition (called a *constructor*) as a value. This comparison function is detailed in a moment.

Another way is to provide a literal function as a parameter. The way this works is that you write your entire `customFunction` right inside the parentheses. You can even put it all on one line if you remember to use semicolons to separate "lines" of code. Ignore the code in the function and just check out the form that this literal technique follows:

```
myArray.sort(function(a,b){return a-b;});
```

Notice that the portion in parentheses (function(a,b){return a-b;}) is almost identical to any other function you can write. Besides being all crammed onto one line, there's no function name. Because this function is used in only one place and not called from other parts of the movie, you don't need to bother naming the function. Regardless of whether you provide a function name (like the first example) or you write the function literally right inside the parentheses, it works the same. The reason to consider the literal technique is that the comparison function is useful only for establishing the "sorting rule," and will likely never have any other use to you. Writing a function separately (like the first way) is not as efficient because Flash makes that function available for the entire movie. In the remainder of this section, you'll see examples of referring to function names only because I think it's easier to read than having the function squeezed into the parentheses.

This function that I'm calling a "comparison function" serves to establish the rules that the sort method uses to decide how to reorder items in the array. The function always accepts two parameters (by convention, called a and b). You can pretend that these two parameters represent two items in the array that are being compared. Two items because when you sort, you look at two items at a time to decide which one goes first. Say that you want to sort numerically. What if a is 10 and b is 12? Naturally, you want 12 to come after 10 (that is, b after a). What if a is 2 and b is 10? In that case, you'll want a to come first. The comparison function provided to the sort() method has one job: to return a positive number, a zero, or a negative number. The idea is that based on how you want the sort to order things, your comparison function returns a positive number when a should come after b, a negative number when a should go before b, or a zero when you don't care (and Flash will just leave the two items in their original order).

Let's look at the finished version of a comparison function that correctly sorts an array numerically (and then we can try some "what-if" numbers):

```
myArray.sort(numerical);
function numerical(a,b){
  if(a>b){
    return 1; //a should come after b
  }
  if (a<b){
```

```
    return -1;//a should come before b
  }
  return 0; //if they get this far, just return 0
}
```

So, just looking at the comparison function called numerical, imagine that a is
10 and b is 5. The function returns 1, which means a should come after b. So far,
so good. If a is 12 and b is 14, -1 is returned, meaning that a should come first. It
works!

In fact, although my example function is easy to read, it's unnecessarily wordy.
Here's a more concise version that (when you try any "what-if" numbers) works
the same:

```
function numerical(a,b){
  return a-b;
}
```

If a is 10 and b is 5, this function returns -5 (which, by being negative, means
that a should go second). As you can see, when you get fancy like this, writing
this whole comparison function right inside the sort() method's parentheses is
more manageable. myArray.sort(numerical) isn't quite as streamlined as
myArray.sort(function(a,b){return a-b;}), especially when you consider
the first way requires you have that numerical function as well.

I hope this exhaustive explanation is clear. There are only so many common sorting requirements (alphabetical, numerical, alphabetical without regard to case,
and so on) and I've provided those later in this chapter. After you have these,
you'll probably never need to *really* understand how sort() works. But when
you want to do some unique sorting, you'll need to write your own comparison
function. For example, you might have a requirement that items in an array are
sorted by value but they could be saved in U.S. dollars, Canadian dollars, euros,
and yen. It's totally possible—albeit complicated—to write a comparison function that translates all the values into one currency before making the comparison. Check out the example below that moves odd numbers to the beginning of
an array for a *taste* of how you can customize the comparison function for any
purpose. The point is that you can do it when you know how sort() works.

Here are a few examples of common sorting needs. You can use any of these in
the form myArray.sort(functionName), where functionName is the appropriate
comparison function. To really grasp the following examples, try some "what-if"
values for a and b and see whether you can determine whether the function
returns a positive number, negative number, or zero.

Handy Formula

Alphabetical without regard to case:

```
function caseInsensitive(a,b){
  return a.toUpperCase() > b.toUpperCase();
}
```

Reverse numerical:

```
function reverseNumerical(a,b){
  return b-a;
}
```

By length (shortest strings first):

```
function byLength(a,b){
  return a.length-b.length;
}
```

Finally, for a slightly odd one…this function (when used with the sort() method) puts the array in numerical order but with all the odd numbers first:

```
function oddFirst(a,b){
  aOdd=a%2; //set aOdd to 1 if a is odd
  bOdd=b%2; //set bOdd to 1 of b is odd
  if (aOdd==0 && bOdd==0){
    return a-b;
  }
  if (aOdd!=0 && bOdd<>0){
    return a-b;
  }
  if (aOdd!=0 && bOdd==0){
    return -1;
  }
  if (aOdd==0 && bOdd<>0){
    return 1;
  }
  return 0;//just in case
}
```

This final example shows that you really can write a comparison function for unique sorting needs.

Associative Arrays

To appreciate associative arrays, you must fully understand the value of arrays generally. You've learned in this chapter that arrays have two general benefits: You can store multiple pieces of data in a single structured variable, and you can perform interesting operations on the contents of arrays. Unlike arrays, which contain multiple single-item values in their indexes, associative arrays have *pairs* of values. That is, a regular array could contain three items (for example, "Phillip," "Kerman," and 37), but an associative array could hold three pairs (say, firstname: "Phillip," lastname: "Kerman," and age: 37). The value for the item in the zero index is `"Phillip"` in either case, but items in any index of an associative array are referred to by their name (also called *property*)—in this case `firstname`. It doesn't matter in which slot the pair `firstname:"Phillip"` resides, you can always find it by referring to `firstname`.

Although associative arrays make your structured data vastly easier to manage (because you'll never need to remember in which index a particular item of data resides), they have one drawback: Associative arrays cannot use the Array object's methods or properties. That includes the `sort()` method (which really isn't interesting since position is irrelevant) and the `length` property (which would be nice). You can, however, loop through an associative array by using the `for in` loop.

The bottom line is that associative arrays are not really "arrays" because the Array object's methods don't work. I prefer to call them "generic objects"—but because this is the "Arrays" chapter, you'll hear me interchange the two terms. Let's first look at how to populate an associative array (oops, I mean, generic object), and then we can look at how to access values within the object.

To create a new object and populate it at the same time, use the following form:

```
myObject={name:"value",nameTwo:"ValueTwo",thingThree:13};
```

Notice that each item in the object is a pair of name and value. The names are always written literally (with no quotation marks). It's weird because you might expect that such names would exist previously as variables. But in this case, `name`, `nameTwo`, and `thingThree` are all created on-the-fly and sit there with no quotation marks. Also, notice that the entire object is surrounded by curly braces (not the square brackets that you saw with regular arrays), and that each item is separated by commas.

You can access a value from within the object in one of two ways. In either case, you need to use the name associated with that value, not the index within the object. For example, `myObject["nameTwo"]` will return `"ValueTwo"`. The thing that freaks me out is that even though `nameTwo` was used verbatim when creating the object, you need to put it within quotation marks when trying to find its value using this (bracket reference) technique. When creating a generic object (associative array), you provide arbitrary names for each item and Flash accepts them. You're really coming up with unique custom property names. When comparing generic objects to arrays, just think of these as names for the indexes. However, when you think of generic objects as objects, think of these names as properties. This should become strikingly obvious when you see the other way to access values of the properties in the object.

I just showed you the bracket reference technique (ObjectName["stringName"]) and said there's another way to access values in the generic object. You can use the familiar `object.property` technique. For example, `myObject.thingThree` returns `13` (the value in the index named `thingThree` in the example earlier). Now it makes sense that names in associative arrays (that is, properties in generic objects—same thing) are not strings.

So, there's no difference between placing a string version of the named item between brackets to access the value of a particular item and using the familiar `object.property` technique. This happens to be identical to the way that you referred to instance names within any timeline. When you knew the instance name, you just used it without quotation marks (such as, `_root.someClip`). When you wanted to refer to a clip dynamically and you could only do it by creating a string, however, you placed that string within brackets (as in `_root["circle_"+curCircle]`). Notice that the `object.property` technique works when you know the clip name; otherwise, you need to use bracket reference. If it doesn't make your brain start melting, realize that every timeline contains an associative array of the clips present in that timeline. Talk about coming around full circle!

We can save some of this discussion of objects for later chapters. Let's step back and look at a few practical examples of building associative arrays (and accessing their contents).

Let's consider another way to store the data from an earlier example:

```
bookOne={title:"Teach Yourself", pageCount:587, price:24.99};
bookTwo={title:"ActionScripting", pageCount:618, price:39.99};
allBooks=[bookOne,bookTwo];
```

Without even considering whether this is the ideal structure, look at how amazingly easy it is to remember which item is which. Earlier, if we wanted to find the price, we had to remember "index 2." The page count was "index 1." (Not exactly intuitive, even if you disregard the zero-based counting.) In this case, when looking at either associative array (bookOne or bookTwo), we can access the price in the form:

```
bookOne["price"];  //or, bookOne.price
```

Is that easy or what? Because allBooks is still a regular array (one that contains two associative arrays), you can access the nested elements in the ways the following examples show.

To access the first book's page count, use:

```
allBooks[0]["price"]; //or, allBooks[0].price
```

To access the second book's title, use:

```
allBooks[1]["title"]; //or allBooks[1].price
```

By the way, in addition to accessing values of any item in an associative array, you can change the values. For example, the following changes the price of the first book to 29.99:

```
allBooks[0]["price"]=29.99; //or, allBooks[0].price=29.99
```

Finally, you can add new items to an associative array as arbitrarily as you created them in the first place. Consider this example:

```
myData={first:"Phillip",last:"Kerman",married:true}
```

Later, I want to add an item:

```
myData["childCount"]=1;  //or, myData.childCount=1
```

At this point, myData equals
{first:"Phillip",last:"Kerman",married:true,childCount:1}. It doesn't even matter whether the additional index was inserted at the end, because you can only refer to it by name (as in myData["childCount"]).

If you're like me, upon first grasping associative arrays, you're probably thinking that regular arrays are practically worthless. Remember, however, that associative arrays don't give you any access to all the fancy methods and the length properties of regular arrays.

INTRO MX

There is one new method for regular arrays that combines associative and regular arrays: sortOn(). Generally, it enables you to sort a regular array; however, if that array contains identically structured generic objects, you can specify those objects to be sorted based on the value for any one property. It's easier than it sounds. In a way, the sortOn() method is limited because you must have an array full of generic objects—and all those objects have to have the same property (on which you're basing the re-ordering). Take, for example, the now-familiar array of data about my books:

```
bookOne={title:"Teach Yourself", pageCount:587, price:24.99};
bookTwo={title:"ActionScripting", pageCount:618, price:39.99};
allBooks=[bookOne,bookTwo];
```

This example follows the rules for sortOn—namely, the allBooks array contains several generic objects and they each have the same properties on which we want to sort. Now, to sort the allBooks array based on the value of the title property of each contained object, use:

```
allBooks.sortOn("title");
```

Notice that "title" is in quotes. Translated, this says to re-order the contents of allBooks based on the value of each item's "title" property. To reorder the main allBooks array based on page count, use:

```
allBooks.sortOn("pageCount");
```

I suppose it would have been logical to discuss sortOn() when we looked at sort(); they both are ways to change the order of a regular array. The trick with sortOn() is that each item in the array has to be a generic object with the same properties (at least they need to contain the property on which you want to sort). Again, it's slightly limited because you're restricted on the structure (for example, you can't have nested arrays), but the performance and convenience of this new method is often worth the effort when appropriate.

Summary

My head hurts! Not from too much technical information, but from being so excited. Arrays are such an eloquent way to store and manipulate data, it's a shame that some people go through life without ever once experiencing their benefits. Seriously, arrays are awesome.

You saw how arrays could be structured to hold lots of discrete data in whatever way you want. Actually, the stage at which you design how to structure your arrays is the most challenging. As far as what you populate your array with, you learned it could be of any data type, including arrays. In this way, you could have an array full of nested arrays. After you populate an array with data, it is a snap to access and see or change any particular item. Looping through an array is a breeze, too.

This chapter detailed how to use every method made for arrays. Without repeating them all now, just remember that you can manipulate your arrays of data in any manner you want.

Finally, just to make things out of this world, we looked at the topic of associative arrays (also known as *generic objects*). Although these arrays lack the methods that regular arrays offer, they give you a way to store name/value pairs within each index of an array. This knowledge also will apply to topics covered in the next two chapters.

Just think, an entire chapter without any puns such as, "Arrays offer an array of great features."

{ Chapter 12 }

Objects

If you've gotten this far in the book, you've seen objects in several places. Instances of Movie Clips are the most basic type of object in Flash, and the best to learn from because you can *see* them onscreen. You've also seen several of the scripting objects (namely, Math, String, Array, Selection, TextField, TextFormat, and the Key object). You've even seen "generic objects" (or "associative arrays"). Although you've already learned a lot about objects, there's more!

The objects introduced in this chapter are not only particularly practical, they all require the formal rules of objects (such as instantiation). In this way, they make some of the previously explored objects seem very forgiving in comparison, because you'll be doing things that were not required in the other objects. Luckily, these objects are well worth the additional effort.

In this chapter, you will:

- Learn the rules of these formal objects.
- Use the Sound object to "attach" sounds that can be manipulated using scripts.
- Use the Color object to color clips on-the-fly.
- Use the Date object to perform any imaginable calculation involving calendars or time.
- Use the `attachMovie` method to effectively drag clips from the Library using ActionScript.
- Create lines, fills, and gradients entirely in script.

Formal Rules of Objects

Most of these concepts will appear familiar. For example, by now you know that objects have properties, which are basically just variables that contain data. Some properties have visual representations, such as a clip's _alpha property. Although the value for this property can be ascertained (as in theClip._alpha) and changed (as in theClip._alpha=10), some properties can be ascertained only. The set of properties for any object type is specific to the object. For instance, only the Movie Clip object has an _alpha property. Other objects have other properties, but they're all the same in that they contain values that can sometimes be modified.

In addition to having properties, objects can have methods, which are functions that are applied to unique instances of an object. Methods are processes, whereas properties are just static attributes. So far, this should be a review. The concept that's a little bit new is that formal objects must be instantiated. In the case of clip instances (that is, Movie Clip objects), you can instantiate them by dragging them from the Library. After objects have been instantiated, they have their own unique set of properties and the potential to have methods, such as nextFrame(), applied to them individually. The formal objects require that you instantiate them using a constructor function. All constructor functions follow this pattern:

```
new Object();
```

This chapter discusses the following constructor functions, each of which instantiates a different formal object type (Sound, Color, and Date, respectively):

```
new Sound();
new Color();
new Date();
```

(By the way, instantiating a new Movie Clip using ActionScript during runtime uses a different technique, which we'll discuss in the "Implications for Movie Clips" section later in this chapter.)

The key to remember with instantiating objects is that you must store the object in a variable; therefore, saying new Sound() doesn't really do anything. However, mySound=new Sound() creates a new instance (in the form of the Sound object) and places it into the variable mySound, whose value is of the Object data type. From this point forward, you can treat mySound like any object—by referring to properties (such as mySound.someProperty) or by using methods (such as mySound.someMethod()) in the same way that you would treat a Movie Clip instance.

Until you build your own objects, that's about all there is to it. The trick is that you must instantiate an object and place it in a variable before you can start doing stuff with it or doing stuff to it. Now we can see the nitty-gritty details of Sound Date, Color, and Movie Clip.

Attaching Sounds

This section probably could be called "The Sound Object." However, if there's one step that's easy to forget when using the Sound object, it's the "attach sound" step, so maybe the section title will help you remember. Here's the process you take in order to use the Sound object.

Sound Object Basics

The idea is that by using ActionScript, you will effectively drag a sound out of the Library and start using it in your movie. Items in the Library that aren't used anywhere in your movie normally don't export when you publish your movie (which is a good thing when you consider that unnecessary sounds will add to the filesize). After you import the sound you intend to "attach" into the Library, you'll need to override the "no-export" feature by setting the Linkage option in the Library's options menu (see Figure 12.1).

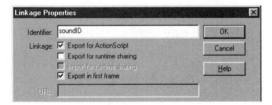

Figure 12.1   *A sound item is set to "Export for ActionScript" (and given an identifier name) through the Library's Linkage option.*

All you need to do is select Export for ActionScript and give it a unique identifier name. (I'll use "soundID" for my examples.) In addition to causing your exported movie's filesize to grow, this sound will now download before the first frame loads.

Now that you have a sound identified, you can start coding. You first instantiate a Sound object and place it in a variable. I'm using the variable name my_sound to trigger code hints. ("_sound" is the specified suffix in the ActionScript code hints configuration file, which is described in Chapter 2, "What's New in Flash MX.")

```
my_sound=new Sound();
```

Before you can start using the Sound object methods, properties, and events (see Figure 12.2), you need to attach the sound item to this object. Events are simply a way for you to automatically trigger a homemade function any time the specified event occurs. By the way, you'll find a lot more detail about events in Chapter 14, "Extending ActionScript."

Figure 12.2   *The list of Sound object methods and properties is short, but powerful.*

The attachSound method enables you to specify which sound (in the Library) you want to associate with this object.

```
my_sound.attachSound("soundID");
```

Notice that "soundID" matches the name you gave the imported sound in the linkage settings. At this point, you can now start playing with the other methods. You'll likely want to start the sound so that you can hear all the changes you might make to the sound later.

```
my_sound.start();
```

This will start the sound playing from the beginning of the sound file. (I always try to use my_sound.play(), which will not work because play() is a method of the Movie Clip object.) Two optional parameters are included in the start() method. If you want to cut in and start the sound (not at the beginning), you can specify the number of seconds into the sound that you want to begin. That is, my_sound.start(10) will start the sound 10 seconds in from the start. (You shouldn't use this to skip past silence at the beginning of your sound; any silence should have been removed before import as it adds unnecessarily to the filesize.) The second optional parameter enables you to specify how many times the sound should loop. To make a sound play almost continuously, use my_sound.start(0,9999999). Notice that you still need something in the first parameter that specifies the delay until start time in order to use the second parameter.

The opposite of start() is obviously stop(). Use my_sound.stop() to stop the sound. This actually "pauses" the sound, although if you later use my_sound.start(), it will start over from the beginning. To create a pause/resume feature, you need to know about a new property of the Sound object: position. My initial thought was that you could (when pausing) save the value of the position property in a variable and then use that as a parameter for the start() method in the resume button. It's actually easier than that. Just use my_sound.start(my_sound.position/1000) for a resume button. The reason position is divided by 1000 is that its value is represented in milliseconds, whereas the start() method accepts seconds. Realize that it doesn't hurt to precede the start() command with a line that performs a stop; otherwise, you can have several sounds playing at once, resulting in a layered effect.

There are only a few other methods and properties (refer to Figure 12.2), so let's look at them all.

Advanced Sound Controls

Although starting or stopping a sound isn't really fancy, you'll likely need to at least start a sound before using the other methods. While a sound is playing, you can easily adjust its volume by using my_sound.setVolume(level), where level is an integer between 0 and 100. Effectively, this is a percent of the volume to which the user has her computer system and speakers set. That is, my_sound.setVolume(100) will play the sound at the full 100 percent of the user's computer settings. Conversely, my_sound.setVolume(0) will make the sound silent. Keep in mind that setVolume(0) is different from stop() because the sound continues to play but at a volume of 0. The default sound level is 100, which you can lower by using setVolume(). If you ever need to ascertain the current level, just use the getVolume() method (for example, theVolume=my_sound.getVolume()).

In addition to changing the volume, you can use pan to affect the balance between the left and right channels. Similar to the way a camera can pan from left to right, you can cause the sound to seem to originate from either the left speaker or the right speaker. The setPan() method accepts a parameter ranging from -100 (to pan all the way to the left) to 100 (to pan all the way to the right). When the sound is sent to both speakers equally, the pan is 0. So, when a sound is playing, you can use my_sound.setPan(-50) to make it sound as though your audio has moved to the left. You can actually set the pan (as you can set the volume) even when a sound isn't playing, but you'll always need a Sound object on which to use the setPan() method. If you ever need to ascertain the current pan, use getPan().

Finally, the last Sound object method is called setTransform() (and its sister, getTransform()). On the surface, this method appears to be very similar to setPan() because it controls how much sound is going to each channel. But it's actually a combination of setting the volume, setting the pan, and determining exactly which portion of the audio goes to each speaker. You specify four factors when using the setTransform() method: how much left-channel sound should go to the left speaker (referred to as ll and ranging from -100 to 100), how much left-channel sound should go to the right speaker (lr), how much right-channel sound should go to the right speaker (rr), and how much right-channel sound should go to the left speaker (rl). The setTransform() method provides you with very fine control. By the way, the changes that you make to volume and pan override the settings that you made previously through the setVolume() and setPan() methods.

Now for the funky part: Specifying the four settings (ll, lr, rr, and rl) would probably be easiest if you simply provided four parameters when invoking the setTransform() method. It doesn't work that way, however. Instead, setTranform() accepts a single parameter in the form of a generic object that has four properties (of pre-designated names). The process involves first creating a generic object in a variable, setting the four properties (ll, lr, rr, and rl, because those are the ones Flash expects), and finally passing that variable as the parameter when calling setTransform(). Here's how you might do it:

```
transObj=new Object();
transObj.ll=100;
transObj.lr=0;
transObj.rr=100;
transObj.rl=0;
my_sound.setTransform(transObj);
```

This script effectively sets the balance to be equal. (The left-channel sound going to left speaker and the right-channel sound going to the right speaker are both 100.)

This assumes that my_sound is already instantiated (and playing if you want to hear anything). After you populate the variable (transObj in this case), you can change any of its four properties and then invoke the last line (my_sound.setTransform(transObj)) to hear the change. Assuming that the transObj exists, you can send all the left channel's audio to the right speaker (and vice versa) by using the following code:

```
transObj.ll=0;
transObj.lr=100;
transObj.rr=0;
transObj.rl=100;
my_sound.setTransform(transObj);
```

To make a stereo sound play as though it were mono, use the following code:

```
transObj.ll=50;
transObj.lr=50;
transObj.rr=50;
transObj.rl=50;
my_sound.setTransform(transObj);
```

Translated, this code says, "Send half of the left-channel's sound to the left speaker, and the other half to the right speaker. Then send half of the right-channel's sound to the right speaker and the other half to the left speaker." The result is that all sounds are distributed evenly to both speakers, and it sounds mono.

Finally, if you need to ascertain the current transform, use getTransform(). The only tricky thing is that this returns another object. If you want to specifically address one of the four properties, you can do so by using the dot-syntax techniques with which you're so familiar. For example, to find out what percent of the left channel is going to the left speaker, use my_sound.getTransform().ll. If you want to access several properties, but don't want to keep calling the getTransform() method, you can store the transform you get in a variable, as follows:

```
curTrans=my_sound.getTransform();
trace("Left speaker is playing "+ curTrans.ll + "% of left channel");
trace("Right speaker is playing "+ curTrans.lr + "% of left channel");
trace("Right speaker is playing "+ curTrans.rr + "% of right channel");
trace("Left speaker is playing "+ curTrans.rl + "% of right channel");
```

Controlling Multiple Sounds

I left out an optional parameter when first introducing the Sound object constructor function (new Sound()). Think of the parameter as the way to attach a sound to a Movie Clip instance. Then that instance and attached sound is independently controllable just like any other property of that clip. The way it works is that you need to provide a reference to a Movie Clip as the parameter, and then the sound's properties will be independently controllable. Otherwise, the volume of all Sound objects will be the same. The following code shows how you can start playing two sounds and then control their respective volume levels:

```
music_sound=new Sound(clip1);
music_sound.attachSound("music");
music_sound.start();
voice_sound=new Sound(clip2);
voice_sound.attachSound("narration");
voice_sound.start();
music_sound.setVolume(50);
voice_sound.setVolume(80);
```

You'll need two clips on the Stage (clip1 and clip2) and two sounds in the Library with linkage set and identifiers ("music" and "narration"). When the sounds start, you'll hear their respective sounds change when calling music_sound.setVolume(toWhat) and voice_sound.setVolume(toWhat). It's weird because you'd think by having the two sound objects stored in two separate variables (music_sound and voice_sound), you'd have independent control. Just remember, though, that you need to attach the sound to a specific Movie Clip instance (by providing the clip as a parameter) to have independent control. Lastly, variables (as always) are indeed part of the timeline where they're created (so you'll need to apply all that you know about addressing if you want to refer to them from other timelines). But interestingly, including a clip reference in the new Sound() constructor has no impact on addressing (so you don't need to worry about it).

Determining a Sound's Position and Duration

The Sound object was pretty awesome when introduced in Flash 5, but it lacked the position and duration properties that are now included. You saw how the position property can help you resume a previously paused sound. The duration property is also quite useful. For example, to create a clip that acts like a progress bar, use the following script in a keyframe:

```
my_sound=new Sound();
my_sound.attachSound("soundID");
my_sound.start();
```

Then attach the following script to a Movie Clip instance that contains a wide rectangle:

```
onClipEvent(enterFrame){
    this._xscale=_parent.my_sound.position/_parent.my_sound.duration*100;
}
```

Let me explain: After you get the sound started in the keyframe, the Movie Clip instance's enterFrame script will execute repeatedly. That script keeps reassigning a value to its own _xscale property. The value is simply the result of the expression "position/duration*100." Because we want to ascertain the position and duration of the sound (which are stored in the variable my_sound in the main timeline), we begin with _parent.my_sound. You can try some "what-if" numbers to see that the scale will go from 0 to 100. (That is, when both the position property and the duration property are the same, the expression will evaluate to 100.) Finally, to make the progress bar appear to grow to the right (rather than evenly in both directions), select the left-center default Registration setting when you first convert the rectangle shape to a Movie Clip (see Figure 12.3).

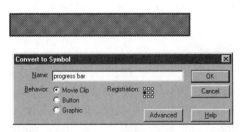

Figure 12.3 *When converting a shape to a symbol, you can select the left-center default Registration setting so that scaling will make it appear to grow to the right.*

To use the Sound object, you just need to remember these steps:

1. Import a sound, and then, in the Linkage Properties dialog box, set the Linkage option to "Export for ActionScript." Also, give the sound a unique identifier.

2. Instantiate the Sound object, and then store it in a variable by using the `new` constructor, `my_sound=new Sound()`.

3. Attach a sound by referring to the identifier name that you provided in Step 1, `my_sound.attachSound("identifier")`.

4. Start the sound with `my_sound.start()` and then use any of the other methods or properties as you wish.

5. Finally, when you're sure that you will no longer need the sound, you can delete the variable containing the object with `my_sound.start()`. Although I don't believe that a few unused sound objects will bring your movie's performance to a crawl, just as with any variables, there's no reason to have more than you're using. (By the way, be sure to `stop()` the sound before you delete the variable, or you'll lose control of the sound.)

Loading Sounds

New to MX

One of the most exciting new features in Flash MX is the fact that you can dynamically load native MP3 sounds (and .jpg images) into your movies at runtime. That is, a tiny .swf can load huge image or sound files upon the user's request. For example, you could create a jukebox that enables users to select to play any song, or a photo gallery that enables them to browse through a collection of images.

Although the capability to load sounds at runtime is a powerful new feature, the process happens to be really simple. After you've instantiated a Sound object (for example, `my_sound=new Sound()`), you can commence downloading by using the following code:

```
my_sound.loadSound("music.mp3",true);
```

The first parameter is simply the MP3's filename. (Relative paths also work fine.) The second parameter is set to `true` (when you want the sound to stream) or to `false` (when you want it to perform like an Event sound). In the case of streaming, the sound will begin playing as soon as it is able. You must start event sounds by using the `start()` method.

The dilemma, however, is that you can't start an Event sound until it's fully downloaded. You can solve this issue in a couple of ways. First, you can (perhaps continually) check whether the sound is fully downloaded by comparing getBytesLoaded() to getBytesTotal(). When they're the same, you know the sound is downloaded. Another way is to link the onLoad event to a homemade function that contains the start() method.

Using the first technique, we can display a progress bar (just like the earlier example that showed position). In a keyframe, start the download with:

```
my_sound=new Sound();
my_sound.loadSound("music.mp3",false);
waiting=true;
```

Then, on a clip with the instance name clip, place the following code:

```
onClipEvent(enterFrame){
  if(_root.waiting){
    this._xscale=_root.my_sound.getBytesLoaded()
    ➥/_root.my_sound.getBytesTotal()*100;
    if(_root.my_sound.getBytesLoaded()==_root.my_sound.getBytesTotal()){
      _root.my_sound.start();
      _root.waiting=false;
    }
  }
}
```

This example is nearly the same as the position indicator from earlier. An additional if statement keeps checking to see if the number of bytes loaded is equal to the total number of bytes; if it is, the start() method is called. The reason I included the waiting variable (which is behaving like a "flag") is that I didn't want the progress bar to start checking and resizing until the downloading had begun.

Instead of continually checking to see whether an Event sound has fully downloaded (before invoking start()), you can link a homemade function to the onLoad event. I'll show you one way to do it here, but realize there's more to learn about extending ActionScript in Chapter 14.

```
my_sound=new Sound();
my_sound.onLoad=beginSound;
my_sound.loadSound("music.mp3",false);
function beginSound(){
  my_sound.start();
}
```

This example is intentionally wordy, as you'll see when you learn more about linking events to functions. The first and third lines should look familiar. In the second line, I'm saying that when the my_sound object triggers its onLoad event (that is, when it fully loads), I want it to trigger the homemade `beginSound()` function. You can see the `beginSound()` code in the last three lines, where it simply starts the sound. There's one important thing to note: Unlike many places in ActionScript, the order of the preceding code is very important. That is, you must specify which function should link with `onLoad` before the loading begins! You're telling Flash what to do when it finishes an operation, but it has to know everything before it starts (including what to do when it's done).

By the way, there's a hidden benefit of using the Sound object with loaded sounds as opposed to imported sounds that have their linkage set. By setting the linkage on any symbol, you force Flash to download that entire symbol before the first frame of the movie displays—even before any graphic progress bar appears! Although you have to manage the download process when using `loadSound()`, it can make the user experience better because you can give him something to look at during the download.

Just so you know, there's another such event that you can link to a function: `onSoundComplete`. It can be used like the `onLoad` function, but to trigger a function when a particular sound finishes playing.

New to MX

Attaching Colors to Clips

Through scripting, you can use the Color object to apply color styles on any named instances the same way you can manually use the Properties panel. That is, you can color anything that you can give an instance name to—clips, buttons, or dynamic or input text. (To color video objects, however, just place them inside a clip). The process is analogous to using the Sound object. The Color object requires that you first instantiate an object through `new Color(instance)`, where `instance` is the clip (or other instance type) that you want to affect. Then use one of the two methods—`setRGB()` or `setTransform()`—to cause the instance to change. It really is that simple. It's just that when you want to perform elaborate effects, there are additional details—as you'll see in the following section, "Using the Color Transform Method."

Simple Coloring

Here's the simple version of coloring a clip using the Color object. First, instantiate the Color object and specify a target instance, as follows:

```
my_color=new Color(theClip);
```

The variable `my_color` now contains the object, so the clip instance named `theClip` will be affected when we do the next step. (Notice that even though the clip is referenced between quotes, you can still use absolute or relative paths as long as you remember the quotes.) At this point, you can color the clip using the `setRGB()` method. To tint it pure red, use

`my_color.setRGB(0xFF0000);`

For green, use

`my_color.setRGB(0x00FF00);`

Notice that the parameter used for the `setRGB()` method is in the form of a hexadecimal color reference. The first two characters (`0x`) act as a warning to Flash that what follows is in the hexadecimal format. That's it! As long as you know the hex value for the color you intend to use, this works great. By the way, if you want to learn more about hexadecimal color references, the easiest way is by exploring Flash's Color Mixer panel when fully expanded (see Figure 12.4).

Figure 12.4   *Flash's Color Mixer panel will display hex values when fully expanded.*

Using RGB Values

In addition to providing a hex value (after `0x`) as the `setRGB()` method's parameter, you can provide a number between 0 and 16,777,215. The following three paragraphs include a detailed explanation of how you can specify colors in an intuitive (RGB) manner. 24-bit color includes 8 bits for each of the three colors: red, green, and blue. This means that there are 256 shades for each color (0–255) because each binary digit is either "on" or "off." Eight binary digits—1, 2, 4, 8, 16, 32, 64, and 128—all "on" adds up to 255. If they're all "off," it adds up to zero. The highest number you can represent with twenty-four binary digits (three 8-bit colors) is 16,777,215.

An interesting method is used to relate 16 million different values to three colors. Blue always gets the first 8 bits (1 through 8 bits, or 0–255). A value of 0 is no blue; a value of 255 is 100 percent blue. A value such as 128 is only 50 percent blue. To add green to the equation, 8 bits are still used, but they start at 9 and go through 16. So instead of ranging from 0 to 255 in one-step increments, green is defined with numbers between 256 and 65,280, which is 256 steps of 256 each. So every notch of green is 256: 256 is one notch of green; 512 is two notches of green; and so on. A number such as 522 is two notches of green and 10 notches of blue. The way to see the breakdown of blue and green is to first extract the round 256 increments. (256 goes into 522 twice; then the left over 10 is used for blue.) It might be easier to see if you imagine that blue went from 0 to 99 (in steps of 1), and that green went from 100 to 1000 (in steps of 100). If you extract the largest steps first and then the remainder, a number such as 600 would be a shade of green 6 units deep (and no blue), but a number such as 630 would be 6 units green and 30 units of blue. It actually works just like this except that instead of being based on 1s and 100s, it's based on 8 bits and 16 bits. Red gets the last 8 bits, of course, which means that it steps from 65,280 to 16,711,680 in 256 steps of 65,536 each. All this means is that it's next to impossible to intuitively specify colors using RGB—but we'll find a way.

The reason the previous concept is so difficult to understand is that we like to think of digits going from 0 to 9 (that is, in base 10). In our base-10 system, the far-right digit is for "ones" (0–9), the second digit is for "hundreds" (0–9 again, but representing how many "hundreds"), and so on. Hexadecimal values do it in three pairs of characters: RRBBGG. For example, the first two characters "RR" represent a number between 0 and 255 for red. The three 256-shade values for R, G, B are in the 24-bit system; they're just hard to derive. If you think in binary, though, it's probably easiest. Using 8 digits (for 8 bits), you can represent any number from 0 to 255. For example, 00000001 is 1, 00000010 is 2, and 00000011 is three. Each position in the 8-digit number represents a bit. To read the previous binary numbers, consider the far-right digit as the "ones" (0–1), the second digit as the "twos" (0–1 representing how many "twos"), the third digit as the "fours," and so on. Therefore, you can count (in binary) 001, 010, 011, 100, 101, 111. Check it out… 1, 2, 3, 4, 5, 6 in binary!

For a 24-bit color, you need to have only 24 binary digits. The eight at the far right represent 0–255 for blue, the middle eight represent 0–255 for green, and the leftmost eight digits represent 0–255 for red (see Figure 12.5).

Figure 12.5   *A binary representation of a 24-bit number includes eight digits for each color.*

Finally, I can show you a quick way to convert RGB values (of 0–255 each) into binary at the same time that they can be used in the setRGB() method. That is, how do you turn r=255, g=255, and b=255 (which is white) into a binary series of 24 ones or zeroes (that can, in turn, be used as the parameter passed when invoking setRGB())? Assuming that r, g, and b are variables containing a number between 0 and 255, you can use a bitwise shift operator to specify how many digits to the left you want the binary number to shift. That is, 5<<8 takes the binary version of 5 (101) and shifts it eight spots to the left (10100000000—that's 101 with eight zeros). This is exactly how to shift the value for green up eight places (or g<<8). Red needs to be shifted 16 places, so r<<16 is used. Finally, the combined form appears in the following handy-dandy formula:

Handy Formula

To supply an RGB value into a single value (as the Color object requires), replace r, g, and b in the formula,

```
my_color.setRGB(r<<16 | g<<8 | b);
```

Notice that b (the value for blue) doesn't need to be shifted. The result of the entire expression in the parentheses is a binary number representing RGB by using eight digits for each color. In practice, you just need to make sure that your values for r, g, and b are between 0 and 255, and then use the previous method call as it appears in the formula.

Using the Color Transform Method

Naturally, you probably aren't satisfied with only 16 million different possible colors; you probably want to change the alpha of a color, too. After all, I said you can use scripting to achieve the same results that you can by using the Properties panel's Color Styles—and just look at all the things you can do with the Advanced Effect dialog box (see Figure 12.6). The setTransform() method enables you to modify any instance associated with the Color object in the same way the Advanced Effect dialog box does. Of course, you could always just use the familiar theClip._alpha=70 if you ever need to change the alpha of a tinted clip—but setTransform() can do even more than that.

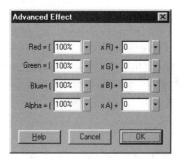

Figure 12.6   *The Properties panel's Advanced Effect dialog box gives you fine control over tinting (especially with bitmaps).*

Actually, if you understand the interface of the Advanced Effect dialog box (which is easiest when applying an effect to a clip containing a raster graphic), you'll better understand how to use setTransform(). Just like using the setTransform() on the Sound object, you need to pass a generic object as a parameter. You first create a generic object, set its properties according to the effect you want, and then pass it when invoking setTransform(). The generic object has eight properties that correlate directly to the eight settings in the Advanced Effect dialog box. Of course we're not using the Properties panel (the manual way)—we're doing this with scripting—but it helps to consider these eight properties in relation to the Advanced Effect dialog box (see Figure 12.7).

Here's a code sequence that you might use to tint a clip 50 percent red and 30 percent alpha:

```
transObj=new Object()
transObj.ra = 50;
transObj.rb = 255;
transObj.ga = 100;
transObj.gb = 0;
transObj.ba = 100;
transObj.bb = 0;
transObj.aa = 30;
transObj.ab = 0;
my_color=new Color(theClip);
my_color.setTransform(transObj);
```

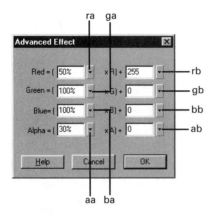

Figure 12.7   *The settings in the Advanced Effect dialog box are the same for the generic object passed to the* setTransform() *method.*

I see setTransform() as having two main benefits: You can change the alpha of a clip, and you can control subtle color shifts that are most apparent when the clip being colored contains a raster graphic (such as a .bmp, .png, or .jpg). Although there are in fact other ways to control the alpha, setTransform() is nice because you can tint and change the alpha in one line (instead of using both setRGB() and the _alpha property). The kinds of effects that you can make on raster graphics are pretty cool, however, and they go way beyond just tinting and changing the alpha.

Before we move on, let me just mention the two other methods: getRGB() and getTransform(). The getRGB() method returns (in base 10) the last color value used on the object referenced. That is, my_color.getRGB() will return the color for the instance associated with the object stored in the variable my_color— specifically, a number between 0 and 16,777,215.

By the way, a handy way to translate that number to binary is by using the toString() method, but by providing a parameter (called a *radix*). That is, my_color.getRGB().toString(2) will return (in the form of a string) the color value represented in binary. You can even use toString(16) to convert the number being operated on to hexadecimal. Check it out by using trace(my_color.getRGB().toString(16)).

Finally, realize that the value returned when you use getTransform() is an object with eight properties. For example, if you want to ascertain the current alpha percentage, use my_color.getTransform().aa, because aa is the property containing the alpha percentage.

The Date Object

The Date object gives you an easy way to store specific dates, ascertain the current date (and time), and find out details about any date (such as its day of the week). For example, I know that I was born on a Wednesday—not because I remember, but because I can check it with the Date object. Basically, I created a new instance of the Date object with my birthday as the initial value, and then I used a method that returns the day of the week. Another interesting application is to repeatedly reassign a variable a new Date object (and use the current date and time for the initial value). Then you can display all the details of the current time (using a clock or calendar). It's even possible to accurately find the difference (in number of days) between two dates, and you don't need to know which are leap years or how many days any particular month "hath." (You know, "Thirty days hath September….")

Instantiating a Date

Similar to the Color and Sound objects, you always start by instantiating the Date object, and then you can use methods on it. The variable you use to hold a Date object contains a snapshot of a moment in time. That is, a variable that contains the Date data type is holding only one moment in time. When you create an instance of the Date object, you can optionally specify that moment (year, month, hour, second, and even millisecond, if you want); or, if you don't specify any date, you're given a date that matches the setting of your user's computer clock. Here's the form to create an instance with the current time:

```
now=new Date();
```

The variable now contains a Date object with the current time. You can provide up to seven optional parameters (to specify year, month, day, hour, minute, second, and millisecond). For example, this is how you create an instance that contains the U.S. Independence Day (July 4, 1776):

```
indyDay=new Date(1776, 6, 4);
```

That is, the year 1776, the month July (counting January as 0, February as 1), the fourth date in the month (which—surprisingly—starts counting with 1). I left out the rest of the optional parameters: hour, which counts from 0 (midnight) to 23 (11 PM); minutes (0–59 for every hour); seconds (0–59 per minute); and, milliseconds (of which there are 1,000 per second). Because the seven parameters are optional, you can leave them off if you want (although the order is important: the first parameter always referring to year, the second to month, and so on).

Manipulating Dates

After you've created a variable that holds your Date object, you can manipulate and view it through the various methods. Although quite a few methods are available (see Figure 12.8), there are only two general types: methods that "get" information from a date, and methods that change (or "set") elements within a date. Let's walk through some operations to get a handle on both types of methods.

Getting Information from Dates

Several methods "get" specific information from a date. For example, the getDay() method returns the day of the week. However, because it returns a number between 0 (for Sunday) and 6 (for Saturday), you might first create an array with all the days of the week, as follows:

```
dayNames=["Sunday","Monday","Tuesday","Wednesday",
➥"Thursday","Friday","Saturday"];
```

Then you can easily determine the day of the week that the U.S. Constitution was signed:

```
trace("Signatures were made on a "+dayNames[indyDay.getDay()]);
```

Because indyDay.getDay() returns a 4, the expression dayNames[4] would return "Thursday". It's almost as though it doesn't matter that getDay() starts counting with Sunday as 0, because when grabbing data from an array, we count the same way. (This isn't to say that it will never mess you up.)

Other methods are similar to getDay() such as getYear() (and its better-half getFullYear()), getMonth(), and getDate() (which returns the number of the day in the month). It's unlikely that you'd really _need_ these to ascertain the year, month, or date for a Date object that you created by specifying the date. However, they can be particularly useful when you're not sure of the date. For example, let's say that you want your Flash movie to display information about the current date in a Dynamic Text field. You can start with:

```
today_date=new Date();
```

Figure 12.8 *Although there are many methods for the Date object, they fall into two general categories: those that get values and those that set values.*

Then, if you have a Dynamic Text field with the instance name message, you can use the following code:

```
monthNum=today_date.getMonth()+1;
dateNum=today_date.getDate();
yearNum=today_date.getFullYear();
message.text=monthNum+"/"+dateNum+"/"+yearNum;
```

By the way, getYear() returns the number of years since 1900 (so if you do a getYear() on a date in the year 2001, you'll get 101). The method getFullYear() returns a 4-digit number (which naturally renders your Flash movie "non-Y10K-compliant"—but I wouldn't worry about it).

If you want to display the date in a format that's a little more wordy than 3/31/2002, you can use a quick-and-dirty technique involving the toString() method. When used on a Date object, toString() returns the full date and time in the form:

Sun Mar 31 00:00:00 GMT-0800 2002

Although this is kind of nice, if you want something more readable, you could use a function such as:

```
function getNiceDate(dateObj){
  var dayNames=["Sunday","Monday","Tuesday","Wednesday",
➥"Thursday","Friday","Saturday"];
  var monthNames=["January","February","March","April","May",
➥"June","July","August","September","October","November","December"];
  var day=dayNames[dateObj.getDay()];
  var month=monthNames[dateObj.getMonth()];
  var date=dateObj.getDate();
  var year=dateObj.getFullYear();
  return (day+" "+month+" "+date+", "+year);
}
```

Just pass an actual Date object for a parameter, and you'll get a string back that follows a more traditional form than what you get with toString(). That is, trace(getNiceDate(indyDay)) will result in "Thursday July 4, 1776" displayed in the Output window.

The data maintained in a Date object is detailed down to the millisecond. However, because instantiating a new Date object (with new Date()) takes a snapshot only of the current time, in order to make a clock (that doesn't appear frozen in time), you'll need to repeatedly re-instantiate the Date object. The ideal place to do this is inside an enterFrame clip event. So, if you have a Dynamic Text field (with an instance name theTime) in a Movie Clip and you attach the following code to the clip instance, you'll have a nice digital clock (see Figure 12.9).

```
onClipEvent (enterFrame) {
  now=new Date();
  seconds=now.getSeconds();
  if (seconds<10){
    seconds="0"+seconds;
  }
  minutes=now.getMinutes();
  if (minutes<10){
    minutes="0"+minutes;
  }
  hours=now.getHours();
  amPm="AM";
  if (hours<10){
    hours="0"+hours;
  }else if (hours>12){
    amPm="PM"
    hours=hours-12;
    if (hours<10){
      hours="0"+hours;
    }
  }
  theTime.text=hours+":"+minutes+":"+seconds+" "+amPm;
}
```

10:45:51 PM

Figure 12.9 *You can easily make this digital clock display with a Dynamic Text field and in a Movie Clip.*

In the preceding code, the now variable is reassigned a new instance of the Date object and then used in most of the subsequent calculations. The seconds variable is set by applying the getSeconds() function to now. If seconds is less than 10, we just add a "0" in front of it so that it still displays using two characters. The minutes variable is similar to seconds. In the case of hours, determining the actual hour is straightforward enough: hours=now.getHours(). I first assume it's AM (by setting amPm to "AM"), but if hours is not less than 10, I check to see whether it's greater than 12, in which case I say amPm is "PM" and then take 12 off; that is, if it's 14:00, you subtract 12 to get 2 PM. (Kind of makes you like the 24-hour system used in most areas of the world.) Finally, I build the string to replace theTime instance's text property.

Naturally, the ugly part of this code is the error checking. That is, I go through extra work to make sure that numbers less than 10 appear with a zero to their left. The important part to remember in this example is that the variable now is continually reassigned a new Date object (12 times a second if the frame rate is set to 12 fps). I don't think you'll see a performance hit from this code executing so frequently—but even if you did, it's a clock, so you'll want it to update frequently.

Setting Values in Dates

So far, we've looked at using the Date object to store a moment in time and then use methods to peek inside. Although we haven't explored all these methods that "get" values returned, there's another set of methods that "set" values. These methods enable you to change any attribute of a date stored in a variable. For example, if you want to take today's date and find out the month and date for a day exactly two weeks from now, you can use the setDate() method. The setDate() method will change the date in the attached object to whichever number you provide as a parameter. If you provide "today plus 14 days" (that is, getDate()+14), you'll find the answer. Here's the code:

```
now=new Date();
fortNight=new Date();
fortNight.setDate(now.getDate()+14);
trace("Two weeks from now is: "+ fortNight.toString());
```

Notice that I could have just used the setDate() method on my original Date object (now)—that is, now.setDate(now.getDate()+14). Instead of getting confused with a variable called "now" that actually contained a date in the future, I came up with another variable name (fortNight). But it's important that before I try setting fortNight's date, I have to instantiate the variable as a Date object (in the second line of code). Simply put, you can only use methods on objects. Another important point is the setDate() method actually changes the object being operated on. This is performing an assignment without the equal sign. Finally, the cool part about setDate() (and all the other "set" methods) is that other elements in the object being operated on automatically update accordingly. That is, if you setDate to today's date plus 40 days (now.setDate(now.getDate()+40)), you'll find that the object's month (found through getMonth()) has changed. Similarly, you'll find that the year changes when you setMonth to the current month plus 13.

There's one last method that I want to describe. When you use the method getTime() on any Date object, the elapsed milliseconds between January 1, 1970 and the object being operated on will be returned. This might seem like a useless piece of trivia, but it might come up on a quiz show some time. It also happens to be the most direct way to determine the difference between two dates. For example, if you knew one person was born five days after January 1, 1970 and another person was born 200 days after January 1, 1970, it's simple to calculate the difference in their two ages as 195 days. It's not that you care how many days apart from January 1, 1970 each birthday is—it's just a common reference point. In the following code sample, you see that we never really take much note as to how many milliseconds have past since 1970, we just find the difference between two dates. In fact, one of the dates used occurred before the magic 1970 date.

```
birthday = new Date(1968, 1, 29);
bicentennial = new Date(1976, 6, 4);
difference = Math.abs(birthday.getTime()-bicentennial.getTime());
millisecondsPerDay = 1000*60*60*24;
difference = Math.floor(difference/millisecondsPerDay);
trace ("Birthday was "+difference+" days before or after the
bicentennial");
```

Notice that no one really cares how many milliseconds have elapsed since January 1, 1970 (or, even that getTime() could result in a negative number if the date being operated on was earlier). Instead of calculating whether a birthday was before or after the bicentennial, I just calculated the absolute value of the difference. The absolute value (Math.abs()) always returns a non-negative number. Finally, to convert milliseconds into days, I divided by 1000*60*60*24 (which is based on the fact that there are 1000 milliseconds every second, 60 seconds every minute, 60 minutes every hour, and 24 hours each day). Instead of just dividing the difference by millisecondsPerDay, I use Math.floor() to make sure to just extract the integer portion of the number. That is, I don't want to know that it's been 3047.95833333333 days—3047 is plenty. Using this same basic technique, you can accurately calculate the difference between any two days. (By the way, leap-day of 1968 isn't really my birthday.)

Implications for Movie Clips

To be perfectly accurate, we've already discussed the Movie Clip object. However, by using the techniques that follow, you can effectively drag instances of clips onto the Stage entirely through scripting. You can even draw lines and fills into Movie Clips using script. In the rest of this chapter, you'll see how to instantiate clip instances at runtime, how to write scripts that get attached to those new clips, and how to draw lines and fills dynamically. Don't think this is the end of what you can do with Movie Clips, however. You'll see Movie Clips make appearances in all the following chapters, too.

Instantiating Clips at Runtime

If you want to use scripting to cause a Movie Clip instance to appear on the Stage during runtime, there are two basic methods: duplicateMovieClip() and attachMovie(). The older method (duplicateMovieClip()) requires that you already have a clip on the Stage; when it gets duplicated, everything on it (that is, scripts) is also duplicated. Personally, I always use the attachMovie() method because I don't have to remember to first place a clip (to be duplicated) on the Stage. However, attachMovie() requires that you first set the linkage for the clip in the Library (as we did for sounds) and come up with a unique identifier. Then, all you do is call the attachMovie() function by using:

```
targetPath.attachMovie("identifier", "newInstanceName", depth);
```

targetPath is a timeline where you want the new clip to reside (for example, _root); "identifier" is the name you gave the clip through its linkage; "newInstanceName" assigns it an instance name (as though you typed it in manually through the Properties panel); and depth is the level number. (Most clips are on level 0, but you can specify higher numbers when loading movies and the clips will appear on top of others.) For example, if I have a clip who's identifier is "box", I can use:

```
_root.attachMovie("box", "box_1",1);
```

This will place an instance of the clip in the Library whose identifier name is set to "box" on the Stage. The clip's instance name will be box_1. The following code will position and change the _alpha property of the clip:

```
_root.box_1._x=190;
_root.box_1._y=33;
_root.box_1._alpha=50;
```

Looks pretty familiar, eh? Well, to explain this any further would probably insult your intelligence. We covered all the bases of Movie Clips in Chapter 7, "The Movie Clip Object." The trick to remember here is the identifier that's set through the Library item's Linkage options.

There are a couple new things to realize. First, the preceding example of first attaching the clip (that is instantiating it) and then setting properties was the only way to create and then modify clips before Flash MX. A fourth optional parameter for attachMovie() is called "init object." Here, you can provide a generic object that contains the properties you want to give to your newly attached clip. For example, instead of following the attachMovie() code with the preceding three lines of code (that set _x, _y, and _alpha), you can do this:

```
myObj = new Object();
myObj._x=190;
myObj._y=33;
myObj._alpha=50;
_root.attachMovie("box","box_1",1,myObj);
```

This code simply constructs the myObj variable with three named properties (that just happen to be built-in to Flash), and that variable is provided as the fourth parameter. By the way, if you want to initialize your attached movie with home-made properties (that is, variables), you can add to the object variable myObj additional homemade properties that don't share a name with Flash's built-in ones. For example, to initialize the clip with an age property, insert the following line before the attachMovie line:

```
myObj.age=36
```

Arguably, providing this fourth parameter is just as much work as setting properties after the clip is instantiated. (It's actually one extra line of code.) However, in Chapter 13, "Homemade Objects," you'll learn about "constructor functions," which simply construct generic objects—but, like all functions, they can do it repeatedly. Just so you can see it here, consider the following code:

```
function constructProps(x,y){
  this._x=x;
  this._y=y;
}
_root.attachMovie("box", "box_1", 1, new constructProps(100,100));
_root.attachMovie("box", "box_2", 2, new constructProps(200,400));
```

Without fully explaining all the ramifications, think of the constructProps() function as simply a way to both create a generic object and set two properties (_x and _y) based on the parameters received. Then, when the two attachMovie() methods are invoked, they in turn invoke our constructProps() function in order to receive back a generic object for that fourth parameter. In the end, two clips are instantiated: box_1 (who's _x and _y are both 100) and box_2 (who's _x is 200 and _y is 400).

Finally, just to show you an application for both loops and the dynamic clip referencing formula you first saw in Chapter 7 (that is path[string clip name]), here's an example that creates 7 clips staggered visually and stacked onto separate levels:

```
for (i=1; i<8;i++){
    _root.attachMovie("box","box_"+i,i);
    _root["box_"+i]._x = i*50;
    _root["box_"+i]._y = i*50;
}
```

Notice that I could have used that init object (fourth parameter) and eliminated the two lines that follow the attachMovie() method. This loop simply takes the iterant i from 1 through 7 and uses i for the clip names ("box_"+i), as well as the level number. Then, when it comes to referring to the current box, a string name is generated ("box_"+i)—but since it's in brackets and follows a path, the clip of that name is addressed. Finally, I just multiply i by 50 to stagger the position of the new clips.

Here are a couple of more things to know about instantiating clips. You can't put more than one clip in the same level. If you attach a clip and specify level 1, you can't put any other clips in that same level (nor can you load movies into that same level). Also, if you want to remove a clip that's been created using the attachMovie() function, you can use removeMovieClip()—which is a *method* of the clip, so the form is:

```
targetPath.instanceName.removeMovieClip();
```

Notice that you apply the removeMovieClip() method on a clip reference—the same way that you use any method—not on the identifier. For example, to remove the clip created previously, use the following:

```
_root.box1.removeMovieClip();
```

Finally, take a quick look at the duplicateMovieClip() method, because it's pretty similar. All you need to specify is the new instance name for the clip and the level number. For example, you can duplicate the instance called original to create one called copy by using:

```
_root.original.duplicateMovieClip("copy", 1 );
```

This method requires that an instance has already been instantiated; otherwise, you'd have no object to apply this method to. The good news, however, is that the duplicateMovieClip() method doesn't require that you've previously specified the linkage and given the Library item an identifier. Also, any scripts attached to the clip that's duplicated are contained in the duplicate. By the way, `removeMovieClip()` works the same way with clips created through the `duplicateMovieClip()` method.

Runtime Drawing Methods

If the `attachMovie()` and `duplicateMovieClip()` methods just aren't enough for you, you'll be happy to see that Flash MX has a new method called `createEmptyMovieClip()`. This was added mainly to work with the new set of runtime drawing methods. However, I can think of ways to use it on its own. For example, I might want to create a single clip on the Stage that contains (has nested inside) two instances of other clips. I can first create an empty clip, and then use `attachMovie()` to place several other clips inside my new clip. For example:

```
//create an empty clip called " myInstance " in the main timeline
_root.createEmptyMovieClip("myInstance",1);
myInstance.attachMovie("box", "boxClip",1);
myInstance.attachMovie("circle", "circleClip",2);
```

The last two lines attach symbols (with linkage "box" and "circle") into the newly created clip. In this way, you can generate clips with dynamic contents.

Like I said, the `createEmptyMovieClip()` method enables you to first create a clip and then draw into that clip. Flash MX's drawing methods let you dynamically create lines, fills, and gradients into any clip. Although you can draw into a clip that contains graphics, the shapes you draw are just that—shapes. Therefore, they are placed underneath everything else. Anyway, the drawing methods appear to be very simple (and they are); however, applying them to do amazing things is more work.

The basic approach is first to create an empty clip, and then start drawing into it. When drawing lines, it's as though you first tell Flash what thickness and color pen you want, where to place it on the canvas, and then where to draw to. The methods are: `lineStyle()` or `moveTo()`, and then either `lineTo()` or `curveTo()` (depending on whether you want a straight line). Consider the following simple example in which I first create an empty clip, set the `lineStyle()`, tell Flash where to place the pen, and then draw a line down 100 pixels:

```
_root.createEmptyMovieClip("clip",1);
_root.clip.lineStyle(3,0x0000FF,100);
_root.clip.moveTo(0,0);
_root.clip.lineTo(0,100);
```

The first line creates an instance called clip into level 1. The second line sets the line thickness to 3, the color to blue, and the alpha to 100 percent. The third line tells the pen to start at 0,0, and the fourth line where to draw to. The only tricky part is the moveTo() method. Think of this as saying, "Pick up the pen and place it down at this point."

Let me complete a drawing of an arrow:

```
_root.clip.lineTo(100,50);
_root.clip.lineTo(0,0);
_root.clip.moveTo(0,50)
_root.clip.lineTo(-100,50)
```

It's easiest to see this code if you look at Figure 12.10.

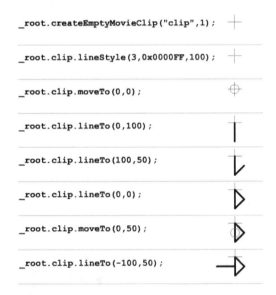

Figure 12.10   _This sequence shows each step of the code to draw an arrow._

In addition to lineTo() (which accepts the x and y coordinates of the destination) there's curveTo(), which also accepts the destination coordinates (called the "anchor" points), but also the control points that influence the shape of the curve. Control points are easiest to understand when you consider how the Pen tool and the Subselection tool draw Bezier curves. You can also check out the sample file "drawing.fla," which is located in the Samples folder ("FLA" sub-folder) adjacent to your installed version of Flash MX. Figure 12.11 shows how control points affect a curve.

Figure 12.11   *A control point is easy to see when using the Subselection tool to modify a hand-drawn line.*

Finally, the last few methods are beginFill(), beginGradientFill(), and endFill(). Basically, you start by saying beginFill(), draw a few lines, and then finish with endFill(). (It's as though Flash took the Paint Bucket tool and filled the shape you drew.) Naturally, your lines have to be enclosed. Also, if you want something that's only fill (that is, no lines), just specify your line style with a zero alpha (lineStyle(0,0x000000,0)). Here's a modified version of the arrow I drew earlier:

```
_root.createEmptyMovieClip("clip",1);
with(_root.clip){
    lineStyle(3, 0x0000FF, 100);
    beginFill(0xFF0000, 100);
    moveTo(0,0);
    lineTo(0,100);
    lineTo(100,50);
    lineTo(0,0);
    endFill();
    moveTo(0,50);
    lineTo(-100,50);
}
```

There are actually two differences between this code and the earlier example. The main thing is that before drawing the triangle, I say beginFill(0xFF0000,100) to indicate that I'm going to be filling with red (0xFF0000) of alpha 100, and then when I'm done with the triangle, I say endFill(). It's important not to forget endFill(); if you do, you might see odd results. In addition, because I was getting tired of typing "_root.clip." before each line (and so that you can see a great usage for the with() command), I just preceded the bulk of code with the line reading with(_root.clip){, and then placed all the code before the ending curly brace. It just means, "with this object... do the following".

Finally, beginGradientFill() is similar to beginFill() in that you call this method before drawing lines and finish with endFill(). However, whereas beginFill()accepts only the color and alpha, beginGradientFill() accepts five parameters—three of which are arrays full of values and one of which is a generic object that has your choice of either six or nine properties. So, really, the number of parameters is unlimited. Without fully explaining complex matrix transformations, let me give you a several pointers to get you started. The form is always:

```
my_mc.beginGradientFill (fillType, colors, alphas, ratios, matrix)
```

Always replace the first parameter (`fillType`) with either `"linear"` or `"radial"` (verbatim, including quotes), depending on the type of fill you want. The following three parameters (`colors`, `alphas`, and `ratios`) are always in the form of an array. That is, you can either type a literal array right in their slots (such as `[1,2,3]`) or refer to a variable previously populated with an array. The arrays for `colors` and `alphas` are relatively straightforward. Consider that your gradient blends from (at least) one color to another. Those two colors need to be identified (by hex value). (Of course, you can use the handy-dandy formula from earlier in this chapter if you want to convert RGB to hex.) To make a gradient go from red to blue, use `[0xFF0000,0x0000FF]`. In addition, the alpha level for each color is specified in the `alphas` array. For example, `[100,100]` will have no transparency at either step of the gradient; `[100,50]` will reach 50 percent at the second color. The `ratios` array is not quite as intuitive. Here, you specify what percentage (of the entire blend) you want completed when a point is reached. You're really affecting the sharpness or smoothness of the falloff. For a two-step gradation (for example, from red to blue), it's pretty simple. You'll often want it 0 percent complete at the first color and then 100 percent complete at the second color. However, for a gradation with three steps, you may or may not want to have a consistent 0 percent, 50 percent, 100 percent progression. You can adjust it to make it look less balanced, perhaps 0 percent, 75 percent, and then 100 percent (see Figure 12.12). The closer in value the percentages are, the less gradual the gradation. Now for the really funky part: where alpha values logically go from 0 to 100, the ratios (that is, the percentage values in the `ratios` array) go from 0 to 255. Therefore, to represent 50 percent, you use 127.5 (half of 255). For example, a consistent three-step blend could have the following values for the first three arrays:

```
colors=[0xFF0000, 0x00FF00, 0x0000FF];
alphas=[100,100,100];
ratios=[0, 127.5, 255];
```

That is, by the time the blend got to green (the second step) it would be 50 percent complete. Naturally, you would have to place the three variables in the proper parameter positions of the `beginGradientFill()` method. Also, these three arrays must all have the same length.

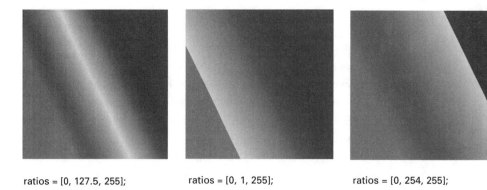

ratios = [0, 127.5, 255];   ratios = [0, 1, 255];   ratios = [0, 254, 255];

Figure 12.12   *These three gradients are identical except for the ratios's array values. Notice how the smoothness of the blend is affected.*

Handy Formula

Many examples, including those in the Flash Help files, use "0x7F" rather than providing 127.5 for 50 percent of 255. That's just the hex equivalent for 127.5. I find myself constantly trying to convert normal numbers (that is, base-10 numbers) to or from hex values (base-16). The following two formulas will simply help you translate:

To express a base-10 number as a hex string, use
`myNumber.toString(16);`

For example, `127.5.toString(16)` becomes 7F (and you just have to remember to add 0x).

To express a hex string as a base-10 number, use:
`parseInt(hexString,10);`

For example, `parseInt(0x7F,10)` will return 127.

At this point, it's necessary to explain the last parameter, `matrix`, because you can't do much without it. It is always a generic object, but you have a choice as to exactly which pre-designated properties that object will have. One format is a, b, c, d, e, f, g, i—the nine values necessary to represent a 3x3 matrix transformation, as visualized here:

```
a       b       c

d       e       f

g       h       i
```

If this looks familiar, you must be a real math-head. It's not so much that these nine values describe how the gradient will appear, but rather you begin with a so called "identity matrix" (zeros in each slot except a, e, and i) and then transform the matrix by scaling, displacing (called *translating*), rotating, skewing, or otherwise "torqueing" it. For example, if you start with a single pixel dot on the edge of the fill and then scale it, the blend will cover more area. If you then translate it, you can move it to the center of the fill area. It's sort of like how you manually use the Fill Transform tool, except it's all done with code. The only problem is that matrix transformations use relatively complex mathematics. (Well, it looks really complex.) Therefore, people tend to write a library of useful functions so that they don't have to do the nitty-gritty work every time. For now, I'll just show you a couple of simple transformations (and then I'll show you where it gets *really* hairy).

First, recall the quick way to both create a generic object and populate it in one line of code: myObj={prop1:"val1", prop2:"val2"}. That's the form I'll use for the matrix parameters that follow.

```
1  _root.createEmptyMovieClip( "grad", 1 );
2  with (_root.grad){
3     colors = [0xFF0000, 0x00FF00];
4     alphas = [100, 100];
5     ratios = [0,255];
6     matrix = {a:1, b:0, c:0, d:0, e:1, f:0, g:0, h:0, i:1};
7     beginGradientFill( "radial", colors, alphas, ratios, matrix );
8     moveto(0,0);
9     lineto(0,600);
10    lineto(600,600);
11    lineto(600,0);
12    lineto(0,0);
13    endFill();
14 }
```

The preceding code will draw a 600x600 box that appears to be all green but is really a tiny 1-pixel dot of red that quickly blends to green. The identity matrix is not much to look at. However, if you want to scale it much larger, replace the sixth line with the following three lines:

```
var xScale=500;
var yScale=500;
matrix = {a:xScale, b:0, c:0, d:0, e:yScale, f:0, g:0, h:0, i:1};
```

Check out Figure 12.13, which shows that the gradation has grown.

Figure 12.13   *After a 500 percent scale transformation, the tiny dot of a gradient looks more substantial.*

The reason this works is that, as everyone knows, the matrix transformation for scaling is described by

xScale	0	0
0	yScale	0
0	0	1

Interestingly, the same brains that brought us the scaling description have found that translation (moving) is performed by the following:

1	0	0
0	1	0
xAmount	yAmount	1

Without whipping out your slide rule, it (seriously) should be easy to see that this doesn't conflict with the two slots for xScale and yScale. So, if you want to both scale and translate the gradation, you could use this (in place of the original line 6 of code):

```
var xScale=500;
var yScale=500;
var xAmount=300;
var yAmount=300;
matrix = {a:xScale, b:0, c:0, d:0, e:yScale, f:0, g: xAmount, h:yAmount,
i:1};
```

This should make the blend appear to grow from the center of the square (see Figure 12.14). Go ahead and try replacing the temporary variables (xScale, yScale, xAmount, and yAmount).

Figure 12.14   *After both a scale and translate transformation, the radial blend now appears in the center of our box.*

We got sort of lucky when combining both scale and translate because none of the 9 slots were shared by both formulas. But in the case of the formula to rotate a transformation, we aren't so lucky. At this point, rather than walking through matrix multiplication, let me first say that it's definitely possible to scale, rotate, and translate a transformation. Second, it's much easier to learn to use the "TransformMatrix.as" library of useful functions. This ships on the Flash MX CD-ROM so that you don't have to "reinvent the wheel." To fully understand how to use this file, you'll want to study the subject of "overriding," which is covered in Chapter 14.

There's still another way to create the `matrix` parameter for the beginGradientFill() method—which you may find easier. Specifically, if the `matrix` object can have five properties (x, y, w, h, r) plus one that's named `matrixType` and always hard-wired as `"box"`. The values for x and y define the horizontal and vertical position of the gradient (relative to the clip's registration point). The w and h are for width and height, respectively. Finally, r is for rotation (in radians). You'll see that since you can't scale x and y differently, the rotation option only makes sense for linear gradients. (That is, you can't make an ellipse, so there's no sense in rotating a circle.) Take the following example (which can just replace the matrix definition in the earlier code):

```
matrix={matrixType:"box", x:150, y:150, w:300,
►h:300, r:(45/180)*Math.PI };
```

You'll also want to change the gradient to linear, as follows:

```
beginGradientFill( "linear", colors, alphas, ratios, matrix );
```

First, notice that `matrixType:"box"` appears verbatim. In this case, we offset the gradient by 150x and 150y, and set both its width and height to 300. Finally, the gradient is rotated by 45 degrees. Because we can't just say 45 for the r property, we use the handy formula to covert degrees to radians. In retrospect, the `"box"` matrix type is a lot more manageable for simple gradients.

In practice, you might find drawing anything more than very primitive shapes and simple blends to be quite difficult. For example, drawing a box or arrow is not too challenging, but suppose you want to rotate or skew the shape you draw? You can apply the same (complex) matrix math used for the gradient transformations to drawing lines. The approach most people take is to first write a few general-purpose functions that accept parameters that are easier to define, and then mix and match these general functions for a particular application. For example, you might write a function that draws rectangles based on four points provided as parameters. Then you could use this rectangle-drawing function in an application that creates a bar graph based on dynamic data. When you learn to use the TransformMatrix.as library, you'll probably get some ideas how to write your own general-purpose functions. Don't feel like you're cheating by starting with the building blocks such libraries provide. Believe me, you'll have plenty of opportunities to come up with creative solutions to challenging problems—even with this code!

Summary

We've looked at three traditional objects made for Flash: Sound, Color, and Date. In each of these, you first need to create an instance of the object (by putting it in a variable), and then you can use any of the object's methods. The three objects introduced in this chapter are a good representation of "formal" objects. So many other objects in Flash have special conditions that let you get away without instantiating them (the Math and String objects, in particular). In addition to Sound, Color, and Date, you saw three ways to instantiate Movie Clips at run-time: (`attachMovie()`, `duplicateMovieClip()`, and `createEmptyMovieClip()`). The important thing to remember when attaching or creating clips is that the master symbol needs to have its linkage set (as does a sound when using the Sound object). On top of all that, you got to play with Flash MX's new drawing methods.

Another key concept you should take away from this chapter is the way a generic object can be populated with values for several named properties and then passed as a parameter. You even saw how a special constructor function can produce such generic objects and even set initial properties. The main thing we did was to populate a variable with values. Both the Sound and Color object's `setTransform()` method requires a generic object with specific properties. (That is, the named properties need to match the arbitrary names designated in Flash's design.) The same basic technique was used in the drawing methods, although often the properties themselves contained multiple values in the form of arrays. We'll fully explore the process of creating generic objects in Chapter 13 when we create our own custom objects that do more than just store data.

If you ever have trouble grasping concepts about objects in general, remember that you can always think about what makes an instance of a clip an object. It has a set of properties that can be varied from instance to instance. And just like any object, there are a host of methods that you can apply to individual instances of clips. The other objects explored in this chapter are still objects; they're just not always visible.

{ Chapter 13 }

Homemade Objects

Now that you've seen a variety of objects built-in to Flash, it's time to make your own objects. You've actually already had to create homemade objects when you made so-called "generic objects" for the purposes of storing multiple values in named properties (similar to arrays, except that each item is named). The homemade objects that you'll make in this chapter go beyond just storing data. They are almost identical to built-in objects such as the Movie Clip, Sound, or Date objects. The instances of homemade objects you create can have properties and methods.

In fact, homemade objects can be more sophisticated than those built-in to Flash because of a special feature called *inheritance*. After you design and build one object, it's possible to design new objects that share certain properties and methods of that object. For example, you could make a "Bank Account" object that includes a method to calculate interest. That same method can be inherited by another object (perhaps a "Certificate of Deposit" object). By using inheritance, you can modularize code to increase your productivity.

The process of creating objects is relatively straightforward and consistent with everything you've learned. Designing a good object, however, is where the challenge lies. The practical examples in this chapter should give you some ideas. Specifically, you will:

- Create simple objects that maintain unique values for properties in each instance.

- Create custom methods for object instances.

- Assign prototype properties so that one object type can inherit properties and methods of another.

- Change properties in "parent" objects so that the values of the same properties in their "children" will reflect the change.

- Learn how to apply objects to practical Flash applications.

Basic Objects

When you see how easy it is to make an object, you'll probably be surprised. In fact, when you created associative arrays (or what I'd call "generic objects") in Chapter 11, "Arrays," and Chapter 12, "Objects," you were actually making objects. Individual objects are just a way to store multiple pieces of data in one variable. A quick way to both create and populate a generic object follows this form (which I call the "one-liner"):

```
myData={age:35,height:72,citizenship:"USA"};
```

From this point, you can access any item using the form:

```
myData["age"]=36;
```

The preceding form tends to look similar to arrays, but it's really easier to consider it a generic object. Let's do the whole thing over, but use a more formal "object way," as follows:

```
myData=new Object();
myData.age=35;
myData.height=72;
myData.citizenship="USA";
```

You can still access individual items (which are probably best called *properties*) the same way as shown earlier (myData["age"]) or by using the preferred dot-syntax with which we are so familiar (myData.age). This just proves that generic objects are associative arrays (and vice versa).

Although I tend to create, populate, and access my generic objects using the "object way" shown above (the second way), it's nice to know both ways. Of particular value is the way you can access the value of a named property when you might not know the exact property name. For example, if all you can do is build a dynamic string (say, `"property_"+n`, where n's value is 1 and you want the value for `property_1`), the only way to access that property is to use the form `myObject[string]` or `myObject["property_"+n]`. This technique should look familiar because it's the same as accessing a clip instance name when you only have a string version of the name, as in `_root["clip_"+n]`. Finally, the form of both creating and populating a generic object in one line of code is nice because it's so quick and easy. Some people call these *short objects* because they don't require the extra step of first declaring that you want to create an object. I still opt for the formal way of declaring the object and then populating it using dot-syntax, but it's good to recognize the options.

Using a Constructor Function

Imagine that you want several variables to contain objects, each of which contains properties for age, height, and citizenship. It would get rather involved to define all three properties every time you wanted to assign this object to a variable. Instead, you can create a function that serves as a constructor function (to instantiate new instances of the object):

```
function MakePerson(age,height,citizenship){
  this.age=age;
  this.height=height;
  this.citizenship=citizenship;
}
```

{ Note }

You may notice that my constructor function (`MakePerson`) appears with the first letter capitalized. This is really just a matter of convention. Programmers capitalize the first letter of a function that will be used as a constructor. Regular functions don't begin with capital letters.

This function accepts three parameters and uses their values to set the values for three (identically named) properties of "this." No rule says that parameter names must match the property names you're setting. (As you know, parameters are just temporary variables that represent values received.) Even though the `MakePerson` function accepts three parameters like a normal function, this function won't make a whole lot of sense if we call it as we would a normal function (`MakePerson(22,68,"Canada")`, for example), because it's only doing stuff to "this." Notice that the three lines inside set three properties of `this`. In Flash, you can use the `this` keyword in one of two ways: either to refer to the current clip (that you're "in"), or (as previously shown) inside a function to refer to the object being created by that function. You're about to see how you create objects (or spawn them) with a function, but not by simply calling the `MakePerson()` function—that won't really do anything. Instead, you're going to use `MakePerson()` as a constructor function (to "construct" an instance of an object). It will be called as follows:

```
canadian=new MakePerson(22,68,"Canada");
```

Basically, we're saying the variable `canadian` will contain a new instance of the object created in the `MakePerson` constructor function, and then we send a few parameters to initialize property values. The reason for `this` in the constructor function is that we don't just want age set to `22`, but rather `canadian`'s age to `22`. The `this` holds the place for the particular instance being created (`canadian` in this example). We can keep calling the constructor function to make as many instances of the `MakePerson` object that we want. For example:

```
mexican=new MakePerson(33,70,"Mexico");
```

We've simply made a constructor function that serves to create multiple instances of an object. All we had to do was define the properties each instance would have automatically (`age`, `height`, and `citizenship`). In the end, you'll have two variables containing objects (`canadian` and `mexican`). Both have a set of three properties each. For instance, `canadian.age` is `22` and `mexican.age` is `33`. Placing all this code in the first keyframe will produce a structure of data visible through the Debugger (see Figure 13.1). Sometimes this might be the only way to verify that your objects are working.

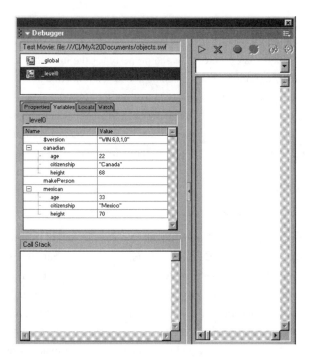

Figure 13.1 *Often the only way to see whether your objects are working is to use the Debugger.*

Making Methods

Now that you know how to create a constructor function, we can move on to creating methods. First, we'll make a method that's hard-wired for just one instance of our `MakePerson` object, and then we'll improve on it.

You can add properties to a single instance by using the following form:

```
instanceVariable.newProperty=newValue;
```

For example, `canadian.favoriteBeer="Lager"` will create a `favoriteBeer` property and set its value to `"Lager"`. This isn't terribly exciting (or anything new, if you recall creating variables that acted like properties of clip instances). What's really wild is that by assigning a property's value to equal a function, you'll actually be making a method. For example, consider this code:

```
function incrementAge(){
  this.age++;
}
canadian.haveBirthday=incrementAge;
```

Because `incrementAge` is really the name of a function, the instance `canadian` now has a method called `haveBirthday()`. Therefore, every time the script `canadian.haveBirthday()` is executed, the age property for the instance `canadian` is incremented. Notice a couple details above. The function `incrementAge` is referred to simply by its name, but not the form `incrementAge()` (as perhaps expected). That's because we don't want to actually call the function (like normal, with the parentheses), we just want to point to it. Also, it's possible to consolidate the two pieces above into one (arguably more confusing) line of code. That is, the following code achieves the same result with one slight advantage:

```
canadian.haveBirthday=function(){this.age++;}
```

The advantage of this consolidated form is that the `incrementAge` isn't sitting around taking up space (in memory). I think the first way is easier, and that's really the only reason I did it that way. Just like variables, if you create a function that only gets used once, you didn't really need it in the first place. It doesn't hurt much, so I'll tend to do it this way for readability. Finally, notice that I never give the function a name in my one-liner above. It actually appears to break the form for functions. To say, "Have birthday equal this function," kind of makes sense, however.

Although making a method for an individual instance is pretty cool, it has the definite drawback of being hard-wired just to the `canadian` instance. Most likely, when you spend the time to develop a method, you'll want to be able to apply it to every instance of a particular type of object. After all, you're allowed to apply the `nextFrame()` method to any instance of a movie clip—so why not be able to apply the `haveBirthday()` method to every instance of the `MakePerson` object? The way we just did it will *not* allow you to use `mexican.haveBirthday()`. We only specified this method for the one instance (`canadian`).

To create a method that will apply to every instance of a particular object, you use a special property, called `prototype`, that's built-in to every object. The `prototype` property is an object, so it has several properties of its own. You can individually specify as many properties of the `prototype` object (so as to create methods) by specifying a function in each one. The methods in the `prototype` object will apply to every instance spawned from the original constructor function. So, in the preceding script, rather than the line:

```
canadian.haveBirthday=incrementAge
```

use the following:

```
MakePerson.prototype.haveBirthday=incrementAge;
```

Translated, this says that the MakePerson object's prototype now includes a property called haveBirthday, which is assigned the value incrementAge. (Because incrementAge is really a function, this means we've made a method called haveBirthday() a method.) And because it's the special prototype property that we just added a property to, all instances created from MakePerson will now have access to this method. Therefore, you can do both canadian.haveBirthday() and mexican.haveBirthday(). The result is that we've made a method for our MakePerson object!

Remember that because the prototype property's data type is an object, it can contain multiple properties of its own. We've added only one property (really a method because it's a function) to the MakePerson's prototype property: haveBirthday. We can add more properties or methods:

```
function growAnInch(){
  this.height+=1;
}
MakePerson.prototype.grow=growAnInch;
```

Notice that this last line doesn't wipe away the haveBirthday method already contained in MakePerson's prototype; we just added a new method (called grow()).

So far, we've talked only about adding methods to your objects. However, if you want to add a property (not a method), you first have to decide whether this new property's value should be the same for each instance or whether it should be maintained individually for each instance. For example, if you decide that your MakePerson object should include an additional property called weight, obviously each instance should have its own value for weight. (That is, the mexican can weigh a different amount than the canadian.) However, if you want to add a property such as species, it makes sense that this has the same value for each instance. A property that's the same for each instance is more accurately called a *constant* (and as such could be written in all capital letters as a matter of convention, such as SPECIES). Let me explain three different ways that you can add properties.

To create a new property for just one instance of an object, use the familiar form `instance.newProp=value`. If you want to create a new property that will be maintained individually for every instance created, you must go back to the original constructor function and add a line such as `this.weight=weightParam`. Finally, if you want to add a property that serves as a constant because it is the same for every instance, you need to add it to the `prototype` property, as follows:

```
MakePerson.prototype.SPECIES="homo sapiens";
```

You might think that you could just hard-wire this `SPECIES` property inside the constructor function (that is, not set `this.SPECIES` to a value passed as a parameter, but just hard-wire `"homo sapiens"`). You could. What's cool about using to the `prototype` property is that later, with one swoop, you could change the value of any property for all instances ever created (including those yet to be created). Just execute the following code:

```
MakePerson.prototype.SPECIES="alien";
```

The previous analogies included physical human characteristics to—hopefully— make some concepts about objects clearer. The problem, however, is that it's nearly impossible to quickly extrapolate this "MakePerson" theme into a practical Flash application. Any time you work with objects (unless they are Movie Clip instances), it can be difficult because while you work, it's still kind of ephemeral. Ultimately, after you build an object, you can use it in conjunction with visual elements that appear onscreen. But the work involved creating clips and graphics can be pretty consuming. My suggestion is that you get very familiar with the Debugger (so that you can watch your variables as they change) and use `trace()` to test what you build every step along the way. For example, I typed the following block of code into the first frame of my movie, and then I opened the Debugger to watch my variables. Finally, I created some buttons so that the values of various expressions would appear in the Output window (see Figure 13.2). This way, I could be sure that all the code I produced was working:

```
1 function MakePerson (age, height, citizenship) {
2   this.age = age;
3   this.height = height;
4   this.citizenship = citizenship;
5 }
6 canadian=new MakePerson(22,68,"Canada");
7 mexican=new MakePerson(33,70,"Mexico");
8 MakePerson.prototype.birthday=incrementAge;
9 function incrementAge(){
10   this.age+=1;
11 }
12 MakePerson.prototype.SPECIES="homo sapiens";
```

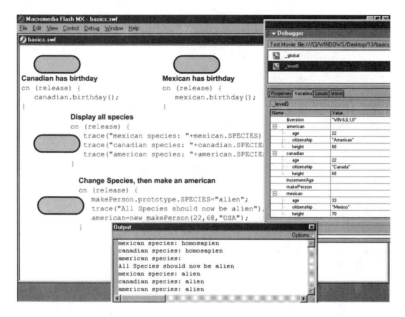

Figure 13.2   *Combining the Debugger and the* trace() *function along with rough buttons enables you to see how your objects are working.*

As a review up to this point, the first five lines are the constructor function that we learned to create earlier in this chapter. Lines 2–4 set properties that can be unique to each instance in the form this.property=value (where value can be passed as a parameter). Actually, the contents of the function itself aren't really important; it's just a regular function. The function becomes a constructor function only when we invoke it by using the new command. We create an instance by saying myInstance=new functionName(), as in lines 6 and 7. Finally, we tapped into the object's prototype property. As an object itself, the prototype property enables us to assign values to as many named sub-properties as we want. To create a method, we simply assign one of the prototype's properties the value of a function, as in line 8. Any other data type, as in line 12, will act like a global property or constant (the value of which will be the same for every instance). Figure 13.3 shows the form for the various maneuvers we've looked at:

- Writing a constructor function.

- Writing a function that will become a method.

- Creating instances of objects by invoking a constructor function.

- Creating a method by creating a property of the prototype property.

- Making a global property (one that is part of every object) instantiated with the constructor function.

```
constructor function:
function obj(param){
  this.prop=param;
}
```

```
function that will become a method:
function doIt(){
}
```

```
creating instances (by invoking "new" constructor):
inst1=new obj("x");          //inst1.prop == "x"
inst2=new obj("y");          //inst2.prop == "y"
```

```
making a method
(by putting a function inside a
property of the object's prototype property)
obj.prototype.myMethod=doIt;   //prototype.myMethod == a function
```

```
making a global property
(by putting any data type--except function--inside a
property of the object's prototype property)
obj.prototype.CONST="value";   //prototype.CONST == a string
```

Figure 13.3   *The syntax for various object-related maneuvers.*

Inheritance

The prototype property can do more than just maintain methods and constants. You're about to see how you can write a generic method for one object, and then recycle that same method in another object. This is similar to the way you can write one generic function that you call from several places in your Movie Clip. It's different, however, because you actually make one object inherit all the properties and methods of another. Consider how a child can inherit a base of attributes from his parent, but then goes on to develop his own. Similarly, we can write a generic object (with a set of methods) that allows other objects to inherit (and thus recycle) the entire set of methods.

In the example that follows, first you'll create a "Bank Account" object that maintains a balance and interest rate for each instance. You'll write a method that compounds the interest on the current balance. Then, you'll make another object: a "Certificate of Deposit" (or "CD") object. Rather than writing a unique method to compound interest on the CD object, you can just use the same method from the Bank Account object. The Bank Account object is the generic template. The CD object inherits all the attributes (that is, the properties and methods) of the Bank Account object (see Figure 13.4).

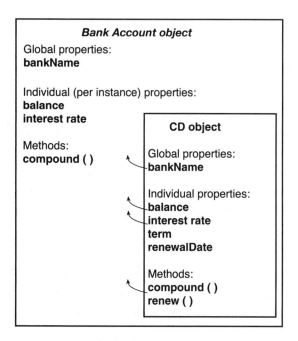

Figure 13.4 *The CD object will have all the same properties and methods of the Bank Account object, plus a few of its own.*

In this way, the CD object is everything that the Bank Account object is—and more. Your head might spin if you consider that you can have a deep hierarchy of objects that inherit attributes of other objects, which, in turn, have inherited attributes from other objects. Although explaining how to do it is easy, applying this knowledge is another matter entirely.

The way you build an object that inherits the methods of a parent object is actually quite simple. Consider the following simple bank account constructor function (BankAct) that you might put in the first keyframe of a movie:

```
function BankAct(startingBalance,interestRate){
  this.balance=startingBalance;
  this.rate=interestRate;
}
```

You probably won't want to start cranking out instances of the BankAct object until you've worked out the methods and inheritance that follow. When you do, however, you'll make an instance (that you store in a variable called primarySavings, for example), by using:

```
primarySavings=new BankAct(5000,.04);
```

To create the `compound()` method for all instances of the `BankAct` object type, use the following two statements:

```
function multiplyAndAdd(){
  this.balance+=(this.balance*this.rate);
}
BankAct.prototype.compound=multiplyAndAdd;
```

In this case, there's no compelling reason to use a different name for the method and function; `multiplyAndAdd` could just as well be called `compound`. In the following section, "A Practical Example of Homemade Objects," I'll show a reason why you might like to keep these names separate. With this method built, you can increase the balance in any instance of the `BankAct` object with a simple call, as follows:

```
primarySavings.compound();
```

This script will cause the object stored in `primarySavings` to increase its `balance` based on interest `rate`. You can type `trace(primarySavings.balance)` before and after the preceding line to verify that the `compound()` method is working.

Now that we have this somewhat simple `compound` method, we might want to use it again for other types of objects. It only makes sense to use the `compound` method on other object types that maintain a balance and interest rate. Let's make a new object (a "CD" object) that will have all the same properties and methods of our `BankAct` object, but that will also have its own set of unique properties and methods. All "certificates of deposit" are "bank accounts," but not all "bank accounts" are necessarily "certificates of deposit." So, here's the constructor function for a CD object:

```
1 function CD(startingBalance,interestRate,lengthOfTermInDays){
2   this.balance=startingBalance;
3   this.rate=interestRate;
4   this.term=lengthOfTermInDays;
5   var now=new Date();
6   this.renewalDate=new Date();
7   this.renewalDate.setDate(now.getDate()+this.term);
8   this.longDate=this.renewalDate.toString();
9 }
```

In addition to initializing the properties `balance`, `rate`, and `term` (based on the parameters received), this function performs some Date object operations to set two other properties (`renewalDate` and `longDate`). Line 5 assigns a local variable (`now`) to the current time, line 6 initializes `renewalDate` as a date object type (that is, its data type is the date object), and line 7 resets `renewalDate` by way of the setDate() method (pushing it out `term` days from now). Finally, last line creates a string version of the `renewalDate` property—really just for readability, because we'll never use this property within a calculation, such as in the following method:

```
function extendDate(){
  this.renewalDate.setDate(this.renewalDate.getDate()+this.term);
  this.longDate=this.renewalDate.toString();
}
CD.prototype.renew=extendDate;
```

Notice that we don't ever *use* `longDate`; we just reassign it after adding `term` to the current `renewalDate`. The last line (outside the function) is the way that we make `extendDate()` become a method (called `renew()`) of the `CD` object.

So far, we've built two objects (`BankAct` and `CD`) and a method for each. At this point, we could duplicate the code for `BankAct`'s `compound()` method and make an identical method for `CD`; however, I hate to repeat code I don't have to. We can specify that the `CD` object should inherit all the properties and methods built-in to the `BankAct` object. Notice that both objects have properties for `balance` and `rate`. When you inherit, all properties and methods are inherited. The fact that both `CD` and `BankAct` objects have some of the same property names doesn't necessarily matter. However, the instant `CD` inherits everything from `BankAct`—it actually overwrites any properties or methods it already has. The point is, the sequence of your code *does* matter. For example, if you store an instance of the `CD` object in a variable and then say, "The `CD` object will inherit everything from the `BankAct` object," the variable already created will be unaffected. (Compare this to how changing the default behavior of a symbol in the Library from Button to Movie Clip will have no affect on instances already on the Stage.) However, if you create a `CD` object after the "inherit now" statement, it will be a child of the `BankAct` object. Unfortunately, saying "inherit now" (the way I'm going to show first) causes all previously defined methods to be wiped away. I'll show some examples later, but first consider the simplicity of the following code, which causes the `CD` object to inherit everything from the `BankAct` object:

```
CD.prototype=new BankAct();
```

That's it. Translated, this simply says the `CD` object is a subset of the `BankAct` object and will inherit all its properties and methods. As you'll recall, defining a method for the `CD` object *added* to its prototype (as in `CD.prototype.methodName=aFunction`). The inherit code above is different in two ways. First, it sets the whole `prototype` equal to *something*—not just by adding a property, but by replacing prototype entirely. Second, prototype is being assigned to a new instance of the BankAct object (notice the word new). You could read the preceding code as "CD's prototype—the whole thing—is now equal to the BankAct constructor and all its properties and methods."

From this point forward, you can create as many CD objects as you want. And if you ever need to compound() the balance, you can do so, as follows:

```
rainyDay=new CD(2000,.08,180);
rainyDay.compound();
```

The first line creates an instance of the CD object and places it in the rainyDay variable. The second line invokes the compound method that was naturally inherited from the BankAct object (with the line CD.prototype=new BankAct();). The only little problem is that when CD inherited everything from BankAct, it wiped away all methods—including the CD object's renew() method. We can solve this problem a couple of ways. Realize the fact that assigning the child object's entire prototype to another object will wipe away methods defined earlier. One easy fix is to simply define any methods for the CD object after the "inherit now" statement. Here's the entire code, with some comments to clear things up:

```
//constructor for BankAct object
function BankAct(startingBalance,interestRate){
  this.balance=startingBalance;
  this.rate=interestRate;
}

//define and create compound() method
function multiplyAndAdd(){
  this.balance+=(this.balance*this.rate);
}
BankAct.prototype.compound=multiplyAndAdd;

//constructor for CD object
function CD(startingBalance,interestRate,lengthOfTermInDays){
  this.balance=startingBalance;
  this.rate=interestRate;
  this.term=lengthOfTermInDays;
  var now=new Date();
  this.renewalDate=new Date();
  this.renewalDate.setDate(now.getDate()+this.term);
  this.longDate=this.renewalDate.toString();
}

//make CDs inherit everything from BankAct
CD.prototype=new BankAct();
//define and create the renew() method (now that it's safe to add to CDs)
function extendDate(){
```

```
  this.renewalDate.setDate(this.renewalDate.getDate()+this.term);
  this.longDate=this.renewalDate.toString();
}
CD.prototype.renew=extendDate;
test=new CD(100,.1,30);
trace ("init: " + test.balance + " "+ test.longDate);
test.compound();
trace ("after compound: " + test.balance + " "+ test.longDate);
test.renew();
trace ("after renew: " + test.balance + " "+ test.longDate);
```

As previously mentioned, the order matters. Notice that I didn't start adding to the `prototype` property of the `CD` object (to create the `renew()` method) until after I said, "Inherit everything from the `BankAct` object." Finally, I threw a few test lines at the end to verify that both the inherited `compound()` method and the `renew()` method were indeed working.

Although my careful attention to the order made the previous example work out, there's another way to inherit. Notice first, though, that the code `child.prototype=new parent()` inherits everything—properties, methods, and constants. For example, even if the `CD` object didn't create the `balance` and `rate` properties; it would still have them because the `BankAct` object does. Basically, anything inside the parent object's constructor becomes part of the child object. The other way to specify inheritance differs because you just say, "Inherit just the methods of the parent object but not any properties in its constructor." The appearance of the code can be intimidating, but it's really not too bad. To understand, first ask yourself: Where are an object's various methods stored? They're stored as named properties inside the object's `prototype` property (for example, `anObject.prototype.method=function`). So, if we want the child object to acquire a parent's set of methods, we just need to point to that parent's `prototype`. We can't just say `child.prototype=parent.prototype`, however, or we'll be overwriting the child's entire `prototype` and, subsequently all its methods. We just want to add to the child's set of methods.

You also need to know about a special built-in property of the `prototype` property: `__proto__` (notice the two underscores on each side). That is, every object automatically gets a `prototype` object into which you can name properties that hold methods. In addition, each `prototype` object has a built-in special property, called `__proto__`, which can optionally point to a parent object's `prototype` to acquire a set of inherited methods. The following code shows how to declare that you want a child object to inherit only the methods of a parent object:

```
child.prototype.__proto__=parent.prototype;
```

For our example, the code would be as follows:

```
CD.prototype.__proto__=BankAct.prototype;
```

That's equivalent to saying `CD.prototype=new BankAct()`. The difference is simply that any code from `BankAct`'s constructor will not be included in all `CD` objects. In this example, that's not a big deal because the following two lines appear in both the `CD` and `BankAct` constructor:

```
this.balance=startingBalance;
this.rate=interestRate;
```

The way I separate the two ways of inheritance is that one simply extends an object (the __proto__ way) and one redefines and overwrites an object (the first way).

A Practical Example of Homemade Objects

For a practical example, let's consider a database full of products for sale through a music and video store. Figure 13.5 shows the start of a rough layout.

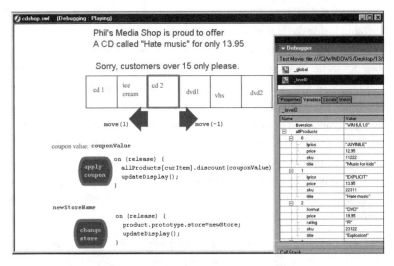

Figure 13.5   *This rough draft of our next exercise will explore every aspect of homemade objects discussed in this chapter.*

The basic features we're going to build include a way to first store the database of products in one big list and then to use the arrow keys to browse one item at a time. The selected product will have details such as its price and title provided in the text above. In addition, a button will enable a person to reduce the price by an amount indicated on a coupon. Finally, to demonstrate a constant (or "global property"), we'll be able to change the store name at any time. Obviously, this isn't the finished product, but it should offer a great way to see how to apply objects. By the way, almost all the scripts are placed in the first keyframe. In addition, there are just a few buttons (such as the "next" and "previous" buttons) that call various functions, such as move(). These are all shown within mouse events (such as on (release)).

First, we will design the objects. The most generic object will be called Product and will contain both a price and a sku (for "Stock Keeping Unit"—a unique number for every stock item). In addition, we'll build a method that allows for a discount to be applied to the price. Here's the code to do what I've specified so far, which can be placed in the movie's first keyframe:

```
function Product(price,sku){
  this.price=price;
  this.sku=sku
}
function coupon(faceValue){
  this.price-=faceValue;
}
Product.prototype.discount=coupon;
```

The first function is the constructor for the Product object; the second function (coupon) turns into a method (called discount()), which, in the last line, is placed in Product's prototype property. The Product object is the most basic form from which all other objects will inherit these properties and methods. (At this point, there's only the discount() method.)

The types of products this store currently sells are audio CDs and videos (in the VHS and DVD formats). Instead of locking those down (and preventing diversification in the future), we'll consider all these products of the type "media." To that end, first we'll design a Media object that inherits everything from the Product object. And then the various objects that follow (CD, DVD, VHS) will inherit everything from the Media object (and, therefore, from Products as well). By placing the following code below the preceding code, we can make the Media object act as a descendant of the Product object:

```
function Media(){
}
Media.prototype=new Product();
```

Notice that the Media constructor doesn't do much. You might expect it to at least set a property or two. In the future, I could make plain Media objects that maintain their own properties, but I have no plans for that now. I could also create a method for the Media object, and all descendants would inherit that as well. (I'm not going to for this example, however.) For now, I just want to ensure that all Media objects (and their descendants) inherit everything from the Product object. (By the way, if you don't want this extra level of hierarchy, you can change the code below that reads new Media() to read new Product(), and it will still work.)

Now we can make a separate object for audio CDs (CD) and one for videos (video) that both inherit everything from the Media object. Each object will be a subset of the Media object (and, therefore, of the Product object), so they'll have the discount() method. In addition, each object will have its own unique set of properties and methods. Let's just make the objects first, as follows:

```
function CD(title,lyrics,price,sku){
  this.title=title;
  this.lyrics=lyrics;
  this.price=price;
  this.sku=sku;
}
CD.prototype=new Media();
```

The last line of the preceding code establishes that CDs inherit everything from the Media object.

The following constructor for Video objects follows a similar form as that of the CD object constructor:

```
function Video(format,title,rating,price,sku){
  this.format=format;
  this.title=title;
  this.rating=rating;
  this.price=price;
  this.sku=sku;
}
Video.prototype=new Media();
```

Now that we have the constructor functions for the Video and CD objects and have established that they inherit everything from Media objects, we can create as many CD or Video instances as we want. First, I would like to write a method that works with either videos or CDs to determine whether the content is approved for children. If a video's rating property is not "R" and not "X," the okayForKids method (that we're about to build) will return true. Similarly, if a CD object's `lyrics` property is not "EXPLICIT," the `okayForKids` method will return true. Initially, you might consider writing the `okayForKids` method for the `Media` object. This makes sense when you consider that you want to be able to use the same method with either object type. However, the decision whether it's "okay for kids" is based on a different property in each object. Instead, let's write two versions of the method. The following start has some problems, which we'll address shortly:

```
function okayForKids(){
  if (this.lyrics ! = "EXPLICIT"){
    return true;
  }else{
    return false;
  }
}
CD.prototype.okayForKids=okayForKids;
function okayForKids(){
  if (this.rating ! = "X" && this.rating<>"R"){
    return true;
  }else{
    return false;
  }
}
Video.prototype.okayForKids=okayForKids;
```

This solution won't work because both the function declarations have the same name. Although it's desirable that both the *methods* are given the same name (so that we can invoke them the same way—`someCD.okayForKids()` or `someVideo.okayForKids()`)—we can't have two constructor *functions* with the same name. Consider the following modified (and usable) solution:

```
function notExplicit(){
  if (this.lyrics ! = "EXPLICIT"){
    return true;
  }else{
    return false;
  }
}
CD.prototype.okayForKids=notExplicit;
function notX_notR(){
  if (this.rating != "X" && this.rating<>"R"){
    return true;
  }else{
    return false;
  }
}
Video.prototype.okayForKids= notX_notR;
```

Earlier in the chapter, I said the function that defines how a method will work can have the same name as the method, but it isn't always desirable. In this case, we made both of them different so that there would be no overlap. Notice, however, that Video objects have an okayForKids() method, and so do CD objects. It's cool that despite checking for slightly different things, they both have the same name. This is called *polymorphism*. Consider how many different professions could have a "get certified" method. It would be called "get certified" regardless of whether you were a building inspector or a lion tamer.

One tiny thing to add is a store name property that can be changed (for all product objects and their descendants) in one move. Although we already have a method for the Product object (discount()), we can add a constant (one that is *not* unique for every object instance) by using the following line:

```
Product.prototype.STORE="Phil's Media Shop";
```

This specifies a STORE property (and its value) for all Product objects (and all descendants).

Finally, we can start using this code to make object instances! From this point forward, we're simply going to use objects in an application—that is, we're done defining the structure. The following discussion is regular "Flash stuff." First, we can make a few objects:

```
cd1=new CD("Music for kids","JUVINILE",12.95, 11222);
cd2=new CD("Hate Music",    "EXPLICIT",13.95, 22311);
cd3=new CD("Musicals",      "MUSICAL", 8.95,  42311);
dvd1=new Video("DVD","Explosion!","R",    19.95, 23122);
dvd2=new Video("DVD","Colors",    "PG-13", 19.95, 2233);
vhs1=new Video("VHS","Horses",    "G",     9.95, 2344);
```

Lastly, we want to store all our objects in an array so that we can step through them one at a time:

```
allProducts=[cd1,cd2,dvd1,vhs1,dvd2,cd3];
```

Now we can do a few exercises. Assume that we want to determine the price for the second product in allProducts:

```
allProducts[1].price;
```

Notice that we can grab the price property of an object by first referring to the array (full of objects).

If we want to discount the price of a product by 1.95, we can use

```
allProducts[1].discount(1.95);
```

The result would be that cd2 now costs 12.

You can see how easy it is to work with this storeful of objects. Let's build two arrow keys that step through each product and display data in a Dynamic Text field. Just make one button containing move(1) (inside a mouse event, of course) and one with move(-1). You should write the move() function and the updateDisplay() function in a keyframe of the main timeline, as follows:

```
function move (direction) {
  curItem -= direction;
  curItem=Math.min(allProducts.length-1, curItem);
  curItem=Math.max(0, curItem);
  updateDisplay();
}
function updateDisplay(){
  descript_txt.text= allProducts[curItem].price;
}
```

Basically, the move() function increases or decreases the value for curItem in the second line. Also, by using Math.min(), curItem is ensured of staying below the highest index in allProducts; by using Math.max(), curItem is ensured of staying at 0 or higher. Then, the last line of the move() function calls the updateDisplay() function, which sets the text property of the field descript_txt to the price of curItem. I didn't just put the code from the updateDisplay() function inside the move() function because I'd like to be able to invoke updateDisplay() from elsewhere as well. Finally, we'll need a Dynamic Text field with the instance name descript_txt. (Be sure to make this field a tall box with multiline and word wrap selected (see Figure 13.6), because we will be adding more information later.)

this will be the description

Figure 13.6 *Because the string we're going to display has a lot of information, make sure to specify multiline and word wrap to accommodate it.*

Notice that the only data being displayed is the price. We'd like to display much more data, however (such as its title, its type of media, and whether it's suitable for children). Check out the replacement version of the `updateDisplay()` function:

```
function updateDisplay(){
  var theObj= allProducts[curItem]
  var str= theObj.store + " is proud to offer \r";
  str=str + "A " + theObj.format;
  str=str + " called " + theObj.title;
  str=str + " for only " + theObj.price;
  descript_txt.text=str;
}
```

We need to call this `updateDisplay()` function every time there's a change (that is, when we call the `move()` function). In addition, however, we should call this function right after we populate the array. The last line of the code in the first keyframe, after `allProducts` is initialized, should include a call to `updateDisplay()`. But it should work.

Now that we have built the structure (and it's sound), we can start adding sophisticated features with ease. For example, if the product is not "okay for kids," we can include an additional warning just by adding the following `if` statement to the end of the `updateDisplay()` function:

```
if (!theObj.okayForKids()){
  descript_txt.text=descript_txt.text + "\r\r
➥Sorry, customers over 15 only please."
}
```

Notice the exclamation point (known as a *logical not*), which changes the meaning of the condition to "if not okay for kids."

You can keep adding features to this with little effort. To change the store name, for example, just combine an Input Text field associated with a variable `newStoreName` with the following code in a button:

```
on (release) {
  Product.prototype.STORE=newStoreName;
  updateDisplay();
}
```

Because `store` is a global property, the preceding code will change the value of `STORE` for every `Product` object, including descendants.

You can do the same thing to let users reduce the price of an item. Just make an Input Text field with the variable `couponValue`, and then make a button with the following code:

```
on (release) {
  allProducts[curItem].discount(couponValue);
  updateDisplay();
}
```

Notice that both these buttons call the `updateDisplay` function.

Although this is pretty complete, I want to add one more variation—for no other reason than to explore another application. Let's assume that our store wants to start selling food as well as media products. I'm going to make another object type equivalent to the hierarchy of the `Media` object and call it `Food`. Later, I could make sub-object types to `Food` (the way CDs and videos were types of media), but I'm not going to go that far. This is all I did:

```
function Food(name,price,sku){
  this.name=name;
  this.price=price;
  this.sku=sku;
}
Food.prototype=new Product();
```

Then, in the place where I instantiated all my objects, I simply created one more: `food1=new("Potato Chips",.55,12223)`. I also made sure to include it when I populated `allProducts`:

```
allProducts=[food1,cd1,cd2,dvd1,vhs1,dvd2,cd3];
```

Everything should still work, except that because the `updateDisplay` function includes the object's `title` and `format`, there's a problem in that `Food` instances have only `name`, `price`, and `sku` properties. We can modify the `updateDisplay` function to say (in pseudo-code), "If it's a media descendant, do what we were doing; otherwise, build a different string." There are a couple of ways to determine an object's parents. It can get pretty hairy because an individual CD is the child of the CD object, which is a child of the `Media` object, and so on. To verify that an object's `__proto__` is equal to another object's `prototype` isn't enough. For our application, we'd have to check whether an object's `__proto__`'s `__proto__` was equal to the media object's `prototype`. (To check whether an object was a descendent of the product object, we'd have to do something to verify that `cd1.__proto__.__proto__.__proto__==Product.prototype` was true.)

New to MX

No thank you! Luckily, Flash MX has added a handy operator, called
`instanceof`. All we need to do is make an expression (such as
`oneObject instanceof otherObject`), and it will evaluate to true or false,
depending on whether `oneObject` is a descendant of `otherObject`. For our
application, we just need to check whether the object in question is an instance
of `Media` or `Food`. To apply this to the `updateDisplay` function, we just need to
make the following adjustment:

```
function updateDisplay(){
  var theObj= allProducts[curItem]
  var str= theObj.store + " is proud to offer \r";
  if (theObj instanceof Media){
    str = str + "A " + theObj.format;
    str = str + " called \"" + theObj.title;
    str = str + "\" for only " + theObj.price;
    if (!theObj.okayForKids()){
      str = str + "\r\r Sorry, customers over 15 only please."
    }
  }

  if (theObj instanceof Food){
    str = str + "A delicious " + theObj.name;
    str = str + " for only " + theObj.price;
  }
  descript_txt.text= str;
}
```

The coolest thing about objects is that after they're built, you can add layers of
features and significantly change your program without having things fall apart.
The hard work is in designing the objects so that they make sense for your application. After they're built, they're easy to modify.

Summary

The truth is that you can live your whole life without once creating an object.
You can also create simply amazing Flash sites without them, too. It's just that
they're so darn convenient as a way to handle complex data. Plus, you're about to
see how to extend Flash's object model to override a built-in object's `prototype`
property. Yes, even the Movie Clip has a `prototype` object full of methods. Not
only can you make your own, but you can re-write Flash commands, such as
`gotoAndPlay()`! The good news is that all the knowledge from this chapter will
help you in Chapter 14, "Extending ActionScript." In the practical example we
built, the code structure wouldn't need to be modified at all if you decided to add
thousands of products. (You'd have to instantiate those thousands of items and

populate the `allProducts` array, of course.) The visual representation of data stored in objects is a bit of work—but then objects aren't supposed to create graphics for you. I see them as a ton of upfront work that pays back only when you can use them repeatedly.

As a quick review:

- You learned how to make custom objects.

- You learned how to create custom methods by using the `prototype` property (which is an object in itself because it has multiple properties).

- Finally, you learned that all attributes are inherited when you associate an object type's `prototype` with another object's `new` constructor function.

{ Chapter 14 }

Extending ActionScript

This chapter covers ways to both extend and re-define ActionScript. Although there is always more than one way to solve a problem, this chapter shows you other ways to use ActionScript. You'll not only get a closer look at the inner workings of Flash, but you'll see how you can adjust the way ActionScript behaves so that it's more under your control. I know that's pretty vague but think of this chapter as one of those car manuals for people who like rebuilding their engines.

Nearly everything in this chapter is new for Flash MX. Despite the fact that every other chapter includes lots of new Flash MX features, there are still many more. While organizing this book, I would often come across an exciting new feature. If I didn't know exactly where to put it, I added it to this chapter! As a result, you'll see that this chapter covers quite a bit of material.

Some of the material is rather advanced. So, instead of spending a lot time studying each topic, I recommend getting the basic idea here and then practicing when you get to the workshop chapters. I'll reference workshop exercises, as appropriate.

In this chapter, you will:

- Write callback functions for buttons and clip events so that you don't have to place scripts right on the instances.

- Make clips act like buttons.

- Register homemade classes and create complex properties based on Movie Clips.

- Fully explore how listeners and watchers can trigger scripts automatically.
- Override built-in methods using the prototype property.
- Trigger functions on schedule using the `setInterval()` command.

The good news about extending ActionScript is that you should be familiar with almost every example in this chapter. ActionScript is very consistent, so you will be able to apply knowledge that you gathered from previous chapters. Things should really start to click!

Callback Functions

The traditional places to write scripts in Flash are in keyframes and on button or clip instances. In the case of buttons and clips, the main instructions would go within a specific mouse event (for buttons) or clip event (for clips). Placing code right on objects this way might seem intuitive because scripts are tied to the objects to which they pertain. However, this technique is limiting—even if it is a good way to learn.

The technique is limiting for several reasons. First, all your code is scattered in a million places. Code is easier to manage when it's centralized. Second, some events (for which you want a script to respond) won't fit neatly into the mouse event or clip event interface. For example, a clip's `data` event is not nearly as clear and concrete as a button's `press` event. It has gotten worse with all the new event triggers added to Flash MX. For example, Movie Clips now have 18 different clip events. Finally, many other types of objects also have events (for example, the TextField object's `onChanged` event). There's no interface to specify text events, however. Fortunately, by using callback functions, you can write scripts to respond to any built-in event—and the same technique works for any object (not just clips and buttons).

Centralizing Code

This "new way" of working means that you can put almost all the code in a keyframe. First let's look at how this differs from the traditional way of placing code right on buttons or clips, and then we can concentrate on the benefits, limits, and applications.

Basically, the form is always:

```
instanceName.eventName=someFunction
```

That is, you're saying for a particular instance that you want a certain event name to trigger the specified function. The function you specify can either be defined separately or appear inline (that is, in *one* line—also called a *function literal*). I'll show both techniques by way of example. This first example shows the myFunction's definition followed by how the button instance my_btn will trigger that function (when it's pressed):

```
1 function myFunction(){
2  trace("You pressed!");
3 }
4 my_btn.onPress=myFunction;
```

The onPress event is listed under Object, Movie, Button, Events in the Actions panel (that is, it's built-in). Notice that we're saying the my_btn instance's onPress callback is the function named myFunction. We're not triggering the function in line 4; rather, we're just assigning the value of the button's onPress event to equal that function. In the preceding example, the function is defined separately, so it's accessible like any function. This means that you can invoke it by saying myFunction(), and you could have another button's onPress event (or any other event for that matter) point to the same function.

In the following example, the function tied to the button's onPress event will be defined all in one line:

```
my_btn.onPress=function(){ trace("You pressed!"); }
```

The effective result is the same as the first example. This time, however, myFunction is *not* available from anywhere else. Actually, it doesn't exist! That brings up something worth noticing: the definition of the function (everything on the right side of the equals sign) looks almost the same as a regular function definition—but no function name is given. When the contents of such a function get longer, it makes sense to space things out and use extra carriage returns. This example shows the same code as the preceding example but with different spacing:

```
my_btn.onPress=function(){
  trace("You pressed!");
}
```

As long as you follow the same form, it doesn't matter how you space out things. Spacing out things in this manner makes a lot of sense when the function includes more than one line of code. (You'll see some examples where this becomes obvious shortly.)

{ Note }

It's a matter of choice whether you define your functions inline or separately. However, when you define them separately, the order is important. You always want the function declaration to appear before the callback points to it. It's actually a logical flow. If you say, "When the event happens, I want you to do this function," one would hope that the function is defined before the event occurs. Take the onData event, for example. You don't want the instructions to follow this order: 1) "When the data loads, I want you to execute the jumper function;" 2) "The jumper function is...." A problem arises if data has loaded while you're still explaining how the jumper function works. Imagine these baking instructions: "Pour the cup of water into the flour. When half a cup of water is still remaining, stop pouring and wait 4 minutes before continuing." You know you should always read all the instructions before you start, of course, but Flash doesn't know that.

Defining the function separately had the advantage that the function could be shared with other parts of your movie. This inline fashion has a few advantages. The main difference is that if you don't expect or need other parts of your movie to trigger the same function, you should certainly use the inline technique. A separate function declaration takes up RAM because it effectively gets copied when identified by an event. In addition, the inline technique enables you to do some fancy stuff with the keyword this. That is, the this in a normal function is the function itself, whereas an inline function's this is the button instance whose event is being defined. Check out this example of a button that moves every time it's pressed:

```
my_btn.onPress=function(){this._x+=10;}
```

It's pretty simple, really: When the press event occurs, the button's _x is increased by 10. This example actually brings out a potentially confusing point. That is, normally, the this of a button is the timeline in which the button is placed. That is, the following code (placed right on the button instance) will have an entirely different result:

```
on(press){
  this._x+=10;
}
```

The result of this code is that the clip in which the button is present (or main timeline) will move to the right. Only when you use callbacks does a button's this mean the button itself. On the one hand, this can be very confusing; however, it's actually rather logical. You can identify callback functions for clip instances (and all the other objects), and this is always the clip (or object) itself.

Now that you know the form, the following examples should give you an idea of what's possible.

First, let's look at an example that uses the mouseMove clip event:

```
1 my_mc.onMouseMove=function(){
2   this._x=_root._xmouse;
3   updateAfterEvent();
4 }
```

This example moves the my_mc clip's "x" to match the location of the mouse in the main (_root) timeline. When working with callback functions, it's almost required that you use this. That is, you can't change line 2 to _x=_root._xmouse; if you do, Flash will think the _x is the main timeline's _x (because this code is in a keyframe of the main timeline). Nor can you change line 2 to this._x=_parent._xmouse. Both changes would have worked fine if the code were attached to the clip itself (inside a clip event); however, here you must be more explicit. By the way, if you wanted to address the _parent timeline, you could change line 2 to this._x=this._parent._xmouse.

Here's an abbreviated version of some code you'll write in Workshop Chapter 4, "Building a Slide Show":

```
1 my_mc.change=-10;
2 my_mc.onEnterFrame=function(){
3   this._alpha+=this.change;
4   if(this._alpha<0 || this._alpha>100){
5     this.change=this.change*-1;
6   }
7 }
```

Basically, the enterFrame script (which executes 12 times a second if the frame rate is 12 fps), changes the clip's _alpha by an amount equal to the value of the change variable (initialized at -10). Then, if the _alpha gets too low (less than 0) or too high (greater than 100), the change variable changes sign (gets multiplied by -1). You might wonder why I didn't use an onLoad callback in this example— that is, change line to read:

```
my_mc.onLoad=function(){this.change=-10;}
```

Although this makes total sense, it doesn't work! In fact, the instance of `my_mc` that I placed on the Stage will trigger its own `load` event *before* this script executes. That is, this script (which defines what's supposed to happen when the clip's `onLoad` event triggers) will never trigger because it's too late—the clip will have already loaded. The `onLoad` event is usable. You just have to place the script in a place where it will be invoked early enough. In the "Registering Custom Classes" section later in this chapter, you'll see how code placed on a frame inside a Movie Clip symbol and inside the `#initclip` and `#endinitclip` keywords will do exactly that: execute before the clip instance loads.

There's more to know about defining callbacks for clips. Because the main timeline is really a Movie Clip too (`_root`), we can identify a callback function for `_root`, as follows:

```
_root.onEnterFrame=function(){my_thing._x++;}
```

Assuming there's a clip, button, or text field with the instance name `my_thing`, this script will move it every 1/12 of a second.

Finally, here's an easy example that helps to introduce the next few sections:

```
my_btn.onRollOver=function(){this._alpha=50;}
my_btn.onRollOut=function(){this._alpha=100;}
```

In this example, the button instance called `my_btn` will drop to `_alpha 50` when you roll over, and come back to `100` when you roll out. This example eliminates the need to edit the contents of the button (to make an Over-state). Interestingly, if the instance called `my_btn` were actually a clip, it would still work. Compare this to editing scripts for clips and buttons using the traditional method (that is, selecting the object and opening the Actions panel). Only mouse events are available for buttons, and only clip events are available for Movie Clips. However, the list of events that can have callbacks identified is the same for buttons and clips (see Figure 14.1).

In my opinion, it's easiest to simply create Movie Clips and treat them as buttons by identifying callbacks for appropriate states (such as `onPress`). As you'll see in the following section, however, other issues arise.

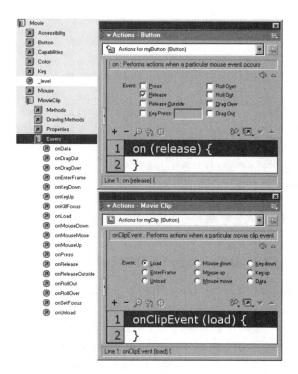

Figure 14.1 *Traditional button and clip events (right) are all available for callbacks functions (left).*

{ Note }

By now you should be familiar with how the keyword `this` refers to the current timeline or, when used inside a function, refers to the function itself. That poses an interesting and confusing issue when defining callbacks. Specifically, the `this` of a callback function refers to the clip or button to which it's assigned, but normally `this` refers to the current timeline. That is, in the callback form `myButton.onPress=function(){trace(this);}`, you'll see the button instance (`myButton`) in the Output window when it's pressed. However, the equivalent conventional code attached right to a button, `on(press){trace(this);}`, will display the timeline where the button resides.

This issue means that you *can't* always add `this` in front of a variable or clip name to explicitly refer to the current timeline. For example, these two code snippets are different:

```
myButton.onPress=function(){
  this.myVariable=100;
  this._alpha=50;
}
```

```
myButton.onPress=function(){
  myVariable=100;
  _alpha=50;
}
```

In the first case, the variable and property affected (`myVariable` and `_alpha`) are both that of the `myButton` instance. But in the second case the variable and property affected are those of whatever timeline where this code resides. It's really not a huge deal when you think about it, but it often messes me up. It's not a bug—after all, you need ways to reference the current timeline or the instance generically. You just can't assume `this` always means "the current timeline."

How a Movie Clip Becomes a Button

Assigning callback functions has several benefits. On the surface, assigning callbacks is mainly just a different approach than putting code right on buttons and clips. It's more than that, however, because other objects have no other alternative (text field instances, sounds, and even data that is loaded externally—to name a few). Even more than serving as an alternative to the traditional way of using buttons and clips, assigning callback functions can make a clip behave like a button. Quite simply, the range of events available to clips includes those once reserved only for buttons. Buttons are (or were) great because they include such events as `press` and `release`, whereas clips have only `mouseDown` and `mouseUp`—and these trigger regardless of where the user clicks. Anyway, it's nice to skip buttons all together by assigning callback functions for whichever event you choose.

Like most things, a few issues crop up. In the preceding section, I showed how you could make a clip act like a button with this code:

```
myClip.onRollOver=function(){this._alpha=50;}
myClip.onRollOut=function(){this._alpha=100;}
```

I'll show you other ways besides an alpha change to treat the rollover effect in a minute. Notice that with just one more line of code, the clip can respond to a mouse press:

```
myClip.onPress=function(){trace("you pressed");}
```

(Naturally, you could replace the `trace` command with some meaningful code.) That works great. What's really interesting is that by simply assigning a callback on a clip to any of those "button-like" events, Flash automatically displays the hand cursor when the user rolls over (just like buttons). It's simple to turn off (for clips or buttons) by setting the `showHandCursor` property to `false`, as the following code shows:

```
myClip.showHandCursor=false;
```

By the way, there's also a similar property, called `enabled`, which not only turns off the cursor, but also causes the button (or clip acting like a button) to be inactive (for example, `my_btn.enabled=false`).

At this point, I've shown you the basics of how a clip can *act* like a button. But there's more—namely, how to make the clip *look* like a button. You should know that traditional button symbols automatically have an Up-, Over-, Down-, and Hit-state (see Figure 14.2). Naturally, if a clip is to replace a button, it will need to have all these states as well.

Figure 14.2 *Traditional buttons symbols have four states: Up, Over, Down, and Hit.*

Unless you're happy with button states that simply change a clip property (like `_alpha` above), you'll want to tap into those four states. To have your clip use the button states, you just need to create frame labels that read (exactly): `_up`, `_over`, and `_down`. (We'll get to the Hit-state in a minute.) That's pretty easy. You'll find out pretty fast that (like any clip with multiple frames) you'll need a `stop()` script in the first frame. But, as long as your symbol has those three frame labels, and somewhere you identify a callback (for at least one mouse event), your clip will do what a button can. What's cool is that you're not limited to one frame per state, although you'll have to place a `play()` script in the labeled frame if you want them to play. Figure 14.3 shows the insides of such a clip.

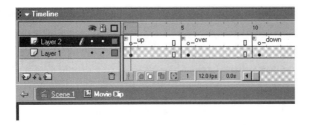

Figure 14.3 *A Movie Clip symbol treated like a button will need the labels _up, _over, and _down to appear like a button.*

Finally, the Hit-state: Inside a button, the graphics in the Hit frame define the shape that's clickable. In clips turned buttons, you can't simply create a label called _hit (which certainly was the first thing I tried). Rather, you have to assign the Hit-state area with a script. The hitArea property defines the clip that will serve as the clickable shape. The form is buttonClip.hitArea=otherClip, where otherClip is an instance name of a clip. (And that other clip doesn't even have to be visible.) For example, suppose that your clip instance in the main timeline (myClip) contains only some text, and you also have a nice big box shape instance (box) placed underneath myClip. The following code (placed in a keyframe) will make the clip act like a button, use the box as the Hit-state, and then make the box invisible:

```
myClip.onPress=function(){trace("it works");}
myClip.hitArea=box;
box._visible=false;
```

The first line just makes the clip behave like a button; that is, the hand cursor and any frames named _up, _over, and _down will work properly. The second line specifies that box will define the clickable area. Then, the third line hides the box.

{ Note }

The process for defining the hitArea clip is fairly straightforward, but I have a couple of warnings. First, you should definitely consider making such a clip even though it's optional. Without it, the default hitArea that gets used is whichever state is currently visible. If the area occupied by the Over-state is significantly different than the Up-state, the result could be that the button will blink (that is, roll over the button—see the Over-state). If that Over-state means that the graphic has moved and is no longer under the button, however, you've really rolled off and you're back to the Up-state (where you roll again)—hence, the blink. This never happens with regular buttons because the last keyframe is always used if no Hit-state is created.

Second, it's likely that you'll want to hide the `hitArea` clip—that's okay. It's also alright to nest that clip inside your "button clip" symbol. However, regardless of whether that `hitArea` clip is visible, it must be present in all the state frames (_up, _over, and _down). Just put it in its own layer. Setting the `hitArea` points to a clip, not just to the shape of that clip; therefore, if it moves or changes, the current shape is used for each state.

Although making your clips act like buttons might look like a little extra work, once you get the hang of it, I'm sure you'll find it convenient. We'll come back to such "clip buttons" in the "Registering Custom Classes" section later in this chapter. For now, let's review and look at a few of the limits to callback functions.

Limits to Callback Functions

Callback functions have a particular limit in that only one function can be defined for any one event on a particular instance. That is, if your button instance named `my_btn` has an `onPress` event assigned to a function that displays "hi," and then you decide to assign a new callback to the `onPress` event (for example, to display "hello"), the old function will be wiped away.

In addition to having only one function per instance, each instance must have its event specified individually. It's not as though two instances can't trigger the same function (that's like the first set of examples where the function name was specified instead of all the code being placed "in line"). However, every instance must have an instance name, and you have to account for each one individually. The name can be verbose (if you have a lot of buttons), but you can always refer to clips dynamically (by using the familiar `path[stringName]` form). For example, the following code assigns a callback function to the buttons `my_btn_1` through `my_btn_10`:

```
for(i=1;i<11;i++){
  this["my_btn_"+i].onPress=function(){_root.play();}
}
```

This looping technique can be particularly useful when you want to disable or enable a bunch of buttons at once—just change the line inside the loop to `this["my_btn"].enabled=false;`.

There's not much more to it than to understand these two limits: Instances can have only one callback per event at a time, and the callbacks of each instance have to be defined individually. If you find yourself wanting an instance to trigger more than one function every time a particular event occurs, you must find another way. The callback function can simply trigger more than one standard function if you want. Another way is to use "listeners." You might recall from Chapter 10, "Keyboard Access and Modifying Onscreen Text," that listeners give you a way to mix and match the response to a particular event. (Listeners are reviewed later in this chapter, too.) The big catch is that most events (to which you can define a callback function) don't work as listeners—but some of them do. (More later.)

In many ways, the limits of callbacks make some tricky code very simple. For example, say you want a toggle button that pauses and plays alternatively. Check out this concise code:

```
1 function stopTime(){
2   stop();
3   my_btn.onPress=pauseTime;
4 }
5 function pauseTime(){
6   play();
7   my_btn.onPress=stopTime;
8 }
9 my_btn.onPress=stopTime;
```

The stopTime() function stops the play head and then reassigns the my_btn instance's onPress event to the other function (pauseTime). In line 5, you see the declaration for the pauseTime() function, which basically does the opposite. Finally, line 9 gets things started by assigning the my_btn instance's onPress event to the stopTime function.

There's no problem in overriding the events in this way. That brings up the fact you can effectively "turn off" a callback by assigning the event to equal null, as in my_btn.onPress=null.

Finally, there *is* a way to automatically assign the same callback function for each and every instance of a particular object type (even if they're not yet on the Stage). We'll discuss this technique more in the "Overriding Built-In Methods" section later, but it's worth showing briefly now.

The form to override an event (or method) is:

```
theObjectType.prototype.theEvent=theFunction
```

The only part used verbatim is `prototype`; everything else is replaced. For example, if you want every button to change its alpha when the user's cursor goes over it, use the following code (but read the follow-up text for warnings):

```
Button.prototype.onRollOver=function(){this._alpha=50;}
```

This should look somewhat familiar to adding methods to the prototype of homemade objects, the way you did in the preceding chapter. However, here we're saying that we want to affect the Button class (that is, the master definition of all buttons). Every button (or any object) has all its methods stuffed in the `prototype` property. Initially, the values for `onPress`, `onRollOver`, and so on are simply undefined. By executing a line of code like the preceding, you're saying that you want every button's initial value for `onRollOver` to be assigned the value of that function (which sets the individual button's `_alpha` to 50). The only warning is that executing this code will wipe away any other functions previously stored in a particular instance. Similarly, any subsequent callbacks assigned to this event will wipe away this one. Think of the preceding code as providing a default value for the `onRollOver` event. (More about this overriding later.)

Registering Custom Classes

Although we looked at a lot of theory and practical uses for homemade objects in the last chapter, the topic of registering custom classes fits well in this chapter. In fact, any time that you create a constructor function, you're really defining a class. However, homemade objects (despite being a lot of fun) are never visualized unless you take steps to affect onscreen clips and text. That is, an object is simply stored in a variable but you don't see anything unless you (by hand) tie it to something onscreen. In fact, no instances of your homemade object (class) exist unless you instantiate them.

The new `registerClass()` method makes it possible to create a class (or definition of your homemade object) that automatically inherits all the features of the built-in Movie Clip class. At the same time, you associate a particular symbol with your class so that every time that symbol is instantiated (dragged out of the Library), you'll be instantiating an object of the homemade class. This means you can design a homemade object that is automatically linked to something visual—and it will behave just like the parent object but with additional methods and properties that you define. For example, you can make a Button class that is just like any other button clip, but which automatically displays a checkmark that toggles on and off. We'll do just that. Not only will the onPress event trigger a callback to display or remove the checkmark graphic, but onPress will also trigger any other function you want—and that function can be different for each instance of the button. That is, we'll effectively get around the fact that one button can have only one onPress event callback. If it sounds to you like the "super button" we're going to create is sort of like a component, you're right. The point is, the registerClass() method is an integral part of how components can supplement your movies without conflicting what's already present.

Basic Form

Even though registerClass() is used extensively in the creation of components, you don't have to be making a component to use it. (And, for that matter, you don't have to use registerClass() if you're making a component.) We won't get into components until it makes sense to do so—both later in this chapter and then again in Chapter 15, "Components."

The three steps to register a custom class are as follows:

1. Define the constructor function for the class.

2. Establish the class is a child of the built-in Movie Clip class (that is, inherit everything from it).

3. Register the class.

Here's a starter script:

```
1 function MyClass () { }
2 MyClass.prototype = new MovieClip();
3 Object.registerClass("symbolID",MyClass);
```

Line 1 is the constructor. You can place initialization scripts in the constructor, but you don't have to (you still need this minimum). (By the way, as a convention, programmers usually capitalize their class names.) Line 2 says that MyClass's prototype property is assigned the value of a new Movie Clip (which is *really* saying that it's a child of the Movie Clip class). Finally, line 3 registers the new class called MyClass (the one we've been fashioning) and ties it to a symbol with identifier symbolID. Remember, an identifier is different than the symbol's name—it's specified from the symbol's linkage setting (accessible from the Library's option menu).

{ Note }

Notice how I defined the constructor for a class:

```
function MyClass () { }
```

This is just like how we made constructors in the preceding chapter. I think it's clearest in this form. However, you may also see programmers use the following code instead:

```
MyClass = function () { }
```

Although it's not exactly the same, it performs the same. It's worth knowing because you'll probably see it both ways.

In practice you'll likely include more code than the minimum. Specifically, you'll define callback functions for any event you desire. The callbacks will be tied to the `prototype` property so that they will be common to all instances of the object you design. Such definitions must appear after the prototype is set equal to a new `MovieClip()` (line 2 above) and before the class is registered (line 3 above) For example, notice the new line of code (line 6) that will cause all instances to move when the `enterFrame` event occurs:

```
1 //constructor:
2 function MyClass () { }
3 //inherit MovieClip class attributes
4 MyClass.prototype = new MovieClip();
5 //override the enterFrame event
6 MyClass.prototype.onEnterFrame=function(){this._x++;}
7 //register the class
8 Object.registerClass("symbolID",MyClass);
```

The form is always "class dot prototype dot event equals function," and `prototype` is used verbatim. You actually don't need to define the callbacks before registering the class. If you define callbacks for the `prototype` of your object in a later script, it still works (it just won't start working until you execute the script). What's really wild is that once the class is registered, you can address it from anywhere in your movie. It's not like how you address a variable name by using the path to the variable. It's just like how you can always say `MovieClip.prototype.onEnterFrame=function(){}` to affect every instance of Movie Clips (and descendants, including instances of the `MyClass` class). Every instance of the symbol with the identifier "symbolID" will automatically be an instance of the `MyClass` class and, thus, be affected by anything you do to that class.

Before I show a practical example, I need to emphasize the importance of the sequence of scripts. If you intend for clip instances to be instances of your custom class, you must register the class *before* any instances are on the Stage. For example, say you place an instance of the symbol with the identifier, "symbolID," on the Stage and give it an instance name of `myInstance`. If in the same frame you execute the three minimum lines of code (from the preceding starter script), you will see that the expression `(myInstance instanceof MyClass)` is false and that `(myInstance instanceof MovieClip)` is true. That is, the instance is part of the `MovieClip` class (not the `MyClass` class). The problem is that if an instance is already on the Stage when you execute the code, that instance's class has already been decided. Imagine you are born in the U.S. to American parents. If later, your parents change their citizenship to another country, you're still an American citizen.

All you need to do is to register the class before any instances are on the Stage. One way is to simply place at least those three lines of code in the first keyframe and then place instances on the Stage in the second frame or later. (To verify that it works, use the `instanceof` operator, as in `trace(myInstance instanceof MyClass)`, which should display `true`.)

The other way to register a class before the symbol is instantiated is by using the `#initclip` *event*. It's not really an event, but it enables you to execute scripts before the symbol is instantiated. The way it works is you place all your code between `#initclip` and `#endinitclip` (sort of like putting code between the opening and closing curly braces). You must place this code in the first frame of a symbol. So, just go inside the master symbol (the one with the identifier "symbolID") and place the following code in the first frame:

```
#initclip
function MyClass() { }
MyClass.prototype = new MovieClip();
Object.registerClass("symbolID",MyClass);
#endiniticlip
```

Now if you place an instance of this symbol on the Stage and give it an instance name `myInstance`, the expression `myInstance instanceof MyClass` will be `true` (and `myInstance instanceof MovieClip` will be `false`). Even more exciting than seeing `true` or `false` in the Output window is the fact that you can execute a line of code like the following to affect every instance of this class (without affecting any regular clips that happen to be present):

```
MyClass.prototype.onEnterFrame=function(){this._x++;}
```

Because I know seeing clips move across the screen might still be less than thrilling, I've created the following practical example of what we've seen so far.

Practical Example: Registering a Class

This example shows a button with an automatic checkmark. (You can download the source files for this example from www.phillipkerman.com/actionscripting.) First I make a new Movie Clip symbol and give it a linkage identifier of "myButton." Then I make three named frames (_up, _over, and _down) where I draw the different states for my button. Still inside the symbol, but in a separate layer (that spans the whole timeline), I draw a shape to become the hit area, convert it to a Movie Clip symbol, and give it an instance name of hitShape. Then I draw a checkmark, convert it to a symbol, and name the instance checkMark. Figure 14.4 shows the clip structure.

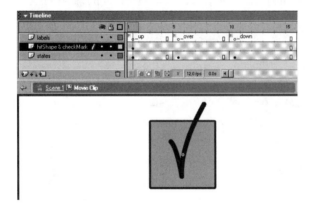

Figure 14.4 *Here are the insides of the clip that will act like a button.*

Finally, I place the following code in the first frame of the button symbol:

```
1 stop();
2 #initclip
3 function MyButtonClass () { }
4 MyButtonClass.prototype = new MovieClip();
5
6 MyButtonClass.prototype.onLoad = function(){
7   this.hitArea = this.hitShape;
8   this.hitShape._visible = false;
9   this.checked = false;
10   this.checkMark._visible=false;
11 }
12
13 MyButtonClass.prototype.onRelease = function(){
```

```
14   this.checked = !this.checked;
15   this.checkMark._visible= this.checked;
16 }
17
18 Object.registerClass("buttonClip",MyButtonClass);
19 #endinitclip
```

Line 1 stops the timeline from continuing to the other frames (for the other
states). Once this clip has a mouse event (onRelease), it automatically will display those frames. Line 2 begins the script that executes before the symbol loads.
Line 3 is the constructor function (not much there, eh?). Line 4 says that this
symbol will inherit all the built-in properties that clips have. Lines 6 and 13
define a couple of callbacks for the prototype property of this class (onLoad and
onRelease). Again, the callbacks are attached to the prototype property because
I want every instance of this class to share them. In onLoad, I do four things:
Line 7 specifies the clip to be used for the hitArea (the clip I named hitShape),
line 8 makes that clip invisible, line 9 sets the homemade variable checked to
false, and line 10 makes the checkMark instance invisible (at the start).

The onRelease callback function first changes the checked variable from false
to true (or true to false) in line 14. Then it sets the _visible property of the
clip checkMark to false or true. Basically, onRelease is just a toggle. Finally,
line 18 registers the class. At this point, I can drag as many instances of the clip
on the Stage, and they all will have an automatic checkmark.

There's nothing wrong with the MyButtonClass. However, there's nothing all that
special about it, either. In fact, it would be easy to pull off the same effect without defining a class. I could put an invisible button inside a clip and do the same
basic thing without much trouble. This was just a start; once you have the class
designed, adding to it is easy. The first thing we should do to this class is to make
it so that the onRelease event can do more than just display or hide a checkmark.
If you have an instance of this clip on the Stage and place code right on the clip,
it won't interfere with the onRelease callback inside the class definition. That is,
the following code works without a problem:

```
on(release){
  trace("do something");
}
```

However, that's the old way (of putting code right on an instance). If the instance
name is myInstance, the following code will actually override the onRelease
event in the class for just that instance (and the checkmark will fail):

```
myInstance.onRelease=function(){trace("do something");}
```

Instead of worrying about overwriting the class's onRelease event, we can just add to the code in the class definition. Specifically, we'll make the onRelease event both display the checkmark *and* invoke a function. However, if we just add a line of code such as _root.myFunction(), every instance will trigger the same function. In order to have multiple instances that do different things, we need to turn the clip into a component. The following chapter explores the process in greater detail, but I'll show you how to apply it here. The idea is that after you drag a particular instance of the symbol onto the Stage, you specify the name of the function you want to be triggered. Here is an extra line of code that goes at the end of the onRelease callback function in the class definition (after line 15, shown earlier):

```
_root[this.handler](this.checked)
```

Although this might not look traditional, it's actually quite simple. The idea is that the name of the function will actually be a string (stored in the variable this.handler). Because we can't just invoke a function with a string name, we use the familiar technique of placing the string in brackets and preceding it with the path to the function. Also, when invoking a function, we have to follow the function name with parentheses. Just to make it more interesting, I'm passing as a parameter the value of the checked variable. Now all we need to do is to define a function in the main timeline of the movie, and then figure out a way to let the author using this symbol specify a unique value for the handler variable. Here's the code you can put in the main timeline:

```
function toggleTime(whichWay){
  if(whichWay==true){
    play();
  }else{
    stop();
  }
}
```

This way toggleTime(true) will make the movie play and toggleTime(false) will make it pause. Again, we could have easily made the main movie stop or play from inside the class definition, but we're going to have only one instance of the button triggering the toggleTime() function. Other buttons can trigger other functions that we declare. All we need to do now is to give the using author a way to specify a different function for each instance of the button. Select the symbol in the Library and choose Component Definition from the options menu. Then, in the dialog box, click the plus button and replace varName with handler. Click OK and the clip becomes a component. At this point, you can select an instance of this symbol on the Stage and, through the Parameters tab in the Properties panel, set the value `toggle time` for `handler` (see Figure 14.5).

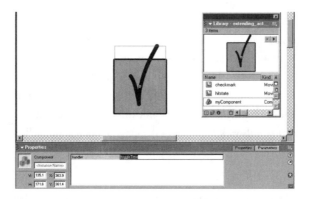

Figure 14.5 *An instance of the component we created can have its* `handler` *variable set via the Properties panel's Parameters tab.*

This was actually a pretty fancy component—but you'll learn more later. The features we add to the button in the next section will work regardless of whether the symbol is actually a component.

{ Note }

Before we move on to adding properties to our custom classes, I should probably note that you can do more than define callback functions for standard events such as `onPress`. When designing your classes, you'll likely want to create methods. These can be accessible from outside scripts (so called *public methods*) or they might be only for use inside the class. Whether they're public or private is just a matter of how they're used. The syntax for methods is the same as that for defining a callback (but you come up with your own name)—something like: `MyClass.prototype.someMethod=function(){//the code}`. The point I'm trying to make is that you're not limited to just extending the built-in features; you can make your own methods. All the knowledge from the preceding chapter can be easily applied here.

Adding "Getter/Setter" Properties

Even though I recommend thinking of homemade variables as homemade properties, they aren't quite the same thing. The syntax to refer to or change them is the same, but they differ in that built-in properties have an immediate (and usually visual) result when they change. That is, change the _alpha property and you see something. That's not the case if you change a homemade variable. All this leads to the fact that when you define classes, you can also define true properties.

These properties are called *getter/setter* properties. You can *get* them (to see their values) and *set* them (to change their values). Flash does not constantly monitor the getter/setter properties. Actually, they are not calculated unless a script tries to set or get them. Anyway, when you make your own properties, you need to define both what should happen when a script sets them and how the value is derived when a script tries to get them. For example, if someone changes the value for the checked variable, aren't you supposed to see something happen? (In the Button class above, if you change an instance's value of checked to anInstance.checked=true, you wouldn't "see" anything happen.)

The basic form of creating a property is:

```
Class.addProperty("property", getFunction, setFunction);
```

The only part that is used verbatim is addProperty. Basically, you name the property you want to create (in quotes) and identify both a function that executes when someone tries to get the value and a function for when he sets the value. You can actually replace getFunction and setFunction with full function definitions "in-line" (but I thought that would be too messy as an example). The form of those two functions is standard, but their jobs are very specific. Namely, getFunction should end with a line that returns the new value of the property. setFunction automatically comes with a parameter (the value of which is the new value for the property at hand). It's probably easiest to see this in a practical example. Suppose that you want to create a new property called _left that contains the left side of any Movie Clip. In this case (and in order to skip all the registerClass() stuff), we'll just extend the built-in Movie Clip class, as follows:

```
1 function getLeft(){
2   var theLeft = this._x - (this._width/2);
3   return theLeft;
4 }
5 function setLeft(toWhat){
6   this._x = toWhat + (this._width/2);
7 }
8 MovieClip.prototype.addProperty("_left",getLeft,setLeft);
```

Notice that line 3 returns the calculated value. That is, if there's a clip instance called myClip and some script says trace(myClip._left), the value returned (after the word `return`) is what appears in the Output window. Also notice that the `setLeft()` function (line 5) expects to receive a parameter (given the name `toWhat` in this case). This is just like a freebie that you get with setter functions. After all, if a script later tries to set the `_left` property (for example, `myClip._left=100`), we need a way to know what value the property is to become (`100`). Finally, the last line uses `addProperty()` to specify that the property name will be `_left`, the getter function will be `getLeft`, and the setter will be `setLeft`. We're using the `addProperty()` method on the Movie Clip's prototype to affect all instances of clips. This is a really useful example. After entering the preceding code, you can set or get any clip's `_left` property. `MyClip._left=100` will move the clip so that its left is at `100`. This example should give you a few ideas of what's possible. (Note that this particular example assumes that the clip's default registration point is the center.)

Here's another practical example. Take the preceding `MyButtonClass` example. It's easy enough to tint the `checkMark` instance, but it will always take two steps (create the Color object, and then use the `setRGB()` method). Let's make a new property called `shade`. You can place the following code right before the `registerClass()` method:

```
MyButtonClass.prototype.setColor=function(toWhat){
  this.c=new Color(this.checkMark);
  this.c.setRGB(toWhat);
}
MyButtonClass.prototype.getColor=function(){
  return this.shade;
}
MyButtonClass.prototype.addProperty("shade",
➥MyButtonClass.prototype.getColor,MyButtonClass.prototype.setColor );
```

By adding the functions `setColor` and `getColor` to the `MyButtonClass`'s prototype (as well as using `addProperty` on the class's prototype), you give every instance of this button clip a `shade` property. If you have an instance called `myInstance`, you can say `myInstance.shade=0xFF0000;` to turn the checkmark red.

Adding properties is a bit more involved than just making up homemade variables. You have to script everything that you expect to happen when the property changes. Once you set things up, however, it can be really fun.

{ Note }

I think this is a good time to demystify the term *polymorphism*. Polymorphism is nothing more than two different classes responding to the same named property or method with different responses. For example, both a circle and a square can have an area property. Calculating area for a circle (PI r^2) is different than calculating area for a square (side^2)—but they both have an "area." A simple definition of *polymorphism* might be "the same result, but derived differently."

One way to apply polymorphism to what we've seen so far would be to create a getter/setter property called shade for an entirely different class. Instead of changing the color of the checkmark, you could have it tint the clip itself. The point is that you would just modify the other class's idea of what "shade" means. Polymorphism really is an easy concept. Applying it to real projects is a little more work.

Inheritance with Classes

We've seen that when creating a custom class, you can make your class automatically inherit the standard methods and properties of a plain Movie Clip. You can take this even further. For example, you can design one class (that inherits Movie Clip attributes), but then make other classes that inherit from the first class (and, thus, they'll inherit from the Movie Clip class as well). That is, you might want several classes that are unique in many ways, but similar in a few ways too. You can define all the ways they're similar in your "parent" class and then let all the different "children" inherit from the parent. Of course, if the parent inherits everything from the Movie Clip class, all the children will do so as well.

To make inheritance work, the parent class is defined first so that when the children say, "Inherit from the parent," the parent already has been defined. All you really need to know is that you can change #initclip to read #initclip 0 and #initclip 1. The lower numbers execute first. To make the children inherit from a homemade class (not from the Movie Clip class), change the part that reads

```
MyClass.prototype=new MovieClip();
```

to

```
MyClass.prototype=new MyParentClass();
```

It's important that MyParentClass has been defined when this executes. (And the #initclip numbers control that.)

Here's a relatively simple example in which the parent clip (with a linkage identifier of "parent") contains the following code in its first frame:

```
#initclip 0
function ParentClass (){}
ParentClass.prototype=new MovieClip();
ParentClass.prototype.setColor=function(toWhat){
    this.c=new Color(this);
    this.c.setRGB(toWhat);
}
ParentClass.prototype.getColor=function(){
    return this.shade;
}
ParentClass.prototype.addProperty("shade",ParentClass.prototype.getColor,
➥ParentClass.prototype.setColor);

Object.registerClass("parent", ParentClass);
#endinitclip 0
```

There's nothing new here except the #initclip 0 (to make sure this code happens first—at least before #initclip 1). You might notice that this example has no methods or callbacks, just a getter/setter property. You can certainly include more than this. Anyway, the code for the child class (which will automatically include the shade property, as well as anything else that you define) looks like this:

```
#initclip 1
function ChildClass (){}
ParentClass.prototype=new ParentClass ();
Object.registerClass("child", ChildClass);
#endinitclip 1
```

The things to notice here are that everything is in initclip 1 (not 0). Therefore, when line 3 executes, the ParentClass has already been defined (so this class has no trouble being a descendant). Finally, this clip's identifier is child. Naturally, you can add more methods, callbacks, or properties to this definition. You don't need to define the shade property, however, because it was automatically inherited from ParentClass in line 3!

Instead of droning on with another example, just wait until Workshop Chapter 9, "Creating a ToolTip Component," where we put some of this to practical use.

Listeners and Watchers

The next couple of sections cover topics not directly related to callbacks and classes. However, both listeners and watchers fit here nicely because they provide things that are either difficult or impossible to achieve with callbacks or classes.

Specifically, the fact that you can have only one callback function defined per event is effectively circumvented with listeners. Although they're not the same as events, listeners are cumulative; therefore, you can have several listeners listening for the same event. Similarly, watchers get around a frustrating fact about getter/setter properties. Specifically, properties are not continuously updated. Only when a script says, "Hey, change this property" or "What's that property's value?" does Flash go and set or get that property. Although this way is more efficient, it's frustrating because you might want to monitor one property's value. If the value ever goes too high, for example, you might want to respond. It's not totally efficient to be continuously checking a property's value—but watchers do that in an efficient way. The truth be told, you can't actually use watchers on getter/setter properties, and you can't use listeners on most events; nonetheless, they're useful and certainly worth studying as a comparison.

Listeners Basics

Listeners enable you to define which function will trigger when a particular event occurs. It's almost the same as callback functions, although the list of events that you can use as listeners does not include every event imaginable. For example, no button events (such as onPress) can be used as a listener. The advantage of listeners is that they're easy to add and remove and they don't conflict with each other. That is, one event (say a text field instance's onChanged event) can be listened for and trigger a particular function. You can easily add more listeners or other events without affecting existing listeners.

To create listeners, you always follow the same basic form: store a generic object in a variable; identify callback functions to events attached to that variable; and then add the listener to the instance to which you want to listen. Here's an example with dummy names:

```
myListener=new Object();
myListener.eventName=function(){trace("event happened");}
someInstance.addListener(myListener);
```

You can use any legitimate variable name in place of myListener. Also, you must replace eventName with one of the event names that may be used for the someInstance object type. Because there are different events for text fields than, say, the Key object, you must use an appropriate event name. Finally, in the last line, you replace someInstance with the instance name you want to listen to. Alternatively, you also can add listeners to classes, such as the Key object class.

In such cases, you just replace someInstance with the class name (for example, Key.addListener(myListener)).

We did a few nice practical examples of listeners in Chapter 10 that applied to the Selection, Key, and TextField objects. Here's an example of using a listener on the Mouse object that requires that you have a clip instance (named "clip") in the main timeline. The following code goes in a frame script:

```
myListener=new Object();
myListener.onMouseMove=function(){
  _root.clip._x=_root._xmouse;
  _root.clip._y=_root._ymouse;
  updateAfterEvent();
  }
Mouse.addListener(myListener);
```

In practice, this example would probably be easier if you typed the following (equivalent) instead:

```
clip.onMouseMove=function(){
  this._x=_root._xmouse;
  this._y=_root._ymouse;
  updateAfterEvent();
}
```

Using listeners always requires at least three steps (creating the generic object, assigning a callback, and then adding the listener). Once you've created the listener, you can modify it in a few ways. If you can add more callback functions to the listener object, the updates appear immediately. For example, using the example above (not the alternative just shown), you could use the following code to make the clip rotate every time the user clicks:

```
myListener.onMouseDown=function(){_root.clip._rotation++;}
```

There are two things to notice. First, adding a new callback to the myListener variable can happen at any time—even after the addListener method. Also, the following code will *not* work because this will be the function itself, not the clip:

```
myListener.onMouseDown=function(){this._rotation++;}
```

Finally, you can also override any callback currently stored in an event of the myListener variable. That is, another line that begins myListener.onMouseDown=... will replace the function already in that event.

Removing a listener is easy, you just say:

```
Mouse.removeListener(myListener);
```

(Replace Mouse with the object or instance to which you added the listener in the first place.) I should mention that in addition to supplementing, overriding, and removing listeners, you can add additional listeners that respond to the same event. For example, even after you have added the myListener listener to the Mouse object, you can fashion a new one and have it respond to the onMouseMove event as well. All you have to do is use a new variable name for your listener object, as follows:

```
myOtherListener=new Object();
myOtherListener.onMouseMove=function(){_root.clip2._x=_root._xmouse;}
Mouse.addListener(myOtherListener);
```

In this case, the other clip instance, clip2, will track the mouse's x coordinate. That you are able to turn listeners on and off at will makes them very convenient. The only trouble with listeners is that there aren't enough of them. (Like I say, you won't find any for clips or buttons.)

Watchers

Setting up a watch on a variable is a way to identify which function you want to execute every time that variable changes. It works only on variables or properties in generic objects, not getter/setter properties—but it's still powerful.

The form gets a little weird, so let's look at it one step at a time. The basic form is as follows:

```
this.watch("myVariable", responseFunction);
```

You can replace this with another address if the variable you're watching is in a different timeline. The variable you're watching (myVariable) appears between quotes (which is weird because you'd normally expect variables to appear without quotes). Finally, responseFunction is replaced with either the name of a function declared elsewhere or (preferably) with an inline version. responseFunction (which can be named anything you want) is interesting because it automatically includes up to four parameters. Here's a sample version (that would have needed to appear above the line of code containing the watch method above):

```
function responseFunction(id, oldVal, newVal, userData){
  trace("var"+id+" changed from "+oldVal+"to"+newVal);
  return newVal;
}
```

Before I explain the parameters, let me point out something important. Namely, the last line within this function should always be something equivalent to `return newVal` (or whatever you use for the third parameter name). That is, if you're watching the variable `variableName` and a script executes `myVariable=10`, you probably want `myVariable` to have the value `10`. If you leave out that last line (`return newVal`), the value of `myVariable` will be undefined. If you do something weird like `return newVal/2`, the code `myVariable=10` will actually assign its value to `5`.

Regarding the parameters, think of these as freebies. Any function identified as a "response function" to a watch will always have up to four parameters. You can name them whatever you want, but they always appear in this order: The first parameter (`id`) is simply a string version of the variable being watched. The second parameter (`oldVal`) is the value of the variable before the imminent change. That is, if `myVariable` were currently 4 and the code myVariable=10 executed, the value for `oldVal` in the response function would be 4. It's kind of weird, but realize that the response function triggers the instant any code tries to change the variable being watched. The third parameter (`newVal`) is the value the variable is trying to become. You can think of this as the value that the variable is about to become, but remember that last line of code can effectively change destiny. Finally, the fourth parameter (`userData`) isn't very important. It's just an optional feature that comes into play only if, when setting the watch, you include an additional value as a third parameter of the `watch` method. For example, you could change the initial `watch` method to read:

```
this.watch("myVariable", responseFunction, 123);
```

Then, once inside the `responseFunction`, the value 123 would be received as the value for the fourth parameter. A practical use for this might be to tell you who set up the watch. That is, you could have two different buttons that set up the same watch (on the same variable). When executing the response function, however, you might want to know who set it up in the first place. (This will show up in the following example.)

Before we look at a practical example, let me mention the `unwatch()` method. The form is pretty simple:

```
this.unwatch("myVariable");
```

Just remember to keep the variable name in quotes.

Applied Example Using Watch

Here's an example of controlling text input. I picked this example having just completed a project in Flash 5 that would have been infinitely easier in Flash MX. In that project, users could enter values into several Input Text fields, each of which limited the range of values the users were allowed to enter. Any time that they entered too high or too low of a value, they were immediately instructed to fix their mistake.

This example will cause a clip to jump to frame 2 when the entered value is above 100, or to frame 3 when the value is below 10. If the value is between 10 and 100, the clip will stay on frame 1. Start by making a clip that has a green circle in frame 1, text that reads "too high" in frame 2, and "too low" in frame 3. Also, place a stop() in the first frame of this clip and give it an instance name of clip. Next, make an Input Text field and associate it with the variable name myField. (Normally, I would recommend using a field's text property rather than the "Var:" option in the Properties panel.) Finally, put the following code in the first frame of the main timeline:

```
1 function checkField(id, oldVal, newVal){
2   _root.clip.gotoAndStop(1);
3   if (newVal>100){
4     _root.clip.gotoAndStop(2);
5   }
6   if (newVal<10){
7     _root.clip.gotoAndStop(3);
8   }
9   return newVal;
10 }
11 this.watch("myText", checkField);
12 myText=10;
```

The first line of interest is line 11, which says that any time the variable myText changes, you want the checkField function to execute. In checkField, line 2 assumes that the value is within range and makes the clip jump to frame 1. Then the two if statements (lines 3 and 6) check whether the new value is above or below the range (and then make the clip jump to the appropriate frame number).

You might think that a simple callback function (for example, the Input Text field's onChanged event) would be enough to pull off the same effect—you'd be right. However, consider that you might give the user other ways to change the variable myText. For example, you might have two buttons: one that increases the myText variable and one that decreases it. (It turns out that the onChanged event would still work, but only because we're using the Var: option with Input Text field.) The point I'm trying to make is that watchers are good for when you don't want to worry about all the different ways a variable can change—you just want to make sure that you know about it when it does.

One thing about the preceding example is that it's sort of hard-wired to the range of 10–100. To show a use for the fourth parameter (userdata), I've made the following modification to the code:

```
 1 function checkField(id, oldVal, newVal, range){
 2   _root.clip.gotoAndStop(1);
 3   if (newVal>range[1]){
 4     _root.clip.gotoAndStop(2);
 5   }
 6   if (newVal<range[0]){
 7     _root.clip.gotoAndStop(3);
 8   }
 9   return newVal;
10 }
11 this.watch("myText", checkField, [10,100]);
12 myText=10;
```

Notice first that an additional value is passed (in line 11)—specifically, an array [10,100]. (Because this option allows for only one extra value to be passed, I cheated and put two values in one!) Then, in line 1, the checkField function refers to that extra parameter as range. Finally, in lines 3 and 6, I extract the values in the first index and zero index to determine the range. You can pass any kind of data you want for that extra parameter—a generic object, for example.

This example should give you some ideas. Keep in mind that watchers are useful for many variables, not just ones that the user types. Remember, also, that you can only watch homemade variables, not getter/setter properties.

Overriding Built-In Methods

We had so much fun earlier writing our own callback functions that I failed to mention that you can also override many of the methods in the built-in objects (such as Array and Movie Clip). It works much the same way as assigning callback functions on the prototype property of homemade classes. The form is still:

```
Class.prototype.methodName=function(){}
```

For example, if you had the twisted thought of reassigning the standard play() command, you could use the following:

```
MovieClip.prototype.play=function(){this.stop();}
```

This works! Not that you'd want to make play() result in the same thing as stop(), but once the preceding code was executed, it would affect your whole movie. More practical situations arise, however. Suppose that you don't like the way charAt() always counts the beginning of the string with 0. You could override the built-in charAt() method (of the String object) with this code:

```
String.prototype.charAt=function(n){
  return this.substring(n-1,n);
}
```

Because the charAt() method accepts a parameter, the function declaration includes the parameter named n. And because charAt() returns a value, you see that the insides of my function return a value. Finally, the keyword this takes the place of whichever string is having its charAt() found. That is, you always precede the function with a particular string, such as "Phillip".charAt(1). If you put the code trace("Phillip".charAt(1)) before the overriding code, you'll see h in the Output window. However, if you place it anywhere after the code, you'll see P instead.

I don't recommend overriding the built-in methods in either of the ways I've shown, but you should understand that you *can* override them. Flash 5 included several particularly slow-working methods, which have all been improved in Flash MX. However, people in the Flash community often rewrite the code to improve one of these slow-performing methods. In addition, you can override built-in methods to make them perform differently or even fix an inherent bug (of which I don't believe there are any). In these cases, it makes sense to override those built-in methods. Also, if some quirky bug arises, it may be worth fixing it in this way.

Keep in mind that perhaps even more powerful than overriding the built-in methods is the fact you can add to the built-in methods. That is, reassigning a method in the object's prototype property wipes away the old method in that place, but adding new methods to the prototype property is no problem at all. For example, say you want all Movie Clips to have a scaleTo() method. You can create such a method with the following code:

```
MovieClip.prototype.scaleTo=function(n){
  this._xscale=n;
  this._yscale=n;
}
```

From this point forward, you could say `myClip.scaleTo(120)` or `myOtherClip.scaleTo(50)`. Actually, perhaps a better idea would be to simply add a property called `_scale` (currently there's only `_xscale` and `_yscale`) using the techniques discussed earlier. That would be good practice (and is something I've included in the source files online). My point here is not to say that these are the specific things you should do; rather, now that you have the foundation skills under your belt, you should feel free to come up with solutions that fit your needs.

Setting Scripts to Trigger on Schedule

All the wild stuff covered in this chapter should have you pretty excited. There's just one more topic that fits here—even though it isn't really an "extension" of Flash. The `setInterval()` command enables you to identify a function that is to be executed automatically, at whatever frequency you desire. Normally, your scripts have to wait until an event triggers them. It's obvious that a script waiting for a mouse press may take a long time before it executes (especially if the user doesn't click), but even events, such as `enterFrame` and `mouseMove`, or simply reaching script in a keyframe are all limited by either how fast the movie's framerate is or how fast the user can move his mouse. That is, an `enterFrame` script that executes every 1/12 of a second might not be often enough. Conversely, if you only want a script to trigger every 4 seconds, it's somewhat difficult to do inside an `enterFrame` script.

For all the reasons listed previously, `setInterval()` is a great new feature. It's super easy to use. Here's the form:

```
setInterval(functionToTrigger, 1000);
```

Replace `functionToTrigger` with either a function's name or an inline version. Replace the second parameter (`1000` in this case) with the interval in milliseconds between each execution. That is, this example will trigger once every second. If you want something to trigger faster, say once every tenth of a second, use `100`. Here's a simple example:

```
setInterval(function(){trace("all's well")},1000);
```

In this case, the function declaration (the first parameter) appears inline. And, just like clockwork, you'll see "all's well" once every second in the Output window. For something a bit more practical, here's the code to make an instance named "clip" blink on and off every half-second:

```
function blink(){
  clip._visible = !clip._visible;
}
setInterval(blink, 500);
```

In this case, I just moved the function declaration out on its own and referred to it by name in the setInterval() command. An optional feature of setInterval() is to pass values as parameters to the function that gets triggered. For example, you might want to recycle the blink() function and make it work for other clips too. You can pass parameters to the function being triggered by including a third parameter in the setInterval() command. Here is a modified example that blinks the circle instance once a second and the box instance once every other second:

```
function blink(what){
  what._visible= !what._visible;
}
setInterval(blink, 1000, circle);
setInterval(blink, 2000, box);
```

Notice that the blink() function now changes the visible property of whatever is passed in as a parameter. Then I set up two intervals that both trigger the same function but at different frequencies and with a different third parameter. The value of what becomes either circle or box.

Finally, although this is cool, you might want to stop the blinking (or whatever interval you design). You can turn off an interval by using the clearInterval() command. It's slightly tricky because Flash needs to know which interval you intend to clear. To identify which interval is which, you must store each inside a variable. Instead of saying setInterval(func,10), you say myInterval=setInterval(func,10). Then, you can later say clearInterval(myInterval). So, in the preceding example, I could change the last two lines to read:

```
circleInterval=setInterval(blink, 1000, circle);
boxInterval=setInterval(blink, 2000, box);
```

Then, in a later script, you could say `clearInterval(boxInterval)` to stop the box from blinking. You could even get tricky and set up a third interval, which might not execute for 10 seconds, but whose job is to clear the other two intervals. For example:

```
function stopBlinking(){
  clearInterval(circleInterval);
  clearInterval(boxInterval);
  clearInterval(stopper);
}
stopper=setInterval(stopBlinking,10000);
```

(Note that this code is added to the previous example.) You can test this script pretty easily. You might want to do some other "clean up" work in the `stopBlinking()` function. For example, you might want to make sure that both the circle and box clips are visible (or not—depending on what you want).

There are two practical situations for using `setInterval()`: either you have a script that you want to execute very infrequently, or you have a script that you want to execute very frequently but bringing out a Movie Clip just to use the `enterFrame` event is too messy. Also, using `setInterval()` along with `clearInterval()` is sort of like cleaning up as you work.

Summary

This chapter covered some cool stuff. Nearly every feature showed you a different way of doing something that could be achieved other ways. Hopefully, you don't feel that the more traditional techniques covered earlier are all wasted now that you know "better" ways to do things. For one thing, these techniques aren't better unless you can make sense of them. Also, they're not better if you have nothing to which to compare them. In any event, I hope you're encouraged to try some out.

It might be overwhelming to put down the book and try all the different features shown in this chapter. My recommendation is that you try to repeat or expand upon the examples in this chapter. Also, if something comes to mind while you're reading this book, I suggest that you try your idea out using more than one technique. For example, if you thought, "Hey, I can make a clip that blinks every time the user types," you should try to achieve that effect using more than one technique. You could try assigning a callback function and then, regardless of whether it worked, go on to try the same exercise using a custom class. I think the hardest thing to learn is how to apply this information. When the material really starts to gel, you'll be able to pick the most appropriate feature. Until then, try as many as you can. Even if you discover a better way, time spent learning is time well spent.

{ Chapter 15 }

Components

Components are a sophisticated and convenient way to encapsulate code snippets in a form that can be shared and reused. (They were first introduced in Flash 5 as "Smart Clips.") A Movie Clip becomes a component when you specify the parameters that you want the author to modify in each instance. Effectively, you're just extending the properties by which Movie Clip instances can vary from the built-in set of properties (such as _alpha and _xscale) to include anything you design.

Although you will see very advanced examples of components in the Components panel when you first launch Flash MX, just because components *can* be very advanced, they don't have to be. For example, you can make a simple component that serves to automate a small portion of just one project. The most important fact to realize is that everyone can make components. (We walk through practical uses for some of the Flash UI (User Interface) components in Workshop Chapter 7, "Adapting Built-In Components.")

In this chapter, you will

- Learn all the steps involved to turn a Movie Clip into a component

- Create adaptable parameters that the author can modify when using your component

- Explore some practical uses for components, such as improving productivity, ensuring consistency, and centralizing code

- Build custom user interfaces (custom UIs) that serve to replace the generic Parameters tab with one you build in Flash

- Create Live Preview files so that your component instances will reflect their settings while authoring (without requiring you to select Test Movie)

- Learn how to distribute and install components so that they appear in the Flash interface

Before beginning this chapter, you should realize that components are used only for authoring. After you build a component, you can use it as many times as you want. You can even share it with others. It makes sense to do so because you might spend a lot of time making the component really useful and adaptable to any situation. Because this means there are two authors, it makes sense to refer differently to the author who builds the original component and the "using author" (that is, the person who uses the finished component while building a Flash movie). After you build a component, you could become the using author. In this chapter, I will distinguish between an "author" and a "using author."

Components Overview

In Chapter 7, "The Movie Clip Object," you learned how to think of variables contained inside clip instances as homemade properties because you access and change them using the same syntax (`clip.property` or `clip.variable`). This concept will help when you create components. The process involves specifying which clip variables (homemade properties) the using author can be initialize. An individual component's initial values are set through the Component Parameters panel or the Parameters tab in the Properties panel (see Figure 15.1). Each component instance has a unique starting value for any variable, just as each instance of a clip can have different starting values for any built-in property. Call them "parameters," "variables," or "homemade properties"—they're all the same. And, components are adjustable to the using author.

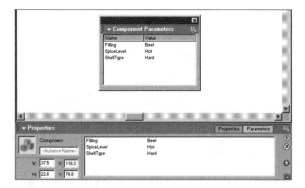

Figure 15.1   *The author can specify variables uniquely for every instance of a component by using either the Component Parameters panel or the Parameters tab in the Properties panel.*

The process of *using* a component is simple: drag an instance on Stage and set the initial values for the parameters (in either the Component Parameters panel or Properties panel). Then, when the movie plays, it's as though each instance has a different onClipEvent(load) event to assign the values for each variable uniquely for each instance. What's the point? You could just write an onClipEvent(load) script for each instance, and you would avoid components altogether. The problem, however, is that it's a lot more work and the process is less intuitive. (For example, you'd have to remember to include assignments for each variable.) Plus, a fully functioning component takes advantage of two features: a custom user interface (custom UI), which replaces the Component Parameters panel with a Flash movie to guide the using author through populating the data, and Live Preview, which enables the using author to see the populated clip while authoring. If nothing else, a component is an error-resistant method for the using author to specify parameters. For example, he can't accidentally double-click the master symbol and modify it.

Ultimately, a component can make you a more efficient programmer. You can write one block of code that behaves differently depending on the values of the variables that have been initialized through the Component Parameters panel. For example, the component could contain Dynamic Text fields of a specific font and layout. If you have specified the values for the text field variables in the Component Parameters panel, each instance will display different text, but the font and layout will remain the same. This is a perfect example of code-data separation (discussed in Chapter 3, "The Programmer's Approach"). In addition, just like any Movie Clip, if you make a change to the master in the Library (for example, you change the font in the Dynamic Text field), you'll see that change in every instance. In this way, a component can serve to establish consistent text styles.

Another simple example is a component that controls the animation of a ball bouncing. The ball will bounce as many times as the using author specifies for the bounceCount variable. He could have several instances of the same component, but each would bounce a different number of times.

Let's first look at a few basic components, and then we'll look at more advanced, practical examples.

Making Components

Similar to a lot of programming, sometimes it's best to start by hard-wiring a prototype and then come back to clean up things, which makes the code more adaptable. Let's go through some (non-component-related) solutions to making individual clips behave differently.

Solutions That Don't Use Components

First, consider a Movie Clip with a 20-frame animation. In the last frame, place a script that reads as follows:

```
loopsRemaining--;
if (loopsRemaining>0) {
  this.gotoAndPlay (1);
} else {
  this.gotoAndStop (1);
}
```

(We'll keep this script for a few examples.) The first line of the preceding code decrements loopsRemaining by 1. Assuming that the variable loopsRemaining is initialized with a value greater than 0, this script will cause the clip to keep looping until loopsRemaining is reduced down to 0. Notice that if loopsRemaining is 0, the condition is false, so it goes to the else part, where gotoAndStop(1) executes. You can place two instances of this clip on the Stage and use the following script on each instance (not *in* the clip, but *on* the instance):

```
onClipEvent (load) {
  this.loopsRemaining=3;
}
```

Just change the value to which you're assigning `loopsRemaining` in each
instance, and they'll repeat a different number of times.

So far, we don't have a component, and you can see the difficulty of writing the
`onClipEvent` script on each instance. Consider that you might not even need a
component but the preceding script is too difficult to trust all your using authors
to execute; a component would be more foolproof. Another (less than ideal) solution would be to first remove the entire `onClipEvent` (previous), name each
instance (`ball_1` and `ball_2`, for example), and then from the first frame in the
main movie, use a script such as the following

```
ball_1.loopsRemaining=3;
ball_2.loopsRemaining=5;
```

We still don't have a component, and you can see this technique has its faults
(namely, you have to name each instance and type the preceding script without
error).

Finally, remove the script in the first frame so that I can show you one other non-
component-related solution. Actually, this solution is not too bad, although it's a
lot of work. It lets us explore a clip property that hasn't been mentioned previously: _name. In the first frame inside the master Movie Clip, we can write the
following script:

```
loopsRemaining=_name;
```

Translated, this says to "set `loopsRemaining` to the instance name of the clip I'm
inside." To use this solution, you'll have to name the clip instances with names
such as 1 or 2 (which is a bad idea because you should never start the names of
variables, clips, or frame labels with a number). In addition, you'll have to
change the script in the last frame to "go to" frame 2 (not 1). Otherwise,
`loopsRemaining` will keep getting reassigned with the previous script. To get
around the first problem, you could use a naming convention (such as `ball_1`)
and use a String method (such as `loopsRemaining=_name.subStr(5)`) to extract
just the portion of the name you need. Plus, you should convert the fifth character
to a number. And then, the whole thing falls apart if you want more than 9 loops
as we're only extracting one digit. Obviously, this is beginning to be a pain and
has definite drawbacks, such as the fact that we can't really use the first frame
inside the clip and that we have to be careful what we name the instance.

Your First Component

Components offer the same basic features explored in all the preceding solutions—but we want the using author to specify the value for `loopsRemaining` in a
very controlled and easy manner (that is, through the Components Parameters
panel). It's really quite simple to convert this clip into a component. A Movie
Clip becomes a component when you access the Component Definition dialog
box. If you first select our Movie Clip that uses the `loopsRemaining` variable and
then choose Component Definition from the Library's Options menu, you'll be
faced with the dialog box shown in Figure 15.2.

Figure 15.2 *The Library's Component Definition dialog box enables you to specify
which variables will be set-able in the component.*

From the Component Definition dialog box, you can use the plus button to add
variables that will be set-able by the using author. For this example, press the
plus button once, click the `varName` that appears in the `Name` column, and then
type `loopsRemaining`. Under the `Value` column, double-click to replace
`defaultValue` with `1` (meaning that if the using author never bothers to access
the Component Parameters panel, `1` will be used by default). Finally, leave the
`Type` column in its default setting—meaning that the data type for this variable
will be either String or Number. (We'll look at the other options shortly.) That's
all you need to do, but I want to mention a couple of other options in this dialog
box before we move on.

Normally, we want the using author to change only the values of variables, not variable names. The Parameters Are Locked in Instances option will prevent the using author from changing the name of the variables being edited through the Component Parameters panel. Although I can't think of many practical reasons for letting the using author change the name of a needed variable, unchecking Parameters Are Locked in Instances will also allow the using author to *add* variables (through the Component Parameters panel) that provide an effective alternative to the onClipEvent(load) option I showed earlier.

Another setting of the Component Definition dialog box worth checking out is the Description field. You can use this field to write a concise explanation of how to use the component. You'll have to first click the Set button and then select Description is Plain Text to type a description. It's a good idea to include information regarding how to set each variable. For example, you could say something such as, "Use the loopsRemaining variable to specify the number of times you want the animation to loop." It's sort of funky for the using author because she'll see the description in the Reference panel only after clicking the Help button (in either the Properties panel or Component Parameters panel). (The Description is a Reference Panel option requires that a modified configuration file was installed at the time the component was installed—a topic touched on later in the "Distributing Components" section.)

Finally, we'll return to the custom UI and Live Preview features later in this chapter.

Just by adding at least one variable through the Component Definition dialog box, we can turn our Movie Clip into a component—evidenced by the new icon in the Library and the fact that the Component Parameters panel is usable and the Properties panel Parameters tab is visible (see Figure 15.3). If you drag three instances of this component on Stage, you can then set loopsRemaining for each one individually very quickly and easily through the Component Parameters panel.

A Practical Example

Let's build another simple component as a quick review and so that you can see a more practical application: a template. Lay out two Dynamic Text fields with placeholder text: one for a title and one for a subtitle. Make sure that the margins are wide enough to accommodate any likely content and pick a nice typeface. Make sure that the title is associated with a variable title and the subtitle with a variable subTitle (see Figure 15.4).

Figure 15.3   *When a Movie Clip turns into a component, its icon changes in the Library (as shown in the second one listed).*

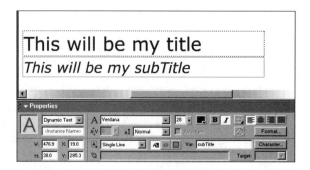

Figure 15.4   *The first practical component that we build will include Dynamic Text fields that we associate to variables.*

Select both blocks of text and convert them into a Movie Clip symbol (F8). Confirm that the layout is satisfactory and use the Info panel to notate the x and y coordinates (making sure to use the center point—indicated by a black box in the Info panel). Go inside the clip you just created and, in the first keyframe, use the following script to specify the initial location for the clip:

```
_x=150;
_y=229;
```

(Use whichever values you found through the Info panel.) Finally, you can make this a component by accessing the Component Definition dialog box. Just add title and subTitle to the Name column for parameters. That's it! Anyone can now drag an instance on Stage and define the content through the Component Parameters panel, and the layout will be perfectly consistent. You can even make a global edit to the layout or font style by editing the master symbol. All the instances in use will retain their values for `title` and `subTitle`. (By the way, you'll need to Test Movie to see anything other than your placeholder text in the two fields—a fact that we'll overcome when we cover Live Preview.)

Other Data Types

Before we move on to some advanced examples of components, let's quickly explore the alternatives to the Default data type found when populating the Component Definition dialog box (refer to Figure 15.2). The other data types are Array, Object, List, String, Number, Boolean, Font Name, and Color.

When you want the using author to populate the clip's variables with strings or numbers, just leave the Type option set to Default. Flash will figure out whether the using author supplied a Number, String, or Boolean data type, and treat it accordingly. You can force Flash to treat the value provided as a String data type or a Number data type. This can be nice when you want `"2"` to be treated as a string. (Flash would normally convert it to a number if you left the data type set to "Default.") Selecting Boolean is kind of cool because the using author will see a drop-down menu from which he can choose only true or false. Realize, however, that setting the data type to String or Number will still permit the using author to type in the wrong data type, and then Flash will consider the value to be `undefined`.

Three of the remaining five data types (Array, Object, and List) are similar in that they enable the using author to supply multiple values for a single parameter's value. The List data type is unique because it really isn't a data type per se. Think of this option as a "drop-down list" where the using author can select from a pre-designated drop-down list that you define. This option enables you to control the using author's input. For example, maybe you want to give the using author a choice among "Jazz," "Rock," and "Classical" for a component that plays music, and those are the only three options available. If you leave the data type as Default, he could enter "Disco" or something that you hadn't expected. When you opt for the List data type, you also need to populate the drop-down list by double-clicking the cell in the Value column (listed as "<none>" by default). The Values dialog box will appear (see Figure 15.5). Click the plus button for each new item, and be sure to click the little check box to indicate the default value (which is selected if the using author never makes a selection).

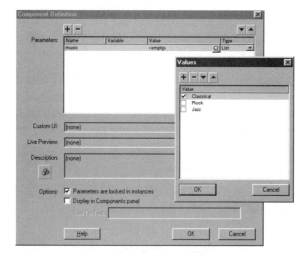

Figure 15.5 *Selecting the "list" type in the Component Definition dialog box (top) gives the using author a limited choice (in the drop-down list at the bottom) when populating component instances.*

Realize that once the using author selects from the drop-down list you populated, the value for the parameter will simply be the item selected in the drop-down. That is, if the using author selects `first` (from Figure 15.6), the `myParam` value will be the string `"first"`. If the using author selects `123`, the value of `myParam` will be the number `123`. In this way, the List data type is similar to the Default data type, except you allow the using author to select from a list.

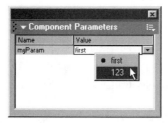

Figure 15.6 *The default data type will automatically turn values into strings or numbers as appropriate.*

The Array data type is a bit more straightforward. Here, you give the using author the capability to populate the parameter with as many values as she wants. For example, the ComboBox Component that ships with Flash uses this option to enable the using author to add as many items as she wants. If you prefer, you can pre-populate the array (through the Values dialog box—not unlike the one shown in Figure 15.5). However, the using author will still be able to add or remove items from the array. In addition, the parameter will have the Array data type, so the component's code will need to access values according to how arrays work (such as using brackets to reference individual items in the array).

Finally, the Object data type should be familiar to you. (We've explored generic objects as a storage mechanism.) Here, the parameter will have multiple *named* values (rather than just multiple values, as in the case of the Array data type). Also, the using author won't be able to add named properties to the object; he'll only be able to set the value for each property. Perhaps you designed a component that requires a generic object to pass to the Color object... or, maybe you've just fallen in love with storing values in named properties. The Object data type enables you to store multiple values in a single variable (with named properties). Just like with the Array or List data types, you'll want to pre-populate the property names (and default values for each) by using the Values dialog box.

Before we discuss more practical uses for each data type, let's look at the remaining two choices: Font Name and Color. These are probably the two most convenient improvements that components have over their "Smart Clip" ancestors. The Font Name data type displays a drop-down list to the using author with all the fonts on his computer (see Figure 15.7). This can be convenient when your component uses the TextField or TextFormat objects (covered in Chapter 10, "Keyboard Access and Modifying Onscreen Text").

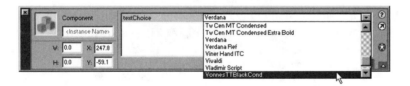

Figure 15.7   *You can present the using author with a selection of the fonts installed on his system.*

The Color data type gives the using author a standard Flash Color Selection dialog box (including the dropper cursor, which can point to any color onscreen). For a super-simple application, draw a shape, convert it to a symbol, and then access its Component Definition dialog box. Add a parameter with the name myColor and the type `Color`, and then click OK. Go inside the master symbol (you'll want to double-click the Library item) and place the following code in the first keyframe:

```
temp_color=new Color(this);
temp_color.setRGB(myColor);
```

The first line instantiates a Color object in the `temp_color` variable that's linked to this clip instance. The second line does a `setRGB()` on the `temp_color` object using the `myColor` variable as the parameter. Drag a few instances on Stage, and then use the Properties panel (Parameters tab) to set the color for each instance. It's pretty convenient, isn't it? You'll see more examples later in this section, but this should give you a taste of how easily you can gather color information from the using author. By the way, the value for the `myColor` variable will range from 0 to 16,777,215. You can use the following formulas to convert this number to a Hex or RGB value.

Handy Formula

To express a base 10 number as a Hex string:
```
myNumber.toString(16);
```

For a practical use of this formula, place the code `trace(myColor.toString(16))` in the first frame of a component that lets the user define `myColor` (as in the code above that exemplifies the Color data type).

To extract the standard values (0–255) for red, green, and blue from a given base 10 color value (0–16,777,215)—shown here as `myColor`:
```
var r=Math.floor(myColor >> 16);
var g=Math.floor(myColor - (r << 16) >> 8);
var b=Math.floor(myColor - (g << 8) - (r << 16));
```

Notice that the formula for g assumes that r has previously been assigned the correct value (and, b assumes both r and b have been assigned). If you want, you could just take the whole formula for r and replace the r in g's formula—although it would get pretty ugly. To reveal the RGB value, add the preceding lines to the component's keyframe, followed by this `trace` statement:
```
trace("R: "+ r +", G: "+g+ ", B: "+b);
```

Before I get carried away with the Color data type, let me show you one last option before we review and move on. The Component Definition dialog box has a column for both "Name" and "Variable." The using author will always see the Name column, and it will appear to him that he is setting its value. Actually, if you leave the Variable column blank, the using author is setting the value for whatever variable is listed under the Name column. It's possible to further separate the using author from the code behind the scene, however. For example, maybe you want to create code that refers to a variable name that might be cryptic to the user. Maybe myColor doesn't really make sense to a novice using author. You can still use myColor inside the component, but let the using author think that he is setting a value for "my favorite color" (which is not a legitimate name for a variable). Simply put, your actual variable in the Variable column and the wordy name for the using author to see in the Name column (see Figure 15.8).

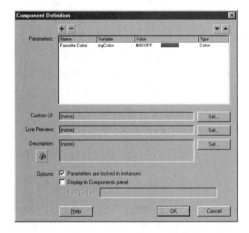

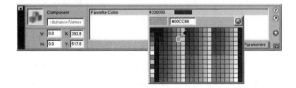

Figure 15.8 *You can insulate using authors from your cryptic variable names by providing a "name" that they will see. (Notice that* myColor *doesn't appear in the Properties panel.)*

As a quick review, we've seen that a component is simply a Movie Clip for which the Component Definition option was used to specify parameters that the using author will be able to manipulate. You also have plenty of choices as to the format for that parameter (Array, Object, List, String, Number, Boolean, Font Name, and Color). Each of the options affects the way and type of values the using author gets to supply. One would suspect that you'll be *using* those variables somehow inside the clip—such as within a Dynamic Text field or in a script that utilizes the value of the variable. Each instance is unique in all the ways the different clip instances can be unique; but, in addition, the using author can change the value of all variables listed in the Component Parameters panel. In this way, the using author makes each instance of a component behave differently because each instance will start off with different values for all its variables.

Advanced Applications for Standard Components

Although the previous example (of using a component like a template to impose a consistent font and layout for text) was indeed practical, it was quite simple. Other practical examples aren't quite as simple. I'm going to call the following examples "standard" components (not "simple") because they don't involve the more advanced features (custom UIs and Live Preview). A *custom UI* replaces the Clip Parameters dialog box (and its rigid-looking Name and Value columns) with a Flash movie that you have to build. It's the job of this other Flash movie (the UI) to set the necessary variables, but it can do so in a very graphic way. The Live Preview is still another Flash movie whose job is to display (during authoring) how the populated component will appear once the movie plays. We'll make both custom UIs and Live Preview files in the following section, but first I want to show some advanced examples of the standard form. You don't need to try to follow along too closely as we explore some of the possibilities.

In Workshop Chapter 3, "Creating a Horizontal Slider," we'll build a slider that lets the user (not just the using author) interact by dragging it from 1 to 100 (see Figure 15.9). After building a somewhat hard-wired version, we'll turn it into a component to allow the using author to specify three properties: the location of 1 (the minimum location for the slider), the location of 100 (the initial location—so that the slider can default to a point other than 1), and the name for a function that the slider will repeatedly call as the user slides the slider. Using a function makes it possible for the slider's value to be used to modify anything on the

Stage—from another clip's alpha level to the overall sound level. A function that a component calls (back in the main movie) can be referred to as a *callback function*.

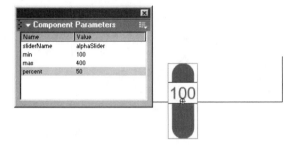

Figure 15.9 *In Workshop Chapter 3, we'll turn a slider into a component so that it can be reused.*

In Workshop Chapter 9, "Creating a ToolTip Component," we'll build a component that will enable the using author to specify the exact string of text that should appear when the cursor rolls over another object. The using author will be able to drag as many instances of this tooltip component as she wants.

Finally, here's an example of a component that I built for use in a real project. I used Flash in a presentation, but wanted another version (that the audience could download) that included speaker notes. The content for the notes would be loaded in from an external file (as you'll learn about in Chapter 16, "Interfacing with External Data") because it wouldn't be written until later—plus, I wanted to be able to modify it at any time. Anyway, I made a component not unlike the tooltip described previously, but rather than making the using author (me) specify *all* the text, I simply specified the section and subsection where it was being used. The loaded data included details as to which section and subsection it applied to, so my component simply displayed (similar to a tooltip) the data appropriate for that section. The result was that users could view the presentation and optionally click a Speaker Notes button to see additional information (see Figure 15.10).

Although these examples are not the only things possible with standard components, I just wanted to make a point that you often don't *need* to build custom UIs or Live Preview files.

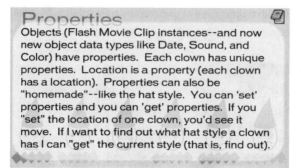

Figure 15.10 *In an actual project, I made a component to display the appropriate speaker notes.*

Replacing the Component Parameters Panel (or the Properties Panel's Parameter Tab) with a Custom UI

One of the most intriguing features of components is the fact that you can assign an interactive Flash movie to play inside, and effectively replace, the Component Parameters panel (or the Properties panel's Parameters tab). The process involves first building a Flash movie, exporting it as an .swf, and then pointing to the .swf through the Component Definition dialog box. You'll have two files: an .fla file with the master component in a Library and an .swf that plays inside the Component Parameters panel. The .swf is called a *custom UI*, and its file-name is specified in the Custom UI field (see Figure 15.11).

By replacing the Component Parameters panel, we have the opportunity to make something more usable. But most components are perfectly suitable without a custom UI. So instead of leaping straight into building custom UIs, we'll first look at how to design them so that we're sure to use them appropriately. You'll see that building a custom UI can be somewhat involved—so it makes sense to make sure that they're necessary.

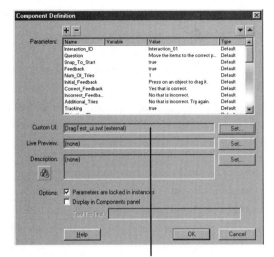

Filename of a custom UI

Figure 15.11   *The Custom UI field of the Component Definition dialog box points to an external file that will be used in place of the Component Parameters panel.*

Designing Custom UIs

Naturally, the process of creating a custom UI is purely technical. To make a *good* custom UI is another matter. I think it's fair to say that the only time to create a custom UI is when the built-in Component Parameters panel is inadequate. There are many situations in which this could occur. For example, making the using author set several variables through the standard Component Parameters panel could be unreasonably tedious. In this case, an easier solution might be a graphic selection device, such as a slider. Or, if he's selecting sounds, you could include a short audio sample. Finally, a perfect situation for a custom UI is when there is a series of complex selections the using author must make. You could build a custom UI that served as a wizard—walking the using author through all the steps involved and even providing online help where appropriate. A good example of this approach can be found in the components included with Flash's Learning Interactions Library (under Window, Common Libraries).

After you've determined that a custom UI is appropriate, you can take steps to design how it will function. The most important consideration is usability. Because the purpose of the custom UI is to provide some benefit not found in the standard Component Parameters panel, you should make sure to make it easy for the using author. I suppose if you're building a component for your own use, you can invest less time designing it (at the expense of usability), but in such a case you probably won't want to build a custom UI at all.

As it turns out, one of the most critical features that will make your custom UI more usable happens to be one of the most difficult to program. It's important for the custom UI to always indicate the current settings. For example, every button should include a highlight to indicate that it's been selected. This highlight should not only provide a clear indication at the time a selection is made, but also the using author should be able to return to the Component Parameters panel and easily ascertain the current setting. After all, she might have several instances of the component and want to check the setting of each one. This round-trip feature (being able to leave and come back to a component) is the difficult programming task. You'll see how to program it in the next section, but realize that it's also a matter of design how you choose to treat the graphic solution. Ultimately, making an intuitive custom UI takes more skill and creativity than just programming it.

Building Custom UIs

Assuming that you've determined a custom UI is really necessary and you have a decent design, you can move on to really building it! First let's make a very simple custom UI, and then add some features. The concentration of this example is on making the custom UI, but we'll need a component for which the custom UI sets properties. You can use the simple bouncing ball Movie Clip that we used in the "Components Overview" section earlier in this chapter. You'll want to create a file (maybe called "host.fla"), make sure it's saved, and then place the following script in the last frame of the Movie Clip:

```
loopsRemaining—;
if (loopsRemaining) {
  gotoAndPlay (1);
} else {
  gotoAndStop (1);
}
```

The job of our custom UI will be to set the loopsRemaining variable. (Arguably, this component doesn't really *need* a custom UI; we're just doing it for practice.) Make sure that your Movie Clip is a component by using the Component

Definition dialog box to specify that loopsRemaining is setable by the using author. Finally, click the Set button adjacent to the Custom UI field, and then select "Custom UI in external .swf file" and type myUI.swf in the Custom UI .swf File field (see Figure 15.12). You can also click the Browse button and point to a file. However, besides the fact that we haven't made the UI yet, this feature always produces an absolute path where—for most situations—the relative path we typed in is more desirable. (By the way, in a workgroup situation, you could keep the custom UI in an absolute path on a server for everyone to share.)

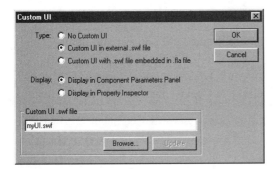

Figure 15.12   *Replacing the Component Parameter panel or the Properties panel's Parameter tab is as easy as identifying a file to use.*

The Custom UI dialog box has a few options that aren't discussed in this example but that are worth exploring. Specifically, the Display options enable you to replace either the Component Parameter panel or the Properties panel's Parameter tab. If you do opt for the Properties Inspector option (that is, the Properties panel), realize that the size provided is 406x72 pixels. The Type choice between "external" or "embedded" is really not terribly complex. Leaving the .swf external will mean that you can edit and re-export the .swf, and the latest version (residing externally) will always be used. Embedding is slightly more convenient because when distributing (to share) the component, you won't have to keep track of two separate files. However, if you need to make an edit to the original custom UI, the "embedded" option requires that you click the "Update" button (which will remain disabled for all Type options other than embedded). Like I say, although this dialog box is fairly intuitive, it's still worth studying. You'll see a very similar dialog box when you make Live Preview files.

Now create a new file and save it as "myUI.fla" in the same folder as the host file. Finally, we can program it. Because we're basically replacing the standard Component Parameters panel, we need to do what it was doing: setting variables. The only catch is that the variables that get exchanged with the host movie's component need to reside in a generic object variable with the name xch. You can have other variables in the UI file, but only the ones in the xch object will become part of the component in the main movie. You can think of the xch object as a surrogate of the actual component; it will contain the necessary variables.

We can make the fastest custom UI in history by creating an Input Text field associated with the variable loopsRemaining and then selecting the text block and converting to the Movie Clip symbol. Finally, just make the Movie Clip's instance name xch and export the movie as myUI.swf in the correct folder. Go back to the host movie and test it out by dragging two instances of the component. In the Clip Parameters panel, you should see the Input Text field where you can specify a number of loops. Also, notice that you can keep the Component Parameters panel open while you alternatively select the two component instances on the Stage. Each should retain its loopsRemaining value. It's easy, really. Although it might not seem as though we created a generic object named xch, we effectively did the same thing by making a clip with the instance name xch. You could reference the loopsRemaining variable as xch.loopsRemaining— the same as if you had an object called xch.

Even if we try to spice it up with gratuitous effects (such as text color), this custom UI is pretty simple. Let's start over so that we can encounter something more challenging. In a new file, create a Dynamic Text field in the main timeline and associate it with the variable showLoops. Also, make a button and create four instances in the main timeline, lined up vertically. Place the following script in each button (changing the 1 to 2, 3, 4 for each button, respectively):

```
on (release) {
  pickLoop(1);
}
```

In the first keyframe of the main timeline, enter the following function:

```
function pickLoop(whatNum){
  _root.xch.loopsRemaining=whatNum;
}
```

This achieves the task of changing the loopsRemaining variable (well, the loopsRemaining property of the xch object variable) to whichever value is passed from the buttons that call pickLoop(). We can export the .swf, and it should work—almost. When we test this from the host movie (the place where we *should* be testing this), two significant problems arise. First, upon making a selection, the user is not given any graphic feedback as to which button was pressed. The other problem is that when a user returns to view the current setting in a component, he has no clue what the value is for loopsRemaining. (However, it should be noted the component does work as far as letting the user set the loopsRemaining variable.) We can produce a highlight on the currently selected button by creating another Movie Clip in the main timeline and calling the instance arrow. Then we just need a script in the pickLoop function to change the _x and _y properties of arrow. Just name each button instance "button_1," "button_2," and so on, and then add the following code to the pickLoop function:

```
arrow._x=this["button_"+whatNum]._x;
arrow._y=this["button_"+whatNum]._y;
```

This simply sets the arrow's coordinates to match the correct button instance. Because we don't know the exact name of the button, we build a string expression ("button_"+whatNum) in brackets preceded by the path to the instance.

Provided that we re-export the myUI.swf, the custom UI should function as far as indicating a selection *after* we make it, but it still fails to appear with arrow in place upon returning to a previously edited component instance. All we need to do is place the following script in an appropriate keyframe so that it executes every time a using author returns to edit the Component Parameters panel:

```
pickLoop(_root.xch.loopsRemaining);
```

Basically, this script sends the current value of loopsRemaining (which is in the xch clip) to the pickLoop function. The problem with our custom UI is not that loopsRemaining is being lost (if we test it, we'll find that it is still there), but that the value of loopsRemaining is unknown when returning to the clip. However, if we place the preceding script in the first frame, it won't work! The issue is that Flash needs some time to send the variables from a component instance to the Component Parameters panel and then to our custom UI. The solution is to move everything in our custom UI out past frame 1, and then invoke a function call (similar to the previous). We'll probably want a stop() command in that frame too. Basically, everything has to move out past frame 1. It's not that funky when

you consider the sequence of events: the user clicks a component that has a previously set variable, it invokes the Component Parameters panel, which then
launches the custom UI .swf, and then the component tells the custom UI the
value of its variables. We just want to make sure that the custom UI waits until
frame 2 before trying to use any variables

Here's the finished code that goes in frame 2 of the custom UI:

```
pickLoop(_root.xch.loopsRemaining);
function pickLoop(whichNum){
  _root.xch.loopsRemaining=whatNum;
  arrow._x=this["button_"+whatNum]._x;
  arrow._y=this["button_"+whatNum]._y;
}
stop();
```

Just remember to name the button instances so that nothing shows up onscreen
until frame 2. (Also, invoke the `pickLoop()` function from each button.) By the
way, my code is pretty sloppy in that I start referring to and assigning
values to properties in the `xch` object before formally instantiating it (as in
`xch=new Object()`). It just so happens that when an .swf is played as a custom
UI (that is, within the Component Parameters panel), the `xch` object is automatically instantiated. It even has all the named properties and default values based
on settings made during the Define Component stage.

Although this example is admittedly simple, a more complex custom UI will
have the same elements. You always need to access and set the component variables through named properties in the `xch` object. And, unless your only means
for the user to see his current settings is a Dynamic or Input Text field, you'll
need to initialize such highlights somewhere other than the first frame. After you
understand these minimum features, you can move on to making more complex
components and custom UIs.

Building Live Preview Files

Components don't "do their thing" until you select Test Movie. It's now possible,
however, to create a separate file that serves as an author-time preview of how
the component will look. In the case of the template component that we built
earlier (in the "A Practical Example" section), the using author could populate
the title and subtitle variables via the Component Parameters panel, but she
wouldn't see her text onscreen (not until she tested the movie). A Live Preview
file will resolve this limitation.

A Live Preview file is similar to a custom UI in that it's a separate file exported as an .swf to which the Component Definition dialog box points. However, its job is to visually represent the forthcoming result of any setting the using author makes to the component instance. It makes the most sense when your component is simply a graphic that appears static. The Live Preview file in this case just needs to display the graphics as they will appear for the component. If your component is more involved—perhaps containing interactive or moving elements—the Live Preview is not just more work, it's less appropriate. Consider that when you drag onto the Stage a component instance that has a Live Preview file on the Stage, you'll actually be watching the Live Preview—not the actual component clip. Then, any time you make a change via the Component Parameters panel, you should immediately see that change reflected on the Stage (really, in the Live Preview). It's just sort of hard (or even distracting) to show something that's moving on the Stage while you're authoring.

Creating a Live Preview file is not all that difficult. Logically, it should contain the same basic elements found in the actual component. The hardest part is making sure the registration is maintained. Follow these steps to make the template (from our earlier example) to utilize a Live Preview file.

First, make the component. Start a new file and save it into a known location. Create two Dynamic Text fields: one associated with the variable title and the other with subTitle. Draw an unfilled box around the text to represent the full size of the template. Use the Info panel to reset the box's width and height to a nice round number. (This will correspond to the Live Preview file's document dimensions.) Select just the box and convert it to a Movie Clip, and then set the instance of this box on the Stage to have an alpha level of 0 (via the Properties panel's Color Styles option). Select everything (the two blocks of text and the now-transparent box instance) and convert to a Movie Clip, making sure to select the top-left default center point, which will help keep things registered. Finally, convert this Movie Clip to a component by selecting Component Definition from the Library. Add two parameters: one for title and the other for subTitle. Leave all the defaults except for Live Preview, and then press the Set button. From the Live Preview dialog box, select the option "Live Preview in External .swf File," and then type template_live.swf into the field (see Figure 15.13). When you click OK, Flash will warn you that this file doesn't yet exist (but that's okay because we're about to make it).

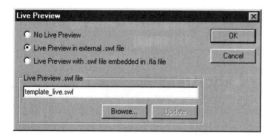

Figure 15.13 *We'll identify the Live Preview file for this component (and then build it later).*

To make the Live Preview file, first enter the master version for the component (via the Library). Select everything onscreen (including the transparent box) and copy. Start a new file and paste. Be sure everything is still selected and use the Info panel's top-left option to align everything to the top-left corner of the Stage. (You can type 0, 0.) Now set the Live Preview's stage size by accessing Modify, Document (Ctrl+J). Set the size to match the dimensions you set for the box. Save this file as "template_live.fla" in the same folder as the component file. Wow, that was just the structure! Now let's discuss the actual code.

The way you make the Live Preview file update any time the using author changes a component variable is by using the onUpdate() function. Basically, whenever the using author makes a change, Flash tries to invoke the function called onUpdate() inside the Live Preview file. All you need to do is put code that handles the refreshing within this function. To apply this to what you just built, simply enter the following code into the first frame of the template_live.fla file:

```
function onUpdate() {
    this.title=this.xch.title;
    this.subtitle=this.xch.subtitle;
}
```

Basically, this just says "set the title variable to equal the title variable contained in the xch object" (and the same with subtitle). Although this might seem pretty easy (it is), there's no rule that says your Live Preview has to be so parallel to the component. You could have a bunch of other stuff that happens whenever this function is invoked. Basically, this is where you put any code that you want to be triggered when the using author makes a change. And, remember that all the variables the using author will be setting are contained as named properties in the xch object.

You should be able to test the example I just outlined. You should notice (provided that you have "Enable Live Preview" selected in the Control menu) that any instances of your component on the Stage will accurately display the values for title and subtitle any time you change them. One way to see what's really happening is to set the font color differently in the main movie's source component. Everything will still work, but you'll see a different color while authoring (the original color, because that's what's in the Live Preview) than the latest color in the component when you select Test Movie. Realize that the tedious steps we took with the transparent box were just to keep the registration accurate.

Finally, it's often desirable to make a component that adapts based on its scale. That is, a component can be "self-aware" of how large it's been scaled and then position contained clips differently based on that scale. In addition to being a fair bit of work for the component, the Live Preview file also needs to make such accommodation. The only catch is the Live Preview file must adjust in real time (as the using author scales it) where a component can do all the layout at runtime. You can see a great example of this kind of behavior in the Bar Chart component in the "Flash Charting Components" available from the Flash exchange site (www.macromedia.com/exchange/flash). When there's enough horizontal space, the bar labels appear horizontally. But when there's not enough room, they rotate 90 degrees to appear vertically (see Figure 15.14). This feat is most impressive when you see the Live Preview adjust as you scale.

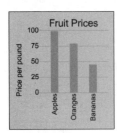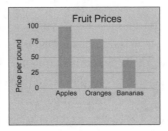

Figure 15.14   *The same component's Live Preview displays labels horizontally (right) when there's enough room.*

In order to make your Live Preview automatically adjust any time the using author scales the component, you need to know about listeners—specifically, the Stage object's onResize listener. Listeners were covered generally in Chapter 14, "Extending ActionScript," and specifically (as applied to the TextField object) in

Workshop Chapter 10 "Creating Timers." Triggering a script in the Live Preview file every time the using author scales the component requires this simple script:

```
myListener=new Object();
myListener.onResize=function(){ //put code here }
Stage.addListener(myListener);
```

Just put code that repositions any clips in place of the "put code here" comment. The only thing really funky about using the Stage's onResize listener is that you'll want the .swf's scale mode to be "no scale." That is, when displaying a .swf (in a browser or as a Live Preview) "no scale" means resizing will only change the window size, not the contained clips. It makes sense when you consider that *you* will be taking care of all the layout as the using author scales the component, so you don't want all the graphics to scale too. Anyway, this call boils down to one extra line of code to accompany the preceding listener code:

```
Stage.scaleMode = "noScale";
```

Basically, this ensures the onResize listener works as intended (and is required any time you use onResize.)

Making Components Affect Other Clips

You might have noticed that some of the built-in Flash UI components can be combined with other clips on the Stage. For example, the ScrollBar component will snap to a text field and let the end user scroll *that* text field. It's actually very simple to make your component snap to another clip.

All you have to do is include, as one of your component's parameters, the variable name _targetInstanceName. In the Define Component stage, just press the plus button and type _targetInstanceName in the Name or Variable column. Then, if the using author has properly snapped a component instance to another object (clip, button, Dynamic Text, or Input Text instance), the value for _targetInstanceName will be a string that matches the instance on the Stage. Even if that instance was never given a name, Flash will give it a default name (such as InstanceName_0). The only thing a bit funky is that _targetInstanceName will store the string version of the instance name. The following formula will convert that string back into a clip reference:

```
target=this._parent[this._targetInstanceName];
```

This simply stores (in the variable target) the actual clip reference. Notice that since we just have a string version, it's placed between brackets preceded by the path (_parent in this case). It's pretty simple, really.

Here's a very quick example of what you can do. Select Insert, New Symbol and make it a Movie Clip. In the first frame of this empty clip, enter the following code:

```
this.onEnterFrame = function() {
    this._parent[this._targetInstanceName]._x += 5;
}
```

This simply assigns a function to occur for the (soon-to-be) component's enterFrame clip event. Inside the function, the target object is addressed and its _x property is increased by 5 pixels—every enterFrame. Finally, you just need to select the clip's Define Component option and add a parameter called _targetInstanceName. Then, just take any clip, button, or Dynamic Text instance on the Stage and drag the component on to its center. You'll see that it snaps to the top-left corner of the object (and the _targetInstanceName parameter is automatically filled). Then, for this weird example, the object automatically moves across the screen.

The point is, it's very easy to let the using author snap a component onto a regular clip instance, and the component's code can affect that target clip. In this way, you can truly separate code from data. The code would be in the component, and the data would be any clip onto which the component is snapped.

Summary

This chapter turned out to be more like a workshop chapter and less like many of the earlier foundation chapters. That's because components are more a feature of Flash than a language element of ActionScript.

The concepts you learned in this chapter included how components enable you to give the using author the ability to set initial values for any property, variable, or homemade property you specify. When you access the Component Definition dialog box, the Movie Clip magically turns into a component. From that point forward, each instance on the Stage maintains its own values for the designated properties. The using author can change individual instance properties through the Component Parameters panel. Additionally, if you go through the work to build a custom UI, you can use this Flash movie to effectively replace the Clip Parameters panel. Finally, for the using author, you can make a Live Preview file to display a component's current values in context.

If you're left with any confusion as to the value of components, don't worry; you'll make plenty of them in the workshop chapters. It's not so much that you sit down and decide, "Today I'm going to make a component." Rather, you can build some code and then say, "Hey, this would be way better as a component because it would be adaptable for multiple instances."

{ Chapter 16 }

Interfacing with External Data

Flash is not an island. Data from outside sources can be included in a Flash movie. This means that even if the data changes after you upload your finished `.swf` file, your movie can reflect those changes, too. You can include timely information or make the movie appear customized to the individual user. The implications for such dynamic Flash sites are infinite.

In this chapter, we'll look at the main ways that Flash can interact with outside applications and data. I should note that there are other Macromedia server products that aren't covered in this chapter. These products integrate with Flash and extend what's possible with Flash alone. For example, at the time I wrote this book, Macromedia had only made announcements of very exciting server technology that let the Flash Player 6 do two-way audio and video, as well as real-time data transfer. Although this chapter won't cover such servers, you can bet that the programming syntax and design approach is consistent with what you learn in this book. In this chapter, we will look only at ways to produce `.swf`s that adapt to outside data.

This chapter includes both detailed information and resources to get you started in the event that you choose to develop your skills elsewhere. Specifically, in this chapter, you will:

- Create external scripts that contain ActionScript code.
- Set Flash variables from within HTML.

- Load data from text files so that you can make changes without having to open Flash.

- Learn how to load data from or send data to server scripts (such as CGI or ASP).

- See how you can incorporate XML structured data into Flash.

- Learn how to use the new Local SharedObject to save data on the user's computer (for later retrieval).

- Use the new LocalConnection feature to give several .swfs access to each other's variables and properties.

External Scripts

In addition to typing your scripts in the Actions panel, you can store your scripts in external text files that are included when you export a .swf. Although all the *other* techniques covered in this chapter involve ways to import data while the movie plays, external scripts become locked inside the movie when you export. (It would be nice if changes to an external script could be reflected in a previously exported .swf, but it doesn't work that way.)

External scripts can still make you more efficient. If the same script is used in several places within one movie, and perhaps even used in several different movies, you can store that script in a single "external script" file. If at any time during production you find that you want to adjust or fix that script, you need to do it in only one place. Movies exported from that point forward would see the change—in every place where the script was used. It's even more powerful when your site structure is broken into several movies (that get loaded via loadMovie()). That way, a change in a single external script will be reflected in every movie that accesses it once you re-export all your .swfs. Basically, it just takes a bit of planning.

An additional benefit of external scripts is that they can be managed using version control software. Such software tracks every change to an external script file and makes it easy to backtrack and find the cause of a newly occurring bug.

Using external scripts is pretty easy. In place of an actual script (that is, in a keyframe, Button instance, or Movie Clip instance), refer to the filename where you plan to store the actual script. Macromedia suggests that you use a file extension of .as, but you can use .txt if you want—it's just a text file. (On my

Windows machine, I've associated the .as file type with the Notepad text editor.) So, in the Actions panel, refer to the file after #include, as in:

```
#include "somefile.as"
```

Notice that you don't put a semicolon at the end of this line. Also, you should realize that the content of this external script can be just a code segment (like the result of an event), or it can be the entire script (including the event). So, attaching the following two scripts to two different buttons is totally legitimate:

One button:

```
on (press){
    #include "code_segment.as"
}
```

Another button:

```
#include "entire_script.as"
```

The only difference is that the file code_segment.as doesn't contain (and shouldn't contain) any mouse events, such as on (press). The file entire_script.as needs to contain the entire mouse event because any scripts on buttons need to be surrounded by events. Actually, the contents of entire_script.as could include more than one mouse event, as follows:

```
on (press){
    pressing=1;
}
on (release){
    pressing=0;
}
```

Just realize that the entire contents of your external file will be placed in Flash exactly where you refer to them. Imagine that the contents of the external script are pasted in place of the line starting #include.

There's not much more to say except to explain some practical concerns and potential applications. If you use Notepad to create your scripts, realize that you won't get all the enhancements (such as syntax coloring and error checking) that you do in Flash. Some third-party and shareware text editors can be customized to do syntax coloring, and because ActionScript is nearly identical to JavaScript, you can use any editor configured to edit JavaScript. It's still probably going to be easier in Flash. You might consider writing the script in Flash first, and then when you identify that using an external script would be more appropriate, just cut the script from Flash, put the `#include` statement in its place , and then paste the code into a text file. That way you not only know that the syntax is correct, but that the code works inside Flash.

Before we move on to the *really* dynamic features, let me suggest a few uses for external scripts. I already mentioned that several different movies within the same site can access the external script. However, you might want to use the same script in several movies in unrelated sites. Of course, it's a slight pain to re-export each `.swf` every time you make a change to the script, but that's much easier (and less prone to errors) than hunting through the file to find where the script was used. Ultimately, external scripts are good for building a code library. This is also a great way to share scripts. As you saw in Chapter 14, "Extending ActionScript," overriding and extending built-in objects simply requires some code in a keyframe. You can get such "prototype" scripts from other program- mers and easily include them in your movies as external scripts. The truth is that storing scripts inside Flash, where you can copy and paste them into new movies, is almost the same thing. Except with external scripts, if you ever find an error in a script you use often, you need only re-export all the movies linked to that script.

I'm sure there are other ways to use the external script feature. In any case, I doubt they'll match the potential power of the other techniques shown in the remainder of this chapter.

Setting Flash Variables from Within HTML

You can easily assign the initial values for variables in your Flash movie by way of HTML. In the following section, "External Data Files," you'll see how to load variables at runtime. That is, you can load variables any time while the movie plays. Setting variables from HTML is different because only the initial values get set (right before the movie starts). It's still a pretty nifty feature because you can place timely data in the HTML file and the Flash movie will have its vari- ables set accordingly.

As a quick example, every morning you could type in a new value for the `wordOfTheDay` variable and visitors to your site would see the day's word. Even better, if the HTML page is generated dynamically (for example, from a Cold Fusion or ASP page), you could set that variable automatically. Just remember that the technique you're about to see sets only the starting value for a variable.

There are two ways to set a Flash variable from within HTML: by tacking the variables onto the end of the `.swf`'s filename or by placing them in the new `FlashVars` tag (supported in the Flash Player 6). All you have to do is identify where your HTML specifies the `.swf`'s filename and concatenate (using a question mark) your variable's name and value. For example, the following shows how to set a variable called `word` through both the `OBJECT` and `EMBED` tags (for Internet Explorer and Netscape, respectively):

```
<OBJECT
<PARAM NAME=movie VALUE="movie.swf?word=skateboarding">
<EMBED src="movie.swf?word=skateboarding"
</EMBED>
</OBJECT>
```

Notice that this is just an excerpt! Also, you can use any legitimate variable name; I just happened to use a variable named `word`. Basically, where you'd normally have just seen `"myMovie.swf"`, you instead see `"myMovie.swf?word=skateboarding"`. That's really about it. There are just a few stipulations. If you want to set additional variables, just separate each variable name/value pair with an ampersand (for example, `"movie.swf?word=skateboarding&color=red"`). If, for some reason, you want to include an ampersand within the value of a variable, you must use the standard URL code `%26` instead. Also, you must use a plus sign (+) in place of any spaces (for example, "myMovie.swf?word=teach+yourself"). You can include a literal plus sign by using the code `%2b`. There are other codes for other special characters (but this is really more of an HTML issue). Notice, however, that the variables' values are always strings. You don't include extra quotation marks around the variables' values—they're always strings.

To give you a quick example of where this type of thing might be helpful, I programmed a site to introduce a new chair: `www.allsteeloffice.com/number19`. The client wanted a total of 7 different entry-paths. That is, some visitors would type in an URL that included one of six different artists' names (and some would use the preceding default address). The visitors who entered by specifying an artist name would default to a part of the site that looked like it was created just for that artist. Instead of making a separate `.swf` for each artist, I made one `.swf` that included all the content for all six artists. (Once the visitors arrived, they were able to view other artists, so it wasn't as though they downloaded unnecessary content.) All I needed was the value for the variable `defaultartist`, and my movie would jump to the correct content. This variable was assigned in the

HTML page. Although the HTML was actually generated by another programmer's ASP script, you can imagine that there were 6 nearly identical HTML files—just the value for defaultartist varied (for example, movie.swf?defaultartist=2 for the second artist). Once inside my movie, I first converted the variable to a number and then used the value accordingly. Here's a simplified version of the code in my first frame:

```
defaultartist=Number(defaultartist);
artistClip.gotoAndStop(defaultartist);
```

New to MX There's really nothing wrong with the preceding technique. However, a new feature was added for the Flash Player 6 that is slightly more elegant: the FlashVars object/embed tag. It follows most of the same rules from the old technique I just showed. However, instead of tacking the variables onto the end of the .swf's name, there's another section in the HTML. Here are the excerpted parts for both Internet Explorer (OBJECT) and Netscape (EMBED):

```
<PARAM NAME=FlashVars VALUE="word=snowboarding&color=blue">

<EMBED FlashVars="word=snowboarding&color=blue">
```

Again, realize that this is an excerpt. (Figure 16.1 shows these changes in the context of the entire HTML.) All the same rules apply regarding spaces (use the plus sign instead), special characters (use URL encoding), multiple values (separate by ampersands), and all values really being strings.

```
<HTML>
<HEAD>
<meta http-equiv=Content-Type content="text/html; charset=ISO-8859-1">
<TITLE>movie</TITLE>
</HEAD>
<BODY bgcolor="#FFFFFF">
<!-- URL's used in the movie-->
<!-- text used in the movie-->
<OBJECT classid="clsid:D27CDB6E-AE6D-11cf-96B8-444553540000"
  codebase="http://download.macromedia.com/pub/shockwave/cabs/flash/swflash.cab#version=6,0,0,0"
  WIDTH="550" HEIGHT="400" id="movie" ALIGN="">
 <PARAM NAME=movie VALUE="movie.swf">
 <PARAM NAME=quality VALUE=high>
 <PARAM NAME=bgcolor VALUE=#FFFFFF>
 <PARAM NAME=FlashVars VALUE="word=snowboarding&color=blue">

 <EMBED src="movie.swf" FlashVars="word=snowboarding&color=blue"
  quality=high bgcolor=#FFFFFF WIDTH="550" HEIGHT="400" NAME="movie" ALIGN=""
  TYPE="application/x-shockwave-flash"
  PLUGINSPAGE="http://www.macromedia.com/go/getflashplayer"></EMBED>
</OBJECT>
</BODY>
</HTML>
```

Figure 16.1   *The additional FlashVars portion of the HTML is highlighted.*

External Data Files

You've seen how to store text files containing ActionScript in external files and how to set initial values for variables through HTML. In both cases, however, after the movie starts to play, no data from the outside world is received. (Actually, in the case of external scripts, once you export the movie, nothing comes into your movie). In the next technique, you'll learn how to store data in external files that aren't loaded until you request them at runtime. Specifically, your script can invoke Flash's loadVariables() method at any time to load variables from an external text file (or another data source, as you'll see in the "Server Scripts" section later in this chapter). By loading variables from a file at runtime, a Flash movie reflects the current values found in the file.

There are several ways to load variables. Naturally, I'll recommend the new "Flash MX way"—the LoadVars object. However I want to point out the other two ways you can do load variables: as a function and as a method of a Movie Clip. Although this may sound like a case of "see how hard it used to be," I'm mentioning the old ways for two reasons: the LoadVars object only works in the Flash 6 player and—perhaps more importantly—because all three syntaxes look similar you should be able to recognize the difference.

As a function, the syntax is either:

```
loadVariables(whatFile,targetClip,optionalMethod);
```

or:

```
loadVariablesNum(whatFile,levelNumber,optionalMethod);
```

The difference between these two forms is simply that the first loads the variables into a named Movie Clip instance and the second loads the variables into a level number. Just replace whatFile with the name of the file containing the variables or with a relative path to that file. Realize that the file is really a URL when the movie's playing on a web server. As such, relative paths use a forward slash (/). Also, although you're allowed to use explicit paths, you're restricted to using paths to files in the same domain where the Flash movie resides (for security reasons). Anyway, it's easiest just to keep the data files in the same directory and simply refer to the filename (which is a relative path). targetClip is replaced with the Movie Clip instance name to where the variables will load. When using loadVariablesNum, you simply specify an integer in place of levelNumber. After the variables load, they will either be part of a clip or a level number. To load variables into the main timeline, use either _root or 0. Finally, we'll look at optionalMethod in the next section.

Consider the following example:

```
loadVariables("data.txt",_root);
```

This will load the data in a file called "data.txt" (which is adjacent to the Flash movie) and place all those variables in the root.

There's nothing particularly wrong with the preceding loadVariables *function*; however, using the following loadVariables() *method* is better—if for no other reason than its syntax is more consistent:

```
clipInstance.loadVariables(theFile);
```

To load variables from a file named "data.txt" into a clip named "myClip," use:

```
myClip.loadVariables("data.txt");
```

To load this same file into a keyframe in the main timeline, use:

```
_root.loadVariables("data.txt");
```

This last example has the same effect as loadVariables("data.txt",_root). And, just so you know, loadVariablesNum doesn't work as a method. (You can use _level0.loadVariables("data.txt") if you want to load into level 0.)

New to MX

Finally, the third (and preferable) way to load variables is by using the new LoadVars object. It takes a few additional steps, but these will look familiar to you and they're certainly worth the extra effort.

To load variables using the LoadVars object, you first need to create an instance of the object, as follows:

```
myVars=new LoadVars();
```

This stores an instance of the LoadVars object type into the homemade variable myVars. From this point forward, you can access and use the various properties and methods of the LoadVars object—on the myVars variable. For example, here's a load() method that starts the download process into the myVars variable:

```
myVars.load("data.txt");
```

In this case, all the data from inside "data.txt" will become named properties of the myVars variable. This is similar to how data loaded into a level number or clip instance (including _root) goes inside the targeted level or clip.

We'll get to the format of this external file soon, but there's a serious consideration when using any of the previous techniques: You must wait for the variables
to fully load. Loading variables takes some time to complete because the data is
actually traveling from your web server into the Flash movie on the user's
machine. The point is that if you start loading variables on, say, the first frame of
the movie, you need a way to know when you can start *using* those variables;
otherwise, you'll get erroneous results.

Waiting for Variables to Load

You can take several approaches to determine whether all the variables you've
started to load have indeed fully loaded. One way is to repeatedly check whether
the last variable in the data file has loaded. This technique is necessary only
when you are delivering to Flash 4 (or, when you load variables into the _root
timeline in Flash 5). Basically, this "polling" technique is not worth the effort.
When loading into a Movie Clip instance, you can take advantage of a second
technique—namely, writing a script triggered by the data clip event. (Similar to
how a load event triggers once when a clip loads, the data event triggers when a
clip has fully loaded data.) Additionally, by using the new LoadVars object, you
can assign the onLoad callback event to trigger a function that you write. Finally,
because all clip events have an equivalent callback function—and because _root
is really a clip—you can use _root.onData the same way onClipEvent(data)
works for a clip. Although it might seem like a million choices, it really just
depends into what clip you want to load variables. Often, when loading variables
into a clip, the first thing I find myself doing (once they've fully loaded) is copying them into the main timeline or into the _global space. Therefore, it's not
always convenient to load data into a clip. I'm going to show three techniques:
the standard data clip event, the onData() callback function (sort of the same
thing), and the new LoadVars object's onLoad callback. Regardless of you do it,
you must ensure that the data has fully loaded before you expect to start using
the loaded values.

Loading Variables into Clips (Using the `data` Clip Event)

When you load variables into a clip (rather than a level number or the _root
timeline), you can place a script within a onClipEvent(data) event
that won't execute until all the data is fully loaded. That is, in a keyframe
of the main timeline, start loading data into a target clip (such as

`myClip.loadVariables("data.txt"))`, and then include a `stop()` to keep the timeline from proceeding. Place a script attached to the clip `myClip`, as follows:

```
onClipEvent(data){
    _root.play();
}
```

Basically, as soon as all the data is loaded, `play()` causes the main timeline to proceed. Just realize that the disadvantage is that you must load variables into a clip instance, not a level number or the main _root timeline. That is, once the data has loaded, you'll find all the variables *in* the `myClip` instance. For example, if one variable is named age, it will really be _root.myClip.age.

Using the `onLoad` Callback Function

As you've seen in several places, many objects can have callback functions trigger when particular events occur. In the case of clip instances, all the events you see listed in the Actions panel can be scripted as callbacks. For example, `onClipEvent(load)` has a matching callback function called `onLoad`. The syntax here is consistent with all callback functions. Say (like before) you start loading variables into a clip (`myClip.loadVariables("data.txt")`) and have a `stop()` in the first frame. You can use the following code (in the first keyframe of the main movie) to cause the main movie to play when the data has fully loaded:

```
myClip.onLoad=function(){_root.play()};
```

This is nearly the same thing as you saw earlier:

```
onClipEvent(data){
    _root.play();
}
```

There are a couple differences, however. First, you don't have to attach any code to the clip instance itself. (You do need to name the instance, of course.) Also, this technique is the only way I can think of to trigger an event when data has fully loaded into the _root timeline. That is, if you begin with `_root.loadVariables("data.txt")`, you won't find a clip instance onto which you place the `onClipEvent(data)` code. Even though you can't attach code to it, _root *is* a clip, and therefore you can do the following:

```
_root.onData=function(){_root.play()};
```

Finally, the only warning about using callback functions is that the sequence of code does matter. In this example, you want to declare the callback function first (that is, what's going to happen when it's fully loaded) and then start loading.

Therefore, the complete code would look like this:

```
_root.stop();
_root.onData=function(){_root.play()};
_root.loadVariables("data.txt");
```

There's more information about callback functions in Chapter 14; it's just being applied here.

Loading Variables into a LoadVars Object

Using the new LoadVars object is more than just a way to show off to your geeky friends. There are some nice new features that make it really worth learning.

The first step is to create a variable that contains an instance of the LoadVars object:

```
myVars=new LoadVars();
```

Then, you can define what you want to occur when data is loaded:

```
myVars.onLoad=function(){_root.play()};
```

Then, simply commence to download the data:

```
myVars.load("data.txt");
```

This looks similar to the callback technique shown earlier, but instead of using a Movie Clip instance as the object, you first create an instance of a LoadVars object and use that instead. (We'll look at why LoadVars is more convenient than loading into clips shortly.) It's important to realize that the variables that eventually load into the movie will be named properties of the myVars variable. That is, if the data contains a variable age, it will be this.myVars.age. This should look identical to loading into clips (where the variables become part of the clip).

Finally, the good stuff. Among the handful of methods and properties in the LoadVars object, the most interesting are getBytesLoaded() and getBytesTotal(), which enable you to easily determine how much has downloaded. Even though your external data shouldn't be particularly huge, it still can take a little while to download. While you're forcing the user to wait for all the data to load, you can accurately report how much has downloaded (by using a visual progress bar, for example). Here's a little snippet of code that will display the amount of data loaded into a text field called message:

```
1 myVars=new LoadVars();
2
3 function myCheck(){
```

```
 4   if ( myVars.getBytesLoaded()==0){
 5     return;
 6   }
 7   var percent=(myVars.getBytesLoaded()/myVars.getBytesTotal())*100;
 8   percent=Math.floor(percent);
 9   message.text="Loaded: "+ percent +"%";
10 }
11 intervalID=setInterval(myCheck,50);
12
13 function done(){
14   clearInterval(intervalID);
15   if (myVars.loaded){
16     message.text="Loaded:100%"
17   }else{
18     message.text="No data file found";
19   }
20 }
21 myVars.onLoad=done;
22
23 myVars.load("http://www.phillipkerman.com/test.txt");
```

Even though this code doesn't show anything particularly, it does warrant a quick walk through. In line 1, I put an instance of the LoadVars object into myVars. Then, notice in line 11 that I use setInterval() to start triggering the myCheck() function (every 50 milliseconds). (I store it in the variable intervalID so that I can clear it later.) Because the myCheck() function will begin checking as soon as line 11 executes, you can see that I placed a quick escape inside the myCheck() function on line 4. That is, if myVars.getBytesLoaded() is absolutely 0, I exit the function. Line 7 inside myCheck() is pretty simple: I set percent equal to "loaded" divided by "total" multiplied by 100. Then line 8 uses Math.floor() to trim the decimal values from percent. Finally, line 9 sets the text property of the message text instance to a string by combining "Loaded: " with percent and "%". Next, notice line 21, which specifies that the done() function should be triggered as the callback function when the myVars.onLoad event occurs. In line 13, the done function simply clears the interval intervalID (so that it doesn't keep executing). Then the done function checks to see whether the LoadVars object's loaded property is true and makes sure the onscreen text displays either a nice round "100%" (in the event that the last myCheck() execution found that less than 100 percent had downloaded) or a warning message. (The onLoad event triggers even when no data file is found.) Now that everything is built, line 23 initiates the load method on myVars. Notice that I'm downloading a sample text file from an actual server. To really *see* this script work, it helps to create a moderately large file and store it on a remote site; otherwise, it will load immediately, and you won't see much onscreen information.

Although the most critical issue is that you wait for data to fully load before using that data, it's also important to account for the possibility that the data never loads. Perhaps the user lost his Internet connection or your server can't find the file (or you've specified a data file with the wrong name). In such situations, it's nice to tell the user what has happened.

Building a timeout feature is really a matter of strategy—it's not like there's a timeout feature. The general approach is always the same: As you're waiting for data to load, pay attention to how much time has elapsed. If the download has not completed after a reasonable amount of time has elapsed, you can tell the user. To adjust the preceding example, just add this line of code before line 23 (where the load begins):

```
shouldBeDone=getTimer()+4000.
```

That is, four seconds from now the download *should* be complete. (You can adjust 4000 to whatever you think is reasonable.) Then change the entire myCheck() function to read as follows:

```
1  function myCheck(){
2    if ( myVars.getBytesLoaded()==0){
3      return;
4    }
5    var percent=(myVars.getBytesLoaded()/myVars.getBytesTotal())*100;
6    percent=Math.floor(percent);
7    message.text="Loaded: "+ percent +"%";
8    if (percent<100 && getTimer()>shouldBeDone){
9      clearInterval(intervalID);
10     message.text="Download is not progressing";
11     myVars.onLoad=null;
12   }
13 }
```

First, notice that only the new stuff appears in lines 8–12. The idea is that every time the myCheck() function executes, I check to see whether the conditions that both percents are less than 100 and the current time is greater than the shouldBeDone variable are met. If so, we've waited too long without the percent reaching 100. In such a case, we clear the interval function, display a message, and set the onLoad callback to null. You can put different code in this area. For example, you might want to give the user an option to continue waiting, or maybe you don't want to clear out the onLoad callback. (If you don't, it will still trigger once the data eventually loads). Anyway, you can vary this basic strategy however you want—but some kind of timeout is a nice feature for the user experience.

Data File Format

At last we're going to look at the contents of the files that get loaded via `loadVariables()` or `myLoadVarsObj.load()`. Although the contents are nothing more than a series of variable assignments, the format is not like ActionScript as you might suspect. That is, the following is *not* a legitimate file format:

```
age=37;
name=Phillip;
```

Instead, the format of the data file must be formatted in what's called *URL-encoded text*—the same format required when you use HTML to initialize Flash variables. This is a standard format about which I'm sure that you can easily find more information. I'll give you the basics here. In URL-encoded text, the preceding data looks like this:

```
age=37&name=Phillip
```

Rather than spaces or returns between variables, an ampersand is used. There are other restrictions on certain characters that cannot be used without first being converted to legitimate URL encoding. It's not so much that returns are not allowed, but consider the following string:

```
age=37
&name=Phillip
```

In this case, age's value is `"37/r/n"`—that is, 37, a return, and a line feed. (Actually, if I used a Macintosh to create this file, I might find that only the return and no line feed appears after 37.) You'll see how you can use the preceding format in a later example. The point I want to make is that age's value isn't wrong, it just includes extra garbage that we don't really want (although we can remove it). If you're using a script to generate the text file automatically, it's probably no big deal to use the standard URL-encoded format (with no spaces). If you're creating the data file by hand, however, it's much more legible if you can include returns. Consider the following two examples.

Example of standard encoding:

```
total=3&page_1=First page&page_2=Page two&page_3=Last page
```

Example with extra lines:

```
total=3
&page_1=First page
&page_2=Page two
&page_3=Last page
```

Obviously, the second example is much more legible.

Another thing to always remember is that (just like the FlashVars object/embed tag) all values are strings. You don't need quotation marks, and even if you type a number (such as 37), it is read in as `"37"`. You can easily convert any variable (after it has fully loaded) to a number version if you want. For example, `age=Number(age)` will reassign the value of `age` to a number version of `age`.

Examples of Using External Data Files

First, let's look at a simple example, and then we can explore ways to make it more sophisticated (and, unfortunately, more complicated).

Let's say you want to make a movie that displays text that's imported from an external text file. Maybe you plan to have several different famous quotations for the user to read and you want to be able to update and add quotes without reopening the source `.fla` file. External data files are perfect for this.

Create a text file called `"quotes.txt"` and type the following text:

```
quote_1=A penny saved is a penny earned
&quote_2=Haste makes waste
&quote_3=It takes two to tango
```

(Notice the ampersand before each variable in the second and third lines.)

Create a new Flash movie and save it in the same directory as the "quotes.txt" file. Into a Static Text field, type `"Loading"`, select the block of text with the Arrow tool, and convert it to a Movie Clip Symbol. Double-click to edit its contents, and then insert a blank keyframe. In this new frame (2), create a Dynamic Text field, set the Line Type to Multiline, and use the margin handle to make the width and height large enough to accommodate a lot of text. Return to the main timeline and attach the following script on the instance of the Movie Clip you just made:

```
onClipEvent (load) {
  this.loadVariables("quotes.txt")
  this.stop ();
}
onClipEvent (data) {
  this.gotoAndStop(2);
  this.allQuotes.text=quote_1 + quote_2 + quote_3;
}
```

It should work great when you test it (see Figure 16.2).

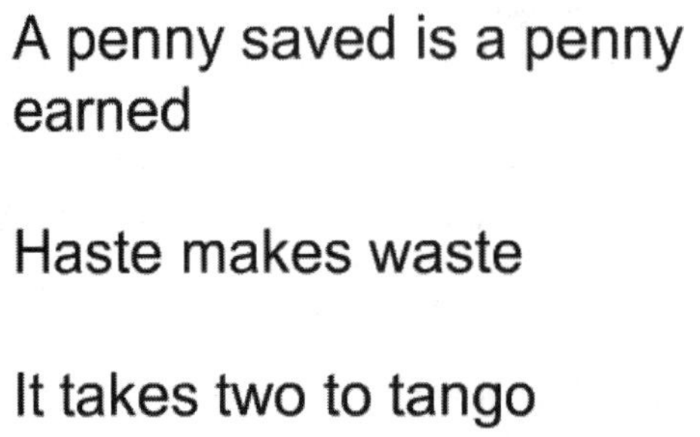

A penny saved is a penny earned

Haste makes waste

It takes two to tango

Figure 16.2 *Loading variables from text files enables you to display their values inside Flash.*

Although this exercise should give you some ideas, there are a few things we need to analyze. Notice that we first go to frame 2 and *then* set the text property of the allQuotes text field. We don't want to change the order (that is, try to set a text property before we're at a frame with the text present). Also, how did we get away with having returns in the text file? Well, when you see the quotations on the Stage, you actually see the words plus an extra return—but that's not a problem because it's at the end of the line. It just so happens that the extra returns don't pose any problems in this situation. Nonetheless, I'll show you how to remove the extra garbage at the end of the lines.

You can also spice up this example slightly by using some skills you acquired earlier. For example, you could include an additional variable in the text file that specifies how many quotes were in the file, as follows:

```
totalQuotes=3&quote_1=A penny saved is a penny earned
&quote_2=Haste makes waste
&quote_3=It takes two to tango
```

Notice that the value for the first variable (totalQuotes) doesn't have the extra return we would otherwise have to deal with. Now you can change the clip to contain just one Dynamic Text field associated with the variable currentQuote. Then, change the instance script to read:

```
onClipEvent (load) {
  this.stop ();
}
onClipEvent (data) {
  this.gotoAndStop(2);
  this.allQuotes.text=quote_1;
  this.currentQuoteNum=1;
}
```

Finally, you can use the clip's `totalQuotes` variable in conjunction with "Next Quote" and "Previous Quote" buttons. For example, here's a script for the "Next Quote" button:

```
1 on (release) {
2   if (currentQuoteNum<totalQuotes){
3     currentQuoteNum++;
4     currentQuote=this["quote_"+currentQuoteNum];
5   }
6 }
```

Basically, knowing the value of `totalQuotes` enables us to make sure that the user doesn't go too far when pressing the "Next Quote" button. Also, line 4 uses the standard bracket reference technique to address a clip or variable with a dynamic string (`path["string"]`). (Chapter 7, "The Movie Clip Object," covered this dynamic referencing technique.)

The quotations example shows the potential of external data files. I have another sample script that does several additional maneuvers, which are not only useful but are also a good way to learn the concepts. In this example, I wanted the text file to include returns after each line to make it easier to read; however, I didn't want those extra returns (and line feeds) to be part of the loaded variable. So, I needed to strip off any returns or line feeds at the end of the line. Here's the contents of the "notes.txt" file that gets loaded:

```
totalNotes=4&note_1=The note for page one is here
&note_2=Here is the note for page two
&note_3=On page three this note appears
&note_4=The fourth page has this for a note
```

I use `totalNotes` so that my Flash movie knows how many `note_` variables to load. Also, instead of remembering to strip off excess returns after the `totalNotes` variable, I figured it was still pretty legible to define `note_1` without first placing a return. The last thing to notice is that all my variables' names (except `totalNotes`) follow the same convention—that is, "note_" followed by a number.

Here's the script that I attached to the clip into, in which the variables were loaded:

```
1 onClipEvent (load) {
2   this.loadVariables("notes.txt");
3 }
4 onClipEvent (data) {
5   totalNotes=Number(totalNotes);
6   for (var i=0; i<totalNotes; i++ ) {
7     var thisOne=this["note_"+(i+1)];
```

```
 8    var lastChar=thisOne.charCodeAt(thisOne.length-1);
 9    while (lastChar==10 || lastChar==13 ) {
10      thisOne=thisOne.substr(0,thisOne.length-2);
11      lastChar=thisOne.charCodeAt(thisOne.length-1);
12    }
13    this["note_"+(i+1)]=thisOne;
14  }
15  //done
16 }
```

Let me explain each line. Because the bulk of the code is in a data clip event, it won't execute until all the variables are loaded. On line 5, I convert the totalNotes variable to a number because all variables loaded will be strings. Next, I start a for loop in line 6 (which encloses everything except the very last line). The for loop sets i to 0 and keeps incrementing i while i is less than the totalNotes variable. Notice the use of var in the for loop statement; I want this variable to be discarded automatically when the function finishes. Inside the loop (and every time the loop iterates), on line 7, I set the temporary variable thisOne to the value of this["note_"+(i+1)] (translated: the first time that I find the value of note_1—because i starts at 0). Because the string note_1 is in brackets preceded by an address (this), it returns the value of note_1. Now, with thisOne containing the value of note_1, I can start stripping return characters or line feeds from it. In line 8, I put the last character into the variable lastChar and begin a while loop on line 9 that will continue "while" lastChar's charCode is either 10 or 13 (the codes for linefeed and return, respectively). Notice that the while loop strips the last character for every iteration (and resets lastChar to the new last character). Line 13 in the for loop re-assigns a value to the current note variable to thisOne (the string that has had its end characters trimmed). Finally, after every "note" variable has gone through the process of stripping excess characters and moving into the root timeline, I have a comment in line 15 where I would put any code I want to execute now that the variables are all fixed. Perhaps this.play() would be appropriate. You can test this script with the Debugger open to verify that it works. It's really cool if you put a breakpoint on line 10 and then step into the code with the Locals tab selected so that you want watch the string get fixed (see Figure 16.3). Try adding a few extra returns into the source notes.txt file to have even more to watch while stepping the code.

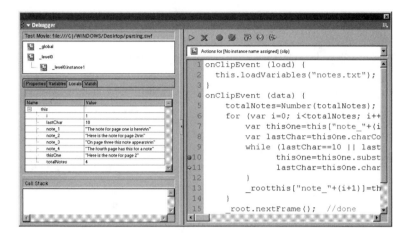

Figure 16.3   *Adding a breakpoint and stepping into the code is a great way to watch the loop do its work.*

Server Scripts

It might seem as though we went through a lot of effort just to load text files that ultimately have to be edited by hand. They're not really *that* dynamic if you have to open the darn text file to make a change. Don't forget, it is indeed dynamic because you don't have to reopen the Flash movie—but we can do even more. For example, many scripting languages (such as CGI, ASP, and Perl) in effect create URL-encoded strings based on dynamic information. Such scripting languages can easily interface with databases to produce different results, depending on the current data in the database. The URL-encoded strings these languages produce can get into Flash in several ways. Practicing with creating your own text files as we did in the previous section is not a waste of time because it mimics the process involved when you make Flash interface with server scripts.

I know just enough about this subject to work productively with others who are experts on the subject. My goal in this section is to give you the tools so that you can make your Flash movies talk to (and listen to) server scripts that someone else produces. Obviously, if you know a server script language, you'll be that far ahead; otherwise, you'll either need to study that subject further or work with someone who has. One big difference between loading variables from text files and loading variables from server scripts is that you can additionally *send* data from your Flash movie to the server script. We'll look at how shortly; for now, let me give you a quick overview of how server scripts work.

Here's my quick explanation. When a user requests an HTML file from your server, the server receives the request and then decides to send the HTML file as well as any embedded images and .swf files to which the HTML refers to the user's machine. Some web pages, however, are produced dynamically. The user requests a web page, and, somehow, the server decides to send the user an HTML file that is created the instant that the user asks for it. Basically, it's as though the user says, "Give me a web page," and the server says, "Hold on one second; let me make a fresh one for you." Often, the server will look at data in a database and deliver a customized HTML file based on timely information. Other times, the web page the user sees is not only customized with timely information, but it reflects the user's personal interests. How does the server know? One way the server knows what the user wants is based on information sent when the user makes a request. For example, if you visit a search engine, type something in the search field, and then press "Search," the text you typed is sent to the server, which processes it and configures a web page just for you.

The two ways (that apply to this section) of getting data to and from the server are called GET and POST. Both have their respective advantages and disadvantages. You might have noticed a telltale sign of the GET technique because it will actually show the variables in the URL's address (for example, http://www.example.com/searchengine.html?searchfor=flashbooks). Check it out: The part after the actual HTML file looks like URL-encoded text—which is exactly what it is! In the case of POST, the data is still sent back to the server, but it's done stealthily; you won't see it in the URL address. Some servers are built around special applications that receive data from the users in the server's own proprietary way. Often you'll see your URL address end in something *other* than an HTML file (such as search.dll or search.cfm). In those cases, the server is still configuring a web page especially for you, but doing so might involve several steps. For example, before sending the user a web page, the server might store information for statistical purposes about what was requested and then send a page back. I'm not going to (nor am I able to) explain all these technologies, but just that realize data is sent from the user to a server, which responds, eventually, with a web page.

Provided that the server has been configured to send URL-encoded text back to Flash, you can easily have Flash ask the server for such a dynamic string of data. Flash taps into the standard GET and POST mechanisms to send data to a server and, optionally, get data back.

Consider the following possibilities:

- Flash can send data to a server.

- Flash can ask a server for data.

- Flash can send data to a server and get data back.

- Flash can jump to another web page at the same time that it sends data to a server.

- A server can send data to an HTML file, which in turn gives all the data to the Flash movie when it initially displays.

Instead of providing examples for each scenario, I can summarize them quite simply. The two gateways to GET and POST are through `getURL()` and `loadVariables()`. When you execute a `getURL()` hyperlink, you can optionally send all the variables currently in the `_root` main timeline by specifying either "GET" or "POST" as a third parameter. For example, `getURL ("other.html", "", "GET")` uses the GET technique. Notice that because the second parameter is for an optional window parameter, if you don't plan to use this parameter, you need to provide at least an empty string in its place. Keep in mind that most likely you'll actually specify a server application file (rather than `"other.html"`), which will not only accept the variables you're sending but, in turn, send an HTML file to the user—for example, `getURL("someapp.php","","GET")`. If you have only one custom variable in your main timeline (say, `username` and its value is currently `"phillip"`), this will perform the same function as typing the following into the URL address: `http://www.example.com/someapp.php?username=phillip`. A good way to test whether the server script is responding correctly is to type the preceding URL into the browser's address bar. (Additional variables are, as with all URL-encoded text, separated with question marks.)

The only catch to notice in preceding example is that only the variables in the main timeline are sent in a URL-encoded string.

The way to load variables from a server into Flash is so simple that you're going to flip. You use the same `loadVariables()` technique explained earlier, but instead of pointing to a text file, you simply point to a server script. For example, `myClip.loadVariables("someapp.cgi")` acts the same as loading from a text file but waits for the server to send URL-encoded variables into Flash. Keep in mind that this technique simply asks the server for variables. If you want to ask

the server for variables by first sending all of what you have in Flash's main
timeline, you simply provide either `"GET"` or `"POST"` as an additional parameter,
as in `myClip.loadVariables("someapp.cgi","GET")`.

Without explaining how to write server scripts, let me say that they can be very
easy. The most effort you'll invest is in deciding which variables will be sent
from Flash (that is, what variables the server script will need) and then which
variables need to be sent back to Flash (that is, which variables the server script
will produce). I highly recommend using either `loadVariables()` in conjunction
with the `data` clip event, or the LoadVars object along with its `onLoad` callback
function (as we did in the preceding section).

Obviously, if you were expecting an extensive explanation of server scripting,
you've been disappointed. However, there are countless resources for topics such
as CGI and the PHP scripting languages. It turns out that macromedia just introduced a new set of protocols called"Flash Remoting" to improve the way Flash
"talks" to servers. In any project, you'll spend a lot of time working in Flash
and—at the same time—the server scripting person will spend a lot of time in her
databases and scripts. But simply getting the data to travel between Flash and a
server is pretty nominal after you learn the proper protocols.

XML

Even though using `loadVariables()` to import data (and `getURL()` to send data
to a server) is quite powerful, the limiting factor is how you must format the data.
Only name-value pairs are supported, which means you can only import or
export variables and their values. Sometimes that is enough, but some types of
data are more complex than that (for example, an object with its properties). In
addition, the techniques we've seen in this chapter require that you carefully plan
the structure of such data and stick to it. After all, Flash needs to know which
variables are coming in, and a server script needs to know which variables are
being sent.

As a format, XML is not very exciting. It's not supposed to be. It's only supposed to be standardized so that data structured as XML in one program can be
interpreted by another. In Flash, XML is interesting for two reasons. First,
because it's extensible; even after you design a data structure, you can add levels
of information without breaking what's already built. Second, it's a standard that

many applications support. For example, any database program worth its salt can export a database in XML format. The exciting part is that through its extensibility, you can design your XML data to be as complex as necessary. Flash can import XML-structured data, make sense of it (that is, parse out the elements it needs), and also modify or create XML data that can be sent to server applications.

Just like the other technologies in this chapter, the difficult part isn't exchanging data (in this case, as XML data), but rather designing an application to fill a particular need. I use an imaginary application to explain the foundation tools available for exchanging XML data. Again, the challenge for you will be to apply this knowledge to your own projects as appropriate.

First, let's look at the way some simple XML data is formatted. In my example, we'll load in data from a text file that contains XML-structured data. (It would be just as easy to load the same data from a server application that provides it in XML format.)

```
<ROSTER>
<STUDENT>
  <NAME>Phillip</NAME>
  <SEX>MALE</SEX>
  <GPA>4.0</GPA >
  <DEGREE>Photography</DEGREE>
</STUDENT>
</ROSTER>
```

XML separates the structure from the data (not unlike the code-data separation concept discussed in Chapter 3, "The Programmer's Approach"). Tags—or, to use an XML term, *nodes*—such as <ROSTER>, <STUDENT>, and <GPA> serve to provide arbitrary names for the data they enclose. For example, the value of the <GPA> node is "4.0". You can have nodes nested inside of nodes; for example, <NAME>, <SEX>, <GPA>, and <DEGREE> are all "children" nodes of the <STUDENT> node (which, in turn, is a child node of <ROSTER>).

In this example, notice that enclosed in the ROSTER node, is a STUDENT. Inside the student node, there are four nodes (NAME, SEX, GPA, and DEGREE), each of which encloses a value. Depending on the level of the hierarchy, you can look at this data in different ways. For example, there's only one student in the roster. The name for the first (and only) student is Phillip, his GPA is 4.0, and so on. You can extend this basic format to include more students provided that they are enclosed between the tags <STUDENT> and </STUDENT>. If they are going to be

elements of the roster as well, additional students must appear before the closing
</ROSTER>. Consider the following example:

```
<ROSTER>
<STUDENT>
  <NAME>Phillip</NAME>
  <SEX>male</SEX>
  <GPA>4.0</GPA >
  <DEGREE>Photography</DEGREE>
</STUDENT>
<STUDENT>
  <NAME>Sally</NAME>
  <SEX>female</SEX>
  <GPA>3.81</GPA >
  <DEGREE>Painting</DEGREE>
</STUDENT>
</ROSTER>
```

This is a very basic XML structure to which you can add additional elements at
will. Not only can you add more children to the ROSTER node (that is more
STUDENTs), but also you can add children to the STUDENT node—perhaps a
GRADUATION_DATE tag. Also, it's possible to add attributes to any node. Think of
attributes like named properties of objects. Attributes are a good solution when
you know how much data is expected. For example, because you don't know the
total number of students, regular nodes would be best. However, if you *know* that
each student will have an ID number, you can create an ID attribute. Compare
nodes to array items—of which you can have any number. Named properties are
like attributes because it's easiest if you know their names. To add an attribute—
in this case a student ID number for each student node—you can change <STU-
DENT> to <STUDENT ID="123">. You can add additional attributes within the tag,
for example _<STUDENT ID="123" YEAR="Sophomore" EXPECTED_GRAD="1989">.
Later, you'll see how easy it is to extract such attribute values.

So far, we've just been formatting the data. There's at least one more detail
that you need to add to an XML data file: a declaration at the top
(<?xml version="1.0"?>). Besides being a requirement, the declaration ultimately means that the first node we care about is really the first child. Notice that
I include only the version property. There are other properties that you can
include in the declaration that generally let you explain the overall structure and
mode of operation—but this one is the minimum necessary.

Here is a complete XML data source used for the following examples (that I'm saving in a file called `"my_data.xml"`):

```
<?xml version="1.0"?>
<CATALOG>
<SONG duration="2:50">
  <TITLE>Alec Eiffel</TITLE>
  <ALBUM>Trompe Le Monde</ALBUM>
  <LABEL>4AD</LABEL>
  <ARTIST>Pixies</ARTIST>
</SONG>
<SONG duration="5:16">
  <TITLE>Optimistic</TITLE>
  <ALBUM>Kid A</ALBUM>
  <LABEL>Capitol</LABEL>
  <ARTIST>Radiohead</ARTIST>
</SONG>
<SONG duration="2:37">
  <TITLE>Brass Monkey</TITLE>
  <ALBUM>Licensed to Ill</ALBUM>
  <LABEL>Columbia</LABEL>
  <ARTIST>Beastie Boys</ARTIST>
</SONG>
<SONG duration="2:43">
  <TITLE>I don't want to grow up</TITLE>
  <ALBUM>Adios Amigos</ALBUM>
  <LABEL>Radioactive Records</LABEL>
  <ARTIST>Ramones</ARTIST>
  <WRITER>Tom Waits</WRITER>
</SONG>
</CATALOG>
```

{ Note }

Before we jump into Flash to learn how to load in all this data, let me point out a couple things. First, XML data needs to be "valid." For example, every < must be balanced with a corresponding >. There are other rules to make valid XML files. If you use a plain text editor, it's easy to make a small typo that will invalidate the XML. When your XML data grows you should probably consider getting a dedicated XML editor. On the simple (and free) end of the spectrum is Microsoft's XML notepad (`http://msdn.microsoft.com/ library/default.asp?url=/library/en-us/dnxml/html/xmlpaddown- load.asp`). On the advanced end of the spectrum, you'll find XML Spy (`http://www.xmlspy.com/`), which will help manage many XML files. I've used both of these Windows-based programs, and they both help create valid XML.

Notice that spaces and returns (like in my XML data) make it more legible. (I'm talking about the spaces between the tags.) While this is totally valid, XML it will pose a problem if you're viewing the Flash movie in a Flash Player prior to version 5.41. (In Workshop Chapter 1, "Ensuring that Users Have the Flash Player 6," you'll learn how to check exactly which version the user has.) In the upcoming scripts, I am careful to take advantage of an XML Object property called `ignoreWhite` (which effectively resolves an issue for earlier Flash Players). Basically, if users have the old Flash Player, blank spaces can be interpreted as nodes; therefore, your first node may be a space character! Because the Flash Player 6 has vastly improved the speed performance of XML parsing, it seems reasonable to require users to have the new Player. Of course, it's possible that you don't want to force the users to download the most-recent Player (although I think you'd be doing them a favor). If that's the case, you can send all the loaded XML data through a recursive function that searches for illegitimate characters and removes erroneous nodes. Basically, clean it up before you try to use it. Flash guru Colin Moock has a nice piece of code that does just that, available at: www.moock.org/asdg/codedepot (under "strip xml whitespace").

To load this data into Flash, we need to use the XML object. The general procedure is to instantiate the object, load data from an XML source, and then parse the data into a form that we can use inside Flash. Just like `loadVariables`, you want to make sure that the data is fully loaded before you start trying to use it—and naturally, there's a way to ensure that it's loaded. Here's a starter script that you could put in the first frame:

```
my_xml=new XML();
my_xml.load("data.xml");
```

This script creates an instance of the XML object, places it in the variable `my_xml`, and then uses the `load()` method to start the import process. By the way, `"data.xml"` could just as easily be a URL address or a server application that returns XML structured data. It's really best that you adjust the preceding code to appear as follows:

```
my_xml=new XML();
my_xml.ignoreWhite=true;
my_xml.onLoad=parse;
my_xml.load("data.xml");
```

The second line sets the ignoreWhite property to true so that blank space between nodes is ignored (as explained earlier). The third line sets the onLoad callback function to trigger the homemade parse() function (which we'll write in a minute) as soon as the data is fully loaded. Notice that we do all of this before we start loading in the fourth line. If you want to advance to the next frame when importing is complete, you could change the line to read:

```
my_xml.onLoad=_root.nextFrame();
```

(Notice that I refer to the _root time absolutely, not by using this example—that would address the my_xml object, which can't go to the next frame.)

So, that's really it! The first line made an object. Next we set the ignoreWhite property, and then specified a function name that we want to execute when it's finished. Then after it was fashioned like we need, we can start loading. Next we can write the parse() function, which will go through all the XML data and extract parts that we can use in Flash. This is a common approach: Structure your data as you want it, load it in, and use only the parts you want. For example, you could make an array full of the XML data's values. You could also load the XML data and extract portions (from the my_xml variable), as needed. Finally, you could send the XML data back to a server (say, after your Flash movie has made adjustments the user has invoked). In the following example, we'll just load in all the data and then parse it into an array full of generic objects—in addition to fashioning a presentable string (to appear onscreen).

Here is the final script that steps through all the XML data, populates an array, and builds a string containing both the node names and the node values:

```
1 function parse(success){
2   if (!success){
3     trace("problem");
4     return;
5   }
6   myCatalog=new Array();
7   var songs=this.childNodes[0].childNodes;
8   for (var s=0; s<songs.length; s++){
9     var thisData= new Object();
10    thisData.duration=songs[s].attributes.duration;
11    for (var t=0; t<songs[s].childNodes.length;t++){
12      thisData[songs[s].childNodes[t].nodeName] =
➥songs[s].childNodes[t].firstChild.nodeValue;
13    }
14    myCatalog[s]=thisData;
15  }
16  doString();
17 }
```

Let me first explain this function's objective and how it works in pseudo-code; then we can walk through each line. In the end, I want an array (myCatalog) that contains a slot for each song. Each song will be in the form of a generic object with named properties (one for duration, for TITLE, and so on). I want to use a generic object for each song because named properties are easier to access. For example, the duration for the first song in my array is returned with the expression myCatalog[0].duration. If I had made an array for each song, I'd have to remember the index for each value (for example, duration could be in slot 0— but I'd have to remember). However, named properties are slightly more difficult to handle when you don't know how many each song will contain. You can see that it gets sort of ugly in the for loop in lines 11–13. (I'll explain them shortly.) If I had known that each song had a value for duration plus four nodes (TITLE, ALBUM, LABEL, and ARTIST), it would have been slightly easier. However, just to mix things up, I added another node for WRITER in the last song. This meant I couldn't do something such as myObject.title=*title* and myObject.album=*album* because I would be locked into the same structure for each song. (Naturally, the italic text would need to be replaced with expressions that resulted in values from the current song's nodes.) So the objective is to make an array of songs, with each song being a generic object with named properties.

As a quick pseudo-code explanation: My function steps through each child node of "catalog." For each song, it first grabs the value for the duration attribute and then steps through each child-node of the song. For each node inside the song, I grab both the name of the node and its value. Sounds easy enough, eh? (I'll explain some techniques to make it fairly easy after the code walkthrough.)

Now for the walkthrough: You should notice in the first few lines that my parse() function expects a parameter (success). The funny part is that I didn't say anything about parameters when I identified the callback function (my_xml.onLoad = parse). Well, the parameter is just a built-in feature of the onLoad event. Because onLoad triggers even when there's a failure, the value for success (either true or false) tells you whether onLoad is triggering because it's really finished loading or because there was a problem. (By the way, as an exercise, you might try to re-work some of the preceding scripts using the LoadVars object's onLoad event; the same "success" parameter works there, too.) Anyway, if there was a problem, I just return out of the function (line 4).

The meat starts on line 6, where I initialize the main array (myCatalog). Line 7 creates a local variable (songs) that contains an array full of all the songs. That is, "this" is the whole XML node and `this.childNodes` is an array of all the children nodes of the whole XML (really, just the `CATALOG` node). The first node of the children (`this.childNodes[0]`) is the first `CATALOG`. In this case, there's only one catalog; however, to get an array of the songs within the first catalog, we grab all the child nodes of that catalog: `this.childNodes[0].childNodes`. In line 8, I define my main loop (looping through all the songs in the catalog). The songs variable is already proving useful, as I use its `length` to calculate the number of times to loop. (My variable s will go from 0 to 3 for four songs.) Line 9 initializes a generic object (`thisData`) into which I will store data about the current song. Notice that line 9 executes for each song, so I create a fresh one each time, and then (on line 14) I stuff it into a slot of `myCatalog` (before looping again). Line 10 simply assigns the `duration` property of my `thisData` variable to the value of the `duration` attribute of this song. Because songs is an array of all songs, `songs[s]` is the first song (if s is 0). That song's `attributes` property (`songs[s].attributes`) contains all the attributes, but since we want only the `duration` attribute, we use `songs[s].attributes.duration`. Then, in order to loop through each node in this song (`songs[s]`), the `for` loop in line 11 sets a variable t to loop through all the `childNodes` (of this song) or `songs[s].childNodes.length`. Line 12 looks sort of ugly—but it's really just long. The pseudo-code is `thisData.currentNodeName=currentNode`'s value. That is, I want to set a property in `thisData` with the same name as the node. The value for that property will be that node's value. As you recall, to access or set properties for which you don't know their actual names, you use `object[string]`. So, the part on the left side of line 12 is simply setting a property name called `songs[s].childNodes[t].nodeName` (that is, the `nodeName` property of this song's current child—if the loop variable t is 0, then the first child). The funky thing (I think) is that you don't just say `songs[s].childNodes[t].nodeValue` to get the node's value, but rather `songs[s].childNodes[t].firstChild.nodeName`. If `songs[0].childNodes[0].nodeName` is `"TITLE"`, then `songs[0].childNodes[0].firstChild.nodeValue` is the `TITLE` tag's value. Think of it this way: The text that appears within the node tag is the value of that node's first child. If you understood all that, you can skip the next paragraph (where I show some tricks to deduce these expressions). Anyway, right outside the loop in line 14, I stuff into `myCatalog` (into slot s) all this data (the value for each node as well as the `duration` attribute). Then, in the last line, I trigger another function: `doString()` (which is discussed later).

If you think I just typed in those long expressions and got it right on the first try, you don't know me very well. I tried a few variations in a `trace` statement. I did it in pieces, always diving down from the top. For example, I initially wanted to know how to address the main catalog. My `parse()` function contained only one line: `trace(this.childNodes[0].nodeName)`. Even that expression could take some time to work out, but once I had a handle on it, I could comment that line (to save it for later), and then move on to trying to express the first song. The point is that once I did such gymnastics, I had a library of expressions that I could grab later. If I needed to address a song, I could grab all or part of one of the `trace` statements I had tested. Such warm-up exercises are a great way to start. Once you know how to access any item in the XML data, you can concentrate on writing the function—looping and populating the array. Occasionally, I'd have to pause and consider how to address another node (or child...or whatever), but I could check my thinking quickly with a `trace` statement.

I should probably mention that there's no requirement that you move your XML data into an array. I usually do it this way because I'm just more comfortable accessing data in arrays and generic objects than nodes and children of XML. Here's a function nearly identical to the `parse()` function. It's what I call in line 17 in the preceding example. The idea simply is to extract data from the XML object and present it onscreen (in a text field called `my_txt`:

```
function doString(){
  var songs=my_xml.childNodes[0].childNodes;
  var theString= "My " + my_xml.childNodes[0].nodeName +
                 " has " +songs.length + " "+
                 my_xml.childNodes[0].firstChild.nodeName +
                 "s \r _____" + "\r";
  for (var s=0; s<songs.length; s++){
    theString += "#"+s+" "+
    my_xml.childNodes[0].firstChild.nodeName + "===="  +"\r"+
    "Duration: "+songs[s].attributes.duration + "\r";
    for (var t=0; t<songs[s].childNodes.length;t++){
      theString += songs[s].childNodes[t].nodeName + " = " +
      songs[s].childNodes[t].firstChild.nodeValue +"\r";
    }
  }
  my_txt.text=theString;
}
```

It might look different, but it's same nested loop structure from the `parse()` function. In this case, though, I'm fashioning a text string. You can see how the finished output looks with content below. Notice that I'm taking advantage of the fact that Flash ignores line breaks. I did it just for legibility. Also, notice that I can't refer to the main XML node using this (as I did in the parse() function). The reason it worked before is that parse was identified as the onLoad callback function for the my_xml instance. Therefore, the "this" was my_xml. The doString() function was invoked in the last line of parse(). There is no "this" for doString(), except the function itself.

Here's the onscreen output from the doString() function:

```
My CATALOG has 4 SONGs
.
#0 SONG====
Duration: 2:50
TITLE = Alec Eiffel
ALBUM = Trompe Le Monde
LABEL = 4AD
ARTIST = Pixies
#1 SONG====
Duration: 5:16
TITLE = Optimistic
ALBUM = Kid A
LABEL = Capitol
ARTIST = Radiohead
#2 SONG====
Duration: 2:37
TITLE = Brass Monkey
ALBUM = Licensed to Ill
LABEL = Columbia
ARTIST = Beastie Boys
#3 SONG====
Duration: 2:43
TITLE = I Don't Want To Grow Up
ALBUM = Adios Amigos
LABEL = Radioactive Records
ARTIST = Ramones
WRITER = Tom Waits
```

To really study all the code in this section, it's best to see it in Flash with syntax coloring. You can download code for this chapter from www.phillipkerman.com/actionscripting. Figure 16.4 shows a visualization of the data from this example.

Hopefully you can see *some* of the potential for XML-structured data. It's easy for me to say that most of the work really isn't *in* Flash, but rather in the way you design the XML solutions. It's true. You'll find your time is spent deciding how the data will be structured and then parsing out just the elements (node values) that you can use. It doesn't hurt, however, to remember the following key points:

- Right before you initiate the load() command, you should identify a callback function to execute when it's finished loading—that is my_xml.onLoad=someFunction. This way you'll know for sure when the data has loaded.

- Extracting nodes, their values, and their properties utilizes one of the following methods: firstChild, which returns an XML object; childNodes, which returns an array of all the nodes nested within a node; or nodeName and nodeValue, which both return strings.

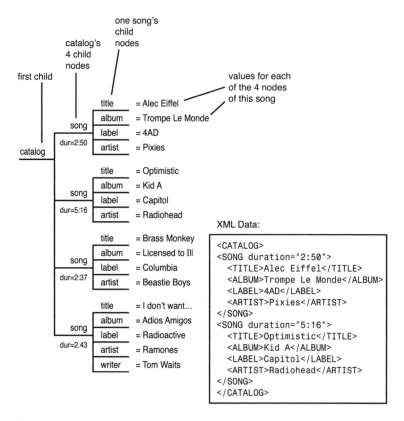

Figure 16.4 *A hierarchical view of the XML data (in the file on the right) shows that values are ascertained only for nodes three levels deep.*

Local SharedObjects

New to MX

It's hard to pick a favorite new feature in Flash MX, but local SharedObjects has got to be one. Basically, local SharedObjects are like HTML cookies—but much more. They enable you to store data (securely on users' hard drives) and then read that data later when they revisit your site. For example, if they've typed in their names the first time they visited your site, you can present them with a "Welcome back..." message when they return. The process is not only simple, but it requires no server technology. Naturally, like most things, coming up with a good strategy on how to use local SharedObjects takes a little more work.

The idea is that you store data in a generic object and then save that object in a special file on the users' hard drives. Even the data types of the values in your generic object are retained. This is a big deal. Numbers are stored as numbers, arrays as arrays, and so on. Compared to all the other techniques that send and receive string-only data (such as `loadVariables()`), this is a major convenience. (In the "Advanced Local SharedObject Examples" section, you'll see how easily different data types are stored .)

The data for your local SharedObject is stored in a text file located in a subfolder of the "Flash Player" folder in a designated location (depending on the user's operating system). The subfolder's name matches your web site's domain, but within *that* folder, you have some control over where the file is saved.

Example: Never See the Intro Again

Here's a simple example that jumps a user who has visited this site ahead to a frame labeled `"post_intro"`:

```
1 my_so= SharedObject.getLocal("myCookie");
2 if (my_so.data.seenIntro){
3   gotoAndPlay("post_intro");
4 }
5 my_so.data.seenIntro=true;
6 my_so.flush();
```

Let me explain each line. Line 1 effectively instantiates a generic object and places it in the homemade variable `my_so`. It's nearly the same as saying `my_so=New Object()`, except that the object we create above automatically includes a named property called `data`, and it's value is in the form of a generic object. As if you had another line of code (`my_so.data=new Object()`), it's just automatic when you use the `getLocal()` method of the local SharedObject. Line 1 also attempts to determine whether there is already a local SharedObject file on this user's machine (in this case, a file called "myCookie.sol"). Finally, line 1 will create such a file if none exists. Anyway, the very first time this runs, the condition for the `if` statement (line 2) is false. That is, `my_so.data.seenIntro` is undefined, so it doesn't evaluate to `true` and they skip down to line 5. At that point, the seenIntro property (of the data property in the my_so object) is set to true. Finally, in line 6, the flush() method forces all new values in the my_so variable to be written to disk. If you type this code into frame 1 of your movie (and make a frame, say, out at frame 10 labeled "post_intro"), the second time you test the movie, it will jump ahead to frame 10.

Details of Local SharedObject Files

There are just a couple of details to know about before I show you a more advanced example. The getLocal() method first looks for a file, and then creates one if none is found. The name of the file matches the parameter plus ".sol" (for, SharedObject Library). The exact location of that file is within the Flash Player folder. And the Flash Player folder is in a different location on every operating system. (You can find details about this location in the readme file in the Configuration folder—adjacent to your installed version of Flash.) Within the Flash Player folder, .sol files are always saved under a folder name that matches your domain (such as phillipkerman.com), or if you're running the movie locally, inside a folder called localhost. Within your domain's folder, additional sub-folders are created to match exactly which part of your web site the user visited. For example, if you're only using local SharedObjects in an .swf that resides in a folder called "flashsite" that sits in the root directory of your domain (say, phillipkerman.com), then .sol files generated by .swfs in the flashsite folder will appear in the folder Flash Player\phillipkerman.com\flashsite\.

This automatic sub-folder creation means that from different parts of your site you could create .sol files with the same name, and you'll have no conflicts. In practice, though, I think this might be complicated—and, besides, it's easy to come up with unique names for the .sol files (it's the first parameter in the getLocal() method). However, if you *want* to share data from .sol files throughout different parts of your site, you can override the default behavior of sub-folder creation. Specifically, an optional second parameter in the getLocal() method enables you to specify a path. For example, getLocal("myCookie", "/") will access the myCookie.sol file in the root directory and getLocal("myCookie","/datafolder") will access myCookie.sol in a subdirectory called datafolder. By the way, .sol files cannot include spaces or any of the following characters: ~ % & \ ; : " ' , < > ? #.

Disk Space Limits

There are a few more miscellaneous details. The flush() method immediately tries to write data to disk. If you never bother to invoke the flush() command, it should do so automatically when the user leaves your site. It still seems safer to invoke it at logical points in time (namely, when the user makes some kind of significant change that you want to save). Notice that I said flush() attempts to write the data to disk. In fact, the amount of data that you're able to store is limited by the user's settings, which are accessible from the Flash Player when they right-click on a Flash movie playing in the browser (or control-click, for Mac users) — see Figure 16.5.

Figure 16.5   *The user will be presented with the Macromedia Flash Player Settings dialog box as soon as a movie attempts to save large amounts of data.*

Actually, the user will see the Macromedia Flash Player Settings dialog box appear any time you attempt to save more data than they have set. (The default is 100KB.) Whatever setting the user makes is permanent. The whole strategy works very well in its automatic form (presenting the dialog box only when necessary, for example). However, you can monitor which setting the user has granted to you. Any time you invoke flush() and your .sol file will exceed the user's current settings, she will see the Macromedia Flash Player Settings dialog box. To trigger a function when she finally answers the dialog box, you can use the onStatus event. Here's an example that you can place after the getLocal() step but before the first flush() occurrence. In this example the text property of a field called `message` will update according to how the user has answered the dialog box:

```
my_so.onStatus= function(info){
  if (info.code=="SharedObject.Flush.Success"){
    message.text="It worked!";
  }
  if (info.code=="SharedObject.Flush.Failed"){
    message.text="It failed."
  }
}
```

Basically, we're just assigning a function as the callback for the `onStatus` event of our my_so object. Notice that the built-in parameter (which I'm calling `info`). It includes a property called `code` containing a string that reports what issue occurred (good or bad). Keep in mind that the above function will never execute nor will the user automatically see the settings in the dialog box unless your `flush()` method is about to pose a problem (go over the quota). To test code like that above, you can include the optional parameter for the flush() method—that is, a "minimum disk space." For example, `flush(100)` will see if it's okay to save 100KB. You might request more space than you really need in order to get the user's approval early instead of finding out later that you can't save all the data you've gathered. You can also force the settings dialog to appear anytime with teh code: `system.showSettings()`. By the way, you can ascertain the current size of your SharedObject instance by using the `getSize()` method, as in `my_so.getSize()`.

One more detail and then you'll see an example that brings it all together. The `flush()` command will actually return information as to the success of the operation. That is, you *can* say `my_so.flush()`, but you can also say `result=my_so.flush()`—and the value of `result` will turn into either `true`, `false`, or (the string) `"pending"`. You'll get `true` when it was a success, `false` when the user has already said "deny" or there was some kind of error, and `"pending"` if the Settings dialog box was forced to appear (and therefore you're waiting for the user's response). Regardless of how fast the user clicks "allow" or "deny," the value returned from `flush()` will stay "pending." A practical situation might be that you want the movie to pause if the Settings dialog box appears. You'll need to stop the movie only if `flush()` returns "pending." To get the movie rolling again, you'll want to use the `onStatus` event (and respond according to the `code` property discussed earlier—that is, according to how the user answered).

Advanced Local SharedObject Examples

It turns out that 100KB is really a fair bit of data. In this next example, I give users the ability to create blocks and then drag them to any location onscreen. When they revisit the site, everything appears as they left it. You'll see that just saving and restoring the local SharedObject data is fairly simple; the majority of the work involves gathering the data while the users interact as well as re-displaying the clips when they return. My basic strategy was to keep count of each new clip the users created. That way, I could name each instance `this["clip_"+count]` and place it in a level number equal to `count`. Then, when it came time to save data, I would loop through 1, through the value of `count`, and gather information about each clip: its location and its color. (Each clip is an instance of the same clip, just colored differently.) Inside the first keyframe of the "dragclip" is the following code:

```
this.onPress=function(){
  dragging=true;
}
this.onRelease=function(){
  _root.updateRecords();
  dragging=false;
}
this.onReleaseOutside=function(){
  _root.updateRecords();
  dragging=false;
}
this.onMouseMove=function(){
  if(dragging){
    this._x=_parent._xmouse;
    this._y=_parent._ymouse;
    updateAfterEvent();
  }
}
```

This code has little to do with local SharedObjects. Notice, however, that whenever the user lets go, I call the custom function `updateRecords()` (which you'll see in a minute). I suppose it might look a bit fancy the way no code is placed on any clips—but since this clip will be spawn by way of `attachMovie`, I couldn't put any code *on* the clip. Anyway, this clip has a linkage identifier of `"dragclip"`.

Next I had three button instances (named red, green, and blue) on the Stage. In addition, I placed the following code in the first keyframe:

```
1 red.onPress=function(){pick(1)}
2 green.onPress=function(){pick(2)}
3 blue.onPress=function(){pick(3)}
4
5 colors=[0xFF0000, 0x00FF00, 0x0000FF];
6 function pick(which){
7   count++;
8   this.attachMovie("dragclip","clip_"+count,count);
9   this["clip_"+count].c=new Color(this["clip_"+count]);
10   this["clip_"+count].c.setRGB(colors[which-1]);
11   updateRecords();
12 }
```

The first three lines cause the three buttons to trigger the pick() function—but with a different value for a parameter each time. Line 5 contains an array full of color values (red, green, and blue). The pick() function (line 6) first increments count (so that the first time it will be 1, then 2, and so on). Then it creates a new instance of the "dragclip" symbol with an instance name clip_1 (or, clip_2—based on count) and places it in a level number matched to count. The next two lines (9 and 10) set the newly created clip's color. Notice that this["clip_"+count] appears in a few places—this is just a dynamic reference to the newly created clip. The first line stores a Color object instance into the variable c (that is part of the clip at hand). The second line sets the RGB of that Color object instance to a color from the colors array, based on the value for the parameter received (which). Finally, the homemade function updateRecords()is called—which you're about to see.

My final code has more stuff *above* the code I just showed you, but it's easiest to look at the code in this order. Anyway, the following code is placed above what you just saw, even though I'm going to explain the updateRecords() function next (despite the fact that it's at the bottom of the following code first):

```
1 my_so= SharedObject.getLocal("locations","/");
2
3 if (my_so.data.count!=undefined){
4   count=my_so.data.count;
5   for(var i=1; i<count+1;i++){
6     this.attachMovie("dragclip","clip_"+i,i);
7     var thisOne=this["clip_"+i];
8     thisOne.c=new Color(thisOne);
9     thisOne.c.setRGB(my_so.data.clipLocs[i-1].c);
10     thisOne._x=my_so.data.clipLocs[i-1].x;
11     thisOne._y=my_so.data.clipLocs[i-1].y;
```

```
12    }
13  }
14  function updateRecords(){
15    my_so.data.count=count;
16    my_so.data.clipLocs=new Array();
17    for(var i=1; i<count+1;i++){
18      var thisOne=this["clip_"+i];
19      var thisData=new Object();
20      thisData.x=thisOne._x;
21      thisData.y=thisOne._y;
22      thisData.c=thisOne.c.getRGB();
23      my_so.data.clipLocs.push(thisData)
24    }
25    my_so.flush();
26  }
```

In line 1, you can that see I'm storing into the variable my_so either a new
instance of the local SharedObject (if there wasn't one already) or a copy of the
old one. Line 3 begins the restoration process automatically, but let's jump down
to line 14 where the updateRecords() is defined. After all, the if statement's
condition (my_so.data.count!=undefined) will most certainly be false the first
time through (count is our variable), so the if statement is skipped. Inside the
updateRecords() function, we start stuffing properties onto the my_so.data
property. Line 15 assigns a property count equal to the movie's count variable,
and then line 16 creates a new array (into a property called clipLocs). The for
loop in line 17 goes through each one-by-one (1 through count). Line 18 creates
a local variable that points to the current clip (so that I can repeatedly type
thisOne rather than this["clip_"+i] in the following lines). Then I make a
generic object (thisData) onto which I'm about to set three named property values (x, y, and c). The clipLocs array will become an array full of generic objects
(one for each clip), and those objects will each have an x, y, and c property.
Lines 20–22 assign values for those three properties, based on the values for the
current clip's _x and _y properties plus the homemade variable c (which contains
a Color object instance). Then line 23 stuffs the generic object onto the end of
the array (using the push() method). Finally, the current value for my_so is written to disk in line 25.

Now that we know how data was saved, we can look through the restoration code
(lines 4–12). Realize lines 4–12 will be executed in the first keyframe, provided
that the condition in line 3 is true—that is, the my_so's data has a count value.
So, if we get to line 4, we know they're returning and we need to restore the variables and display. Line 4 shows the only variable we really need from the local

SharedObject file: count. That is, we need to make sure that count starts where they left off. The rest involves creating instances, putting them in the right location, and coloring them all according to values in the clipLocs array (which is a property of the data property of the my_so instance). Line 6 creates a new clip, and line 7 stores a local variable to save typing in the next few lines. Line 8 makes a new instance of the Color object into a variable c (of the current clip). Line 9 sets RGB (based on the c value found in the current position of the clipLocs array). Notice that the portion my_so.data.clipLocs[i-1] appears in several places. This simply returns the value in a particular slot of the clipLocs array (namely, the i-1 slot because i goes from 1 to count and arrays count starting at 0). The value in that slot of the clipLocs is itself a generic object (with three named properties). Looking at line 10 and 11 is somewhat intimidating unless you break it down or read it backwards: We're setting this one's _x and _y equal to the x property of the generic object in the current slot of the myLocs array (which itself is a property of the data property of the my_so instance). Believe it or not, I think it was easier to write than it is to read. If the details of this code are fuzzy, try to first understand the overall objectives and sequence. You can also download this file (from www.phillipkerman.com/actionscripting) or try to write it from scratch yourself. Hopefully, it will give you some ideas, too.

This chapter is already long, so adding one more paragraph can't hurt. After building the preceding file, I realized it was tiresome for me to keep deleting the .sol file while testing. I thought the user might want to clear everything. Well, I just added a button (instance name clear) and placed the following code in my first keyframe (see if you can find the bug):

```
1 clear.onPress=function(){
2   for(var i=1; i<count+1;i++){
3     this["clip_"+i].removeMovieClip()
4   }
5   count=0;
6   updateRecords();
7 }
```

Although this code is totally logical (and not very far off), line 3 has a bug. The problem is that this is the button instance itself. You can fix this bug by changing this to _root. While outside of the onPress callback function, this["clip_"+i] would indeed refer to the clip called clip_1 (if i were 1), but it doesn't work here because this is the button! (If you like finding bugs, you'll love Workshop Chapter 18, "Fixing Broken Scripts.")

The LocalConnection Object

I guess all the new Flash MX features are my favorite because this one is pretty cool too! The Local Connection object enables two separate Flash movies to communicate with each other. Think of it this way: This feature lets one movie trigger functions that are written in another movie. The applications for this are really quite vast. You can have different .swfs in HTML table cells or different frames triggering events in each other. Perhaps, one .swf that contains code and music is placed in a hidden frame, and then when the visitor navigates to different parts of your web site, the music continues to play. Scripts in various other movies can trigger sound effects to play in that hidden movie. Not only does the audio download just once, you won't hear any breaks in the music as different pages load. This is just one example; I can also see doing something where a pop-up HTML window containing an .swf could trigger scripts present in other windows—perhaps a master controller to play or stop other movies. Again, the hard part is coming up with an idea; the code for LocalConnection objects is really quite simple.

To work through the upcoming code, you need to consider a few things. We're going to have two movies: receiver.swf and transmitter.swf. We'll write a function inside receiver.swf and then let transmitter.swf trigger that code. Inside receiver.fla, make a text field with the instance name message, and then put the following code in the first frame:

```
lc = new LocalConnection();
lc.onMessageTime=function(param){
    message.text=param;
}
lc.connect("receiver");
```

The first line stores an instance of the LocalConnection object into the variable lc. Then, you need to define all the functions to which the other movie will be given access—in this case, just one function called onMessageTime. When the other movie invokes onMessageTime(), it will also send a single parameter (param) and we'll be able to see its value in the message text field. Finally, the last line invokes the LocalConnection object's connect() method. The name I provided ("receiver") is just an arbitrary name I came up with; the other movie will need to refer to this same name.

In the other movie (`transmitter.fla`), create a button with the following code on it:

```
on (press){
  lc = new LocalConnection();
  lc.send("receiver", "onMessageTime", getTimer());
  lc.close();
  delete lc;
}
```

This code first makes an instance of the LocalConnection object. (Because this code is in another file, however, it's not as though `lc` is the same variable.) Next, the LocalConnection object's `send()` method is invoked. The syntax is `send(theName, theFunction, parameterValue)`, where `theName` matches the name provided in the other movie's `connect()` method; *theFunction* is the function we plan to trigger; and `parameterValue` is the parameter being sent. It's almost as though this code were `onMessageTime(getTimer())`—but it doesn't work this way because `onMessageTime` is really a callback event attached to the other movie's `lc` instance; in addition, it's in another movie, so instead we address the name that the other movie connected to. The only thing I find difficult is that the syntax doesn't follow other addressing techniques we've seen. Finally, the `lc` variable (in the transmitter movie) is deleted, as we're done sending messages to the other movie and no longer need to be connected. When you export and launch both movies, you will be able to click the button in `transmitter.swf` and see a number change in the `receiver.swf` file (see Figure 16.6).

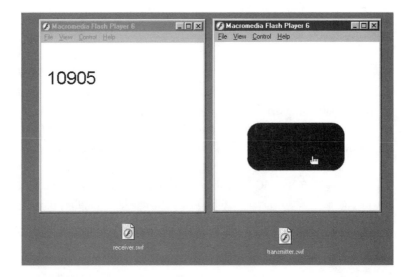

Figure 16.6 *Two separate* `.swf`*s can send messages via the LocalConnection object.*

I'm not going to work through an advanced example here; you will see one in Workshop Chapter 17, "Using the LocalConnection Object for Inter-Movie Communication." I will, however, mention a few more details about the LocalConnection object. First, it's easy to send additional parameters to your receiver movie—just separate them with commas. For example, you could trigger the onMultiFunction event and send three parameters (p1, p2, and p3) by using the following code:

```
lc.send("receiver", "onMultiFunction", p1, p2, p3);
```

Also, as with any function, you can pass any sort of data type that you want. It might be confusing because since the send() method's second parameter is always a string version of the callback name, the parameters' data type is retained. For example, you could pass an array or an object in addition to a number or a string.

One thing that I didn't really mention earlier is that the order of the code in the receiver movie is important. Notice that the first bit of code had three steps: instantiate the LocalConnection object, declare the callbacks, and *then* connect.

```
lc = new LocalConnection();
lc.onMessageTime=function(param){
   message.text=param;
}
lc.connect("receiver");
```

The point is, you want to be sure to define all the callbacks (in this case, only onMessageTime) before you connect. You can have many more callbacks, just be sure to put them before connect().

Finally, the LocalConnection object has only three methods: (open(), send(), close() (plus the System Object's allowDomain() method). They actually return a value, so you could use result=lc.open("somename"). Although they always return either true or false, the result can be different than you might expect. You might think that true means the connection was successful and that false means it was a failure. However, open() returns true if the named connection *isn't* already open, and both send() and close() return true if the named connection *is* open. It kind of makes sense: The result just tells you whether everything seems to be in order. However, additional information can be useful; namely, whether the send() method was successful. You need to define a callback function for the onStatus event. Unfortunately, I can't seem to make it work for an individual LocalConnection instance (such as

`lc.onStatus=function(){}`). However, you can overwrite one super `onStatus`
callback for the LocalConnection object itself. For example, you can place the
following code inside the transmitter movie, and it will display either `"error"` or
`"status"` (the two possible values for the LocalConnection's `onStatus` event)
into a text field called `message`:

```
LocalConnection.prototype.onStatus = function(info) {
  message.text=this.info.level;
}
```

This is just like the way we overwrote events of the Movie Clip and Array
objects in Chapter 14. It's also similar to the `onStatus` callback function we
wrote for the local SharedObject. In this case, however, the parameter received
has the interesting data hidden inside the property called `level` (rather than the
`code` property). By the way, if you want a single `onStatus` callback function like
this, but for the local SharedObject, you can change `my_so.onStatus` to read
`SharedObject.prototype.onStatus` in the definition earlier.

Summary

What can I say? This was a long chapter! It's the last one in the Foundation section, and we're about to move on to some fun workshop exercises. Hopefully,
you are beginning to see things synthesize. For example, adding callbacks to the
topics in this chapter was relatively easy because you already understand callbacks generally. At this point, you should feel comfortable in any programming
language; you haven't just been learning Flash, you've been learning programming. (Congratulations, you're now a programming geek!)

Seriously, this chapter showed you many of the ways in which Flash can interact
with the world around it. We started by including linked scripts when exporting a
movie. Then we saw how Flash can read in data from text files. The same format
was used when we learned how Flash can read data sent to it via a server script.
The advantage to server scripts is that Flash can also send data (that is, all its
variables) to the server. Although the standard technique (`loadVariables()` and
`getURL()`) used the URL-encoded format, we also took a dive into XML-structured data. We rounded out the chapter with a good look at two new Flash MX
features: local SharedObjects (to save data between sessions) and the Local
Connection Object (to let multiple `.swf`s talk to each other). Although you might
not have an immediate need for all the material in this chapter, you should have a
clear idea of what's possible.

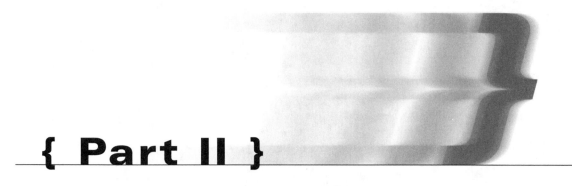

{ Part II }

Workshops

{Workshop} Introduction

Now we really get to apply the knowledge gained in the first part of the book. I can't imagine that you haven't touched Flash since starting the book, but in any case, you will now.

The first thing that I feel compelled to mention is that the code you'll find in the workshop chapters ranges from flat-out bad to really good. The bad stuff is just there for educational purposes (so that we can fix it up). Even the good stuff should not always be considered the "best." There's always more than one way to achieve a result. I would never fault code if it worked. Certainly you shouldn't write code that's unmanageable, but there's a good argument for code that's clear to you. Often the examples shown are presented in a way that makes the most sense. I didn't make sacrifices just to make the code look pretty, but I didn't spend an inordinate amount of time streamlining it either. The workshop chapters are intended to teach you a process of development as well as offer a chance to apply the topics covered in the first part of the book. (Please don't call me when you find a better way to do the same thing—consider that I'd be proud and leave it at that.)

Anyway, let me offer this quick overview of all the workshop chapters.

1. "Ensuring that Users Have the Flash Player 6." This no-nonsense workshop chapter discusses some of the ways to make sure that your audience is equipped to see your Flash 6 creation. We also walk through an exercise using Flash itself as a way to determine player version.

2. "Creating Custom Cursors." After two simple steps to make a custom cursor, this workshop chapter goes on to make a component and then a custom UI for that component. This workshop chapter is pretty involved. You learn that you can't use buttons (even invisible ones) because they would conflict with any buttons that you try to place this component over.

3. "Creating a Horizontal Slider." In this workshop chapter, we make a slider component that can work for anything from volume control to video playback. We make this component as generic and universal as possible.

4. "Building a Slide Show." In addition to the slide show application that you build, you get your first introduction to using the `onEnterFrame` event as well as disabling buttons.

5. "Mapping and Scripted Masks." The general technique of mapping is applied to a contrived exercise, but in a way that enables you to apply it to other situations. Bring your math "thinking cap" to this one.

6. "Working with Odd-Shaped Clickable Areas." Although buttons are great, this workshop chapter shows how Movie Clips (along with the `hitTest()` method) can serve as alternatives to buttons.

7. "Adapting Built-In Components." Not only does this exercise show you how to adapt the look and feel of the ComboBox component that ships with Flash, you also learn a bit about the process involved in looking through someone else's code.

8. "Creating a Currency-Exchange Calculator." We turn a simple currency-exchange calculation into a really usable application. This workshop chapter includes some fancy string maneuvers and a simple use of the new LoadVars object.

9. "Creating a ToolTip Component." The basic concepts from Workshop Chapter 2, "Creating Custom Cursors," come into play, but we use `getTimer()` for the first time to add an optional delay.

10. "Creating Timers." In this workshop chapter, we use the `getTimer()` function in a most typical way—to make three separate timers: a digital stopwatch, a traditional analog display, and a countdown timer (like a sand hourglass). The code for the first two parts is nearly identical.

11. "Using Math to Create a Circular Slider." The result of this workshop chapter doesn't look much different than a regular slider—it just follows a circular path. However, to calculate angles and draw arcs, we use several trigonometry functions from the Math object.

12. "Developing Time-Based Animations." In a simple example, we see how to use `getTimer()`to ensure perfect synchronization—and how to effectively drop frames if the animation is not keeping up.

13. "Drawing Graphs." This workshop chapter uses the new drawing functions to create graphs based on dynamic data. Then we go on to label the graph using the TextField object and add a colored mask using the new `setMask()` method.

14. "Offline Production." We'll build an animation and then save the coordinates of each step so that it can be used in a time-based application.

15. "Creating a Dynamic Slide Presentation." Here we build an XML application that dynamically loads data (including images) to build a slide show with bullet points. This workshop chapter is an exercise in using XML-structured data as well as general template design.

16. "Using the Local SharedObject to Remember User Settings." In this workshop chapter, we build a language-selection interface so that users can specify their language preferences.

17. "Using the LocalConnection Object for Inter-Movie Communication." Perhaps the most under-appreciated new feature in Flash MX is the LocalConnection object, which lets two Flash movies communicate. In this workshop chapter, we use the LocalConnection object to build a help system.

18. "Fixing Broken Scripts." This workshop chapter challenges you to fix 10 faulty Flash files (that you download from `www.phillipkerman.com/actionscripting`). For each one, you'll be given a clue and the solution to make things right.

Naturally, each of these workshop chapters involves many details that require you to use additional parts of ActionScript. After completing all the workshop chapters, consider trying to rebuild them from scratch (without the book). I'll bet that many of you will find quicker or better ways to get them running.

{ Part IIA }

Basic Workshops

{ Chapter 1
Workshop }

Ensuring That Users Have the Flash Player 6

It's safe to say that most everything covered in this book is specific to Flash MX. This means that your audience must be equipped with Flash Player 6 or later. Although it's possible to target older Flash Players using the Publish Settings (see Figure W1.1), selecting any option lower than Flash 6 causes much of the scripting capabilities to be off-limits. It's actually possible to work in Flash MX and deliver to Flash 4 or Flash 3; there are just so many details that we're not even going to discuss it. The fact is that at the beginning of 2002, about 98 percent of all Internet users had at least the Flash Player 3; even the relatively new Flash Player 5 has reached 85 percent. Although your Flash 6 movies might not work for these users, the solution outlined in this workshop will easily identify those users with anything less than the Flash Player 6 and provide alternatives for them. These alternatives range from a link to Macromedia (so that they can upgrade) to channeling them to a different version of your web page. The technique you'll learn in this workshop uses Flash to identify which version of Flash the user has.

Naturally, using Flash to test which version of Flash is installed assumes that users have at least *some* version of Flash. To provide a seamless experience for those 2 percent of users without any Flash Player, you have a host of alternatives. Unfortunately, I don't think any solution is 100 percent foolproof. I'm not saying that the alternatives I'm about to present have inherent flaws; it's just that they also rely on technology that may not be functional. For example, if you try to use JavaScript to determine whether the user has the Flash Player, it's possible that the user has turned off JavaScript in her browser. Anyway, there *are* some near ironclad solutions to reach *any* users, even if they don't have Flash.

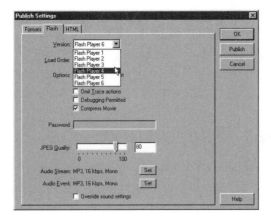

Figure W1.1   *You can target old versions of Flash using the Publish Settings, but you won't be able to use most Flash MX features.*

First I'll provide a quick rundown of two non-Flash solutions, and then walk through exactly how to use Flash to check which version of Flash is installed.

The non-Flash solutions use what's commonly called a "sniffer" script—an HTML file with scripts that attempt to sense which version of the Flash Player is installed (if any). The sniffer script is a file that serves as a gateway to redirect users to the appropriate content. Every user who visits your site always starts by visiting this gateway file. The file tries to determine whether the user can see Flash. If the user has Flash, he goes to the Flash version of your site (another page); if the user doesn't have Flash, he goes to the non-Flash version of your site. You can even send a user to a third place if he has Flash, but needs to upgrade to the latest version. The non-Flash site can be as simple as a page that provides the user a link to Macromedia, where he can download the Flash Player. The non-Flash site can also be as complex as the whole site built in HTML. The point is that the sniffer or gateway page sends the user to one of two places: the Flash site or the non-Flash site.

Macromedia has a nice set of instructions and sample files that can help you produce a sniffer page. The Flash Deployment Kit (which you can download for free
from `www.macromedia.com/software/flash/download/deployment_kit/`)
includes a gateway page (`enter.html`) and scripts in both JavaScript and
VBScript, as well as plenty of documentation. Although there are a lot of features, they all come down to how you use the "dispatcher." Basically, you just
provide the appropriate parameters to the `MM_FlashDispatch()` JavaScript function. You specify the URL for where your Flash content resides (the page where
users with the appropriate Flash Player automatically go), the minimum version
of the Flash Player required (for example, version 6,0,23), whether you want to
require the revision number (for example, 23) or just the major version number
(such as 6), the alternative URL for those users who don't have Flash, the
upgrade URL for those who have Flash but not the required version (this can be
the same as the alternative URL), and finally, whether you want to remember (by
way of a JavaScript cookie) when a user says she doesn't want to upgrade so that
you don't even bother with this whole scenario the next time and instead automatically jump to the alternative URL. So really, you just specify the web
addresses to which you want to send users in different situations, and you're
done. As you might expect, there are more details in the documentation that
comes with the Flash Deployment Kit.

{ Note }

> By the way, there's another nice set of scripts included in the Flash
> Deployment Kit called the Flash Dispatcher behaviors. It's really a
> set of Dreamweaver behaviors. The same dispatcher code from the
> Flash Deployment Kit is included in the behaviors (but made espe-
> cially for Dreamweaver). A big advantage of installing the Flash
> Dispatcher for Dreamweaver is that the code comes in the form of
> a Macromedia extension. By using the free Macromedia Extension
> Manager program, you can easily manage various extensions
> (including this one). The reason I mention it is that you can make
> Flash extensions that are also managed through this tool. It's nice
> for users because they can download and install components,
> Flash libraries, and Dreamweaver behaviors and manage them all
> through the Extension Manager.

Before we get into the main workshop, I want to mention a suitable alternative to Macromedia's set of sniffer scripts. Colin Moock has produced the Moock Flash Player Inspector (Moock FPI), which provides a similar set of alternatives to the Flash Deployment Kit. You can download the Moock FPI from www.moock.org/webdesign/flash/detection/moockfpi/.

Because this is a workshop, we're going to step through an exercise. The following exercise assumes that your user has at least the Flash Player 2. We'll create a Flash sniffer that redirects the user if he has anything less than Flash Player 6. This exercise is based on a Flash file that comes in the Flash Deployment Kit called detectFlash.fla. We'll build our own version of this file by following these steps:

1. In a new file, select File, Publish Settings. Under the Formats tab, make sure that Flash is selected. Select the Flash tab and select Flash 4 from the Version drop-down menu (refer to Figure W1.1) and click OK. After making this change, notice that many of the ActionScript components are highlighted in yellow, meaning that they're unavailable because you changed the Publish Settings to Flash Player 4.

2. In frame 1, place the following script:

   ```
   atLeastFlash4 = "1";
   ```

   This script sets a variable, which will be ignored in any version of Flash lower than 4. That's because Flash 4 was the first version to introduce variables.

3. Insert a blank keyframe in frame 2 and place the following script:

   ```
   if (Number(atLeastFlash4)==1) {
     } else {
       tellTarget ("flashThreeButton") {
       gotoAndStop (2);
     }
     stop ();
   }
   ```

   Basically, if the variable atLeastFlash4 is indeed 1 (as we just set it in frame 1), nothing really happens, and we'll proceed like normal to frame 3. Because versions prior to Flash Player 4 don't support if statements, this script effectively will be ignored. Actually, Flash Player 3 and earlier versions don't totally ignore if statements; they execute only the else part of the statement. Why, I don't know. What happens is that any version before Flash 4 will execute the tellTarget() and stop() methods contained in the else portion of the statement. The tellTarget() method is the old way to attach a method to an individual instance. Translated to Flash 6, the script says this.flashThreeButton.gotoAndStop(2). We'll make a clip with the instance name flashThreeButton that will jump to frame 2 for

these (less than Flash 4) users. Finally, the `stop()` method just prevents
our main timeline from going any further.

4. Let's build the clip for users of Flash 3 (and earlier). Select Insert, New
Symbol. Select Movie Clip and name it "Flash3."

5. You should be inside the Flash3 symbol. In frame 2, insert a keyframe and
draw the shape for a button. Convert the shape to a button symbol (select
it, press F8, and select Button). Attach the following script to the button:

```
on (release) {
  getURL ("http://www.macromedia.com/shockwave/download/index.cgi?
[ccc]P1_Prod_Version=ShockwaveFlash", "_blank");}
```

Notice that the web address should appear on a single line. The idea is that
if the user doesn't even have Flash 4, he'll see this button, which will take
him to Macromedia where he can upgrade. You may also want to center
the button instance within the Flash3 symbol.

{ Note }

This movie must work in Flash 3, so we can't assign a callback function
to the button instance. However, because I think it's such a great way to
work, we will use that technique in all the rest of the workshops.

6. In frame 1 of the Flash3 symbol, place a `stop()` script. Now the clip will
normally sit in frame 1 (effectively as an invisible clip) and jump to frame
2 only when the button appears. You can place more content in frame 2,
such as the message, "Click the button to upgrade" (using Static text). If
you want the user to automatically jump to the Macromedia site, you can
take the `getURL()` code from the button and place it in frame 2. However,
if you do this, it might be unclear to the user what is happening.

7. Go back to the main timeline, and drag an instance of the Flash3 symbol
that we just made into frame 2. (Remember, we just did a New Symbol
and not a Convert to Symbol, so there's no instance on the Stage yet). Give
this invisible clip an instance name of `flashThreeButton`.

8. Now that we've taken care of the sub-Flash 4 users, let's see whether the
user has Flash 6. Insert a blank keyframe in frame 3 and place the following script in that frame:

```
playerVersion = eval("$version");
revision = substring(playerVersion, 5, 1);
if (Number(int(revision))<Number(int(6))) {
  tellTarget ("lessThanSixButton") {
  gotoAndStop (2);
  }
} else {
  getURL ("flash_six_content.html", "_self");
}
 stop ();
```

The first line assigns the variable `playerVersion` equal to the old `$version` variable that was introduced during the Flash 4 era. Unlike most variables, you can't just say `playerVersion=$version`; the dollar sign is not a legitimate way to start a variable name. The `eval()` function evaluates the value of the built-in `$version` variable. The form returned to the `playerVersion` variable looks like this: `"WIN 6,0,23,0"` (see Figure W1.2).

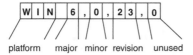

Figure W1.2 *The* `$version` *variable contains five key elements.*

The `$version` variable is a very specific string with information about the platform, the major version, the minor version (which is rarely if ever updated), the revision (also sometimes called the "patch" version, which is occasionally updated to provide added features and bug fixes—for example, the `ignoreWhite` XML property was introduced in `5,0,41`), and the last number (which isn't even used). What might mess you up is that we assign the variable `revision` using the `substring()` *function* (not the preferred—and only available in Flash MX—`substring()` *method* of the String object). This function behaves differently, as discussed in Chapter 9, "Manipulating Strings." The `if` statement in line three just checks whether an integer version of `revision` is less than 6. If it is, we tell the `lessThanSixButton` clip (that we're about to build) to go to frame 2, where the user will see a button to upgrade. Otherwise (if the version number is not less than 6), we do a `getURL()` to jump the user to our "real" HTML page with Flash 6 content. Just replace `flash_six_content.html` with the name of the HTML file that contains your Flash 6 content.

{ Note }

If you ever need to use the Flash 4 `substring()` function to ascertain the revision number, use `substring(playerVersion, 9, 2)`. An issue that might really freak you out is that the `$version` variable wasn't released with the very first version of Flash Player 4. The earliest versions of the Flash Player 4 won't recognize this variable. That's not a problem, however, because the `if` statement in line three will still work. Also, notice that the `int()` function is used to convert the `version` string to a number that can be used in a conditional statement. That's simply because Flash 4 didn't have the `Number()` function.

9. Now let's make the `lessThanSixButton` clip. Just duplicate the symbol called Flash3 (and rename it Flash4), and then change any Flash3-specific text contained in the symbol. Make a new layer and drag an instance of the Flash4 symbol onto the Stage. It doesn't matter that this instance will start in frame 1; it just must be present at the time `tellTarget()` is called. Make sure to give the symbol an instance name of `lessThanSixButton`.

10. At this point, you can export or publish the `.swf`.

We have just made a Flash 4 movie that acted like a sniffer to sense for sub-Flash Player 6 users. Those folks with Flash, but not Flash 6, are redirected. Those users with Flash 6 won't notice much at all because they'll jump to the right page.

There's one last task you may have to resolve: making sure that your Flash Player 6 users have the latest revision of the Flash Player 6. For example, you might really *need* to take advantage of a new feature (or lack of bug) in a later release. For example, the current release is 6,0,29,0 (6,0,21,0 in the authoring tool), but for all I know, some bug will be found in this Player and fixed in a later revision. It may be important to ensure the user has a later revision. Once you know the user has Flash 6, it's easy to check for the actual revision number (and tell the user if it's not new enough).

You can use any of the `String` object methods on either the built-in `$version` variable (which, unlike in Flash 4, can be used as-is and doesn't require the `eval()` function) or the new `version` property of the System object (which looks like `System.capabilities.version`). Consider these five expressions to extract key portions of the `$version` variable:

```
//form:  WIN 6,0,21,0
platform=$version.substr( 0, 3 );
major=$version.charAt(4);
minor=$version.charAt(6);
revision=$version.substr(8,2);
unused=$version.charAt(11);
```

These `String` object methods should look familiar if you've read Chapter 9. Basically, I just came up with five custom variables to represent each portion of the `$version` variable. Most likely, you'll just need the line `revision=$version.substr(8,2)` to extract the revision number of the Player (because this is the portion that is updated most often). By the way, you can replace `$version` with `System.capabilities.version` in any of the preceding code.

Personally, I'm a paranoid person. The preceding scripts are not guaranteed to work if the Flash version numbering system ever changes. For example, what if there's a Flash 10? Although most web sites created today will probably need an overhaul that far in the future, here are a couple of alternatives to parsing individual elements from the $version variable. By using the indexOf() method, we can find the location of the commas and then set our minor, revision, and unused variables:

```
var startMinor=$version.indexOf(",",5)+1;
var endMinor=$version.indexOf(",",startMinor);
minor=$version.substring(startMinor,endMinor);

var startRevision=$version.indexOf(",",endMinor)+1;
var endRevision=$version.indexOf(",",startRevision);
rev=$version.substring(startRevision,endRevision);

var startUnused=endRevision+1;
var endUnused =$version.length;
unused=$version.substring(startUnused, endUnused);
```

If nothing else, this example provides a good reminder of how to use the indexOf() method. Notice that all the expressions shown with the $version (string) variable return strings. You can always use the Number() function if you need to.

Now that you're familiar with the ways to ensure that your users have the Flash Player 6, we can move on to much more fun workshop chapters! I included this workshop chapter because I really wanted to concentrate on Flash MX. All the great Flash MX movies you make will go unrecognized if you can't upgrade your users.

{ Chapter 2
Workshop }

Creating Custom Cursors

Flash lets you make fairly sophisticated buttons with very little effort. However, despite the new control to turn off the hand cursor (`myButton.useHandCursor =false`), you really just have two options for cursors: the hand or no hand. In this workshop chapter, you'll learn how to create custom cursors. Custom cursors not only tell users that a button is clickable, they also provide clues about the type of button users are presented with. A custom cursor can tell users whether they're supposed to drag the button or just slide it to the left or right.

This workshop chapter shows you how to make a custom cursor in just a few steps. Then, the workshop takes what you built and creates a component so that you can incorporate cursors in any movie you make. Finally, the workshop guides you through the steps to create a custom UI (User Interface).

1. To start, we need a Movie Clip that contains the graphics for your cursor. Just draw something and convert it to a Movie Clip symbol named "Cursor Graphic" (see Figure W2.1). In this figure, the symbol is a hand with a pointing finger. Give the instance on the Stage an instance name of "hand".

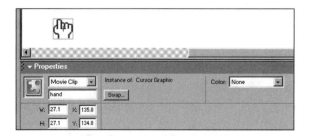

Figure W2.1 *Any graphic you place in a Movie Clip can become a cursor.*

2. Now we're going to write a script that we'll attach to the hand instance on the Stage. On the mouseMove event, we want the script to position the clip at the same point as the mouse. Although there's a property called _xmouse that can help us out in this script, it's important to understand that this property returns the location of the cursor relative to a particular timeline. For example, if your cursor is at the top-left corner of the Stage, _xmouse has an _xmouse and _ymouse of 0 (relative to the Stage). Relative to a clip whose center point is 0x, 0y, the cursor may be something quite different. So the script we write says to "set the location of this clip to the location of the cursor within the main timeline":

```
onClipEvent (mouseMove) {
  _x=_root._xmouse;
  _y=_root._ymouse;
  updateAfterEvent();
}
```

Notice that I included an updateAfterEvent(), which is best understood by testing what happens without this line (the clip won't play as smoothly).

3. Notice that the center of the hand instance coincides perfectly with the user's mouse. If you want to adjust the location of the cursor symbol, edit the master version of the symbol and move all the contents to a different location relative to the center (see Figure W2.2). The center will still coincide with the user's mouse, but the graphics contained in the clip will appear in an offset location.

In a minute, we'll use Mouse.hide() to make the user's cursor disappear. The drawback to having a cursor present all the time in Flash is that the cursor remains onscreen when the user moves the mouse out of Flash's window. We want to make the custom cursor appear only when the user places the mouse pointer over an object (a button or a draggable item) and then restore the original cursor when the user rolls off the object. Although that may sound like a single action, it's really two: In addition to hiding and restoring the cursor, you must make sure that the hand instance is displayed or hidden accordingly. We'll do all that through a function.

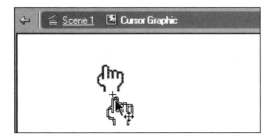

Figure W2.2 *Moving the Movie Clip's contents relative to the center (the plus sign) affects where the graphic appears.*

4. Draw a square (with no stroke) and convert it to a Movie Clip called "Hot Area." You can set the clip's alpha so that it appears to be semitransparent. Also, give it an instance name of "hot." We will use this shape to define the area in which the cursor will appear. An invisible button (discussed in Chapter 1, "Flash Basics") would be a convenient solution because it has built-in mouse events for rollOver and rollOut (the events we'd like to trap). However, if we ever place an invisible button on top of another button, the script for the button underneath will be ignored. Because we'd like to be able to use this component anywhere (including on top of other buttons), we'll use the instance of hot to define what area is "hot"—the area where the cursor should change. (By the way, even if we use a Movie Clip instead of a button, as soon as we assign an onRollOver or onRollOut callback, the clip can't be used on top of actual buttons.) Because we want both the hot area and the hand to stick together and we're eventually going to make this a component, select both the hot instance and the hand instance, choose Insert, Convert to Symbol, call the symbol "Cursor Clip," and then select the Movie Clip behavior.

5. If we test the movie, we'll find that it's broken; the hand instance doesn't match the cursor. That's because the instance of hand is now inside another clip. The script attached to the hand instance (_x=_root._xmouse) is wrong now; we actually want _x to be assigned to the _xmouse within the Cursor Clip symbol. To fix the problem, we could simply replace _root with _parent in the code attached to the instance of Cursor Clip symbol. Instead of fixing the code, however, I think we should move it to the first frame of the Cursor Clip symbol where we can consolidate other code as well. While we're moving code, we can call a function that we're about to write that will hide or reveal the cursor when the mouse is over the hot clip. The function, which we'll call check(), will also reside in the first frame of the Cursor Clip symbol. Therefore, remove all the code attached to the instance hot and type the following (similar) code in the first frame of the Cursor Clip symbol:

```
hot.onMouseMove=function() {
  check();
  this._x = _xmouse;
```

```
  this._y = _ymouse;
  updateAfterEvent();
}
```

The only thing that sort of freaks me out here is that the lines referring to
this._x and this._y are addressing the hot instance. However, the lack of
addresses in front of check(), _xmouse, and _ymouse naturally addresses
the timeline of the Cursor Clip symbol—that is, the timeline where this
code is placed. Normally, having no address is the same as saying
"this"—but not with callbacks.

6. Let's write the check() function. We can do it in steps. The pseudo-code is
   simply this: "If the mouse is on top of the hot clip, hide the real mouse
   and make the hand clip visible; otherwise, reveal the real mouse and make
   the hand clip invisible." That's a lot to dive right into. Let's worry about
   how to determine whether the mouse is on top of the hot instance last.
   Here's a start for our check() function that resides in the first keyframe of
   the Cursor Clip symbol:

```
check();
function check(){
  onHot=true;
  if (onHot){
    Mouse.hide();
    hand._visible = true;
  }else{
    Mouse.show();
    hand._visible = false;
  }
}
```

The first line calls the function so that we start checking even before the
mouse starts moving. The function itself either hides the mouse—
Mouse.hide() is a built-in function—and sets the _visible property of the
hand instance to true, or shows the mouse using Mouse.show() and makes
the hand instance invisible. This script is entirely dependent on the value of
onHot, which must be replaced with an actual expression that results in
true or false, depending on whether the mouse is on the hot instance.
Notice that the hard-wired line onHot=true causes the condition to be true
always. We can test it now and if it works, change that line to read
onHot=false. This is a great way to make sure that this part of our script
works before we add complexity.

7. There happens to be a built-in Movie Clip method called hitTest().
   Although we'll use hitTest() in Workshop Chapter 6, "Working with
   Odd-Shaped Clickable Areas," we won't use it now. It's a shame we can't
   use the method because hitTest() can easily tell us when the mouse is on
   top of the hot instance. We can't use that method because we need to make
   the hot instance invisible, and hitTest() doesn't work with invisible clips.

Instead, we'll first gather information about the size and location of hot, store it in a variable, and then make hot invisible. (By the way, hitTest() will work with clips set to _alpha 0, so we could do that, but we'll use a different solution anyway.)

The good news is that we get to explore another method: getBounds(). This method returns a rectangle of any given clip instance. Because there isn't a "rectangle" data type, getBounds() returns a generic object with four properties: xMax, xMin, yMax, and yMin. The coordinate values for the four extremes are relative to the timeline you provide as a parameter. Within the Cursor Clip symbol, the coordinates of hot are different than the coordinates of hot within the main _root timeline. Type the following script directly above the check() function in the first frame of Cursor Clip symbol:

```
rect=hot.getBounds(this);
hot._visible=false;
```

The variable rect contains the coordinates of hot relative to the current timeline (Cursor Clip). For example, rect.xMax contains the coordinate of the left side of the hot instance (as measured within the Cursor Clip symbol). The second line of code makes the hot instance invisible because we want it to disappear as soon as the movie plays.

8. Now we can finish the check() function. Remove the line onHot=true from the script that we wrote in step 6, and then replace the if statement's onHot condition with the following expression:

```
_xmouse>rect.xMin&&_xmouse<rect.xMax&&_ymouse>rect.yMin&&_ymouse
<rect.yMax
```

This expression says that if _xmouse is greater than the xMin of rect and less than xMax and if _ymouse is greater than yMin and less than yMax, then the mouse is within the rectangle defined by the hot instance. This statement doesn't look pretty, but it works perfectly.

9. At this point, we can drag instances of Cursor Clip into any movie, placing the semitransparent shape from the hot instance wherever we want a cursor to appear (see Figure W2.3). If we resize any instance of Cursor Clip, however, (for example, if we have a larger or smaller area over which we want the cursor to appear), the Cursor Graphic clip will resize accordingly because it's inside the Cursor Clip we resized. This is not just annoying— the Cursor Clip isn't very useful unless we're allowed to resize it as needed.

10. Let's think about what we need to do to resolve the resizing issue. Basically, we want the hand instance to resize itself in inverse proportion to the scale of the clip in which it resides. For example, if the instance of Cursor Clip on the Stage is resized to be really big, we want the hand instance to compensate by resizing itself really small, and vice versa. The problem is a lot easier to solve when thought of it in those terms. We can

add the following code to the first frame of Cursor Clip—above the check() function:

```
hand._xscale=(100/this._xscale) * 100;
hand._yscale=(100/this._yscale) * 100;
```

The way this code sets hand's scale to the inverse of the Cursor Clip's scale is based on the fact that no scaling has an _xscale and _yscale of 100. Let's try some "what-if" numbers to see how this formula works: If _xscale of Cursor Clip is 100, we want hand._xscale to be 100 as well. ((100/100) * 100 equals 100.) If Cursor Clip is scaled down by 50 percent, we want hand to be 200 percent. ((100/50)*100 equals 200.)

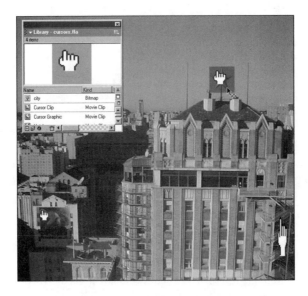

Figure W2.3 *You can use several copies of the clip to create cursors in different areas.*

11. The Cursor Clip appears to work great. Now is a good time to test it in a real-life situation. You may notice that if you place more than one instance of the Cursor Clip in a movie, only one will actually hide the cursor (although it blinks). The problem is that our script says, "Hide the cursor," but another instance of the Cursor Clip has code that says, "If you're not within my rectangle, show the cursor." Because the instances are in different areas, you will indeed be outside one clip's rectangle when you're within another's. We have to add a script that lets each clip reveal the cursor only once. In the current script, we are repeatedly hiding or showing the mouse. If we restore the cursor with Mouse.show() once (only when exiting a clip's rectangle), the problem will be resolved. Again, it would be more convenient if we were using the mouse event rollOut, but we're not.

To fix this bug, we'll use a custom variable we'll call `flag`. Programmers commonly need a variable that is switched on or off once or infrequently, and they call it a "flag." Think of the flag on some mailboxes that indicates whether you have outgoing mail. As soon as the mail carrier takes the mail, the flag goes down. The flag is a toggle for an event that occurs infrequently; the flag should not constantly go up and down. Outside of our `check()` function, we need a script that initializes `flag` to `false` (flag=false) so that `flag` is `false` at the start. Also, in place of where `Mouse.show()` is used in the `false` condition part of the `check()` function, we need an `if` statement such as the following:

```
if (!flag){
  Mouse.show();
  flag=true
}
```

With the preceding code, only if `flag` is `false` will the mouse be shown. Then we set `flag` to `true` so that it won't happen again until `flag` is `false` once more.

Finally, we must reset `flag` to `false` any time the cursor is indeed within this clip's rectangle. So right before the `else` in the `true` condition of `check()`, we add the line `flag=false`. Here's the finished script for the frame inside Cursor Clip:

```
hand.onMouseMove=function() {
  check();
  this._x = _xmouse;
  this._y = _ymouse;
  updateAfterEvent();
}

this.rect=hot.getBounds(this);
hot._visible=false;
hand._xscale=(100/this._xscale) * 100;
hand._yscale=(100/this._yscale) * 100;
flag=false;
check();

function check(){

  if (_xmouse>rect.xMin&&_xmouse<rect.xMax&&_ymouse>
➥rect.yMin&&_ymouse<rect.yMax){
    Mouse.hide();
    hand._visible = true;
    flag=false
  }else{
    if(!flag){
      flag=true;
      Mouse.show();
      hand._visible = false;
    }
  }
}
```

Now the script is quite solid. As long as you place the Cursor Clip symbol on top of buttons, the button scripts will execute, and you'll see only the custom cursor graphic. You can do some other refinements, such as positioning the hot instance within Cursor Clip so that its top-left corner is centered. With this adjustment, when the author scales Cursor Clip, it appears to stretch to the right and down rather than scaling equally in all directions the way a clip with its contents centered will. Maybe you can think of more refinements; we're about to do many in the next section.

Now let's convert the Cursor Clip symbol into a component that enables the author using the clip to select from a variety of cursors. Keep in mind that we made the cursor in just two steps—it took several more steps to make the cursor really useful. The state it's in now is totally usable—it's complete. Converting the cursor into an adaptable component will take more work. In a real project, this investment is worth the additional time only if you can use the component many times. Of course, it's worth the time now because we're learning.

1. First, save what you've created so far (call it symbol_version.fla), and then do a Save As so that you can start with the component (call the file component_version.fla). Then, go inside the Cursor Clip symbol and delete the hand instance.

2. We need a few cursors from which the using author can select. I created four: finger, grab, left-right, and up-down (see Figure W2.4). Make four unique Movie Clips now, even if that means that you just draw something quickly.

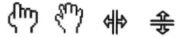

Figure W2.4   *We'll give the using author a choice of cursors.*

At this point, you shouldn't have any instances of the Movie Clips (finger, grab, left-right, or up-down) anywhere on the Stage. Inside Cursor Clip there's just the hot instance and code in the first frame. If you ever want to use the component we're building in other projects, or if you want to share the component, you're going to want to know about a great trick that ensures that all the necessary pieces (including the four cursors we just made) are copied into other movies. Inside the Cursor Clip, make a Guide layer and place one instance of each clip on that layer. Even though objects in a Guide layer are not exported with the movie (and are not visible while you're working), placing objects in a Guide layer ensures that they are copied whenever you drag Cursor Clip into another movie. You can call the Guide layer "Just so they get copied."

3. We're going to use `attachMovie()` to create the `hand` instance. In order for `attachMovie()` to work, each cursor must have a unique identifier name. Individually set the linkage for each cursor in the Library (finger, grab, left-right, and up-down). In the Linkage setting, select the Export for ActionScript option and give it an identifier name identical to the symbol name (see Figure W2.5). We select this option not so much because we need to export the clips (which will happen), but because `attachMovie()` requires an identifier name.

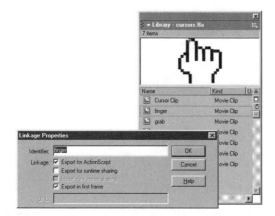

Figure W2.5 *To use* `attachMovie()`, *each clip must have an identifier name.*

4. Now we can write the script that decides which of the four cursors to use. The using author will ultimately specify this by setting a value for a variable. We can use the custom variable `pointerName` that we'll hard-wire at first and then have the using author specify using the Clip Parameters panel. Instead of trying to do it all in one step, we'll first try to make the variable work with a hard-wired script. At the beginning of the first frame in Cursor Clip (above all other code), add the following two lines:

```
pointerName="grab";
this.attachMovie( pointerName, "hand", 1 );
```

The first line hard-wires `pointerName`. The second line (including the four cursors we just made) "attaches" a new clip instance called `hand`. Basically, this just replaces the one we just deleted with one of the four cursor choices. Test it out!

5. Next, we just have to remove or comment out the line in which we hard-wired `pointerName` and make the using author set this for us. Type `//` in front of the first line we added in step 4 so that it will be ignored. From the Library, select Component Definition for the Cursor Clip symbol.

6. Click the plus sign in the upper-left corner of the Component Definition dialog box, and then double-click varName to select it. Type `pointerName`. Instead of making the author remember the names of the four possible cursor choices, let's use the `List` data type (double-click `Default` under the Type column and select `List`). After selecting `List`, you should be able to double-click under the Value column and populate the list. Add the four names given as identifiers in step 3: finger, grab, left-right, and up-down (see Figure W2.6).

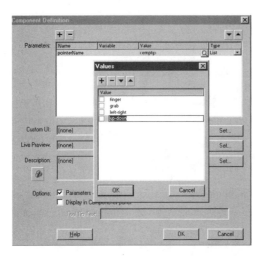

Figure W2.6   *The* `List` *data type enables the using author to select from a predefined list of cursor types.*

It's done! Yep, that was a lot of work, but check it out. Drag an instance of Cursor Clip—which is now a component—into any movie you have. Using the Parameters tab in the Properties panel, select the cursor of your choice. Use as many cursors as you want and mix and match the cursor choices. You can even resize the Cursor Clip, and the cursor won't get all whacked out of scale.

This particular component is a good candidate for either a custom UI or a Live Preview movie (or both). For example, instead of making the using author select from a list of cursor names, you can show pictures of the cursors. You also can use a Live Preview movie to show the current cursor choice. Generally, the purpose of a Live Preview movie is to show the content that will be presented (without requiring a test movie). The following steps show how to extend this component to include a custom UI.

//

In addition to a tiny bit of math and some addressing issues, most of this workshop chapter involves Flash features—namely, the _xmouse and _ymouse properties, the Mouse.hide() and Mouse.show() functions, the getBounds() and attachMovie() Movie Clip methods, as well as components. We covered components in Chapter 15, "Components," but this is your first chance to make something practical. We'll make more components in upcoming workshop chapters, including the Workshop Chapter 3, "Creating a Horizontal Slider." Remember that there are usually two steps involved: First make the clip work, even if it's hard-wired, and then convert it to a component.

We need to build a Flash movie that lets the using author select from the different cursor choices. Specifically, we want the user to set the value for pointerName. When this Flash movie is finished, we can export it as an .swf and use it in place of the Parameters tab in the Properties panel.

1. Leave open the file you used to create the Cursor Clip component and make sure that the Library is open. Start a new file by pressing Ctrl+N. Drag an instance of Cursor Clip into the new file. Save the original file as cursorSC.fla and then close it. Save the new file as ui.fla in the same folder as cursorSC.fla. The ui.fla file has four buttons, one for each of the four cursor choices. Ultimately, we'll use our plain Cursor Clip component on top of those buttons. For now, delete the instance of the Cursor Clip. (Don't worry; it's safe in the Library of the new file.) Set the dimensions for ui.fla to 406X72 (through Modify, Document). This size will match the space provided in the Properties panel. As you learned in Chapter 15, custom UIs require at least one frame to initialize. Therefore, create a keyframe at frame 2 and create four horizontally aligned buttons as graphically as you want (see Figure W2.7).

2. On each button, place a version of this script:

```
on (release) {
  selectPointer(1);
}
```

For each button, change the parameter to read 1, 2, 3, or 4.

3. Draw some kind of highlight that will be used to indicate which cursor is currently selected. A simple orange square just bigger than the buttons will work fine. Convert this highlight graphic to a Movie Clip and name the instance on the Stage highlight.

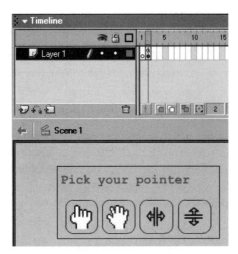

Figure W2.7   *The custom UI has four buttons that won't appear until frame 2.*

4. Now we can write the `selectPointer()` function that the act of selecting each button invokes. The function sets `pointerName` and moves the `_highlight` instance. To complete this function, we need something that translates the number (provided in the parameter sent when `selectPointer()` is invoked) to a name (which is needed in our component for the value of `pointerName`). Yay! It's time for an array like the one you remember from Chapter 11, "Arrays." In the keyframe at frame 2, start with this script:

```
stop();
names=["finger","grab","left-right","up-down"];
```

The first line prevents us from looping back to frame 1. The `names` array makes it easy to find any particular name. For example, if we want to know the name for the second `pointerName`, we just find the value in index 1.

5. We might as well make an array to contain the four locations for the `highlight` instance. You can position the `highlight` instance by hand in each spot and note the Info panel's x coordinate to acquire the clip's center. After you gather the values, leave `highlight`'s vertical position so that it matches the buttons, but move it either to the left or right, way off the Stage. In frame 2, add this line of code below what you've got so far:

```
locs=[35, 88.3, 141.6, 194.9];
```

Use whichever values you found for your `highlight` instance. For example, `35` is the location in my movie when the `highlight` instance surrounds the first button. Because the vertical location is the same for all the buttons, the script has to change only the `highlight`'s `_x` property.

6. Now for the function. The previous two lines just sit in a keyframe script, so they execute only when that frame is reached. We want the `selectPointer()` function to move the highlight and store the value for `pointerName`. To make it easier when we get to making this custom UI restore old values, it's best to also store a value for `pointerNumber`. You'll see why this is important in step 8, when we make this custom UI restore the old settings. Here's the `selectPointer()` function:

```
function selectPointer(whichOne){
  highlight._x=locs[whichOne -1];
  xch.pointerName=names[whichOne -1];
  xch.pointerNum=whichOne;
}
```

The first line in the function is the easiest: It just sets the _x property of `highlight` to the value found in the appropriate index of the `locs` array. Similarly, the second line sets the value of `pointerName` to the appropriate name. Actually, it looks like I'm setting the value of `pointerName` inside a clip instance or generic object variable called `xch`. Yep, custom UIs must store all the variables you want to be variables of the component in a clip as properties of a generic object you call `xch`. Finally, `xch.pointerNum` is saved for later.

7. Normally, you can't start referring to or setting properties in a generic object variable if it's undefined (which it will be the way it is now). However, once this movie becomes the custom UI, it will work fine as is. My natural tendency is to place the following error correction script above the function:

```
if (xch==undefined){
     xch=new Object();
}
```

Basically, if the variable is undefined, it gets initialized as a generic object. For good practice, you should place the preceding code above the function.

8. To visually display a previously selected value for `pointerNum`, place the following script at the bottom of frame 2, below the `selectPointer()` function:

```
selectPointer(xch.pointerNum);
```

This line invokes the `selectPointer()` function the first time frame 2 is reached and supplies as a parameter the value of `pointerNum` currently stored in the `xch` variable. The statement makes sense only if `xch.pointerNum` has a value, which it will when the using author has previously chosen a cursor. Note that the statement doesn't cause any problems if this value is `undefined`, which it will be the first time.

9. Finally, go ahead and drag the Cursor Clip component on top of the four buttons. Use the Parameters tab in the Properties panel to choose an appropriate cursor. Don't get confused here! There's certainly no requirement that you use a plain non-custom UI component while you're producing the UI. I just thought it would be cool to put our component to the test. This custom UI can have any element you want; simply setting the value for `pointerName` is enough.

10. Save the file, and then export an `.swf` by selecting Control, Test Movie. Close this file so that nothing gets mixed up and reopen `customSC.fla`. Select Cursor Clip from the Library window and then select Component Definition. Click the top Set button (adjacent to "Custom UI"), select "Custom UI in External File" and "Display in Property Inspector," and then type the name of the movie we just exported—in this case, `ui.swf`— and click OK (see Figure W2.8) Now you can drag instances of the finished Cursor Clip component, and for each one use the Parameters tab of the Properties panel to select the cursor of your choice (see Figure W2.9).

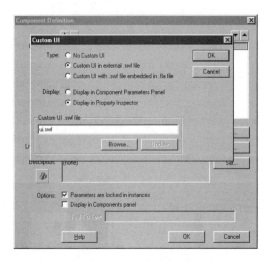

Figure W2.8 *Here are the settings to link to a custom UI.*

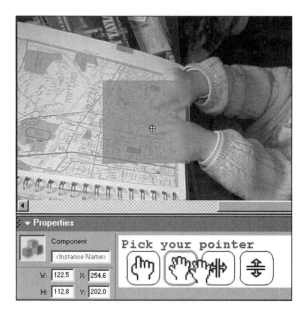

Figure W2.9 *When completed, our component uses a custom UI.*

This workshop chapter shows that you can take a task that's easy to program and refine it—with a ton of work—to make it something really usable. Please realize that the purpose of this workshop chapter was not *just* to make a cursor component, but to explore and learn.

{ Workshop

Chapter 3 }

Creating a Horizontal Slider

This workshop explores a popular user interface control: the slider. Many users prefer to specify a number by using the seemingly continuous scale offered by a slider rather than by typing into a field. Some tactile learners may respond better to the sense of touch provided by a slider. Another benefit of using sliders is that you can adjust them without taking your hand off the mouse.

This workshop has two parts. First we make a perfectly acceptable plain slider, and then we convert it into a more useful component.

Creating a Quick-and-Dirty Slider

1. Create a shape that will serve as the slider the users are supposed to grab. Convert it to a Movie Clip symbol called "Simple Slider." Perhaps you'll want to use a vertical rectangle with rounded corners.

2. Making the slider movable is easy enough—but we just need it to move horizontally, and only while users are dragging it. To move the slider only while users are dragging it, we'll set a homemade variable (`active`) to `true` when they press and then `false` when they let go. Then, for every `mouseMove` event, we'll only move the clip if the active variable is `true`. First name the instance of clip to `slider`, and then put the following code in the frame of the main timeline:

```
slider.onPress=function(){
  this.active=true;
}
```

```
slider.onRelease=function(){
  this.active=false;
}
slider.onReleaseOutside=function(){
  this.active=false;
}
```

Notice that there are two ways to "unclick": onRelease and onReleaseOutside. That is, if users press the mouse on the slider and keep holding their mouse until it's outside the Flash window, only onReleaseOutside will capture that event.

3. Now you can add the code for an onMouseMove callback function (anywhere in this same frame):

```
slider.onMouseMove=function(){
  if(this.active){
    this._x=_xmouse;
    updateAfterEvent();
  }
}
```

Now, any time the mouse moves, this code sets the clip's _x (this._x) to the mouse's _x (provided that the variable active is true).

You can test the movie now and see we're getting pretty close. It would be nice to set some limits for the high and low points, and to see a percentage displayed as it slides. The limits are pretty easy. We'll start by setting arbitrary (and hard-wired) values, and then improve on it later.

4. First determine the minimum and maximum x positions for the slider instance. You can draw a few vertical lines and then snap the slider to those lines—taking note as to what is displayed in Info panel. (Remember to use the center point option when gathering this information instead of the top-left option.) In my case, I decided upon a minimum of 50 and maximum of 250 (yes, to make it easier later)—but you can use any numbers you want. Because I know I'm going to need access to the minimum and maximum values later, they should be stored in a variable. Here are two lines of code that can precede everything else you've written:

```
slider.minX=50;
slider.maxX=250;
```

I decided to store my two variables inside the slider instance itself.

5. Now we can adjust the onMouseMove callback so that the slider never goes past the limits. There are often two ways to approach this issue: to prevent the slider from ever going past the limits, or to let it go past the ends but fix it before anyone sees anything. I'm going to opt for the second choice—that is, if the code places the slider past the end points, I'll fix it. You can see the code I came up with is pretty wordy but easy to follow. Use this replacement for the onMouseMove callback:

```
slider.onMouseMove=function(){
  if(this.active){
    this._x=_xmouse;
    if(this._x>this.maxX){
      this._x=this.maxX;
    }
    if(this._x<this.minX){
      this._x=this.minX;
    }
    updateAfterEvent();
  }
}
```

Those two if statements just say, "If it's greater than the max, set it to the max; if it's less than the minimum, set it to the minimum." I find this "fix it when there's a problem" approach is usually easier than trying to avoid any possibility of users breaching the limits. Users won't see anything refresh onscreen until this function is complete, so it doesn't matter.

6. Now we can display the percentage. Double-click the slider instance to edit the contents of the Simple Slider symbol. Create a Dynamic Text field and give it an instance name percent. Make sure the margins are wide enough to display 100 (actually, just type 100 into the field). You can position it next to or on top of the slider shape. (See Figure W3.1.) Now go back up to the main timeline so that we can edit the scripts.

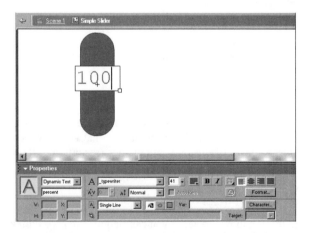

Figure W3.1 *A Dynamic Text field inside the Simple Slider symbol will display a percentage.*

The formula for percentage is simply "current position divided by the total distance." Actually, that formula will yield percentages from 0 to 1. For example, if the current position is the same as the total, you'll get 1. Multiplying by 100 gives us the right formula: current/total*100. You can try a few "what-if" numbers to confirm this formula. Now, translating that formula to our application is not very difficult at all. First, let's try a few easy examples to deduce a formula. My minimum was 50 and my maximum was 250. What would the percentage be if the current position was 150? Sketch it out and I'll bet you know it's 50 percent. That's because the total difference is 200 (250-50) and the current position (150) was really an "elapsed" distance of 100 (because it started at 50). So the current position is 150-50. By replacing those numbers with dynamic expressions based on our variables, the percentage is returned from the expression:

```
(_x-minX) / (maxX-minX) *100
```

Replace the variables and replace _x with 150 and you have:

```
(150-50) / (250-50) *100
```

It helps to make up nice numbers when testing such formulas.

7. Now we can add one line of code to complete our onMouseMove callback:

```
 1 slider.onMouseMove=function(){
 2   if(this.active){
 3     this._x=_xmouse;
 4     if(this._x>this.maxX){
 5       this._x=this.maxX;
 6     }
 7     if(this._x<this.minX){
 8       this._x=this.minX;
 9     }
10     this.percent.text=
       ➥(this._x-this.minX)/(this.maxX-this.minX) *100;
11     updateAfterEvent();
12   }
13 }
```

Notice line 10, which set the text property of the percent instance. If you test it now, you'll see the percent is displaying decimal values, which is really more than we need. To display only the integer portion of the value found, change line 10 to:

```
this.percent.text=
➥Math.floor((this._x-this.minX)/(this.maxX-this.minX) *100);
```

Go ahead and test the movie to see if you can find anything you think we should fix. There are just a couple minor touches that I think are worth fixing before we convert it to a component. First, I don't like the way the slider always snaps a tiny bit unless I grab it right by the center. The problem is that the slider is being placed at the exact _xmouse location. Also, the slider doesn't display the correct percentage until I start sliding it. Finally, it would be nice if this slider *did* something—such as control the _alpha level of another clip or the volume of a sound.

Although fixing the snap issue is pretty easy, it's important to fully understand the problem and exactly what you want it to do differently. The problem is that the slider centers itself to where the mouse is. Say you click on
the right side to start dragging. We'd like (as the slider gets dragged) for it
to position itself to where the mouse is minus a little bit. When you click
on the left, we want the slider to be where the mouse is plus a little.
Exactly how much extra is added or subtracted depends on how far off
center you click. So the fix is two-part: First, use a variable to save how far
off center they click. Then, use that variable's value when moving the
slider.

8. To fix the snap issue, change the onPress callback by adding one line of
   code so that it reads as follows:

```
slider.onPress=function(){
  this.offSet=this._x-_xmouse;
  this.active=true;
}
```

The second line simply stores (into the variable offSet) the difference
between the slider's _x and the _xmouse.

9. Now, adjust the third line inside the onMouseMove callback (from earlier) so
   that when you set the _x of the slider you set it to the _xmouse plus offSet:

```
this._x=_xmouse+this.offSet;
```

10. To make the slider display the correct percentage at the very beginning,
    place the following code below all the other code:

```
slider.percent.text=
➥Math.floor((slider._x-slider.minX)/(slider.maxX-slider.minX)*100);
```

Basically, this is the same code from inside the onMouseMove callback (line
10 shown previously), but I changed all the this's to address slider. I
realize it's sort of ugly and long, but we'll fix this later (when converting
to a component).

11. Finally, to make this slider do something, we'll just invoke a function and
    send the current percent as a parameter. We can define this function in the
    same frame with all the rest of the scripts:

```
function doit(howMuch){
  slider._alpha=howMuch;
}
```

This function sets the _alpha of the slider to whichever value is received as
a parameter. You can change the code inside the function to affect any clip
you want, in any way. For example, you might have another instance called
dial that you want to rotate. You could change the code to:

```
dial._rotation=(howMuch/100)*360;
```

12. To trigger the doit() function (and send the percentage), we'll add an extra line to the onMouseMove callback. Because we need to both display percentage and send it as a parameter, I decided to add a local variable p. Notice that where I used to set the text of percent, I now do three things (lines 10–12): calculate the percentage and save it in a variable p, set the text property, and trigger the doit() function:

```
1 slider.onMouseMove=function(){
2   if(this.active){
3     this._x=_xmouse+this.offSet;
4     if(this._x>this.maxX){
4       this._x=this.maxX;
5     }
6     if(this._x<this.minX){
7       this._x=this.minX;
8     }
9     var p=
      ➥Math.floor((this._x-this.minX)/(this.maxX-this.minX)*100);
10    this.percent.text=p;
11    doit(p);
12    updateAfterEvent();
13  }
14 }
```

This is a pretty solid slider now. You could probably spend more time refining it even further, but (for better or worse) other issues will arise when converting it to a component, so it makes sense to move on (and deal with the other issues if and when they arise). Sometimes just knowing which issues remain is all that's necessary; they sometimes fix themselves or become moot. Anyway, we're moving on to make this a component.

Converting the Slider into a Component

We're about to make our slider slightly better. The limiting issues with the slider we built in the first part of this workshop include the following:

- All the code is in the main timeline. The problem is that we can't drag additional instances of this clip from the Library without copying and pasting the code and naming the slider instance. If there were a bug in the code, it could get duplicated and would have to be fixed for each case.

- The minX and maxX variables are hard-wired. Our component will allow each instance its own minX and maxX values, plus an additional variable for the starting percentage.

Here are the steps for making our pretty good slider into a very good component that addresses the preceding issues:

1. The first step is to encapsulate all the code and graphics into a single symbol. Select all the code (in the first frame) and cut it. Then, double-click the slider instance to edit the master symbol. Paste the code into the first frame inside the Simple Slider symbol. Now we just have to adjust it a bit.

2. Because we are now inside the slider instance, you can change the code to say this anywhere it currently says slider. There's actually one other replacement that you may notice in the finished code that goes inside the clip:

```
 1 this.minX=0;
 2 this.maxX=330;
 3
 4 this.onPress=function(){
 5   this.offSet=this._x-_parent._xmouse;
 6   this.active=true;
 7 }
 8 this.onRelease=function(){
 9   this.active=false;
10 }
11 this.onReleaseOutside=function(){
12   this.active=false;
13 }
14
15 this.onMouseMove=function(){
16   if(this.active){
17     this._x=_parent._xmouse+this.offSet;
18     if(this._x>this.maxX){
19       this._x=this.maxX;
20     }
21     if(this._x<this.minX){
22       this._x=this.minX;
23     }
24     var p=
   ➥Math.floor((this._x-this.minX)/(this.maxX-this.minX)*100);
25     this.percent.text=p;
26     doit(p);
27     updateAfterEvent();
28   }
29 }
30 function doit(howMuch){
31   this._alpha=howMuch;
32 }
33 this.percent.text=
   ➥Math.floor((this._x-this.minX)/(this.maxX-this.minX)*100);
```

Notice in lines 5 and 17 that _xmouse changed to _parent._xmouse because the hierarchy has changed. This code is much better even if we don't make a component because now we can drag as many instances of the Simple Slider onto the Stage and each will perform independently. You don't even need to give them instance names!

3. Now we can convert to a component. First, we need to decide which variables are going to be set by the using author. Actually, we can add more later, but we already know that minX and maxX should be specified by the using author. In addition, the initial percentage should be set-able by the using author. Let's call that variable initialVal.

4. To make this a component (and give the using author access to the three variables minX, maxX, and initialVal), open the Library, select the Simple Slider symbol, and then select Component Definition from the options menu. Click the Plus button three times, and then change the three names ("varName") minX, maxX, and initialVal. In the Value column, change "defaultValue" to 0 for minX, 400 for maxX, and 50 for initialVal. These are just in case the using author never populates these values. You can see how the Component Definition dialog box looks in Figure W3.2. Click OK when you're done.

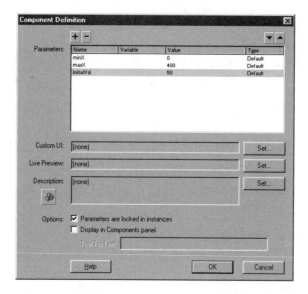

Figure W3.2   *Our slider becomes a component after we configure the Component Definition dialog box.*

5. Now that the using author will set minX and maxX, we don't need the first two lines of code inside the symbol. Go ahead and comment out (with //) the first two lines of code inside our component—where minX and maxX are

assigned. By the way, you can't just double-click an instance of Simple Slider now that it's a component (that's to prevent authors using this component from accidentally editing it). Edit it either via the Library or by selecting "Edit in Place" in the menu that appears when you right-click the instance (Control-click on a Mac).

6. While we're editing the code in the component, we can change the line of code that determines the initial percent. We will change the last line of code in our current script (the part that sets the `text` property of the `percent` field). Instead of calculating percent, we'll just display the value provided by the using author. Change that line of code (the one that begins "`this.percent.text=...`") to read:

```
this.percent.text=this.initialVal;
```

That was pretty easy. My idea is that the using author sets the current `percent`. If he sets `50`, the slider initially appears at 50 percent. Displaying `50` is easy. Now we have to actually position the slider in the correct location. The code is really a backwards version of how we calculated `percent`. Here, we know `percent` and have to calculate where the slider goes.

7. At the end of your script, add the following line of code:

```
this._x=this.minX+(this.maxX-this.minX)*this.initialVal/100;
```

Translated, this says: Set the `_x` to the minimum plus the total (max-min) times `percent`. If the minimum is `50` and the maximum is `250`, an initial value of `50` should place the slider at `150`. Try a few "what-if" numbers if you like.

The only thing that remains is to replace the hard-wired `doit()` function with one provided by the using author. That is, I think it would be most useful to let the using author specify a function name, and we'll call it as the slider moves.

8. First, we need to add an additional parameter to the Component Definition dialog box. Through the Library window, select Component Definition for the Simple Slider symbol. Add one more parameter (press the plus sign) and call it `functionName`. You can leave all the defaults as they are, and then click OK.

9. Just so we can test this out, drag one instance of the component to the main timeline and set its `functionName` parameter to `changeRotation` (through the Parameters tab in the Properties panel). Also, in the main timeline, draw a square, convert it to a Movie Clip, and give it an instance name `box`. Finally, place the following code in a frame of the main timeline:

```
function changeRotation(toWhat){
  this.box._rotation= (toWhat/100)*360;
}
```

The idea is that the using author would do all the things we just did in this step: Drag an instance of the component onto the Stage, set the parameters (including `functionName`), and then write that function (to accept a parameter—called `toWhat` in this case).

10. Now we can make our component trigger the function provided as a parameter. Mainly, we have to just replace the code that currently reads `doit(p)` (line 26 way back in Step 2). The only trick is that you can't just say `_parent.functionName(p)` because `functionName` is a variable. Actually, its value is a string. The fact that you can address variables or properties by using strings can come in handy here, too. Just replace the line (`doit(p)`) with the following code (and then I'll explain it):

```
_parent[this.functionName](p);
```

The value of `functionName` is a string, so we precede it with the path to the function. (By design, the function will reside in the same timeline where the slider component is placed.) Finally, the really weird part is at the end: (p). Just realize that to invoke a function, you always say the function name followed by parentheses for parameters. The first part (`_parent[this.functionName]`) is, in fact, the function name; we're just following it with the parentheses as normal. We're passing the value of `p` because that function needs to know where the slider is currently set.

11. The last step involves triggering the `functionName` function when the component first loads. Add the following line of code below all the rest of the code:

```
_parent[this.functionName](this.initialVal);
```

Like the code from Step 10, this triggers the `functionName` provided by the using author—except this time we pass the value of `initialVal`.

That's it! Although I'm sure you'll find it a rather useful component, hopefully you will have ideas for making it even better.

Summary

This workshop chapter explored how to write a relatively simple script and then convert it into a component. The process involved first creating a hard-wired script that worked to our satisfaction. Then we identified the aspects of the script that were not ideal—especially the fact that all the code was in the main timeline and there were several hard-wired numbers. We also tried to think of generic applications for this component, such as allowing the author to specify an initial percentage.

For more information about relative references, refer to Chapter 1, "Flash Basics," and Chapter 4, "Basic Programming in Flash." You can find general information about how to identify ways to improve scripts in Chapter 3, "The Programmer's Approach." Writing functions was discussed in Chapter 8, "Functions." Finally, Chapter 5, "Programming Structures," covered `if` statements and how to write expressions such as our formula that determines percentage.

{ Chapter 4

Workshop }

Building a Slide Show

After the last couple of workshop chapters, this one will seem like a breeze. That doesn't mean that the results won't be impressive. In this workshop, you'll see how a little code can create a really nice effect. We're going to build a slide show that lets the user step through a series of images in a Movie Clip. Although the user can step forward and back in the slide show, instead of simply jumping to the next frame, we'll make the current page fade out and the next one fade in.

In addition to creating a slide show, you'll learn two general techniques: First, you'll use the enterFrame event to continuously make changes to the _alpha property of the current slide. You'll also look at how you can deactivate buttons and display a dim version so that when users view the first slide, they can't click the "Page Back" button. Similarly, when users are on the last page, they shouldn't be able to click the "Page Forward" button. Although these two techniques are useful for *this* workshop, they'll also prove helpful in many of the workshops to come.

1. First you'll create a Movie Clip with a separate image on each frame. Create a new Movie Clip, insert blank keyframes as you import pictures or just draw something onto each frame. Put the script stop(); in the first frame so that the clip appears to be paused on frame 1 from the start (see Figure W4.1).

Figure W4.1   *Our slide show will be a simple Movie Clip with several frames.*

2. Drag an instance of this clip onto the Stage and give it an instance name of `slides`.

3. In the main timeline, draw a triangle that points to the right and convert it to a Button symbol. Make a copy of the Button symbol and rotate the copy 180 degrees (see Figure W4.2).

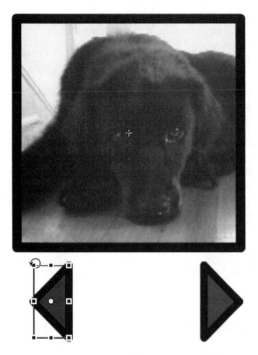

Figure W4.2 *The same Button symbol is used in two places, just rotated 180 degrees.*

4. Give the two buttons instance names of forward and back, respectively. Then place the following code in the first frame of the main timeline (which is where all the code for this workshop will go):

```
back.onPress=function(){
  goPage(-1);
}
forward.onPress=function(){
  goPage(1);
}
```

In a minute, we'll write the goPage() function in the main timeline. Just make sure that for the "Forward" button, you use 1 for the parameter. The preceding script uses -1 because it's the "Back" button.

5. Now we can write the goPage() function. Even though it's not going to be terribly complex, I'd much rather keep the buttons as simple as possible and place all the code in a function. This way there won't be any repeated code. Type this version of the function in the first frame of the movie:

```
function goPage(whichWay){
  slides.gotoAndStop(slides._currentframe+whichway);
}
```

This code just uses the `gotoAndStop()` method to make the `slides` clip jump to a frame equal to its current frame plus either 1 or -1.

6. The clip basically works, but we're going to make the clip fade out first and then jump to the destination frame. To start, add the following script to the frame in the main timeline:

```
slides.onEnterFrame=function(){
  this._alpha+=this.alphaChange;
}
```

If the homemade variable `alphaChange` were 0 or `undefined`—as it will be if we never assign it—this script would have no effect. That is, if on every `enterframe` we assign the `_alpha` to be 0 more than it is, nothing happens visually. Recall from Chapter 5, "Programming Structures," that saying `_alpha+=alphaChange` is the same as saying `_alpha=_alpha+alphaChange`.

7. Return to the `goPage()` function in the first keyframe and add the following line of script:

```
slides.alphaChange=-5;
```

Although many bugs remain, it's amazing how close to the finish we are. First, notice that regardless of the value of the `whichWay` parameter received in the `goPage()` function, we always want the `slides` instance's `alphaChange` variable to be negative. Also notice that `goPage()` is premature in making `slides` jump to a new frame—we don't want the page to advance until it has faded out completely. Finally, if you debug the movie and watch the properties for the `slides` instance, you'll see that once `alphaChange` is set to -5, the `_alpha` property continues to drop indefinitely.

8. Change the `goPage()` function so that it appears in its revised form, as follows:

```
function goPage(whichWay){
  slides.alphaChange=-5;
  slides.destinationframe=slides._currentframe+whichway;
}
```

Instead of actually making the `slides` clip "go to" a page, we set a variable in `slides` called `destinationFrame` (which won't be used until the clip is ready to advance).

9. Now we can adjust the `onEnterFrame` callback on `slides`. The first line is fine. We just need to keep checking to see whether `_alpha` has gotten low enough (say 0) at the point when we want to jump to the destination frame (either the next or the previous frame), and then change `alphaChange` to a positive 5 so that it starts to fade back up. Check out the final version:

```
slides.onEnterFrame=function(){
  this._alpha+=this.alphaChange;
  if (this._alpha<0){
```

```
      this.alphaChange=this.alphaChange*-1;
      this.gotoAndStop(this.destinationFrame);
    }
  if (this._alpha>100){
    this.alphaChange=0;
    this._alpha=100;
  }
}
```

Basically, if _alpha ever goes below 0, we jump to the destination frame and set alphaChange to 5 so that the frame will start "unfading." The last if statement prevents _alpha from going past 100.

//

You might not think there's any harm in letting the clip's _alpha increase past 100. However, if you let several seconds pass as it keeps increasing above 100 (to, say, _alpha 300), the next time the user clicks "Forward" or "Back," it will take just as long to come back down from 300 and then below 100, where you'll see the clip fade out again.

One other note: You just as easily could have written the two conditions for the if statements as _alpha==0 and _alpha==100. Although that might work fine, I think the solution presented in the preceding script is "safer." What would happen if the _alpha skipped past 0 or 100? It won't now with alphaChange being -5 and 5, but it could jump past such round numbers if you decided to start alphaChange at -3. Personally, I always prefer an if statement condition using > or < instead of == (when doing so makes sense, of course).

This slide show works pretty well. Now we're going to add a feature that deactivates the appropriate buttons when the user reaches the beginning or end of the slide show. It turns out that the current version doesn't break when the user tries paging past either end because the gotoAndStop() method is ignored when you provide a frame number below 1 or above _totalframes. I point out the fact that Flash doesn't break only because you can often save yourself from writing error-checking scripts (for instance, one that makes sure there's a next or previous frame to go to). Instead of writing such an error check, in this exercise we will write a script that simply deactivates the buttons—thus eliminating the issue entirely.

In Flash MX it's really easy to just set a button's enabled property to true or false, as appropriate. Although we'll do that first, you'll see that the technique for making the button look like it's not enabled is a bit trickier. I'll show two solutions for making the button look dim. One way involves changing the _alpha of the button when it's inactive. Another way is just to move the button offscreen to reveal a dim looking graphic that was underneath the whole time (see Figure W4.3). In many ways, this is the easier of the two solutions.

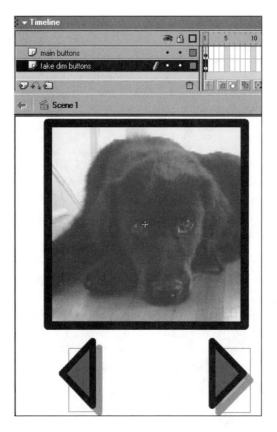

Figure W4.3   *An alternative to "un-enabling" a button is to move it offscreen to reveal a fake button underneath.*

A more involved solution involves creating a new object class, which is really just a Movie Clip acting like a button—but with an additional getter/setter property that we could call "active." I'll show the solution for that later so that you can see a good application for the addProperty() command. Let's do the easy way first.

10. We need to add code that will lower the _alpha and enabled properties to false for the Forward button (when on the last page) and the Back button (when on the first page). Add two if statements to the goPage() function so that it appears as follows:

```
 1 function goPage(whichWay){
 2    slides.destinationFrame=slides._currentframe+whichway;
 3   slides.alphaChange=-5;
 4   if(slides.destinationFrame>=slides._totalframes){
 5        forward.enabled=false;
 6        forward._alpha=50;
 7   }
 8   if(slides.destinationFrame<=1){
 9        back.enabled=false;
10        back._alpha=50;
11   }
12 }
```

The two if statements (lines 4 and 8) check to see whether the frame number we're headed to (destinationFrame) is at either end. Notice that I don't just say "greater than total frames" but rather "greater than or equal to total frames." It just seems much safer this way.

11. It turns out this code is pretty good, but it fails to ever restore the buttons. You could work out an else statement to the two if statements, but I think it's easiest just to add the following six lines of code *before* the two if statements:

```
forward.enabled=true;
forward._alpha=100;
back.enabled=true;
back._alpha=100;
forward.gotoAndStop(1);
back.gotoAndStop(1);
```

It might seem weird to go ahead and set everything to enabled=true and _alpha=100; however, it's simple, it works, and the two if statements fix any problems before anyone see anything. If we didn't include those last two lines, there would still be some weirdness when the buttons become inactive (that is, when they stay in their Over state).

That solution works pretty well. You can probably figure out that you could have plain graphics underneath the two buttons, and rather than setting the _alpha and enabled states, just change the _x or _y property to move them offscreen to leave the graphic behind. There are countless ways to make buttons look inactive.

Just for fun, I worked out a totally different solution that first involved creating a Movie Clip that would replace the two buttons. Inside this clip, I created four keyframes: _up, _over, _down, and _inactive. The first three keyframes make the clip act like a button, but the last one was my idea. I used the two instances of my new clip in place of the Back and Forward instances. Finally, I placed the following code in the first frame of the movie:

```
 1 function setActive(toWhat){
 2    this.enabled=toWhat;
```

```
3   if (toWhat){
4      this.gotoAndStop("_up");
5   }else{
6      this.gotoAndStop("_inactive");
7   }
8 }
9 function getActive(){
10   return this.active;
11 }
12 MovieClip.prototype.addProperty("active", getActive, setActive);
```

Basically, this makes an `active` getter/setter property for all Movie Clips. (You can learn more about how to create getter/setter properties using the `addProperty()` command in Chapter 14, "Extending ActionScript.")

12. With the new `active` property in place, I can change the `goPage()` function to the following:

```
1 function goPage(whichWay){
2    slides.destinationFrame=slides._currentframe+whichway;
3    slides.alphaChange=-5;
4
5    forward.active=true;
6    back.active=true;
7
8    if(slides.destinationFrame>=slides._totalframes){
9        forward.active=false;
10       forward._alpha=50;
11   }
12   if(slides.destinationFrame<=1){
13       back.active=false;
14       back._alpha=50;
15   }
16 }
```

The point is that setting `active` to `true` or `false` (in lines 5, 6, 9, and 13) takes care of both the `enabled` property and jumping to a fourth keyframe (`_inactive`) when appropriate. Arguably, the first solution (step 11) is easier, but this is a great example of how a little extra code can make something even better.

13. Finally, the Back button is active at the beginning. To fix that, just put some code outside the rest of the code in frame 1 (that is, not inside a function or callback). The following code is all you need:

```
back.active=false;
```

The workshop is pretty complete now. There are a few things you might consider adding. One would be a Dynamic Text Field inside the clip that displays a message such as "Page 1 of 5" (or something similar). You could place the following statement in the `onEnterFrame` callback (right after the `gotoAndStop()` script):

```
this.myField.text="Page "+this._currentframe+" of "+this._total
frames;
```

Naturally, you'll need a field with the instance name `myField`.

Another cool idea is to add some background music and have it fade down and up to match the `_alpha` of the `slides` clip. Provided you have a sound in your Library with a Linkage of "music" you can start the music with these three lines of code:

```
my_sound = new Sound();

my_sound.attachSound("music");

my_sound.start(0,999999);
```

This is boiler-plate Sound Object code, which was covered in Chapter 12, "Objects."

Finally, add the following line of code inside the `onEnterFrame` callback function (after `_alpha` is set—line 2 from step 9):

```
_root.my_sound.setVolume(this._alpha);
```

Now the volume will always match the `slide`'s `_alpha`. There are tons of other things you might want to try. I have a few variations online that you can check out.

The main thing that you learned in this workshop chapter was how to use the `enterFrame` event to make changes repeatedly (in this case, to the `_alpha` property). In other workshops, including Workshop Chapter 10, "Creating Timers," and Workshop Chapter 12, "Developing Time-Based Animations," you'll learn how to use `enterFrame` to make changes only when necessary or desired instead of repeatedly, as you did in this workshop. Notice that one flaw of this exercise is that the speed of the alpha change is tied directly to the movie's frame rate. If you change the frame rate, the fade speed also changes. In upcoming workshop chapters, you'll learn ways to make animations based on time rather than on frame rate.

You also learned how to inactivate buttons—both by simply setting the `enabled` property and also by extending the Movie Clip class (by adding a property).

I think the best part of this workshop chapter was that we created something that looks really cool, works really well, and takes very little work. It just proves that simple solutions are sometimes best.

Chapter 5

Mapping and Scripted Masks

In this workshop chapter, you'll learn a valuable technique even though the exercise has limited practical value. Although mapping is a good concept to understand, this exercise involves a specific design that may or may not ever arise in the projects you build. The result is pretty cool, but the idea is to learn more than just a special effect.

Mapping is the technique of translating coordinates from one space (such as a tiny map) to another space (such as the territory represented by the map). Mapping is like those mechanical tracing arms that let you trace and scale at the same time. In this workshop chapter, you'll do it with ActionScript.

Practical applications for mapping do exist. You might have a giant map of a city as well as a smaller one that the user can click on. By using mapping, you can calculate the location that was clicked and move the giant map proportionally to display the correct area. You can also use this technique with an assortment of sliders so that you can calculate the portion of a tall text field that should appear based on the location of a scroll bar. Finally, a really cool example of mapping is to make a magnifying glass that can be moved around the Stage. In this workshop, we'll do an adaptation of part of a real project I worked on. The "boards" section of the 1999 www.m-three.com web site included a mechanism that "zoomed in" on a snowboard graphic (see Figure W5.1). When users move the crosshairs to the left, they "zoom in" on the left side of the large version of the board; when they move the cursor to the right, the board moves to the left to reveal the right side. The effect was pretty cool, but it didn't take a whole lot of work to program (to design, yes, but to program, no).

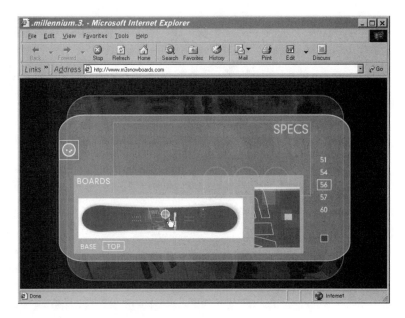

Figure W5.1   *In the original M3 web site, users could inspect close-up views of the snowboards in a Flash movie that used mapping. Screen shot courtesy of Paris France Inc., Copyright © 1999 by MLY Snowboards.*

Here are the steps for mapping one image to another:

1. Either import a photograph or draw a large rectangle that contains a variety of colors and shapes (see Figure W5.2). Convert the rectangle to a Movie Clip. Name the instance now on the Stage `big`.

2. Copy the `big` instance and paste it into a new layer. Resize the copy so that it's much smaller and can fit on the Stage. Name this instance `small`.

3. Draw a perfect square and scale it so that its width is a little less than half the height of the large rectangle (`big`). This square will define the viewable area. Place this square in a layer just above the layer containing `big`. To control how the layers interact, select the Layer Properties (Modify, Layer...) for each layer as follows. Set the layer containing the square to Mask. Make sure that the layer that contains the `big` instance is set to Masked and the layer containing `small` is set to Normal (see Figure W5.3).

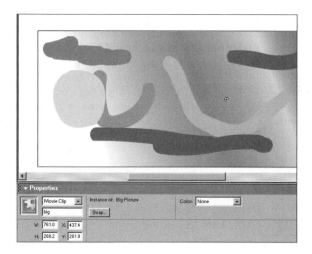

Figure W5.2   *A very large graphic or picture is turned into a Movie Clip with an instance name of* big.

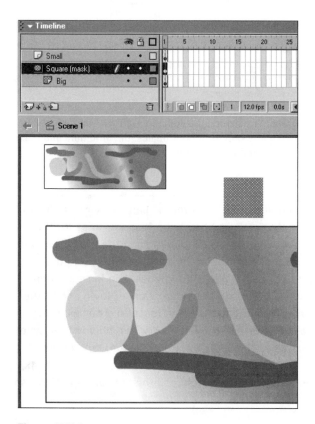

Figure W5.3   *The* small *instance is in a Normal layer, and the square shape is masking the* big *instance in the lowest layer.*

4. At this point, successively grab the big clip by each corner and use the Info panel to ascertain the x and y coordinates for all four extremes. (Be sure to use the center point option in the Info panel.) Note the x and y values when big is moved all the way down and to the right (when big's top-left corner snaps to the square's top-left corner, as shown in Figure W5.4). Repeat this for the other three corners: when big's top-right corner snaps to the square's top-right corner, when big's bottom-right corner snaps to the square's bottom-right corner, and when big's bottom-left corner snaps to the square's bottom-left corner.

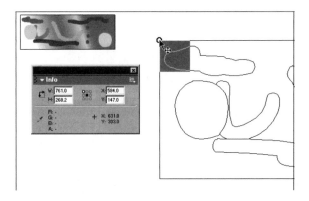

Figure W5.4   *We need to successively snap each corner of* big *to the square shape to gather the coordinates of the four extremes.*

5. Regardless of what you named the eight coordinates you gathered in step 4, there are really only four coordinates: the minimum and maximum x plus the minimum and maximum y.

The terms "minimum" and "maximum" can easily be confused. Consider Figure W5.5, which shows the four extremes for the mouse (a, b, c, and d in the small rectangle at the top left) and the four extreme locations for the big rectangle (a, b, c, and d in the rectangles at the bottom). When the mouse is in location a on small, the instance big should be in location a (down and to the right). Similarly, when the mouse is in location d on small, big should be moved up and to the left (shown as d below). So when the mouse is at what I'd call a "minimum x" and "minimum y" (location a on small), the big instance should be moved to 584x, 147y (location a)—which you might call the "maximum" because those numbers are large. However, we're going to call these values the "minimum" because they correspond to when the mouse is in the "minimum" corner (a). You can call the numbers whatever you want, but just realize that clicking the top-left corner of `small` should move the `big` clip down and to the right.

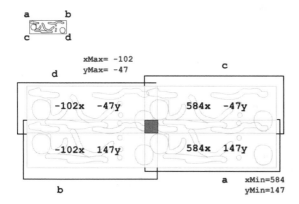

Figure W5.5 *This figure demonstrates how the four corners of the* `small` *rectangle are mapped to four extreme positions of the* `big` *rectangle.*

6. Now that we've gathered the four extremes for `big`, we can store those values in variables. Pick a frame in the main timeline to type the following code (and, for that matter, all the code for this workshop):

```
b=new Object();
b.xMin=584;
b.xMax=-102;
b.yMin=147;
b.yMax=-47;
b.width= b.xMax- b.xMin;
b.height= b.yMax- b.yMin;
```

Naturally, you should use your own gathered values for the four variables. We certainly could have just had 6 separate variables, but I decided to store the values as 6 properties in a generic object b. That will help with consistency later because we'll have other variables with the same name. It's actually going to be easier to say b.xMin than xMin. Notice that I went ahead and created the properties width and height to save some typing later.

7. Because we're going to be calculating a proportional location of the cursor (on top of `small`), we should gather some variables containing the coordinates of the four sides of `small`. Luckily, we can use the getBounds() method, which was first discussed in Workshop Chapter 2, "Creating

Custom Cursors." If we assign a variable (say s) to the getBounds() method of small, the variable s will become an object with four properties: s.xMin, s.xMax, s.yMin, and s.yMax. Conveniently, we used similar names to contain the information about big. We just have to remember that b.xMin is for big and s.xMin is for small. This is no problem provided that we can just keep them straight. Add the following script below the code you have in the first frame:

```
s=small.getBounds(_root);
s.width=s.xMax- s.xMin;
s.height=s.yMax - s.yMin;
```

Notice that the first line assigns values to the four properties in the variable s. That is, using getBounds(), we get the left, right, top, and bottom location of small (in the _root timeline)—but they're stored in 4 properties (xMin, xMax, yMin, and yMax). The last two lines just add two new properties (width and height) to the variable s.

8. It turns out that writing an expression to place the big clip in the proportional location doesn't take quite as many variables as we gathered. For any given mouse location (on top of small), we want to move big so that the mask reveals the correct (mapped) location. There's two parts: writing the script and putting it in an event so that it gets triggered at the right time. The event is easy: mouseMove (or any time the mouse moves). The expression is easiest to deduce using what-if numbers. What if the mouse is in the middle of small? In that case, the _x location of big should be its minimum plus half its width. More generally, big should always appear at its minimum plus the percentage times its width—the percentage being the mouse location relative to small. You can calculate that value by taking the mouse location minus the left side of small divided by small's width. You can use some easy numbers to check that expression. If small is 100 pixels wide and it's left side is 200, a mouse position of 250 is indeed 50 percent—(250-200)/100. Anyway, here's the code that goes beneath all the rest of the code you've written:

```
1 _root.onMouseMove=function(){
2    var percentX=(_root._xmouse - s.xMin )/ s.width;
3    var percentY=(_root._ymouse - s.yMin )/ s.height;
4    big._x=b.xMin+ (percentX*b.width);
5    big._y=b.yMin+ (percentY*b.height);
6    updateAfterEvent();
7 }
```

The _root.onMouseMove callback gets called any time the mouse moves. You can see in lines 2 and 3 that the percentages are calculated by subtracting the left side (or top, for _y) of small from the mouse location and then dividing by the width (or height for _y). Then that percentage is multiplied by the width (or height) of big and added to the left side (or top) of big. Finally, updateAfterEvent() makes it play smoothly. Select Control, Test Movie, and you should see it work very nicely.

There are a few other things you might want to add. For example, a few `if` statements could ensure that `big` never moves out of view of the mask. Something such as, "If `big`'s position is about to be less than its minimum, then set it to the minimum." We won't do that yet, however. One thing that is worth doing is to make `big` move only while the user drags (instead of all the time). One way to do that is to set a variable (to `true` when the user clicks and to `false` when he releases), and then put all the code in the `mouseMove` within an `if` statement so that it executes only while the user is clicking.

9. Replace the old `onMouseMove` callback with the following code:

```
_root.onMouseDown=function(){clicking=true;}
_root.onMouseUp=function(){clicking=false;}
_root.onMouseMove=function(){
  if(clicking){
    var percentX=(_root._xmouse - s.xMin )/ s.width;
    var percentY=(_root._ymouse - s.yMin )/ s.height;
    big._x=b.xMin+ (percentX*b.width);
    big._y=b.yMin+ (percentY*b.height);
    updateAfterEvent();
  }
```

At this point, the movie should work fine regardless of whether you use those last few enhancements. However (as always), there's one subtle issue I think we should fix. Note that when you click once on the `small` instance, nothing happens. Only when you click *and* drag does the `big` clip start moving. You *could* just copy the entire code inside the `if` statement in the `mouseMove` event (see Figure W5.6) and paste it into the `mouseDown` event. Doing that, however, places the same code in two locations—yuck! Yes, a function is the solution.

```
_root.onMouseMove=function(){
  if(clicking){
    var percentX=(_root._xmouse - s.xMin )/ s.width;
    var percentY=(_root._ymouse - s.yMin )/ s.height;
    big._x=b.xMin+ (percentX*b.width);
    big._y=b.yMin+ (percentY*b.height);
    updateAfterEvent();
  }
}
```

Figure W5.6   *You can move this portion of code to a function.*

10. Select the code shown in Figure W5.6 in the `onMouseMove` event and cut it (don't delete). In its place, type `moveBig()`, which calls a function we're about to write. Inside the `onMouseDown` callback, type `moveBig()` below where `clicking` gets set to `true` so that the `mouseDown` event executes the same function. The two callbacks should look like this:

```
_root.onMouseDown=function(){
  clicking=true;
```

```
    moveBig();
  }
  _root.onMouseMove=function(){
    if(clicking){
      moveBig();
      updateAfterEvent()
    }
  }
```

11. Finally, we just have to paste our code inside a function called `moveBig()`
(placed anywhere in that first keyframe):

```
function moveBig(){
  var percentX=(_root._xmouse - s.xMin )/ s.width;
  var percentY=(_root._ymouse - s.yMin )/ s.height;
  big._x=b.xMin+ (percentX*b.width);
  big._y=b.yMin+ (percentY*b.height);
}
```

Notice that we create only the framework for the function (`function
moveBig(){}`) and then paste the code that we cut in step 10 in between the
curly brackets.

Now your movie should be complete!

Just for fun, I want to show you how easy it is to convert this entire workshop
into something different. Flash MX enables you to script the movement of
masks, so why not move the mask with the mouse? If you place `big` on top of
`small` (but keep everything in the same layers) and then move the mask, you'll
see a zoomed-in version of `small`. Follow these steps.

1. Resize `big` (if necessary) to make it significantly larger than `small`. Center
`big` on top of `small`. Be careful to leave all the layers in the same arrangement as before (see Figure W5.7).

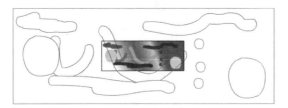

Figure W5.7   *By positioning* big *on top of* small *(and moving only the mask), you can
create a different effect.*

2. Now just convert the shape in the mask layer to a Movie Clip and give it an instance name of mag (for "magnifier").

3. Finally, we're going to write a replacement mouseMove script. Instead of trashing what you have, however, you can just rename it with an "X" at the start: "X_root.onMouseMove…." Here's a new mouseMove script to use:

```
_root.onMouseMove=function(){
  mag._x=_root._xmouse;
  mag._y=_root._ymouse;
  updateAfterEvent();
}
```

That was almost too easy! It's a neat effect, but there's something wrong. Because big is so much bigger, you have to move way off to either side (way past the edge of small) to see the edge of big. We can use mapping to fix this. The idea is that not only will we move the mask (exactly the way it behaves now), but we'll also move big so that it appears in a logical spot. big should move like it did before, but with different minimums and maximums.

4. Re-gather big's four coordinates for b.xMin, b.xMax, b.yMin, and b.yMax. This time, however, snap big's top-left corner to small's top-left corner, big's bottom-left corner to small's bottom-left corner, and so on. Then take part of the code from the old onMouseMove script and place it in the new mouseMove script. (See why we didn't trash it?) Here is how it should look:

```
_root.onMouseMove=function(){
  mag._x=_root._xmouse;
  mag._y=_root._ymouse;

  var percentX=(_root._xmouse - s.xMin )/ s.width;
  var percentY=(_root._ymouse - s.yMin )/ s.height;
  big._x=b.xMin+ (percentX*b.width);
  big._y=b.yMin+ (percentY*b.height);
  updateAfterEvent();
}
```

The new stuff it at the top, and the old stuff at the bottom. This will work great if you gathered and set the new values for b's properties (such as b.xMin).

There's one other tiny thing that makes this look sort of rough. When you go past the edges, the big clip moves so far that you can see through to the small clip underneath (see Figure W5.8). It's easy enough to fix that.

5. Place the following four if statements right before the updateAfterEvent() line in the current onMouseMove callback:

```
if(big._x<b.xMax){
  big._x=b.xMax;
```

```
}
if(big._x>b.xMin){
  big._x=b.xMin;
}
if(big._y<b.yMax){
  big._y=b.yMax;
}
if(big._y>b.yMin){
  big._y=b.yMin;
}
```

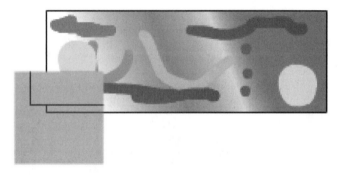

Figure W5.8   *The magnifier effect is lost when the cursor goes past the edges.*

It might appear as though I made a typo, but realize that b.xMin is a large number and b.xMax is a small number.

It turns out that we could have skipped re-gathering the coordinates of big (in step 4). That is, we can write expressions based on the coordinates of small. As long as you place the following code after the s variable is assigned, it will save you a lot of manual work. In addition, you can move small to anywhere on the Stage and everything still works:

```
b=new Object();
b.xMin=s.xMin+(big._width/2);
b.xMax=s.xMax-(big._width/2);
b.yMin=s.yMin+(big._height/2);
b.yMax=s.yMax-(big._height/2);
b.width=b.xMax-b.xMin;
b.height=b.yMax-b.yMin;
```

You might consider trying to do this workshop again with a photograph. You'll get the best results if big is not scaled. That is, import a large photo and put it in clip with the instance name of big. Then drag another instance of this clip from the Library and scale it to be smaller—with the instance name small. This way, the magnified version that is revealed will look nice and sharp (see Figure W5.9). In this figure, I set the brightness lower for the small instance.

Figure W5.9 *By using a photograph (scaled down for the* small *clip), you can create a really nice-looking magnifier effect.*

This workshop chapter involved many specific steps. We used some hard-wired values that we gathered as well as some values that we calculated with the getBounds() method. Then we used those values to gather coordinates and determine proportional locations of the mouse compared to the small clip.

{ Chapter 6
Workshop }

Working with Odd-Shaped Clickable Areas

Flash buttons are the easiest way to trap mouse clicks. Buttons are simple and powerful. It's easy to include Over-and Down-states and even to define an odd shape that's clickable in the Hot-state. Placing a script on a button opens up a variety of mouse events to which you can respond.

For all their greatness, buttons are fixed in their feature set: As soon as you want more, they become limited. In addition, the fact that Movie Clips can now trap mouse events (once reserved for buttons) means that you can avoid buttons completely. Movie Clips give you access to clip events such as mouseDown, mouseUp, and mouseMove. The only catch is that clips respond to all mouse events regardless of where the event occurs; for example, the mouseDown event will be received regardless of where you click. However, if we use clips in conjunction with the Movie Clip object method hitTest(), we can determine whether the user has clicked on a particular clip. You'll see that the alternative (to use a mouse event, such as onPress, on a clip) is not always ideal because it makes the clip start acting like a button—including making the hand cursor appear.

This workshop chapter involves a situation in which there are many individual shapes—representing the outlines of various European countries—that you want to become clickable (see Figure W6.1). Instead of making each shape a separate

button, we'll use Movie Clips. And instead of naming each instance and assigning a unique callback function to each one, we'll just write a single `for` loop that
checks whether the user is rolling over the shape.

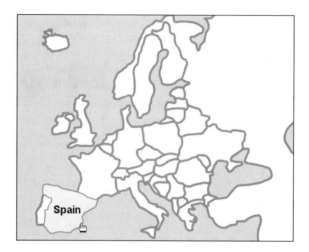

Figure W6.1   *You might need odd-shaped clickable areas when letting a user select*
individual countries.

In addition to exploring the `hitTest()` method, this workshop chapter exposes
you to a technique which stores references to all the clips in the movie in an array.

Here are the steps for creating and managing odd-shaped clickable areas:

1. Draw a large, filled square. Set Stroke to at least 5 and use the Pencil tool
   with Pencil Mode set to Ink to draw squiggly lines (of a different color
   than the fill) to divide the square into sections (see Figure W6.2).

2. Select everything you've drawn and choose Modify, Shape, Convert Lines
   to Fills. Then carefully select and delete the lines you just drew. The result
   is that you are chopping up the original square into sections. Pretend that
   these are the borders of countries.

3. Individually select each section and convert it to a Movie Clip (F8). This
   is the one time when you can use the default "Symbol 1" name. In this
   example, we won't even name the instances!

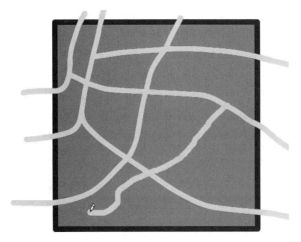

Figure W6.2   *We'll make odd shapes by drawing thick lines through a square.*

//

Normally, you'd probably prefer to address clips by name when setting their _alpha or using the hitTest() method. We're not going to
name the clips. Instead, we'll write a script that loops through all the
"objects" on the Stage (that is, all the instances); for the objects that
happen to be Movie Clips, we'll place a reference of that clip in an
array. Consider if we did name the clips country1, country2, and so
on. If we simply populated an array with a statement such as
allClips=[_root.country1,_root.country2], we could later address
any individual clip using an expression such as allClips[1]._alpha=50.
Even though we're not going to name our clip instances, we can still
populate the array with references to those clips. Specifically, we'll
step through the built-in array for _root, which contains all objects
on the Stage.

4. We're about to write the script that checks whether the mouse is on top of
    any clips. Instead of writing a script for each instance, we'll just put the
    code in an onMouseMove callback function for the main timeline. This way
    we can monitor all the different clips in one place. First, we can store all
    the Movie Clip instances in an array in the main timeline. In the frame of
    the main timeline (where all the code will go), type the following code:

```
allClips= new Array();
  for (i in _root){
    if (_root[i] instanceof MovieClip){
      allClips.push(_root[i]);
  }
}
```

The variable `allClips` is an array. The `for in` loop checks each object in the _root array and, if it's an `instanceof` the `MovieClip` class, it pushes an object reference onto the end of the `allClips` array. (We discussed the `instanceof` operator in Chapter 13, "Homemade Objects.") Notice that not only is _root an address of a clip (the main movie's timeline), it also happens to contain an associative array with references to all the clips. Here, we're addressing each clip in _root not by an index in an array, but rather by the name of the sub-object in an object. That is, `myArray[0]` pulls something out of the array in index `0`, but `myObject[myProperty]` pulls `myProperty` out of a generic object (even though it looks nearly the same). The fact that it's weird is not an issue because once the `allClips` array is populated, we step through it using the same `for in` technique used to create the array. You can learn about `for` loops in Chapter 5, "Programming Structures," and about how generic objects (AKA *associative arrays*) compare to arrays in Chapter 11, "Arrays."

5. Now that the `allClips` array is populated, we can write script that runs every time the mouse moves. Below the initialization script you wrote in step 4, type the following code:

```
_root.onMouseMove=function(){
  for(i in allClips){
    allClips[i]._alpha=30;
  }
}
```

If you test this, you should see all the clips dim down to 30 percent alpha as soon as you move the mouse. Incidentally, you could change the `for in` loop to a regular for using the following code in the second line above: `for(i=0;i<allClips.length;i++){`.

6. Obviously, we want only one clip to dim out: The one with the mouse on it. The `hitTest()` method can help us figure out which clip that is. The form for `hitTest()` is `targetClip.hitTest(x,y,flag)`, where `targetClip` is the clip you're checking, x and y are the coordinates of the point in question, and `flag` must be either `0` (when you only want to check whether the coordinates are within the square boundary of the clip) or `1` (when you want to check whether the coordinates are on top of the clip's outline—just its shape, as we're doing in this case). Finally, this method returns either `true` or `false` depending on whether the coordinates are within the clip's shape or bounds. To apply this logic to our function, we can put an `if` statement inside the `for in` loop with the condition `allClips[i].hitTest(_xmouse,_ymouse,1)`. If that condition is `true`, we can set _alpha to `30`. Just for fun (and because we're so close to finishing), try the following replacement for the `onMouseMove` callback and see whether you can figure out the minor bug:

```
_root.onMouseMove=function(){
  for(i in allClips){
    if(allClips[i].hitTest(_root._xmouse,_root._ymouse,1)){
      allClips[i]._alpha=30;
    }
```

```
    }
    updateAfterEvent();
}
```

If you test this movie, you'll see that it works alright. However, once a clip's _alpha is set to 30, it never comes back up to 100. You can add an else clause to the if statement to solve the problem:

```
_root.onMouseMove=function(){
  for(i in allClips){
    if(allClips[i].hitTest(_root._xmouse,_root._ymouse,1)){
      allClips[i]._alpha=30;
    }else{
      allClips[i]._alpha=100;
    }
  }
  updateAfterEvent();
}
```

By the way, because allClips[i] addresses a clip, you can set any other property or use any other method with the form allClips[i].property or allClips[i].method(), respectively.

This script works perfectly. However, it can be streamlined in several ways. Although it's not a problem, notice that we're addressing the current clip by using allClips[i] in three places. It's actually more efficient to first store the reference in a local variable and then refer to that local variable several times. We can just add the line var thisClip=allClips[i] as the first line inside the for loop, and then use thisClip in the three places where we currently use allClips[i]. Although this refinement is arguably useless, I wanted to point out that you can store references to clips in variables just as allClips already includes several references. Check out this finished alternative:

```
_root.onMouseMove=function(){
  for(i in allClips){
    var thisClip=allClips[i]
    if(thisClip.hitTest(_root._xmouse,_root._ymouse,1)){
      thisClip._alpha=30;
    }else{
      thisClip._alpha=100;
    }
  }
  updateAfterEvent();
}
```

7. Finally, we'll add a feature that determines which clip, if any, the user has clicked when the mouse button is pressed. Add this script below the rest of your scripts:

```
_root.onMouseDown=function(){
  for(i in allClips){
    var thisClip=allClips[i]
```

```
        if(thisClip.hitTest(_root._xmouse,_root._ymouse,1)){
          trace ("You clicked "+ thisClip._name);
          thisClip._xScale-=10;
          thisClip._yScale-=10;
          return;
        }
      }
    }
```

Although this workshop (and this function in particular) might have little practical value the way it is, we can take away several lessons. In the onMouseDown callback, notice that because we're doing something only to the clip that matches (but nothing to all the other clips), we can use return to stop looping as soon as something is found. In the onMouseMove callback, we had to set every clip's _alpha to either 100 or 30. As it turns out, even when you have to loop through the entire array, the process goes quite quickly. After you learn more about getTimer() in Workshop Chapter 10, "Creating Timers," and Workshop Chapter 12, "Developing Time-Based Animations," you'll be able to test the impact that different script approaches have on performance. For example, I suggested that you could place the value of allClips[i] into the variable thisClip rather than constantly referring to allClips[i]. This change would certainly be worth the effort if performance noticeably increased because of the change. If you make 200 copies of the clips on the Stage, you'll start to see a slowdown. In my tests, for example, I found that when I had 200 instances on the Stage, the loop took as long as 100 milliseconds (1/10 of one second) to complete. By trying different scripts, I reduced the loop to half that time. The point is that looping through an array is fast, but trying different scripts can often make it faster.

Remember that one of the main lessons in this workshop chapter was to store references to clip instances in an array variable so that you can use the variable when you want to address instances. We also got to use a for loop as well as hitTest().

Adapting Built-In Components

By now you should have enough skill to create your own components. First of all, they don't need to be complex. Even if you do need to invest a lot of work to create a component, as we did in Workshop Chapter 2, "Creating Custom Cursors," you can often reuse the code so many times that you'll quickly see a return on your investment. Just because you *can* make a component, however, doesn't mean that you have to reinvent the wheel.

Flash MX comes with several components, and countless others are available from the Flash community at the Macromedia Exchange for Flash (`www.macromedia.com/exchange/flash`). Most of these preexisting components can be used as-is. However, you'll often find that you need to adapt them for your own purposes. If nothing else, you'll always need to populate the component with your own data. For example, the preinstalled ComboBox component (in the Components panel under "Flash UI Components") appears blank until you populate it with items. It's similarly easy to specify a function you want triggered every time the user makes a selection from this component. In this workshop chapter, we'll quickly walk through how to populate this component.

Sometimes just populating the component might not be enough. You might want to change the way it works. For example, the ComboBox component triggers the function you specify every time a selection is made—maybe you want the function to trigger only when the user selects a new item (that is, you don't want anything to happen when she reselects the same item). For this adjustment, you just modify how your function works. Other times, however, you'll need to snoop through the component's scripts to see if you can make a change. In this workshop chapter, we'll make a few fine-tune adjustments to some of the newer components to make them drag smoother.

Finally, perhaps the most fundamental way to edit a component is by replacing skins. A *skin* is the set of graphics used in the component (not your content). Think of a skin as a set of colors and graphics. For example, we'll change the appearance of the little down arrow that appears in the ComboBox component. I suppose "skinning" a component is less drastic than changing its scripts—but it *looks* like you've made a bigger change. In any event, we'll do all three things: populating components, editing their scripts, and skinning.

Populating Components

1. First, let's populate a ComboBox component. (We can skin it later.) From the Components panel, drag an instance of the ComboBox component onto the Stage. From the Parameters tab in the Properties panel, click to enter values into the Labels parameter. Click the plus button and enter three values—such as "Macromedia," "Microsoft," and "New Riders" (see Figure W7.1).

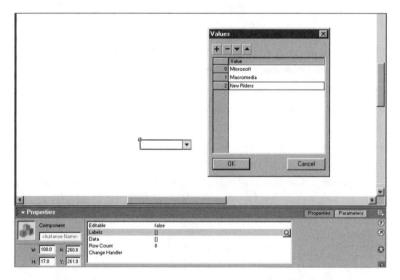

Figure W7.1 *Parameters that contain multiple values are populated through this dialog box.*

2. Next, populate the Data parameter with three URLs to match the three items entered as labels (for example, `http://www.macromedia.com`, `http://www.microsoft.com`, and `http://www.newriders.com`).

3. Finally, specify the Change Handler to read `jumpTime`. We'll have to also write this function. (Some programming tools use the term "handler" to mean "function.") Anyway, in the first frame of the main timeline, type this `jumpTime()` function:

```
function jumpTime(who){
  trace(who.getValue());
}
```

If you test the movie, you'll see the URL any time an item is selected from the ComboBox component. Even though we didn't specify a parameter for the `jumpTime()` function, this component automatically passes a reference to the component that triggers the function. That's nice in this case because we won't have to name the instance. If you had several ComboBox instances on the Stage, you'd probably want to know which one triggered the function (instead of, perhaps, making a different function for each one). Anyway, I found the `getValue()` method under FlashUIComponents, FComboBox in the Actions panel. It returns the currently selected value (not just item number).

Obviously, you could change the `trace` statement to do a `getURL` (for example, `getURL(who.getValue())`). Before you do that, I'll just show a solution to making this ComboBox component trigger only when the user changes the selected item.

4. To modify the way the ComboBox component works, we won't really change the component but rather how our function responds to it. Check out this finished version of the `jumpTime()` function:

```
function jumpTime(who){
  if (lastTime==who.getSelectedIndex()){
    return;
  }
  lastTime=who.getSelectedIndex();
  getURL(who.getValue())
}
```

Now you can't navigate to the same place twice in a row. For example, if the user makes a selection, and then selects the menu and decides not to change anything, it won't take them anywhere (the way it did before). The code stores the last selected item number in the `lastTime` variable. Then, every time this function is triggered, we first check to see whether the current selected index (using another ComboBox method, `getSelectedIndex()`) is the same; if it is, we `return` and skip the rest of the code. This is just one solution. We'll come back to this ComboBox component to add a new skin. Now let's go and tweak the code in some of the other components.

To follow the next section, you need to download and install the Extension Manager and the Flash UI Components Set 2. You can find them both at `www.macromedia.com/exchange/flash`.

Editing Scripts in Components

The Flash UI Components Set 2 came out only days after Flash MX was released, and they're pretty sweet. For example, the DraggablePane component is similar to the ScrollPane component that is installed with Flash MX. Both these components enable you to identify a symbol (by its linkage "identifier") and it automatically appears inside a scrollable window. This is great for when an image is larger than the space you want to allot to it. The DraggablePane component adds features for dragging, resizing, and collapsing. However, those extra features seem to be a tad sluggish, especially when your movie's framerate is low. Let me walk you through how to adjust this component—not as a way to "dis" an otherwise great component, but to practice our bug-finding skills.

1. Import a photograph or draw a large graphic. Convert it into a Movie Clip symbol. Access the Linkage settings for the Movie Clip you just created (from the Library's options menu). Click the Export for ActionScript option and set the Identifier to read myPicture (see Figure W7.2). You can trash any clips or photos on the Stage. (They're both safe in the Library.)

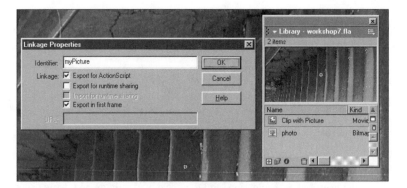

Figure W7.2   *You need to set a linkage identifier for clips used with the DraggablePane component*

2. Drag a DraggablePane component onto the stage. You might need to change the currently visible set of components (to view "Flash UI Components Set 2") by clicking the little arrow inside the Components panel. With the instance on the Stage selected, use the Parameters tab of the Properties panel to specify a value for Scroll Content—that is, make it read myPicture.

3. Set the movie's frame rate to 3 fps, and then select Control, Test Movie. You should notice that whereas scrolling the image is very snappy, dragging and resizing it (from the bottom-right corner of the window) is very sluggish. We can try to fix this.

   Back in Flash, we'll need to snoop through the code in the component. Even if we mess up, the original component won't be affected (just the one in this movie). Anyway, there's a ton of code, so let me walk you through the way I found to fix these issues.

4. Because you can't just double-click a component instance, you have to select it and then choose Edit, Edit In Place. Nearly all the code for this component is in the first layer: "Actions : Class." Even though there are nearly 700 lines of code, we can get to what we want very quickly by using the Find button. I know that scripts that include the ActionScript fragments _xmouse, mouseMove, or startDrag likely affect dragging. Select the first frame and then open the Actions panel. Click the Find button and search for mouseMove. The first instance I found was on line 494. This is line 494:

   ```
   this.onMouseMove = this.controller.dragResizeCursor;
   ```

   We don't have to know everything this says except that we're assigning a callback for the onMouseMove event—namely, the function called dragResizeCursor. We'll find dragResizeCursor defined on line 502. (It's so close, you don't have to search for it.)

5. The key problem with the definition of dragResizeCursor is that there's no updateAfterEvent() script. Insert a line of code before the closing curly brace (in line 506) that reads:

   ```
   updateAfterEvent();
   ```

   When you test the movie, the resizing feature should be very smooth despite having a low frame rate. (That was an easy fix.)

6. Now to fix the dragging issue. If you continue to search for likely drag-related-scripts, you'll find that startDrag appears around line 561. This is an older Flash feature. Just replace the line of code (this.controller.startDrag()) with the following:

   ```
   this.controller.onMouseMove=function(){
     this._x=_root._xmouse;
     this._y=_root._ymouse;
     updateAfterEvent();
   }
   ```

   Notice that right after what you see here, there should be a closing curly brace (for the titleTrackBegin definition of which we are currently inside). Also, there are two lines of code that appear above what I just told you to insert. You're just replacing the one startDrag() line of code. Notice that we didn't say this.onMouseMove; we said

```
this.controller.onMouseMove because the line we replaced said
this.controller.startDrag.
```

7. A few lines after where startDrag() used to be, you'll find the stopDrag() command. (It's in the titleTrackEnd definition.) Replace that line with the following:

```
this.controller.onMouseMove=null;
```

This stops our code from functioning (at the same instance that the old stopDrag() was doing its thing).

If you test the movie now, you'll see that it's much smoother—although it looks as though you're always dragging from the top-left corner. That's because the center of the component is that top-left corner and our code says to position the _x and _y to where the mouse is—meaning the "center" of the clip goes to where the mouse is. We need something here like the extra touch we did in Workshop Chapter 3, "Creating a Horizontal Slider."

8. To use an offset, change the two lines that set the _x and _y (in the code that replaced the startDrag() code) so that those lines appear as follows:

```
this._x=_root._xmouse+this.offsetX;
this._y=_root._ymouse+this.offSetY;
```

This just says "move to where the mouse is plus the offset variables" (that we're about to define).

9. To assign the values for our offset variables, add the following code anywhere in this frame script (except inside another function):

```
FDraggablePaneClass.prototype.onMouseDown=function(){
  this.offsetX=this._x-_root._xmouse;
  this.offsetY=this._y-_root._ymouse;
}
```

Put simply, when the user clicks, this script figures out how far off center the mouse is and stores that information in the two variables (offsetX and offsetY).

Test it out. It works pretty well. One thing you probably want to do is test to see that the changes we made didn't break anything else. By the way, you might try your hand at fixing the same issue in the MessageBox component; the fix is nearly the same as what we just did.

Generally, you won't need to change the code in a component; I just thought it would be good practice. Skinning a component makes a much more visually striking change (provided that the component creator made it "skin-able"). In the most basic sense, skinning is nothing more than replacing the contents of various clips used in the component. It's just that there are a few details worth understanding. Let's walk through how to make a few graphic and color changes to a simple component.

Skinning a Component

1. Drag a few instances of the PushButton component and one ComboBox component into a new movie. Populate the ComboBox component with a few labels (like you did in the first part of this workshop chapter). Test the movie. You should see the default _sans typeface.

2. You can change the font choice for all components in just one move. Open the Library window and notice the folder structure shown in Figure W7.3. Navigate to the Component Skins folder and then to the Global Skins folder, and finally double-click to edit the FLabel symbol.

Figure W7.3 *All the skins for components that ship with Flash are contained in a single folder.*

3. Once inside the FLabel symbol, unlock the layers and select the text field on the Stage. Use the Properties panel to select a different font and font size. Test the movie again. Depending on the font choice, you might want to return to the FLabel symbol and click the Character button so that you can select to Embed Font Outlines for All Characters (see Figure W7.4).

Figure W7.4 *Embedding all characters with a text field will often make the text appear clearer (although this also adds to the filesize).*

Although we changed only the font, you can also change any graphic element in the component. For example, in the FPushButton Skins Library folder you'll find a symbol called fpb_up. That's basically the button in its Up state. Replacing graphical elements in components can be tedious because there are often skin elements. The PushButton component has five separate skin elements (independent instances within the component).

Because skinning a component can be a bit of work, you certainly don't want to do it for every movie. However, once you complete one component "makeover," you can save it to use later. In the remaining steps, I'll show you how to save the modified PushButton component.

4. To make components available to other movies, you need to confirm two things: that the source .fla is saved in Flash's Configuration folder and that the component is set to display in the Components panel. Select the PushButton component symbol in the Library of your working file. (It should be in a folder called Flash UI Components.) Select Component Definition from the Library options menu and verify that the Display in Components panel check box is selected (see Figure W7.5).

5. Next we need to save a copy of our working file inside Flash's Configuration folder. This folder's location varies based on your operating system. You can find the exact location in the readme.html file located in the Configuration folder adjacent to your installed version of Flash MX. On Windows 98, for example, you'll find the Configuration folder inside C:\WINDOWS\Application Data\Macromedia\Flash MX\. Inside the Configuration folder are several subfolders, including the Components folder. It is into this folder that you should save the working file containing the modified component. Save the file as myComponents.fla.

Figure W7.5 *Before a component will appear in the Components panel, you must select the Display in Components panel option in the Component Definition dialog box.*

6. Quit Flash and restart the program to implement the changes (that is, so that the component will appear in the Components panel). Now, you'll find an additional sub-menu item in the Components panel based on the file-name you provided in Step 5 (see Figure W7.6).

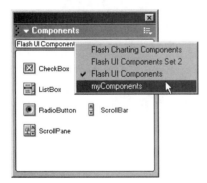

Figure W7.6 *Components that you add to Flash's Configuration folder appear in the Components panel.*

//

After you save a .fla file inside the Components folder (inside the Configuration folder), you will not be able to edit it from Flash. If you need to make an edit, just copy the folder to another location, make the edit, and then return it to the Components folder.

The intention of this workshop chapter was not to show you the "ultimate" component; rather, the purpose was to show you some of the ways that you can modify existing components. You should also have learned some ways to analyze the work of others. In particular, the hundreds of lines of code in the DraggablePane component are not that terrible if you study only a part at a time. Actually, looking through all the components is a great way to learn. Not only do they show some fancy class inheritance (introduced in Chapter 13, "Homemade Objects," and Chapter 14, "Extending ActionScript"), they exhibit elements of good programming style (as discussed in Chapter 3, "The Programmer's Approach").

{ Part IIB }

Intermediate Workshops

{ Chapter 8

Workshop }

Creating a Currency-Exchange Calculator

The first seven workshop chapters were relatively basic. Sure, there were plenty of new concepts and unique solutions to problems, but there wasn't all that much complex math or string manipulation, any interfacing with external data, and just one optional custom class. If the first seven workshop chapters were "basic," this workshop and the next four will be "intermediate" workshops. As such, some of the steps are not explained as fully as they have been in the first workshops. Instead, I'll try to reference where the topics were first covered. Don't worry, the remaining workshop chapters won't be impossible, they'll just involve different topics.

In this workshop chapter, we'll build a currency-exchange calculator. The user will be able to input any value and, based on the exchange rate, calculate the equivalent cost in another currency. As is true with many of the workshop chapters, the finished product is not necessarily something you'll use as-is, but the process of working through the exercise will teach you some very valuable techniques. If you've read all the chapters in the "Foundation" section of this book, you'll no doubt recall the several times I referred you to this workshop. A lot is covered here. Specifically, you'll do some simple math and some slightly more complex math. You'll encounter some of the challenges when you have to convert between numbers and strings. You'll also look at ways to improve the user experience by adding a feature that enables the user to select from predefined exchange rates for different countries. Just to make it easy for us (and because exchange rates vary daily), we'll make it possible to load in the current exchange rates from external sources. Although you may never have to build a currency-exchange calculator again, I'll be willing to bet that you'll be able to use all of the topics covered here!

Consider the following description as the specification for this workshop chapter. As you learned in Chapter 3, "The Programmer's Approach," after you have a detailed "spec," programming is almost routine.

Provide the user with a way to convert values in one currency to the equivalent value in another currency. The user will be able to type any number into one field, adjust the exchange rate by typing into the "rate" field, and then see the resulting equivalent value appear in a third field. Additionally, you must format the value displayed in the standard money format: with at least one 0 to the left of the decimal, two decimal places shown at all times, and all fractional values rounded off to the nearest cent (the one-hundredth decimal place). Finally, the calculator must allow the import from an external source of several countries' exchange rates from U.S. dollars. The user will be able to select any country, and that country's exchange rate will automatically fill the "rate" field. Additionally, after any country's exchange rate has been selected, the user must be allowed to toggle between dollars and the other currency. For example, if the current rate is for British pounds, the user should be able to toggle from "dollars to pounds" and from "pounds to dollars." See Figure W8.1 for a rough layout. Finally, feel free to improve the interface for utmost usability, where appropriate.

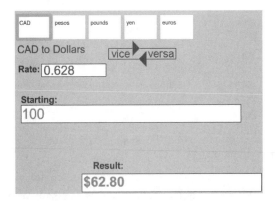

Figure W8.1 *We'll build a calculator based on a specification that includes this mock-up.*

Although this is a rather big task, realize that all great things are done in pieces. For example, we're not going to jump right in and have everything done after writing one script. Rather, we'll break things down and build each piece as we go. The whole time, we'll keep an eye out for approaches that might conflict with a future task. Luckily, this spec has been organized in a logical order with the simple tasks first. It will serve as the guide for the following steps:

1. Place two Input Text fields onscreen, give one an instance name of `rate_txt` and the other an instance name of `original_txt`. Make sure that both fields have nice wide margins. Using the Text Options panel, set the Maximum Characters option to something high, such as 20. You might also opt for the Show Border Around Text option so that the field remains outlined and easy to see. It's important that we allow the user to input only numbers and a period for decimals into these two fields; therefore, click the Character button, and then click the Only radio button and the Numerals check box. In the "And these characters" field, type a period (see Figure W8.2). You can label these fields by using additional plain Static Text fields.

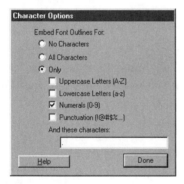

Figure W8.2   *You can limit input to just numbers plus individually identified characters.*

2. Create a Dynamic Text field (not an Input Text field because this field will be used to display the results) and give it an instance name of `result_txt`. Click the Character button and select the No Characters option.

3. Now we can start to put code in a frame script. We can use listeners to calculate the result field's text. Type in this script:

```
1 myListener=new Object();
2 myListener.onChanged=convert;
3 rate_txt.addListener(myListener);
4 original_txt.addListener(myListener);
5 function convert(){
6   result_txt.text=original_txt.text * rate_txt.text;
7 }
```

We have a currency-exchange calculator! Pretty simple, eh? The first two lines create a generic listener that triggers the convert function. Then lines 3 and 4 add that listener to the rate_txt and original_txt fields so that if either one changes, the convert() function triggers. Finally, the convert function multiplies the text in original_txt by rate_txt to display a value in result_txt. By the way, I could have defined the convert() function inline at the end of line 2, but I figure I might want to trigger convert() from another place (specifically, when the user clicks a preset or when the movie begins). Having the convert() function standing by itself will make this possible.

If you type .70 into the rate_txt field and 10 into the original_txt field, you'll see 7 into the result_txt field. Thank you, and good night!

//

Not so fast. Although the preceding steps create a working calculator, we have more to consider. Try a rate_txt like .7 on an original_txt value such as 10.95. No doubt, the bug tester will determine that we're not rounding off to the nearest cent. We just need to write a round() function. Because the Math object already has a round() method, however, let's not use the same name for our function. We cannot use Math.round() directly because that function rounds to the nearest whole number. Consider the result of 0.7*10.95. Currently, we're getting a result of 7.665, but we want it to round to 7.67. If you change the assignment to result_txt.text=Math.round(original_txt.text * rate_txt.text), you'll find that 7.665 rounds to 8. However, we can still use Math.round() if we apply a fairly simple trick. Consider what happens if you first multiply result by 100 (you'd get 766.5), round that off (you'd have 767), and then divide by 100 (you'd get 7.67, which is what we want). Consider this verbose solution:

```
result_txt.text=original_txt.text *rate_txt.text;
result_txt.text =result_txt.text *100;
result_txt.text =Math.round(result_txt.text);
result_txt.text =result_txt.text /100;
```

Although we could do this math in a slightly easier way, I think rounding off to specific decimal places might prove to be a useful utility for other projects (if not later in this workshop chapter). Consider how this works: We used 100 to multiply and then divided by 100 because we wanted 2 decimal places. To round off to 3 places, we would use 1000. We'd use 10 for 1 decimal place.

4. Consider the relationship described in the preceding note as you type this
   homemade `rnd()` function into frame 1:

```
function rnd(num, places){
  var multiplier = Math.pow(10, places);
  var answer = Math.round(num*multiplier);
  return answer/multiplier;
}
```

This function accepts two parameters: `num` (for the number being rounded
off) and `places` (for the number of decimal places). First we determine
what we're going to multiply by (10, 100, 1000, or whatever). The
`Math.pow()` method accepts two parameters—base and exponent—so
that the first number is raised to the power of the second number. In this
example, if `places` is 2, 10^2 is 100. We then round off `num` multiplied by
`multiplier` and place it in another temporary variable answer. Finally, we
return the answer we just found divided by `multiplier`. This is exactly the
process we need, and because it's now a function, we can use it any time.

5. To test the function we just wrote, change the script for the `convert()`
   function to read as follows:

```
function convert(){
  rate=Number(rate_txt.text);
  original=Number(original_txt.text);
  result_txt.text=rnd(original * rate,2);
}
```

Notice that because I was getting real tired of typing "`rate_txt.text`"
every time I wanted to refer to the rate, I just created two new variables:
`rate` and `original`. Also, because I'm paranoid, I made sure they're number versions of the text in those two fields (by using the `Number()` function).
Also notice that instead of preceding with `var` (to make local variables), I
figured we might want to know what the `rate` is in another script. From this
point forward, just think of `rate` and `original` as the values in those fields.
The last line of code does three things: multiplies the two variables, rounds
them off, and then places the result in the `result_txt` field. I suppose that I
could have written this formula in two steps by first setting
`result_txt.text` to `original*rate` and then reassigning `result_txt.text`
to `rnd(result_txt.text,2)`. The solution shown isn't too difficult if you
remember that multiplication is performed first.

//

At this point, you might find that the rnd() function still doesn't work! 7.665 rounds off to 7.66, but it *should* be 7.65. There's nothing wrong with the logic used in the rnd() function; rather, you're seeing an inherent problem with all computers when using floating-point numbers (decimal values). It's called the *rounding error*, and it's unavoidable. Although we humans have no problem looking at a fraction such as 1/2 and deriving the accurate decimal equivalent of 0.5, computers sometimes have problems. It's obvious when you consider a fraction such as 1/3, because the computer will need to round off a decimal like 0.333... (with repeating threes). But even fractions that should be expressed in simple decimals (such as 7.665) will exhibit the problem. Our case of 10.95*0.7 exhibits the rounding error because the computer considers the answer to be 7.66499999.... You won't see it in Flash if you execute the script trace(10.95*.7), but you will see it if you execute the equivalent code in JavaScript—alert(10.95*.7) (see Figure W8.3).

Figure W8.3   *This pop-up box shows the full number.*

If you investigate this subject, you'll find that there's actually a lot to it. You can avoid the issue entirely by using integer numbers only. However, dividing one integer by another will often create a floating-point number. The common practice is to avoid floating-point numbers as long as you can (through all your calculations) and at the very end, display decimal values onscreen. For example, the exchange rate of 0.7 can be expressed as an integer if you use 7 and remember to divide the final answer by 10. We're not going to go through that effort in this workshop chapter, but it's worth considering. Instead, we'll use a quick-and-dirty trick. Just realize that the user doesn't care what's going on behind the scenes if, in the end, he sees the correct numbers onscreen.

6. The rounding error is small, but quite annoying. To address it, I've developed this quick-and-dirty solution. Change the `convert()` function to read as follows:

```
1 function convert () {
2   rate=Number(rate_txt.text);
3   original=Number(original_txt.txt);
4   var decimals=1;
5   decimals+= (original.length- 1) - original.lastIndexOf( "." );
6   decimals+= (rate.length- 1) - rate.lastIndexOf( "." );
7   fudge=1/Math.pow(10,decimals);
8   result_txt.text=rnd ((original*rate)+fudge,2);
9 }
```

This fix adds a very small "fudge factor" to the floating-point product of `original*rate` that is always smaller than the total number of decimal places for both `original` and `rate`. In line 4, I initialize the local variable `_decimals` to `1`. (If no decimals are found, my fudge factor will still be `.1`, which will have no effect.) In line 5, `decimals` is increased by the difference between the length of original (minus 1) and the last index of `"."` So, if the original was 10.95, I would subtract 2 (the index where the last `"."` is found) from 4 (the length of `"10.95"` minus 1) to determine that the number of decimal places is 2. In line 6, the number of decimals in `rate` is added to the `decimals` variable using the same expression. Finally, in line 7, I assign the `fudge` variable to the inverse of 10 to the power of all the decimals (`1/Math.pow(10,4)` returns `1/10000` or `.0001`, for example). That `fudge` variable is added to the product of `original*rate` that is used in the `rnd()` function. Wow. All that work, and I still can't promise that you'll never encounter the rounding error!

Although our homemade `rnd()` function works great, we still don't have displays that look like currency. We need "trailing" zeros to two decimal places and at least one zero that "pads" to the left of the decimal. Oh, and we need a dollar sign, too, but that's a piece of cake: `result="$"+result`. (Don't insert this code yet.) It turns out that our needs are not all that uncommon.

7. In addition to `rnd()`, here are two other utility functions I've used for years in Director. They're translated here into ActionScript. We'll use both of them, so type them into the frame script:

```
function pad(num, places){
  theString=String(num)
  for(i=0;i<places;i++){
    if (theString.length<places){
      theString="0"+theString;
    }
  }
  return theString;
}
```

```
function trail(num, places){
  var theString=String(num)
  for(i=0;i<places;i++){
    if (theString.length>=places){
      break;
    }else{
      theString=theString+"0";
    }
  }
  return theString;
}
```

These two functions help you turn a number into a string with a minimum number of digits. For example, you can use the pad() function to ensure that a number has at least 5 digits. For example, pad(18,5) takes 18 and returns a five-digit number. Returned, you'll have 00018. Naturally, you use a variable for the first parameter. Similarly, the trail() function ensures that your string has a minimum number of digits, but it adds zeros at the end.

> I had an occasion to use the pad() function in a project that listed product numbers from a client's clothing catalog. Most items had three-digit product numbers, but several used only two digits. The items were supposed to be displayed as 004, 089, or 102. Item numbers less than 100 had to be padded with zeros. I just used the pad() function like this: stringVersion=pad(itemNum,3).

Both the pad() and trail() functions loop through each character in the string. Until the desired number of places has been reached, the string "0" is concatenated to the end or beginning of the string that is returned. We'll use both of these functions within the currency() function that we're about to write to ensure that all decimal values have two digits.

8. Let's get started writing the currency() function. Although this function has to do several things, I know that all dollars should be at least one digit and that all decimals should be two digits. Type this function in the first keyframe:

```
function currency(num){
  //round it and make it a string
  var theString=String(rnd(num,2));

  //find where the decimal is
  var decimalLoc=theString.indexOf(".");

  //separate dollars portion from decimal
  var dollars=theString.substring( 0, decimalLoc );
```

```
  var cents=theString.substring(decimalLoc+1);

  //trail cents, pad dollars
  cents=trail(cents,2);
  dollars=pad(dollars,1);

  //return a nice string
  return "$"+dollars+"."+cents;
}
```

First we round off the number supplied as num and turn it into a string.
Then we get the indexOf the decimal (that is, the location of the decimal).
We use two local variables to store dollars and cents, respectively.
Finally, we use the pad() and trail() functions to ensure that we have the
minimum number of digits, using zeros if we don't. The whole thing is
concatenated to return a nice-looking string with a dollar sign.

9. Now change the last line in the convert() function to read

```
result_txt.text=currency((original*rate)+fudge);
```

This way, the new currency() function will be called (instead of just the
rnd() function).

If you test this script, it appears to work only intermittently. Actually, if
you didn't have the attitude of a cynic, you could easily think that the
script works fine. Perhaps all the what-if numbers you've provided work
out fine. But just try something as simple as a rate of .5 and an original
value of 10. I get a result of $0.50—that can't be right! The solution is
found in the fact that indexOf() returns -1 when the pattern being
searched for (in this case ".") is not found. Therefore, our currency()
function works only when the rounded number includes a decimal. Without
a decimal, the decimalLoc variable starts off at -1 and the rest of the function falls apart.

10. To fix this bug, use this adjusted version of the currency() function:

```
 1 function currency(num){
 2   //round it and make it a string
 3   var theString=String(rnd(num,2));
 4
 5   //find where the decimal is
 6   var decimalLoc=theString.indexOf(".");
 7   var dollars;
 8   var cents;
 9   if (decimalLoc==-1){
10     dollars=theString;
11     cents="00";
12   }else{
13     dollars=theString.substring( 0, decimalLoc );
14     cents=theString.substring(decimalLoc+1);
15   }
16
```

```
17    //trail cents, pad dollars
18    cents=trail(cents,2);
19    dollars=pad(dollars,1);
20    //return a nice string
21    return "$"+dollars+"."+cents;
22 }
```

This version of the function considers that when there's no decimal, the entire theString must be whole dollars; therefore, cents must be "00".

There's one last feature that I suggest adding to the currency() function: When the dollars value goes above 999, it would be nice if commas appeared to separate every thousand. For example, $43009.95 should appear as $43,009.95. Instead of walking through the *entire* process of writing such a script, you can simply replace the last line in the preceding currency() function (line 21, starting return…) with this code:

```
var actualDollars="";
var thousands=Math.floor((dollars.length)/3);
var extra=(dollars.length)%3;
if (extra>0){
  actualDollars=actualDollars+dollars.substr(0,extra);
}
if (thousands>0){
  if (extra>0){
    actualDollars=actualDollars+",";
  }
  for (i=1;i<=thousands;i++){
    theseThree=dollars.subStr( extra + ((i-1)*3) ,3);
    actualDollars=actualDollars+theseThree;
      if (i<thousands){
          actualDollars=actualDollars+",";
      }
  }
}
//return a nice string
return "$"+actualDollars+"."+cents;
```

This code is gnarly, but let me explain the basic process. First we initialize the actualDollars variable that will ultimately contain the dollars portion of the result. Then we determine how many times 3 can be evenly divided into the length of our string and place the result in thousands. The variable extra is then assigned to the remainder of dividing our string's length by 3. For example, if the string is "10000", thousands becomes 1 (the integer part of 5/3) and extra becomes 2 (the remainder of 5/3). If extra>0, we initialize actualDollars to equal just the first few characters of the string. For example, with the string "10000", the first 2 characters are placed in actualDollars (those characters are "10"). Then, provided that there is at least one set of thousands (that extra>0), we place a comma after the actualDollars variable. In the example of the string "10000", actualDollars is now "10". At this point, we're about to start the for loop that keeps extracting the next three characters from our original dollars and attaches them to the end of the actualDollars string we're building. At the end of each loop, a comma is added, provided that we have more loops to go (if extra>0). Finally, we build our string using actualDollars, which now has commas appropriately inserted, and the original cents variable. For a good challenge, try to extract this "comma-insertion" code and create a function that can be called any time.

Now that the main functionality of the currency-exchange calculator is working, let's move on to loading preset rates from an external source.

11. Create a text file containing the following text and save it as rates.txt in the same folder as your working Flash file:

```
name_1=CAD
&name_2=pesos
&name_3=pounds
&name_4=yen
&name_5=euros
&rate_1=0.628
&rate_2=0.11
&rate_3=1.43
&rate_4=0.0075
&rate_5=0.878
```

The five name_ variables describe the currencies; the five rate_ variables contain the exchange rates from dollars to those currencies. The form is URL encoded. We'll have to eliminate the extraneous return characters at the end of each line. (You can find a discussion of URL encoding in Chapter 16, "Interfacing with External Data.") Now we can load these variables into Flash.

12. Currently, our movie is only one frame long. Select the first keyframe and then move it to frame 2 (see Figure W8.4). In frame 1, type the following script:

```
stop ();
rates=new LoadVars();
rates.onLoad = function() {
  _root.nextFrame();
}
rates.load("rates.txt");
```

This script stops the movie from reaching frame 2, initializes a LoadVars object, defines the onLoad callback (which takes the user to the next frame), and then starts loading variables from the rates.txt file created in the last step. This script will accurately make the user wait on frame 1 until all the data is loaded. Once the data is loaded, however, we should remove the extra carriage returns. While we're doing that, we might as well move the variables (rate_1, rate_2, and so on) from inside the rates variable to the main timeline. We can do all of that before the nextFrame() method is invoked.

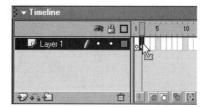

Figure W8.4   *We can move everything that we've built so far to frame 2.*

13. I have a function that will remove redundant characters from the end of a string. Because we have several strings (one for each variable loaded), we'll process one at a time. Here's the generic function that you should type into the first frame script:

```
function removeExtra(fromString){
  var lastChar=fromString.charCodeAt(fromString.length-1);
    while (lastChar==10 || lastChar==13 ) {
      fromString=fromString.substr(0,fromString.length-2);
      lastChar=fromString.charCodeAt(fromString.length-1);
    }
  return fromString;
}
```

This function just removes any carriage returns or line feeds from the end of a line—as we did in Chapter 14, "Extending ActionScript." Because it's a function, we'll be able to call it from anywhere. All we need to do to fix a variable's value is to use:

```
myVariable=removeExtra(myVariable)
```

14. In order both to clean up the loaded variables and to move them into the main timeline, change the `onLoad` callback definition for the `rates` object to read as follows:

```
 1 rates.onLoad = function() {
 2   var thisRate="something"
 3   var i = 0
 4   while(true) {
 5     i++;
 6     var thisName=this["name_" + i];
 7     thisRate=this["rate_" + i];
 8     if (thisRate==undefined){
 9       break;
10     }
11     thisName=_root.removeExtra(thisName);
12     thisRate=_root.removeExtra(thisRate);
13     _root["name_"+ i]=thisName;
14     _root["rate_"+ i]=Number(thisRate);
15   }
16   _root.nextFrame();
17 }
```

This code looks worse than it is. Basically, the while loop keeps sending each variable through the removeExtra() function, and then creates a duplicate (same-named) variable in the _root timeline. Line 2 initializes the thisRate variable to a dummy string. Notice that the while loop on line 4 tries to loop forever. Our "escape route" is on line 8. That is, if thisRate is ever undefined, we break out of the loop. Line 2 just makes sure that thisRate is something at the start. In order to have an incrementing variable, line 3 initializes i to 0 (and then line 5 increments on every loop). Then, inside the loop, you can see the bulk of code. The variables thisName and thisRate temporarily hold the value of a dynamically referenced name (lines 6 and 7). Therefore, thisRate is never "something" by the time we get to line 8. However, if the dynamic expression in line 7 (this["rate_"+i]) turns out to be undefined, we break out of the loop. Assuming that everything's legitimate, lines 11 and 12 reassign the two local variables (thisRate and thisName) to a cleaned-up version. Then lines 13 and 14 assign same-named variables in the _root timeline. Finally, you see the nextFrame() method is called once the loop is finished. By the way, a plain old for loop might have been easier, but I'd have to know exactly how many rates were being loaded. The while(true) loop will stop as soon as it tries to process a variable that doesn't exist—but it does require a bit more work.

You can use the Debugger to see the "before" and "after" results. That is, the rates object has a bunch of variables, including carriage returns and line feeds. The same-named versions of those variables in the main timeline should be nice and clean (see Figure W8.5). Actually, this makes me think that the very first line of code in frame 2 should read delete rates to remove that variable. (By the way, you can't delete the rates variable from inside its onLoad callback.)

We're done with frame 1. We'll add the remainder of our graphics and scripts to frame 2.

15. Let's make a clip (of which we'll have 5 instances) that enables the user select a preset exchange rate. First draw a box with a bright thick stroke. Select just the stroke and convert it to a Movie Clip—this will be our "selected" highlight. Give this new clip an instance name of highlight, and then move it offscreen.

16. Place a Dynamic Text field on top of the remaining box shape and give the text an instance name of thisName. Select both the text and box and convert to a Movie Clip. Give the instance of your new clip the name select_1. Make 4 copies of this clip and name them select_2, select_3, and so on (see Figure W8.6).

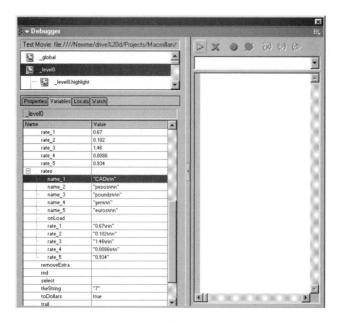

Figure W8.5   *A quick look with the Debugger reveals that our variables have loaded, but with "trailing garbage."*

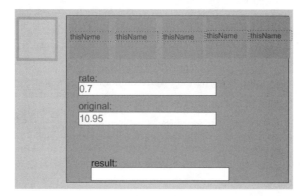

Figure W8.6   *Five instances of a clip containing Dynamic Text will provide a way for the user to select preset exchange rates.*

17. In order for these five buttons to display a currency name and to trigger a function that displays the highlight, type this code into frame 2 of the main timeline:

```
select_1.onPress=function(){select(1);}
select_1.thisName.text =this.name_1;
select_2.onPress=function(){select(2);}
select_2.thisName.text =this.name_2;
```

```
select_3.onPress=function(){select(3);}
select_3.thisName.text =this.name_3;
select_4.onPress=function(){select(4);}
select_4.thisName.text=this.name_4;
select_5.onPress=function(){select(5);}
select_5.thisName.text=this.name_5;

function select(whichOne){
    highlight._x=this["select_"+whichOne]._x;
    highlight._y=this["select_"+whichOne]._y;
}
```

The first 10 lines set a callback for each button as well as the text displayed in the thisName field. The select() function will do more, but for now it just displays the highlight in the same location as the button that invoked the function. For a decent challenge, try writing a loop to fill each clip's thisName text field. You should be able to test the movie and see each button's label and the highlight move when you click a button.

18. Now we can add a bit more code to the select() function. The main thing we want to have happen when the user clicks a preset is for the appropriate rate to be selected. Add the following two lines anywhere inside the select() function:

```
rate_txt.text=_root["rate_"+whichOne];
convert();
```

The idea is that we change the rate_txt field's contents and then trigger the convert() function (which automatically triggers only when the user changes that field).

At this point, I'd say the project is pretty complete. It's certainly done enough to send it out for testing. In addition to at least one minor bug, the main results that will come out if you test this are features to make it more useful. Test it out a bit and try to think of what you'd like to add. Here's my list (and the things we'll address in the rest of this workshop):

- A text message that reads "CAD to Dollars" (or something similar) should appear so that it's clear which kind of conversion is taking place.

- A Toggle button should be added so that the user can quickly change from "CAD to Dollars" to "Dollars to CAD."

- The highlight, text message, and Toggle button should all disappear as soon as the user edits the rate_txt field (or it could be an inaccurate representation). Naturally, they should all reappear when the user selects a preset exchange rate again.

These refinements really aren't too terrible and are well worth the effort to implement. With the exception of the one bug-fix that I know we need to make, the edits to add the preceding features shouldn't mess up what we already have. That is, adding layers of features can be easy and safe if you're careful not to change the core code. You'll see that we won't really tamper with the main functions already in place.

19. For the text message, create a Dynamic Text field with the instance name of message _txt. Then add the following line of code to the select() function:

```
message_txt.text=_root["name_"+whichOne]+" to Dollars";
```

That's a pretty straightforward way to display a dynamic message. We'll need to adjust this code once the Toggle button is pressed so that it says either "Dollars to CAD" or "CAD to Dollars," for example.

20. For the Toggle button, just create a button and name the instance on the Stage toggle_btn. Then write this callback (in frame 2 of the main movie) for when the button is pressed:

```
toggle_btn.onPress=function(){
    rate_txt.text=1/rate_txt.text;
    convert();
}
```

This is pretty simple in that it just fills in the rate_txt field with a reciprocal of the current value, and then triggers the convert() function to reset the display.

At this point, there are a couple of problems with the two added features. First, the Toggle button fails to change the message_txt field. Also, the user can change the value in the rate_txt field and the message remains onscreen. A listener will be the easiest way to "listen" for any changes in the rate_txt field and then clear the message_txt (and move the highlight too). Even though there's already a listener set up for the rate_txt field (that triggers the convert() function), there's no problem adding more listeners to the same field.

21. To add another listener to the rate_txt field, add the following code (near where you set up the other listeners way back in step 3):

```
listenChangeRate=new Object();
listenChangeRate.onChanged=function(){
  message_txt.text="";
  highlight._x=-9000;
}
rate_txt.addListener(listenChangeRate);
```

Unlike the other listener, this listener's onChanged callback function is defined right inline. If it turns out that I want to execute the code in this function (which effectively hides the message and highlight), I might take it out into a function so that other scripts can trigger it. Notice that now, as soon as the user changes the `rate_txt` field, the highlight and message text disappear.

Now to fix the contents of the `message_txt` field. I know that I'll use one of the two scripts (not both), depending on which direction the conversion is taking:

```
message_txt.text=_root["name_"+whichOne]+" to Dollars";
message_txt.text="Dollars to "+_root["name_"+whichOne];
```

We just have to figure out which one (and replace `whichOne` with a number tied to the currently selected preset). My thinking is that either the user is converting "to dollars" or not. It's worth storing a variable that says `toDollars=true` when the user first clicks a preset and then toggle between `true` and `false` every time she clicks the Toggle button. In addition, we'll have to save the `whichOne` variable passed to the `preset()` function if we expect to use it later (including every time the user clicks the Toggle button). Because the message display will have to update when the user clicks both a preset and the Toggle button, I'm going to move the following code into a separate function.

22. Write the following function somewhere in frame 2's script:

```
function updateDisplay(){
  if (toDollars){
    message_txt.text=_root["name_"+curPreset]+" to Dollars";
  }else{
    message_txt.text="Dollars to "+_root["name_"+ curPreset];
  }
}
```

Basically, any time `updateDisplay()` is triggered, the message text will refresh with one or the other expressions, depending on the value of `toDollars`. Naturally, we'll have to initialize this variable and change it as necessary. Notice, too, that this code relies on a variable called `curPreset`. We'll have to make sure that is assigned whenever the user clicks a preset. Follow the next two steps to fully implement the `updateDisplay()` function.

23. Change the `select()` function to read as follows:

```
function select(whichOne){
  highlight._x=this["select_"+whichOne]._x;
  highlight._y=this["select_"+whichOne]._y;
  rate_txt.text=_root["rate_"+whichOne];
  toDollars=true;
  curPreset=whichOne;
  updateDisplay();
  convert();
}
```

Basically, we removed the code that was assigning `message_txt`'s text property (that's handled in the `updateDisplay()` function). In addition, we assigned the variables `toDollars` and `curPreset` that are needed elsewhere.

24. To make the Toggle button work, use this revised code:

```
toggle_btn.onPress=function(){
  toDollars=!toDollars;
  rate_txt.text=1/rate_txt.text;
  updateDisplay();
  convert();
}
```

The only difference is that `toDollars` is toggled (between `true` and `false`) and the `updateDisplay()` function is triggered.

At this point, you can really pound on this application, and it should work pretty well. There are two tiny bugs that are worth fixing. Basically, the `currency()` function (added back in step 10) is not perfect. For one thing, if the user clears either the `rate_txt` or `original_txt` fields, you'll see "NaN" in the `result_txt` field. ("NaN" means "not a number.") Anyway, we should change it so that the `result_txt` field appears blank instead. Also, the dollar sign is cool and all, but it really doesn't belong there when the user is not converting "to dollars." Both these issues are easy to resolve, but because they involve changing the `currency()` function, we have to be careful to fully test what we add.

25. First let's fix the `NaN` issue (which is not a non-issue). Just inside the `currency()` function, add this code:

```
if (isNaN(num)){
  return "";
}
```

The parameter received is `num`. So, if the `isNaN()` function returns `true` (that is, `num` is not a number), we return an empty string. Not only will that string be used in the `result_txt` field, but `return` means that the rest of this function will be bypassed. If you wanted, you could change the code here to read `return "enter a number"`.

26. The dollar sign issue is not quite as easy. Way down at the bottom of the currency function, use the following code to replace the last line (the line that currently reads `return "$"+actualDollars+"."+cents`):

```
if (toDollars){
  var prefix="$";
}else{
  var prefix=_root["name_"+curPreset]+": ";
}
return prefix+actualDollars+"."+cents;
```

This just displays either a dollars sign or the actual currency name (*name_x*). Even though this basically works, there's still a problem with the dollar sign issue. (You should be able to find it when you do a Test Movie.) The issue is that once the user edits the rate_txt field, the toDollars variable doesn't change—nor does the curPreset value. That is, if the user clicks a preset, clicks the Toggle button, and then edits the rate_txt field, the result_txt field will erroneously display the most recent currency name. There are several ways to fix this. I tried several things that didn't work. Adding the following line of code to the listenChangeRate.onChanged callback sort of works: toDollars = true. As soon as you click the Toggle button, however, the problem reappears. (And I really liked that fix as it required so little code—oh well.)

27. The solution I came up with involves two steps. First, add the following line of code to the listenChangeRate.onChanged callback function:

```
curPreset=undefined;
```

28. Then, change the added code in the currency() function (which we just added in step 30) to read as follows:

```
var prefix=""
if(curPreset<>undefined){
  if (toDollars){
    prefix="$";
  }else{
    prefix=_root["name_"+curPreset]+": ";
  }
}
return prefix+actualDollars+"."+cents;
```

Basically, I start by setting prefix to an empty string, and then I do only the dollar sign (or other) code if curPreset is defined. I know that curPreset is undefined any time the user edits the rate_txt field (because I just added it to the callback).

That's it! If that wasn't fun, I don't know what is. Welcome to the more advanced workshop chapters. Actually, this one was not only advanced, but long. The upcoming workshop chapters won't be so involved. Keep in mind that we created a lot of code that we later needed to fix. This is typical.

Here's a quick rundown of the techniques, both new and familiar, that came up in this workshop chapter:

- We used Math.round()to round off and Math.floor() to find the integer portion of a number. You can learn more about the Math object in Chapter 5, "Programming Structures."

- We exploited the `length` property, the `subStr()` method, and the ever-popular concatenation operator (+). Chapter 9, "Manipulating Strings," covers many details of the String object.

- We used operators such as `%` (modulo) and `!` (logical NOT). These operators are touched on in Chapter 5.

- We discussed the dynamic referencing of clips. Dynamic referencing is covered in Chapter 7, "The Movie Clip Object."

- We loaded data from external sources like we learned to do in Chapter 16, "Interfacing with External Data."

- We defined callback functions for buttons, as covered in Chapter 16. We also used listeners, which are discussed in Chapter 10, "Keyboard Access and Modifying Onscreen Text," and Chapter 16.

- We reviewed some general approaches to programming and debugging techniques. These techniques are covered in Chapter 3, "The Programmer's Approach," and Chapter 6, "Debugging," respectively.

{ Workshop

Chapter 9 }

Creating a ToolTip Component

In Workshop Chapter 2, "Creating Custom Cursors," you learned how to position a clip instance precisely where the mouse moved. You also learned how to turn a clip instance into a component. This workshop chapter is similar to that one in that we're going to move an instance to the mouse location, but it will be a text field rather than a cursor graphic. The result is a feature commonly known as a *tooltip*.

No doubt you've encountered tooltips in many software applications, including Flash. In this workshop chapter, we'll add several features to our tooltip, including those common to system-level tooltips plus a few extra features that will make our tooltip unique. Naturally, the exact feature set for each instance of our component will be adjustable through the Parameters tab in the Properties panel.

Like most workshop chapters, this one starts off really easy and builds in complexity as we add specific features. Here are the steps:

1. Create a Dynamic Text field containing the text "test." Give it an instance name of `tip`.

2. Draw a square shape, select it, and then convert it to a Movie Clip symbol. Give the instance of the square shape left behind an instance name of `hotspot`. After we finish building the component, the using author will resize `hotspot` on top of the area for which he wants a tooltip to appear. Change the alpha of the `hotspot` instance (using the Properties panel) to something semi-transparent to make it easier for the using author to position on top of other objects.

3. Select both `tip` and `hotspot` and convert to a Movie Clip symbol. Name the symbol "ToolTip Component."

4. Double-click to edit the inside of the ToolTip Component symbol. Type this beginning code in the first frame:

```
this.onRollOver=function(){
  this.tip._x=_xmouse;
  this.tip._y=_ymouse;
}
this.onRollOut=function(){
  this.tip._x=-5000;
}
```

Now any time the user rolls over an instance of this symbol, the `tip` instance appears at the mouse location. When the user rolls out, it moves offscreen.

5. To modify what's "hot" (that is, which shape triggers the rollover), add the following line underneath the existing code:

```
this.hitArea=this.hotspot;
```

This line of code specifies the `hitArea` to be the shape that triggers the rollover (with the instance name `hotspot`).

6. Finally, in order for shape to be visible only when authoring, add this line of code:

```
this.hotspot._visible=false;
```

It still works, but the user won't see that shape.

At this point you can test the ToolTip Component symbol. (Just pretend that the word "test" can be changed—it's dynamic text, after all.) I've found two significant issues with what we have thus far:

- When the user resizes an instance of the ToolTip Component symbol, the text gets scaled as well.

- The `onRollOver` and `onRollOut` events will interfere with the code assigned to other buttons in the same area (that is, you can't place the component on top of buttons).

Naturally, there are a few other minor things, but these two issues will require a significant overhaul. In addition, I'd prefer to use the TextField and TextFormat objects (to create and format text on-the-fly) so that the using author can specify any attribute of the ToolTip Component symbol that she prefers.

7. Trashing time. Delete the text instance inside the ToolTip Component symbol and remove all the code from the frame. Also, let's position the
hotspot instance so that its top-left corner is centered inside the clip.
(Just use the Info panel's top-left option and type 0 and 0 for x and y
respectively—see Figure W9.1.) This way, the using author can resize by
dragging the right or bottom of the clip, and it will grow in just one direction at a time.

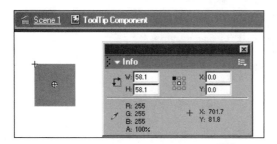

Figure W9.1   *Placing the* hotspot *instance in this location makes scaling easier.*

8. The first thing I'd like to build is an alternative to the rollOver and
rollOff mouse events (because they'll conflict with other buttons).
Instead, we can make an onMouseMove callback that checks whether the
coordinates of the mouse are in the area of the hotspot clip. Because I
think a custom class might be appropriate, we'll start building on top of the
basic skeleton for classes. First, give the ToolTip Component symbol a
linkage identifier of tooltip (through the Library item's Linkage option),
and then type the following code into the first frame:

```
#initclip
function TipClass(){}
TipClass.prototype=new MovieClip();

Object.registerClass("tooltip", TipClass);
#endinitclip
```

This is pretty much the minimum code necessary to make a custom class
(in this case one called TipClass). The remainder of the code that we'll
write for this entire workshop will go after the first three lines and before
the last two.

9. Now for the alternative to onRollOver and onRollOut. First, we need to
gather the coordinates of the hotspot instance, so type this onLoad callback for the class:

```
TipClass.prototype.onLoad=function(){
    this.bounds=this.hotspot.getBounds(_root);
    //this.hotspot._visible=false;
}
```

This just stores in the variable bounds the coordinates of the hotspot symbol (in relation to the main _root timeline). Later, when we use _xmouse, we'll just use the same coordinate space (_root._xmouse, that is). By the way, we'll come back to add more to the onLoad callback (including uncommenting the last line).

10. Now create another callback, this time for onMouseMove:

```
1 TipClass.prototype.onMouseMove=function(){
2   if(_root._xmouse>this.bounds.xMin &&
3     _root._xmouse<this.bounds.xMax &&
4     _root._ymouse>this.bounds.yMin &&
5     _root._ymouse<this.bounds.yMax){
6     if (this.wasOff){
7       this.wasOff=false;
8       trace("rolled on "+this._name);
9     }
10  }else{
11    if (!this.wasOff){
12      this.wasOff=true;
13      trace("rolled off");
14    }
15  }
16 }
```

Notice that lines 2–5 are just and extension of the if statement's condition (spread out for readability). The wasOff variable is simply there as a flag. That is, if the user rolls into the area and then keeps moving the mouse (within the hotspot), we don't want this script to keep thinking that she's rolling on. The user can rollOver only once until she rollOffs again. So, after you know whether she's in the space, you can check to see whether she *used* to be out of the area. Anyway, you can test this with a couple of instances on the Stage. Give them different instance names, and the Output window will display accurate information as you roll on and off the shape.

11. Instead of displaying the (yet-to-be-created) ToolTip Component text right when the user rolls over the hotspot, it would be nice to have a short delay. That is, most tooltips don't appear until your cursor has been hovering over an area for a second or so. The approach we'll take is to assign an onEnterFrame callback function (that keeps checking the time) when the user rolls over. (We'll clear that callback when the user rolls out.) We'll just change the two lines of code that have trace statements in the preceding onMouseMove callback. Replace line 8 with the following two lines:

```
this.expiration=getTimer()+1000;
this.onEnterFrame=check;
```

Also, change line 13 to

```
this.onEnterFrame=null;
```

Basically, a new variable `expiration` will contain a time 1 second later than when the user rolls over. Also, the `check` function will start executing every `enterFrame`. We'll define `check` next. For readability, I decided not to define the function "inline" (where the word `check` appears)—but I could have.

12. Here's the code for the `check` function:

```
function check(){
  if (getTimer()>this.expiration){
    trace("show time");
    this.onEnterFrame=false;
  }
}
```

Obviously, we'll change the `trace` statement later so that it actually shows the ToolTip Component text. Notice that once the `if` statement is `true`, we clear the `onEnterFrame` callback because we don't need to keep checking if it's time to show the text. (You can learn more about `getTimer()` in Chapter 4, "Basic Programming in Flash.")

We're pretty much done with the triggers. There are a few more touches, but we'll move on to displaying the text and then come back to fix an issues that may arise. (You know something's bound to come up.)

//

When creating the actual TextField object, we have options as to where to put it. Originally, I tried to create a TextField object inside the ToolTip Component symbol, but I ran into a few problems related to scaling. I had to un-scale the text proportionally to how much the symbol had been scaled and then calculate the position (for the text) based on the cursor location in the main timeline. These problems were not impossible to overcome, but the main reason I'm going to suggest the following method (putting the new text field in the main timeline) is that in the end, we'll have only one text field. The file could get bogged down if a using author places many instances of this symbol in his movie. It just makes sense to have one text field. After all, the user should be able to see only one tip at a time.

13. To create a TextField object, place the following code in place of the `trace` statement in the `check` function (that currently reads: `trace("show time")`):

```
1 //make Text field:
2 _root.createTextField("tip",1,0,0,0,0);
```

```
 3 _root.tip.background=true;
 4 _root.tip.autoSize=true;
 5 _root.tip.selectable=false
 6 _root.tip.backgroundColor=0xFFFF00;//hw
 7 _root.tip.text="this is a tip";//hw
 8
 9 //format
10 var format=new TextFormat();
11 format.font="_typewriter"; //hw
12 format.color=0xFF0000;//hw
13 format.size=18;//hw
14
15 //apply
16 _root.tip.setTextFormat(format);
17
18 //position
19 _root.tip._x=_root._xmouse+10;
20 _root.tip._y=_root._ymouse+10;
```

Basically, this code creates a TextField object in the main timeline called
tip. It sets a few properties and then creates a format object to apply to the
field. Then it positions it in the location of the mouse. The lines ending
//hw, which currently are hard-wired, will be replaced with variables by
the using author (as they populate this component—after it's a component).
Notice the last four parameters in the createTextField() command are all
0. (They're supposed to define the location and size of the TextField
object). This doesn't matter, however, because in line 4 the autoSize property effectively overrides those settings. (Chapter 10, "Keyboard Access
and Modifying Onscreen Text," covers the rest of the code.)

This should work pretty well if you test it out. All we need to do now is
come up with variable names to replace the hard-wired values (lines 6, 7,
11, 12, and 13). Then, we'll turn this into a component so that the using
author can specify how he wants it to appear.

14. Change lines 6, 7, 11, 12, and 13 of the preceding script to read as follows:

```
 6 _root.tip.backgroundColor=this.backcolor;
 7 _root.tip.text=this.tipText;

11 format.font=this.fontface;
12 format.color=this.forecolor;
13 format.size=this.fontsize;
```

This just replaces the hard-wired values with variables to which we'll give
the using author access.

15. To give the using author access to these variables (and to turn this into a
component), select the ToolTip Component symbol in the Library and
access the Component Definition dialog box (from the Options menu). All
you have to do is press the plus button (in the upper-left corner) five times,
and then replace each "varName" with one of the five preceding variables.

In the case of `backcolor` and `forecolor`, set the Type to Color. Change `fontface`'s Type to Font Name. The results should resemble Figure W9.2. Be sure to come up with reasonable default values (for example, make sure that `forecolor` and `backcolor` provide a good contrast).

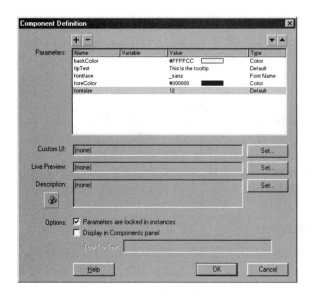

Figure W9.2   *The five parameters in this component use a variety of type choices.*

16. It works great, but there are two minor things worth fixing. Remember, to edit the component, you'll have to select Edit, Edit in Place (not just double-click it). Anyway, uncomment the line in the `onLoad` callback to appear as follows:

```
this.hotspot._visible=false;
```

This just makes the `hotspot` instance disappear when the movie runs.

17. Finally, add one more callback to the class definition:

```
TipClass.prototype.onMouseDown=function(){
    _root.tip._x=-90000
}
```

Like "real" tooltips, ours will now disappear when the user clicks.

That's it! At this point, you should be able to place the ToolTip Component on top of any element in any movie and even stretch it from the right or the bottom to cover areas of different sizes (see Figure W9.3). You can even come up with a variable to replace the 1000 (used when assigning a value to expiration in the onMouseMove callback). That way you can give the using author access to how much of a delay she wants until the clip appears.

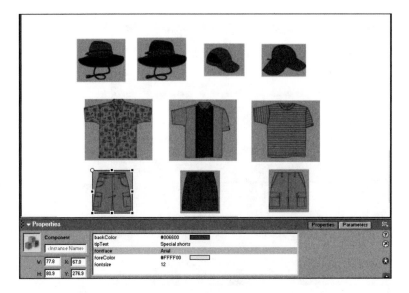

Figure W9.3 *Our handy ToolTip Component will work great in any movie you make.*

I can safely say that the TextField and TextFormat objects not only made this workshop better than what was possible in Flash 5, but it's much easier too. For example, the same basic exercise in the first edition of this book was twice as long! (Don't worry; I made up for it by having longer chapters in the "Foundation" section.)

{ Workshop

Chapter 10 }

Creating Timers

Using Flash's `getTimer()` function the way we did in Workshop Chapter 9, "Creating a ToolTip Component," is quite common. We saved the current `getTimer()` in a variable, and then kept checking to see whether "enough" time elapsed by rechecking `getTimer()` and comparing that to the variable we saved at the start. In this workshop chapter, we'll make several timers that the user can start, stop, and pause. To give the timers their functionality, we'll save the current `getTimer()` when the user starts the timer. Then, in every `enterFrame` event, we'll see how many milliseconds have elapsed since the start. We can then easily convert this value into hours, minutes, seconds, and even fractions of seconds.

This workshop chapter should teach two concepts in particular: how to translate numbers between different formats (milliseconds into hours, for example) and how to use `getTimer()` in conjunction with the `enterFrame` event. In the end, of course, we'll have a digital timer (see Figure W10.1). You'll also see how easy it is to convert the timer to an analog timer. Finally, in the third section of this workshop chapter, we'll build a timer that counts down.

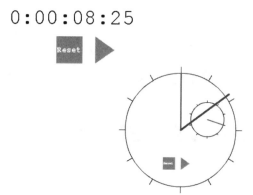

Figure W10.1 *The digital timer (left) and the analog timer (right) use the same code base.*

Creating a Digital Timer

Here are the steps to follow to create a digital timer:

1. Create a new Movie Clip symbol called Timer. Basically, we want to make a clip that we can place in any other movie.

2. Inside Timer (where you'll stay for the rest of this workshop chapter), create a Dynamic Text field with an instance name of display. Make the field wide enough to accommodate about 10 characters based on whichever size of font you use. I recommend the font _typewriter or another monospace font because fonts that have variable widths make the timer jump around as it keeps changing.

3. Draw a small box for the Stop button and draw a triangle for the Play button, and leave them as shapes (see Figure W10.2).

Figure W10.2 *The square will become the Stop button and the triangle will become the Play button.*

4. Draw a square shape that will become an invisible button. Make it an invisible button by first converting it to a button and then moving the square shape (from the Up frame of the button) to the Hit frame of the button. Come back to the Timer clip and create two instances of the invisible button. Place them on top of the square (for Stop) and triangle (for Play). Finally, give the two invisible button instances names of `stop_btn` and `play_btn`, respectively (see Figure W10.3).

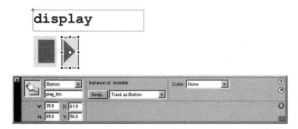

Figure W10.3   *Invisible buttons (*`stop_btn` *and* `play_btn`*) are placed on top of plain shapes.*

5. Now we can spend some time in the frame script for the Timer symbol. First, let's just try to make the `display` update as the movie plays. Type the following code into the frame script:

```
this.onEnterFrame=function(){
    display.text=getTimer();
}
```

Naturally, this lacks several features, but it succeeds in continuing to change the `display` field's `text` property. Because I know we'll want Timer to turn on and off, we'll be assigning the `onEnterFrame` callback to `null` (when we want it to stop). It will be slightly easier if we change the preceding code to point to a function (rather than defining it inline, as shown).

6. Change the code to read

```
this.onEnterFrame=updateTimer;
function updateTimer(){
    display.text=getTimer();
}
```

This is really the same thing, but this way it will be easy to change the `updateTimer()` function—as we have a lot to do there.

7. Rather than walking through how to revise the `updateTimer()` function, just use this code as-is and I'll explain it below:

```
1 function updateTimer () {
2     elapsedTime = getTimer();
```

```
3    // hours:
4    var elapsedH = Math.floor(elapsedTime/3600000);
5    var remaining = elapsedTime-(elapsedH*3600000);
6    // minutes:
7    var elapsedM = Math.floor(remaining/60000);
8    remaining = remaining-(elapsedM*60000);
9    if (elapsedM<10) {
10     elapsedM = "0"+elapsedM;
11   }
12   // seconds:
13   var elapsedS = Math.floor(remaining/1000);
14   remaining = remaining-(elapsedS*1000);
15   if (elapsedS<10) {
16     elapsedS = "0"+elapsedS;
17   }
18   // hundredths:
19   var elapsedFractions = Math.floor(remaining/10);
20   if (elapsedFractions<10) {
21     elapsedFractions = "0"+elapsedFractions;
22   }
23   // build the nice display string:
24   display.text=
     ➥elapsedH+":"+elapsedM+":"+elapsedS+":""+elapsedFractions;
25 }
```

This code looks much worse that it is. Line 2 places the elapsed milliseconds (`getTimer()`) into our `elapsedTime` variable. (Actually, we'll come back to adjust this line later.) Then, line 4 calculates the full hours that have elapsed by placing into the variable `elapsedH` just the integer portion of `elapsedTime` divided by `3600000` (the number of milliseconds in an hour). Then we have to calculate the remaining milliseconds.
Suppose that 2 hours and 10 minutes have passed. If you know that there have been 2 whole hours, you need only the remaining 10 minutes' worth of milliseconds to calculate the remainder. The `remaining=elapsedTime - (elapsedH*3600000)` statement in line 5 subtracts the total number of hours just calculated (`elapsedH`) multiplied by the number of milliseconds in an hour from the original `elapsedTime`. For the remaining values—`elapsedM`, `elapsedS`, and `elapsedFractions`—first we calculate how many full minutes or seconds or fractions remain, and then we subtract that number of milliseconds from the remaining variable so that each subsequently smaller value is based on what's leftover. In addition, on lines 9, 15, and 20, we check each value; if the value is less than 10, we insert a `0` in front of the value. (By the way, you could probably figure out a way to use the `%` modulo operator to calculate the remaining variable in all the preceding cases.) Finally, a nice string is fashioned with colons in line 25, where the `display` field's `text` property is assigned.

Timer should work pretty well at this point. However, it starts timing from the start only. Let's write some callback functions for the `onPress` events for the two buttons.

8. To let the user control things with the buttons, cut the line of code added in step 6 (`this.onEnterFrame=updateTimer`) and in its place type this code:

```
play_btn.onPress=function() {
  this.onEnterFrame=updateTimer;
}
```

The idea is that when the user clicks the button `play_btn`, the `onEnterFrame` callback will point to the `updateTimer` function. However, it fails because `this` is the button itself. You must change it to read:

```
play_btn.onPress=function() {
  _parent.onEnterFrame=updateTimer;
}
```

9. Next, let's get the Stop button working:

```
stop_btn.onPress=function() {
  _parent.onEnterFrame=null;
  display.text="0:00:00:00"
}
```

Notice that the second line will make the display appear cleared when the user presses the Stop button. (Otherwise, the Stop button would behave more like a Pause button.) It works pretty well now except when the user first clicks the Play button, Timer shows how much time has elapsed since the beginning of the movie—not from the time the button was pressed. (You can test the movie and wait a few seconds before pressing Play to see what I mean.)

10. The problem with the `updateTimer()` function is that it reports the elapsed time from the start of the movie. We want to know how much time has passed since the Play button was pressed. All we need to do is store in a variable the time at which the Play button is `pressed` and subtract that from the calculations in `updateTimer()`. There are two steps: First, change the `onPress` callback for the `play_btn` button to read as follows:

```
play_btn.onPress=function() {
  startTime=getTimer()-elapsedTime;
  _parent.onEnterFrame=updateTimer;
}
```

11. Next, change the first line of code inside the `updateTimer()` function (that currently reads `elapsedTime = getTimer()`) to read as follows:

```
elapsedTime = getTimer()-startTime;
```

Now the updateDisplay() function will base its calculations on the amount of time that has passed since the user pressed the Play button. It's still not finished, though. Now the Stop button fails to start things over. That is, if the user clicks Play, then Stop, then Play again, the timer appears to pick up from when the Stop button was pressed. To remedy that, add this line of code to the Stop button's callback:

```
elapsedTime=0;
```

Okay, it finally works without fail. But I want more features! We basically had a "pause" feature by mistake, so it'd be nice if the user could pause and then resume. All we need to do is make a new button and use the pause code placed on the Stop button by mistake. Let's do that.

12. Create a new shape for the Pause button and place an instance of the invisible button on top of it. Give the invisible button an instance name of `pause_btn`. Finally, place this code in the frame script:

```
pause_btn.onPress=function() {
    _parent.onEnterFrame=null;
}
```

Pretty simple, eh? At this point, I think a usability issue is worth addressing. I don't think the user should be able to pause unless Timer is currently timing, or play unless Timer is currently paused or stopped. It's really quite easy. We'll put both blocks of the code from the Pause and Play buttons into one button. We'll need a variable to tell us whether Timer currently paused so that we know which block to execute. We'll get to the graphics in a second, but first let's just trash the Pause button and make the Play button really a Play/Pause button.

13. Trash the invisible `pause_btn` instance and remove the callback for `pause_btn`'s onPress event. Here is the revised code for the `play_btn`'s callback:

```
1 play_btn.onPress=function() {
2   paused=!paused;
3   if (paused){
4     _parent.onEnterFrame=null;
5   }else{
6     _parent.onEnterFrame=updateTimer;
7     startTime=getTimer()-elapsedTime;
8   }
9 }
```

This code reflects both the Pause button's code (line 4) and the Play button's code (lines 6 and 7). They just appear exclusively based on the value of the variable `paused`. I just made up the `paused` variable, so we have not only to toggle its value every time the user presses Play/Pause (line 2), but we need to set it to `true` both initially and any time user presses the Stop button.

14. Instead of having the same code in two places (namely, everything the Stop button does), let's take the code from the Stop button and put it in a function that we can also call at the start of the movie. Change the `stop_btn`'s onPress callback to read:

```
stop_btn.onPress=function() {
  init();
}
```

Then create the init() function as follows:

```
function init(){
  display.text="0:00:00:00"
  elapsedTime=0;
  _parent.onEnterFrame=null;
  paused=true;
}
```

This is the same as before, with the addition of the paused variable.

15. Finally, let's trigger the init() function at the very start. Outside of any functions, just type the following:

```
init();
```

16. Now we just have to make the Pause/Play button *look* like it's toggling. Select the triangle shape (not the Play button) and convert it to a Movie Clip. Double-click this new clip and insert a new keyframe in frame 2. Draw two vertical rectangles for the Pause button's look. Go back to the Timer clip and give the instance of this new symbol the name pp (for "Pause/Play").

17. Finally, add the following line of code to the init() function:

```
pp.gotoAndStop(1);
```

This way, the clip will appear to be stopped on frame 1 initially (and any time the user presses the Stop button).

18. Finally (and I promise this is the last "finally"), place the following line of code in front of everything else inside the play_btn's onPress callback:

```
pp.gotoAndStop(1+paused);
```

The idea is that when the user presses Play, if paused is true, the pp clip will jump to frame 2 (true is evaluated as 1). Otherwise, the clip jumps to frame 1. You could certainly write a more verbose solution involving an if statement, if you wanted.

It's really done. The scripting turned out to be relatively easy compared to how cool the result looks. You'll be thrilled to learn that you can use the bulk of this code in the following section of this workshop chapter, "Creating an Analog Timer."

If you want a challenging exercise, try adding a "lap" function. Like a stopwatch, the lap() function would enable the user to click to stop the display from changing, but the timing would continue in the background. When the user clicked to proceed, the display would catch up and keep displaying the elapsed time since the user originally clicked to play. I added that feature to the downloadable version of this file (at www.phillipkerman.com/actionscripting/) so that you can see one possible solution.

Creating an Analog Timer

Turning the digital timer you just made into an analog timer is little more than adding a few graphics. In addition to a few clips (for the arms of the clock's face), we'll need to translate the values calculated in the updateTimer() into degrees of rotation. It's an easy task! We'll use the Sound object for some "clicking" sound effects.

1. Let's start by drawing some graphics in the Timer symbol. Delete the display text field. For the clock's face, draw a large circle with no fill. If you want "hash marks" at 30-degree increments (see Figure W10.4), you can add them, but it is not necessary. Convert the entire shape to a Movie Clip called Face (Be sure to use the center registration option.)

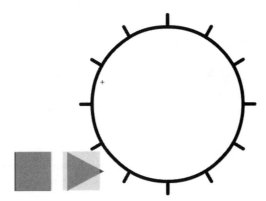

Figure W10.4   *The circle that will become the stopwatch face can include hash marks every 30 degrees.*

2. While still inside the Timer symbol, draw a vertical line with a thick stroke. Convert the line to a Movie Clip called Hand—but this time, select the bottom-middle option for registration (see Figure W10.5).

Figure W10.5 *The bottom-middle registration point will make the hand rotate like a regular clock hand.*

3. Make a total of four instances of the Hand symbol. Give them instances names of h, m, s, and f, respectively.

4. Snap the bottom of the h clip to the center of the instance of the Face symbol. Adjust the clip's length by scaling it so that it's a little longer than the radius of the instance of Face. In order not to accidentally move this instance, send it to the back by choosing Modify, Arrange, Send to Back.

5. Snap the bottom of the m clip to the center of the instance of Face and adjust the length of the clip so that it's about the same length as the radius of the instance of the Face symbol. Use the Properties panel to tint this instance so that you can keep the different hands straight. Send this clip to the back.

6. Snap the s clip to Face in the same way as you did the m clip and send it to the back.

7. Rather than snapping the f clip to the center of the instance of the Face symbol, first make a copy of the Face symbol. Reduce the scale of this copy and place it on top of the larger instance of Face (see Figure W10.6).

Figure W10.6 *The fractional seconds will be displayed on the smaller instance of the Face symbol.*

Believe it or not, we're almost done. We're done building all the graphics; we just need to translate the values calculated in the updateTimer() function to _rotation values for the various hand clips.

8. Inside the updateTimer() function, remove or comment out each if statement. Remember that these if statements add a 0 in front of values less than 10. We'll need numbers, not strings, to calculate the rotation for the clock face. Remove or comment out the following parts of the updateTimer() function:

```
if (elapsedM<10) {
  elapsedM = "0"+elapsedM;
}
if (elapsedS<10) {
  elapsedS = "0"+elapsedS;
}
if (elapsedFractions<10) {
  elapsedFractions = "0"+elapsedFractions;
}
```

9. Also, in the updateTimer() function, remove the line where display is assigned and replace it with these three lines:

```
h._rotation=elapsedH*30;
m._rotation=elapsedM*6;
s._rotation=elapsedS*6;
f._rotation= elapsedFractions*3.6;
```

We multiply minutes and seconds by 6 based on the fact that there are 60 of each per 360 degrees: 360/60 is 6. Try the what-if number 30 for minutes: 30*6 is 180, and that's exactly how many degrees we need the minute hand to rotate on the circle of the clock. Because one revolution should equal 12 hours, I divided 360 by 12 to get 30 (that is, how many degrees per hour). In the case of fractions that are 1/100 of a second, consider that we want the f hand to go 360 degrees every second. Every 1/100 of a second must be multiplied by 3.6 or 360/100 because it takes 100 hundredths to make a whole second, or a whole circle in this case.

//

At this point, the movie works pretty well, but I know that on fancy stopwatches, the fractional second hand precisely displays a round fractional number. On the small clock face, the hand we've built for fractional seconds appears accurately, but the hand can often appear in odd locations, such as between hash marks. Start and pause the timer a few times to see what I mean (see Figure W10.7). We can't just change the hash marks because we'd need 100 marks around the circle. Even if we did, the hand wouldn't touch each one because screen updates won't appear that frequently. Even if you cranked the frame rate up to 100 fps, it still wouldn't work.

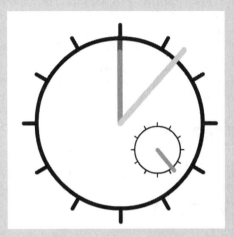

Figure W10.7 *The fractional seconds displayed don't always correspond to the hash marks on the small clock face.*

10. To address the fractional seconds issue, change the line in the updateTimer() function that assigns the f clip's _rotation to read as follows:

```
f._rotation= Math.round(elapsedFractions/10) * 36;
```

With this version of the formula, we'll always find the closest tenth of a second and set the rotation to 36 times that tenth because there are 10 36-degree units in a circle. The only problem now is that your hash marks may not represent tenths of a second. You can either make another version of the Face symbol and move the hash marks to every 36 degrees, or change the expression to this version:

```
f._rotation= Math.floor(elapsedFractions*.12) *30;
```

This version first calculates a round number of one-twelfth seconds and then multiplies by 30, which is the number of degrees in the hash marks added in step 1 to match our standard clocks with 12 hours per revolution.

11. One last touch is to modify the init() function to look like this:

```
function init(){
    h._rotation=0;
    m._rotation=0;
    s._rotation=0;
    f._rotation=0;
```

```
elapsedTime=0;
_parent.onEnterFrame=null;
paused=true;
}
```

To make things interesting, let's add some audio for the seconds and fractional seconds. To do these next steps, you'll need one very short sound clip such as a click sound. (I included one in the downloadable version of this workshop available at www.phillipkerman.com/actionscripting/.)

12. We can use the Sound object to make the click sound play once every second. Import a short sound and give it a linkage identifier name of sec—as you learned to do in Chapter 12, "Objects" (see Figure W10.8).

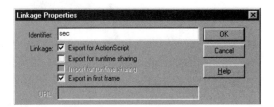

Figure W10.8   *To play the sound using scripting, we have to set its linkage.*

13. Inside the init() function, add these lines of code:

```
sec=new Sound(this);
sec.attachSound("sec");
```

Notice that these statements won't actually start the sound; they just place the sound inside the variable called sec. The fact that we're attaching the sound to the this clip means that you can have multiple instances of the Timer clip, each of which can maintain its own sound.

14. Anywhere inside the updateTimer() function *after* you set elapsedS, place the following if statement:

```
if (elapsedS<>lastS){
  sec.start();
  lastS=elapsedS;
}
```

This statement uses the start() method on the sec instance of the Sound object. It does not call start() every time the updateTimer() function executes because updateTimer() executes many times a second based on the enterFrame event. As long as elapsedS is not equal to lastS (another variable we are introducing), start() starts the sound. It then sets lastS to the value of elapsedS so that the next time this function executes, it will again be able to compare the new elapsedS and see whether it's truly a new value. Depending on your frame rate, the updateTimer() function will be executed many times per second.

At this point, you could take another, even shorter sound and follow steps 12–14 to make it play 10 times a second, or whatever the fractional display is displaying. However, I think this is a good example of where "faking it" is perfectly acceptable and more believable. We don't really have to make a sound play every tenth of a second. Instead, we can just record a loop that plays 10 clicks per second. Then, whenever the timer is running, we'll make that loop play; when the timer is stopped, we'll stop the sound. You just need a nice looping sound that makes 10 clicks a second when it's playing.

15. Import the looping sound and give it an identifier name of `loopingClick` in the same way you named the sound in step 12.

16. In the `init()` function, add the following three lines:

```
loop=new Sound(this);
loop.attachSound("loopingClick");
loop.stop();
```

This code simply creates another instance of the Sound object in the variable called `loop`. The reason we stop it at the end is that the Stop button also triggers the `init()` function (and we'll want the sound to stop then).

17. Now all we have to do make the looping sound start and stop when the user plays or pauses. Change the `play_btn`'s `onPress` callback to read as follows:

```
1 play_btn.onPress=function() {
2   paused=!paused;
3   if (paused){
4     _parent.onEnterFrame=null;
5     _parent.loop.stop();
6   }else{
7     _parent.onEnterFrame=updateTimer;
8     startTime=getTimer()-elapsedTime;
9     _parent.loop.start(0,9999999);
10  }
11 }
```

Notice line 9, where the sound starts (and loops many times) and line 5, where the sound stops.

That's it. It's kind of amazing that the fake way of just starting or stopping a loop is more believable than forcing Flash to carefully play a click sound for every fraction of a second. If you don't believe me, try it out. Just follow the steps to make the `sec` Sound object play, but do it for fractions of seconds, which is related to the `elapsedFractions` variable.

Creating a Countdown Timer

Whereas the analog timer built upon code created in the digital timer section, the countdown timer is more like the horizontal slider we made back in Workshop Chapter 3, "Creating a Horizontal Slider." Because it uses getTimer(), however, I figured it fits well in this chapter.

The countdown timer will act like a kitchen timer: simply start it timing and it will go off after the elapsed time has expired. In this exercise, a filled rectangle will empty a little bit at a time until it's totally empty, and then a sound will play and another function will get invoked. After getting the main functionality working, you can add refined graphics to make any effect you want—for example, an hourglass effect (see Figure W10.9).

Figure W10.9 *Although we don't walk through all the steps to make the hourglass timer, you'll be able to figure it out after doing this exercise.*

Follow these steps to create a countdown timer:

1. In a new file, draw a wide rectangle (with both a fill and a pretty thick stroke). Select everything and convert it to a Movie Clip called Timer. Double-click to edit Timer and then select just the fill and convert it to a Movie Clip symbol called Strip. Name the layer Frame.

2. Select the instance of the Strip symbol, cut it, insert a new layer, and then select Edit, Paste in Place. Name this instance bar. Name this new layer Strip and lock it so that it doesn't get messed up during the next few steps.

3. Create a third layer and Paste in Place again to create another instance of the Strip symbol. Name this new layer Mask, set the layer properties to Mask, and lock that layer, too.

4. Arrange the layers so that Frame is on top, Mask is in the middle, and the original Strip layer is under Mask (see Figure W10.10). Make sure that the Strip layer's properties are set to Masked.

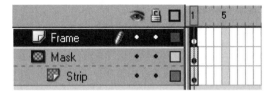

Figure W10.10 *The arrangement of layers is shown here.*

// The Mask layer will reveal the bar only in the area currently covered. So, if we move the bar, the bar will be hidden. The Frame layer provides an outline so that the user can see the whole size of the timer bar. You could build a simpler arrangement by foregoing the mask and changing the `bar` instance's `_xscale` (rather than its `_x` coordinate, as we're about to do). The masking technique is easier for irregular shapes, such as the hourglass that you'll see at the end.

5. Click the Frame layer (to make it active) and create a button. Give the instance the name of `start_btn`.

6. Now we can put some code in the frame script of this layer (where we'll stay for the rest of the workshop chapter). Begin with a few variables that will help to calculate percentages:

```
howLong=10;
max = bar._x;
min = max - bar._width;
total = max-min;
bar._x = max;
```

The first line hard-wires a value for `howLong`. We'll remove this line when we convert the Timer clip to a component. The variable `max` just contains the end point (or "maximum") for the `bar` instance. The `min` variable is where the `bar` is positioned when all the way to the left (that is, where it is now—`max`—minus its width). The `total` variable is the difference. Finally, the last line places the `bar` instance in its minimum position initially.

7. Now, to add the callback function so that the button will commence a timing function, we'll write

```
start_btn.onPress=function(){countDown()}
```

This triggers the `countDown()` function when the button is pressed.

8. Now for the `countdown()` function:

```
 1 function countDown(){
 2   var totalTime = howLong*1000;
 3   var startTime = getTimer();
 4   this.onEnterFrame=function(){
 5     percent = (getTimer()-startTime)/totalTime;
 6     bar._x = max-(percent*total);
 7     if (percent>1) {
 8       this.onEnterFrame=null;
 9     }
10   }
11 }
```

Line 2 creates the `totalTime` variable based on `howLong` (which is represented in seconds) multiplied by 1000 because `getTimer()` uses milliseconds. Line 3 saves the current time in `startTime`. You see `startTime` again in line 5, which calculates `percent` by taking the *elapsed time* (`getTimer()` minus `startTime`) divided by `totalTime`. Notice that in line 4 the `onEnterFrame` callback is assigned for `this` timeline (the Timer's). That callback's definition isn't finished until line 10. What's sort of weird is that we're replacing the same `onEnterFrame` callback inside the `if` statement on line 8. Anyway, everything between lines 4 and 10 happens repeatedly (every `enterFrame`). Line 5 calculates `percent` (really a number between 0 and 1). Then line 6 positions the `bar` instance at its `max` minus the percent times total. Finally, if, in line 7, `percent` is higher than 1, we clear out the `onEnterFrame` callback so that it stops working. Line 8 is also where we'll put code that gets triggered once—when time's up.

The timer should work pretty well now. There are countless enhancements that we can add—but let's just add two: First, we'll a sound effect when the time is up, and then we'll turn the whole thing into a component so that the using author can specify both a total time and a function to trigger when the time is up.

9. To add a sound effect, drag into your movie's Library the "Smack" sound from the Sounds library (Window, Common Libraries, Sound). Set the linkage for the sound to "smack." Then, type the following code within the `if` statement of the callback function defined in step 8 (above or below line 8):

```
s=new Sound();
s.attachSound("smack");
s.start();
```

Now the sound effect plays once when the timer finishes.

10. To convert this into a component, just select Timer in the Library and access the Component Definition option. Click the plus button twice and replace one "varName" with `howLong` and the other with `functionName`. It makes sense to provide a default value for `howLong` as well. When you click OK, the dialog box should look something like Figure W10.11.

Figure W10.11 *The completed Component Definition dialog box gives the using author two variables to assign.*

11. Then go into the master symbol for Timer and comment out the very first line of code, where howLong was initialized way back in step 6. We don't need to assign this value because the using author will.

12. Finally, in the onEnterFrame callback (anywhere near where you made the sound effect play), add this line of code:

```
_parent[functionName]();
```

This simply executes a function in the main timeline based on a string name provided in the variable functionName. (We first discussed this trick in Workshop Chapter 3.)

That's it. The using author should be able to place instances of this component in any movie and specify both a howLong parameter and a functionName.

There are a lot of variations you can try out. For example, you can show the user the number of seconds remaining by placing a text field (say, with an instance name of display_txt) and adding the following code right after you set bar's _x (in the callback):

```
display_txt.text=Math.floor(howLong+1-(howLong*percent));
```

You can also make the bar *fill* the frame by changing the one line that sets bar's _x to read:

```
bar._x = min+(percent*total);
```

For both enhancements, you'll want to modify or add to the initialization scripts (the code placed right in the frame in step 6). The fact that you can make the bar fill the frame just as easily as making it empty the frame means you can do the hourglass example I mentioned before. Just have two bars with different instance names, in different layers, with different masks. Then, when you set one bar's _x to fill the frame, set the other one to empty the frame. Figure W10.12 shows the basic arrangement of layers, but you'll have to figure out how to program it on you own. (Or, download the finished piece from my web site: www.phillipkerman.com/actionscripting.)

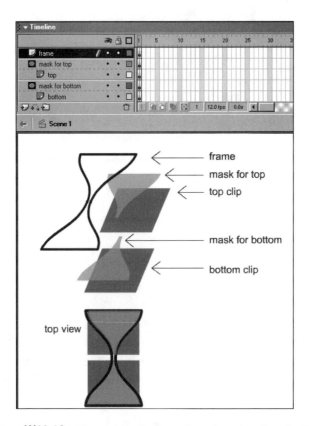

Figure W10.12   *The work involved to make an hourglass timer is all in the layers and masks.*

Summary

This was a pretty fun (triple) workshop that extended the use of our `getTimer()` function. You lucked out in the analog timer section; calculating the angles for the Hand instances was fairly straightforward. In Workshop Chapter 11, "Using Math to Create a Circular Slider," and to a lesser degree in Workshop Chapter 12, "Developing Time-Based Animations," you'll have to calculate angles based on trigonometry and the related issues of degrees versus radians—which are discussed in Chapter 5, "Programming Structures."

Naturally, there's a ton more you can do with `getTimer()`.

{ Workshop

Chapter 11 }

Using Math to Create a
Circular Slider

By now, you're probably quite familiar with calculating percentages based on minimum and maximums. You're also probably quite comfortable writing scripts for the `enterFrame` and `mouseMove` events. This workshop chapter involves using just a few trigonometry concepts to calculate angles and to specify locations around a circular path. Suppose that you have two known points, such as the center of a clip and the current position of the mouse. Calculating the angle of a line drawn through those points is the main task in this workshop. Although the applications of such a trick can include creating eyeballs that appear to follow the mouse movements (see Figure W11.1), we can actually use this knowledge for something more practical: a slider that moves along a curved path.

Figure W11.1 *Making eyeballs follow the mouse is one of the fun things you can do with math.*

It turns out that the actual math involved in this workshop chapter isn't *that* bad. However, if you want, you can brush up on some of the Math object methods— especially Math.atan2(), the first trigonometry function I learned to love—by reviewing Chapter 5, "Programming Structures."

Here are the steps for creating a curved slider:

1. First, to get a sense of the formula we'll be using, create an eyeball shape: Draw a small dark circle inside a larger light circle, and make the dark circle touch the inside edge of the right side of the light circle (see Figure W11.2).

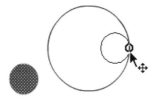

Figure W11.2   *Position the small dark circle inside the right edge of the larger circle.*

2. Select everything and convert it to a Movie Clip called "Eyeball." Attach the following code to the Movie Clip instance:

```
onClipEvent (mouseMove) {
  var radians =
➡Math.atan2(_root._ymouse-this._y, _root._xmouse-this._x);
  var degrees=radians/(Math.PI/180);
  this._rotation=degrees;
  updateAfterEvent();}
```

Every time the mouse moves, this code will first assign the variable radians to the result of the Math.atan2() method. The two parameters provided to Math.atan2() are the x and y difference between where the mouse is and the center of the Eyeball clip. (For example, the y difference is _root._ymouse - this._y.) As you recall from Chapter 5, the Math.atan2() function returns an angle based on the length of the sides of a right triangle, even if those lengths are negative. Realize that for any angle you can draw vertical and horizontal lines to create a right triangle. Those two sides are provided for by the parameters in the Math.atan2() function. Also remember from Chapter 5 that the angle returned is in the form of radians.

The second line of this script uses a standard formula to convert radians to degrees. Those degrees are used to set the angle of the Eyeball clip.

It's kind of cool: You can copy as many instances of the Eyeball clip as you want, and they'll all calculate the correct _rotation to follow the mouse pointer.

So we can make eyeballs, so what? For our slider, this bit of math will come in handy. While the user drags, we can calculate the angle from any known point—such as the center of the circle around which the user is dragging—to the mouse (see Figure W11.3).

Figure W11.3 *We're going to make a draggable slider that follows the radius of a circle.*

With that angle in hand, we can calculate where the slider should be positioned. We want the user to be able to grab a small circle (think of the moon); as the user drags that circle, we position it in the correct place along a larger circle (think of the moon's orbit).

Actually, we could solve this exercise just by placing the moon off center within a clip (similar to the way the pupil was off center within the Eyeball symbol). However, this seemingly easier approach would require that any adjustments to the radius be made by editing the contents of our moon symbol. Besides, we've already learned how to rotate an off-center symbol (the Eyeball). Positioning a clip on a circular path is entirely different.

3. In the main timeline, draw a large circle and convert it to a Movie Clip. Give it an instance name of theCircle. It is the perimeter of this instance that we'll use for the draggable clip's path.

4. Copy and paste the instance of theCircle, scale it down, tint it, and then change its instance name to slider. You can also snap its center to a point on the edge of the theCircle instance.

5. Now go to the frame script in the main timeline (where we'll put all the remaining code for this exercise) and type the following script to initialize some variables:

```
centerX=theCircle._x;
centerY=theCircle._y;
radius = theCircle._width/2;
```

To calculate the angle (between the center of the theCircle clip and the mouse), we need to know the center of the circle. Also, to position the slider instance in the correct location, we need to know the radius of the circle (that is, half its width). These variables just save a bit of typing later.

6. Before we actually start calculating angles and positioning the slider instance, let's get the triggers in place. All we'll do is assign an onMouseMove callback to the slider instance when the user presses on it. In addition, we'll clear this callback when the user releases the mouse. Type the following code below what you already have:

```
slider.onPress=function(){slider.onMouseMove=dragTime}
slider.onRelease=function(){slider.onMouseMove=null}
slider.onReleaseOutside=function(){slider.onMouseMove=null}
```

The function dragTime will be defined in a second. Naturally, in place of the word dragTime we could have defined the function right there—but for readability we'll do it next. Quite simply, this code says that while the user is dragging (that is, after an onPress event), the dragTime function will be tied to every mouseMove. Then, when the user lets go of the mouse, there will be no onMouseMove callback.

7. The dragTime() function will have one primary objective: to position the slider instance. It will take a couple of steps, of course, so first write the following skeleton into which we'll add one line at a time:

```
function dragTime(){
}
```

8. We can use the atan2() method to determine the angle between the center of the circle and the mouse pointer. Here, we'll store the angle in a variable called radians (which goes inside the dragTime() function):

```
var radians =
➥Math.atan2(_root._ymouse-centerY, _root._xmouse-centerX);
```

Note that this is the same code that we used in the Eyeball example.

9. With the angle stored in the radians variable, we can now position the slider. Interestingly, because we're not rotating anything (that is, setting its _rotation property), we may never need to convert to degrees. Actually, doing so prematurely would mess us up. Check out these two lines that go right below the radians assignment:

```
this._y = centerY+Math.sin(radians)*radius;
this._x = centerX+Math.cos(radians)*radius;
```

First look at the code to the right of the plus sign. When provided with an angle (in radians), the `Math.sin()` method returns the vertical proportion. Remember that sine returns the "opposite/hypotenuse." So, if you imagine a triangle that varies from 0 degrees to 90 (see Figure W11.4), you should see that "opposite/hypotenuse" is 1 at 90 degrees (because the opposite and hypotenuse are equal). At 0 degrees, sine returns 0 because the opposite is 0 height. Anyway, all variations between 0 and 1 are some percentage. The reason we multiply the sine (in line 1) by `radius` is because at 90 we want the _y to be the full radius (vertically). When at 0 degrees, we want the _y to be zero. The entire first line says, "set the _y to the center of the circle plus the appropriate proportion of the radius based on the sine." If that doesn't make sense, you can read more about this topic in Chapter 5. Also notice that we don't bother converting to degrees. The `Math.atan2()` method returns radians, and both `Math.cos()` and `Math.sin()` accept radians, so there's no need to bother with the "degrees" middleman, if you will.

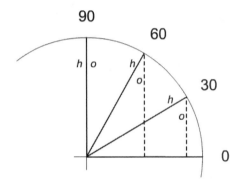

Figure W11.4 *Visualizing trigonometry functions helps deduce the expressions you write.*

10. Throw in an `updateAfterEvent()` below the three lines you've added to the `dragTime()` function.

    We're done early, so let's add a feature that will calculate what percentage the way around the circle the slider is currently positioned. Perhaps you want to make this control the volume or some other effect.

11. To display the percentage, place a Dynamic Text field on the Stage and give it an instance name of `percent_txt`.

12. Because I know the forthcoming discussion will be easier for you if we go back to degrees, add the following lines of code inside the `dragTime()` function:

```
var degrees = radians/(Math.PI/180);
_root.percent_txt.text=degrees;
```

After converting to degrees, we set the text in the `percent_txt` field to display the degrees as we drag. Notice that when you test the movie, dragging clockwise from nine o'clock increases `degrees` from `0` to `180`, whereas moving counterclockwise reduces a negative number from `0` to `-180`. I suppose it makes sense. My idea was to display `0–100`. I'd expect to at least see `0–360`, but no dice. We'll need to adjust the display.

13. We can make the display of degrees range from 0 to 360 by inserting an `if` statement between the two statements you inserted in Step 12:

```
var degrees=radians/(Math.PI/180);
if (degrees<0){
  degrees=360+degrees;
}
_root.percent=degrees;
```

This code simply says that if `degrees` is less than `0`, set `degrees` to `360` plus `degrees` (which is negative). That is, `-180` (three o'clock) turns to `180`; `-90` (six o'clock) changes to `270`; and so on (see Figure W11.5).

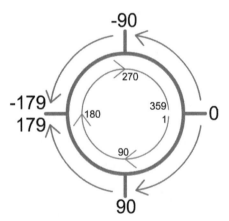

Figure W11.5   *The original degree values on the outside of the circle, including negative numbers, can be converted to all positive numbers as shown on the inside of the circle by using a simple formula.*

14. To make the `percent` variable show a number between `0` and `99`, we can change the last line of the script to read as follows:

```
_root.percent_txt.text=Math.floor(100*degrees/360);
```

This statement says that `360` divided into `degrees` times `100` gives us a percentage. You can add `1` outside the `Math.floor()` method if you want to display values from `1` through `100`.

You can just as easily use these calculations to set any property of any other clip. For example, if you have a clip named `it`, you can add this line of code:

```
_root.it._alpha= Math.floor(100*degrees/360);
```

15. If you don't like the fact that the scale starts at three o'clock, you can use the following technique to adjust the degrees found by any amount you want. Suppose that we want to add 90 degrees from every value to make twelve o'clock become the zero point. After all, before we converted to an actual percentage, twelve o'clock was displaying 90 (refer to Figure W11.5). To accomplish this task, add what you want (90 in this case), and our current `if` statement will adjust for any negative numbers. Place the following code right before the line starting `if (degrees<0)`...:

```
degrees+=90;
```

All this does is add 90 from `degrees` so that twelve o'clock is the zero point. As long as you do this *before* that `if` statement, you can subtract any value from the degrees calculated.

This discussion was a little easier for you to read and for me to write after we converted to degrees. However, unless you are setting `_rotation`, which is the one part of Flash that requires numbers in degrees, you probably will never need to convert to degrees. If you remember that there are `2*Math.PI` radians in a circle, you can perform any of the code in steps 12–15. For example, here is the same exact code without ever translating radians to degrees:

```
radians+=(Math.PI/2);
if (radians<0){
  radians=(2*Math.PI)+radians;
}
_root.percent_txt.text=Math.floor(100*radians/(2*Math.PI));
```

Notice that this code has one less line than the original version because we're not translating to degrees. The first line effectively adds 90 degrees from the `radians` found because `Math.PI/2` is equivalent to 90 degrees. If `radians` is less than `0`, we subtract `radians` from `2*Math.PI` in the same way we subtracted `degrees` from 360 earlier. Finally, to figure out the percentage, we divide `radians` by `2*Math.PI` instead of dividing `degrees` by 360.

With the exception of a little bit of math, this workshop turned out to be pretty easy. We'll use some of the same knowledge in Workshop Chapter 12, "Developing Time-Based Animations," to rotate a clip and make it follow a path. The main goal of that workshop chapter, however, is to make sure that the clip rotates at a perfect rate, regardless of frame rate or the computer's performance. You will get to use some of the same math, though.

{ Chapter 12

Workshop }

Developing Time-Based Animations

Flash is a frame-based animation tool. As you know, just because you set the frame rate to 120 frames per second, that doesn't mean Flash will really display that many frames in one second. The frame rate you specify is more of a top end that Flash will not exceed. Even if you keep your frame rate down in the normal range of 20 fps, there's a good chance that Flash will occasionally take longer than one-twentieth of a second to display a frame. The standard practice is to just make sure that your movie performs adequately on a slow machine, although there's still no guarantee.

If you use audio set to stream, Flash will drop frames to maintain a constant rate of sound. However, this approach to maintaining a particular speed has its drawbacks as well. This workshop chapter explores ways you can write your own code that effectively drops frames to keep up with a predetermined rate. This doesn't mean that you can actually reach the mythical 120 fps (Flash's maximum), but rather that you can make sure that your graphics stay on time. For example, you can designate that a circle will rotate fully in 10 seconds. On a super-slow machine, the circle might display only four times: at 0, 90, 180, and 360 degrees. On a fast machine, however, the circle might display at all 360 discrete angles. Regardless of the machine speed, however, one second after the clip starts, the circle will have made a full revolution. You'll learn how to accomplish this feat in this workshop chapter.

We're actually going to make circles rotate as well as revolve around other circles. The techniques learned, however, can also be applied to animations that aren't so predictable and geometric. For example, in Workshop Chapter 14, "Offline Production," you'll first learn how to collect data for any kind of animation offline and then apply the time-based animation knowledge from this workshop chapter.

This workshop chapter starts our animation efforts with circles:

1. Start a new movie and set the frame rate to 24 fps.

2. Draw a circle that will become a graphic of the earth. Make sure that you include additional graphical elements that will enable you to see when this graphic rotates (see Figure W12.1).

Figure W12.1 *Draw some shapes in the "earth" circle so that you'll notice when the circle rotates.*

3. Convert the circle to a Movie Clip and name the instance `earth`. Place the following code in the first frame of the Movie Clip (where you'll put all the code for this workshop chapter):

```
1 rpm = 60;
2 degreesPerSecond = (rpm*360)/60;
3 fps=24;
4 degreesPerFrame=degreesPerSecond/fps;
5 earth.onEnterFrame=function(){
6   this._rotation += degreesPerFrame;
7 }
```

This code isn't going to exhibit perfect synchronization. The `rpm` variable in line 1 is hard-wired to the number of times per minute the clip should rotate. We will use this variable to specify how fast, based on time, this clip should rotate. Line 2 translates revolutions per minute into the number of `degreesPerSecond`. Lines 3 and 4 become problematic. First, hard-wiring `fps` is going to prove to be a hassle—and anyway, this movie should play the same regardless of the frame rate we specify. Line 4 accurately calculates the number of `degreesPerFrame`, but bases its calculation on `fps`, which could easily slow down. Finally, the `onEnterFrame` callback makes perfect sense *provided that* it is indeed executed 24 times a second.

//

> You can prove that this code doesn't work by first testing it and getting a feel for what 60 rpm looks like on your machine. Then change both the movie's frame rate and the fps value to, say, `120`. The movie won't play quite as fast unless you have a *really* fast computer. This approach, which simply adds to _rotation in every enterFrame event, assumes that each frame is entered on time.

4. Change the `onEnterFrame` callback to read as follows:

```
earth.onEnterFrame=function(){
  now=getTimer();
  this._rotation+=degreesPerSecond/(1000/(now-lastTime));
  lastTime=now;
}
```

The first thing you may notice is that because the variables `fps` and `degreesPerFrame` are no longer used, only the first two (of the four) lines that appear before the `onEnterFrame` callback are needed. Within the `onEnterFrame` callback, we first put the current `getTimer()` in a variable called `now`. Then we add the result of an expression to _rotation. Try the slow motion what-if possibility that we're supposed to rotate only 10 degrees per second: If it's been two seconds since the last time we rotated, we should rotate 20 degrees. If it's been only 0.5 second since we rotated, we need to rotate just 5 degrees. To calculate how long it's been since the last time we rotated, we subtract `lastTime` from `now`. The formula works like this: If `lastTime` was five past the hour and `now` is six past the hour, we know that one minute has elapsed—but we're using milliseconds. If we divide 1000 into the number of milliseconds that have elapsed, we know how many seconds have passed. Then we divide that value into the number of degrees per second. (I think this formula is easiest to see when you try a few numbers.) Anyway, after we set the _rotation, we can save the current `now` into the variable `lastTime` so that the next time around we can calculate how long it's been since the last rotation.

It should work really well. Try changing the movie's frame rate to 10 fps or 90 fps. The movie might play smoother or clunkier, but it always stays "on time."

5. We can extend this workshop to practice both our math and our skills with time-based animation. Draw another circle to represent the sun. Convert it to a Movie clip and name the instance `sun`.

6. Before we change the `onEnterFrame` callback, we need to come up with different variable names. For example, if we want the earth to both rotate on its axis and revolve around the sun, the variable `rpm` could be confusing. (Is it "revolutions per minute" or "rotations per minute?") In any event,

we'll need two variables, so start over with the following initialization script. (We'll do the onEnterFrame callback next.)

```
1 rotationsPerMinute = 60;
2 degreesPerSecond = (rotationsPerMinute*360)/60;
3 revolutionsPerMinute=20;
4 radiansPerSecond=(revolutionsPerMinute*Math.PI*2)/60;
5 orbitRadius=Math.sqrt(Math.pow ( Math.abs(sun._x-earth._x),2) +
➥Math.pow ( Math.abs(sun._y-earth._y), 2 ))
```

Notice that the first two lines are the same as before, but I changed rpm to rotationsPerMinute. Lines 3–5 set up the variables for positioning earth along a path. After hard-wiring a desired revolution speed (in line 3), radiansPerSecond is calculated. This is really the same as calculating degreesPerSecond; however, because I expect to use radians, I consider one revolution to be Math.PI*2 (rather than 360 as in the case of degrees). Finally, line 5 calculates the distance between the sun and earth clips (that is, the radius) using a formula based on Pythagoras' theorem.

Handy Formula

By the way, you can use the following handy-dandy formula any time you want to calculate the distance between two points:

```
Math.sqrt(Math.pow(Math.abs(x1-x2),2)+Math.pow(Math.abs(y1-y2), 2 ));
```

In this syntax, x1 and y1 are the coordinates of one point, and x2 and y2 are the coordinates of the other point. For those of you who were awake in high-school Math class, this formula is based on Pythagoras' theorem (which, yes, *does* come up in everyday life). Pythagoras said that with a right triangle, the square of the length of one side added to the square of the length of the other side will equal the square of the third side. For any two points, we can easily find the difference in x and the difference in y so that we can draw the straight sides of a triangle. We can then raise those values to the second power (that is, square them), and then add them together. Finally, we know that that sum is the square of the diagonal line connecting the two points; when we take the square root of that sum, we end up with the actual length. Figure W12.2 shows how the formula is derived. Notice that when finding the difference between two points, I use Math.abs() to ensure that the value is not negative. It turns out that this shouldn't matter because when you square a negative number, the result should be positive. I'm leaving in that formula, however, because it always shows distance as a positive number.

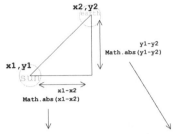

$$\text{Math.pow}\,(\,_{\text{Math.abs}(x1-x2)}\,,2\,)\ +\ \text{Math.pow}\,(\,_{\text{Math.abs}(y1-y2)}\,,2\,)$$

$$\text{Math.sqrt}\,(\text{Math.pow}(\text{Math.abs}(x1-x2),2)\ +\ \text{Math.pow}(\text{Math.abs}(y1-y2),2)\,)$$

Figure W12.2 *Based on Pythagoras' theorem, this diagram shows you how to determine the distance between any two points.*

7. Now replace the onEnterFrame script:

```
1 earth.onEnterFrame=function(){
2    now=getTimer();
3    this._rotation+=degreesPerSecond/(1000/(now-lastTime));
4
5    radians= lastRad+radiansPerSecond/(1000/(now-lastTime));
6    this._x = sun._x+Math.cos(radians)* orbitRadius;
7    this._y = sun._y+Math.sin(radians)* orbitRadius;
8
9    lastRad=radians;
10   lastTime=now;
11 }
```

Lines 1–3 are the same—only the variable names have been changed. To understand line 5, realize that in line 3 we say "add to rotation" and we want to effectively say "add this many radians to the angle used to position the earth on its orbit." The earth instance doesn't have a "radians" property, however, and adding involves knowing where the earth instance was the previous time. That's why we add to lastRad (the variable assigned in line 9 to hold the last time around). Imagine if you were responsible for positioning the hour hand on a clock one hour ahead (that is, 1/12 of a circle more)—you'd have to know where the hand *was* when you started (just like our code needs to know where the earth instance was positioned the last time). Once we know at what angle (in radians) the earth instance should be positioned, we use lines 6 and 7 to assign the _x and _y properties accordingly. (These two lines are just formulas used in Workshop Chapter 11, "Using Math to Create a Circular Slider.")

The result is pretty neat. Notice that you can position the earth instance in any location, and it will determine the circular path to follow based on a circle drawn with its center at the sun instance and its radius equal to the distance between sun and earth instances. Also notice that you can change the frame rate to anything you want, and the movie will always keep perfect synchronization (although the movie is sometimes jumpy when the frame rate is very low). You can also change the values for rotationsPerMinute and revolutionsPerMinute to effect how it rotates and revolves.

We have successfully created an animation that is based entirely on time, not on frame rate. Originally, I thought this exercise would be perfect for setInterval(); however, I'm not so sure that it makes much difference.

8. To see how you can use setInterval() as an alternative, first change the onEnterFrame callback to look like a function—that is, so that the first line reads

```
function update(){.
```

In addition, change the three cases of this to earth.

9. Finally, add the following code somewhere outside the function:

```
setInterval(update,50);
```

You can change the 50 to anything you want. There really isn't much difference in this approach. If, however, you really believe that setInterval will trigger the update() function every 1/20th of a second (based on 50 milliseconds) without fail (which it won't), you can forgo most of the code we came up with in this workshop. That is, you could have something as simple as this version:

```
function update(frequency){
    earth._rotation+=degreesPerSecond/(1000/frequency);
    radians= lastRad+radiansPerSecond/(1000/frequency);

    earth._x = sun._x+Math.cos(radians)* orbitRadius;
    earth._y = sun._y+Math.sin(radians)* orbitRadius;

    lastRad=radians;
}
setInterval(update,50,50);
```

First, notice that anything to do with getTimer() is gone (including the now variable). In place of (lastTime=now), I just use the parameter frequency, which contains how frequently this function is being called. That is, the third parameter for setInterval() is a value that gets sent to the function it triggers. You can learn more about setInterval() in Chapter 14, "Extending ActionScript." Realize that the preceding code assumes setInterval() is working perfectly. A true time-based solution uses getTimer() to check to see how much time has elapsed since the last execution. Only this last bit of code (after step 9) exhibits a non–time-based solution.

What if you want to make an animation that's not based on math, but you still want to make the animation time-based? We'll do that in Workshop Chapter 14,

"Offline Production." In brief, there are two basic steps to making a time-based animation that's not based on math: First you gather the coordinates for where the graphic you're animating should be at key moments in time, and then you use those values in an `enterFrame` event that keeps checking `getTimer()`. I know that explanation isn't complete, but you'll see how it's done in Workshop Chapter 14.

{ Part IIC }

Advanced Workshops

{ Workshop

Chapter 13 }

Drawing Graphs

In this workshop chapter, you'll draw graphs using the new drawing methods of the Movie Clip object. Without a clip on the stage, you'll create a bar chart that displays dynamic data. If you need to change the graph, you can just change a few variables. Figure W13.1 shows what you'll have at the end of this workshop.

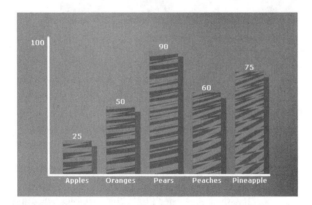

Figure W13.1 *You'll learn how to dynamically draw a graph, make shadows, fill with a pattern, and place text labels anywhere you please.*

This workshop chapter is broken into two sections. First, you'll prepare and draw the graph using the drawing methods. Next, you'll add a few extra features (such as labels) using the TextField and TextFormat objects.

Using the Drawing Methods

In Chapter 12, "Objects," you learned all the Movie Clip's drawing methods. These methods make anything that's imaginable possible. The difficulty, however, lies in the "imagining" part. Everything in our graph is going to be drawn using code, so it will take some pre-visualization as we work. I guess all this is leading to my recommendation to draw a rough layout for your graph by hand in order to work up a few expressions to use when coding. That's how we'll start—we'll draw something in draft form (see Figure W13.2).

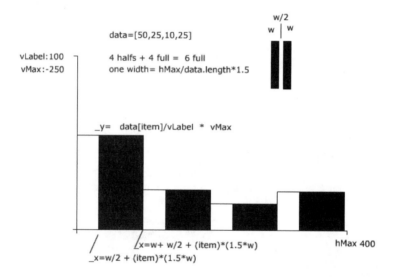

Figure W13.2   *A rough layout can help you to deduce the expressions you'll need to draw the graph.*

Follow along these first few steps even though you won't type any code until later.

1. Go ahead and draw a rough layout for the graph. We can identify a few variables that we will need. If we consider the bottom-left corner to be the graph's origin, to specify its size, we need only the variables vMax and hMax (refer to Figure W13.2). Actually, vMax will always be a negative number.

2. Because we're going to be calculating the height of each bar, we're going to need a scale. That is, if a bar reaches the maximum height (vMax), what number will that represent? If vMax is -250 (for a graph that is 250 pixels tall), is that the same as 250 units? What if the numbers in my graph just range from 0–100? I just need another variable (which I'll call vLabel) that contains a number for that maximum height position.

3. Regarding the widths of the bars (and the space between each bar), I want to leave that calculation dependent on the number of bars I draw. That is, if I draw only three bars, they'll be wide; if I draw additional bars, they'll be thin. In any event, I want the space between each bar to be half the width of one bar. To make the calculation a tad easier, I decided that the sequence from left to right will be: "space, bar, space, bar, and so on" (rather than "bar, space, bar"). For example, for 3 bars we'll need space for 3 full bars and 3 half bars (the space)—for a total of 4.5 bar widths. Based on the variables for both totalBars and hMax (the graph's width), we can use the following formula for the width of a single bar (w):

```
w=hMax/(totalBars*1.5);
```

Simply put, totalBars times 1.5 must fit evenly into the space for the whole graph.

4. We'll use that formula for w in a minute, but how will we come up with totalBars? Instead of assigning its value, we'll just assign one variable (data) that will be an array full of values. Each item in data will be repre-sented as a bar in the graph. Therefore, we can use data.length in place of totalBars in the formula for w. By the way, because we don't know where all these handy formulas are going to go, we just type them into text on the Stage. This also makes subsequent formulas easier to deduce.

5. Now we just have to write four general expressions, and then this graph will come to life very quickly. Specifically, in order to draw a filled shape, we need to express dynamically the coordinates for the four corners of any bar. We want to use an expression that is as dynamic as possible. The first bar's left side will appear at w/2 (the size of a space). The right side will appear at w + w/2 (the width of a bar plus the width of a space). However, subsequent bars will appear farther out. The expression for the _x of any bar (that is, the left side) looks like this:

```
w/2 + (item * (1.5*w))
```

That is, assuming the variable item starts at 0 for the first bar, we can mul-tiply one bar and space (1.5*w) times the item number.

To express the right side of any bar (that is, its _x), we use the same formula, plus w:

```
w + w/2 + (item * (1.5*w))
```

Notice that the two expressions are exactly what I mentioned previously (w/2 and w+w/2) if item is 0, and therefore much of the formula turns to zero. You can peek ahead at Figure W13.3 to see these formulas right on the graph.

6. Now, for the height of each bar. It's all based on the value in the current index of data. Remember that the height of the graph (vMax) is nearly always a negative number, and then check out this expression:

```
(data[item]/vLabel) * vMax
```

Dividing the value (in the `item` index of `data`) by `vLabel` is like calculating a percentage, although it will range from 0 to 1. Multiply that by `vMax`, and you have the pixel location for the top of any bar. Figure W13.3 shows all four corners of a bar that uses these expressions.

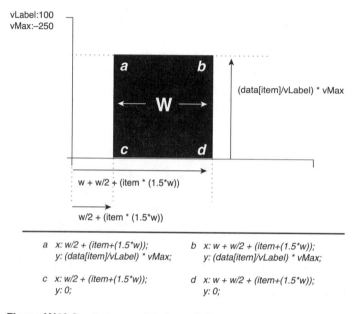

a x: w/2 + (item+(1.5*w));   b x: w + w/2 + (item+(1.5*w));
    y: (data[item]/vLabel) * vMax;   y: (data[item]/vLabel) * vMax;

c x: w/2 + (item+(1.5*w));   d x: w + w/2 + (item+(1.5*w));
    y: 0;   y: 0;

Figure W13.3 *A closeup of the layout helps you to visualize the expressions.*

7. It might seem as though preparing our expressions has taken a long time, but that will pay off in the speed it takes to write this code. In a new Flash movie, type in this code into the first frame:

```
this.createEmptyMovieClip("graph",1);
graph.itemData=[25,50,100];
graph.vLabel=100;
graph.vMax=-250;
graph.hMax=400;
graph.w= graph.hMax/(graph.data.length*1.5)
graph._x=0;
graph._y=graph.vMax*-1;
```

First we create a new clip instance called `graph`. Then we store all the variables discussed earlier inside the `graph` clip itself. This just saves some typing later because we'll be "in" the `graph` instance when we draw. You can change the values for `data`, as this example shows that three bars will be drawn. Also, you can adjust `vMax` and `hMax` to whatever size of graph you want to make. Finally, you can see in the last line that we move the graph down (as far as it is tall); otherwise, it would appear at 0,0 by default.

8. Now we can draw the graph. We need to draw a bar for each item in item
    data, so we'll use a loop. Check out the following code, which follows
    what you have so far:

```
 1 with (_root.graph){
 2   for (var i=0; i<data.length; i++){
 3     lineStyle(0,0x000000,0);
 4     beginFill(0x000000,100);
 5     moveTo(w/2+(i*1.5*w) , 0);
 6     lineTo(w/2+(i*1.5*w) ,(data[i]/ vLabel)*vMax);
 7     lineTo(w+w/2+(i*1.5*w),(data[i]/vLabel)* vMax);
 8     lineTo(w+ w/2+(i*1.5*w), 0);
 9     lineTo(w/2+(i*1.5*w) , 0);
10     endFill();
11   }
12 }
```

It's almost as though I don't have to explain this code because we
calculated all the values already. Notice that the iterant of the `for` loop is `i`
(not `item` as used in my formulas). Other than that, it's pretty simple: Line
3 sets the line style to `0` thickness and `0` alpha, line 4 begins the fill (feel
free to change the color from black), line 5 moves to the bottom left, line 6
draws a line to the top left, line 7 draws a line to the top right, line 8 to the
bottom right, and then line 9 goes back to the bottom left to enclose the
shape. It really is simple once you write the expressions.

9. To draw the graph's outline, add the following code after line 11's curly
    brace and before line 12's curly brace:

```
lineStyle(4,0x000000,100);
moveTo(0,0);
lineTo(0,vMax);
moveTo(0,0);
lineTo(hMax+10,0);
```

Notice that the line thickness is 4. Also, the last line goes 10 pixels beyond
the right side of the graph. (I think it looks better that way.)

At this point, it's pretty complete. If you want, you can add a few more
touches before the next section (where we label the graph). Try the next
couple of steps, but realize that they're optional; you might not like the
effect created.

10. There are many ways to add a shadow under the bars. Basically, we'll just
    draw more bars with a lower alpha. To make it easy, just add the following
    code right inside the `for` loop in step 8 (before the main bars are drawn in
    line 3). That is, instead of figuring out where to draw the shadow and
    where not to, we'll just draw the shadow and then draw the regular bars on
    top. Here's the extra code:

```
beginFill(0x000000,30);
moveTo(w/2+(i*1.5*w) , 0);
```

```
lineTo(w/2+(i*1.5*w),(data[i]/vLabel)*vMax+10);
lineTo(w+w/2+(i*1.5*w)+10,(data[i]/vLabel)* vMax+10);
lineTo(w+ w/2+(i*1.5*w)+10, 0);
lineTo(w/2+(i*1.5*w) , 0);
endFill();
```

Notice that this is a repeat of the other code, except the alpha is 30 (for a shadow effect), and the height is 10 pixels greater (meaning it's visually lower) and 10 pixels to the right. The base doesn't change, only the top-left point, top-right point, and bottom-right _x.

The shadow is a bit fancy, but this next effect is downright gratuitous. Even though the drawing methods can do some interesting effects, they often can be more work than they're worth. For example, drawing a pattern on top of the graph's bars is certainly possible, but if the pattern has a company logo or something, it would be tedious to re-create using code. In this next step, I'll show you how to use setMask() before drawing a second set of bars so that the new bar's color will show through only where the mask appears. It's a lot like batik (where you die cloth a light color and then add wax before dyeing it with darker and darker colors).

11. Create a Movie Clip with a dense pattern of shapes (see Figure W13.4). The clip should not appear on the Stage; instead, set its linkage to pattern. Start with this code (typed below everything else so far):

```
1 this.createEmptyMovieClip("graphYellow",2);
2 graphYellow._x=0;
3 graphYellow._y=graph.vMax*-1;
4 this.attachMovie("pattern","pattern",3);
5 pattern._x=0;
6 pattern._y=graph.vMax*-1;
7 graphYellow.setMask(pattern);
```

The first three lines just make another graph clip, called graphYellow. This is the same as the graph instance, but it's placed into level 2. Line 4 creates an instance of the pattern symbol and gives it an instance name of pattern. There's no problem in having a symbol's linkage match an instance name. Then, after positioning the new pattern clip, line 7 designates that pattern will be the mask for (the now empty clip) graphYellow.

12. Now, we just need to draw the bars (for graphYellow) the same way we did for graph, but in a different color (and we don't need to bother with the shadows, either). Here is the code, which is nearly identical to what we typed in step 8:

```
1 with (_root.graphYellow){
2   var g=_parent.graph;
3   for (i=0; i<g.data.length; i++){
4     lineStyle(0,0x000000,0);
5     beginFill(0xFFFF00,100);
6     moveTo(g.w/2+(i*1.5*g.w) , 0);
7     lineTo(g.w/2+(i*1.5*g.w) ,(g.data[i]/g.vLabel)*g.vMax);
```

```
 8    lineTo(g.w+g.w/2+(i*1.5*g.w),(g.data[i]/g.vLabel)* g.vMax);
 9    lineTo(g.w+ g.w/2+(i*1.5*g.w), 0);
10    lineTo(g.w/2+(i*1.5*g.w) , 0);
11    endFill();
12  }
13 }
```

First, notice that line 2 stores (into the temp variable g) a reference to the graph clip. As you recall, we stored the variables vLabel, data, and w in the graph instance. Because this code uses those variables, we can now just precede each reference with "g.". Notice, also, that we're using the iterant variable i as-is. Finally, the only difference is that the color specified in line 5 is yellow.

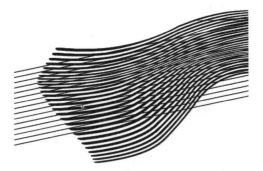

Figure W13.4   *This dense pattern (inside a symbol) will serve as the mask for the second set of colored bars that we draw.*

It's a pretty cool effect, as you can see in Figure W13.5. If you wanted, you could add more layers of color—although you first might try to figure out a loop rather than just adding more and more code (as I had you do in this step).

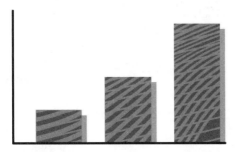

Figure W13.5   *You certainly could draw a pattern like this using only the drawing methods, but a mask is much easier.*

Dynamic Text Labeling

Perhaps it was premature to start creating shadows and patterns of color before the graph had labels. I don't know which teacher told me, but a graph with no labels means nothing. In this part of the workshop chapter, you'll place labels on the vertical axis (one for vLabel and one for each bar) so that the user can see its value.

1. To place a dynamically generated Text Field, you'll need to start with the graphing code from the first part of this workshop. Actually, you really only need the code through at least step 9. You'll start by creating an instance of the TextFormat object. Place the following four lines above all the rest of the code in the file:

```
myFormat= new TextFormat();
myFormat.size=12;
myFormat.font="_sans";
myFormat.bold=true;
```

You can use whichever font, size, and style you want. Just realize that the myFormat variable will be stored in the _root timeline.

2. To display the value of vLabel on the graph, place the following code right inside the first with() statement (it should start with with(_root.graph){—as you can see in line 1 of step 8 earlier):

```
1 targ=_root.graph;
2 targ.createTextField("myLabel",1, 0 ,0,0,0);
3 targ.myLabel.autoSize=true;
4 targ.myLabel.text=vLabel;
5 targ.myLabel.setTextFormat(_root.myFormat);
```

The first line just specifies an absolute address for all subsequent addresses. Line 2 makes a new TextField instance (called myLabel) and places it in level 1 of the graph clip. Line 3 sets autoSize to true so that the margins adapt automatically. In line 4, I set myLabel's text to reflect the value of vLabel. Finally, the last line applies the myFormat format defined in step 1.

3. The text should appear but in the wrong location. Its _y location should be the same as the variable vMax. To set the _x position, we can effectively make it right justified by moving the text to the left a value equal to its width. Here are two more lines of code that go right after the scripts added in step 2.

```
targ.myLabel._y=vMax;
targ.myLabel._x= -1*targ.myLabel._width;
```

You could actually subtract another 2 or 3 pixels to move the _x position a little farther if you think the right edge is too close to the graph.

4. Before we add code inside the `for` loop to display a text field for each bar, realize that the `createTextField()` method specifies a level number into which the text resides. We now have text in level 1, so we should start with a higher level and keep placing each text field into new level numbers. The following code will label each bar. Place it anywhere *inside* the `for` loop inside the `with()` code (that is, after the line that reads: `for (i=0; i<data.length; i++){`—line 2 in step 8 noted previously):

```
1 targ.createTextField("bar_"+i ,i+2, 0 ,0,0,0);
2 var thisText=targ["bar_"+i];
3 thisText.autoSize=true;
4 thisText.text=data[i];
5 thisText.setTextFormat(_root.myFormat);
6 thisText._y=0;
7 thisText._x=w+(i*1.5*w)- thisText._width/2;
```

Line 1 just creates a new text field with an instance name of `bar_0` (and then `bar_1`, and so on). Notice, however, that the new text field is placed in a level number `2` greater than the value of the iterant `i` because the `vLabel` text is in level `1`. Then, in line 2, I store a reference to the current text field (into `thisText`) using the standard bracket reference so that I can save typing in the following five steps (where I format and then position it). The last line is just a modified version of the code used for calculating the bar's locations. I subtract half the width of the text field to make it appear center justified. (I could have set the `_root.myFormat` align property to `"center"`, but then I'd have to remember to set it back if I expected it later to be, say, `"left"`.)

5. The horizontal spacing is great, but those labels really should appear right on the bar. (If we want labels on the base of the bars, we could do that separately.) Change the line where `thisText`'s `_y` is set to read as follows:

```
thisText._y=(data[i]/vLabel)*vMax;
```

Again, I just stole some code from where the bars are being drawn. It actually works great, but if the text is the same color as the graph, you won't see it! To fix that, you can just pick a different color for the `myFormat` format (such as `_root.myFormat.color=0x00FFFF;`). Realize, however, that if you change the color before the `myLabel` instance has the `setTextFormat()` method applied (in step 2), you will color it too. Another alternative to make the text visible is to change the fill color in the bars.

6. Regardless of whether you changed the color orientation, I think it makes sense to move the labels. Try this final version for how `thisText` gets its `_y` set:

```
thisText._y=(data[i]/vLabel)*vMax - thisText._height;
```

By simply moving the text up a value that matches its height, it appears on top of each bar.

I'm sure we could spend a lot more time fine-tuning, but I want to show you one issue that will arise if you try to place both labels at the base of each bar and the values on top. The issue has to do with the level into which you instantiate the text fields. That is, using an expression such as i+2 works fine for the labels we've drawn, but it's slightly more complex when you make two labels for each iteration. Try the following two steps to see what I'm talking about.

7. First, outside the `with()` statement, find where you set the values for the data variable (step 7 in the first section of this workshop chapter). Add this line of code right underneath:

```
graph.labels=["Apples", "Oranges", "Pears"];
```

The idea is that for each item in the data array, you now have an equivalent text label in the `labels` array.

8. Then, back inside the `for` loop that's inside the `with()` statement (where you created the value labels), add the following code:

```
targ.createTextField("label_"+i ,i+1+100, 0 ,0,0,0);
var thisText=targ["label_"+i];
thisText.autoSize=true
thisText.text=labels[i];
thisText.setTextFormat(_root.myFormat);
thisText._y=0
thisText._x=w+(i*1.5*w)- thisText._width/2;
```

This looks pretty much the same, except in the fourth line, we grab a value out of the `labels` array (instead of `data`). Oh, and don't worry that we're storing a different reference in `thisText`. As long as we redefine that value before using it for the value text (`bar_0` and so on), there's no problem. The key thing to notice is that in the first line, we're placing these new text fields way up in level `100` and greater. This solution falls apart when we have more than 100 bars. Perhaps you can figure out an expression that automatically places these "label" fields into even-number levels and the "value" text fields into odd-number levels.

This workshop chapter was a good exercise into practical uses for the drawing methods. As you have other ideas come to mind, it will be only a matter of applying the skills you have to solve the challenges. For example, because the graph is drawn dynamically, the data for the various points could be imported from a text file or online database. By the way, you can make an animated effect by repeatedly drawing slightly different graphs. You have to redraw *everything* for every step of the animation, so it might start bogging down, but you might be surprised with the performance.

The key concept I hope you take away from this workshop is that once you write all your various expressions, you can very easily apply them to complex drawing tasks. That is, the time upfront is well worth the investment.

{ Workshop

Chapter 14 }

Offline Production

This workshop chapter combines offline production with time-based animation. As discussed in Chapter 3, "The Programmer's Approach," *offline production* is any procedure that's executed only during authoring. The process of collecting coordinates for the mapping exercise—which we covered in Workshop Chapter 5, "Mapping and Scripted Masks"—is an example of offline production. In this workshop chapter, we will build a data string and output it using the `trace()` command. Then we'll take the text that appears in the Output window to another file and use it in a time-based animation sequence. Making one file that gathers data and another file that uses that data might seem like extra work, but you'll see that both files can be quite simple. The file that acquires data has one simple job: to gather data; the file that uses that data also has a simple job: to use the data.

Think about how a player piano accepts a roll of paper that has holes punched out of it. Imagine now that there was a special piano that punched the holes as you played on the keyboard. We're going to build a special Flash movie that produces the data for an animation and another movie that uses the data. After the data is produced, the offline movie that produced it can be discarded or saved for future jobs because it will have done its job.

1. Create a new file and save it as `offline.fla`. Set the movie's document properties to 8 fps. Draw a circle, convert it to a Movie Clip called Circle, and give the instance the name `circle`.

2. Make a simple animation using the `circle` instance in the main timeline and put a `stop()` script in the last frame. For this example, I made a tween that follows a Motion Guide (see Figure W14.1).

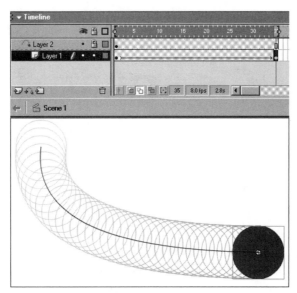

Figure W14.1 *Any animation will do, but I used a Motion Guide for this example.*

3. Type the following code into a frame script of the main timeline:

```
1 xLocs = new Array();
2 yLocs = new Array();
3 flag = 0;
4 circle.onEnterFrame=function(){
5    xLocs.push(this._x);
6    yLocs.push(this._y);
7    if (_root._currentframe == _root._totalframes && flag == 0) {
8      flag = 1;
9      trace("xLocs=["+xLocs.toString()+"]");
10     trace("yLocs=["+yLocs.toString()+"]");
11   }
12 }
```

Lines 1–3 initialize two empty arrays that will hold _x and _y locations plus the `flag` variable (which gets set to 1 after all the data has been gathered). Notice that the `onEnterFrame` callback function (line 4) contains two primary lines of code (lines 5–6) that execute once every time a new frame is displayed. The current position of the `circle` clip gets pushed onto the end of each array. Then the `if` statement in line 7 will only execute once—namely, when the _root timeline's _currentframe matches _totalframes (that is, the last frame) *and* the `flag` variable is still equal to 0. If that condition is true, the flag is set to 1 (therefore the `if` statement is never true again). Also, two `trace` commands display a nicely formed string in the Output window.

I say the string is nicely formed because it will be able to be used as-is to populate both array variables `xLocs` and `yLocs` in the second movie. The string includes three basic components: First, the variable name, an equal sign, and an open bracket: `xLocs=[`. Second, a string version of the array, which, incidentally, separates each value with a comma: `xLocs.toString()`. Finally, a closing bracket: `]`. Figure W14.2 shows what appears in my Output window. (By the way, you don't need to use the `toString()` method; Flash automatically converts the array's contents to a string form when executing a `trace()` command—it doesn't hurt to be explicit, however.)

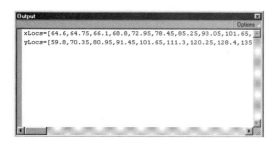

Figure W14.2 *The Output window displays the string as we formatted it.*

4. Test this movie and copy the contents of the Output window to the Clipboard. Return to the movie and open the Library window.

It turns out that if you have a lot of data in the Output window— and I mean a *lot*—you might not be able to copy it all. I've noticed that this condition happens on the Macintosh more often than on Windows machines. Usually, you can get around this problem by using the Output window's Save to File option. At the worst, you can shorten your animation for this workshop. In a real-world situation, you might have to gather the data in stages, maybe 100 frames at a time.

5. Create a new file called `online.fla`. Drag the Circle symbol from the old file's Library onto this file's Stage. Close the Library window.

6. Give the instance of the Circle in the new file the name `circle`.

7. Before we forget, paste the contents of the Clipboard (from Step 4) into the frame script of `online.fla` (where all the rest of our code will go) so that you have two lines of script that populate the two array variables (`xLocs` and `yLocs`).

8. To see where we're headed, type the following simple script underneath where the two arrays are initialized:

```
_root.onEnterFrame=function(){
  frame++;
  circle._x=xLocs[frame];
  circle._y=yLocs[frame];
}
  circle._x=xLocs[0];
  circle._y=yLocs[0];
```

As soon as the movie begins, this script executes once every 1/12 of a second (based on your frame rate). The last two lines just position the `circle` clip in its initial location. This code is slightly sloppy because I'm relying on the fact that `frame` (a homemade variable with no value) will evaluate as 0 the first time. The only significant problem with this example is that it's still tied to the frame rate—that is, if you increase the frame rate, the `circle` clip will animate faster.

In addition to making this time-based rather than frame-based, I want to make the `circle` clip play its animation once every time the user clicks; therefore, we won't define the `onEnterFrame` callback until the user clicks.

9. First let's make it animate only after the user clicks. Replace all but the two lines that initialize the two arrays with the following code:

```
 1 _root.onMouseDown=function(){
 2   frame=-1;
 3   this.onEnterFrame=function(){
 4     frame++;
 5     circle._x=xLocs[frame];
 6     circle._y=yLocs[frame];
 7     if (frame>=xLocs.length){
 8       this.onEnterFrame=null;
 9     }
10   }
11 }
```

This code is a bit circular, but it makes sense. When the user clicks, the `frame` variable is initialized to `-1`, and then an `onEnterFrame` callback is created (lines 3–10) that contains the same basic code we used before to position the `circle` clip. In addition, an `if` statement is triggered when the `frame` variable reaches the end of the `xLocs` array. If that `if` statement's condition is `true`, the `onEnterFrame` callback is cleared.

Now that the `circle` clip moves only after the user clicks, we can move on to apply a time-based script. Although we'll keep the `onEnterFrame` callback, we can calculate a value for `frame`. This way, `frame` will neither increase too fast nor ever fall behind. This time-based approach requires that we store the current time when the user clicks and then continually check to see how much time has elapsed.

10. To make a time-based solution, we need to decide on an effective frame rate. This way, the original animation will always play the same even if we crank up the frame rate. Because our offline animation was created at 8 fps, we'll need some calculation to make it play the same inside the 12 fps online version. Type the following code inside the first frame (but not in any callback functions):

```
fps=8;
milPerFrame= (1000/fps);
```

Basically, because we'll be checking to see how many milliseconds elapse between each `enterFrame` event, we'll need to know how many are supposed to elapse. To save a variable, you could replace `fps` in the second line with 8—but it's clearer this way.

11. Now that we know how many milliseconds are in 1/8th of a second, we can use the following modified version of the two callback functions:

```
1  _root.onMouseDown=function(){
2    startTime=getTimer();
3    frame=0;
4    this.onEnterFrame=function(){
5      now=getTimer();
6      elapsed=now-startTime;
7      frame=Math.floor(elapsed/milPerFrame);
8      circle._x=xLocs[frame];
9      circle._y=yLocs[frame];
10     if (frame>=xLocs.length){
11       _root.onEnterFrame=null;
12     }
13   }
14 }
```

The first difference appears in line 2, which stores the starting time. Then, instead of having one line of code that increments `frame`, lines 5–7 first figure out how much time has elapsed, and then line 7 calculates an integer value for `frame` based on the elapsed time divided by how many milliseconds per frame should have elapsed. That's all!

What's really cool about this workshop is that you can set the frame rate in the online movie to anything you want, and the animation will always play the same! Sure, if you lower the frame rate to something lower than what was used in the offline movie, the online movie will skip frames to keep on time—but that's a good thing.

Consider how you might use this technique to "record" your mouse movement. You could make another version of the offline movie that includes a draggable clip. As you drag the clip, the script records where the clip has been dragged. The only thing to remember is that you'll have to output all the variables gathered before you finish testing the movie. If you return to the authoring environment before you do that, all your variables will be reset. (This "record" version appears in the downloadable version, which you can find at www.phillipkerman.com/actionscripting.)

The technique discussed in this workshop is quite versatile. For example, you can use other programs to create the variables for the online version of the movie. Most animation tools have some sort of scripting capability to make that possible. You can even determine synch points in an audio file to use in Flash. When there's not a whole lot of data, you can just create the array of locations by hand. If it's just a simple animation, doing it by hand is easy. Actually, in Workshop Chapter 15, "Creating a Dynamic Slide Presentation," we'll create a short array that contains the location for a text bullet point that animates onto the Stage. No tweening necessary! Finally, realize that the array full of data doesn't have to be limited to x and y locations. You can automatically gather data about a clip's scale, alpha, or any other property.

{ Workshop

Chapter 15 }

Creating a Dynamic Slide Presentation

In this workshop chapter, we'll explore three advanced topics: loading structured data in XML format, loading JPEG images (using `loadMovie()`), and creating a dynamic screen layout on-the-fly. The project is to create a slide presentation that includes text and bullet points. Each "slide" is based on the same template, but the content of each will vary. In this project, every slide will have a title; a photograph; a variable number of bullets; some "permanent content" (such as the title), which stays on the screen while the slide is visible and the bullet points change; and some "post content," which appears after the last bullet point (see Figure W15.1).

Structuring the data in XML format is only part of the task. We have to import that data, parse it, and then use it in an interactive Flash movie. When we're finished, the Flash movie will adapt itself to any XML file that has the format we design. With this approach, you can update the presentation just by editing the XML file and replacing JPEG images. This workshop chapter isn't terribly intense, but surprisingly, designing the XML structure is probably the easiest part.

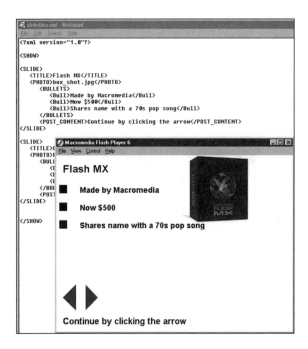

Figure W15.1 *In this workshop chapter, we'll make a dynamic slide show that reads structured data from a file.*

1. First, let's structure the XML. For each slide, we need a title, a photo, permanent content, post content, and a variable number of bullets. So actually, the bullets node will include child nodes. Here's the starter format to consider:

```
<SLIDE>
<TITLE>title goes here</TITLE>
<PHOTO>somephoto.jpg</PHOTO>
  <BULLETS>
    <Bull>first bullet</Bull>
    <Bull>second bullet</Bull>
    <Bull>third bullet</Bull>
  </BULLETS>
<POST_CONTENT>this appears at the end</POST_CONTENT>
</SLIDE>
```

   Notice that the "values" for the first child of TITLE, PHOTO, and POST_CONTENT are all strings. The value for the first child of BULLETS, however, is a series of BULL children, which each have a value.

2. Use a text editor to create a file that contains several slides, such as the one in Step 1, but start the file with the following text:

```
<?xml version="1.0"?>
<SHOW>
```

This code declares the file as XML and then starts the first tag SHOW. Each of our SLIDEs will be children of SHOW. After this line, place several SLIDEs that follow the form shown in Step 1. For the PHOTO tag, specify the file-names for a few JPEG files you have handy.

3. After the last </SLIDE>, insert a line that reads </SHOW>. This tag closes the <SHOW> tag that we opened in the second line.

4. Save the XML file as slidedata.xml. You can find details about how to create and format XML files in Chapter 16, "Interfacing with External Data." Be sure to place your sample JPEG files in the same location as the XML file.

   Loading the XML data into Flash is easy enough, but we'll parse it once it's loaded. Although it's possible to load XML data and just leave it in its native XML format, we will store the data in arrays designed for easy access within Flash. We will modify the parsing script developed in Chapter 16, so the parsing won't be a ton of work. Besides, I want to remove all extraneous null nodes caused by white space in the XML file.

5. Open Flash and immediately save the default Flash file right next to your slidedata.xml file. Place some text onscreen that says "Loading...". In the first keyframe, place the following script:

```
stop();
my_xml=new XML();
my_xml.ignoreWhite=true;
my_xml.onLoad=parse;
my_xml.load("slidedata.xml");
```

   The first line stops the timeline from proceeding. Then we create an XML object, set the ignoreWhite property to true, identify that the parse() function will trigger when the XML data is fully loaded (onLoad), and finally, commence loading in the last line. Next, we'll need to define the parse() function.

6. The parse() function is a monster. It's actually a modified version of the script that's fully explained in Chapter 16. As we progress, I'll point out some of the differences between this version and the original. For now, this script goes below what you've already typed into the first frame of the movie:

```
 1 function parse(success){
 2   if (!success){
 3     trace("problem");
 4     return;
 5   }
 6   allSlides=new Array();
 7   var slides=this.childNodes[0].childNodes;
 8   for (var s=0; s<slides.length; s++){
 9     var thisData= new Object();
10     var nodesInSlide=slides[s].childNodes.length;
```

```
11      for (var n=0; n< nodesInSlide;n++){
12        var thisNodeName=
⮡slides[s].childNodes[n].nodeName.toUpperCase();
13        if(thisNodeName=="BULLETS"){
14          var theVal=new Array();
15          totalBullets=slides[s].childNodes[n].childNodes.length;
16          for (var b=0;b<totalBullets;b++){
17            theVal.push(slides[s].childNodes[n].childNodes[b].
⮡firstChild.nodeValue);
18          }// for "b"
19        }else{
20          var theVal=slides[s].childNodes[n].firstChild.nodeValue;
21        }//if
22        thisData[slides[s].childNodes[n].nodeName]=theVal;
23      }//for "n"
24      allSlides[s]=thisData;
25    }//for "s"
26    _root.nextFrame();
27 }
```

This function differs from the parse() function in Chapter 16 in two ways: The hierarchy in this version is one step deeper in the case of the BULLETS node. The second difference is that when all the loops are finished, we just jump to the next frame (where the slide show will begin). Just because this was covered earlier doesn't mean it's crystal clear. Let me describe the various loops and point out specific differences.

The error check at the beginning is really just for our testing. You can replace the trace() command (in line 3) to take users to another frame that contains a warning. Before we step through the rest, it might help to understand the structure we're going to end up with. In the end, the allSlides array will contain values for each slide. The value in each index will be a generic object with properties named the same as each of the nodes (TITLE, PHOTO, BULLETS, and POST_CONTENT). The value for each property will be a string, except for BULLETS, which will have an array for a value. Figure W15.2 can help you visualize how the allSlides array gets populated:

```
allSlides =[
  { title:"txt",  photo:"a.jpg", post:"txt",  bullets: ["a","b","c"] },
  { title:"txt2", photo:"b.jpg", post:"txt2", bullets: ["x","y","z"] },
  { title:"txt3", photo:"c.jpg", post:"txt3", bullets: ["a","b","c"] },
]
```

Figure W15.2   *Visualizing the structure of the* allSlides *array will help when we need to extract portions of the array.*

The reason this structure will be so nice is that later we'll be able to, say, find the name of the photo for the first slide with an expression such as allSlides[0].photo.

The loops work as follows: Line 7 stores all the `slides` by first taking the first child of the XML file `this.childNodes[0]` (that's the same as the `SHOW` node) and then taking the `childNodes` of that. If you notice, `slides` shows up many times later, so line 7 mainly saves typing. Line 8 starts a loop that goes through all the slides. Then line 9 initializes a temporary variable that will store all the data for one slide at a time. After gathering everything for the first slide, `thisData` is copied into the `allSlides` array (line 24) and then is used again. Line 10 just makes line 11 more readable as we begin to loop through all the nodes within the current slide. In the old version, we then just created a new property for the `thisData` variable (like the start of line 22) and simply assigned its value like line 20. This version, however, needs to account for `BULLETS`, which contains nested `BULL`s. If it weren't for this fact, we could replace lines 12 through 22 with this one line:

```
thisData[slides[s].childNodes[n].nodeName]=
➥slides[s].childNodes[n].firstChild.nodeValue;
```

Basically, that's the first part of line 22 followed by the second part of line 20; again, it sets a property (matching the `nodeName`) to equal the `nodeValue`. Because each slide is not just a series of names with matching values, we need to treat `BULLETS` uniquely. Line 12 stores an uppercase version of the current node's name, and then line 13 checks whether it matches `"BULLETS"`. If not, lines 20 and 22 execute as described earlier (and like in Chapter 16). If the current node *is* a bullet, lines 14–18 create a new array in the variable `theVal` and loop through all the `BULL`s to `push()` each value onto the end of the array variable `theVal`. Notice that line 22 executes in all cases; it's just how the value of `theVal` gets populated that varies. Finally, in line 24 (after all the nodes in the current slide are processed), the temp variable `thisData` is pushed onto the end of `allSlides`.

All this work to structure and parse the XML data is worth it. For one thing, you can use this slide presentation even if the data changes. As you're about to see, it's easy to do the rest of the work in Flash because we have a very nice array: `allSlides`.

7. Insert a blank keyframe into frame 2 by pressing F7.

8. Just for a test, type this code into the frame script for frame 2 (where we'll put all of the rest of the code for this workshop):

```
trace(allSlides[0].title);
trace(allSlides[0].photo);
trace(allSlides[0].bullets[0]);
trace(allSlides[0].post_content);
```

You should see the values from the various nodes (including just the first `Bull`). If you don't, you can try to find the problem. (You can also just download my file that's online at www.phillipkerman.com/actionscripting, of course.) Generally, you want to do a test like the `trace()` commands every step along the way to confirm that your code is working.

9. Now that we know the data has loaded alright, we can move on to displaying it. Start by placing two Dynamic Text fields on the Stage in frame 2—one with the instance name of `title_txt`, positioned at the top of the Stage and another with the instance name of `post_txt` at the bottom of the Stage. Leave room for the bullets and the photo in the middle of the screen. (We'll get to those in a minute.)

10. To let the user step through the different slides, you can make arrow buttons. Place two instances on the Stage and rotate one of them 180 degrees. Give the two buttons instance names of `back_btn` and `forward_btn`, respectively.

11. Replace the script in frame 2 with the following:

```
back_btn.onPress=function(){ goPage(-1)}
forward_btn.onPress=function(){ goPage(1)}
currentPage=-1;
goPage(1);
```

We'll write the `goPage()` function next, but these 4 lines first assign callbacks to the two buttons (so that they both trigger `goPage()` but with different parameters). Then, `currentPage` is initialized to `-1` so that when `goPage(1)` executes (page forward) the first time, it lands on the first page. (Remember, arrays start counting with zero).

12. Here's the starter version for the `goPage()` function that you can type into the frame script:

```
function goPage(direction){
  currentPage+=direction;
  title_txt.text=allSlides[currentPage].title;
  post_txt.text=allSlides[currentPage].post_content;
}
```

Test it out; it's pretty amazing how easy it is. All we do is increment or decrement `currentPage` and then set the `text` property appropriately for the text fields. We'll add a few more lines to this function.

13. We can easily make the photos show up by first making a clip into which the photos will load. So, draw a box that matches the approximate size of your photos, select it, and then convert to a Movie Clip—but be sure to select the default top-left registration point option (see Figure W15.3). Name the instance of your clip `thePhoto`.

Figure W15.3   *The clip's registration point establishes where the top-left corner of a loaded JPEG will appear the loadMovie() method is invoked.*

14. Next, add the following line of code somewhere inside the goPage() function, but after where currentPage is assigned:

    ```
    thePhoto.loadMovie(allSlides[currentPage].photo);
    ```

    This extracts the photo property of the current item and uses it as the parameter for loadMovie(). In the downloadable version of this project, I've added a feature that will display a progress bar while the JPEG loads.

    To add the bullet functionality, we need a couple of more pieces. Because we don't know how many bullets might appear on a slide, we'll make one Movie Clip and use the attachMovie() method to create as many instances as necessary. Alternatively (and perhaps as a good exercise), we could use createEmptyMovieClip(), draw a bullet (using the drawing methods), and then create a TextField object—all with code. Instead, we'll manually create a clip containing a hand-drawn bullet and text formatted by hand.

    After the text and bullet graphic are created, we'll let the user click anywhere onscreen to see the next bullet. That is, clicking the arrows will jump to the next slide (as it does now), but the way to advance through the bullets is just to click anywhere onscreen.

15. Inside the goPage() function, add these two lines of code:

    ```
    bullNum=-1;
    nextBullet();
    ```

    Basically, every time a new page is displayed, bullNum is set to -1 and the nextBullet() function gets invoked. (We'll write that function in a minute.)

16. Start by creating a wide Dynamic Text field using left-justified formatting. Put some sample text that represents a typical bullet point but make sure the margins are set wide enough to accommodate the longest bullet. Name the instance bullet_txt. Draw a box or circle as your bullet-point graphic and place it to the left of the bullet_txt instance.

17. Select both the bullet-point graphic and the bullet_txt instance and convert them to a Movie Clip named "Animated." (Be sure to keep the top-left registration option). Note the symbol name.

18. Actually, we'll remove every instance of the Animated symbol, but before that, we can do some offline animating. Position this symbol in its destination position (assuming it's the first bullet to appear).

19. Copy the instance, and then select Edit, Paste in Place. Press the down arrow on your keyboard until the space between the two bullets looks good. Use the Info panel to note both the y coordinate of the first bullet and the difference between the two bullets. If the top bullet's y is 66 and the second bullet's y is 106, you know the separation is 40 pixels. Based on this information, let's initialize some variables. Create the start for the nextBullet() function with the following code, placed below everything else in the second keyframe:

```
function nextBullet(){
  var topY=66
  var spacing=40;
}
```

This code will come in handy in a minute when we position each new bullet.

20. I'd like to see the bullets animate onscreen, but really snappy. So, use the left and right arrow buttons to position the top bullet all the way off the left side of the Stage. (You can hold down the Shift key to make it jump in bigger steps.) Note the x coordinate. Move it to the right so that it's about halfway to its destination, and then note the x location again. Continue by gathering coordinates for the text, as follows: when moved 10 or 20 pixels to the right of the destination, when moved to the left of the destination about 5–10 pixels, and, finally, in its destination (which, I suppose, you could have gathered earlier—but the idea of this step is that you're "animating" by just gathering coordinates). The final effect I'm thinking of will zoom the text onscreen (actually a bit too far), and then it will bounce back and finally settle in place. Now enter the following line to place those values in an array that gets assigned inside the nextBullet() function:

```
var steps=[-400, -163, 27, 1, 7];
```

21. Delete both instances of the Animated symbol on the Stage. Select the symbol in the Library and set its linkage to animated. Now we can use the attachMovie() method.

22. Finish the nextBullet() function so that it appears as follows:

```
1 function nextBullet(){
2   var topY=66;
3   var spacing=40;
4   var steps=[-400, -163, 27, 1, 7];
5   bullNum++;
6   _root.attachMovie("animated","bull_"+bullNum,bullNum);
7   var thisOne=_root["bull_"+bullNum];
8   thisOne._x=-9000;
9   thisOne._y=topY+( bullNum*spacing );
```

```
10   thisOne.bullet_txt.text=
➥allSlides[currentPage].bullets[bullNum];
11   thisOne.steps=steps;
12   thisOne.curStep=0;
13   thisOne.onEnterFrame=function(){
14     this._x=this.steps[this.curStep];
15     this.curStep++;
16     if(this.curStep>=this.steps.length){
17       this.onEnterFrame=null;
18     }
19   }
20 }
```

After the three lines of variables, we increment bullNum. Line 6 creates a new instance of the Animated symbol, gives it an instance name of bull_x (where x is bullNum), and puts it in the level number one greater than bullNum. (We don't want to use level_0 because it would wipe out our main movie.) Line 7 just stores the newly created instance in a variable to save typing. Line 8 moves it way off to the left. Line 9 basically sets the _y location to match topY but adds a space for every bullNum greater than 0 (that is, multiplying the spacing by bullNum results in 0 when bullNum is zero). Line 10 is a bit uglier than the rest, but all it's doing is setting the text property of the field bullet_txt (inside the new instance) equal to the value of the first bullet (just like we did with the trace() command in step 8).

Lines 11–19 get a bit hairy. To set up the animation, the new clip is given its own copy of the steps array and has a new variable stepNum (which gets incremented in line 15) initialized to 0. Line 13 defines an onEnterFrame callback for the new clip (thisOne). Line 14 sets the clip's _x property to a value in the appropriate index of steps. The part that's a bit wild is inside the if statement (which is checking to see whether stepNum has reached the end of the steps array). The new clip's onEnterFrame callback is cleared on line 17.

23. Now we can let the user trigger more bullets. (Currently, only the first one shows up when each new slide appears.) Add this simple callback outside of any other functions:

```
_root.onMouseDown=function(){nextBullet()};
```

This just triggers the nextBullet() function whenever the user clicks anywhere. Now when the program runs, there seems to be a million problems: two bullets animating at a time, bullets not disappearing, and more! We can attempt to fix only one thing at a time.

The first step to fixing this is to determine exactly what's happening. The main issue is that even when pressing a button, the user is also triggering the onMouseDown callback. By placing two separate trace() commands in the two functions (goPage() and nextBullet()), I determined that nextBullet() is executing first—or more specifically, that onMouseDown occurs before onPress. An amazingly simple solution is to just remove all bullet instances on the Stage when the goPage() function runs. A for in loop can go through all the clips on the Stage, and if we just check that their name starts with "bull_", we know it's a bullet and can remove it.

24. To remove all the instances of the Animated symbol, add this function to the frame script:

```
function removeAll(){
  for (i in _root){
    if(i._name.substr(0,5).toUpperCase()=="BULL_"){
      this[i].removeMovieClip();
    }
  }
}
```

This function just checks each object in the main timeline; if the first five characters match "BULL_", it gets removed. (I like to use the toUpperCase() method as a safety precaution whenever checking strings for exact matches because "bull_"=="BULL_", for example, is false.)

25. Now just trigger the removeAll() function from within the goPage() function by adding

```
removeAll();
```

This works pretty well for fixing most of the problems. It's not totally elegant because every time the user clicks the page forward button, a new bullet starts to animate but then gets wiped away instantly. It works, but if you have a better idea, feel free to use it.

There are only two tasks remaining: to stop the bullets from appearing once the last one is displayed, and not to reveal the post_content until the last bullet displays.

26. To stop the bullets from appearing, place the following code right beneath the line that reads bullNum++ inside the nextBullet() function:

```
if(bullNum>=allSlides[currentPage].bullets.length){
  return;
}
```

This code bypasses the rest of the nextBullet() function, provided that bullNum has reached or exceeded the length of the bullets property (an array) in the current slide's data.

27. It turns out that the last step will help us with our final objective: to display the post_content, only once all the bullets have displayed. In the goPage() function, find the line that sets the post_txt field's text (it reads: post_txt.text=allSlides[currentPage].post_content;). First, copy the

line (because we're going to paste it somewhere else), and then change it to read

```
post_txt.text="";
```

This clears the `post_txt` field any time `goPage()` is triggered.

28. Finally, add the following code to the `nextBullet()` function (somewhere below the `if` statement you just created):

```
if(bullNum>=allSlides[currentPage].bullets.length-1){
  post_txt.text=allSlides[currentPage].post_content;
}
```

Notice that the third line is the same code you copied from the `goPage()` function.

Now you should be able to run the presentation. After you put the final touches on some graphics, you can export a `.swf` and never need to touch Flash again. That is, you can make new slide presentations just by editing the XML file and replacing the JPEG images. You might consider adding a feature to disable the back button when on the first slide or the forward button when on the last slide.

This workshop was a lot of work, but realize that you can use the results of it over and over. For example, you can make a giant XML file full of whatever data or bullet points you want. You can also add other elements to this presentation, such as pictures and sounds. Generally, the work to make this project even better lies in good template design: You want something that's usable, expandable, and visually appealing.

{ Chapter 16

Workshop }

Using the Local SharedObject to Remember User Settings

A common reaction to a long, drawn-out Flash introduction is to quickly click the Skip Intro button. Actually, the site `www.skipintro.com` exaggerates the issue. It doesn't have to be this way, however. You can use the new local SharedObjects to store information about a user's activities and preferences, and then retrieve that data later to adjust your Flash actions to that specific user.

The scenario for automatically skipping an intro animation might work like this: The first time the user sees the intro animation, you write a local SharedObject; then, for subsequent visits, you can check to see whether the local SharedObject is present and, if so, skip the intro for the user.

In this workshop chapter, we'll use a Flash movie to let the user specify his language of preference; we'll store that selection in a local SharedObject file. If the user ever revisits your site, the preferred language will be restored automatically. When we're done, I'll show you some other uses for local SharedObjects.

This exercise requires very little programming; most of the work is design, as you'll see:

1. Draw a button, and then create six instances of the button, stacked vertically and spaced evenly (see Figure W16.1).

Figure W16.1   *Draw six buttons and space them evenly apart.*

2. On top of each button, place some text to specify a language choice. If this weren't a workshop, you'd actually spell out the name of each language in the native language—that is, you'd write *Español* rather than *Spanish*. However, this is just an exercise, so don't waste your time fumbling for your Swahili dictionary.

3. Arbitrarily establish that the top button is language 1, the second button is language 2, and so on, and then give each button an instance name lang_1, lang_2, and so forth.

4. To make a highlight (that indicates which button is selected), copy one of the language buttons. Select it and choose Modify, Break Apart. Set a really thick stroke by using the Ink Bottle, and then remove the fill. Select the outline and convert it to a Movie Clip. Give it an instance name of highlight. Then move it off the Stage.

5. Start with the following code in the first frame of the movie:

```
lang_1.onPress=function(){pick(1)}
lang_2.onPress=function(){pick(2)}
lang_3.onPress=function(){pick(3)}
lang_4.onPress=function(){pick(4)}
lang_5.onPress=function(){pick(5)}
lang_6.onPress=function(){pick(6)}
```

This code just assigns a callback to each button to trigger the pick() function (but with a parameter for each language).

6. Next we can define the pick() function. Although we'll add more later, here's the start:

```
function pick(whichOne){
  language=whichOne;
  redisplay(whichOne);
}
```

After setting the language variable, this function just goes and triggers another function: redisplay(). The redisplay() function will handle all the display issues, including placing the highlight in position. We want to separate that job from the pick() function because we'll need to do it both when the user clicks a language button as well as when she resumes.

7. To make a separate function to handle the highlight display, write this function:

```
function redisplay(whichOne){
  highlight._x=this["lang_"+whichOne]._x;
  highlight._y=this["lang_"+whichOne]._y;
}
```

This code positions the highlight in the same location as the appropriate language button. If you want more things to happen when the user selects a language or returns to the site, you can add extra code inside the redisplay() function. For example, maybe you have a background image that relates to the selected language. You could display that graphic in this function too.

8. Now for the local SharedObject issue. We'll need to both write the language preference when the user clicks a button as well as check (at the beginning) to see whether there is an existing value for language. We'll write the code to read in any existing language choice. Type the following code above all the rest of the code already in place:

```
my_so=SharedObject.getLocal("language_choice","/");
if (my_so.data.language!=undefined){
  redisplay(my_so.data.language);
}
```

Because this code isn't inside any function or callback, it executes when the movie first plays. The first line does three things at once! It places an instance of SharedObject in the variable my_so; it checks for the existence of an .sol (shared object local) file named language_choice and creates one if it doesn't exist; finally, it sets all the variables contained in the built-in data property (provided that an old file exists). Then the if statement checks to see whether the value for language (within the data property of my_so) is not undefined—it will be undefined the first time, but for subsequent visits the redisplay() function is invoked because the condition will be true. You can learn more details and the full syntax for local SharedObjects in Chapter 16, "Interfacing with External Data."

9. To write this local SharedObject file (or, more importantly, to save the user's language choice in that file), just modify the pick() function, as follows:

```
function pick(whichOne){
  my_so.data.language=whichOne;
  my_so.flush();
  redisplay(whichOne);
}
```

Instead of placing our language variable in the _root timeline, this code places it as a property inside the data property. Naturally, my_so needs to be an Object data type before we can set the values of properties—but the getLocal() method handles that in the first line (of step 7). Also, this example uses only one variable, but you can store as many as you want. Each variable just needs to be saved as a property of the data property. Finally, the flush() method immediately writes the data to disk.

If, by chance, this workshop is not working for you, confirm that your Flash settings allow you to write movies to disk. Just right-click (or Control-click on Macintosh) while testing the movie. You'll want to make sure the slider (accessed when you click the second tab labeled Local Storage) is set above 0 (see Figure W16.2). Normally, these settings can be different for each domain you visit; however, there's one "local" setting for movies you view when selecting Control, Test Movie.

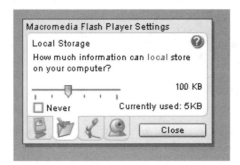

Figure W16.2   *Users can change how much Flash local SharedObject data is stored on their computer.*

That's it! I feel guilty that this was such a piece of cake. As most of the workshop chapters illustrate, you can accomplish equivalent tasks much easier with Flash MX than you could with Flash 5. For example, saving the user's language preference in the past would require writing JavaScript cookies. Not only was that more work, but it would fail on some browsers. Furthermore, cookies contain only the String data type, whereas SharedObjects enable you to store any data type, including, as in the case of our language variable example, the Number data type. You can even store arrays. In addition to this workshop, you'll find a sample at www.phillipkerman.com/actionscripting that lets the user drag shapes around the screen and save their positions (see Figure W16.3).

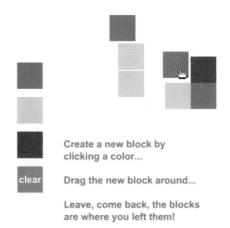

Create a new block by
clicking a color...

Drag the new block around...

Leave, come back, the blocks
are where you left them!

Figure W16.3   *Local SharedObjects enable you to save complex data, such as the arrays for this drag-and-drop interaction.*

Just so that we explore another feature of local SharedObjects, consider a scenario in which you plan to store a lot of data in a SharedObject. It turns out that the default setting of 100KB is plenty big enough for most applications, although you might still want more—perhaps to let users store huge databases of information locally. Although users can take it upon themselves to select the Settings dialog box and crank up the Local Storage option, they won't normally see that dialog box automatically unless you try storing more data than they currently have set (which is likely 100KB because that's the default). However, you can use the System object's showSettings() method to force the user to see this dialog box. For example, the following code will display the settings dialog box:

```
System.showSettings(1);
```

The optional parameter (1 in this case) specifies which tabbed panel will initially appear (0-3 correspond to the four different panels in the dialog box).

Anyway, you probably don't want to let users spend a lot of time interacting with your movie if, in the end, they don't want to let you store data locally. It would be nice if, before you get rolling, you give users the option to save a lot of data; if they decline, you offer them a different experience.

{ Chapter 17

Workshop }

Using the LocalConnection Object for Inter-Movie Communication

The new LocalConnection object lets one movie trigger functions in another. The steps covered in Chapter 16, "Interfacing with External Data," were straightforward: multiple movies create instances of the LocalConnection object using a common name, and then the "listening" movie specifies which functions will be available to the other Flash movies. Although the steps might be simple, you really need to see a practical application to begin to understand how powerful the LocalConnection object really is.

In this workshop chapter, we'll build an application that uses the LocalConnection object for a help system. Users will be able to open an additional browser window and get help for any other part of the web site they visit (see Figure W17.1). Ideally, this workshop chapter will inspire other ideas. Although this example is powerful, it's rather simple. Seeing what's possible, however, should spark more ideas.

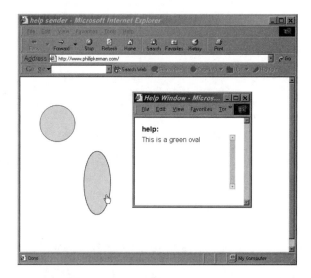

Figure W17.1   *The movie in the background will send messages to the "help" window in front.*

Here are the steps to follow:

1. First we'll create the help window. Because this movie will receive function calls from other movies, it will be the most complex file. Resize the document properties (Ctrl+J) so that the Stage is 300X200.

2. Create a Dynamic Text field that's almost 300 pixels wide and about 180 pixels tall. Give this field an instance name of `display_txt` and be sure that the line type is set to Multiline.

3. Just in case more text needs to be displayed, drag the ScrollBar component onto the `display_txt` Dynamic Text field.

4. Finally, you can add some static text such as "Help Info" above the field.

5. Into the first keyframe of this movie, type the following code:

```
1 my_lc = new LocalConnection();
2 display_txt.text="Help will appear here.";
3 my_lc.displayHelp = function(param) {
4     display_txt.text=param;
5 }
6 my_lc.connect("incoming");
```

This code should look familiar. Line 1 instantiates an instance of the LocalConnection object (into the variable `my_lc`). Line 2 just puts some starter text into the text field. Lines 3–5 specify that other movies connected to this movie (through a common LocalConnection name, in this case, `incoming`) will get access to the `displayHelp` function.

If `displayHelp` were a regular function (it isn't), it would appear like this:

```
function displayHelp(param){
  display_txt.text=param;
}
```

However, in order for other movies to have access, it must appear as a call-back, as originally shown. Notice that line 6 is where we get "connected" to the incoming name. That step must appear below all the functions to which we're giving other movies access.

6. Save this movie as `help.fla`, and then select Control, Test Movie to publish an .swf. Start a new file (named `help_sender_a.fla`) and save it in the same location as `help.fla`.

7. Draw a few shapes in the `help_sender_a` movie—perhaps a circle and a square. Individually, convert each to a Movie Clip. Give one an instance name of `circle` and the other an instance name of `square`.

8. Place the following code in the first frame of the movie:

```
 1 function triggerHelp(message){
 2   var my_lc = new LocalConnection();
 3   my_lc.send("incoming", "displayHelp", message);
 4   delete my_lc;
 5 }
 6 circle.onRollOver=function(){
 7   triggerHelp("This is a circle")
 8 }
 9 square_btn.onRollOver=function(){
10   triggerHelp("This is a square")
11 }
```

Notice that we consolidate some work by creating the `triggerHelp()` function that each clip will invoke. Adding more shapes later will be easy. Inside the `triggerHelp()` function in quick succession a LocalConnection instance is created (`my_lc`), the function `displayHelp()` (in the other movie) gets triggered, and then the LocalConnection instance is deleted. The fact that we named the variable `my_lc` is unimportant. (The other movie can have the same named variable without incident.) However, what is significant is that line 3 executes the `send` method and specifies three parameters: `"incoming"` (the same name as in the other movie), `"displayHelp"` (a string version of the function name in the other movie), and `message` (the value of the parameter passed to `triggerHelp()`, which, in this movie, gets passed as a parameter to the `displayHelp()` function in the other movie). Finally, you can see at the end that each clip invokes the `triggerHelp()` function with a parameter that contains a helpful string.

9. Create an .swf by selecting Control, Test Movie. Finally, find the folder where the two movies (`help.swf` and `help_sender_a.swf`) reside. Double-click each one and position the windows so that you can see both movies. Rollover the circle and square shapes to see help appear in the small help window.

At this point, you can make a copy of help_sender_a and change the text messages and appearance of the shapes. Users will be able to launch any combination of movies; if the help.swf is running, they'll see the text change, as appropriate. Of course, if you want this to run in a browser, you'll have to create an HTML file for each file. If you add a bit of JavaScript, you can even make the help window appear as a pop-up that stays on top of other windows.

You can think of help.fla as the source version of a function that's shared among several other files. As long as you don't expect to receive additional parameters, you won't ever need to adjust the various "help_sender" movies.

10. Just for fun, let's add some (arguably gratuitous) features to the help.fla. Go back to the source file and import a short sound. (I just copied a sound from Window, Common Libraries, Sounds.) Set the linkage identifier for the imported sound to chime. Next, add the following code above everything else in the first frame of help.fla:

```
s=new Sound();
s.attachSound("chime");
```

This creates a Sound object instance in the variable s.

11. Now just insert the following line of code within the displayHelp() definition (above or below line 4 in step 5):

```
s.start();
```

Now when you test the movie, a sound effect will play every time the help text changes to prompt the user.

This strategy can be very effective in other projects that have a similar structure. For example, if you plan to display several Flash movies in separate HTML table cells or framesets, one movie can contain all the audio. As the user navigates to different parts of the site, new movies can appear to contain sounds (even though they don't) and they'll load fast. This way, you could have one movie (such as "help") with all the sounds as well as a lot of small "send_help" files that cause sounds to play (even though they don't contain sounds).

Chapter 18

Fixing Broken Scripts

In Chapter 6, "Debugging," you learned some of the ways to debug movies.
In this workshop chapter, you're given the chance to put those skills to work.
Your task is to download the "broken" Flash files (from
`www.phillipkerman.com/actionscripting/`) and fix the errors that I have
purposely included in them. None of these files will work without adjustment.
Most of the fixes are simple—after you track them down.

The files you'll work with in this workshop chapter either don't work at all or
they work incorrectly. For each file, you'll find a description of what's *supposed*
to happen in the following sections. Then, if you choose to peek, you'll find a
clue to the problem. Finally, I provide the solution and a short explanation. The
difficulty of the problems in these files ranges from simple to quite difficult. (It's
actually hard to gauge how difficult it is to find and fix a bug.)

One thing to remember in your real projects is that most bugs require only a simple fix. Sometimes the fix is very involved, but usually, it's just a minor oversight
you made while programming. In this workshop chapter, the "harder" bugs to fix
usually require a little more digging to find. For example, you might have to edit
the script in a keyframe nested inside another clip. For every bug you find, you
should feel *really* good about your debugging skills. If nothing else, you'll be
rewarded with a movie that functions.

Card Flip

The file ("01_card_flip.fla") is just the start of a card-game movie that could evolve to be three-card monte. Although this file will take many steps to finish, the current version is supposed to allow the user to click on any card. The card then animates by reducing its _yscale until it reaches 0. Then it's supposed to increase its _yscale until it reaches the normal 100 again, where it stops. Don't worry about showing the face of the card—we have bigger problems! The current version appears to scale down alright, but then it seems to scale up forever! All the code is in a keyframe inside the Card Movie Clip (so that it's automatically duplicated for each instance). See whether you can find and fix the bug.

Hint

The error is probably different than it appears. If you edit the master version of the Card symbol and place an odd graphic shape inside the rectangle shape (see Figure W18.1), you'll see that the next time you test the movie, the error is *not* that the _yscale increases too much, but rather that it starts to decrease and keeps decreasing below 0 (where it will appear upside down). Don't worry about _yscale going above 100; make sure that it never goes below 0, and you'll be on the right track.

Figure W18.1   *Placing a splotch on one part of the card provides a clue to the exact problem.*

Solution

The problem can be found in the two if statements contained inside the onEnterFrame callback:

```
if (this._yscale==0){
  this.direction=12;
}
```

```
if (this._yscale==100){
  this.onEnterFrame=null;
}
```

The variable `direction` starts at `-12` and is supposed to turn to `12` when the
`_yscale` reaches `0`. However, the `if` statements check to see whether `_yscale` is
equal to `0` or `100`. The problem is that if `_yscale` jumps by `12` for each
`enterFrame` event (while it's animating), it will jump right past `0`. Change the
first condition from `this._yscale==0` to `this._yscale<0`. Test the movie, and
you'll see that the other `if` statement must be fixed, too. Change its condition to
`this._yscale>100`. Finally, you'll want to make one more touch. In addition to
clearing the `onEnterFrame` callback (within the `if(this._yscale>100)` statement), add one line that reads `this._yscale=100`. This ensures that when
`_yscale` goes past `100`, it is set back to `100`. Here is the final script:

```
this.onPress=function(){
  this.direction=-12;
  this.onEnterFrame=function(){
    this._yscale+=this.direction;
    if (this._yscale<0){
      this.direction=12;
    }
    if (this._yscale>100){
      this._yscale=100;
      this.onEnterFrame=null;
    }
  }
}
```

By the way, another solution would be to change both values for `direction` (`12`
and `-12`) to a number that divides evenly into `100`—perhaps `10`. I think that's a
poor solution for this workshop, however, because it will change the "speed" of
the animation. Besides, even if did work, it's always safer to use a conditional
like < or <= than == (when appropriate).

Card Snap

In this broken file ("02_card_snap.fla"), I've added quite a bit to the preceding
Card Flip file (although we're not playing three-card monte yet). We're successfully assigning a unique random number to each "card" instance's `cardNum` variable. I even threw in a Dynamic Text field just for testing purposes. (We don't
want the user to know the value of `cardNum` for each card.) The randomization

works, as does the animation, but we want the card to reveal its face in the middle of the animation. The instant the _yscale reaches its minimum (index 2 of the tweenLocs array), we want to make the instance called card jump to a frame within its 11-frame movie. We think most of it is built right, but we never see the card's value!

Hint

Code appears in both the first frame of the movie and in the first frame of the symbol named Clip w-Card. Because the randomization is working fine, you don't need to bother with the code in the main timeline.

The solution involves an easily misunderstood fact about the keyword this. Namely, when you say this inside a clip, you're addressing the clip; when you say this inside a function, you're addressing the function; and when you say this inside a callback, you're addressing the clip to which the callback is attached. If all that makes sense, you should look for places in the code that don't use this but should.

Solution

It's much easier to fix this file than it is to understand why the fix works. All you need to do is make sure the ActionScript editor preferences are set to display line numbers and then change line 21 from how it currently reads:

```
gotoAndStop (destination+1);
```

to instead read

```
this.gotoAndStop (destination+1);
```

Including this addresses the card instance (the one with all the card faces). The way it was (without this), the code was addressing the timeline of the symbol Clip w-Card (which had only one frame). I've said in the past that if a clip address doesn't begin with _root, _parent, or this, you can always add this (because Flash will anyway). What's confusing in this case is that the this that Flash inferred is the timeline where the code is placed—not the timeline of the card instance. The lesson here (besides that the keyword this can be confusing) is that it's best to be explicit.

Circle Move

This is a pretty easy one, but it's likely to trip up even the most experienced
ActionScripter. In the file ("03_circle_move.fla"), you'll find three instances of
the *same* Movie Clip—but only two bounce back and forth when you test the
movie. Naturally, all the code is inside the master symbol so that it's not duplicated. That makes it doubly frustrating because you would expect the same code
to behave the same. That is, when you fix the script, you'll have to fix it in only
one place. For some unknown reason, the green circle never bounces back the
way the red and blue instances do. What's so different about the green clip? How
can you fix it so that all the circles bounce back and forth?

Hint

Drag another instance of the Circle symbol and chances are very good that it will
be broken too. Here's another clue: Review the solution for the "Card Flip" broken script, earlier in this workshop chapter.

Solution

The reason both the red and green instances bounce back and forth is because I
carefully placed their x coordinates at 210 and 100, respectively. Because they're
moving by 10 or -10 each enterFrame, both will eventually reach precisely 550
and 0, which are the two extremes. We don't really want to check whether the _x
position *equals* 550 or 0; we care only whether it's above 550 or below 0. The if
statement should use a greater-than and less-than comparison operator. The following is the finished version:

```
this.direction=10;
this.onEnterFrame=function(){
  this._x+=this.direction;
  if(this._x>550){
    this.direction=this.direction*-1;
  }
  if(this._x<0){
    this.direction=this.direction*-1;
  }
}
```

It's true that I was being deceptive by artificially making the red and blue circle
work when, in fact, almost any clip would fail with this script. However, you'll
quite often write a script that appears to work for your conditions—and *only* for

your conditions. As soon as you take a script that works fine under certain conditions to another situation, errors often pop up. So, in fact, this kind of thing will probably happen to you eventually. However, if your tests are exhaustive, you should find such bugs.

Multiple Choice

The file ("04_multiple_choice.fla") is a great example of a dynamic multiple-choice quiz. You just assign the variables `question`, `answer1`, `answer2`, `answer3`, and `correctNum`, and the text is displayed onscreen. This code could be expanded to load questions from a server or a text file. You can have a lot of questions and even report the score at the end of a quiz. If only it worked! It's a shame it doesn't because we even have a highlight for the button that the user clicks, and a way to color the Dynamic Text field for `feedback` using the new TextFormat object. The only problem is that *any* answer is considered correct. Here's a free hint: Salem is the capital of Oregon. Please fix my quiz.

Hint

The entire problem is one missing character that should be included somewhere in the `attempt()` function. Okay, the problem is found in the `if` statement's condition.

Solution

This one gets me *all* the time! The `if` statement condition should use the comparison operator `==`, not the assignment operator `=`. The way it is now, `whatNum` is assigned to `currectNum` every time. I don't know whether the bug would have been easier to solve if I had placed the code that moves the highlight at the end. If I did that, the highlight would always move to the correct choice, not to the button the user clicked.

Rotating Box

Don't ask me what the practical use of this movie is—maybe a *Wheel of Fortune* game? If you open and then test the file "05_rotating_box.fla," you'll find that you can set the box in motion by clicking either arrow button. When you click the Stop button, the next time the `_rotation` reaches a point that's evenly divisible by `90`, the box should stop (see Figure W18.2). I added some visual feedback for when the user clicks the Stop button—much like how a public bus might have a lighted sign that says "Stop requested" so that riders don't keep requesting the bus to make the next stop. That's just a little touch that makes this movie more usable. The problem seems to be related to "seltzer"—I can't seem to make the box stop on it. Actually, if you start by pressing the left button, you won't be able to stop it on "apples" either. Obviously, when you investigate the solution, don't get hung up on the "seltzer" and "apples" choices. Try to determine why the box isn't working generally.

Why can't I stop it on seltzer?

Figure W18.2   *Despite having little or no practical value, the goal of this movie is to enable the user to stop the box in one of four rotations.*

Hint

Set the movie's frame rate down to 2 fps (Ctrl+J) and debug the movie. Then select the box instance and Properties tab of the Debugger so that you can monitor the box's _rotation property. This should answer why the long-winded condition in the if statement (_rotation==0||_rotation==90||_rotation==180||_rotation==270) isn't working. Here's another clue: The solution requires a different condition in the if statement. Consider the modulus operator (%) and re-read the phrase "evenly divisible by 90" in the preceding movie description.

Solution

Like most solutions, the one I'm going to give you isn't the only one. All you need to do is to change the condition in the if statement to this._rotation%90==0. In pseudo-code, this condition says, "The remainder of 90 divided into _rotation is equal to 0." Here's the finished version of the enterFrame event:

```
box.onEnterFrame=function(){
  this.stopLight._visible=stopRequested;
  this._rotation+=direction;
  if (stopRequested){
    if (this._rotation%90==0){
      direction=0;
      stopRequested=0;
    }
  }
}
```

Word Float

I'm not really sure where I'm headed with this project, but the "06_word_float.fla" file doesn't seem to let me get any further than where I am. All I want is for the five instances (word_1, word_2, word_3, word_4, and word_5) to contain the five individual words in my arrayOfWords array variable. The entire script is in frame 1, but it doesn't seem to work right. Please help!

Hint

This bug is almost too easy for a hint, but here's one: The first index in an array is 0.

Solution

The easiest solution is to change the instance names from word_1 through word_5 to word_0 through word_4. When setting the text property of the fields being addressed dynamically (_root["word_"+w].text), the w iteration variable is going from 4 down to 0. (Remember that for-in loops effectively count back-ward, which doesn't have much to do with the problem but is an interesting tidbit.)

If, for whatever reason, you don't want to rename the instances (maybe you're using those names elsewhere or it's too much work to change them), there is another solution. Unfortunately, changing the statement that assigns the text property to read _root["word_"+w].text=arrayOfWords[w-1] won't work. The w iteration variable is not exactly usable as-is. Instead, you could initialize a variable such as counter and then increment it within the loop. See if you can find the error in the following code:

```
counter=0;
for (w in arrayOfWords){
  counter++;
  this["word_"+counter].text=arrayOfWords[w];
}
```

You'll see the problem if you test it: counter is going from 1 to 5, and w is going in the opposite direction—from 4 to 0. Here's one of many possible alternatives that work:

```
counter=arrayOfWords.length+1;
for (w in arrayOfWords){
  counter--;
  this["word_"+counter].text=arrayOfWords[w];
}
```

And here's still another version using the TextField object that works without any text fields onscreen:

```
for (w in arrayOfWords){
  _root.createTextField("word_"+w,w+1,0,0,50,50);
  targ=_root["word_"+w];
  targ.text=arrayOfWords[w];
  targ._x=100+(w*50);
  targ._y=100+(w*50);
}
```

Yellow Box

Here's another practically useless project as it is, but wait until you see it run! Right now, if you open and test the file "07_yellow_box.fla," nothing happens. When you fix the syntax errors, however, the yellow box will rotate constantly and, as you move the mouse, it will change its _xscale and _yscale based on where the mouse goes. Please make it work. There's only a tiny bit of code.

Hint

Make sure that the Syntax Coloring option is selected from the ActionScript Editor tab of the Preferences dialog box(see Figure W18.3).

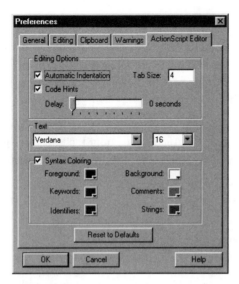

Figure W18.3   *If the Syntax Coloring option is selected, you'll have an easier time fixing the bug.*

Solution

The solution is pretty easy. The _xmouse property appears incorrectly as xmouse. (In addition, the underscore is missing from _ymouse and _rotation.) Notice, however, that unless the _rotation property appears as this._rotation, the entire Stage rotates rather than just the box clip—the way I had wanted. (Try it both with and without this to see the difference.) This exercise just underscores the importance of using correct syntax.

Click and Hold

The file "08_click_and_hold.fla" should let the user either click once or click and hold to move the box left and right. It used to work fine when there was just a forward and backward button (which reacted to single clicks). After I added the click-and-hold feature and moved some code around, however, the single-click feature stopped working. Although there are a number of ways to fix the single-click buttons, try to do so without making a new function. That is, I don't want another version of the moveBox() function.

Hint

Again, the fix in this file is related to the keyword `this`. That is, notice that `moveBox()` is triggered both as a regular function *and* as an `onEnterFrame` callback. Try placing the script `trace(this);` somewhere inside the `moveBox()` function for a clue.

Solution

Because using the keyword `this` inside `moveBox()` function will address the main timeline (when triggered normally) and the box clip (when triggered as a callback), we need to use something more specific. Just change the `moveBox()` function to read as follows:

```
function moveBox(){
  box._x+=box.direction;
}
```

Objects

Don't worry, the broken script in the "09_objects.fla" file doesn't have much to do with objects. Instead, it deals with a common problem that arises when using objects. In this movie, I want a representation for each wheel of each vehicular homemade object that gets instantiated. In the first frame, you can see that I'm trying to put instances of my vehicle object in the variables `bicycle`, `car`, `unicycle`, and `truck`. Then I want to use `attachMovie()` to both place an instance of the Vehicle Shell symbol for each vehicle and, inside each vehicle, place an instance of the `Wheel` symbol for each wheel in that vehicle.

Just to see how the movie is working (or not working), I created a generic object (`clickObj`) onto which I assigned an `onClick` callback function. That generic object gets passed as the fourth parameter of `attachMovie` for each wheel (line 25 of the code). The problem is that I seem to get only one wheel for each vehicle—but I want to see as many wheels as necessary (see Figure W18.4). The thing that kills me is that when I debug the movie, all my objects are instantiated properly (as Figure W18.4 shows). Please make the wheels appear to spread out horizontally. Consider peeking at the hint because you'll still be left with a nice challenge; even when you know *where* the script has to be adjusted, there's still a lot of work to do the adjusting.

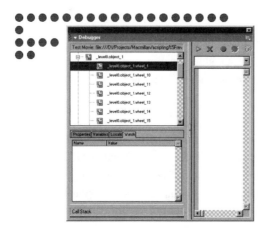

Figure W18.4   *When the file is corrected, you should see a circle for every wheel in every object.*

Hint

Right after you execute the `attachMovie()` method for each wheel inside the `for` loop (`for (var w=1; w<allObjects[i].wheels+1; w++)`), you must reposition the newly created wheel by setting its _x property. Right now, all the clips are indeed appearing, but they all have the same x coordinate, so they're stacked. It's the same basic thing that happens in scripts that set the _y property of each vehicle or `object_x` clip. Study this line of code for an idea of what you have to do:

```
this["object_"+objectCount]._y=30*objectCount;
```

We want to set the _x property of the newly created `wheel_x` instance. With dynamic referencing, however, it's not so simple.

Here's another hint: The pseudo-code for the statement you have to write is: "Set the x of the new wheel inside the current vehicle to 20 pixels more than the last one," or "set the x of the correct wheel instance (`"wheel"+wheelCount`) inside the correct object (`object_+objectCount`) to 20 times `wheelCount`."

Solution

Right underneath line 25 (which begins
`this["object_"+objectCount].attachMovie(...)`, place the following statement:

```
this["object_"+objectCount]["wheel_"+wheelCount]._x=30*wheelCount
```

Pretty ugly, eh? Re-read the pseudo-code provided in the "Hints" section, if necessary.

Move Multiple

How can so little code have so many errors? The "10_move_multiple.fla" file has two buttons that simply call my move() function, which is supposed to move each circle 10 pixels in the direction requested. I'm sure I'm targeting the correct circle_ clip because I re-read the "Dynamic Referencing" section of Chapter 7, "The Movie Clip Object." However, I can't even test the movie without the Output window rearing its ugly head. Make it go away and make the circles move.

Hint

After you fix the syntax error by putting semicolons in place of the commas in the for loop, you have two more fixes to make! I'll give you one: We're supposed to be changing the _x property of each circle. Add ._x after this["circle_"+i] and you'll only have one more fix to make.

Solution

First, change the commas to semicolons in the for loop. (I mistakenly use commas all the time.) Next, notice that although we're targeting the correct circle_ clip, we're not specifying which property we want to change. It's likely that we want to change the _x property. Finally, the loop doesn't loop enough times. More specifically, it loops only when i is less than 4. We want it to keep looping while i is less than or equal to 4. There are a few other fixes you could make to solve this problem, but changing < (less than) to <= (less than or equal to) will do it. Here's the finished version of the move() function:

```
function move(direction){
  total=4;
  for(i=1;i<=total;i++){
    this["circle_"+i]._x += direction*10;
  }
}
```

Summary

That was fun wasn't it? I sure had fun *breaking* the scripts. Fixing them should be quite rewarding and very educational. I tried to expose some of the common problems that programmers have with ActionScript. Errors in the following categories are common: addressing (both for variables and properties), syntax, logic flow, and array indexes. There are countless ways to solve any problem, of course, but you must realize that there are even more ways to do it incorrectly! ActionScript is not easy to program, but with deliberation and patience, you have proven that you can do it!

{ Index }

Symbols

assigning

  values to arrays, 267

  variables, 77-78

assignment operators, 95-98

associative arrays, 282-284. *See also*

 generic objects

  accessing values, 283-284

  managing, 282

  manipulating, 282

asterisk slash (*/), 51

atan2() method, 594

attaching sounds

  instances, 294

  Sound objects, 291

attachMovie(),

  init object, 312-313

  function, 314

  method, 483

attachSound method, 290

audio, streaming, 599

authors, 388

authortime sharing, 28

Auto Completion, new features of

 Flash MX, 31-32

auto-formatting code, 62

B

background music, adding, 511

balance, sounds, 292, 294

balancing parentheses, 87-88

balancing errors, 131

beginFill() method, 316

beginGradientFill() method, 316

  matrix parameter, 318

behavior, Actions, 67

behaviors, symbols, 17

  modifying, 18

binary RGB values, converting to, 301

binary operators, 88

blank keyframes, 22-23

  managing, 23

book conventions, 41-42

Boolean data types, 73

braces, curly ({ }), 58

bracket access (array items), 266-267

break statements, 123-124

breakpoints (debugging), 143

bugs

  analyzing, 134-135

  defining, 130-135

  documenting, 134-135

  fixing, 135-137

  intermittent, 133

  preventing, 137-138

  recreating, 134

  resolving offline, 137-138

  searching, 130-135

  tracking, 134

building

  nesting symbols, 8

  UIs, custom, 404-407

built-in

  functions, 184-187, 204

   format, 204

   values, returning, 185

  methods

   adding to, 381

   overriding, 380-381

HOW TO CONTACT US

VISIT OUR WEB SITE

WWW.NEWRIDERS.COM

On our web site, you'll find information about our other books, authors, tables of contents, and book errata. You will also find information about book registration and how to purchase our books, both domestically and internationally.

EMAIL US

Contact us at: **nrfeedback@newriders.com**

- If you have comments or questions about this book
- To report errors that you have found in this book
- If you have a book proposal to submit or are interested in writing for New Riders
- If you are an expert in a computer topic or technology and are interested in being a technical editor who reviews manuscripts for technical accuracy

Contact us at: **nreducation@newriders.com**

- If you are an instructor from an educational institution who wants to preview New Riders books for classroom use. Email should include your name, title, school, department, address, phone number, office days/hours, text in use, and enrollment, along with your request for desk/examination copies and/or additional information.

Contact us at: **nrmedia@newriders.com**

- If you are a member of the media who is interested in reviewing copies of New Riders books. Send your name, mailing address, and email address, along with the name of the publication or web site you work for.

BULK PURCHASES/CORPORATE SALES

The publisher offers discounts on this book when ordered in quantity for bulk purchases and special sales. For sales within the U.S., please contact: Corporate and Government Sales (800) 382-3419 or **corpsales@pearsontechgroup.com**. Outside of the U.S., please contact: International Sales (317) 581-3793 or **international@pearsontechgroup.com**.

WRITE TO US

New Riders Publishing
201 W. 103rd St.
Indianapolis, IN 46290-1097

CALL/FAX US

Toll-free (800) 571-5840
If outside U.S. (317) 581-3500
Ask for New Riders
FAX: (317) 581-4663

New Riders

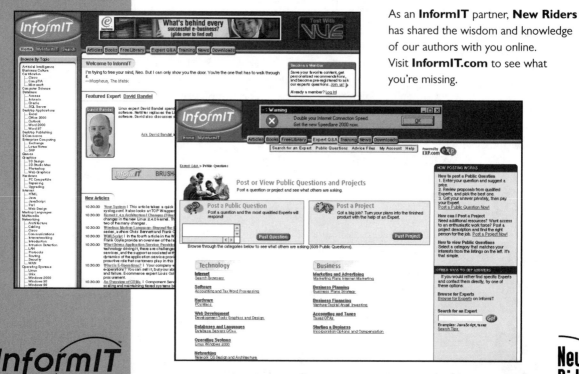

VIEW CART 🛒 | | search ⊙

▸ Registration already a member? Log in. ▸ Book Registration

OUR AUTHORS

PRESS ROOM

| web development | design | photoshop | new media | 3-D | server technologies |

EDUCATORS

ABOUT US

CONTACT US

You already know that New Riders brings you the **Voices That Matter**.

But what does that mean? It means that New Riders brings you the

Voices that challenge your assumptions, take your talents to the next

level, or simply help you better understand the complex technical world

we're all navigating.

Visit **www.newriders.com** to find:

- ▸ *Discounts* on specific book purchases
- ▸ Never before published chapters
- ▸ Sample chapters and excerpts
- ▸ Author bios and interviews
- ▸ Contests and enter-to-wins
- ▸ Up-to-date industry event information
- ▸ Book reviews
- ▸ Special offers from our friends and partners
- ▸ Info on how to join our User Group program
- ▸ Ways to have your Voice heard

New
Riders

WWW.NEWRIDERS.COM